Emerging Applications of Natural Language Processing:

Concepts and New Research

Sivaji Bandyopadhyay
Jadavpur University, India

Sudip Kumar Naskar
Dublin City University, Ireland

Asif Ekbal
University of Heidelberg, Germany

Information Science
REFERENCE

Managing Director:	Lindsay Johnston
Editorial Director:	Joel Gamon
Book Production Manager:	Jennifer Romanchak
Publishing Systems Analyst:	Adrienne Freeland
Development Editor:	Myla Merkel
Assistant Acquisitions Editor:	Kayla Wolfe
Typesetter:	Lisandro Gonzalez
Cover Design:	Nick Newcomer

Published in the United States of America by
Information Science Reference (an imprint of IGI Global)
701 E. Chocolate Avenue
Hershey PA 17033
Tel: 717-533-8845
Fax: 717-533-8661
E-mail: cust@igi-global.com
Web site: http://www.igi-global.com

Library of Congress Cataloging-in-Publication Data

Emerging applications of natural language processing: concepts and new research / Sivaji Bandyopadhyay, Sudip Kumar Naskar, and Asif Ekbal, editors.
    p. cm.
  Includes bibliographical references and index.
  Summary: "This book provides pertinent and vital information that researchers, postgraduate, doctoral students, and practitioners are seeking for learning about the latest discoveries and advances in NLP methodologies and applications of NLP"--Provided by publisher.
  ISBN 978-1-4666-2169-5 (hardcover) -- ISBN 978-1-4666-2170-1 (ebook) -- ISBN 978-1-4666-2171-8 (print & perpetual access) 1. Natural language processing (Computer science) 2. Natural language processing (Computer science)--Research. I. Bandyopadhyay, Sivaji, 1963- II. Naskar, Sudip Kumar, 1979- III. Ekbal, Asif, 1977-
  QA76.9.N38E54 2012
  006.3'5--dc23
                            2012019631

British Cataloguing in Publication Data
A Cataloguing in Publication record for this book is available from the British Library.

All work contributed to this book is new, previously-unpublished material. The views expressed in this book are those of the authors, but not necessarily of the publisher.

Table of Contents

Section 1
Text Analytics

Section 2
Machine Translation

Section 6
Speech Processing

Detailed Table of Contents

Section 1
Text Analytics

This chapter presents a survey of research in Multiword Expressions (MWEs). The chapter starts with definition(s) of MWEs, describes some MWEs classes, and goes into more specific detail on a particular MWEs class called Verb-Noun Constructions (VNCs). Outlining several approaches to VNC representation in lexicons, the chapter explains the formalism of Lexical Function as another possible approach to VNC representation.

This chapter presents the basic concepts of Word Sense Disambiguation (WSD) and discusses different approaches to solving this problem. The chapter discusses both general purpose WSD and domain specific WSD. The first part of the chapter focuses on existing approaches to WSD, including knowledge-based, supervised, semi-supervised, unsupervised, hybrid, and bilingual approaches. The latter part of the chapter presents a greedy neural network inspired algorithm for domain-specific WSD and compares its performance with other state-of-the-art algorithms for WSD.

The chapter discusses different approaches to tackling the problem of domain adaptation for part-of-speech tagging and presents a case study that has achieved significant accuracy rates in tagging journalistic and scientific texts.

This chapter introduces the rationale behind SMT, describes the state-of-the-art approaches in SMT, and presents a number of emerging approaches (tree-based SMT, discriminative SMT). The chapter starts with the word-based approach to SMT that forms the basis for more advanced approaches. The general phrase-based approach is discussed, along with a number of components that are commonly used within this approach and the standard algorithms used to perform translation (decoding) as well as to estimate the weights of the model components (tuning). Then, the chapter presents more recent models that use linguistic information at different stages of phrase-based approaches, including pre- and post-processing stages. The chapter also describes more advanced hierarchical and syntax-based and discriminative models. It also gives an overview of popular metrics for automatic evaluation of SMT systems. The chapter concludes by providing a number of future research directions in this field.

This chapter outlines a computational framework for a cognitive model of human translation. The authors investigate the structure of the translators' keystrokes and gaze data, discuss possibilities for their classification and visualization, and explain how a translation model can be grounded and trained on the empirical user activity data. This chapter starts by outlining the current translation process theories. Then it describes the translators' user activity data. The chapter then introduces translation progression graphs, a visualization method, and discusses the coarse structure of human translation processes. The next section looks into more details of the user activity data, their segmentation, and classification. The chapter then provides an overview of cognitive architectures. Two models of human translation processes, one based on ACT-R and the other a statistical approach, are then discussed.

This chapter presents a paradigm for advanced question answering, which mainly includes how-to, why, evaluative, comparative, and opinion questions. The first part of the chapter discusses the different parameters at stake in answer production, involving several aspects of cooperation. The second part discusses text semantics aspects relevant for answering questions. The last part of this chapter introduces <TextCoop>, a platform for discourse semantics analysis for answering complex questions, in particular how-to and opinion questions.

Chapter 7

Natalia Konstantinova, University of Wolverhampton, UK
Constantin Orasan, University of Wolverhampton, UK

This chapter presents the state-of-the-art in the field of Interactive Question Answering (IQA). It also briefly presents dialogue systems and question answering, since IQA inherits a lot of features from them. The chapter starts with a description of the characteristics of human dialogues and the basic concepts behind dialogue systems, followed by a brief introduction of question answering focusing on the concepts that are used in IQA. Then it presents the most important approaches used by the IQA systems and the challenges in evaluating such systems. The chapter finishes with a description of some large projects that developed and integrated IQA features.

Section 4
Multilingual Information Access

Chapter 8

Vasudeva Varma, IIIT Hyderabad, India
Aditya Mogadala, IIIT Hyderabad, India

This chapter starts with a discussion highlighting the importance of cross-lingual and multilingual information retrieval and information access. The chapter then discusses the distinctions between Cross-Lingual Information Retrieval (CLIR), Multilingual Information Retrieval (MLIR), Cross-Lingual Information Access (CLIA), and Multilingual Information Access (MLIA). The chapter subsequently outlines issues and challenges in these areas and various approaches, including machine learning-based and knowledge-based approaches, to multilingual information access. It also describes various subsystems of an MLIA system ranging from query processing to output generation. Then evaluation aspects of the MLIA and CLIA systems are discussed at the end of the chapter.

Chapter 9

Víctor Peinado, ETSI Informática, Spain
Álvaro Rodrigo, ETSI Informática, Spain
Fernando López-Ostenero, ETSI Informática, Spain

This chapter focuses on Multilingual Information Access (MLIA), a multidisciplinary area that aims to solve accessing, querying, and retrieving information from heterogeneous information sources expressed in different languages. The chapter starts by presenting the idea of an information retrieval system supporting MLIA, breaking up the three different stages a Cross-Language Information Retrieval system is made up of, namely: (1) processing and indexing the document collection; (2) translation and techniques to overcome the language gap; and (3) matching queries and documents. It also provides details about difficulties and problems dealing with multiple languages. The subsequent section focuses on Question Answering, a more sophisticated form of IR systems, along with the most successful cross-lingual approaches reported in the field. Then it presents a user's perspective with the difficulties associated to conduct and evaluate user-centered experiments: the most relevant results on interactive TREC and CLEF, along with an introduction to user-generated search logs analysis.

Section 5
Digital Content Management

Chapter 10

Rafael E. Banchs, Institute for Infocomm Research, Singapore
Carlos G. Rodríguez Penagos, Barcelona Media Innovation Centre, Spain

This chapter presents a general overview of the most relevant applications of text mining and natural language processing technologies evolving and emerging around the Web 2.0 phenomenon along with the main challenges and new research opportunities that are directly and indirectly derived from them. The chapter starts with providing definitions and general discussions on social media and user-generated content analysis. Some fundamental issues regarding Web 2.0, social media, and natural language processing technologies are covered. Then it presents the main issues and technical challenges related to processing user-generated content in the context of the Web 2.0, namely encoding, chatspeak, emoticons, ungrammaticality, normalization, co-referencing, spamming, multilingualism, communication structure, and user roles. It also discusses the important point of deciding how much natural language processing is warranted for each task, and when the emerging regularities in vast amounts of data allow for the use of language-independent statistical methods. Next, it presents applications related to user-generated content analysis. These applications include: automatic categorization, document summarization, question answering, dialogue systems, opinion mining and sentiment analysis, outlier identification and misbehavior detection, and social estimation and forecasting. Then, it presents a section on future trends and research opportunities related to processing and analysis of user-generated content in the context of Web 2.0. The chapter concludes with a discussion of ethical and legal issues concerning privacy and proprietary rights that arise when processing and using user-generated content.

Chapter 11

Lyne Da Sylva, University of Montreal, Canada

This chapter describes the issues relating to the task of managing a digital library, explores various NLP applications, which can be applied to the task, and identifies new research problems related to these issues.

Section 6
Speech Processing

Chapter 12

Preety Singh, Malaviya National Institute of Technology, India
Vijay Laxmi, Malaviya National Institute of Technology, India
M. S. Gaur, Malaviya National Institute of Technology, India

This chapter discusses audio-visual speech recognition, an emerging research topic. The chapter describes in detail the various steps involved in the processing of the audio and visual cues for better recognition. It first discusses speech processing using audio signal only. Then it concentrates on the various steps involved in visual signal processing, including face detection, lip segmentation, and extraction of lip features. Subsequently, it discusses the recognition methods that are usually employed for classification of these two types of signals, and the fusion of the audio and visual streams. The chapter also provides a brief discussion on some of the available audio-visual databases. The authors then present their proposed methodology for a visual speech recognition system. They conclude the chapter by mentioning the factors affecting the performance of lip-reading.

Foreword

It is my great pleasure to write a few remarks about this wonderful collection of very timely and significant chapters on Natural Language Processing (NLP), covering both the research directions and the emerging applications of NLP. The editors (Sivaji Bandyopadhyay (SB), Sudip Kumar Naskar (SKN), and Asif Ekbal (AE), have provided us with a collection of very timely and comprehensive chapters on many of the key aspects of NLP written by a set of international scholars, who are active in their respective sub-areas of NLP. The areas covered in this volume, such as Text Analysis, Machine Translation, Question Answering Systems, Content Management, and Speech Processing, very nicely survey the current major NLP research and development areas. From this perspective, this collection is being published just at the right time! The editors (SB, SKN, and AE) have also provided us with a very helpful preface useful for active researchers as well as for those who are planning to enter this very exciting field. They are to be congratulated for undertaking the very significant task of presenting this volume to all of us in the NLP community.

Aravind K. Joshi
University of Pennsylvania, USA
February 23, 2012

Aravind K. Joshi *is the Henry Salvatori Professor of Computer and Cognitive Science in the Department of Computer and Information Science at the University of Pennsylvania. He received his Ph.D. in Electrical Engineering from the University of Pennsylvania in 1960. His early research was in information theory and communication theory. Since 1958, he has been working almost continuously on problems that overlap computer science and linguistics. Much of this research can be classified under formal linguistics, natural language processing, artificial intelligence, and cognitive science. In his professional career, he has been in many responsible positions, such as the Chair of the Department of Computer and Information Science, University of Pennsylvania (1972-1985), Co-Director, Institute for Research in Cognitive Science, University of Pennsylvania. His professional awards include the Life Time Achievement Award from ACL, Research Excellence Award from IJCAI, Honorary Doctorate from University of Paris, and the Franklin Medal for Cognitive Science, among others. He was elected fellow of both the IEEE and ACM, member of the advisory panel of NSF, fellow of the AAAI, and member of the International Joint Committee of Computational Linguistics (COLING).*

Preface

Natural Language Processing (NLP) deals with computational techniques to fully automate any kind of human-like processing of natural language content. The field of NLP has witnessed a phenomenal growth of interest in recent years, both in the academic research space and in the industry scene; the NLP research and development community is thriving today. Important applications of NLP include Machine Translation, Question-Answering, Information Retrieval, Information Extraction, Summarization, Dialogue Systems, Speech Processing, Word Sense Disambiguation, Sentiment and Emotion Analysis, Text Mining, etc. A comprehensive account of all NLP methodologies and applications is beyond the scope of any textbook. In this edited volume, some of the important applications of NLP have been discussed.

It has been observed during several years of teaching and research and development in NLP that some areas of NLP are slowly maturing themselves. These research topics have attracted huge interests, resulted in new workshops and evaluation tracks, and contributed significantly in terms of research publications in recent NLP conferences and journals. However, there are hardly any books collating related readings on such research topics, other than journal publications, workshop / conference proceedings, and evaluation track notes. This book aims to provide relevant theoretical frameworks and the latest empirical research findings in the emerging areas of NLP. Future research directions along with an extensive reference sections on each research topic have also been included.

This edited volume is intended for established NLP researchers who want to improve their understanding of the state-of-the-art in NLP and broaden their research spheres, as well as information-hungry budding researchers looking for related information. The main beneficiary will be the postgraduate and doctoral students' community who have just stepped into the world of NLP research and are looking for new research problems. A basic background in computational linguistics is expected.

The volume has been divided into six sections. Section 1 contains chapters on text analytics. Section 2 has been devoted to machine translation. Section 3 deals with advanced question answering, while Section 4 presents works on multilingual information access. Digital content management is discussed in Section 5. Finally, Section 6 is on speech processing.

Alexander Gelbukh and Olga Kolesnikova present a survey of contemporary NLP research on Multiword Expressions (MWEs) in Chapter 1. MWEs pose a huge problem to precise language processing due to their idiosyncratic nature and diversity of their semantic, lexical, and syntactical properties. The chapter begins by considering MWE definitions, describes some MWE classes, indicates problems MWEs generate in language applications and their possible solutions, presents methods of MWE encoding in dictionaries and their automatic detection in corpora. The chapter goes into more detail on a particular MWE class called Verb-Noun Constructions (VNCs). Due to their frequency in corpus and unique characteristics, VNCs present a research problem in their own right. Having outlined several approaches to VNC representation in lexicons, the chapter explains the formalism of Lexical Function as a possible VNC representation. Such representation may serve as a tool for VNCs automatic detection in a corpus. The latter is illustrated on Spanish material applying some supervised learning methods commonly used for NLP tasks.

In Chapter 2, Pushpak Bhattacharyya and Mitesh Khapra present the basic concepts of Word Sense Disambiguation (WSD) and discuss different approaches to solving this problem. The chapter discusses both general purpose WSD and domain specific WSD. The first part of the chapter focuses on existing approaches to WSD, including knowledge-based, supervised, semi-supervised, unsupervised, hybrid, and bilingual approaches. The latter part of the chapter presents a greedy neural network inspired algorithm for domain specific WSD and compares its performance with other state of the art algorithms for WSD.

In Chapter 3, Miriam Lúcia Domingues and Eloi Luiz Favero discuss different approaches to tackling the problem of domain adaptation for part-of-speech tagging and present a case study that has achieved significant accuracy rates on tagging journalistic and scientific texts.

Lucia Specia provides a comprehensive account of Statistical Machine Translation (SMT) in Chapter 4. The chapter introduces the rationale behind SMT, describes the state-of-the-art approaches in SMT, and presents a number of emerging approaches (tree-based SMT, discriminative SMT). The chapter starts with the word-based approach to SMT that forms the basis for more advanced approaches. The general phrase-based approach is discussed along with a number of components that are commonly used within this approach and the standard algorithms used to perform translation (decoding) as well as to estimate the weights of the model components (tuning). Then the chapter presents more recent models that use linguistic information at different stages of phrase-based approaches, including pre- and post-processing stages. The chapter also describes more advanced hierarchical and syntax-based and discriminative models. It also gives an overview of popular metrics for automatic evaluation of SMT systems. The chapter concludes by providing a number of future research directions in this field.

Michael Carl outlines a computational framework for a cognitive model of human translation in Chapter 5. The author investigates the structure of the translators' keystrokes and gaze data, discusses possibilities for their classification and visualization, and explains how a translation model can be grounded and trained on the empirical user activity data. This chapter starts by outlining the current translation process theories. Then it describes the translators' user activity data. The chapter then introduces translation progression graphs, a visualization method, and discusses the coarse structure of human translation processes. The next section looks into more details of the user activity data, their segmentation, and classification. The chapter then provides an overview of cognitive architectures. Two models of human translation processes, one based on ACT-R and the other a statistical approach, are then discussed.

In Chapter 6, Patrick Saint-Dizier presents a paradigm for advanced question answering, which mainly includes how-to, why, evaluative, comparative, and opinion questions. These types of questions require quite a lot of discourse semantics analysis and domain knowledge. The first part of the chapter discusses the different parameters at stake in answer production, involving several aspects of cooperation. The second part discusses the text semantics aspects relevant for answering questions. The last part of this chapter introduces <TextCoop>, a platform for discourse semantics analysis for answering complex questions, in particular how-to and opinion questions.

Natalia Konstantinova and Constantin Orasan present the state-of-the-art in the field of Interactive Question Answering (IQA) in Chapter 7. The chapter also briefly presents dialogue systems and question answering, since IQA inherits a lot of features from them. The chapter starts with a description of the characteristics of human dialogues and the basic concepts behind dialogue systems, followed by a brief introduction to question answering, focusing on the concepts that are used in IQA. Then it presents the most important approaches used by the IQA systems and the challenges in evaluating such systems. The chapter finishes with a description of some large projects, which developed and integrated IQA features.

A large variety of research challenges related to advanced question answering have been presented in Chapter 6. The author focuses on mainly two emerging areas, i.e., developing informative and cooperative answers and using accurate discourse analysis in order to be able to identify well-formed text portions, which are the answer to those questions. These two areas will remain quite challenging for a number of years, in spite of the rapid evolution of the language processing technology. The main focus in Chapter 7 is on Interactive Question Answering (IQA) that has emerged as a research field at the intersection of question answering and dialogue systems, and which allows users to find the answers to questions in an interactive way. The dialogue system plays an important role in IQA, and it initiates dialogues with the user in order to clarify missing or ambiguous information, or suggest further topics for discussion.

Vasudeva Varma and Aditya Mogadala present an account of the issues and challenges in building multilingual information access systems in Chapter 8. The chapter starts with a discussion highlighting the importance of cross-lingual and multilingual information retrieval and information access. The chapter then discusses the distinctions between Cross-Lingual Information Retrieval (CLIR), Multilingual Information Retrieval (MLIR), Cross-Lingual Information Access (CLIA), and Multilingual Information Access (MLIA). The authors subsequently outline issues and challenges in these areas and various approaches, including machine learning-based and knowledge-based approaches, to multilingual information access. It also describes various components of an MLIA system ranging from query processing to output generation. Then evaluation aspects of the MLIA and CLIA systems are discussed at the end of the chapter.

In Chapter 9, Víctor Peinado, Álvaro Rodrigo, and Fernando López-Ostenero survey Multilingual Information Access (MLIA), a multidisciplinary area which aims to solve accessing, querying, and retrieving information from heterogeneous information sources expressed in different languages. The chapter starts by presenting the idea of an Information Retrieval system supporting MLIA, breaking up the three different stages of the Cross-Language Information Retrieval system, namely: (1) processing and indexing the document collection; (2) translation and techniques to overcome the language gap; and (3) matching queries and documents. It also provides details about the difficulties and problems when dealing with multiple languages. The subsequent section focuses on Multilingual Question Answering, a more sophisticated form of IR systems, along with the most successful cross-lingual approaches reported in the field. Then the authors present interactive information retrieval from the user's perspective with the difficulties associated to conduct and evaluate user-centered experiments: the most relevant results on interactive TREC and CLEF, along with an introduction on user-generated search logs analysis.

While Chapter 8 discusses the issues and challenges in MLIA, Chapter 9 focuses on system architectures that perform Information Retrieval involving MLIA. Chapter 9 also presents Multilingual Question Answering and Interactive Information Retrieval to satisfy users' information needs.

In Chapter 10, Rafael E. Banchs and Carlos G. Rodríguez Penagos present a detailed introductory account of the most relevant applications of text mining and natural language processing technologies evolving and emerging around the Web 2.0 phenomenon along with the main challenges and new research opportunities that are directly and indirectly derived from them. The chapter starts with providing definitions and general discussions on social media and user-generated content analysis. Some fundamental issues regarding Web 2.0, social media, and natural language processing technologies are covered. Then it presents the main issues and technical challenges related to processing user-generated content in the context of the Web 2.0, namely encoding, chatspeak, emoticons, ungrammaticality, normalization, co-referencing, spamming, multilingualism, communication structure, and user roles. It also discusses the important point of deciding how much natural language processing is warranted for each task, and when the emerging regularities in vast amounts of data allow for the use of language-independent statistical methods. Next, the authors present applications related to user-generated content analysis. These applications include automatic categorization, document summarization, question answering, dialogue systems, opinion mining and sentiment analysis, outlier identification and misbehavior detection, and social estimation and forecasting. Then, the chapter presents a section on future trends and research opportunities related to processing and analysis of user-generated content in the context of Web 2.0. The chapter concludes with a discussion on ethical and legal issues concerning privacy and proprietary rights that arise when processing and using user-generated content.

Lyne Da Sylva offers a detailed overview of digital library management in the perspective of NLP in Chapter 11. The chapter describes the issues relating to the task of managing a digital library, explores various NLP applications, which can be applied to the task, and identifies new research problems related to these issues.

Preety Singh, V. Laxmi, and M. S. Gaur conclude the volume with a presentation on audio-visual speech recognition, an emerging research topic, in Chapter 12. The chapter describes in detail the various steps involved in the processing of audio and visual cues for better recognition. It first discusses speech processing using audio signal only. Then it concentrates on the various steps involved in visual signal processing, including face detection, lip segmentation, and extraction of lip features. Subsequently, it discusses the recognition methods that are usually employed for classification of these two types of signals, and the fusion of the audio and visual streams. The chapter also provides a brief discussion of some of the available audio-visual databases. The authors then present their proposed methodology for a visual speech recognition system. They conclude the chapter by mentioning the factors affecting the performance of lip-reading.

Each chapter included in this edited volume reports a detailed literature survey and provides information about existing techniques, including the state-of-the-art, tools, evaluation tracks, and shared tasks organized on the specific NLP topic discussed. It is expected that early career researchers will find the chapters informative and useful and asa gateway to the world of NLP.

Sivaji Bandyopadhyay
Jadavpur University, India

Sudip Kumar Naskar
Dublin City University, Ireland

Asif Ekbal
University of Heidelberg, Germany

Section 1
Text Analytics

Chapter 1
Multiword Expressions in NLP:
General Survey and a Special Case
of Verb–Noun Constructions

Alexander Gelbukh
National Polytechnic Institute, Mexico

Olga Kolesnikova
National Polytechnic Institute, Mexico

ABSTRACT

This chapter presents a survey of contemporary NLP research on Multiword Expressions (MWEs). MWEs pose a huge problem to precise language processing due to their idiosyncratic nature and diversity of their semantic, lexical, and syntactical properties. The chapter begins by considering MWEs definitions, describes some MWEs classes, indicates problems MWEs generate in language applications and their possible solutions, presents methods of MWE encoding in dictionaries and their automatic detection in corpora. The chapter goes into more detail on a particular MWE class called Verb-Noun Constructions (VNCs). Due to their frequency in corpus and unique characteristics, VNCs present a research problem in their own right. Having outlined several approaches to VNC representation in lexicons, the chapter explains the formalism of Lexical Function as a possible VNC representation. Such representation may serve as a tool for VNCs automatic detection in a corpus. The latter is illustrated on Spanish material applying some supervised learning methods commonly used for NLP tasks.

1. INTRODUCTION

Many NLP applications deal with a natural language text as a "bag of words" where each string of letters between spaces, or a token, is viewed as an individual word associated with its proper semantics and syntactical functions. In *John sud-* denly kicked the ball, the tokens *John, suddenly, kicked, the, ball*, are words contributing their own meaning to the overall meaning of the utterance. Thus, the semantics of the whole utterance is a composition or a "sum" of elementary meanings conveyed by each word in the utterance. However, the semantics of *John suddenly kicked the bucket*

DOI: 10.4018/978-1-4666-2169-5.ch001

cannot be considered a "sum" of elementary meanings represented by individual words. Although *kicked the bucket* consists of three words, this expression functions semantically as one word denoting the meaning *died*. Phrases like *kick the bucket*, *put on airs*, *bee in bonnet*, *up the creek* are called phraseological expressions, or idioms. Such linguistic phenomenon presents a challenge for natural language processing because they cannot be interpreted by a fully compositional analysis. The degree of cohesiveness between words in idioms is very high; the choice of such words is unmotivated and therefore cannot be predicted. For this reason, idioms are better viewed as a single word.

Sometimes, the degree of cohesiveness in expressions is not so strong as in idioms, and the semantics of a phrase is more transparent, though not completely clear, for example, for non-native speakers or language learners. *Mailing list*, *sign up*, *traffic light*, *kindle excitement* belong to such expressions. It has been a trend in NLP to group expressions with varying degree of cohesiveness under a single term "Multiword Expressions" (MWEs).

The main characteristic of MWEs is a lack of compositionality, though other features are put forward in alternative definitions of MWEs mentioned in Section 2. Section 3 presents MWEs classification, Section 4 discusses some problems posed by MWEs in NLP and their possible solutions. In Section 5, MWEs resources are described alongside with different encoding used to represent MWEs features in such resources. In Section 6, we consider statistic, rule-based and hybrid approaches to MWE automatic detection as well as evaluation methods used to estimate performance of MWE extraction techniques. Section 7 gives more detail on Verb-Noun Constructions (VNCs). Due to their frequency in corpus and unique characteristics, VNCs present a research problem in its own right. Having outlined several approaches to VNC representation in lexicons, Section 7 goes on explaining the formalism of Lexical Function as a

possible VNC representation. Such representation may serve as a tool for VNC's automatic detection in a corpus. Section 8 illustrates the latter on Spanish material referring to results showed by some well-known supervised learning methods on the task of VNC automatic recognition while VNC was represented by means of the lexical function formalism. Section 9 concludes the chapter.

2. DEFINITIONS

Although MWEs are understood quite easily by intuition and their acquisition presents no difficulty to native speakers (though it is usually not the case for second language learners), it is hard to identify what features distinguish MWEs from free word combinations. Concerning this issue, such MWE properties are mentioned in literature: reduced syntactic and semantic transparency; reduced or lack of compositionality; more or less frozen or fixed status; possible violation of some otherwise general syntactic patterns or rules; a high degree of lexicalization (depending on pragmatic factors); a high degree of conventionality (Calzolari, Fillmore, Grishman, Ide, Lenci, MacLeod, & Zampolli, 2002).

No convention exists so far on the definition of MWEs but almost all formulations found in research papers emphasize the idiosyncratic nature of this linguistic phenomenon. Here are some definitions that are most frequently referred to in papers; we marked in boldface those concepts and properties that we think serve as the criteria for distinguishing MWE from compositional phrases:

- MWE are "recurrent combinations of words that co-occur more often than expected by chance and that correspond to arbitrary word usages" (Smadja, 1993);
- MWE are "idiosyncratic interpretations that cross word boundaries (or spaces)" (Sag, Baldwin, Bond, Copestake, & Flickinger, 2002);

- MWE are "a sequence of words that acts as a single unit at some level of linguistic analysis,. ... they are usually instances of well productive syntactic patterns which nevertheless exhibit a peculiar lexical behavior" (Calzolari, et al., 2002);
- "An MWE is composed of two or more words that together form a single unit of meaning, e.g., *frying pan*, *take a stroll*, and *kick the bucket*. Semantic idiosyncrasy, i.e., the overall meaning of an MWE diverges from the combined contribution of its constituent parts" (Fazly & Stevenson, 2007);
- "We take idiomaticity as the key feature for the definition and classification of MWE. Idiomaticity could be described as a nondiscrete magnitude, whose "value," has turned to depend on a complex combination of features such as institutionalization, noncompositionality and lexico-syntactic fixedness" (Gurrutxaga & Alegria, 2011).

3. MWE CLASSES

MWEs include a vast dominion of diverse language expressions. It was mentioned in Section 2 that it is problematic to lay strict borders to the MWE realm. Structural, semantic, and lexical diversity also makes it difficult to elaborate a complete and comprehensive MWE classification which could generalize and embrace all MWE instances, that is why researches usually speak of "some" MWE classes and types not daring to suggest an "overall" typology.

We have considered various MWE classifications and made an attempt to collate them in a single scheme presented further in this section taking the taxonomy in Sag *et al.* (2002) as a basic framework. MWE classes are illustrated with examples, no explanation is given due to space

limits, but definition and detailed discussion of MWE classes can be found in papers referenced in this section. Here we mention the following classes:

- Lexicalized phrases:
  - Fixed expressions: *by and large*, *in short*, *kingdom come*, *ad hoc*, including conjunctions (*as well as*) and prepositions (*in front of*, *next to*)
  - Semi-fixed expressions (see below)
  - Syntactically-flexible expressions (see below)
- Institutionalized phrases: *traffic light*, *fresh air*, *kindle excitement* (described accurately in Agirre, Aldezabal, & Pociello, 2006).

Semi-fixed expressions can be further classified into the following classes:

- Nondecomposable idioms
  - Opaque idioms *(kick the bucket, shoot the breeze)*
  - Figurative idioms *(rack one's brain)*
- Certain compound nominals, or noun compounds
  - nominals: *car park*, *attorney general*; see subtypes in Calzolari *et al.* (2002)
- Proper names or named entities (other than compound nominals): *the San Francisco 49ers*

Syntactically-flexible expressions can in turn be classified into the following classes:

- Verb-particle constructions or phrasal verbs: *write up, find out*
- Decomposable idioms: *let the cat out of the bag*
- Verb-noun constructions: *give confidence, make a living* (further classification according to the level of compositionality

by Fazly and Stevenson [2007]; alternative classification by Diab and Bhutada [2009]).

- Collocations. This category intersects with verb-noun constructions. The latter in fact are collocations of the syntactical pattern.

  ○ According to syntactic structure, collocations are classified into groups sharing the same pattern, e.g., "adjective as modifier + noun," "verb + noun as direct object" (verb-noun constructions in 1.3.3), "verb + adverb."

  ○ According to the degree of compositionality, collocations are classified into semi-compositional combinations and compositional combinations with lexical restriction. The former are combinations in which the noun keeps its literal meaning, whereas the verb acts as a support verb (*to make a decision*) or has a meaning which is specific to that combination (*to launch a project*). The latter are combinations in which it is not possible to substitute the verb with its synonyms, or that present a clear statistical idiosyncrasy in favor of a given synonym choice (*to express solidarity, to confirm a commitment*).

  ○ According to the level of abstraction, collocations are classified into grammatical collocations (consist of a content word and a preposition, infinitive, clause, etc., e.g., report to, coincident with, a proposal that) and lexical collocations (consist of more than one content words, e.g., decomposable idioms in 1.3.2).

The categories of opaque idioms, figurative idioms, collocations are presented in Gurrutxaga and Alegria (2011). Details on the dichotomy of grammatical and lexical collocations can be found in Benson, Benson, and Ilson (1986). Lexical representation of Verb-Noun Constructions (VNC) and their subclasses are discussed in more detail in Section 7. Section 8 presents our experimental results on VNC classification applying supervised machine learning methods. The experiments were carried out on Spanish text documents.

4. PROBLEMS AND POSSIBLE SOLUTIONS

Apart from the problem of identifying clear boundaries that distinguish MWEs from free word combinations, MWEs pose such difficult problems for computational processing so that Sag *et al.* (2002) call MWEs "a pain in the neck for NLP."

Two principal approaches are applied to interpret MWEs in NLP: compositional analysis and word-with-spaces analysis. However, compositional methods of linguistic analysis do not have power to grasp the idiosyncratic nature of MWEs completely thus producing two principal problems.

Firstly, text generation system will suffer overgeneration problem (Sag, et al., 2002). For example, the rule "adjective + noun" will produce normal combinations like *big house, heavy bag, high mountain*, but it will also generate grammatically correct combinations *big rain, *heavy temperature, *high number*. The solution is to build filters for eliminating phrases, which do not agree with lexical choices, restrictions, and frequencies characteristic for MWEs. Taking the above examples into account, the output of a filtering module must be only *heavy rain, high temperature, big number*. For verbal expressions in medical domain, Xiao & Rösner (2004) suggested to evaluate a proper multiword verb candidate based on the domain-specific named entity knowledge, syntactic and statistical information. Chikara (2004) proposed to elaborate a more fine-grained typology of verbal compounds according to their linguistic properties and specify verbal classes in syntactic patterns for generation.

Secondly, fully compositional analysis is obstructed by the idiomaticity problem: how to predict, for example, that the grammatically well-formed expression *kick the bucket* has a meaning unrelated to the meanings of *kick*, *the*, and *bucket*. The simplest solution is to make an entry for each idiom in a lexicon presenting it as words-with-spaces. However, this method does not capture MWE variability and lacks generalization. On the other hand, Deksne, Skadiņš, and Skadiņa (2008) suggest to generalize MWEs syntactic structures and morphological restrictions on their constituents in various rules. One rule is capable to describe ten, hundreds or even thousands of items. However, some rules are complicated and require a lot of manual work for their construction. Diaconescu (2004) shows how the idiomaticity problem can be treated using Generative Dependency Grammar with Features. Sag *et al.* (2002) attempt to resolve the same problem on the basis of the constraint-based Head-driven Phrase Structure Grammar (HPSG) formalism. Ramisch, Villavicencio, Moura, and Idiart (2008) show on the material of verb-particle combinations that MWE statistical properties together with their linguistic properties can be used to distinguish idiomaticity from compositional cases.

Word-with-spaces analysis mentioned in the previous paragraph is another approach to MWEs processing which treat them as one word. For example, in WordNet 1.7 (Fellbaum, 1998), 41% of the entries are multiword (cited from Sag, et al., 2002). Although simple string-type listing of MWEs in a dictionary fails to capture MWE variability and is unable to recognize MWE morphological and syntactic modifications, it is appropriate for fixed MWEs like *ad hoc*, *by and large*, *in the main* (Hore, Asahara, & Matsumoto, 2005).

A vivid interest to MWE problems in academic NLP research as well as in language processing software development has been the driving force in organizing annual workshops dedicated to a wide range of MWEs endorsed by the Special Interest Group on the Lexicon of the Association for Computational Linguistics (SIGLEX). Since 2003 up to present, MWE workshops have been an authoritative forum for NLP researchers working on this topic around the world, and the proceedings are published on the MWE Workshop website (see References). NLP-oriented journals publish special issues on the MWE problems, for example, a special MWE issue of *Computer Speech and Language* (Volume 19 Issue 4, October, 2005) included 10 articles. Researchers are eager to elaborate MWE solutions in languages other than English such as Basque (Alegria, Ansa, Xabier, Ezeiza, Gojenola, & Urizar, 2004), Bengali (Chakraborty, Das, & Bandyopadhyay, 2011), Chinese (Piao, Sun, Rayson, & Yuan, 2006), Dutch (Grégoire, 2007), Italian (Calzolari, et al., 2002), Portuguese (Villavicencio, Ramisch, Machado, de Medeiros Caseli, & Finatto, 2010), and Japanese (Baldwin & Bond, 2002), among others.

5. SOME MWE ENCODINGS AND RESOURCES

It will not be overestimating to say that all researches agree with the importance of finding adequate means to represent MWEs in lexicons and of building MWE repositories accessible by NLP techniques. Yet no single approach to MWE encodings in such lexicons is acknowledged to be most appropriate for dealing with MWE in natural language research and applications. A number of MWE encodings have been suggested that include Frame Semantics, Generative Lexicon, Lexical Functions and Lexical Conceptual Structure.

Frame semantics (Fillmore & Baker, 2001) associates a word with other relevant concepts (world knowledge) which form the word's background scene or frame indispensable for understanding what the word means. The famous example *kick the bucket* is listed as a lexical unit and indexed as DEATH-concept together with *asphyxiate.v, croak it.v, croak.v, death.n, decease.v, demise.n, die.v, drown.v, expire.v, kick the bucket.v, mortality.n, pass away.v, perish.v, starvation.n, starve.v, suffocate.v, suffocation.n, terminator.n.* The words in this frame describe the death of a Protagonist. A Cause of DEATH may also be expressed obliquely. For comparison, let us view the entry for *kick the bucket* in WordNet 2.1 (2005) where it is placed together with its synonyms, the gloss and examples: *die, decease, perish, go, exit, pass away, expire, pass, kick the bucket, cash in one's chips, buy the farm, conk, give-up the ghost, drop dead, pop off, choke, croak, snuff it* (pass from physical life and lose all bodily attributes and functions necessary to sustain life; "She died from cancer"; "The children perished in the fire"; "The patient went peacefully"; "The old guy kicked the bucket at the age of 102"). Its hypernyms are *change state, turn,* and *change.* The advantage of FrameNet is that similar concepts expressed by nouns are located together with the verbs of the same idea and semantic roles are indicated. This makes it easier to recognize MWEs in syntactical patterns. However, WordNet lists more MWEs with the meaning *die* though without specifying if these expressions can or cannot occur in varying syntactic structures.

Another representation method is suggested in Generative Lexicon (Pustejovsky, 1995) whose purpose is to encode selectional knowledge in a language. The encoding comprised of four elements: lexical typing structure, argument structure, event structure, and qualia structure. This type of encoding has been used in SIMPLE lexicons (Lenci, et al., 2000) where lexical entry includes information on typical collocations. EAGLES (Expert Advisory Group for Language Engineering Standards) initiative (Calzolari, McNaught, & Zampolli, 1996) and subsequent ISLE (International Standards for Language Engineering) project (Calzolari, Zampolli, & Lenci, 2002) have the objective of developing multilingual computational lexicons according to specified representation standards for MWE (Calzolari, et al., 2002; Calzolari, 2004). Likewise, the XMELLT

(Cross-lingual Multi-word Expression Lexicons for Language Technology) project (Calzolari, et al., 2002) attempts to design the guidelines for MWE lexicographic representation, but up to now no common standard has been accepted in NLP community.

Lexical Function (LF) is an alternative MWE representation (Mel'čuk, 1996). It is a mapping from the MWE headword to the semantically dependant constituent. Lexical function is a formalism, which attempts to encapsulate semantic and syntactic structure of MWEs. For example, LF Magn has the value of *dark* for *night, high* for *temperature, heavy* for *rain,* or using LF notation, Magn(*night*) = *dark,* Magn(*temperature*) = *high,* Magn(*rain*) = *heavy.* The meaning of Magn (from Latin *magnus* 'big,' 'great') is *intensive,* and all MWEs have the syntactic structure 'adjective + noun.' Note that different nouns choose unpredictably different words in the same semantic function as intensifier.

Lexical Conceptual Structure (Jackendoff, 1990) is another attempt to incorporate lexical, semantic, and pragmatic data with world knowledge. It is based on language-independent features and therefore can serve as interlingual representation of text meaning applicable for example in machine translation. It has been developed to explain varieties of linguistic phenomena including lexical derivations, the construction of compounds and verb alteration.

Finally it could be noted, that all representations considered in this section are capable of encoding different but significant lexical and syntactic aspects of MWEs, so the objective of finding an appropriate MWE representation which absorbs every advantage of existing encodings is another important issue in MWE research.

6. MWE AUTOMATIC DETECTION

The task of MWE automatic detection attracts attention of computational linguists and natural language engineers both as an independent problem in its own right and as a subtask for resolving other issues including semantic role labeling, word sense disambiguation, POS-tagging, parsing, machine translation, information retrieval, and others. Usually, the task is formulated as a binary classification problem, i.e., the class variable is assigned two values: MWE or non-MWE.

Although MWE has no "standard" definition accepted by the whole linguistic and NLP community, it has been implicitly agreed, for practical purposes of automatic detection, that the principal feature distinguishing MWEs from free word combinations is a special type of relation between MWE components termed in some papers as institutionalized relations. The same idea is expressed when the main MWE characteristic is said to be institutionalization.

Institutionalized relations are modeled statistically and measured using various metrics that aim to estimate the strength of association between MWE components. Evidently, these cooccurrence techniques will produce higher values if a group of words is a MWE, and lower values in case of free word combinations. It is not rare to observe that some authors do not argue on theoretical principles of MWE definition or simply skip the topic; nevertheless, it becomes clear that when they make their choice of a particular association measure to be employed in the extraction process, they implicitly acknowledge that institutionalization is the critical and decisive MWE feature.

As a rule, the process of MWE automatic detection is accomplished in two stages. First, MWE candidates are extracted using an association measure or a combination of association measures. Then, the obtained candidate phrases are checked if they are MWE and the precision of the extraction method used is evaluated. Now, we will consider each of two stages separately and discuss various ways of extracting and evaluating MWEs.

6.1. Extraction: Statistical Methods

Like for any NLP task, MWEs extraction begins with developing a new MWE model or adopting an existing one. Statistical models are most commonly used language models in computational projects because they use raw corpora where a selected language unit (word, type or lemma, phrase, sentence, document) is viewed as a data item. Statistical modeling is attractive since conclusions are derived out of data in a way that seems much more objective, and thus scientific, than linguistic interpretations and theories based on a linguistic expert's introspection and intuition. Moreover, statistical analysis is language-independent.

However, statistical methods work under certain assumptions, for example, that data items "obey" certain well-studied distributions, for example, normal, binomial, χ^2 or other. We do not know actually how real life linguistic data is distributed but in any case our mathematical constructs can be justified by the golden principle of pragmatics: it works therefore it is true. Without further philosophical discussion, we will consider statistical metrics most effectively used for MWE detection, namely, mutual information, log-likelihood ratio, and φ^2 statistic. All these measures test independence of word occurrences.

In many cases, before calculating a predetermined association measure, n-grams are extracted from corpus. Usually, they are word combinations of a chosen syntactic pattern, e.g., "adjective + noun," or "verb + preposition" depending on the preferred MWE structural type. In order to do this, corpus is lemmatized, POS-tagged and/or parsed. Evidently, this preprocessing is language-dependent. Another feature used for n-grams extraction is window size, typically from ±1 to ±5.

After n-grams are extracted, the association strength between constituents is computed according to some statistical metric. Such metrics used in MWE extraction process are termed association measures because they compute the degree of cohesion or association between MWE components.

A comprehensive list of 82 association measures can be found in Pecina and Schlesinger (2006), and of 84 measures (Pecina, 2008). The latter papers are best works known to summarize statistical tests unitized in MWE detection.

In this chapter, we will consider three association measures known to be very effective in MWE identification. We provide formulas and explanation for the case of two-word MWEs, but they can be easily generalized to MWEs of more components. All three metrics test independence of word occurrences. For the purpose of such statistical analysis, words (w_1 and w_2) in bigrams (remember, the formulae can be generalized to n words) are viewed as two random discrete variables. The next step is to put forward two hypotheses: the null hypothesis (w_1 and w_2 are independent and cooccur by chance, in other words, their co-occurrence is statistically insignificant) and the MWE hypothesis (w_1 and w_2 are MWE components).

In these statistical tests, the following data is taken into account: frequency $f(w)$, is the number of occurrences of word w in a corpus; probability $P(w)$ is frequency $f(w)$ compared with the corpus size N (number of language units, i.e., tokens, types, sentences, documents, etc.). Therefore, $P(w) = f(w)/N$. Frequencies observed for each combination of w_1 and w_2 are organized in a contingency table. The term *contingency table* was first used by Karl Pearson in 1904. We give a table for two words w_1 and w_2, any word other than w_1 is symbolized $\sim w_1$.

It is seen from Table 1 that

$$f(w_1) = f(w_1, w_2) + f(w_1, \sim w_2);$$
$$f(\sim w_1) = f(\sim w_1, w_2) + f(\sim w_1, \sim w_2);$$

$$f(w_2) = f(w_1, w_2) + f(\sim w_1, w_2);$$
$$f(\sim w_2) = f(w_1, \sim w_2) + f(\sim w_1, \sim w_2);$$
$$f(N) = f(w_1) + f(\sim w_1) = f(w_2) + f(\sim w_2).$$

Frequencies $f(w_1)$, $f(\sim w_1)$, $f(w_2)$, $f(\sim w_2)$ are called marginal totals, and $f(N)$ is grand total.

Mutual Information

MI is a well-known information-theoretic notion used to judge about dependence of two random variables. Its application as an association measure for MWE extraction was suggested by Church and Hanks (1990). MI is an estimation of how much one word, e.g., w_1, tells about the other word w_2, computed according to the formula

$$MI = \log_2 \frac{P(w_1, w_2)}{P(w_1)P(w_2)},$$

where the probabilities are calculated using data from Table 1: joint probability of w_1 and w_2 cooccurrence $P(w_1, w_2) = f(w_1, w_2)/N$; and individual, or marginal, probabilities of w_1 and w_2 $P(w_1) = f(w_1)/N$; $P(w_2) = f(w_2)/N$. As it is seen from the formula for MI, the MWE hypothesis is expressed as the probability $P(w_1, w_2)$ actually observed in a corpus, and the null hypothesis suggests that w_1 and w_2 are independent therefore the probability of cooccurrence $P(w_1, w_2) = P(w_1)P(w_2)$. If MI = 0, the null hypothesis is proved, if MI > θ, where θ is a threshold estimated experimentally, then w_1 and w_2 are associated as constituents of a candidate MWE.

Strictly speaking, the metric we have just considered, is point-wise mutual information. But in

Table 1. Two-way contingency table of word cooccurrences

	w_2	$\sim w_2$	Sums
w_1	$f(w_1, w_2)$	$f(w_1, \sim w_2)$	$f(w_1)$
$\sim w_1$	$f(\sim w_1, w_2)$	$f(\sim w_1, \sim w_2)$	$f(\sim w_1)$
Sums	$f(w_2)$	$f(\sim w_2)$	$f(N)$

NLP literature it is referred to as simply *mutual information* according to the tradition started in Church and Hanks (1990) since we are interested not in mutual information of two random variables over their distribution, but rather in mutual information between two particular points.

Having compared the effectiveness of 84 association measures, Pecina (2008) demonstrates experimentally that point-wise mutual information works as the best association measure to identify collocations. However, this metric becomes problematic when data is sparse and also it is not accurate for low-frequency MWEs.

Log-Likelihood Ratio

The alternative terms for this measure found in literature are *G*-test and maximum likelihood statistical significant test. Log-likelihood ratio is computed with the formula

$$LR = -2\sum_{ij} f_{ij} \log \frac{f_{ij}}{f_{ij}^{expected}},$$

where f_{ij} is frequency in a cell of i x j contingency table, on our example of *2* x *2* table (Table 1), the cells are $f_{11} = f(w_1, w_2), f_{12} = f(w_1, \sim w_2), f_{21} = f(\sim w_1, w_2),$ $f_{22} = fr(\sim w_1, \sim w_2)$. The expected frequency is computed as if data items were independent, i.e., according to the formula given for the case of our contingency table

$$f_{ij}^{expected} = f(dataItem_1)f(dataItem_2) / N,$$

where *dataItem* is either w_1, w_2, $\sim w_1$ or $\sim w_2$ depending on what cell is considered.

Phi-Squared Test (φ^2 Statistic)

This measure is a χ^2-like statistics proposed by Church and Gale (1991) computed according to the formula

$$\phi^2 = \frac{(f(w_1,w_2)f(\sim w_1,\sim w_2) - f(w_1,\sim w_2)f(\sim w_1,w_2))^2}{f(w_1)f(w_2)f(\sim w_1)f(\sim w_2)},$$

where all frequencies *f* are taken from the contingency table. The values of φ^2 are bounded between 0 and 1. It is significant that φ^2 measure takes into account the values of $f(\sim w_1, w_2)$ and $f(w_1, \sim w_2)$ unlike χ^2 metric (Person's chi-squared test) whose formula is given now for comparison:

$$\c^2 = \sum_{ij} \frac{(f_{ij} - f_{ij}^{expected})^2}{f_{ij}^{expected}}.$$

Classification of Association Measures

Evert (2005) proposes an excellent classification of association measures. Besides, they can be calculated using UCS toolkit, software written in Perl of the same author. He identified the following classes of association measures:

- **Likelihood Measures:** Multinomial-likelihood, binomial-likelihood, Poisson-likelihood, the Poisson-Stirling approximation, and hypergeometric-likelihood;
- **Exact Hypothesis Tests:** Binomial test, Poisson test, Fisher's exact test;
- **Asymptotic Hypothesis Tests:** Z-score, Yates' continuity correction, t-score (which compares the observed co-occurrence frequency O_{11} and the expected co-occurrence frequency E_{11} [Wermter, 2008, p. 89] as random variates), Pearson's chi-squared test, Dunning's log-likelihood (a likelihood ratio test);
- **Point Estimates of Association Strength:** MI (mutual information, mu-value), logarithmic odds-ratio logarithmic relative-risk, Liddell's difference of proportions, MS (minimum sensitivity), gmean (geometric mean) coefficient, Dice coefficient (aka "mutual expectation"), Jaccard coefficient;

Table 2. Candidate selection rules from Kim and Kan (2009)

Criteria	Rules
Frequency	(**Rule 1**) *Frequency heuristic*: frequency ≥ 2 for simplex words vs. frequency ≥ 1 for NPs
Length	(**Rule 2**) *Length heuristic*: up to length 3 for NPs in non-*of-PP form* vs. up to length 4 for NPs in *of-PP form* (e.g. *synchronous concurrent program vs. model of multiagent interaction*)
Alternation	(**Rule 3**) *of-PP form alternation* (e.g. *number of sensor = sensor number, history of past encounter = past encounter history*) (**Rule 4**) *Possessive alternation* (e.g. *agent's goal = goal of agent, security's value = value of security*)
Extraction	(**Rule 5**) *Noun Phrase = (NN|NNS|NNP|NNPS|JJ|JJR|JJS)¤(NN|NNS|NNP|NNPS)* (e.g. *complexity, effective algorithm, grid computing, distributed Web-service discovery architecture*) (**Rule 6**) *Simplex Word/NP <u>IN</u> Simplex Word/NP* (e.g. *quality of service, sensitivity of VOIP traffic (VOIP traffic extracted),* *simplified instantiation of zebroid (simplified instantiation extracted))*

- **Conservative Estimates of Association Strength:** MIconf (a confidence-interval estimate for the mu-value);
- **Measures from Information Theory:** MI (pointwise mutual information), local-MI (contribution to average MI of all cooccurrences), average-MI (average MI between indicator variables);
- **Heuristic Measures:** Cooccurrence frequency, MI2 and MI3 (variants of MI), random selection,

6.2. Extraction: Rule-Based and Hybrid Methods

Statistical approach requires large collections of data, otherwise estimations of frequencies and probabilities of word cooccurrences become imprecise and untrustworthy. However, the Zipf's Law asserts that frequency of a word in a corpus is inversely proportional to its rank in the frequency table. Therefore, a great deal of words (from 40% to 60% of large corpora, according to Kornai, 2008, p. 72) are *hapax legomena*, i.e., they are used only once in corpus. Low-frequency phenomenon also extends to MWEs. Baldwin and Villavicencio (2002) indicate that two-thirds of

verb-particle constructions occur at most three times in the overall corpus. An example of rule-based approach can be found in Kim and Kan (2009). The authors use candidate selection rules for keyphrase extraction from scientific articles. Keyphrases are simplex noun or noun phrases that represent the key ideas of the document. Examples of rules are presented in Table 2.

On the other hand, rule-based approaches usually depend on language and lack flexibility. The latter characteristic harms the extraction of semi-compositional expressions and collocations, which permit syntactic variation. In addition, making hand crafted rules is time consuming. Moreover, such rules have limited coverage and will hardly discover new MWE appearing in language. To combat these disadvantages, hybrid approaches are proposed. The latter used rules to extract candidate MWEs and apply statistical methods to improved the obtained results. For example, in Hazelbeck and Saito (2010), machine learning is used together with simple patterns to identify functional expressions in Japanese. Their experiments show that the hybrid method doubles the coverage of previous approaches to resolving this issue, at the same time preserving high values of precision.

6.3. Evaluation

Upon obtaining a list of MWE candidates, evaluation or interpretation of the list must be done to check what candidate word combinations are true MWE. Evaluation can be manual or automatic. Results are presented in terms of conventional precision and recall. Given a finite set of word combinations, precision is the number of word combinations correctly identified as MWEs by the method under evaluation compared to all word combinations identified as MWEs by the method, recall is the same number of correctly identified MWEs compared to all MWEs in the set.

$$Precision = \frac{\# \ correctly \ identified \ as \ MWE}{\# \ identified \ as \ MWE};$$

$$Recall = \frac{\# \ correctly \ identified \ as \ MWE}{\# \ MWE}.$$

Manual evaluation is fulfilled using three methods. The retrieved list of MWE candidates is ordered and the first *n*-best candidates (with highest values of association measure applied in the extraction process) can be

- Checked by a native speaker who has sufficient training in linguistics or by a professional lexicographer.
- Compared against a dictionary; however, the evaluation results will depend on quality and coverage of the dictionary.
- Evaluated using hand-made gold standard (a list of MWEs manually identified in a corpus).

Although manual evaluation is very accurate, it suffers certain limitations. If MWE candidates are evaluated by human experts, they may have disagreements on the status of some expressions. This is due to lack of formality in MWE definitions as well as to the nature of MWE, since there are no clear-cut boundaries among MWE types and between MWE and free word combinations. On the other hand, when evaluation is performed against a dictionary, the scope of work is restricted by the MWE inventory in the selected dictionary. However, when MWEs are extracted from very large corpora, the list of MWE candidates is much bigger than the expressions found in the dictionary, therefore, a good portion of true MWEs might be lost in the evaluation process. Concerning hand-made golden standard, the limit is time and financial resources because manual word is always costly in both senses. A very serious limitation of manual evaluation is the impossibility to estimate recall for very large lists of MWE candidates. It may seem that the problem may be solved with the data size reduction (to 50-200 samples), but association measures do not work well on small data sets.

To overcome the drawbacks of manual evaluation, automatic evaluation methods have been proposed. A well-known and widely used method is developed by Evert and Krenn (2001). Instead of manually annotating only a small (in the sense of automatic language processing) number of *n*-best MWE candidates, Evert and Krenn suggest to compute precision and recall for several *n*-best samples of arbitrary size comparing them against a golden standard of about 100 MWEs (True Positives, TPs). Then, precision is the proportion of TPs in the *n*-best list, and recall is the proportion of TPs in the base data that are also contained in the *n*-best list, the base data being an unordered list of all MWE candidates extracted.

7. MORE DETAIL ON VERB NOUN CONSTRUCTION AS A SPECIAL CASE OF MWE

Verb Noun Constructions (VNCs) is a class of MWEs, which vary in compositionality and predictability (Diab & Bhutada, 2009). Though the meaning *fail at an early stage* of the VNC *fall at the first fence* is not predictable from the semantics of *fall, first* and *fence*, however, *take a walk* is related to *to walk* in a very explicit way. Therefore, *fall at the first fence* is a non-decomposable VNC, and *take a walk* is a decomposable VNC. It is important for precise language processing to distinguish decomposable VNCs from non-decomposable or idiomatic expressions. Besides, Cook, Fazly, and Stevenson (2008) report that over 40% cases of VNCs in text correspond to literal usage. A good example of research aimed at diagnosing idiomatic VNCs apart from literal expressions is Diab and Bhutada (2009) referenced above.

VNCs whose meaning is determined by the noun functioning as the complement of the verb like the above *take a walk* (= *to walk*), also *give an example* (= *to exemplify*), *impose a fine* (= *to fine*), are referred to as Light Verb Constructions (LVCs) in the linguistic literature (e.g., Butt, 2003). Tan, Kan, and Cui (2006) give a broad survey of light verb construction detection and suggest new syntactic features for machine learning of LVCs.

One of the obstacles to accurate NLP processing of VNCs is a lack of lexical-semantic relations in wordnets. This is what Boyd-Graber, Fellbaum, Osherson, and Schapire (2006) see as a weakness of the Princeton WordNet: "WordNet, a ubiquitous tool for natural language processing, suffers from sparsity of connections between its component concepts (synsets)." Lemnitzer, Wunsch, and Gupta (2008) report that the number of 68,000 relation instances connecting 53,312 synsets and 76,563 lexical units in GermaNet is surprisingly low and needs to be increased. They assume that similar ratios between objects and relations characterize many wordnets.

7.1. Lexical Functions (LFs) as a Source of Lexical-Semantic Relations for VNC Annotation in Lexicons

In was mentioned in Section 5 that LF is an alternative MWE representation developed in the frame of the Meaning-Text Theory (Mel'čuk, 1996) and it is defined as a mapping from the MWE headword (the noun in VNCs, for example, *announcement*) to the semantically dependant constituent called the LF value (the verb in VNCs, *to make* for the headword *announcement*). To prevent confusions on what depends on what, it should be noted here that though the noun makes its choice of the verb and therefore is semantically dominating, the verb is the head of VNCs at syntactic level.

We will illustrate the concept of lexical function by some examples. As it is mentioned in the previous paragraph, LF is a mapping from the noun to the verb. This mapping is further characterized by its meaning. For example, for the headword *announcement*, the LF denoted as 'Oper$_1$' gives the value *make*. 'Oper' is from Latin *operari*, to 'do,' 'perform,' 'carry out.' That is, to express the meaning 'to perform an announcement,' one says in English *to make an announcement*. The subscript 1 in Oper$_1$ means that the agent of *announcement* is the grammatical subject in utterances: *He* (agent) *has made an announcement*. Using the notation of lexical function, this collocation can be re-written as Oper$_1$(*announcement*) = *make*. Other examples of Oper$_1$ are *to break the news, to narrate a story, to deliver a message, to perform a drama, to give a smile, to lend support, to mount resistance, to have authority, to exercise power*. All these collocations share the common semantic pattern 'to do the <noun>.'

As a further example, let us consider the word *importance*. The value of Oper$_1$ for *importance* is *to have* (*to have importance*). Another LF termed Oper$_2$ means 'to undergo what is expressed by the <noun>' and it gives the following value for *importance*: Oper$_2$(*importance*) = *to get* (*to get importance*). The lexical function IncepOper$_1$ has the meaning 'to begin performing the <noun>,' so IncepOper$_1$(*importance*) = *to acquire* (*to acquire importance*). CausFunc$_1$ is the label for the semantics 'to cause the existence of the <noun>,' therefore, CausFunc$_1$(*importance*) = *to give* (*to give importance*).

About 20 LFs capture VNCs. In this section and elsewhere LFs are characterized by their semantics, but LF notation is not explained in detail. We only mention here that a LF name is an abbreviated Latin word with the meaning identical to the semantics of LF in question, and numbers in subscripts are used to identify syntactic functions of semantic roles of the noun in a VNC. A comprehensive presentation of the LF formalism and notation can be found in Mel'čuk (1996).

It can be observed from the examples given in the previous paragraphs that LFs generalize VNC semantics and may be used as tags of lexical-semantic relations between the noun and the verb. Such cross-categorial connections of synsets in wordnets will enrich these databases commonly used in NLP. It will be also possible to group verbs and nouns with similar semantic relations thus capturing lexical similarities and variations in VNCs.

In fact, LFs represent semantic classes of collocations that are characterized by typical semantic patterns. Thus, collocations with common generalized semantics are subsumed under one class with the semantics of the respective LF. Returning to the example given above, we say that collocations *to break the news*, *to narrate a story*, *to deliver a message* are of the semantic class 'do,' which is the meaning of $Oper_1$.

7.2. Automatic Detection of Lexical Functions in Verb Noun Combinations

Wanner (2004) and Wanner, Bohnet, and Giereth (2006) suggest to regard the task of LFs automatic detection as a task of VNCs classification according to LF typology. They completed experiments on two groups of Spanish VNCs: those with emotion nouns and others with field-independent nouns applying four machine learning techniques: nearest neighbor technique, Naive Bayesian network, tree-augmented network classification technique and a decision tree classification technique based

on the ID3-algorithm. Each VNC was to be classified as one of the eight LFs chosen for the experiments. For learning LFs, hypernyms of the Spanish part of EuroWordNet (Vossen, 1998) were used as features together with Base Concepts and Top Concepts—items of two respective ontologies implemented in EuroWordNet. The highest F-measure achieved for field-independent VNCs was 0.766, and the average F-measure over all experiments was about 0.700.

Alonso Ramos, Rambow, and Wanner (2008) proposed an algorithm to retrieve VNCs of the type 'support verb + object' from the semantically annotated FrameNet corpus of examples (Ruppenhofer, Ellsworth, Petruck, Johnson, & Scheffczyk, 2006). Their interest was to see whether the collocations they extracted were of $Oper_n$ (with the meanings 'to realize, perform, carry out the <noun>,' to undergo the <noun> and the like). The authors assumed that certain syntactic, semantic and collocation annotations in the FrameNet corpus could signal that a particular VNC belonged to $Oper_n$. The proposed algorithm was tested on 208 instances and showed the accuracy of 76%.

8. EXPERIMENTS ON DETECTION OF LEXICAL FUNCTIONS IN VERB NOUN COMBINATIONS

8.1. Data

Our experiments were carried out on about one thousand Spanish VNCs retrieved from Spanish WebCorpus via SketchEngine, the Web-based software for automatic text processing (Kilgarriff, et al., 2004). Spanish Web Corpus includes 116,900,060 tokens and is compiled of texts found in the Internet. The texts are not limited to particular themes so the corpus can be considered to represent the general Spanish lexis. Other tools can also be used for extracting Verb Noun Constructions (Sidorov, 1996).

VNCs were annotated manually with LFs and Spanish WordNet senses (Vossen, 1998; Spanish WordNet online). The resulting dataset is available in the public domain *(Spanish Verb-Noun Lexical Functions Dataset)*. Dataset instances are exemplified in Table 3 which also presents the meaning of LFs under study, the number of VNCs for each LF specified in the second column of the table (the overall number of examples is 608), and English translation of Spanish examples.

8.2. VNC Modeling for Machine Learning

The meaning of each VNC was modeled as a set of all hypernyms of the verb and all hypernyms of the noun. Hypernyms were extracted from the Spanish WordNet referenced in Section 8.1. Each of eight lexical functions was assigned its training set. All eight training sets included the same 608 VNCs. For a particular lexical function, "yes" class was assigned to positive instances of this function, and "no" class, to the rest of the instances.

To submit the data to machine learning techniques, we used vectorized binary representation of the hypernym sets to model VNC semantics. Each hypernym was considered as an attribute; so vectors of VNCs were of the size equal to the sum of all hypernyms. When a particular hypernym was present in a given VNC, the respective attribute acquired the value of 1; otherwise its value was 0.

WEKA 3-6-2 toolkit (Hall, Frank, Holmes, Pfahringer, Reutemann, & Witten, 2009; WEKA download) was used for experimenting with many supervised learning algorithms. The training sets of eight LFs were supplied to 68 classifiers and predictions of the positive class on the same sets were evaluated by applying the 10-fold cross-validation technique.

Table 3. Lexical functions (LFs) in our dataset

LF	#	LF meaning	Spanish VNC	English translation
$Oper_1$	266	to carry out the <noun>, to experience the <noun>	*prestar atención* *tener una duda* *celebrar la reunión*	to pay attention to have doubt to have a meeting
$Oper_2$	28	to undergo the <noun>, to be source of the <noun>	*obtener beneficio* *sufrir un ataque* *recibir la respuesta*	to get a benefit to have an attack to get the answer
$IncepOper_1$	24	to begin to do, perform, experience, carry out the <noun>	*asumir la responsabilidad* *iniciar un proceso* *tomar la iniciativa*	to take on the responsibility to start a process to take the initiative
$ContOper_1$	16	to continue to do, perform, experience, carry out the <noun>	*mantener el contacto* *seguir el curso* *guardar silencio*	to keep in contact to follow the course to keep silent
$Func_0$	16	the <noun> exists, takes place, occurs	*la posibilidad existe* *el día pasa* *la duda cabe*	the possibility exists the day passes by a doubt arises
$CausFunc_0$	109	the agent of the <noun> causes the <noun> to occur	*poner un ejemplo* *dar explicación* *provocar la reacción*	to give an example to give an explanation to provoke a reaction
$CausFunc_1$	89	a person/object, different from the agent of the <noun>, causes the <noun> to occur	*dar importancia* *abrir paso* *producir daño*	to give importance to make way to inflict damage
$Real_1$	60	to fulfill the requirement of the <noun>, to act according to the <noun>	*utilizar la herramienta* *corregir el error* *alcanzar el nivel*	to use a tool to correct an error to reach a level

Table 4. Best classifiers on LF prediction

LF	Classifier	F
Oper1 266	BayesianLogisticRegression	0.873
	Id3	0.870
	SMO	0.864
Oper2 28	J48	0.706
	LogitBoost	0.686
	LADTree	0.667
IncepOper1 24	Prism	0.774
	NNge	0.727
	SMO	0.722
ContOper1 16	DecisionTable	0.833
	FilteredClassifier	0.800
	Ridor	0.783
Func0 16	BFTree	0.696
	HyperPipes	0.636
	AttributeSelectedClassifier	0.636
CausFunc0 109	JRip	0.725
	EnsembleSelection	0.699
	REPTree	0.695
CausFunc1 89	END	0.762
	LogitBoost	0.756
	AttributeSelectedClassifier	0.733
Real1 60	FT	0.598
	NNge	0.593
	Id3	0.587
# total 608	Average best:	0.746

8.3. Experimental Results and Discussion

As it is mentioned in Section 8.2, the performance of the supervised learning algorithms implemented in WEKA was evaluated in terms of F-measure using 10-fold cross-validation technique. Table 4 presents the results of the three best classifiers for each LF, F stands for F-measure, and the highest F-measure for each LF is in bold-face. The number of LF positive instances is indicated after LF names for convenience of further discussion.

As it is seen from Table 4, no single classifier is the best one for detecting all LFs. For each LF, the highest result is achieved by a different classifier. The maximum F-measure of 0.873 is achieved by BayesianLogisticRegression classifier for Oper$_1$. The lowest best F-measure of 0.598 is shown by FT for Real$_1$. The average best F-measure (calculated over only the eight best results, one for each LF) is 0.746.

No correlation was observed between the number of instances in the training set and the results obtained from the classifiers. For example, a low result of 0.598 is shown for Real$_1$ which has more positive instances (60) than $ContOper_1$ (only 16), but for $ContOper_1$ a high result of 0.833 was attained. At the same time, $Func_0$ with the equal number of positive instances as $ContOper_1$ (16) was detected with the F-measure of 0.696 which is low. Similar results were showed for $CausFunc_1$ (F-measure of 0.762) and $IncepOper_1$ (F-measure of 0.774), though $CausFunc_1$ has 89 positive instances and $IncepOper_1$, only 24.

It can be observed in Table 4 that the best classifiers for all LFs except for $Oper_1$ are symbolic. J48, the best method for detecting $Oper_2$, is a rule-based classifier algorithm that generates C4.5 decision trees, which in their turn implement ID3 algorithm. Prism, the best classifier for $IncepOper_1$, is based on the inductive rule learning and uses separate-and-conquer strategy. DecisionTable, the best for $ContOper_1$, is an induction algorithm whose task is to find the optimal list of attributes such that the decision table created from this list will have the lowest possible error on the training data. BFTree, the best method for $Func_0$, is a best-first decision tree learner – an alternative approach to standard decision tree techniques such as C4.5 algorithm since they expand nodes in best-first order instead of a fixed depth-first order. JRip, the best algorithm for $CausFunc_0$, implements a propositional rule learner RIPPER. END, the best for $CausFunc_1$, is a meta-classifier for handling multi-class datasets with two-class classifiers by building an ensemble of nested dichotomies. FT, the best for $Real_1$, is a classifier for building functional trees, which are classification trees that could have logistic regression functions at the inner nodes and/or leaves. More details on WEKA classifiers can be found in (Witten & Frank, 2005).

Since almost all best classifiers for LF detection are symbolic, we can suppose that VNC semantics is better distinguished by rules and trees (in some cases in combination with probabilistic knowledge) than on the basis of pure probabilistic information learned from the training data. Purely statistical methods are limited by the assumption that all features in data are equally important in contributing to the decision of assigning a particular class to an example and also independent of one another. This is a rather simplified view of data, because in many cases data features are not equally important or independent and this is certainly true for linguistic data, especially for such a language phenomenon as hypernyms. Graphically, hypernyms form a hierarchic structure called a tree where every hypernym has its ancestor (except for the hypernym at the root of the tree) and daughter(s) (except for hypernyms at the leaves of the tree).

We are in no position to compare our results with the results obtained in Wanner (2004) and Wanner *et al.* (2006) mentioned in Section 7.2, because our experiments were not done on the same dataset though on analogous VNCs with field-independent nouns. Unfortunately, the data used in Wanner (2004) and Wanner *et al.* (2006) is no longer available (Wanner, personal communication). However, we will mention here that data representation in our work was different from that of Wanner (2004) and Wanner *et al.* (2006) who used hypernyms, Base Concepts and Top Concepts from EuroWordNet to learn LFs. Only hypernyms were included as features in our data sets; nevertheless, the hypernym information on its own distinguished LFs quite well.

Table 5 shows the performance of classifiers commonly used for text mining: Naive Bayes, C4.5 decision tree learner, nearest-neighbor instance-based learner, and support vector machine. In this table, the numbers are values of F-measure, BLR stands for Bayesian Logistic Regression, DT stands for Decision Table. The column 'Best' presents the best result achieved in our research by classifiers specified after the symbol "|". The best values are derived from Table 4 and displayed here for the sake of more comfortable viewing. It can be seen from Table 5 that the value of F-measure averaged over four classifiers for each LF is significantly lower than the best result for this LF with the only exception of $Oper_1$ for which the difference between the average result and the best result is not so great (0.760 vs. 0.873).

Table 5. LF prediction of some classifiers commonly used in NLP

LF	NB	J48	IB1	SMO	Average		Best
$Oper_1$	0.711	0.844	0.620	0.864	**0.760**	0.873	BLR
$Oper_2$	0.000	0.706	0.327	0.595	**0.407**	0.706	J48
$IncepOper_1$	0.000	0.571	0.357	0.722	**0.413**	0.774	Prism
$ContOper_1$	0.000	0.800	0.333	0.750	**0.471**	0.833	DT
$Func_0$	0.000	0.636	0.348	0.583	**0.392**	0.696	BFTree
$CausFunc_0$	0.308	0.609	0.387	0.643	**0.487**	0.725	JRip
$CausFunc_1$	0.077	0.762	0.462	0.681	**0.496**	0.762	END
$Real_1$	0.040	0.533	0.364	0.627	**0.391**	0.598	FT
Average:					**0.477**	0.746	

It is rather surprising that Naive Bayes classifier performed so poorly except for $Oper_1$ (F-measure of 0.711). Naive Bayes was not able to predict $Oper_2$, $IncepOper_1$, $ContOper_1$, and $Func_0$ at all. Such results seem to support the observation made earlier in this section that symbolic methods work better on LF prediction than classifiers based only on probabilistic featured learned from linguistic data.

8. CONCLUSION

It is widely acknowledged that MultiWord Expressions (MWEs) are "pain in the neck for NLP" (Sag, et al., 2002) due to their idiosyncratic nature. Besides, it is difficult to identify the clear-cut boundaries of MWEs; therefore, the exact MWE definition is still to be worked on. Existing definitions reviewed in this chapter attempt to capture some important MWE features. The same problem hinders a comprehensive and exhaustive consideration of MWE classes though MWE types we discussed here represent very large groups of MWE to be found in texts of various domains and genres.

Another important issue in MWE research is how to represent these sometimes capricious constructions in lexicons. Again, several methods of MWE lexical representation have been proposed, though none of them are recognized as standard. As we looked at these representations, it could

be noted that all of them are capable of encoding different but significant lexical, syntactic, and pragmatic aspects of MWE, so the objective of finding an appropriate MWE representation which absorbs every advantage of existing encodings is another important issue in MWE research.

Three approaches to MWE automatic detection have been considered, namely, statistic, rule-based, and hybrid. Undoubtedly, the statistic approach is more common in developing language applications due to its robustness and language-independent nature; however, rule-based approach is more effective for low-frequency MWE. Hybrid approaches aim at combining the advantages of two previous approaches seeking to improve performance of MWE extraction techniques.

A class of MWEs termed Verb Noun Constructions (VNCs) was discussed in more detail. Lexical Functions (LFs) were explained as one of the methods of VNCs encoding. The explanation was accompanied with our experimental results on supervised machine learning of LFs in Spanish VNC. The average F-measure achieved in the experiments is 0.746. Therefore, it is feasible to predict LFs by supervised learning methods using hypernyms as features for LF learning, since hypernym data was exploited in our experiments to distinguish among eight LFs. Symbolic learning methods showed a significantly higher F-measure on LF prediction than purely statistic classifiers like Naive Bayes.

REFERENCES

Agirre, E., Aldezabal, I., & Pociello, E. (2006). Lexicalization and multiword expressions in the Basque WordNet. In *Proceedings of Third International WordNet Conference*. Jeju Island, Korea: WordNet.

Alegria, I., Ansa, O., Xabier, A., Ezeiza, N., Gojenola, K., & Urizar, R. (2004). Representation and treatment of multiword expressions in Basque. In *Proceedings of the ACL Workshop on Multiword Expressions,* (pp. 48–55). Barcelona, Spain: ACL.

Alonso Ramos, M., Rambow, O., & Wanner, L. (2008). Using semantically annotated corpora to build collocation resources. In *Proceedings of the International Language Resources and Evaluation Conference (LREC),* (pp. 1154–1158). Marrakesh, Morocco: LREC.

Baldwin, T., & Bond, F. (2002). Multiword expressions: Some problems for Japanese NLP. In *Proceedings of the 8th Annual Meeting of the Association for Natural Language Processing,* (pp. 379–382). Keihanna, Japan: Natural Language Processing.

Baldwin, T., & Villavicencio, A. (2002). Extracting the unextractable: A case study on verbparticles. In *Proceedings of the Sixth Conference on Computational Natural Language Learning (CoNLL 2002),* (pp. 99–105). CoNLL.

Benson, M., Benson, E., & Ilson, R. (1986). *The BBI combinatory dictionary of English*. Amsterdam, The Netherlands: John Benjamins.

Boyd-Graber, J., Fellbaum, C., Osherson, D., & Schapire, R. (2006). Adding dense, weighted connections to WordNet. In *Proceedings of the Third International WordNet Conference*. Brno, Czech Republic: Masaryk University.

Butt, M. (2003). The light verb jungle. *Workshop on Multi-Verb Constructions*. Retrieved from http://ling.sprachwiss.uni-konstanz.de/pages/home/butt/main/papers/harvard-work.pdf

Calzolari, N. (2004). Computational lexicons and corpora: Complementary components in human language technology. In van Sterkenburg, P. (Ed.), *Linguistics Today – Facing a Greater Challenge* (pp. 89–108). Amsterdam, The Netherlands: John Benjamins.

Calzolari, N., Fillmore, C., Grishman, R., Ide, N., Lenci, A., MacLeod, C., & Zampolli, A. (2002). Towards best practice for multiword expressions in computational lexicons. In *Proceedings of the Third International Conference on Language Resources and Evaluation (LREC 2002),* (pp. 1934–1940). Las Palmas, Spain: LREC.

Calzolari, N., McNaught, J., & Zampolli, A. (1996). *EAGLES final report: EAGLES editors' introduction*. Pisa, Italy: EAGLES.

Calzolari, N., Zampolli, A., & Lenci, A. (2002). Towards a standard for a multilingual lexical entry: The EAGLES/ISLE initiative. *Lecture Notes in Computer Science, 2276,* 264–279. doi:10.1007/3-540-45715-1_25

Chakraborty, T., Das, D., & Bandyopadhyay, S. (2011). Semantic clustering: An attempt to identify multiword expressions in Bengali. In *Proceedings of the Workshop on Multiword Expressions: From Parsing and Generation to the Real World (MWE 2011),* (pp. 8-13). Portland, OR: MWE.

Chikara, H. (2004). *A computational treatment of V-V vompounds in Japanese*. (Ph.D. Dissertation). Kobe Shoin Graduate School of Letters. Kobe, Japan.

Church, K. W., & Gale, W. A. (1991). Concordances for parallel text. In *Proceedings of the Seventh Annual Conference of the UW Centre for the New OED and Text Research,* (pp. 40–62). UW Centre.

Church, K. W., & Hanks, P. (1990). Word association norms, mutual information and lexicography. *Proceedings of 27th Association for Computational Linguistics, 16*(1), 22–29.

Cook, P., Fazly, A., & Stevenson, S. (2008). The VNC-Tokens dataset. In *Proceedings of the LREC Workshop on Towards a Shared Task for Multiword Expressions (MWE 2008)*. Marrakech, Morocco: LREC.

Deksne, D., Skadiņš, R., & Skadiņa, I. (2008). Dictionary of multiword expressions for translation into highly inflected languages. In N. Calzolari, K. Choukri, B. Maegaard, J. Mariani, J. Odjik, S. Piperidis, & D. Tapias (Eds.), *Proceedings of Proceedings of the Sixth International Language Resources and Evaluation (LREC 2008)*. Marrakech, Morocco: European Language Resources Association (ELRA).

Diab, M. T., & Bhutada, P. (2009). Verb noun construction MWE token supervised classification. In *Proceedings of the Workshop on Multiword Expressions: Identification, Interpretation, Disambiguation and Applications, (ACL-JICNLP 2009)*, (pp. 17–22). Singapore: ACL-JICNLP.

Diaconescu, S. (2004). Multiword expression translation using generative dependency grammar. In *Proceedings of ESTAL 2004 – España for Natural Language Processing*. Alicante, Spain: ESTAL.

Evert, S. (2005). *The statistics of word cooccurrences: Word pairs and collocations*. (Ph.D. Thesis). University of Stuttgart. Stuttgart, Germany.

Evert, S., & Krenn, B. (2001). Methods for the qualitative evaluation of lexical association measures. In *Proceedings of the 39th Annual Meeting on Association for Computational Linguistics*, (pp. 188–195). ACL.

Fazly, A., & Stevenson, S. (2007). Distinguishing subtypes of multiword expressions using linguistically motivated statistical measures. In N. Grégoire, S. Evert, & B. Krenn (Eds.), *Proceedings of the ACL 2007 Workshop on a Broader Perspective on Multiword Expressions*, (pp. 9–16). Prague, Czech Republic: ACL.

Fellbaum, C. (Ed.). (1998). *WordNet: An electronic lexical database*. Cambridge, MA: MIT Press.

Fillmore, C. J., & Baker, C. F. (2001). Frame semantics for text understanding. In *Proceedings of WordNet and Other Lexical Resources Workshop*. Pittsburgh, PA: NAACL.

Gelbukh. (2012). *Spanish verb-noun lexical functions*. Retrieved from http://www.Gelbukh.com/lexical-functions

Grégoire, N. (2007). Design and implementation of a lexicon of Dutch multiword expressions. In N. Grégoire, S. Evert, & B. Krenn (Eds.), *Proceedings of the ACL 2007 Workshop on a Broader Perspective on Multiword Expressions*, (pp. 17–24). Prague, Czech Republic: ACL.

Gurrutxaga, A., & Alegria, I. (2011). Automatic extraction of NV expressions in Basque: Basic issues on cooccurrence techniques. In *Proceedings of the Workshop on Multiword Expressions: From Parsing and Generation to the Real World*, (pp. 2-7). Portland, OR: Association for Computational Linguistics.

Hall, M., Frank, E., Holmes, G., Pfahringer, B., Reutemann, P., & Witten, I. H. (2009). The WEKA data mining software: An update. *SIGKDD Explorations*, *11*(1), 10–18. doi:10.1145/1656274.1656278

Hazelbeck, G., & Saito, H. (2010). A hybrid approach for functional expression identification in a Japanese reading assistant. In *Proceedings of the Workshop on Multiword Expressions: From Theory to Applications (MWE 2010)*, (pp. 80-83). Beijing, China: MWE.

Hore, C., Asahara, M., & Matsumoto, Y. (2005). Automatic extraction of fixed multiword expressions. *Lecture Notes in Computer Science*, *3651*, 565–575. doi:10.1007/11562214_50

Jackendoff, R. (1990). *Semantic structures*. Cambridge, MA: The MIT Press.

Kilgarriff, A., Rychly, P., Smrz, P., & Tugwell, D. (2004). The sketch engine. In *Proceedings of EURA-LEX,* (pp. 105–116). Lorient, France: EURALEX.

Kim, S. N., & Kan, M.-Y. (2009). Re-examining automatic keyphrase extraction approaches in scientific articles. In *Proceedings of the 2009 Workshop on Multiword Expressions, ACL-IJCNLP 2009,* (pp. 9–16). Singapore: ACL and AFNLP.

Kornai, A. (2008). *Mathematical linguistics*. London, UK: Springer-Verlag Limited. doi:10.1007/978-1-84628-986-6

Lemnitzer, L., Wunsch, H., & Gupta, P. (2008). Enriching germanet with verb-noun relations - A case study of lexical acquisition. In *Proceedings of the 6th International Language Resources and Evaluation*. ACL.

Lenci, A., Bel, N., Busa, F., Calzolari, N., Gola, E., & Monachini, M. (2000). SIMPLE: A general framework for the development of multilingual lexicons. *International Journal of Lexicography, 13*(4), 249–263. doi:10.1093/ijl/13.4.249

Mel'čuk, I. (1996). Lexical functions: A tool for the description of lexical relations in a lexicon. In Wanner, L. (Ed.), *Lexical Functions in Lexicography and Natural Language Processing* (pp. 37–102). Amsterdam, The Netherlands: Johm Benjamins.

Pecina, P., & Schlesinger, P. (2006). Combining association measures for collocation extraction. In *Proceedings of the 21th International Conference on Computational Linguistics and 44th Annual Meeting of the Association for Computational Linguistics (COLING/ACL 2006),* (pp. 651–658). COLING/ACL.

Piao, S. L., Sun, G., Rayson, P., & Yuan, Q. (2006). Automatic extraction of Chinese multiword expressions with a statistical tool. In *Proceedings of the Workshop on Multi-Word-Expressions in a Multilingual Context held in Conjunction with the 11th Conference of the European Chapter of the Association for Computational Linguistics (EACL 2006),* (pp. 17–24). Trento, Italy: EACL.

Pustejovsky, J. (1995). *The generative lexicon*. Cambridge, MA: The MIT Press.

Ramisch, C., Villavicencio, A., Moura, L., & Idiart, M. (2008). Picking them up and figuring them out: Verb-particle constructions, noise and idiomaticity. In A. Clark & K. Toutanova (Eds.), *Proceedings of the Twelfth Conference on Natural Language Learning (CoNLL 2008),* (pp. 49–56). Manchester, UK: Association for Computational Linguistics.

Ruppenhofer, J., Ellsworth, M., Petruck, M., Johnson, C. R., & Scheffczyk, J. (2006). *FrameNet II: Extended theory and practice*. Retrieved from http://framenet.icsi.berkeley.edu/book/book.pdf. ICSI

Sag, I., Baldwin, T., Bond, F., Copestake, A., & Flickinger, D. (2002). Multiword expressions: A pain in the neck for NLP. In *Proceedings of the 3rd International Conference on Intelligent Text Processing and Computational Linguistics (CICLing-2002),* (pp. 1–15). Mexico City, Mexico: CICLing.

Sidorov, G. (1996). Lemmatization in automatized system for compilation of personal style dictionaries of literature writers. In *Word of Dostoyevsky* (pp. 266–300). Moscow, Russia: Russian Academy of Sciences.

Smadja, F. (1993). Retrieving collocations from text: Xtract. *Computational Linguistics, 19,* 143–177.

Spanish WordNet. (2012). *Website*. Retrieved from http://www.lsi.upc.edu/~nlp/web/index.php?Itemid=57&id=31&option=com_content&task=view

Tan, Y. F., Kan, M.-Y., & Cui, H. (2006). Extending corpus-based identification of light verb constructions using a supervised learning framework. In *Proceedings of the EACL Workshop on Multi-Word Expressions in a Multilingual Contexts,* (pp. 49–56). Trento, Italy: Association for Computational Linguistics.

Villavicencio, A., Ramisch, C., Machado, A., de Medeiros Caseli, H., & Finatto, M. J. (2010). Identicação de expressões multipalavra em domínios especícos. *Linguamática, 2*(1), 15–34.

Vossen, P. (Ed.). (1998). *EuroWordNet: A multilingual database with lexical semantic networks*. Dordrecht, The Netherlands: Kluwer Academic Publishers.

Wanner, L. (2004). Towards automatic fine-grained classification of verb-noun collocations. *Natural Language Engineering, 10*(2), 95–143. doi:10.1017/S1351324904003328

Wanner, L., Bohnet, B., & Giereth, M. (2006). What is beyond collocations? Insights from machine learning experiments. In *Proceedings of the EURALEX Conference*. Turin, Italy: EURALEX.

WEKA. (2012). *The University of Waikato computer science department machine learning group*. Retrieved from http://www.cs.waikato.ac.nz/~ml/weka/index_downloading.html

Wermter, J. (2008). *Collocation and term extraction using linguistically enhanced statistical methods*. (Ph. D. Thesis). Friedrich-Schiller-Universität Jena. Retrieved from http://deposit.ddb.de/cgi-bin/dokserv?idn=993920594&dok_var=d1&dok_ext=pdf&filename=993920594.pdf

Witten, I. H., & Frank, E. (2005). *Data mining: Practical machine learning tools and techniques* (2nd ed.). San Francisco, CA: Morgan Kaufmann.

WordNet. (2010). *WordNet release 3.1*. Retrieved from http://wordnet.princeton.edu

Workshops, M. W. E. (2012). *Website*. Retrieved from http://multiword.sourceforge.net/PHITE.php?sitesig=CONF

Xiao, C., & Rösner, D. (2004). Detecting multiword verbs in the English sublanguage of MEDLINE abstracts. In *Proceedings of the 20th international conference on Computational Linguistics (COLING 2004)*. Stroudsburg, PA: Association for Computational Linguistics.

Chapter 2
Word Sense Disambiguation

Pushpak Bhattacharyya
Indian Institute of Technology Bombay, India

Mitesh Khapra
Indian Institute of Technology Bombay, India

ABSTRACT

This chapter discusses the basic concepts of Word Sense Disambiguation (WSD) and the approaches to solving this problem. Both general purpose WSD and domain specific WSD are presented. The first part of the discussion focuses on existing approaches for WSD, including knowledge-based, supervised, semi-supervised, unsupervised, hybrid, and bilingual approaches. The accuracy value for general purpose WSD as the current state of affairs seems to be pegged at around 65%. This has motivated investigations into domain specific WSD, which is the current trend in the field. In the latter part of the chapter, we present a greedy neural network inspired algorithm for domain specific WSD and compare its performance with other state-of-the-art algorithms for WSD. Our experiments suggest that for domain-specific WSD, simply selecting the most frequent sense of a word does as well as any state-of-the-art algorithm.

1. INTRODUCTION

Word Sense Disambiguation (WSD) is the problem of finding the correct sense (*i.e.*, meaning) of a word by looking at the context in which it appears. It is one of the central challenges in NLP and is ubiquitous across all languages. Almost every language that we know has polysemy (*poly* means *"many"* and *semy* means *"signs"* or *"meanings"*) to a certain degree. For example, consider the two different meanings of the word *bank* in English:

*I am going to the **bank** to withdraw money.*

*I am going to take a walk along the river **bank**.*

In the first sentence, the word 'bank' refers to a *"financial institution"* whereas in the second sentence it refers to a *"sloping land beside a water body (river, in this case)."* When a human being reads the first sentence, he sees the words *"withdraw"* and *"money"* in the context and uses his world knowledge to decide that the word *bank* here refers to a *"financial institution."* Similarly, he sees the word *"river"* in the second sentence and easily infers that the word *bank* here refers

DOI: 10.4018/978-1-4666-2169-5.ch002

to a *"sloping land near the river."* Identifying the correct meaning of a word can serve as a building block for many Natural Language Processing (NLP) tasks, such as Information Retrieval (IR), Machine Translation (MT), Information Extraction (IE), and more recently for Subjectivity and Sentiment Analysis. In IR, WSD can help in identifying the correct sense of a word in the query and thereby improve the precision of the results fetched (Harman, 2005). In MT, identifying the correct sense of a word in the source language can help in selecting its appropriate translation in the target language (Carpuat & Wu, 2007). Similarly, in IE, knowing the correct sense of every word in a document may help in doing an accurate analysis of the text. More recently, Balamurali *et al.* (2011) have shown that WSD can help in improving the performance of document level sentiment classifiers.

The above-mentioned applications of WSD suggest that distinguishing between different senses of a word is indeed important, but, *how do we train a machine to acquire the necessary world knowledge required to perform such distinction or how do we even make a machine aware that a word has such multiple senses or meanings?* The first question brings out the *hardness* of the problem and it is a commonly accepted notion that WSD is an AI-complete problem, *i.e.* it is as hard as any other AI problem (Navigli, 2009). In fact, several studies (Snyder & Palmer, 2004) have shown that WSD is a hard problem even for human beings. Specifically, these studies have shown that given the task of assigning senses to a large set of words by looking at their context, the agreement in the senses assigned by two humans is only 78%. Considering the difficulty of the task, its importance, and its ubiquitous nature, much work has been done in this area. In this chapter, we describe some of the popular algorithms, which have been proposed to perform WSD and highlight that in some specific conditions, such as when the corpus is restricted to a specific domain, it is possible to achieve near human performance on WSD.

The second question, *i.e., "how do we make a machine aware of the different senses of a word"* brings us to the concept of a *sense repository* or a *knowledge base*. A sense repository is a lexical resource which lists down the different senses of a word. The most popular sense repository used for WSD is *WordNet* (Fellbaum, 1998) which is a hierarchical lexical database where the basic unit of storage is a synset (short for *synonymy set*). As the name suggests, each synset contains a *set* of words, which together define a concept. From now on, we use the words synset and sense interchangeably. In addition to storing the *gloss, examples* and *members* for each synset, *a* wordnet also stores *semantic relations* between the synsets, *e.g.*, hypernymy/hyponymy (IS-A), holonymy/meronymy (PART-OF), troponymy (TYPE-OF), *etc.* Below, we give examples of two synsets from the English wordnet along with their relations.

Synset: (v) walk (use one's feet to advance; advance by steps) *"Walk, don't run!"; "We walked instead of driving"; "She walks with a slight limp"; "The patient cannot walk yet"; "Walk over to the cabinet"*
- ○ {direct troponym}
- ○ (v) tramp down, trample, tread down (walk on and flatten) *"tramp down the grass"; "trample the flowers"*

Synset: (n) car, auto, automobile, machine, motorcar (a motor vehicle with four wheels; usually propelled by an internal combustion engine) *"he needs a car to get to work"*
- ○ {direct hyponym}
- ○ (n) bus, jalopy, heap (a car that is old and unreliable) *"the fenders had fallen off that old bus"*
- ○ (n) cab, hack, taxi, taxicab (a car driven by a person whose job is to take passengers where they want to go in exchange for money)

Apart from Wordnet, other popular sense inventories or *Machine Readable Dictionaries* (MRD) exist and are used as knowledge sources by several WSD algorithms. One such popular MRD is Roget's thesaurus wherein words are arranged into categories like *Sports*, *Finance*, *Animals/Birds*, and *Machinery*. For example, the word *crane* would appear in two categories, *viz.*, *Animals/Birds* and *Machinery*. These categories serve as different senses of words. Given such a repository of senses (*i.e.*, WordNet, Thesaurus or any other MRD), WSD can be viewed as a classification problem wherein the different senses of a word listed in the repository serve as the *class labels* and the evidences extracted from the *context* of the word serve as features. This evidence can be in the form of part-of-speech of the word, collocations, contextual words, semantic relations with other words in its neighborhood, *etc*. For example, in the first example sentence containing the word *bank* the contextual words *withdraw* and *money* provide sufficient evidence to identify the correct sense of the word. Similarly, in the second example sentence the collocation *river bank* provides sufficient evidence needed to identify the correct sense of the word.

Depending on the type of evidence or knowledge sources used, existing algorithms for WSD can be classified into two broad categories, *viz.*, knowledge-based approaches, and machine learning-based approaches. Machine learning based approaches can be further divided into supervised (require sense tagged corpus), unsupervised (require untagged corpus) and semi-supervised approaches (bootstrap using a small amount of tagged corpus and a large amount of untagged corpus). Apart from these, there are a few hybrid, Web-based, and bilingual approaches for WSD. Figure 1 gives a summary of the various approaches for WSD. In the forthcoming sections, we will give a primer to the different algorithms falling under each of these categories. A more detailed discussion on the existing approaches for WSD can be found in Ide and Véronis (1998) and Navigli (2009).

The remainder of this chapter is organized as follows. In section 2, we discuss knowledge-based

approaches for WSD. In sections 3, 4, and 5, we discuss supervised, semi-supervised, and unsupervised approaches, respectively. In section 6, we discuss hybrid, Web-based, and ensemble approaches for WSD. In section 7, we discuss some bilingual approaches for WSD. In section 8, we present some evaluation metrics which are commonly used for evaluating the performance of WSD engines. Finally, in section 9, we present a case study in domain-specific WSD.

2. KNOWLEDGE-BASED APPROACHES

These approaches rely only on knowledge sources such as lexical databases (*e.g.*, Wordnet or Thesaurus). They do not use any information from any corpus (tagged or untagged). These approaches can be further classified into 3 types, *viz.*, (1) overlap based approaches, (2) approaches using similarity measures, and (3) graph-based approaches.

- **Overlap-Based Approaches:** These approaches essentially calculate the overlap between the features describing a sense and the features describing a word in a given context. For example, consider a word *w* appearing in a context *C* and having *n* senses as listed in a lexical database. The features describing each sense of the word are extracted from a lexical database to form *n sense bags* (each sense bag is thus a bag-of-words, which captures the behavior specific to that sense). Similarly, the features describing the word in the given context *C* are extracted to form a *context bag* (the context bag is thus a bag-of-words, which captures the behavior exhibited by the word in the given context). The correct sense of the word in the given context can thus be identified by finding the *sense bag*, which has the maximum overlap with the *context bag*. Different algorithms falling

Figure 1. A taxonomy of monolingual approaches for WSD

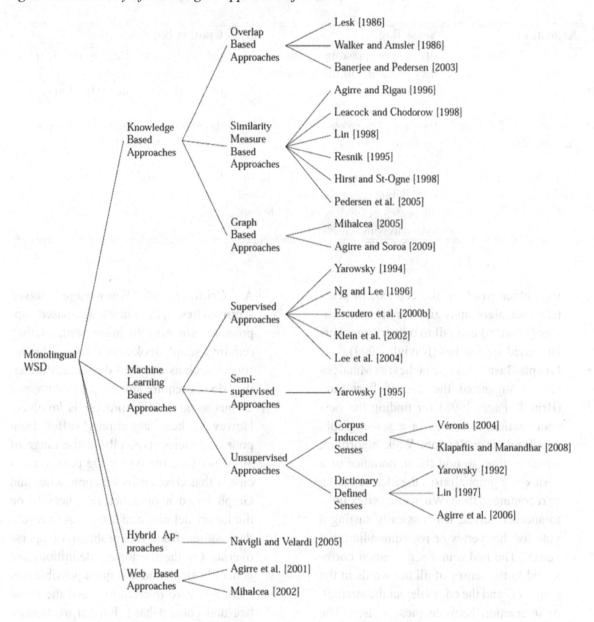

in this category differ only in the features used for constructing the sense bag and the context bag. Some popular overlap based approaches along with their sense bags and context bags are summarized in Table 1.

- **Using Semantic Similarity Measures:** Several semantic similarity measures, which exploit the hierarchical and graph based structure of Wordnet have been used

for WSD. The most popular ones include the measures proposed by Agirre and Rigau (1996), Leacock and Chodorow (1998), Lin (1998), Resnik (1995), Hirst and St-Ogne (1998), and Pedersen et al. (2005). The modus operandi of WSD algorithms based on semantic similarity measures is to select that sense of a word, which maximizes its semantic similarity

Table 1. Sense bags and context bags used by different overlap based approaches for WSD

Algorithm	Sense Bag	Context Bag
Lesk [Lesk, 1986]	the words appearing in the dictionary definition of the i-th sense	the words appearing in the dictionary definition of all the senses of all the words appearing in the context
Walker [Walker and Amsler, 1986]	the thesaurus category to which the i-th sense belongs	the thesaurus category of each sense of each context word
Extended Lesk [Banerjee and Pedersen, 2003]	the words appearing in the dictionary definition of the i-th sense and all senses related to it (*i.e.*, hypernyms, hyponyms, *etc.*)	the context words

with other words in the context. In practice, such algorithms give very low accuracies (30-40%) and fail to outperform overlap-based approaches (Navigli, 2009).

- **Graph-Based Approaches:** Mihalcea (2005) suggested the use of PageRank (Brin & Page, 1998) for finding the best combination of senses in a sense graph. PageRank is a Random Walk algorithm, which is used to find the importance of a vertex in a graph. It uses the idea of voting or recommendation. When one vertex links to another vertex, it is basically casting a vote for that vertex or recommending that vertex. The nodes in a sense graph correspond to the senses of all the words in the context C and the edges depict the strength of interaction between these senses. The weight *Wij* of the edge between two nodes, *Si* and *Sj*, is proportional to the overlap between the definitions of senses *Si* and *Sj* as found in the Wordnet. The problem is thus reduced to performing a PageRank calculation over a connected graph. This method collectively disambiguates all the words in the context C by selecting that sense for each word, which has been assigned the highest score by the PageRank formula.

- **A Critique of Knowledge Based Approaches:** All knowledge-based approaches are easy to implement, as they require a simple lookup of a knowledge resource such as a lexical database. Further, they do not require any tagged or untagged corpus as no training process is involved. However, these algorithms suffer from poor accuracies (typically in the range of 30-55%). One reason for the poor accuracies is that Overlap based approaches and Graph based approaches rely heavily on dictionary definition of senses. As a result, they suffer from the problem of sparse overlap (as the dictionary definitions are generally small and it is quite possible that there is a zero overlap between the sense bag and context bag). Further, dictionary definitions do not provide enough cues about the selectional preferences of different senses of a word. For example, we would expect the words *cigarette* and *ash* to co-occur as they are semantically related. However, the dictionary definitions of these words do not contain a reference to each other. Due to the failure of dictionary definitions to capture such distributional properties, there is often very little overlap between the *definition of a sense* and the *context of a word*.

Furthermore, approaches based on similarity measures such as Conceptual Density (Agirre & Rigau, 1996) assume that different senses of a word belong to different categories or different sub-trees. This assumption is valid in most cases (for example, the two senses of the word bank - one belonging to the concept *geological formation* and the other belonging to the concept *institution*) but might fail for some fine-grained senses of a word (for example, the two senses of the word *drug*—both belonging to the concept *medicine*).

In summary, complete dependence on a single knowledge source (*i.e.*, lexical database) limits the performance of knowledge-based approaches. This led to the idea of using corpus-based approaches (*i.e.*, using corpus evidence) instead of relying on dictionary evidence as discussed in the subsequent sections.

3. SUPERVISED APPROACHES

Supervised learning algorithms for WSD are mostly word specific classifiers, e.g., WSD using SVM (Lee, et al., 2004), exemplar-based WSD (Ng & Lee, 1996), and decision list-based algorithm (Yarowsky, 1994). They require a training corpus where several instances of an ambiguous word are manually annotated with the contextually appropriate sense. Using this training corpus, a classifier is built to disambiguate new instances of the ambiguous word. The annotated senses act as the class labels and various features extracted from the context provide the necessary evidence for training. These models thus learn a mapping from *(word, context)* → *sense*. Different supervised machine learning algorithms have been tried for word sense disambiguation, some of which are discussed below.

- **Naive Bayes:** Naive Bayes is one of the simplest and most widely used machine-learning algorithm. Here, WSD is formulated as the problem of finding the sense of a word which is most likely given the features exhibited by the word and its context (Escudero, et al., 2000b). In mathematical terms, we are interested in finding the sense, s^*, which maximizes $P(s \mid V_w)$, *i.e.*,

$$s^* = \arg\max_s P(s \mid V_w)$$

where Vw is the feature vector consisting of information about and around the word w. Applying Bayes rule and naive independence assumption (*i.e.*, assuming that the features are independent of each other) we get,

$$s^* = \arg\max_s P(s) * \prod_{i=1}^{n} P\left(V_{w_i} \mid s\right)$$

The parameters in the above equation, *viz.*, P(s) and $P\left(V_{w_i} \mid s\right)$ can be easily estimated from a sense annotated corpus using Maximum Likelihood Estimation (MLE).

- **Decision Lists:** Yarowsky (1994) suggested that the *"one-sense-per-collocation"* property of words can be exploited for WSD. The idea is to use an annotated corpus to learn the mappings between *(word, collocation)* → sense. Such mappings or rules are arranged in a list (known as decision list) such that the collocations having the highest log likelihood for a given sense appear at the top of the list. For example, consider the word *crane*, which has two senses, *viz.*, *bird* and *machinery*. In the *bird* sense, it has the following collocations: *fly, fish, dive, beak, etc.*, whereas in the *machinery* sense, it has the following collocations: *lift, drop, move, etc.* The log likelihood of a given collocation (say, *beak*) is calculated using the following formula:

$$LL\left(beak\right)_{bird\ sense} = \log \frac{P(bird\ sense| beak)}{P(machinery\ sense| beak)}$$

Once such an ordered list of mappings or rules is constructed from an annotated corpus, a test instance of the word *crane* can be disambiguated by extracting its collocations from the given context, matching it against all the rules in the decision list, and selecting the sense corresponding to the highest matching rule.

- **k-NN:** Another simple approach to supervised sense disambiguation is to assign a sense to a word appearing in a given test context by looking at its nearest neighbors in the training data (Ng & Lee, 1996). This algorithm is popularly known as the *k*-Nearest Neighbor algorithm. During the training phase each instance of an ambiguous word *w* (say, *bank*) in the training data is represented as a vector of features (*e.g.*, part-of-speech of the word and its neighboring words, collocations, contextual words, semantic relations, *etc.*). Now, given a test instance containing the ambiguous word, it is again represented as a vector using the same features. This vector corresponding to the test instance is then compared to every training instance. The *k* nearest training examples is selected. The sense which occurs the maximum number of times in these *k* nearest training examples is then selected as the winner sense (*i.e.*, we select the most prevailing sense among the *k* nearest training examples).
- **SVM:** Support Vector Machine (SVM) (Boser, et al., 1992) is another widely used machine-learning algorithm, which has been applied to the problem of WSD (Lee,

et al., 2004). SVM is a binary classifier, which finds a hyperplane that separates training examples into two classes with the largest possible margin. A test example is classified depending on the side of the hyperplane it lies on.

- **A Critique of Supervised Approaches:** Supervised approaches give better accuracies (typically in the range of 65-75%) than other approaches. However, these high accuracies come at the cost of requiring a significant amount of training data. The main factor responsible for the high WSD accuracies is that these algorithms use corpus evidence instead of relying on dictionary definitions. Specifically, distributional similarity between words like *ash* and *cigarette*, which are not captured in a dictionary, can be captured from a corpus. The downside of supervised approaches is that they require a large training corpus and hence are not directly suitable for many resource scarce languages. Only a few sense annotated datasets are available publicly (a few important ones are summarized in Table 2). Some of these datasets include hand labeled instances for all words, whereas others include instances for only a few target words. As is evident from Table 2, there are very few language-domain pairs for which sense annotated data is publicly available thereby restricting the applicability of supervised approaches to a few languages and domains.

4. SEMI-SUPERVISED APPROACHES

Semi-supervised or minimally supervised algorithms use a small amount of training data as seed to train an initial model for WSD. This model is then applied to an untagged corpus and the instances which are classified with a high confidence are

Table 2. A summary of a few publicly available datasets

Source	Popular Name	Language	Domain	Type
Miller et al. [1993]	SEMCOR	English	General	all words
Ng and Lee [1996]	DSO	English	General	target words
Weeber et al. [2001]	MEDLINE	English	Medical	all words
Van et al. [2002]	-	Dutch	Children's books	all words
Navarro et al. [2003]	Cast3LB	Spanish	General	all words
Bentivogli and Pianta [2005]	MultiSemCor	Italian	General	all words
Koeling et al. [2005]	-	English	Sports, Finance	target words
Khapra et al. [2010]	-	English, Hindi, Marathi	Health, Tourism	all words

then added to the initial seed data. A new model is then trained using this larger training set and the above process is repeated until all the instances in the untagged corpus are classified with a high confidence. Yarowsky (1995) describes a semi-supervised version of the decision list algorithm described in section 3. This algorithm starts by using seed collocations to identify a relatively small number of training examples representative of that sense. Seed collocations should accurately distinguish the senses. For example, *life* and *manufacturing* can be used as seed collocations for the two senses of *crane*. Once the seed collocations have been identified, we collect all the sentences, which contain the seed collocations. These sentences act as the initial seed data for creating a decision list, which is used to classify all the unlabeled instances of *crane* in the corpus. The instances which are assigned to the *bird* or *machinery* sense with a high confidence are then added to the training data. For example, we started out with the seed collocations *life* and *manufacturing*. Using these seed collocation, we collect unlabeled examples which are assigned to one of the two senses with high confidence. Now, these examples might contain some other collocations such as *species* and *equipment*, which are strong indicators of the two senses of *crane*. The decision

list is then reconstructed using this larger training data and the above process is repeated until all the instances are classified with high confidence or until the residual set (*i.e.*, the set containing the instances, which cannot be classified with high confidence) becomes constant.

5. UNSUPERVISED APPROACHES

Unlike supervised or semi-supervised algorithms, unsupervised algorithms do not require any tagged data. Hence, they do not face the knowledge acquisition bottleneck faced by these algorithms. Unsupervised approaches can be further classified into two types, *viz.*, (1) approaches which use dictionary defined senses (*e.g.*, Lin's algorithm [Lin, 1997] and Yarowsky's algorithm [Yarowsky, 1992]) and (2) approaches which induce senses from an untagged corpus (*e.g.*, Véronis, 2004; Manandhar & Klapaftis, 2009).

- **Lin's algorithm (Lin, 1997):** This algorithm is based on the idea that *"Two different words are likely to have similar meanings if they occur in identical local contexts."* However, instead of using a simple bag of neighboring words as local context, Lin used the syntactic dependencies between the ambiguous word and other words in the sentence as local context. For example, consider the sentence,

The facility will employ 500 new employees.

Here *facility* is an ambiguous word, which has 5 different senses1 (*viz., installation, proficiency, adeptness, readiness, and toilet*). By looking at the local context we observe that in this sentence *facility* is the subject of the verb *employ* (*i.e.*, there is a syntactic dependency between *facility* and *employ*). We now look at an untagged corpus and list all the words which have the same syntactic dependencies with a high likelihood (*i.e.*, we list down all the words that happen to be the subject of the word *employ*). These words, which have the same syntactic dependencies as the target words, are called *selector* words. In this case, *ORG, plant, company, industry,* and *unit* act as *selector* words as all these words appear as the subject of *employ* in an untagged corpus. Since these selector words are more similar to the *installation* sense of *facility* as compared to any other sense of factory we conclude that here the *installation* sense of *facility* is being used.

- **Yarowsky's Algorithm:** Yarowsky (1992) suggested the use of Roget's categories as classes for WSD. Sense disambiguation is done by selecting the category, which is most probable given the surrounding context. The algorithm begins by extracting neighboring words for each word belonging to a particular thesaurus category. From this list of neighboring words, the most salient words, *i.e.*, the words which co-occur frequently with the words belonging to this thesaurus category are identified and weighted using the following formula

$$Weight(word) = Salience(word)$$
$$= \frac{P(word \mid category)}{P(word)}$$

Now, given a test sentence containing an ambiguous word, its appropriate sense is predicted using the weights of the words in its context.

$$category^* = argmax_{category}$$
$$= \sum_{w \in context} \frac{P(w \mid category) * P(category)}{P(w)}$$

- **Unsupervised Word Sense Induction (WSI):** The main motivation for unsupervised WSI (Manandhar & Klapaftis, 2009; Agirre & Soroa, 2007) comes from the observation that hand-crafted dictionary definitions contained in lexical databases (such as Wordnet) sometimes fail to reflect the exact meaning of a target word appearing in a corpus. WSI aims to overcome these limitations by extracting the different senses of a word from the corpus itself instead of relying on a fixed-list of definitions as contained in a lexical database. Under this paradigm, graph based algorithms (Véronis, 2004; Agirre, et al., 2006; Klapaftis & Manandhar, 2008), which induce corpus senses by partitioning the co-occurrence graph of a target word, have shown promise. Here, every word appearing in the context of a target word is represented as a vertex. Two vertices are connected if they co-occur with each other. Once such a co-occurrence graph is constructed, standard graph partitioning algorithms are used to partition the graph. Each partition of the graph corresponds to words, which are indicative of a particular *corpus-sense* of the target word. A test instance of a target word can then be classified based on the semantic relatedness of its contextual words with the words in the different partitions of the graph.

One drawback of these approaches is that they require a large number of untagged instances for every target word to induce meaningful partitions in the co-occurrence graph. Such untagged instances are obtained by using a Web-based semi-automatic method by issuing queries containing the target word to commercial search engines (such as Bing, Yahoo, and Google). However, such an approach of collecting target-word specific data will not be applicable (especially in an all-words scenario) for resource poor languages which have a very poor Web presence.

- **A Critique of Semi-Supervised and Unsupervised Approaches:** Unsupervised and semi-supervised algorithms are capable of performing almost at par with supervised algorithms when tested on a specific set of target words. However, it is difficult to build general-purpose broad coverage classifiers since most semi-supervised and unsupervised algorithms, which perform well, are word specific classifiers (*e.g.*, Yarowsky, 1995; Véronis, 2004; Klapaftis & Manandhar, 2008), which need a large number of untagged examples for every target word. As mentioned earlier, even collecting unlabeled instances for *all words* is a difficult proposition for resource poor languages, which have poor Web presence. On the other hand, even though broad coverage unsupervised algorithms that exploit syntactic dependencies between words (*e.g.*, Lin, 1997) are able to perform large scale disambiguation (*i.e.*, they can be used for *all-words* WSD), their accuracies are much lower when compared to supervised algorithms.

6. MISCELLANEOUS APPROACHES

In this section, we discuss some miscellaneous approaches for WSD.

6.1. Web-Based Approaches

Some approaches exploit monosemous synonyms of polysemous words to automatically acquire sense labeled data from the Web. The sentences containing these monosemous words can be used as additional training data for building classifiers for their polysemous synonyms (Mihalcea, 2002). Such data can also be used for constructing topic signatures for capturing the behavior of a word in a particular sense (Agirre, et al., 2001). For example, if u is a monosemous synonym of a polysemous word v in sense S then the words which co-occur with u act as the signature (clues) for identifying sense S of word v. Such methods of acquiring automatically sense labeled data from the Web have shown promise (Mihalcea, 2002) but are not suitable for resource poor languages, which have very poor Web presence.

6.2. Hybrid Approaches

Hybrid approaches like WSD using Structural Semantic Interconnections (Navigli & Velardi, 2005) use combinations of more than one knowledge sources (WordNet as well as a small amount of tagged corpora). This allows them to capture important information encoded in WordNet (Fellbaum, 1998) as well as draw syntactic generalizations from minimally tagged corpora. *These methods which combine evidence from several resources seem to be most suitable in building general purpose broad coverage disambiguation engines.*

6.3. Ensemble Approaches

Some studies (Klein, et al., 2002) have shown that the accuracy of word sense disambiguation can be increased by combining different classifiers. Some popular approaches of combining different classifiers include majority voting, weighted voting, rank based voting, AdaBoost (Freund & Schapire, 1999), *etc.* (see Klein, et al., 2002 for further details).

7. BILINGUAL APPROACHES FOR WSD

The failure of monolingual approaches to deliver high accuracies for all-words WSD at low costs created interest in bilingual approaches, which aim at reducing the annotation effort. Here again, the approaches can be classified into two categories, *viz.*, (1) approaches using parallel corpora and (2) approaches using non-parallel corpora. Figure 2 provides a summary of the various bilingual approaches for WSD.

7.1. Using Parallel Corpora

The approaches to WSD which use parallel corpora rely on the paradigm of *Disambiguation by Translation* (Gale, et al., 1992; Dagan & Itai, 1994; Resnik & Yarowsky, 1999; Ide, et al., 2001; Diab & Resnik, 2002; Ng, et al., 2003; Tufi, et al., 2004; Apidianaki, 2008). Such algorithms rely on the frequently made observation that a word in a given source language tends to have different translations in a target language depending on its sense. Given a sentence-and-word-aligned parallel corpus, these different translations in the target language can serve as automatically acquired sense labels for the source word. Hence, instead of relying on human annotated data these algorithms rely on the information encoded in the lexical choices made by human translators. Although these algorithms give high accuracies, the requirement of a significant amount of bilingual parallel corpora may be an unreasonable demand for many language pairs (perhaps more unreasonable than collecting sense annotated corpora itself). Furthermore, some of these algorithms require bilingual pre-processing tools such as word-aligners (for aligning transla-

Figure 2. A taxonomy of bilingual approaches for NLP

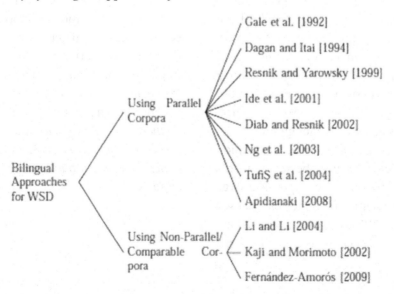

tion equivalents in parallel texts) which is again a tall task for many resource poor language pairs.

7.2. Using Non-Parallel Corpora

These approaches do not use parallel corpora but rely on in-domain corpora from two languages, as discussed below.

- **Li and Li (2004):** Li and Li (2004) proposed a bilingual bootstrapping approach for the more specific task of Word Translation Disambiguation (WTD) as opposed to the more general task of WSD. This approach does not need parallel corpora and relies only on in-domain corpora from two languages. However, their work was evaluated only on a handful of target words (9 nouns) for WTD and has not been tried for all-words WSD.

- **Kaji and Morimoto (2002):** Another approach worth mentioning here is the one proposed by Kaji and Morimoto (2002) which aligns statistically significant pairs of related words in language *L1* with their cross-lingual counterparts in language *L2* using a bilingual dictionary. This approach is based on two assumptions: (1) words which are most significantly related to a target word provide clues about the sense of the target word and (2) translations of these related words further reinforce the sense distinctions. The translations of related words thus act as cross-lingual clues for disambiguation. This algorithm when tested on 60 polysemous words (using English as *L1* and Japanese as *L2*) delivered high accuracies (coverage=88.5% and precision=77.7%). However, when used in an all-words scenario on our dataset this algorithm performed poorly (F-score = 9-12%).

- **Fernández-Amorós (2009):** More recently, Fernández-Amorós (2009) proposed a preliminary approach, which uses comparable corpora and aligned wordnets (Eurowordnet [Vossen & Letteren, 1997]) to perform WSD using cross-lingual clues for disambiguation. Phrases appearing in the context of a target word in language *L1* are automatically aligned to their counterparts in another language *L2* using bilingual comparable corpora. These translated contextual clues then help in identifying the correct sense of the target word by filtering out the inappropriate senses from the aligned Wordnets. However, they reported a recall of 2.74% on the SemCor corpus, which is very low for any practical utility.

In summary, like most problems in NLP, word sense Disambiguation faces the dilemma of choosing between cost on one hand and accuracy on the other hand. In situations where high WSD accuracy is desired for all words, one has to settle for supervised approaches and bear the associated cost of annotating data.

8. EVALUATION METRICS

There are 4 measures (*viz.*, Coverage, Precision, Recall, and F-score) which are used for evaluating the performance of WSD systems. These measures are borrowed from Machine Learning and Information Retrieval and are described below.

$$Coverage\,(C) = \frac{no.\ of\ words\ disambiguated}{total\ no.\ of\ words\ in\ the\ test\ corpus}$$

$$Precision\left(P\right)$$
$$= \frac{no.\ of\ words\ disambiguated\ correctly}{total\ no.\ of\ words\ disambiguated}$$

$$Recall\left(R\right)$$
$$= \frac{no.\ of\ words\ disambiguated\ correctly}{total\ no.\ of\ words\ in\ the\ test\ corpus}$$

$$F - score\left(F\right) = \frac{2 * P * R}{P + R}$$

Following standard practice, for all the results reported in this chapter, we use *Precision, Recall, and F-score* as the evaluation metrics. Note that we exclude monosemous words while evaluating the performance of our algorithms. Also note that, for systems which produce a sense label for every word in the test corpus $P = R = F$.

9. A CASE STUDY IN DOMAIN-SPECIFIC WSD

Recently there has been a lot of interest in domain-specific WSD. A testimony to this is the inclusion of the task on *"All-words Word Sense Disambiguation on a Specific Domain"* in the recently concluded SEMEVAL 2010 workshop which acknowledges that, *"...the behavior of WSD systems on domain specific texts is largely unknown"* (Agirre, et al., 2009a). Despite its importance and profound implications, a large-scale study of domain specific WSD has not been possible due to the lack of domain-specific all-words sense marked corpora. In this section, we present a case study in domain specific WSD on a large all-words sense tagged corpora (Khapra, et al., 2010). The aim of this study is to understand the importance of different parameters/features used for WSD. Specifically, we wanted to establish

that for domain specific WSD, sense distribution is the only parameter which matters and other parameters do not contribute much. We first introduce these parameters in the next section and then propose a scoring function, which combines these parameters to rank the different senses of an ambiguous word.

9.1. Parameters Essential for WSD

Intuitively, a number of parameters can play a crucial role in WSD. To appreciate this, consider the following example:

The river flows through this region to meet the sea.

The word *sea* is ambiguous and has three senses as given in the Princeton Wordnet (PWN):

S1: (n) sea (a division of an ocean or a large body of salt water partially enclosed by land)
S2: (n) ocean, sea (anything apparently limitless in quantity or volume)
S3: (n) sea (turbulent water with swells of considerable size) "heavy seas"

The first parameter is obtained from *Domain specific sense distributions.* In the above example, the first sense is more frequent in the tourism domain (verified from manually sense marked tourism corpora). Domain specific sense distribution information should be harnessed in the WSD task.

The second parameter arises from the *dominance of senses in the domain.* Senses are expressed by synsets, and we define a dominant sense as follows:

A synset node in the wordnet hypernymy hierarchy is called dominant if the synsets in the sub-tree rooted at the synset frequently occur in the domain corpora.

A few dominant senses2 in the Tourism domain are *{place, country, city, area}, {body of water}, {flora, fauna}, {mode of transport},* and *{fine arts}*. In disambiguating a word, that sense which belongs to the sub-tree of a domain-specific dominant sense should be given a higher score than other senses. The value of this parameter (θ) is decided as follows:

- $\theta = 1$; if the candidate synset is a dominant synset
- $\theta = 0.5$; if the candidate synset belongs to the sub-tree of a dominant synset
- $\theta = 0.001$; if the candidate synset is neither a dominant synset nor belongs to the sub-tree of a dominant synset.

The third parameter comes from *Corpus Co-Occurrence*. This is calculated as *P(Si|Sj)* where *Si* is the candidate sense for the word being disambiguated and *Sj* is the sense of an already disambiguated contextual word. The intuition here is that co-occurring monosemous words as well as *already disambiguated words* in the context help in disambiguation. For example, the word *river* appearing in the context of sea is a monosemous word. The frequency of co-occurrence of *river* with the "water body" sense of *sea* is high in the tourism domain and hence it is a good indicator of this sense. Corpus co-occurrence is calculated by considering the senses, which occur in a window of 10 words around a sense.

The fourth parameter is based on the *semantic distance* between any pair of synsets in terms of the shortest path length between two synsets in the wordnet graph. An edge in the shortest path can be any semantic relation from the wordnet relation repository (*e.g., hypernymy, hyponymy, meronymy, holonymy, troponymy, etc.*).

For nouns, we do something additional over and above the semantic distance. We take advantage of the deeper hierarchy of noun senses in the wordnet structure. This gives rise to the fifth and final parameter, which arises out of the

conceptual distance between a pair of senses. Conceptual distance between two synsets *S1* and *S2* is calculated using Equation (1), motivated by Agirre and Rigau (1996).

$$ConceptualDistance\left(S_1, S_2\right) = \frac{Length\ of\ the\ path\ between\ S_1\ and\ S_2\ in\ terms\ of\ hypernymy\ hierarchy}{Lowest\ common\ ancestor\ of\ S_1\ and\ S_2\ in\ the\ wordnet\ hierarchy}$$

(1)

The conceptual distance is proportional to the path length between the synsets, as it should be. The distance is also inversely proportional to the height of the common ancestor of two sense nodes, because as the common ancestor becomes more and more general the conceptual relatedness tends to get vacuous (e.g., two nodes related through *entity*, which is the common ancestor of EVERYTHING, does not really say anything about the relatedness).

To summarize, the various parameters used for domain-specific WSD are:

- *Wordnet-dependent parameters*
  - o *Belongingness-to-dominant-concept*
  - o *Conceptual-distance*
  - o *Semantic-distance*
- *Corpus-dependent parameters*
  - o *Sense distributions*
  - o *Corpus co-occurrence*

Note that unlike many other approaches we do not use word based parameters, such as, part of speech tags of neighboring words, word collocations, *etc.* in our scoring function. Even though our algorithms do not use word based features (*i.e.,* pos tags, collocations, *etc.*), we still wanted to evaluate the performance of these features in order to ensure that our case study is exhaustive. We do so by using a state of the art supervised algorithm which uses such word based features (see section 9.4).

The parameters listed above have been used in previous works on WSD (*e.g.,* conceptual distance is used by Agirre and Rigau [1996], semantic distance is used by Navigli and Velardi [2005], and so on). Our main contribution lies in combining these parameters in an intuitive manner as described below.

9.2. A Scoring Function for Ranking Senses

Based on the above parameters, we desired a scoring function which:

1. Uses the strong clues for disambiguation provided by the monosemous words and the already disambiguated words
2. Uses sense distributions learnt from a sense tagged corpus
3. Captures the effect of dominant concepts within a domain, and
4. Captures the interaction of a candidate synset with others synsets in the sentence.

We have been motivated by the Energy expression in Hopfield network (Hopfield, 1982) in formulating a scoring function for ranking the senses. Hopfield Network is a fully connected bidirectional symmetric network of bi-polar (0/1 or +1/-1) neurons. We consider the asynchronous Hopfield Network. At any instant, a randomly chosen neuron (a) examines the weighted sum of the input, (b) compares this value with a threshold, and (c) gets to the state of 1 or 0, depending on whether the input is greater than or less than or equal to the threshold. The assembly of 0/1 states of individual neurons defines a state of the whole network. Each state has associated with it an energy, E, given by the following expression

$$E = \theta_i V_i - \sum_{i=1}^{N} \sum_{j>i}^{N} W_{ij} V_i V_j \qquad (2)$$

where, N is the total number of neurons in the network, i and j are the activations of neurons i and j respectively and Wij is the weight of the connection between *ith* and *jth* neurons. Energy is a fundamental property of Hopfield networks, providing the necessary machinery for discussing convergence, stability and such other considerations.

The energy expression as given above cleanly separates the influence of self-activations of neurons and that of interactions amongst neurons to the global macroscopic property of energy of the network. This fact has been the primary insight for equation (3), which was proposed to score the most appropriate synset in the given context. The correspondences are as follows:

- *Neuron→ Synset*
- *Self-activation→ Corpus Sense Distribution*
  Weight of connection between two neurons→ Weight as a function of corpus co-occurrence and Wordnet distance measures between synsets

$$S^* = \operatorname*{argmax}_i \left(\theta_i * V_i + \sum_{j \in J} W_{ij} * V_i * U_j \right) \qquad (3)$$

where,

$J = Set\ of\ disambiguated\ Words$

$\theta_i = Belongingness To Dominant Concept(S_i)$

$V_i = P\left(S_i \mid word\right)$

$U_j = P\left(sense\ assigned\ to\ word_j \mid word_j\right)$

$W_{ij} = Corpus Cooccurences\left(S_i, S_j\right)$

$* \dfrac{1}{WN Conceptual Distance(S_i, S_j)}$

$* \dfrac{1}{WN Semantic Graph Distance(S_i, S_j)}$

The component $\theta_i \cdot V_i$ is the energy due to the self-activation of a neuron and can be compared to the corpus specific sense of a word in a domain. The other component $W_{ij} \cdot V_j \cdot V_j$ coming from the interaction of activations can be compared to the score of a sense due to its interaction in the form of corpus co-occurrence, conceptual distance, and wordnet-based semantic distance with other words in the sentence. The first component thus captures the rather *static corpus sense*, whereas the second expression brings in the *sentential context*.

9.3. WSD Algorithms Employing the Scoring Function

We now put the scoring function (and thereby the parameters) to test by using it to perform monolingual WSD. For this, we propose 2 graph based algorithms which use the above scoring function to arrive at sense decisions. The first is a greedy iterative algorithm, and the second is a brute force algorithm, which performs an exhaustive search to find the best path in a sense graph constructed using contextual words in a sentence. Each of these algorithms are described in detail below.

Algorithm 1: Iterative WSD (IWSD)

The steps involved in our greedy iterative algorithm are summarized below:

Algorithm 1: performIterativeWSD(sentence)
1. Tag all monosemous words in the sentence.
2. Iteratively disambiguate the remaining words in the sentence in increasing order of their degree of polysemy.
3. At each stage select that sense for a word which maximizes the score given by Equation (3)

Monosemous words are used as the seed input for the algorithm. Note that they are left out of consideration while calculating the precision and recall values. In case there are no monosemous words in the sentence, the disambiguation starts with the first term in the formula, which represents the corpus bias (the second term will not be active as there are no previously disambiguated words). The least polysemous words are disambiguated first and then act as the seed input to the algorithm.

IWSD is clearly greedy. It bases its decisions on already disambiguated words, and completely ignores words with higher degree of polysemy. For example, while disambiguating bisemous words, the algorithm uses only the monosemous words and ignores completely the trisemous words and higher order polysemous words appearing in the context. This is illustrated in Figure 3. As shown in Figure 3, Word3 is the polysemous word currently being disambiguated. The algorithm only considers the interaction of its candidate senses with already disambiguated words and monosemous words in the context (shown in dark circles). Word4 (which is more polysemous than Word3) does not come into picture.

Algorithm 2: Exhaustive Graph Search Algorithm

Suppose there are *n* words W1, W2, W3,...,Wn in a sentence with m1, m2, m3,...,mn senses respectively. WSD can then be viewed as the task of finding the best possible combination of senses from the possible $m_1 \cdot m_2 \cdot m_3 \cdot \ldots \cdot m_n$ combinations.

Each of these combinations can be assigned a score, and the combination with the highest score gets selected. The score of each node in the combination can be calculated using Equation (4).

$$score(node_i) = \theta_i * V_i + \sum_{\substack{j \in allWords \\ j \neq i}} W_{ij} * V_i * U_j$$

(4)

Figure 3. Greedy operation of IWSD

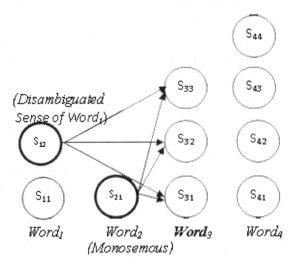

The terms on the right-hand-side have the same meaning as in equation (3). Note that the summation in the second term is performed over all words as opposed to IWSD where the summation was performed only over previously disambiguated words. Thus unlike IWSD, this algorithm allows *all* the words, already disambiguated or otherwise, to influence the decision for the current polysemous word.

The score of a combination is simply the sum of the scores of the individual nodes in the combination.

$$score\left(combination\right) = \sum_{i \in all\ nodes} score(node_i)$$

(5)

Note: The second term is halved to account for the fact that each term in the summation is added twice.

As shown in Figure 4, there is an edge between every sense of every word and every sense of every other word which means that every word influences the sense decision for every other word. Contrast this with IWSD where Word4 had no say in the disambiguation of Word3. In addition,

the objective here is to select the best combination at one go as compared to IWSD which disambiguates only one word at a time. Note that each combination must contain at most and at least one sense node corresponding to every word. A possible best combination along with the connecting edges is highlighted in Figure 2. This is definitely not a practical approach as it searches all the possible $m_1 \cdot m_2 \cdot m_3 \cdot \ldots \cdot m_n$ combinations to find the best combination and hence has exponential time complexity. However, we still present it for the purpose of comparison.

9.4. Other State-of-the-Art Algorithms for WSD

This case study on monolingual WSD would be incomplete without comparison with the current state of the art algorithms. In this section, we briefly discuss the best performing algorithms in each genre (knowledge based, supervised and unsupervised) and later on present the results for each of these algorithms on our dataset (in section 9.6).

Figure 4. Exhaustive operation of graph search method

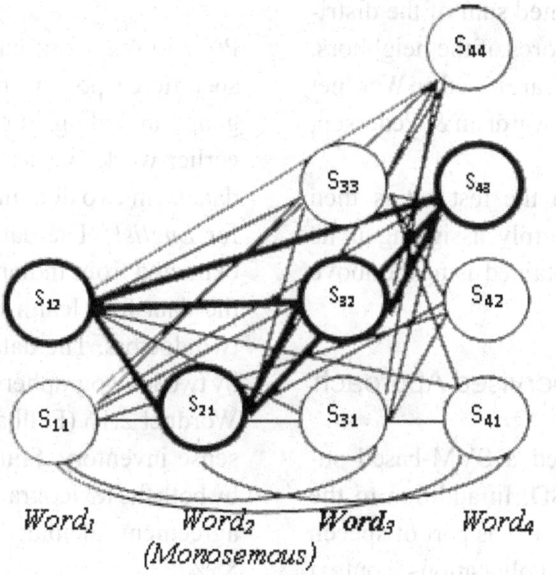

A State-of-the-Art Knowledge-Based Approach

The knowledge-based approach proposed by Agirre et al. (2009b) is known to give good accuracies (even better than supervised approaches) when tested on specific domains (for a set of chosen target words). This algorithm involves the following steps:

1. Represent Wordnet as a graph where the concepts (*i.e.*, synsets) act as nodes and the relations between concepts define edges in the graph.
2. Apply a context-dependent *Personalized PageRank* algorithm on this graph by introducing the context words as nodes into the graph and linking them with their respective synsets.
3. These nodes corresponding to the context words then inject probability mass into the synsets they are linked to, thereby influencing the final relevance of all nodes in the graph.

We used the publicly available implementation of this algorithm3 for our experiments.

A State-of-the-Art Unsupervised Approach

The unsupervised algorithm proposed by McCarthy et al. (2007) for predicting the domain-specific predominant senses of a word is known to give the best performance amongst all unsupervised algorithms. We implemented their method using the following steps:

1. Obtain a domain-specific untagged corpus (we crawled a corpus of approximately 9M words from the Web).
2. Extract grammatical relations from this text using a dependency parser4 (Klein & Manning, 2003).
3. Use the grammatical relations thus extracted to construct features for identifying the *k* nearest neighbors for each word using the distributional similarity score described in Lin (1998).

4. Rank the senses of each target word in the test set using a weighted sum of the distributional similarity scores of the neighbors. The weights in the sum are based on Wordnet Similarity scores (Patwardhan & Pedersen, 2003).

5. Each target word in the test set is then disambiguated by simply assigning it its predominant sense obtained using the above method.

A State-of-the-Art Supervised Approach

Lee *et al.* (2004) proposed a SVM-based supervised classifier for WSD. In addition to the commonly used features (such as part of speech tag of neighboring words, collocations, context words, *etc.*) they introduced the following syntactic features depending on the part-of-speech tag of the word.

1. **Nouns:** If *w* is a noun then its parent headword (*h*), the POS of *h*, the voice of *h* (*i.e.*, active or passive if *h* is a verb or *null* if *h* is not a verb) and the relative position of *h* with respect to *w* are used as syntactic features.

He turned his head (NN) towards the television.

<turned, VBD, active, left>

He turned (VBD) his head towards the television.

<he, turned, PRP, NN, VBD, active>

The white ball was kept in a red (JJ) box.

<box, NN>

These syntactic features are extracted using a statistical parser (Lee, et al., 2004). We used the publicly available implementation5 of this algorithm for all our experiments.

9.5. Dataset

Prior to our work large scale all words domain specific corpora were not available in any language including English. Hence, as part of our earlier work, we set upon the task of collecting data from two domains, *viz.*, *Tourism* and *Health* for *English*. The data for Tourism domain was extracted from Indian Tourism websites whereas the data for Health domain was obtained from two doctors. The data was then sense annotated by two lexicographers adept in English. Princeton Wordnet 2.16 (Fellbaum, 1998) was used as the sense inventory. Some files were sense marked by both the lexicographers and the inter-annotator agreement calculated from these files was around 85%.

This was a first of its kind effort at collecting all-words domain specific sense marked corpora. This data is now freely available for research purposes to help advancing research in domain-specific all-words WSD.

We now present different statistics about the corpora. Apart from the Tourism and Health domain data collected we also used the publicly available SemCor corpus for some of our experiments. Hence, we present the statistics of this corpus also. Tables 3 and 4 summarize the number of polysemous and monosemous words per category in each domain. Table 5 gives the number of unique polysemous words per category in each domain. Table 6 gives the number of instances per polysemous word per category in each domain. Finally Tables 7 and 8 summarize the average degree of wordnet polysemy and corpus polysemy of the polysemous words in the corpus. Wordnet polysemy is the number of senses of a word as listed in the Wordnet, whereas corpus polysemy is the number of senses of a word actually appearing in the corpus. As expected, due to the domain-specific nature of the corpora, the average degree of corpus polysemy (cf. Table 8) is much less than the average degree of Wordnet polysemy (cf. Table 7). Further, the average degree

Table 3. Number of polysemous words per category in each domain

	Tourism	English Health	SemCor
Noun	62636	53173	66194
Verb	30269	31382	84815
Adjective	25295	21091	24946
Adverb	7018	6421	11803
All	125218	112067	187758

Table 4. Number of monosemous words per category in each domain

	Tourism	English Health	SemCor
Noun	25345	19400	17642
Verb	1413	1189	4467
Adjective	13318	9952	8969
Adverb	4449	5070	7704
All	44525	35611	38782

Table 5. Number of unique polysemous words per category in each domain

	Tourism	English Health	SemCor
Noun	4307	3185	5921
Verb	1804	1560	3135
Adjective	1738	1602	2559
Adverb	310	281	454
All	8159	6628	12069

Table 6. Average number of instances per polysemous word per category in each domain

	Tourism	English Health	SemCor
Noun	14.54	16.69	11.18
Verb	16.78	20.12	27.05
Adjective	14.55	13.17	9.75
Adverb	22.64	22.85	26.00
All	15.35	16.91	15.56

Table 7. Average degree of wordnet polysemy of polysemous words per category in each domain

	Tourism	English Health	SemCor
Noun	3.74	3.97	3.55
Verb	5.01	5.31	4.28
Adjective	3.47	3.57	3.26
Adverb	2.89	2.96	2.72
All	3.93	4.15	3.64

Table 8. Average degree of corpus polysemy of polysemous words per category in each domain

	Tourism	English Health	SemCor
Noun	1.68	1.57	1.90
Verb	2.06	1.99	2.44
Adjective	1.67	1.57	1.70
Adverb	1.81	1.75	1.79
All	1.77	1.68	1.99

of corpus polysemy in the two domains is less than that in the mixed-domain SemCor corpus, which is again expected due to the domain specific nature of the corpora.

9.6. Results

We now report the performance of the above algorithms on two domains, *viz.*, *Tourism* and *Health* for English. For each domain, we did a 4-fold cross validation. Note that even though we reported the number of monosemous words in each domain in Table 4, we do not consider these words during evaluation. These words are only used as seed input to the algorithm. Since monosemous words do not need any disambiguation, it would be obviously unfair to use them while calculating the precision and recall values. We follow this practice of not including monosemous words during evaluation for all the results reported in this chapter. We report the P, R, and F-scores obtained by employing the following algorithms:

1. **IWSD:** the iterative word sense disambiguation algorithm described in section 9.3.
2. **EGS:** the exhaustive graph search algorithm described in section 9.3.
3. **PPR:** a state of the art knowledge based approach described in section 9.4.
4. **SVM:** a state of the art supervised approach which uses a SVM based classifier for sense disambiguation (described in section 9.4).
5. **McCarthy *et al.* (2007):** a state of the art unsupervised approach described in section 9.4.
6. **RB:** randomly selects one of the senses of the word from the Wordnet.
7. **WFS:** assigns the first sense of the word from the Wordnet.
8. **MFS:** assigns the most frequent sense of the word as obtained from an annotated corpus.

The first two results (IWSD and EGS) give an idea about the performance of the proposed scoring function in 2 different settings (greedy v/s iterative). The next three results (PPR, SVM, and

Table 9. Precision, recall, and f-scores of different WSD algorithms

Algorithms	Tourism			Health		
	P%	R%	F%	P%	R%	F%
SVM	78.82	78.76	78.79	79.64	79.59	79.61
IWSD	77.00	76.66	76.83	78.78	78.42	78.60
MFS	77.60	75.20	76.38	79.43	76.98	78.19
WFS	62.15	62.15	62.15	64.67	64.67	64.67
PPR	53.1	53.1	53.1	51.1	51.1	51.1
[McCarthy et al., 2007]	51.85	49.32	50.55	-	-	-
RB	25.50	25.50	25.50	24.61	24.61	24.61

Table 10. Precision, recall, and f-scores of IWSD and EGS on a restricted set of sentences

Algorithms	Tourism			Health		
	P%	R%	F%	P%	R%	F%
IWSD	77.00	76.66	76.83	78.78	78.42	78.60
EGS	74.03	74.03	74.03	75.81	75.81	75.81

McCarthy *et al.* [2007]) provide a comparison with other state of the art algorithms for WSD. The final three results provide a comparison with typically reported baselines for WSD. Since EGS is essentially a brute force method it was computationally infeasible to run it on the entire dataset. Hence, we ran it only on those sentences for which the total number of sense combinations (*i.e.*, $m_1 \cdot m_2 \cdot m_3 \cdot .... \cdot m_n$) was less than 50000. For comparison purposes, the results of IWSD and EGS on this restricted dataset are provided separately in Table 10, while the results of the other 7 algorithms on the entire dataset are summarized in Table 9.

9.7. Discussions

We now discuss the results presented in Tables 9 and 10.

9.7.1. Comparison with Other State-of-the-Art Approaches

We first present a comparison with the state of the art approaches described in section 9.4. It is to be

noticed that it is unfair to compare our supervised approach with knowledge based and unsupervised approaches but we still present this comparison for the sake of completeness and for putting the results in the right perspective.

- **Knowledge-Based Approach:** The results, as summarized in Table 9, show that the performance of the PPR algorithm comes nowhere close to any of the supervised approaches (*i.e.*, IWSD, EGS, SVM, and MFS). This is expected as this algorithm relies only on the relations between concepts in a Lexical Knowledge Base (wordnet, in this case) and does not use any evidence extracted from a corpus (tagged or untagged). For the same reason, the performance of the algorithm is poor when compared to the WFS baseline, which relies on sense counts derived from the SemCor corpus. The performance of the PPR algorithm is good as compared to the random baseline. The results clearly indicate that this algorithm falls in the category of *low cost low accuracy* algorithms and is not suitable in situations where a high accuracy is desired for all words.

- **Unsupervised Approach:** McCarthy *et al.* (2004) reported that the best results were obtained using *k=50* neighbors and the Wordnet similarity *jcn* measure (Jiang & Conrath, 1997). Following them, we used *k=50* and observed that the best results for nouns and verbs were obtained using the *jcn* measure and the best results for adjectives and adverbs were obtained using the *lesk* measure (Banerjee & Pedersen, 2002). Accordingly, we used *jcn* for nouns and verbs and *lesk* for adjectives and adverbs. Each target word in the test set is then disambiguated by simply assigning it its predominant sense obtained using the above method.

The results, as summarized in Table 9, show that the performance of this algorithm is very poor when compared to any of the supervised approaches (*i.e.*, IWSD, EGS, SVM, and MFS). In fact, the performance of the algorithm is better than only the random baseline and is poor when compared to the WFS baseline also. This is expected as this algorithm relies only on an untagged corpus and does not rely on sense distributions learned from an annotated corpus. Apart from the poor results, this approach has two severe drawbacks, (1) it requires a large amount of untagged corpus (of the order of 2 to 9 million words) and (2) it needs a dependency parser. Collecting even an untagged corpus of this magnitude could be an unreasonable demand for some languages and domains. We could test this approach only on Tourism domain for English due to unavailability of large untagged corpus in Health domain. Furthermore, dependency parsers are not available for many languages, which renders this approach infeasible. The results indicate that these algorithms, while suitable for a small set of target words (McCarthy, et al., 2004), do not scale well when applied to an all words scenario.

- **Supervised Approach:** The performance of our algorithm is comparable (within 1-2%) to that of the SVM approach proposed by Lee *et al.* (2004). This is appreciable since our algorithm does not use any word-based features or syntactic features, which require a statistical parser (Charniak, 1999). As is evident from Table 9, such rich features do not contribute much to WSD. In fact, the performance of the 3 supervised algorithms (*i.e.*, IWSD, EGS, and SVM) is very close to that of MFS which suggests that for domain-specific WSD simply picking up the most frequent sense of the word is sufficient to get high accuracies and other features (whether word-based or sense based) do not contribute much to the overall accuracy. Our observations about the importance of domain-specific sense distributions are in line with similar results reported by other researchers (Escudero, et al., 2000a; Magnini, et al., 2002).

9.7.2. Comparison of the 2 Algorithms that use our Scoring Function

The greedy search performed by IWSD does better (around +3%) than the brute force search done by EGS. This shows that taking decisions based on semantic relatedness with all words in the context can sometimes be misleading. Instead, a greedy approach which relies more on *self merit* and less on *contextual merit* can deliver better results. This is mainly because of the dominance of the sense distributions ($P(Si|word)$) in the overall performance. These results (along with the results for SVM) clearly prove that domain-specific sense distributions are what really matter in WSD and other features do not contribute much to the performance. Even though there is not much quantitative difference between the algorithms, we present a qualitative comparison of these 2 algorithms below.

Figure 5. A spectrum showing the position of different WSD algorithms

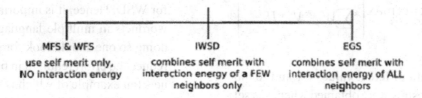

MFS and WFS lie at one end of the spectrum (see Figure 5) as they rely only on the self energy of the node (in terms of ranking in corpus and ranking in wordnet respectively) and completely ignore the interaction with other senses in the context. EGS lies at the other end of the spectrum as it combines the self energy with the interaction energy derived from the interaction with all words in the context. IWSD lies somewhere at the middle of the spectrum as it combines the self energy of a node with its interaction energy based on interaction with only few (previously disambiguated) words in the context. However, given that the performances of the algorithms are very close to each other, it does not matter whether one performs an exhaustive search or a greedy search over the synset graph.

9.7.3. Ablation Test to determine the Contribution of Each Parameter

The results presented in Table 9 clearly suggest that the parameter $P(Si|word)$ is the most important parameter for high accuracy WSD. To conclusively establish this fact, we performed an ablation test where we disabled one parameter at a time in the scoring function and calculated the corresponding changes in performance. A parameter is disabled by setting its value to a constant k (0.0001) for all the candidate synsets so that it cannot play any discriminating role. The results of this ablation test are summarized in Table 11.

As expected, the drop in the F-score was maximum when the parameter $P(Si|word)$ was disabled. Disabling the other parameters does not have much impact in the overall F-score. This test consolidates the fact that $P(Si|word)$ is indeed the most crucial parameter for high accuracy WSD.

At this point, the importance of $P(Si|word)$ is clearly established, but for the sake of completeness we performed a set of experiments to determine the contribution of the two terms in the scoring functions (*i.e.*, *self energy* and *interaction energy*). For this, we used a weighted version of the scoring function proposed in Equation 3 as shown below,

Table 11. Results for ablation test indicating the contribution of each parameter

Ablation Parameter (*i.e.*, the parameter which was set to 1 for all candidate synsets)	Tourism			Health		
	P%	R%	F%	P%	R%	F%
θ_i	77.85	66.39	71.67	79.66	67.98	73.36
$P(S_i|word)$	22.21	19.54	20.79	21.18	18.71	19.87
$CorpusCooccurrence(S_i, S_j)$	76.91	76.57	76.74	78.76	78.39	78.57
$WNConceptualDistance(S_i, S_j)$	77.01	76.60	76.80	78.80	78.31	78.55
$WNConceptualDistance(S_i, S_j)$	77.61	75.28	76.43	79.42	77.10	78.24
Using all parameters	77.00	76.66	76.83	78.78	78.42	78.60

$$S^* = \underset{i}{\operatorname{argmax}}\,\underset{i}{\operatorname{argmax}}\begin{pmatrix} \lambda * \theta_i * V_i + (1 - \lambda) \\ * \sum_{j \in J} W_{ij} * V_i * U_j \end{pmatrix}$$

We tried with different values for and found that the worst results were obtained when was set to a very low value (0.00001, which is as good as disabling *P(Si|word)*). Since the findings of this particular set of experiments (performed by varying the value of) do not add anything more to the already made observations, we do not present the details here.

9.8. Key Observations from the Case Study on Domain-Specific WSD

The important observations made from this case study are summarized below.

1. Domain specific sense distributions (or counts) are very important for WSD thereby highlighting the importance of sense-annotated corpora. In the absence of such sense-annotated corpus in a particular language, one should device means of porting the sense counts learned from one language to another.

2. Wordnet based parameters do not contribute much to the performance of WSD engines. One reason for this could be the failure of Wordnets to capture distributional properties of words. For example, the word *cigarette* could help in disambiguating the meaning of *ash*, but there is no relation between the synsets of *cigarette* and *ash* in the Wordnet. Perhaps a richer ontology would help in increasing the contribution of the second term (i.e., interaction energy) in the scoring function. However, the importance of wordnet as a sense repository cannot be undermined. By acting as a sense repository

it provides the most elementary resource for WSD. Hence, it is important to develop wordnets in multiple languages and while doing so one should look for smart ways to reduce the effort required in building wordnets (an example of which is the expansion approach for building wordnets [Mohanty, et al., 2008]).

3. Word based features such as part of speech tags, collocations do not contribute much to the performance of WSD. Even richer features such as syntactic dependencies extracted using sophisticated syntactic parsers are not of much help. Further, in resource-constrained scenarios it is not possible to use such features due to the unavailability of such parsers for many resource poor languages.

10. SUMMARY

In this chapter, we discussed the basics of Word Sense Disambiguation and gave a primer to some popular approaches used for solving this problem. These algorithms range from low cost, low accuracy knowledge-based approaches on one hand to high cost, high accuracy supervised approaches on the other hand. We then addressed the problem of domain specific Word Sense Disambiguation and highlighted that when restricted to specific domains it is possible to get very high performance on WSD by simply selecting the most frequent sense as estimated from a sense tagged corpus.

REFERENCES

Agirre, E., Ansa, O., & Martinez, D. (2001). Enriching wordnet concepts with topic signatures. In *Proceedings of the NAACL Workshop on WordNet and Other Lexical Resources: Applications, Extensions and Customizations*. NAACL.

Agirre, E., de Lacalle, O. L., Fellbaum, C., Marchetti, A., Toral, A., & Vossen, P. (2009). Semeval-2010 task 17: All-words word sense disambiguation on a specific domain. In *Proceedings of the Workshop on Semantic Evaluations: Recent Achievements and Future Directions*, (pp. 123–128). Morristown, NJ: Semantic Evaluations.

Agirre, E., de Lacalle, O. L., & Soroa, A. (2009). Knowledge-based WSD on specific domains: Performing better than generic supervised WSD. In *Proceedings of IJCAI*. IJCAI.

Agirre, E., Martínez, D., de Lacalle, O. L., & Soroa, A. (2006). Two graph-based algorithms for state-of-the-art WSD. In *Proceedings of the 2006 Conference on Empirical Methods in Natural Language Processing, EMNLP 2006*, (pp. 585–593). Stroudsburg, PA: EMNLP.

Agirre, E., & Rigau, G. (1996). Word sense disambiguation using conceptual density. In *Proceedings of the 16th International Conference on Computational Linguistics (COLING)*. COLING.

Agirre, E., & Soroa, A. (2007). Semeval-2007 task 02: Evaluating word sense induction and discrimination systems. In *Proceedings of the Fourth International Workshop on Semantic Evaluations (SemEval 2007)*, (pp. 7–12). Prague, Czech Republic: SemEval.

Agirre, E., & Soroa, A. (2009). Personalizing pagerank for word sense disambiguation. In *Proceedings of the 12th Conference of the European Chapter of the Association for Computational Linguistics*, (pp. 33–41). Morristown, NJ: EACL.

Apidianaki, M. (2008). Translation-oriented word sense induction based on parallel corpora. In *Proceedings of LREC*. LREC.

Balamurali, A. R., Joshi, A., & Bhattacharyya, P. (2011). Harnessing wordnet senses for supervised sentiment classification. In *Proceedings of the 2011 Conference on Empirical Methods in Natural Language Processing*, (pp. 1081–1091). Edinburgh, UK: Empirical Methods in Natural Language Processing.

Banerjee, S., & Pedersen, T. (2002). An adapted lesk algorithm for word sense disambiguation using wordnet. In *Proceedings of the Third International Conference on Computational Linguistics and Intelligent Text Processing*, (pp. 136–145). London, UK: CICling.

Banerjee, S., & Pedersen, T. (2003). Extended gloss overlaps as a measure of semantic relatedness. In *Proceedings of the 18th International Joint Conference on Artificial Intelligence*, (pp. 805–810). San Francisco, CA: IEEE.

Bentivogli, L., & Pianta, E. (2005). Exploiting parallel texts in the creation of multilingual semantically annotated resources: The multisemcor corpus. *Natural Language Engineering, 11*, 247–261. doi:10.1017/S1351324905003839

Boser, B. E., Guyon, I. M., & Vapnik, V. N. (1992). A training algorithm for optimal margin classifiers. In *Proceedings of the Fifth Annual Workshop on Computational Learning Theory, COLT 1992*, (pp. 144–152). New York, NY: COLT.

Brin, S., & Page, L. (1998). The anatomy of a large-scale hypertextual web search engine. In *Proceedings of the Seventh International Conference on World Wide Web 7, WWW7*, (pp. 107–117). Amsterdam, The Netherlands: WWW.

Carpuat, M., & Wu, D. (2007). Improving statistical machine translation using word sense disambiguation. In *Proceedings of EMNLP-CoNLL*. EMNLP.

Chapman, R. (1977). *Roget's international thesaurus* (4th ed.). New York, NY: Thomas Y. Crowell Company.

Dagan, I., & Itai, A. (1994). Word sense disambiguation using a second language monolingual corpus. *Computational Linguistics, 20,* 563–596.

Diab, M., & Resnik, P. (2002). An unsupervised method for word sense tagging using parallel corpora. In *Proceedings of the 40th Annual Meeting on Association for Computational Linguistics, ACL 2002,* (pp. 255–262). Morristown, NJ: ACL.

Escudero, G., Màrquez, L., & Rigau, G. (2000a). An empirical study of the domain dependence of supervised word sense disambiguation systems. In *Proceedings of the 2000 Joint SIGDAT Conference on Empirical Methods in Natural Language Processing and Very Large Corpora,* (pp. 172–180). Morristown, NJ: SIGDAT.

Escudero, G., Màrquez, L., & Rigau, G. (2000b). Naive bayes and exemplar-based approaches to word sense disambiguation revisited. In *Proceedings of ECAI,* (pp. 421–425). ECAI.

Fellbaum, C. (1998). *WordNet: An electronic lexical database.* WordNet.

Fernández-Amorós, D. (2009). *Word sense disambiguation using English-Spanish aligned phrases over comparable corpora.* In *Proceedings of CoRR.* CoRR.

Freund, Y., & Schapire, R. E. (1999). A short introduction to boosting. In *Proceedings of the Sixteenth International Joint Conference on Artificial Intelligence,* (pp. 1401–1406). IEEE.

Gale, W., Church, K., & Yarowsky, D. (1993). A method for disambiguating word senses in a large corpus. *Computers and the Humanities.* Retrieved from http://nlp.cs.swarthmore.edu/~richardw/papers/gale1993-method.pdf

Harman, D. (2005). Beyond English. In Voorhees, E. M., & Harman, D. (Eds.), *TREC: Experiment and Evaluation in Information Retrieval* (pp. 153–181). Cambridge, MA: MIT Press.

Hirst, G., & St-Ogne, D. (1998). *Combining local context and WordNet similarity for word sense identification.* Cambridge, MA: MIT Press.

Hopfield, J. J. (1982). Neural networks and physical systems with emergent collective computational abilities. *Proceedings of the National Academy of Sciences of the United States of America, 79*(8), 2554–2558. doi:10.1073/pnas.79.8.2554

Ide, N., Erjavec, T., & Tufi, D. (2001). Automatic sense tagging using parallel corpora. In *Proceedings of the 6th Natural Language Processing Pacific Rim Symposium,* (pp. 212–219). Pacific Rim.

Ide, N., & Véronis, J. (1998). Introduction to the special issue on word sense disambiguation: The state of the art. *Computational Linguistics, 24*(1), 1–40.

Jiang, J. J., & Conrath, D. W. (1997). Semantic similarity based on corpus statistics and lexical taxonomy. In *Proceedings of the International Conference on Research in Computational Linguistics,* (pp. 19–33). Research and Computational Linguistics.

Kaji, H., & Morimoto, Y. (2002). Unsupervised word sense disambiguation using bilingual comparable corpora. In *Proceedings of the 19th International Conference on Computational Linguistics, COLING 2002,* (vol 1), (pp. 1–7). Stroudsburg, PA: COLING.

Khapra, M., Shah, S., Kedia, P., & Bhattacharyya, P. (2010). Domain-specific word sense disambiguation combining corpus based and wordnet based parameters. In *Proceedings of the 5th International Conference on Global Wordnet.* WordNet.

Klapaftis, I. P., & Manandhar, S. (2008). Word sense induction using graphs of collocations. In *Proceeding of the 2008 Conference on ECAI 2008: 18th European Conference on Artificial Intelligence*, (pp. 298–302). Amsterdam, The Netherlands: ECAI.

Klein, D., & Manning, C. D. (2003). Accurate unlexicalized parsing. In *Proceedings of the 41st Annual Meeting of the Association of Computational Linguistics*, (pp. 423–430). ACL.

Klein, D., Toutanova, K., Ilhan, H. T., Kamvar, S. D., & Manning, C. D. (2002). Combining heterogeneous classifiers for word-sense disambiguation. In *Proceedings of the ACL-02 Workshop on Word Sense Disambiguation: Recent Successes and Future Directions, WSD 2002*, (vol 8), (pp. 74–80). Stroudsburg, PA: WSD.

Koeling, R., McCarthy, D., & Carroll, J. (2005). Domain-specific sense distributions and predominant sense acquisition. In *Proceedings of the Conference on Human Language Technology and Empirical Methods in Natural Language Processing*, (pp. 419–426). Morristown, NJ: HLT.

Leacock, C., & Chodorow, M. (1998). *Combining local context and WordNet similarity for word sense identification*. Cambridge, MA: MIT Press.

Lee, K. Y., Ng, H. T., & Chia, T. K. (2004). Supervised word sense disambiguation with support vector machines and multiple knowledge sources. In *Proceedings of Senseval-3: Third International Workshop on the Evaluation of Systems for the Semantic Analysis of Text*, (pp. 137–140). Senseval.

Lesk, M. (1986). Automatic sense disambiguation using machine readable dictionaries: How to tell a pine cone from an ice cream cone. In *Proceedings of the 5th Annual International Conference on Systems Documentation*. Systems Documentation.

Li, H., & Li, C. (2004). Word translation disambiguation using bilingual bootstrapping. *Computational Linguistics, 30*, 1–22. doi:10.1162/089120104773633367

Lin, D. K. (1997). Using syntactic dependency as local context to resolve word sense ambiguity. In *Proceedings of the 35th Annual Meeting of the Association for Computational Linguistics (ACL)*, (pp. 64–71). ACL.

Lin, D. K. (1998). Automatic retrieval and clustering of similar words. In *Proceedings of the 17th International Conference on Computational Linguistics*, (pp. 768–774). Morristown, NJ: ACL.

Magnini, B., Strapparava, C., Pezzulo, G., & Gliozzo, A. (2002). The role of domain information in word sense disambiguation. *Natural Language Engineering, 8*(4), 359–373. doi:10.1017/S1351324902003029

Manandhar, S., & Klapaftis, I. P. (2009). Semeval-2010 task 14: Evaluation setting for word sense induction & disambiguation systems. In *Proceedings of the Workshop on Semantic Evaluations: Recent Achievements and Future Directions, DEW 2009*, (pp. 117–122). Stroudsburg, PA: DEW.

McCarthy, D., Koeling, R., Weeds, J., & Carroll, J. (2004). Finding predominant word senses in untagged text. In *Proceedings of the 42nd Annual Meeting on Association for Computational Linguistics*, (p. 279). Morristown, NJ: ACL.

McCarthy, D., Koeling, R., Weeds, J., & Carroll, J. (2007). Unsupervised acquisition of predominant word senses. *Computational Linguistics, 33*(4), 553–590. doi:10.1162/coli.2007.33.4.553

Mihalcea, R. (2005). Large vocabulary unsupervised word sense disambiguation with graph-based algorithms for sequence data labeling. In *Proceedings of the Joint Human Language Technology and Empirical Methods in Natural Language Processing Conference (HLT/EMNLP)*, (pp. 411–418). HLT/EMNLP.

Mihalcea, R. F. (2002). Bootstrapping large sense tagged corpora. In *Proceedings of the 3rd International Conference on Language Resources and Evaluations (LREC)*, Las Palmas, Spain: LREC.

Miller, G. A., Leacock, C., Tengi, R., & Bunker, R. T. (1993). A semantic concordance. In *Proceedings of the Workshop on Human Language Technology*, (pp. 303–308). Morristown, NJ: HLT.

Mohanty, R., Bhattacharyya, P., Pande, P., Kalele, S., Khapra, M., & Sharma, A. (2008). Synset based multilingual dictionary: Insights, applications and challenges. In *Proceedings of the Global Wordnet Conference*. Wordnet.

Narayan, D., Chakrabarti, D., Pande, P., & Bhattacharyya, P. (2002). An experience in building the indo wordnet - A wordnet for Hindi. In *Proceedings of the First International Conference on Global WordNet*. WordNet.

Navarro, B., Civit, M., Martí, A. M., Marcos, R., & Fernández, B. (2003). Syntactic, semantic and pragmatic annotation in Cast3LB. In *Proceedings of SProLaC*, (pp. 59–68). SProLaC.

Navigli, R. (2009). Word sense disambiguation: A survey. *ACM Computing Surveys*, *41*(10), 1–69. doi:10.1145/1459352.1459355

Navigli, R., & Velardi, P. (2005). Structural semantic interconnections: A knowledge-based approach to word sense disambiguation. *IEEE Transactions on Pattern Analysis and Machine Intelligence*, *27*(7), 1075–1086. doi:10.1109/TPAMI.2005.149

Ng, H. T., & Lee, H. B. (1996). Integrating multiple knowledge sources to disambiguate word sense: an exemplar-based approach. In *Proceedings of the 34th Annual Meeting on Association for Computational Linguistics*, (pp. 40–47). Morristown, NJ: ACL.

Ng, H. T., Wang, B., & Chan, Y. S. (2003). Exploiting parallel texts for word sense disambiguation: An empirical study. In *Proceedings of the 41st Annual Meeting on Association for Computational Linguistics, ACL 2003*, (vol 1), (pp. 455–462). Morristown, NJ: ACL.

Patwardhan, S., & Pedersen, T. (2003). *The CPAN WordNet: Similarity package*. Retrieved from http://search.cpan.org/ sid/wordnet-similarity/

Pedersen, T., Banerjee, S., & Patwardhan, S. (2005). *Maximizing semantic relatedness to perform word sense disambiguation. Research Report UMSI 2005/25*. Minneapolis, MN: University of Minnesota Supercomputing Institute.

Resnik, P. (1995). Using information content to evaluate semantic similarity in a taxonomy. In *Proceedings of the 14th International Joint Conference on Artificial Intelligence*, (vol 1), (pp. 448–453). San Francisco, CA: IEEE.

Resnik, P., & Yarowsky, D. (1999). Distinguishing systems and distinguishing senses: New evaluation methods for word sense disambiguation. *Natural Language Engineering*, *5*, 113–133. doi:10.1017/S1351324999002211

Snyder, B., & Palmer, M. (2004). The English all-words task. In R. Mihalcea & P. Edmonds (Eds.), *Senseval-3: Third International Workshop on the Evaluation of Systems for the Semantic Analysis of Text*, (pp. 41–43). Barcelona, Spain: Senseval.

Tufi, D., Ion, R., & Ide, N. (2004). Fine-grained word sense disambiguation based on parallel corpora, word alignment, word clustering and aligned wordnets. In *Proceedings of the 20th International Conference on Computational Linguistics, COLING 2004*. Stroudsburg, PA: COLING.

Van, A., Hendrickx, I., & Van Den Bosch, A. (2002). Dutch word sense disambiguation: Data and preliminary results. In *Proceedings of Senseval-2, Second International Workshop on Evaluating Word Sense Disambiguation Systems*, (pp. 13–16). Senseval.

Véronis, J. (2004). Hyperlex: Lexical cartography for information retrieval. *Computer Speech & Language, 18*(3), 223–252. doi:10.1016/j.csl.2004.05.002

Vossen, P., & Computer Centrum Letteren. (1997). Eurowordnet: A multilingual database for information retrieval. In *Proceedings of the DELOS Workshop on Cross-Language Information Retrieval*, (pp. 5–7). DELOS.

Walker, D., & Amsler, R. (1986). The use of machine readable dictionaries in sublanguage analysis. In Grishman & Kittredge (Eds.), *Analyzing Language in Restricted Domains*, (pp. 69-83). LEA Press.

Weeber, M., Mork, J. G., & Aronson, A. R. (2001). Developing a test collection for biomedical word sense disambiguation. In *Proceedings of the AMAI Symposium*, (pp. 746–750). AMAI.

Yarowsky, D. (1992). Word-sense disambiguation using statistical models of Roget's categories trained on large corpora. In *Proceedings of the 14th Conference on Computational Linguistics, COLING 1992*, (vol 2), (pp. 454–460). Stroudsburg, PA: COLING.

Yarowsky, D. (1994). Decision lists for lexical ambiguity resolution: Application to accent restoration in Spanish and French. In *Proceedings of the 32nd Annual Meeting of the Association for Computational Linguistics (ACL)*, (pp. 88–95). ACL.

Yarowsky, D. (1995). Unsupervised word sense disambiguation rivaling supervised methods. In *Proceedings of the 33rd Annual Meeting on Association for Computational Linguistics*, (pp. 189–196). Morristown, NJ: ACL.

ENDNOTES

[1] Source: Princeton Wordnet.

[2] These dominant senses were identified from a sense tagged Tourism corpus.

[3] http://ixa2.si.ehu.es/ukb/

[4] We used the Stanford parser—http://nlp.stanford.edu/software/lex-parser.shtml

[5] http://nlp.comp.nus.edu.sg/software

[6] http://wordnetweb.princeton.edu/perl/webwn

Chapter 3
Domain Adaptation in Part-of-Speech Tagging

Miriam Lúcia Domingues
Federal University of Pará, Brazil

Eloi Luiz Favero
Federal University of Pará, Brazil

ABSTRACT

Many Natural Language Processing (NLP) applications rely on accuracy of the part-of-speech taggers. Although many taggers have good accuracy for the domain in which they were trained, their accuracy typically is not portable to new domains due to problems, such as different linguistic structures or presence of new words. The need for domain adaptation has emerged as a new challenge for part-of-speech tagging and in most NLP tasks. The goal of this chapter is to highlight solutions that handle labeled and unlabeled data, methods that deal with such data to solve the domain adaptation problem, and to present a case study that has achieved significant accuracy rates on tagging journalistic and scientific texts.

INTRODUCTION

Many state-of-the-art Natural Language Processing (NLP) applications based on supervised learning have good accuracy for the domain or genre in which they were trained; however, most of them exhibit a lack of portability to new domains due to problems such as different linguistic structures or the presence of new words. As a result, domain adaptation, which is the ability to exhibit good performance on both the training (source) and the new (target) domains, has emerged as a new challenge. This challenge arises in many NLP tasks, such as Part-Of-Speech (POS) tagging, Named

Entity (NE) recognition, parsing, Word Sense Disambiguation (WSD), and relation extraction.

Published literature has addressed the importance of domain adaptation in NLP tasks by applying machine learning methods, such as supervised (Chelba & Acero, 2006; Daumé, 2007), unsupervised (Blitzer, McDonald, & Pereira, 2006; Jiang & Zhai, 2007; Huang & Yates, 2010), and ensemble methods (Daumé III & Marcu, 2006).

Jiang and Zhai (2007) cited several examples of domain adaptation problems. The first example is POS tagging, where the source domain being tagged is journalistic data and the target domain is scientific data. The second example is NE

DOI: 10.4018/978-1-4666-2169-5.ch003

recognition, where the source domain being annotated is news articles and the target domain is personal blogs. The third example is personalized spam filtering, where many labeled spam and ham emails from publicly available sources must be adapted to an individual user's inbox because of the specificities of the user distribution of emails and the individual notions of what constitutes a spam.

The objective of this chapter is to present state-of-the-art domain-adaptation problems focused on solutions in POS tagging, an important preprocessing task in many NLP applications. Specifically, we present experiments with the adaptation of a hybrid POS tagger, which improves tagging accuracy by reducing errors in new or Out-Of-Vocabulary (OOV) words and by making adjustments to the tagger to handle different data distributions in the source and in the target domains. This tagger has been trained with Portuguese texts to generate similar levels of accuracy on texts from two different domains: journalistic and scientific.

In the following sections, we first describe basic concepts of POS tagging and its main approaches. Then, we present the current state of the art in domain adaptation, including any related issues and problems. We highlight solutions using NLP systems that handle labeled and unlabeled data, taking the perspectives adopted by researchers working on NLP. There is also a brief overview of domain adaptation solutions in POS tagging. We then present a case study with a Portuguese POS tagger, followed by a discussion of future research directions and the conclusions of this chapter.

PART-OF-SPEECH TAGGING

POS tagging is the basic task of labeling a word or a token in a sentence with its grammatical category, such as noun, adjective, or verb. Punctuation marks are usually tagged as well. When a suitable automatic tagging algorithm is given a string of words and a specified tag set, the tagger outputs annotated results such as the following:

- A/ART casa/N é/V grande/ADJ ./. (*The house is big.*)
- Maria/NPROP casa/V hoje_à_noite/ADV ./. (*Maria marries tonight.*)

The tags of the examples are from the MacMorpho tag set (Aluísio, et al., 2003) and are described as the following: ART=article, N=noun, V=verb, ADJ=adjective, NPROP=proper noun, ADV=adverb and the punctuation mark .=.

A word is ambiguous when it has more than one grammatical category, such as the word "casa" in the example. (In Portuguese, the word "casa" may refer to the noun *house* or to the verb *to marry*.) The tag with the correct grammatical category will be assigned according to the context of the word in the sentence. For disambiguation, taggers use a large set of methods and techniques with different approaches to tag the words with the greatest accuracy possible. Tags may include more lexical attributes, such as gender, number, verbal mood, tense, and person. For example, the word "casa" may be tagged as NFS, a noun (N) that is feminine (F) in gender and singular (S) in number.

NLP applications rely on taggers that have high accuracy. State-of-the-art taggers have achieved, for example, an accuracy of 97.24% for the English language (Toutanova, Klein, Manning, & Singer, 2003) and an accuracy of 96.75% for the Brazilian Portuguese language (dos Santos, Milidiú, & Rentería, 2008).

Main Approaches for POS Tagging

Researchers working on POS tagging have focused on three main approaches: rule-based, probabilistic, and hybrid.

Rule-Based

The rule-based approach was earlier implemented using hand-coded rules (Klein & Simmons, 1963; Greene & Rubin, 1971) and was later implemented by the use of semi-automated approaches (Heikkilä, 1995). In general, these approaches involve a dictionary containing words and a list of their potential tags and then apply large sets of hand-coded rules to disambiguate the words. The Constraint Grammar (CG) architecture is a well-known example of this method (Karlsson, Voutilainen, Heikkilä, & Anttila, 1995; Bick, 2000). In the CG paradigm, sets of tags are assigned to words based on a lexicon and morphological analysis, and tags are then eliminated according to contextual rules, such as *"the current word is not a verb if the preceding word is a determiner"* (Abney, 1996).

The performance of rule-based taggers is reported to be at least as good as that of other approaches. However, a problem with rule-based taggers is that the amount of effort necessary to write the disambiguation rules is high; additionally, a good performance is not always repeatable with new text data because performance is sensitive to changes in word sets, such as neologisms and words that fall into disuse.

Probabilistic

The probabilistic approach applies machine-learning techniques to tag words in a sentence with the most likely sequence of tags occurring among the potential candidates. These methods assume that each word has a finite set of possible tags that can be searched in a dictionary or in an electronic corpus. Given a sequence of words, these methods can determine the optimal sequence of POS tags, even when the words can potentially be tagged with more than one option (Nugues, 2006).

Some well-known probabilistic methods for POS tagging include single Hidden Markov Models (HMMs), combinations of HMMs and decision trees, the maximum entropy model, cyclic dependency networks, and Conditional Random Fields (CRFs).

Many studies of POS tagging are based on Hidden Markov Models (HMM) (Church, 1988; Kempe, 1993; Brants, 2000). According to Jurafsky and Martin (2000), for a given word sequence, HMM taggers choose the sequence of labels that maximizes the formula (1):

$$P(\text{word}|\text{tag}) * P(\text{tag}|\text{previous } n \text{ tags}) \qquad (1)$$

HMM-based taggers choose a sequence of tags for an entire sentence rather than for a single word. In general, they use the Viterbi algorithm (Viterbi, 1967) to choose the most probable sequence of tags for each sentence. Most of these models are first-order (bigram) or second-order (trigram) Markov Models, which have difficulty estimating small probabilities accurately when the amount of training data is limited.

Many methods have been proposed to avoid this sparse data problem. The tagger TreeTagger (Schmid, 1994, 1995), for instance, performs a method that combines HMM and decision trees to avoid the sparse data problem. The TreeTagger, similar to the conventional HMM taggers, models the probability of a tagged sequence of words, in the case of a trigram, recursively by formula (2):

$$P(w_1 w_2 ... w_n, t_1 t_2 ... t_n):$$
$$= P(t_n \mid t_{n-2} t_{n-1}) P(w_n \mid t_n) P(w_1 w_2 ... w_{n-1}, t_1 t_2 ... t_{n-1}) \qquad (2)$$

The advantage of TreeTagger compared to the other methods is that TreeTagger replaces the Maximum Likelihood Estimation (MLE) with a binary decision tree to estimate the transition probability $P(t_n|t_{n-2} t_{n-1})$. This replacement can improve the performance in cases where the training set is small. The MLE principle is modeled by formula (3):

$$P\left(t_n \mid t_{n-2}t_{n-1}\right) = \frac{F\left(t_{n-2}t_{n-1}t_n\right)}{F\left(t_{n-2}t_{n-1}\right)} \qquad (3)$$

where $F(t_{n-2}t_{n-1}t_n)$ refers to the number of occurrences of the trigram $t_{n-2}t_{n-1}t_n$ in the training corpus and $F(t_{n-2}t_{n-1})$ refers to the number of occurrences of the bigram $t_{n-2}t_{n-1}$.

According to Schmid (1995), assigning a tag based on the sequence of its preceding tags is a classification problem in which we are given a set of features (preceding tags) and we ask for the most likely class of the item (the tag of the next word). Decision trees are a well-known method for solving this classification problem. Each non-terminal node in the tree is the examination of a feature, whereas terminal nodes contain information about the class. The decision tree must be binary because while splitting the set of training items into as many subsets as there are tags, some subsets may be large and others may be empty; thus, the result is that no prediction is possible. Binary tests in the decision tree are provided to produce non-empty subsets, which avoid having the information gain of the test be zero. The algorithm prunes the tree when the weighted information gain at a terminal node is below a threshold. Besides the decision tree, there are other techniques among the set of TreeTagger methods that improve lexical probability estimates in small corpora. Two of these methods, yield significantly elevated tagger performance (Schmid, 1995):

- Smoothing with equivalence classes
- Treatment of sentence-initial words

Smoothing with equivalence classes assumes that words with the same set of possible tags have similar probability distributions. Therefore, estimating probabilities for rare words from equivalence class probabilities may produce reasonable results, whereas frequent words can have their tag probabilities based on corpus frequencies.

The *treatment of sentence-initial words* is to search for a capitalized word at the beginning of a sentence and for its identical uncapitalized word in the lexicon. If both are found, then the probability vectors are weighted by the relative frequency of the corresponding forms, and the weighted frequencies are summed. An example is the word "Nova" in the sentence "*Nova negociação está marcada para terça-feira.*" (*New negotiation is scheduled for Tuesday*), which is more likely to be tagged as a noun than as a proper noun, as in "*Cidade de Nova York*" (*New York City*).

Another frequently used model in POS tagging is the maximum entropy model (Ratnaparkhi, 1996), which uses an unrestricted and rich contextual feature set to predict a tag. This model, whose objective is to maximize the entropy of a distribution subject to certain constraints, uses feature templates to generate the space of features by scanning each pair (h_i, t_i), where h_i is defined as the history (the set of possible word and tag contexts) available in the training data when predicting the tag t_i. An example of a feature template is the following: "*if a word w_i occurs, then the previous tag $t_{i-1}=X$, and the tag $t_i=T$.*"

Feature-rich POS tagging was also explored by Toutanova *et al.* (2003), who presented a tagger that improved performance using bidirectional inference with both preceding and following tag contexts in a cyclic dependency network representation. Additional techniques in this tagger are lexical features that include joint conditioning on multiple consecutive words, effective use of priors in conditional log-linear models, and fine-grained modeling of OOV word features. This tagger achieved one of the best results for English, with an accuracy of 97.24% on *Wall Street Journal* texts from the Penn Treebank III.

Ekbal, Haque, and Bandyopadhyay (2007) proposed a POS tagger for Bengali based on a CRF framework using diverse features to tag words. CRFs are undirected graphical models used to calculate the conditional probability of values on the output nodes given values on the input nodes.

This tagger has improved accuracy for Bengali using a set of features containing the following: a context word feature; prefix and suffix lengths up to three; NE information on current and previous words; POS information for the previous word; digit and symbol features; and gazetteer lists. The tagger also introduced word suffix features, a NE recognizer, and a lexicon for handling OOV words.

Hybrid

A third approach, "hybrid," is a combination of the first two approaches. The hybrid approach was presented by Brill (1995), who proposed a machine-learning method known as Transformation-Based error-driven Learning (TBL) for corpus-based NLP applications. This approach has been used successfully to learn rules in tasks, such as POS tagging, prepositional phrase attachment disambiguation, and text chunking.

In general, TBL has two main steps:

* The initial tagging
* The automatic learning of an ordered list of rules

In the initial tagging step, an unannotated corpus is annotated with a tagging method, for example, by using a robust probabilistic tagger, by tagging all words with their most likely tag in accordance with the training corpus, or by tagging all words as nouns.

In the second step, the output of the first step is compared with a previously manually annotated version that is used as gold standard data. The algorithm learns an ordered list of transformations (rules) that are applied to the output, trying to approximate its output to the gold standard data, based on the errors of the initial tagging. The learned rules then become available to tag new texts.

For the learning step, it is necessary to specify a set of rule templates that provide space for allowable transformations in the tagging process

and to specify an objective function for comparing the corpus to the gold standard data and for choosing a transformation. A transformation has two components: a rewrite rule and a triggering environment. A rewrite rule, for example, can be as follows (Brill, 1995): *Change the tag from verb (V) to noun (N)*. An example of a triggering environment is as follows: *The preceding word is an article (ART)*. The transformation combines the two components in the rule: *Change the tag from verb to noun, if the preceding word is an article*.

Brill (1995) describes two context-sensitive versions of templates for POS tagging:

* Non-lexicalized
* Lexicalized

Non-lexicalized templates do not make reference to specific words. They focus on contextual structures (the tags), as in this example: *Change tag adverb (ADV) to tag adjective (ADJ) when the preceding word is tagged verb (V)*.

Lexicalized templates find relationships between the words and the tags, adding contextual rules to the model that can make reference to the words and the POS tags. An example is: *Change tag preposition (PREP) to tag adverb (ADV) when the current word is "Em" (In) and the following word is tagged adverb (ADV)*.

To tag OOV words, the initial tagging step of TBL assigns the most likely tag for words, which is a proper noun if capitalized and a noun otherwise. Then, a set of transformations can be applied, for example: *Change the tag of the OOV word "loco" from noun (N) to foreign adverb (ADV\EST) if word "in" ever appears immediately to the left of the word "loco."*

According to Brill (1995), an advantage to TBL is that the transformations list is used as a postprocessor and not as a classifier, which renders it suitable to any tagging system. In this way, learning transformations from mature systems used in the initial tagging step of the TBL provides a readable description of errors of those systems that may contribute to their refinement. Many studies have recognized the advantages of the TBL approach (Lager, 1999; Finger, 2000; Ngai & Florian, 2001; Kinoshita, Salvador, & Menezes, 2007; Ning, Yang, & Li, 2007; dos Santos, et al., 2008).

DOMAIN ADAPTATION FOR NLP

In recent years, statistical natural language processing models have been increasingly required to manage textual information that has been digitally stored. Many of these models are based on supervised learning, which requires a large amount of manually labeled data. However, variations in texts from different domains and the human efforts in creating labeled training data for each different domain rules out direct application of supervised learning to NLP tasks in new domains (Jiang, 2008). The domain adaptation problem has emerged as a new challenge in NLP tasks, for example, POS tagging, NE recognition, parsing, WSD, and others, motivating the development of new techniques and models to adapt classifiers to perform well in different domains.

Thus, most state-of-the-art NLP tasks have faced the problem of domain adaptation, which occurs when these applications fail to perform well when applied to data of a new domain. According to Blitzer (2007):

Domain adaptation addresses the situation in which we possess a large amount of labeled data from a source domain to train a model but little or no labeled data from a target domain where we wish to apply the model (p. 79).

Jiang and Zhai (2007) cited some examples of domain adaptation problems, such as POS tagging, where the source domain being tagged is journalistic data and the target domain is scientific data. Another example is NE recognition, where the source domain being annotated is news articles and the target domain is personal blogs.

A third example is personalized spam filtering, where many labeled spam and ham emails from publicly available sources must be adapted to an individual user's inbox because of the specificities of the user distribution of emails and individual notions of what constitutes a spam.

The notion of domain is not restricted to different textual genres, such as journalism and science, but can include other situations where the new data has a different distribution compared to the data of the training corpus. Examples include child language versus adult language domains and source-side re-ordering of words versus target-side word-order domains of a statistical machine translation system (Daumé, Deoskar, McClosky, & Plank, 2010).

Notations of the Domain Adaptation Problem

In this section, for a better understanding of the domain-adaptation problem, we present the following notations introduced by Jiang (2008). The training domain where labeled data is abundant is referred to as the source domain, and the test domain where labeled data is not available or is available only in a very small amount is referred to as the target domain.

Let the input variable X be a feature space (an observation), and let the output variable Y be the set of class labels. Then $P(X, Y)$ is the true underlying joint distribution of X and Y, which is unknown. In domain adaptation, this joint distribution in the target domain differs from the distribution in the source domain. Thus, $P_t(X, Y)$ is the true underlying joint distribution in the target domain, and $P_s(X, Y)$ is the true underlying joint distribution in the source domain. The true marginal distributions of Y and X in the target and the source domains are denoted, respectively, by $P_t(Y)$, $P_s(Y)$, $P_t(X)$, and $P_s(X)$. In the same way, $P_t(X \mid Y)$, $P_s(X \mid Y)$, $P_t(Y \mid X)$, and $P_s(Y \mid X)$ are the true conditional distributions in the two domains. Let the lowercase x be a specific value of X, and let the lowercase y be a specific class label. A specific x is also referred to as an observation, an unlabeled instance, or simply an instance. A pair (x, y) is referred to as a labeled instance. Here, $x \in X$, where X is the input space, that is, the set of all possible observations, and $y \in Y$, where Y is the class label set. Without any ambiguity, $P(X = x, Y = y)$ or $P(x, y)$ should refer to the joint probability of $X = x$ and $Y = y$. Similarly, $P(X = x)$, $P(Y = y)$, $P(X = x \mid Y = y)$, and $P(Y = y \mid X = x)$ also refer to probabilities rather than to distributions. It is assumed that in the source domain, there is a relatively large amount of *labeled* data, and $D_s = \{(xi_s, yi_s)\}i_{1...Ns}$ denotes this set of labeled instances in the source domain. In the target domain, it is assumed that there is access to a large amount of *unlabeled* data, and $D_{t,u} = \{(xi_{t,u})\}i_{1...Nt,u}$ denotes this set of unlabeled instances. Any labeled data from the target domain, which can sometimes be present in a small amount, is denoted as $D_{t,l} = \{(xi_{t,l}, yi_{t,l})\}i_{1...Nt,l}$. In the case where $D_{t,l}$ is not available, that is, $N_{t,l} = 0$, the problem is referred to as *unsupervised domain adaptation*, whereas when $D_{t,l}$ is available, the problem is referred to as *supervised domain adaptation*.

Methods for Domain Adaptation Problems

Domain adaptation has been the subject of several studies in both the machine learning and the NLP communities, which have applied different methods, with different motivations behind them. Some methods are applicable to unsupervised domain adaptation problems where others are applicable to supervised domain adaptation problems. There are also ensemble methods that combine a set of models to construct a complex classifier for a classification problem. In the following sections, we present a brief overview of these methods according to the categorization proposed by Jiang (2008, p. 96).

Unsupervised Methods for Domain Adaptation Problems

Unsupervised methods work when there is no labeled data available. The methods using unsupervised domain adaptation can be included in the following approaches:

- Change of Representation
- Instance Weighting
- Semi-supervised Learning

The difference between $P_t(X, Y)$ and $P_s(X, Y)$ is the cause of the domain adaptation problem because the representation of Y is fixed and the representation of X can change with the use of different features. This *change of representation* for X can affect both the marginal $P(X)$ and the conditional $P(Y|X)$ distributions. Thus, it can be assumed that under some representation of X, $P_t(X, Y)$ and $P_s(X, Y)$ will become the same. This idea is explored, for example, in Blitzer et al. (2006), who proposed a Structural Correspondence Learning (SCL) method that uses unlabeled instances from the target domain to infer a good feature representation, which is regarded by Jiang and Zhai (2007) as weighting the features. The SCL method is based on the idea of using pivot features that are frequent and have similar behavior in both the source and the target domains. Blitzer et al. (2006) demonstrated the effectiveness of SCL on the tasks of POS tagging and parsing.

Instance weighting is an approach used to solve the domain adaptation problem by assigning instance-dependent weights to the loss function when minimizing the expected loss over the distribution data. There are two lines of work in this perspective: class imbalance that assumes $P_s(X \mid Y = y) = P_t(X \mid Y = y)$ for all $y \in Y$, but $P_s(Y) \neq P_t(Y)$, a method explored by Chan and Ng (2005) in the WSD task; and covariate shift that assumes $P_s(Y \mid X = x) = P_t(Y \mid X = x)$ for all $x \in X$, but $P_s(X) \neq P_t(X)$, a method studied by Bickel, Brückner, and Scheffer (2007) on spam filtering, text classification and landmine detection problems.

In *Semi-Supervised Learning* (SSL) domain difference is ignored. The labeled instances from the source domain are treated as labeled data, and the unlabeled data from the target domain are treated as unlabeled data. There are two differences between SSL and domain adaptation. First, there is a small amount of labeled data in SSL, whereas the total amount of labeled data is large in domain adaptation. Second, SSL has reliable labeled data for all of its data, whereas in domain adaptation, the labeled data may be noisy if it is not assumed that $P_s(Y \mid X = x) = P_t(Y \mid X = x)$ for all x. Among the studies that exemplify this semi-supervised perspective, there is one proposed by Dai, Xue, Yang, and Yu (2007) that focuses on an Expectation-Maximization (EM)-based algorithm used in the text classification task. It estimates the trade-off parameter between the labeled and the unlabeled data using the Kullback-Leibler divergence between the two domains. There is also the study by Jiang and Zhai (2007) that proposes to include weighted source-domain instances in addition to weighted unlabeled instances from the target domain in training. They evaluated their instance-weighting method in three NLP tasks: POS tagging, entity type classification, and personalized spam filtering.

Supervised Methods for Domain Adaptation Problems

Supervised methods only work when there is some labeled data available. The methods using supervised domain adaptation can be included in the following approaches:

- Bayesian Prior
- Multi-Task Learning

Bayesian prior is a method applied when the target domain has a small amount of labeled data available. By using the Maximum A Posterior

(MAP) estimation approach for supervised learning, some prior knowledge about the classification model can be encoded into a Bayesian prior distribution that can be drawn from the source domain in domain adaptation studies. An example is the Chelba and Acero (2006) study for the task of adapting a maximum entropy capitalizer to different domains, which uses the parameters of the maximum entropy model learned from the source domain as the means of a Gaussian prior to training a new model on the target data.

In *multi-task learning* or transfer learning, there is initially a single observation $P(X)$ and a number of different output variables $Y_1, Y_2, ..., Y_M$, that correspond to M different tasks. Thus, there are M joint distributions and the class label sets are different for these M different tasks, which are assumed to be related. Domain adaptation differs from multi-task learning in the fact that there is only a single task and different domains. Thus, domain adaptation can be treated as a special case of multi-task learning because there are two tasks, a task in the source domain, and a task in the target domain, which have the same class label sets. An example is the study of Daumé III (2007) that proposed a method based on the idea of transforming the domain adaptation problem into a standard supervised learning problem to which any standard algorithm may be applied. Their transformation consisted on augmenting the feature space of both the source and target data and use the result as input to a standard learning algorithm. This method was tested on the following NLP tasks: NE recognition, shallow parsing, and POS tagging.

Ensemble Methods

Another type of learning algorithm is called the *ensemble method*, which combines a set of models in a complex classifier for a given classification problem. These methods include bagging, boosting, and mixture of experts. For example, Daumé III and Marcu (2006) proposed a model in which

Table 1. Some research on different approaches of domain adaptation problems in NLP tasks

Research	Method						NLP task
	Unsuperv.			Superv.		(6)	
	(1)	(2)	(3)	(4)	(5)		
Chan and Ng (2005)	-	x	-	-	-	-	WSD
Blitzer et al. (2006)	x	-	-	-	-	-	POS tagging, parsing
Chelba and Acero (2006)	-	-	-	x	-	-	capitalization
Daumé and Marcu (2006)	-	-	-	-	-	x	mention type classification, mention tagging, recapitalization
Blitzer (2007)	x	-	-	-	-	-	sentiment classification, POS tagging
Daumé (2007)	-	-	-	-	x	-	POS tagging, NE recognition, shallow parsing
Dai et al. (2007)	-	-	x	-	-	-	text classification
Jiang and Zhai (2007)	-	-	x	-	-	-	POS tagging, entity type classification, spam filtering
Bickel et al. (2007)	-	x	-	-	-	-	POS tagging

(1) change of representation, (2) instance weighting, (3) semi-supervised learning, (4) Bayesian prior, (5) multi-task learning, (6) ensemble methods.

the data from the source and the target domains are generated from a mixture of the truly source domain distribution, the truly target domain distribution and the general domain distribution. This method improved performance on three NLP tasks: mention type classification (a subcomponent of the entity mention detection task), mention tagging, and recapitalization.

In Table 1, we include studies that present different approaches of domain adaptation problems in POS tagging and in other NLP tasks.

DOMAIN ADAPTATION IN POS TAGGING

Critical Issues and Problems

When conducting a corpus-based study to improve POS tagging accuracy, there are critical issues and problems with which we need to be concerned. These issues, if not properly tackled, may prevent

taggers from achieving high accuracy, and thus may affect domain adaptation.

- Textual Genre or Domain
- Size of the Training Corpus
- Amount of Labeled Data in the Target Domain
- Presence of Noise
- Out-of-Vocabulary Words
- Domain Adaptation Approach for POS Tagging

The textual genre or domain is an important issue because some structures in the textual data are characteristic of a particular genre. Some structures are recognizable based on simple patterns, whereas others are more complex.

The size of the training corpus is an important issue related to high-accuracy tagging. A large corpus (approximately one million words) is more representative of a domain because it contains more linguistic information than a small corpus (Berber Sardinha, 2004). However, constructing a large corpus requires much effort for the annotation. Banko and Moore (2004) predicted growth in the use of relatively unsupervised methods to reduce the need for expensive human annotation of data.

The amount of labeled data in the target domain poses a problem when it is small or absent because taggers can be prevented from extracting the specific patterns of the domain. Corpora containing a small amount of data are available and may be used as training data for the target domain, but many of these corpora have been automatically annotated and have not always been manually reviewed by human experts. This circumstance also prevents the evaluation of POS taggers because annotated test sets are required to measure the tagging accuracy rates. In this way, the construction and revision of annotated corpora for as many domains as possible should continue contributing significantly to the development of NLP applications.

Even though a large corpus for machine learning is recommended, it is very difficult for human experts to completely review a large corpus to remove noise; this constraint affects the quality of the corpus and the NLP tasks. For example, the presence of noise in the training data affects the performance of taggers based on the TBL method because the system may learn rules that correct false errors. Even when the review of the corpus is divided among several linguists, noise may occur because the specialists may hold different views about the annotation of certain categories of words. Banko and Moore (2004) reported some factors that cause noise, such as the occurrence of mistagged words in the training corpus; all title words being tagged as proper nouns, which create noise for many closed-class words; and frequently occurring words being labeled with infrequently occurring tags. These sources of noise make it difficult for HMM taggers to perform well and are common factors in many available corpora.

The presence of OOV words in the target domain has been the focus of several studies.

Because such words are very influential to the overall accuracy of taggers, an appropriate solution must be devised. These words are typically open-class words, which include a potentially infinite set of words that can receive new units where appropriate. The main categories are the nouns, the adjectives, the verbs, and the adverbs.

As has been discussed so far, there is a broad range of approaches and methods for domain adaptation in POS tagging already proposed in the NLP literature. Choosing the best approach for a given application requires learning about the methods that are emerging, and conducting many experiments.

Solutions and Recommendations

In this section, we identify some solutions and recommendations for dealing with the issues and problems presented in the preceding section. This chapter covers textual genres or domains with different linguistic structures in the source and in the target domain. As has been presented here, there are several methods that have been applied to the domain adaptation problem. Nevertheless, many questions remain about how to better solve this problem in POS tagging and in other NLP tasks.

The size of the training corpus, the amount of labeled data in the target domain, and the presence of noise can be handled effectively with the use of *active learning* algorithms. These algorithms deal with an initial set of training data of reduced size that increases as a sampling strategy for creating annotated data is applied. This approach requires less time and effort from human specialists and produces annotated data of high quality. In the active learning approach, a model is trained with the help of an oracle that can be a human. The algorithm has the following steps (Ringger, et al., 2007): 1) trains a tagger with initial training data; 2) applies the model to unannotated data; 3) computes potential informativeness of each sentence; 4) removes the top *n* sentences with the most potential informativeness from the unannotated data and gives it to the oracle; 5) adds the *n* sentences annotated by the oracle to the training data; 6) retrains the model; and 7) if a stop condition is reached, returns to step 2. Active learning has provided good accuracy in many state-of-the-art studies (Ringger, et al., 2007; Tsujii Laboratory, 2010).

Many methods have been proposed in the literature for handling OOV words. In the context of POS tagging, Toutanova et al. (2003, p. 178) have included the use of character *n*-gram prefixes and suffixes and have included the detection of features of words, such as capitalization, hyphens, and numbers. With their ideas following from Ratnaparkhi (1996), they have suggested the addition of a NE recognizer as a preprocessor to the tagger. As we cited earlier, Schmid (1995, p. 5) has described the method of smoothing with equivalence classes that was developed to improve poor lexical probability estimates obtained from small corpora. Banko and Moore (2004, p. 558) have constructed a lexicon from tagged versions of the full training corpus, which takes advantage of the knowledge of what tags are possible for each word in the lexicon.

In the context of domain adaptation, Umansky-Pesin, Reichart, and Rappoport (2010) have presented a Web-based algorithm for tagging OOV words, suitable for multi-domain tagging that requires no information about the target domain, and does not need domain-specific corpora or external dictionaries. This algorithm searches the Web to collect contexts of a given OOV word; the contexts are used to improve computations of the tag probability by the tagger. The three types of contexts used are as follows: all neighboring words, the words on the left, and the words on the right. For an OOV word, the algorithm executes three queries for each of its test contexts: replacement, left-side, and right-side. For example, the word "H2O2" in a right-side query has the following words and frequencies as result: in comparison (3), on Fe (1), treatment by (1), cause an (1), and does not (1). This algorithm is integrated into the maximum entropy tagger (MXPOST) of

Ratnaparkhi (1996) and improves the OOV word tagging quality of this tagger.

Recently, unsupervised solutions to the domain adaptation problem in POS tagging have become more frequent. An example is the study of Huang and Yates (2010) that proposed a representation-learning approach, which explores the discovering of stable features across domains that are predictive in both the source and the target domain. The method applies multi-dimensional clustering to discover many latent categories for each word. Then, these latent categories become useful and domain-independent features for supervised learning, which is performed with a CRF POS tagger that is trained on data annotated with the learned features.

Experiments with Domain Adaptation for the Portuguese POS Tagger

In this section, we explore domain adaptation for POS tagging in a case study that takes advantage of existing software and data resources using the Brazilian Portuguese language to gain insight into the adaptation problem.

Experimental Resources

Public resources available on the Web were used in the tagging model we developed. The TreeTagger tool was chosen to perform the probabilistic step and the μ-TBL system was chosen to learn rules automatically. Annotated data from the Mac-Morpho corpus was used to train the tagger and data from Mac-Morpho, Bosque CETENFolha and Selva Científica corpora were used as test sets of the target domains.

TreeTagger (Schmid, 1994, 1995) is a multilingual probabilistic tagger, which uses lexical information to tag a new text provided by a *parameter file* that contains information about the language. Unlike many taggers that require only a training corpus file to construct the parameter file, the parameter file of TreeTagger, in turn, is composed of three files: 1) a *lexicon*, which contains the words and their possible tags extracted from the training corpus; 2) *the training corpus*, containing annotated texts; and 3) an *open-class file*, which contains possible tags to OOV words. TreeTagger lets the user configure a series of parameters for training, for example, the context length (bigram, trigram, and so on), minimum decision tree gain, equivalence class weight, affix tree gain, and the end-of-sentence-POS tag, among others.

The *μ-TBL* (Lager, 1999) is an alternative system based on the TBL method (Brill, 1995) that supports a compositional formalism of rules/templates and presents three TBL algorithms, which are Brill, simple, and lazy, that can be adapted to different learning tasks (Lager, 1999). A template for POS tagging can search five previous words and five following words from the current word in a window of eleven. In the experiments of this study, 26 Brill templates available in μ-TBL were used, which were divided into eleven nonlexicalized templates that focused on the contextual structures (tags) and fifteen lexicalized templates that focused on the relation between words and tags (Brill, 1995). The system allows the user to configure parameters of the sequence of rules to be learned, for example, the algorithm, the set of templates, and the minimum threshold for score and accuracy desired (Lager, 1999). At the end of the tagging process, μ-TBL generates a file that contains the tagging errors in the context of the sentences in which they have occurred.

Mac-Morpho is a closed corpus, which was first annotated by the parser Palavras (Bick, 2000), mapped onto the tag set of the Lácio-Web Project (Lácio-Web, 2007) and manually revised for POS tags by specialists. Mac-Morpho contains 1.2 million words. The tag set (Aluísio, et al., 2003) has 78 POS tags 22 of which are regular, 18 of which are punctuation marks, and 38 of which are combined with complementary tags.

CETENFolha (Linguateca, 2007) is a large corpus with over 28 million words of Brazilian Portuguese texts from the Folha de São Paulo newspaper that were automatically annotated by the parser Palavras (Bick, 2000). This large corpus contains a subset with about 80,000 words called *Bosque CETENFolha* (Bosque CF), which has been reviewed by experts. The tag set of the corpus is reported by Afonso (2006) and contains 18 POS tags.

Selva Científica is a subcorpus of the Selva corpus (Linguateca, 2009) that contains texts from reports of Banco Central do Brasil and Banco Central Europeu and chapters of theses and articles from Wikipedia collected in September 2008 on topics related to science. Selva was automatically annotated by the parser Palavras (Bick, 2000) and is a partially reviewed corpus. It contains 141,361 words. In this study, to make the accuracy metric simpler, we adjusted the tags of some words to be the same as in the CETENFolha because the tag sets are very similar. In addition, Selva has a "n-adj" tag that is assigned to words that can be either a noun or an adjective. In order to have an accurate model for measuring the tagger accuracy, we have manually reviewed the corpus for POS tags.

POS Tagging Approach

The POS tagging model we have explored is based on the TBL method, which results in a model that combines probabilistic tagging with rule-based tagging and performs these steps in a pipeline. Public tools have been integrated into this model to perform the steps of the tagging process. For the probabilistic step of this model, we chose TreeTagger, based on its good performance in cases of small training sets. For the rule-based step, we chose μ-TBL to provide a set of rules automatically learned from the training corpus. The rule-based step also contains sets of hand-coded rules that we have developed and added to the model to correct errors. The addition of hand-coded rules to the TBL approach was also used by Finger (2000). To minimize tagging errors on OOV words, we have applied a strategy that takes advantage of the lexicon file used in the TreeTagger training. The strategy is to use a lexicon containing not only the lexical entries (the words and their possible tags) of the training corpus but as many lexical entries as possible from other domains. The use of a lexicon in a fashion similar to that described by Banko and Moore (2004, p. 558), which explores the knowledge of what tags are possible for each word in the lexicon, provided good results for the POS tagging accuracy.

The steps of our tagging model are as follows: 1) text preprocessing to convert text into the appropriate format required by the taggers; 2) initial tagging, in which unlabeled text is tagged with the TreeTagger; 3) tagging proper nouns, in which a lexicon of 60,000 proper nouns is consulted to tag proper nouns that were incorrectly tagged in the previous step; 4) tagging with an intermediate hand-coded rule set that is applied to the previous output to correct errors; 5) tagging with μ-TBL rules, in which a set of automatically obtained rules

are applied to correct the errors of the previous steps; 6) tagging with a post-correction hand-coded rule set that is applied to the previous output to correct the remaining errors; 7) comparing gold standard data with results, and if a pre-annotated test set is available, comparing it with its equivalent result from our tagging process; and 8) calculating the accuracy of the system and computing the statistics. In Figure 1, we present the tagger architecture, which includes the training step of the model.

Methodology

The case study includes both labeled data and unlabeled data that are used for semi-supervised domain adaptation. Data from the source domain are labeled data and data from the target domain are unlabeled data.

The experimental methodology to test the effectiveness of our domain adaptation model

Figure 1. POS tagger architecture

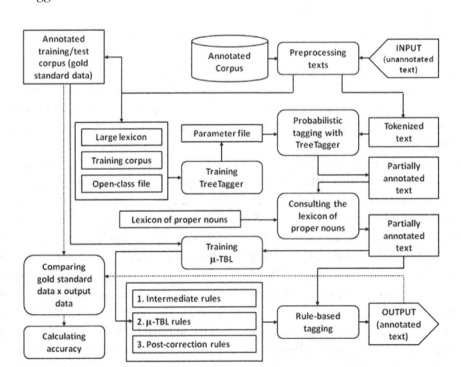

for Brazilian Portuguese consists performing the following steps and measuring the accuracy of each: 1) apply the hybrid tagger that was originally developed from journalistic texts (source domain) to tag unlabeled texts of the same genre, to obtain baseline accuracy rates; 2) tag unlabeled texts in the scientific genre (target domain); 3) extract the lexical entries from the labeled result of the previous step, insert them into the TreeTagger lexicon, retrain the tagger, and then tag the texts of the target domain again; 4) evaluate the results, observe the tagging errors due to the domain differences, and provide solutions to increase accuracy; 5) tag the texts of the target domain again; and 6) having gathered the results for the scientific genre, tag the test sets for the journalistic genre again and reevaluate the results.

The results of ten experiments, E1 to E10, show the evolution of the tagging accuracy after the completion of each step. The experiments differ in the test sets that are tagged and the size of the lexicon file used in the TreeTagger training.

Baseline Accuracy Rates

To evaluate the tagger accuracy, a set of 496,281 words from the Mac-Morpho corpus was divided into two disjoint sets, a training set containing 90% of the corpus (446,676 words) and a test set containing 10% of the corpus (49,605 words), the latter of which was not used in the training process. In this test set, 5.96% of the words are OOV words. These training and test sets had equal proportions of texts from each journalistic section of the corpus. Accuracy rates were calculated as the

sum of all the correctly tagged instances divided by the total number of words tagged.

In experiments E1 to E4, corresponding to the first step of the methodology, two test sets from the journalistic genre were tagged: the Mac-Morpho test set and the Bosque CF. In E1 and E2, TreeTagger was trained with a lexicon of 35,000 entries extracted from the full Mac-Morpho corpus. In E3 and E4, new lexical entries were extracted from the CETENFolha corpus and added to the TreeTagger lexicon so that the tagger was trained with a lexicon of 379,335 entries. Comparing the results shown in Table 2, we note that the strategy of using a large TreeTagger lexicon in training significantly reduced the number of tagging errors on OOV words. These results have been taken as baseline values for the following experiments.

Results in the Target Domain

In E5 and E6, corresponding to the second and third steps of the methodology, the Selva Científica corpus was tagged. In E5, TreeTagger was trained with the lexicon of 379,335 entries and achieved overall accuracy of 96.41%. In E6, the lexical entries of the Selva Científica were extracted from the result of the previous tagging step and were included in the lexicon file of TreeTagger, which resulted in a lexicon of 422,411 entries. In Selva corpus, 15.45% of the words are OOV words to the training set of the source domain. In that instance, an overall accuracy of 97.21% was achieved. In E6, we observed an accuracy improvement of 4.93% in OOV words when compared with E5 due to the enlargement in the lexicon size.

Table 2. POS tagging accuracy on Mac-Morpho and Bosque CF

Exp	Test set	Overall acc. (%)	Acc. known words (%)	Acc. OOV words (%)
E1	Mac-Morpho	97.50	97.73	93.55
E2	Bosque CF	97.56	98.38	88.41
E3	Mac-Morpho	98.05	98.01	98.65
E4	Bosque CF	98.27	98.47	96.05

Adjusting the Tagger

Because the overall accuracy rates in E5 and E6 were lower than those of the baseline (over 98% for journalistic texts) for the target domain of the Selva Científica, in the fourth step, the tagging errors were analyzed to determine what caused these problems. Many problems occurred due to different data distributions in the target domain. One example is that, in the scientific genre, the personal pronoun "se" in an enclitic expression such as "observa-se" (*is observed*) was tagged as a subordinating conjunction, which was the most frequent tagging error. This error was not frequent in the journalistic genre, because such enclitic cases are rare in that domain. We observed corpora differences that have since helped us minimize the number of errors. In Mac-Morpho, the verb before a personal pronoun separated by a hyphen; for example, "usa-se" (*is used*) is tokenized without the hyphen (usa/V|+ se/PROPESS), which creates difficulties in the disambiguation of the word "se." The rule we first codified covered only verbs that occurred in Mac-Morpho and could fail when tagging OOV verbs. In Selva, the verb is tokenized including the hyphen (usa-/v-fin se/pron-pers[1]). This observation led us to codify a more comprehensive post-correction rule that inspects if the final letter of a current word in the input is followed by a hyphen (for example, *a-, e-, m-, r-, s-,* etc.) to disambiguate the next word "se." This adjustment reduced these errors significantly, from 342 to 12 occurrences.

Because we needed annotated corpora with the purpose of measuring the tagger accuracy, in this stage we also made efforts to adjust the tagger to support differences of the corpora tag sets and their tokenization of words.

Evaluating the Final Accuracy Rates

At the fifth step, in E7 and E8, due to the described adjustments, the tagger was retrained using the TreeTagger lexicons of 379,335 entries and 422,411 entries, respectively, and the accuracy rates were re-calculated for the Selva Científica test set. The results in Table 3 show an improvement in the accuracy of the tagging. The errors that remained from E7 and E8 show the tagging problems that could not yet be resolved, which include problems with closed-class[2] words or problems at the semantic level of the language that require information not provided by the tag set of these experiments.

Finally, in the sixth step, in E9 and E10, we tagged the Mac-Morpho test set and the Bosque CF, respectively, after the modifications that were performed in Selva, and we re-evaluated the tagger. We used the TreeTagger lexicon of 422,411 words (including the words from Selva in the lexicon for TreeTagger). The results improved slightly, as shown in Table 4, because errors that occurred more frequently in the target domain were less frequent in the source domain.

Table 3. POS tagging accuracy on the Selva corpus after tagger adjustments

Exp	Overall acc. (%)	Acc. known words (%)	Acc. OOV words (%)
E7	97.50	97.93	95.13
E8	98.07	97.98	98.49

Table 4. POS tagging accuracy on the Mac-Morpho and Bosque CF Corpora after the tagger adjustments

Exp	Test set	Overall acc. (%)	Acc. known words (%)	Acc. unknown words (%)
E9	Mac-Morpho	98.06	98.00	99.00
E10	Bosque CF	98.30	98.43	96.93

FUTURE RESEARCH DIRECTIONS

For future work on domain adaptation, there should be more research on methods that handle unsupervised approaches and on methods that deal with unlabeled data in conjunction with labeled data in semi-supervised approaches. These approaches are now emerging as promising solutions for NLP applications that perform well in many different domains. Web-based algorithms (Umansky-Pesin, et al., 2010) are in the range of these solutions.

However, it is important to develop primary resources for supervised approaches: annotated corpora of various domains with the minimum possible noise. In this way, active learning techniques can be explored to increase the amount of labeled data and to reduce noise in corpora. Ringger et al. (2007) explored where to focus manual tagging efforts to achieve annotation of the highest quality and planned to evaluate an active-learning cost metric of annotating one sentence at a time or one word at a time. These authors incorporate costs into a model in search of a highly accurate system.

As discussed by Daumé III et al. (2010), semi-supervised adaptation with no available annotated data in the new domain is more difficult than supervised domain adaptation when a limited amount of annotated data in the new domain is available. Many questions remain as how to provide better solutions.

CONCLUSION

POS tagging plays an important role in NLP applications. Most state-of-the-art taggers have good accuracy for the domain in which they were trained, but perform poorly in new domains due to problems such as different linguistic structures or the presence of new or Out-Of-Vocabulary (OOV) words. Thus, the need for domain adaptation poses a new challenge in NLP tasks. Many recent studies have proposed supervised or unsupervised solutions. Some of them have good performance in up to three NLP tasks, whereas others perform well in one task, but not in another task. In this chapter, we present the state of the art in the domain adaptation problem, and we highlight the main approaches presented in the literature that handle labeled and unlabeled data in NLP tasks, with focus on POS tagging. We present a case study of a hybrid Portuguese POS tagger and describe how to handle the presence of OOV words in the target domain by including words of the new domain in the lexicon of the probabilistic tagger in the training step, and by making adjustments to the tagger to support differences in domains. Favorable results, with an overall accuracy rate over 98%, were achieved when tagging three Portuguese test sets of scientific and journalistic domains.

REFERENCES

Abney, S. (1996). Part-of-speech tagging and partial parsing. In Young, S., & Bloothooft, G. (Eds.), *Corpus-Based Methods in Language and Speech Processing* (pp. 118–136). Dordrecht, The Netherlands: Kluwer Academic Publishers.

Afonso, S. (2006). *Árvores deitadas: Descrição do formato e das opções de análise na floresta sintá(c) tica*. Retrieved from http://www.linguateca.pt/documentos/Afonso2006ArvoresDeitadas.pdf

Aluísio, S. M., Pelizzoni, J. M., Marchi, A. R., Oliveira, L. H., Manenti, R., & Marquiafável, V. (2003). An account of the challenge of tagging a reference corpus of Brazilian Portuguese. *Lecture Notes in Computer Science, 2721*, 110–117. doi:10.1007/3-540-45011-4_17

Banko, M., & Moore, R. C. (2004). Part of speech tagging in context. In *Proceedings of the 20th International Conference on Computational Linguistics*, (pp. 556-561). ACL.

Berber Sardinha, T. (2004). *Lingüística de corpus.* Barueri, Spain: Manole.

Bick, E. (2000). *The parsing system palavras – Automatic grammatical analysis of Portuguese in a constraint grammar framework.* Aarhus, Denmark: Aarhus University Press. Retrieved from http://beta.visl.sdu.dk/pdf/PLP20-amilo.ps.pdf

Bickel, S., Brückner, M., & Scheffer, T. (2007). Discriminative learning for differing training and test distributions. In *Proceedings of the 24th Annual International Conference on Machine Learning,* (pp. 81-88). IEEE.

Blitzer, J. (2007). *Domain adaptation of natural language processing systems.* Retrieved from http://john.blitzer.com/papers/adaptationthesis.pdf

Blitzer, J., McDonald, R., & Pereira, F. (2006). Domain adaptation with structural correspondence learning. In *Proceedings of the 2006 Conference on Empirical Methods in Natural Language Processing,* (pp. 120-128). ACL.

Brants, T. (2000). TnT – A statistical part-of-speech tagger. In *Proceedings of the Sixth Applied Natural Language Processing Conference,* (pp. 224-231). ACL.

Brill, E. (1995). Transformation-based error-driven learning of natural language: A case study in part-of-speech tagging. *Computational Linguistics, 21*(4), 543–565.

Chan, Y. S., & Ng, H. T. (2005). Word sense disambiguation with distribution estimation. In *Proceedings of the 19th International Joint Conference on Artificial Intelligence,* (pp. 1010-1015). IEEE.

Chelba, C., & Acero, A. (2006). Adaptation of maximum entropy capitalizer: Little data can help a lot. *Computer Speech & Language, 20*(4), 382–399. doi:10.1016/j.csl.2005.05.005

Church, K. W. (1988). A stochastic parts program and noun phrase parser for unrestricted text. In *Proceedings of the Second Conference on Applied Natural Language Processing,* (pp. 136-143). ACL.

Dai, W., Xue, G., Yang, Q., & Yu, Y. (2007). Transferring naive Bayes classifiers for text classification. In *Proceedings of the 22nd AAAI Conference on Artificial Intelligence,* (pp. 540-545). AAAI.

Daumé III, H., (2007). Frustratingly easy domain adaptation. In *Proceedings of the 45th Annual Meeting of the Association for Computational Linguistics,* (pp. 256–263). ACL. Retrieved from http://www.aclweb.org/anthology-new/P/P07/P07-1033.pdf

Daumé III, H., Deoskar, T., McClosky, D., & Plank, B. (2010). *ACL 2010 workshop on domain adaptation for natural language processing (DANLP).* Retrieved from http://sites.google.com/site/danlp2010/call-for-papers

Daumé III, H., & Marcu, D. (2006). Domain adaptation for statistical classifiers. *Journal of Artificial Intelligence Research, 26*(1), 101–126.

dos Santos, C. N., Milidiú, R. L., & Rentería, R. (2008). Portuguese part-of-speech tagging using entropy guided transformation learning. *Lecture Notes in Computer Science, 5190,* 143–152. doi:10.1007/978-3-540-85980-2_15

Ekbal, A., Haque, R., & Bandyopadhyay, S. (2007). Bengali part of speech tagging using conditional random field. In *Proceedings of the 7th International Symposium of Natural Language Processing,* (pp. 131-136). ACL.

Finger, M. (2000). Técnicas de otimização da precisão empregadas no etiquetador Tycho Brahe. In Nunes, M. G. V. (Ed.), *Anais do V Encontro para o Processamento Computacional da Língua Portuguesa Escrita e Falada* (pp. 141–154). Atibaia, Spain: ICMC/USP.

Greene, B. B., & Rubin, G. M. (1971). *Automatic grammatical tagging of English. Technical Report.* Providence, RI: Brown University.

Heikkilä, J. (1995). A TWOL-based lexicon and feature system for English. In Karlsson, F., Voutilainen, A., Heikkilä, J., & Anttila, A. (Eds.), *Constraint Grammar: A Language-Independent System for Parsing Unrestricted Text* (pp. 103–131). Berlin, Germany: Mouton de Gruyter. doi:10.1515/9783110882629.103

Huang, F., & Yates, A. (2010). *Exploring representation-learning approaches to domain adaptation.* Retrieved from http://www.cis.temple.edu/~yates/papers/2010-danlp-lvlms-for-domain-adaptation.pdf

Jiang, J. (2008). *Domain adaptation in natural language processing.* Retrieved from http://hdl.handle.net/2142/10870

Jiang, J., & Zhai, C. (2007). Instance weighting for domain adaptation in NLP. In *Proceedings of the 45th Annual Meeting of the Association for Computational Linguistics,* (pp. 254–261). ACL. Retrieved from http://www.aclweb.org/anthology/P/P07/P07-1034.pdf

Jurafsky, D., & Martin, J. (2000). *Speech and language processing: An introduction to natural language processing, computational linguistics, and speech recognition.* Upper Saddle River, NJ: Prentice-Hall.

Karlsson, F., Voutilainen, A., Heikkilä, J., & Anttila, A. (1995). *Constraint grammar: A language-independent system for parsing unrestricted text.* Berlin, Germany: Mouton de Gruyter. doi:10.1515/9783110882629

Kempe, A. (1993). *A probabilistic tagger and an analysis of tagging errors.* Stuttgart, Germany: Research Report, Institut für Maschinelle Sprachverarbeitung. Universität Stuttgart.

Kinoshita, J., Salvador, L. N., & Menezes, C. E. D. (2007). CoGrOO - An OpenOffice grammar checker. In *Proceedings of the Seventh International Conference on Intelligent Systems Design and Applications,* (pp. 525-530). Washington, DC: IEEE Computer Society.

Klein, S., & Simmons, R. F. (1963). A computational approach to grammatical coding of English words. *Journal of the ACM, 10*(3), 334–347. doi:10.1145/321172.321180

Lácio-Web. (2007). Lácio-Web manuals. In *Compilação de Córpus do Português do Brasil e Implementação de Ferramentas Para Análises Lingüísticas.* Retrieved July 02, 2007, from http://www.nilc.icmc.usp.br/lacioweb/english/manuais.htm

Lager, T. (1999). The μ-TBL system: Logic programming tools for transformation-based learning. In *Proceedings of the 3rd International Workshop on Computational Natural Language Learning,* (pp. 33-42). Retrieved from http://acl.ldc.upenn.edu/W/W99/W99-0705.pdf

Linguateca. (2007). CETENFolha. In *Linguateca.* Retrieved February 12, 2007, from http://www.linguateca.pt/CETENFolha/

Linguateca. (2009). Material que compõe a Floresta Sintá(c)tica. In *Linguateca.* Retrieved February 12, 2009, from http://www.linguateca.pt/Floresta/material.html

Ngai, G., & Florian, R. (2001). Transformation-based learning in the fast lane. In *Proceedings of the Second Conference of the North American Chapter of the Association for Computational Linguistics,* (pp. 40-47). ACL.

Ning, H., Yang, H., & Li, Z. (2007). A method integrating rule and HMM for Chinese part-of_speech tagging. In *Proceedings of the 2nd IEEE Conference on Industrial Electronics and Applications,* (pp. 723-725). IEEE Press.

Nugues, P. M. (2006). *An introduction to language processing with Perl and Prolog: An outline of theories, implementation, and application with special consideration of English, French, and German.* Heidelberg, Germany: Springer.

Ratnaparkhi, A. (1996). A maximum entropy model for part-of-speech tagging. In *Proceedings of the Conference on Empirical Methods in Natural Language,* (pp. 133-142). ACL. Retrieved from http://acl.ldc.upenn.edu/W/W96/W96-0213.pdf

Ringger, E., McClanahan, P., Haertel, R., Busby, G., Carmen, M., & Carroll, J..... Lonsdale, D. (2007). Active learning for part-of-speech tagging: Accelerating corpus annotation. In *Proceedings of the Linguistic Annotation Workshop,* (pp. 101–108). Retrieved from http://www.aclweb.org/anthology-new/W/W07/W07-1516.pdf

Schmid, H. (1994). Probabilistic part-of-speech tagging using decision trees. In *Proceedings of the International Conference on New Methods in Language Processing,* (pp. 44-49). ACL.

Schmid, H. (1995). Improvements in part-of-speech tagging with an application to German. In *Proceedings of the EACL SIGDAT Workshop,* (pp. 47-55). EACL.

Toutanova, K., Klein, D., Manning, C. D., & Singer, Y. (2003). Feature-rich part-of-speech tagging with a cyclic dependency network. In *Proceedings of the 2003 Conference of the North American Chapter of the Association for Computational Linguistics on Human Language Technology,* (vol 1), (pp. 173-180). ACL.

Tsujii Laboratory. (2010). Domain adaptation of part-of-speech taggers. In *Research on Advanced Natural Language Processing and Text Mining: aNT.* Retrieved June 30, 2010, from http://www-tsujii.is.s.u-tokyo.ac.jp/aNT/domain-pos.html

Umansky-Pesin, S., Reichart, R., & Rappoport, A. (2010). A multi-domain web-based algorithm for POS tagging of unknown words. In *Proceedings of the 23rd International Conference on Computational Linguistics,* (pp. 1274-1282). ACL. Retrieved from http://www.aclweb.org/anthology/C10-2146.

Viterbi, A. J. (1967). Error bounds for convolutional codes and an asymptotically optimal decoding algorithm. *IEEE Transactions on Information Theory, 13*(2), 260–269. doi:10.1109/TIT.1967.1054010

Yoshida, K., Tsuruoka, Y., Miyao, Y., & Tsujii, J. (2007). Ambiguous part-of-speech tagging for improving accuracy and domain portability of syntactic parsers. [IJCAI.]. *Proceedings of, IJCAI-07,* 1783–1788.

ADDITIONAL READING

Ando, R., & Zhang, T. (2005). A framework for learning predictive structure from multiple tasks and unlabeled data. *Journal of Machine Learning Research, 6,* 1817–1853.

Angeli, E., Wagner, J., Lawrick, E., Moore, K., Anderson, M., Soderland, L., & Brizee, A. (2010). *General format.* Retrieved from http://owl.english.purdue.edu/owl/resource/560/01/

Ben-David, S., Blitzer, J., Crammer, C., & Pereira, F. (2007). Analysis of representations for domain adaptation. *Advances in Neural Information Processing Systems, 19,* 137–144.

Blitzer, J., Crammer, K., Kulesza, A., Pereira, F., & Wortman, J. (2008). Learning bounds for domain adaptation. *Advances in Neural Information Processing Systems, 20,* 29–136.

Carlberger, J., & Kann, V. (1999). Implementing an efficient part-of-speech tagger. *Software, Practice & Experience, 29*(2), 815–832. doi:10.1002/(SICI)1097-024X(19990725)29:9<815::AID-SPE256>3.0.CO;2-F

Cutting, D., Kupiec, J., Pederson, J., & Sibun, P. (1992). A practical part of speech tagger. In *Proceedings of the Third Conference on Applied Natural Language Processing*, (pp. 133-140). ACL.

Dagan, I., & Engelson, S. P. (1995). Committee-based sampling for training probabilistic classifiers. In *Proceedings of the International Conference on Machine Learning*, (pp. 150-157). IEEE.

Dahlmeier, D., & Ng, H. T. (2010). Domain adaptation for semantic role labeling in the biomedical domain. *Bioinformatics (Oxford, England), 26*(8), 1098–1104. doi:10.1093/bioinformatics/btq075

Dai, W., Yang, Q., Xue, G., & Yu, Y. (2007). Boosting for transfer learning. In *Proceedings of the 24th Annual International Conference on Machine Learning*, (pp. 193-200). IEEE.

Jiang, J., & Zhai, C. (2007). A two-stage approach to domain adaptation for statistical classifiers. In *Proceedings of the Sixteenth ACM Conference on Information and Knowledge Management*, (pp. 401-410). ACM Press.

Lafferty, J., McCallum, A., & Pereira, F. (2001). Conditional random fields: Probabilistic models for segmenting and labeling sequence data. In *Proceedings of the Eighteenth International Conference on Machine Learning*, (pp. 282 – 289). IEEE.

Lewis, D., & Gale, W. (1994). A sequential algorithm for training text classifiers. In *Proceedings of the 17th Annual International ACM SIGIR Conference on Research and Development in Information Retrieval*, (pp. 3-12). ACM Press.

Li, X., & Bilmes, J. (2007). A Bayesian divergence prior for classifier adaptation. In *Proceedings of the Eleventh International Conference on Artificial Intelligence and Statistics*. IEEE.

Manning, C. D., & Schütze, H. (1999). *Foundations of statistical natural language processing*. Cambridge, MA: The MIT Press.

Mansour, Y., Mohri, M., & Rostamizadeh, A. (2009). Domain adaptation with multiple sources. *Advances in Neural Information Processing Systems, 21*, 1041–1048.

Marcus, M. P., Santorini, B., & Marcinkieewicz, M. A. (1994). Building a large annotated corpus of English: The Penn treebank. *Computational Linguistics, 19*(2), 313–330.

McClosky, D., Charniak, E., & Johnson, M. (2010). Automatic domain adaptation for parsing. In *Proceedings of the Human Language Technologies: The 2010 Annual Conference of the North American Chapter of the Association for Computational Linguistics*, (pp. 28-36). ACL.

Pradhan, S. S., Ward, W., & Martin, J. H. (2008). Towards robust semantic role labeling. *Computational Linguistics, 34*(2), 289–310. doi:10.1162/coli.2008.34.2.289

Pyysalo, S., Salakoski, T., Aubin, S., & Nazarenko, A. (2006). Lexical adaptation of link grammar to the biomedical sublanguage: A comparative evaluation of three approaches. *BMC Bioinformatics, 7*(3), 1–9. doi:10.1186/1471-2105-7-S3-S2

Rai, P., Saha, A., Daumé, H., III, & Venkatasubramanian, S. (2010). Domain adaptation meets active learning. In *Proceedings of the NAACL HLT 2010 Workshop on Active Learning for Natural Language Processing*, (pp. 27-32). NAACL.

Roark, B., & Bacchiani, M. (2003). Supervised and unsupervised PCFG adaptation to novel domains. In *Proceedings of the 2003 Conference of the North American Chapter of the Association for Computational Linguistics on Human Language Technology*, (vol 1), (pp. 126–133). ACL.

Satpal, S., & Sarawagi, S. (2007). Domain adaptation of conditional probability models via feature subsetting. In *Proceedings of the 11th European Conference on Principles and Practice of Knowledge Discovery in Databases*, (pp. 224–235). IEEE.

Settles, B. (2010). *Active learning literature survey*. Computer Sciences Technical Report 1648. Madison, WI: University of Wisconsin–Madison. Retrieved from http://www.cs.cmu.edu/~bsettles/pub/settles.activelearning.pdf

Tsuruoka, Y., & Tsujii, J. (2005). Bidirectional inference with the easiest-first strategy for tagging sequence data. In *Proceedings of the Conference on Human Language Technology and Empirical Methods in Natural Language Processing*, (pp. 467-474). ACL.

Wallach, H. M. (2004). *Conditional random fields: An introduction*. Technical Report MS-CIS-04-21. Retrieved from http://people.cs.umass.edu/~wallach/technical_reports/wallach04conditional.pdf

KEY TERMS AND DEFINITIONS

Annotated Data: Data labeled with their grammatical categories or other lexical attributes, used to train a model (training data) or to measure the accuracy of a model (test data).

Domain Adaptation Problem: When the accuracy in the target domain is poor compared with that of the source domain.

Lexicon: A list of words or lexical entries, which may be of a specific content category, such as proper nouns. The words in a lexicon may also have many entries, each with a part of speech or other lexical attributes.

Natural Language Processing: A subarea of Computational Linguistics that deals with the study of language with the purpose of constructing computational tools.

Part-of-Speech Tagging: A task applied in many preprocessing NLP applications to disambiguate a word in the context of a sentence and assign the word its appropriate part-of-speech tag.

New Words or Out-of-Vocabulary Words: Words that appear in the target data that are not present or are rare in training data.

Noise: Mistagged words in the training data.

Semi-Supervised Domain Adaptation: When labeled data are available to train a model in the source domain, but there is no labeled data in the target domain.

Supervised Domain Adaptation: When labeled data are available to train a model in the source domain, and there are small amounts of labeled data in the target domain.

Unsupervised Domain Adaptation: When only unlabeled data are available in both source and target domains.

ENDNOTES

[1] The tags v-fin and pron-pers are from the CETENFolha tag set and refer to finite verbs and personal pronouns, respectively.

[2] Closed-class words are more stable classes of words, and the evolution of language rarely adds new members to them. Examples include determiners, pronouns, prepositions, conjunctions, and numerals.

Section 2
Machine Translation

Chapter 4
Statistical Machine Translation

Lucia Specia
University of Sheffield, UK

ABSTRACT

Statistical Machine Translation (SMT) is an approach to automatic text translation based on the use of statistical models and examples of translations. SMT is the current dominant research paradigm for machine translation and has been attracting significant commercial interest in recent years. In this chapter, the authors introduce the rationale behind SMT, describe the currently leading approach (phrase-based SMT), and present a number of emerging approaches (tree-based SMT, discriminative SMT). They also present popular metrics to evaluate the performance of SMT systems and discuss promising research directions in the field.

1. INTRODUCTION

Statistical Machine Translation (SMT) is an approach to automatically translate text based on the use of statistical models and examples of translations. Although Machine Translation (MT) systems developed according to rule-based approaches are still in use, SMT is the dominant research paradigm today and has recently been garnering significant commercial interest. The core of SMT research has developed over the last two decades, after the seminal paper by Brown et al. (1990). The field has progressed considerably since then, moving from word-to-word translation towards phrase-to-phrase translation and other more sophisticated models that take sentence structure into account. A trend observed in recent years is the shift from using pure statistical information extracted from large quantities of data to incorporating linguistic information about the source and/or the target language.

The idea of SMT is related to the late 1940's view of the translation task as a cryptography problem where a decoding process is needed to translate from a foreign "code" into the English language (Hutchins, 1997). This is the basis for the fundamental approach to SMT proposed in the early 1990s through the application of the *Noisy*

DOI: 10.4018/978-1-4666-2169-5.ch004

Figure 1. The noisy channel model

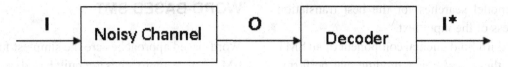

Channel Model (Shannon, 1949) from the field of Information Theory. This model had proved to be successful in the area of Speech Recognition and was thus adapted to MT.

The use of the Noisy Channel Model for translation assumes that the original text has been accidentally scrambled or encrypted (using a different alphabet, for example) and the goal is to find out the original text by "decoding" the encrypted/scrambled version, as depicted in Figure 1. According to this model, the message I is the input to the channel (text in a native language). I gets encrypted into O (text in a foreign language) using a certain coding scheme. The goal is to find a decoder that can reconstruct the input message as faithfully as possible into $I*$.

In a probabilistic framework, finding $I*$, i.e., the closest possible text to I, can be stated as finding the argument that maximizes the probability of recovering the original input given the noisy text, i.e.:

$$\underset{\text{noise-free text}}{\text{argmax}}\ P(\text{noise-free text} \mid \text{noisy text})$$

This problem is commonly exemplified as the task of translating from a *foreign* language sentence f into an *English* sentence e. Given f, we seek the translation e that maximizes $P(e \mid f)$, i.e., the most likely translation:

$$\underset{e}{\text{argmax}}\ P(e \mid f)$$

This problem can be decomposed in smaller and simpler problems applying the Bayes Theorem:

$$\underset{e}{\text{argmax}}\ P(e \mid f) = \underset{e}{\text{argmax}}\ \frac{P(f \mid e)P(e)}{P(f)}$$

Since the source text f, i.e., the input for the translation task is constant across all possible translations e, $P(f)$ can be disregarded:

$$\underset{e}{\text{argmax}}\ P(e \mid f) = \underset{e}{\text{argmax}}\ P(f \mid e)P(e)$$

The process of decomposing the problem of translation into smaller problems and modeling each step individually is motivated by the fact that more reliable statistics can be collected for the smaller problems. The modeling of each smaller problem with probability distributions followed by their combination to find a model that best explains the data complies with a type of statistical learning called *generative modeling*. The generative models resulting from the decomposition of $P(e \mid f)$ correspond to two of the fundamental components of a basic SMT system: the *translation model* $P(f \mid e)$ and the *language model* $P(e)$. The translation model is used to search for the best translation given an input text. While mathematically it represents the inverse translation probability, i.e., the probability of the source text given the target text, in practice the initial direction, i.e., the probability of the target text given the source text, can be estimated in the very same way using the same data, as we will discuss later. In most SMT systems, both probability directions are used. The decomposition is relevant mostly to isolate the language model component from the translation model. The language model searches for the best translation regardless of the input text.

The third fundamental component of an SMT system, the *decoder*, is a module that performs the search for the best translation e given the space of all possible translations (or a subset of it) based on the probability estimates $P(\mathbf{e})$ and $P(\mathbf{f} \mid \mathbf{e})$. These are major components of the basic word-to-word SMT approaches proposed in the early 1990s. The state-of-the art SMT approaches, however, use extra components to provide additional information to translate phrases or hierarchical structures, and discriminative methods to combine such models by weighting them according to their relevance to discriminate between good and bad translations. This chapter concentrates on such advanced approaches to SMT.

In the remainder of this chapter, we start by briefly presenting the word-based SMT approach, which forms the basis for more advanced approaches presented in Section 2. In Section 3, we describe the general phrase-based approach, along with a number of components that are commonly used within this approach and the standard algorithms used to perform translation (decoding) as well as to estimate the weights of the model components. In Section 4, we move to more recent models using linguistic information at different stages of phrase-based approaches, including pre- and post-processing stages. We then describe more advanced hierarchical and syntax-based models (Section 5), as well as an alternative approach that treats the translation problem as a fully discriminative machine-learning task (Section 6). In Section 7, we introduce popular metrics for automatic evaluation of SMT systems. We finish by discussing some research directions in the field of SMT (Section 8).

2. WORD ALIGNMENT AND WORD-BASED SMT

Word-based approaches are the simplest form of SMT. These approaches are built based on *word-alignment models*, which also constitute a fundamental module in the more advanced approaches based on other units like phrases or syntactic trees to be discussed in this chapter. In order to build word-alignment models, the most important resource is a *parallel corpus*, i.e., a corpus that contains a text in one language f and its translation in another language e . This corpus first needs to be aligned at the sentence level, i.e., it needs to contain information about the correspondence between sentences in both languages. Common algorithms for sentence alignment are based on heuristics such as sentence length and anchor word pairs (Brown, et al., 1991; Gale & Church, 1991).

The parallel corpus can be pre-processed in several ways after sentence alignment. Common techniques include cleaning the corpus to remove sentence-pairs, which are very different in length (i.e., number of words), performing word segmentation / tokenization, lowercasing, and sometimes word lemmatization in order to allow models to cover form variations and therefore better generalize the data. Depending on the type of SMT approach, other pre-processing steps might be performed to incorporate linguistic information, such as morphological features, Part-Of-Speech (POS) tags, or syntactic structures. In this section, we assume that no such linguistic features are used.

Once sentence alignment and the necessary pre-processing steps are performed, the next step is to estimate translation probabilities. According to the noisy channel formulation of the SMT problem, given the input sentence f , the aim is to estimate a general model for $P(\mathbf{f} \mid \mathbf{e})$, i.e., the inverse translation probability, by looking at the parallel corpus with examples of translations between e and f . However, extracting probability estimates for the whole sentences **f** and **e** is not feasible, since it is unlikely that the corpus would contain repeated occurrences of complete sentences, particularly for long sentences. Therefore, shorter portions of the sentences need to be considered. The smallest translation unit that is normally considered is a *word*.

In order to estimate word translation probabilities, the first step is to word-align the corpus, i.e., to identify the correspondences between the two languages at the word level. This can be done by using *word alignment models*. In what follows we outline a simple model, which is based on lexical translation probability distributions to align words in isolation, regardless of their position within the parallel sentence or any additional information. This model can be used as a basic word-to-word translation model. It is part of a set of five generative models proposed by Brown et al. (1990, 1993), which came to be known as the *IBM Models* for word alignment and are the basis for more advanced models proposed later, such as Vogel *et al.* (1996).

The translation probability of a source sentence $\mathbf{f} = (f_1, ..., f_J)$ of length J being translated into a target sentence $\mathbf{e} = (e_1, ..., e_I)$ of length I is modeled in terms of the alignment between individual words e_i and f_j according to the alignment function $a : i \rightarrow j$, i.e.:

$$P(\mathbf{e}, a \mid \mathbf{f}) = \frac{\varepsilon}{(J+1)^I} \prod_{j=1}^{I} P_l(e_j \mid f_{a(j)})$$

The parameter ε is a normalization constant to guarantee a probability distribution for $P(\mathbf{e}, a \mid \mathbf{f})$. $(J+1)^I$ are all possible alignments that map $(J+1)$ (source words can be aligned to zero target words, resulting in the addition of one more token, *NULL*) source words into I target words. The lexical translation probabilities $P_l(e_j \mid f_{a(j)})$ can be estimated using the Expectation Maximization (EM) unsupervised algorithm

(Dempster, et al., 1977) as follows (Koehn, 2010a, p. 88):

1. Initialize the model, typically with uniform distributions. This means that each input word f in a source sentence is assumed to be aligned with equal probability to any target word e from its parallel target sentence.

2. Apply the model to the parallel corpus (expectation step). This means applying the alignment model with the current probability distributions to words in all sentence pairs and accumulating these probabilities for each possible word pair.

3. Learn the model from the data, i.e., maximize the likelihood of the model given the data (maximization step). This means updating the probability distributions by considering the actual frequencies of different possible alignments. This can be done by defining the new alignment probability for each *target given source* word pair as the sum of all current alignment probabilities for that pair, divided by the number of occurrences of the *source* word (Maximum Likelihood Estimation).

4. Repeat steps 2 and 3 until convergence, i.e., until the probabilities are stable: no more updates happen in step 3, or the updates are smaller than a certain threshold.

By using such a model for translation, the best translation will be the one that maximizes the lexical alignment a between **f** and **e**; in other words, the translation that maximizes the probability that all words in **e** are translations of words in **f**. This alignment/translation model is very simple and has many flaws. More advanced models take into account other information, for example, the fact that the position of the words in the target sentence may be related to the position of the words in the source sentence (*absolute* *reordering* or *distortion* model), the fact that some source words may be translated into multiple target words (*fertility* of the words), or the fact that the position of a target word may be related to the position of the neighboring preceding words (*relative distortion* model). An implementation of all IBM models, along with a few further developments for word alignments, are provided in the GIZA++ toolkit (Och & Ney, 2003).[1]

3. PHRASE-BASED SMT

State of the art SMT systems such as *Moses* (Koehn, et al., 2007) modify the noisy channel generative modeling approach initially proposed by adding a number of other model components and learning the relative importance (weight) of each component by discriminative training. The discriminative training approach directly maximizes translation performance by learning to discriminate between good and bad translations and adjusting the models to prefer good translations (Section 3.4).

The two main model components mentioned earlier, i.e., the translation model and language model, are still essential. However, these models are among a number of other components, or *feature functions*, that represent specific properties of candidate translations, i.e., alternative translations for a given input text. A common strategy is to combine these features using a *log-linear model*.

Log-linear models for SMT have the following general form:

$$P(\mathbf{e} \mid \mathbf{f}) = f(x) = \exp \sum_{i=1}^{n} \lambda_i h_i(x)$$

where the overall probability of translating the source sentence f into a target sentence e is given by a combination of several model components $h_i(x)$ to be used during the decoding process, weighted by parameters λ_i estimated for each

component. With discriminative training, weights for each component are learnt in a way that reflects their relevance to the translation problem. In other words, components are weighted in a way that helps the model discriminate between good and bad translations. During the decoding process, the best translation can then be found by maximizing this log-linear model.

Log-linear models allow a natural way to include additional model components in the form of feature functions, as well as to provide weights for different components according to their relevance. For practical reasons, most systems are restricted to a few features, not exceeding 10-12. Some of the recent work on discriminative learning focuses on using a much larger set of features, such as the actual phrases that can be used in the translation (see Section 6), but their development and use is still heavily hampered by scalability issues.

The units of translation in the log-linear framework can vary: words, flat phrases, gapped phrases, hierarchical representations, or syntactic trees. For most language pairs, the state of the art performance is achieved with *Phrase-Based SMT* (PBSMT) systems (Koehn, et al., 2003), i.e., systems that consider a sequence of words as their translation unit. In the next sections, we describe the standard pipeline necessary to build such systems, as well as a number of commonly used model components, and the procedures for tuning the weights of these components and decoding. Most of the description is based on the functioning of the *Moses* system,[2] the most popular and freely available open-source PBSMT system. Interested readers are referred to Koehn (2010a) for a more detailed description.

3.1. Phrase Extraction and Scoring

When translating a sentence, it is common for continuous sequences of words to be translated as a unit. To account for that, most of the current SMT systems are *phrase-based*, i.e., they use phrases as their basic translation unit. In SMT, a phrase is simply a continuous sequence of words, as opposed to a linguistically motivated set of words. A phrase dictionary in such systems, usually called *phrase table*, contains non-empty source phrases and their corresponding non-empty target phrases, where the lengths of a given source-target phrase pair are not necessarily equal. These phrase-based models implicitly allow the local context of the phrase-internal words being translated to be taken into account. The longer the phrases that can be extracted from the corpus, the more context can be used.

A source sentence can be split into many different phrases. A simple and common method is to identify valid splits of a sentence by applying simple heuristics to extract phrase pairs, which are consistent with its word alignment to the target sentence. Since the parallel corpus can be handled in both directions (i.e., $f \rightarrow e$ and $e \rightarrow f$), it is trivial to generate word alignments in both directions. By intersecting two such alignments, one can get a high-precision alignment with high-confidence alignment points. By taking the union of the two alignments, one can get a high-recall alignment with additional alignment points. For example, consider the word alignments in both directions and their intersection/union for the English-Spanish sentence pair in Figure 2, based on the example by Callison-Burch and Koehn (2005).

Figure 2. Word alignments in both directions and their intersection (black points) and union (black and grey points)

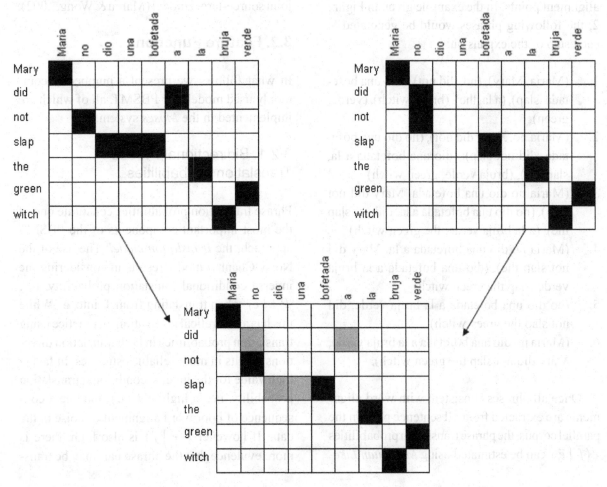

A phrase pair $(\bar{f}, \bar{e})$ is consistent with an alignment a if all words $f_1, ..., f_m$ in $\bar{f}$ that have alignment points in a have these alignment points with words $e_1, ..., e_n$ in $\bar{e}$ and vice-versa. Based on this heuristic, a phrase pair can be created if the words in the phrases are only aligned to each other, and not to words outside that phrase.

In the heuristics used in *Moses*, the phrase extraction process loops over all possible target phrases and finds the minimal source phrase that matches each of them in a consistent way. Given an alignment matrix like the one in Figure 2, starting from the intersection of the two certain word alignments, a new alignment point that exists in the union of two word alignments can be added provided that it connects at least one unaligned word. The algorithm expands first to directly adjacent alignment points, and then adds non-adjacent alignment points. In the example given in Figure 2, the following phrases would be generated at each step of the expansion:

1. (Maria, Mary), (no, did not), (dio una bofetada, slap), (a la, the), (bruja, witch), (verde, green)
2. (Maria no, Mary did not), (no dio una bofetada, did not slap), (dio una bofetada a la, slap the), (bruja verde, green witch)
3. (Maria no dio una bofetada, Mary did not slap), (no dio una bofetada a la, did not slap the), (a la bruja verde, the green witch)
4. (Maria no dio una bofetada a la, Mary did not slap the), (dio una bofetada a la bruja verde, slap the green witch)
5. (no dio una bofetada a la bruja verde, did not slap the green witch)
6. (Maria no dio una bofetada a la bruja verde, Mary did not slap the green witch).

Once all phrases consistent with word alignments are extracted from all sentence pairs in the parallel corpus, the phrase translation probabilities $\phi(\bar{f}_i \mid \bar{e}_i)$ can be estimated using *Maximum Like-*

lihood Estimation (MLE), i.e., counts of such phrase pairs in the corpus:

$$\phi(\bar{f} \mid \bar{e}) = \frac{count(\bar{e}, \bar{f})}{\sum_{\bar{f}_i} count(\bar{e}, \bar{f}_i)}$$

All extracted phrase pairs are usually stored in a *phrase table*, which is similar to a bilingual dictionary of phrase pairs, along with associated translation probabilities and optionally other information about each phrase pair, depending on the feature functions used (Section 3.2).

Phrase extraction and scoring can also be done simultaneously and directly from a sentence-aligned parallel corpus. Similar to word alignment, it is possible to use the EM algorithm to produce phrase alignments and their probabilities with a joint source-target model (Marcu & Wong, 2002).

3.2. Feature Functions

In what follows we present a number of commonly used models for PBSMT, all of which are implemented in the *Moses* system.

3.2.1. Bidirectional Phrase Translation Probabilities

Phrase translation probabilities constitute one of the most important components of the PBSMT approach, the *translation model*. The use of the Noisy Channel model results in considering the inverse conditional translation probability, i.e., $P(\mathbf{f} \mid \mathbf{e})$ when translating from $\mathbf{f}$ into $\mathbf{e}$. While this has a theoretical motivation, in practice using translation probabilities in both translation directions results in more reliable estimates. In fact, a high value for the inverse conditional translation probability, i.e., a high $\phi(\bar{f} \mid \bar{e})$, may be a consequence of poor word alignment or noise in the data. If however $\phi(\bar{e} \mid \bar{f})$ is also high, there is more evidence that the phrase pair may be translation of each other. Therefore, most systems use translation probabilities in both translation directions as feature functions, i.e.: $\phi(\bar{f} \mid \bar{e})$ and $\phi(\bar{e} \mid \bar{f})$. The probability estimates $\phi(\bar{e} \mid \bar{f})$ can be obtained in the very same way as for $\phi(\bar{f} \mid \bar{e})$, using word alignments in the opposite direction.

3.2.2. Language Model

The language Model (LM) is the second major component of SMT since its initial formulation. It estimates how likely a given target language sentence is to appear in that language. The intuition is that common translations are more likely to be good translations. This component models fluency, and it does not take the source sentence into account. It is estimated based on relative frequencies of sentences in a (preferably very large) monolingual corpus of the target language.

Formally, the language model component $P(\mathbf{e})$ for a sentence with m words is defined as the joint probability of a sequence of all words in that sentence:

$$P(\mathbf{e}) = P(w_1, w_2, ..., w_m)$$

The chain rule can then be applied to decompose such joint probability in a series of conditional probabilities:

$$P(\mathbf{e}) = P(w_1)P(w_2 \mid w_1)P(w_3 \mid w_1 w_2)$$
$$P(w_4 \mid w_1 w_2 w_3)...P(w_m \mid w_1...w_{m-1})$$

However, given the variability of human language, the chances of finding a significant number of occurrences of a given new sentence to be translated, and hence its possible translations, are very small, even in a very large corpus. Therefore, instead of looking for a complete sentence, the language model component usually computes frequencies of parts of such sentences, more specifically, *n-grams*, or sequences of up to n

words. The larger the n, the more information about the context of the specific sequence (larger discrimination). The smaller the n, the more cases will have been seen in the training data, and therefore the better the statistical estimates (more reliability). In practice, n can be varied according to the size of the corpus: the larger the corpus, the longer the n-grams that can be reliably counted. Common lengths of n vary between 3 and 7.

N-gram language models are formalized by applying the *Markov* assumption that one can approximate the probability of a word given its entire history by computing the probability of a word given the last few words. For example, a *bigram* language model considers only one previous word:

$$P(\mathbf{e}) = P(w_1)P(w_2 \mid w_1)P(w_3 \mid w_2)$$
$$P(w_4 \mid w_3)...P(w_m \mid w_{m-1})$$

while a *trigram* language model takes into account two previous words:

$$P(\mathbf{e}) = P(w_1)P(w_2 \mid w_1)P(w_3 \mid w_1 w_2)$$
$$P(w_4 \mid w_2 w_3)...P(w_m \mid w_{m-2} w_{m-1})$$

The probability of a word w given a number of previous words can be estimated using MLE, i.e., as the count of occurrences of the entire sequence of words *n*, divided by the count of the *n-1* previous words. For example, for *trigrams*:

$$P(w_3 \mid w_1 w_2) = \frac{count(w_1 w_2 w_3)}{count(w_1 w_2)}$$

Smoothing techniques can be applied to avoid having zero-counts for a given *n-gram* and as a consequence having $P(\mathbf{e}) = 0$ for previously unseen sequences. The simplest technique consists of adding *one* to all the counts of n-grams. For example, the MLE counts for unigrams would become:

$$P(w_i) = \frac{count(w_i) + 1}{N + V}$$

where N is the number of tokens in the corpus, and V the vocabulary, i.e., all different words seen in the corpus. Off-the-shelf language modeling toolkits such as SRILM (Stolcke, 2002) are used by many SMT systems and they provide a number of more advanced smoothing strategies.

3.2.3. Bidirectional Lexical Probabilities

In order to obtain reliable translation probabilities, in addition to phrase translation probabilities, one can decompose phrases into their word translations, i.e., consider the lexical weighting of the phrases. This is motivated by the fact that rare phrase pairs will have very high phrase translation probability: if they are seen only once or a few times, but are not aligned to anything, then their probability in both directions will be close to one. This often overestimates how reliable rare phrase pairs are, and can thus be problematic, especially if the phrases are extracted from noisy data. One can therefore also use the probability distributions for lexical translations, for which the statistics are usually more reliable.

The computation of lexical probabilities relies directly on word-alignment information within phrases. The lexical translation probability of a phrase $\bar{e}$ given the phrase $\bar{f}$ can be computed as Koehn (2010a):

$$lex(\bar{e} \mid \bar{f}, a) = \prod_{i=1}^{length(\bar{e})} \frac{1}{|\{j \mid (i,j) \in a\}|} \sum_{\forall (i,j) \in a} w(e_i \mid f_j)$$

where each target word e_i is produced by an aligned source word f_j with the word translation probability $w(e_i \mid f_j)$, as extracted using word-alignment models. e_i may be aligned to multiple source words, and in that case the average of the corresponding translation probabilities is taken.

e_i may also be aligned to the *NULL* token (if it is not aligned to any source token), which is also counted as a *word*. Similar to the phrase translation probabilities, both translation directions can be considered, i.e.: $lex(\bar{e} \mid \bar{f}, a)$ and $lex(\bar{f} \mid \bar{e}, a)$.

3.2.4. Word Penalty

The language model component results in a multiplication of many probabilities, i.e., numbers smaller than one. It therefore has a bias towards shorter translations, since the fewer the n-grams, the higher the global language model score. To compensate for this bias and also to allow the control of the translation length in terms of the source text length, it is common to introduce a word penalty component ω, where $\omega < 1$ increases the scores for shorter translations, and $\omega > 1$ increases the scores for longer translations. The value for word penalty function is usually pre-defined, as opposed to learned from the corpus.

3.2.5. Phrase Penalty

When translating a sentence, there are usually many possible ways of segmenting this sentence into phrases, given the multiple possible translations in the phrase table. Only the combination of the phrase probabilities of a given segmentation with other feature functions can determine the best choices for the input sentence segmentation. Intuitively, one can think that the system should prefer longer and fewer phrases, since they include more context and therefore are more likely to be correct. On the other hand, longer phrases are less frequent and can thus be statistically less reliable. In order to bias the choice towards longer or shorter phrases, it is common to introduce a phrase penalty factor ρ. $\rho < 1$ increases the scores for fewer and longer phrases, while $\rho > 1$ increases the scores for shorter and more phrases. Likewise for the word penalty component, the value of ρ is pre-defined.

3.2.6. Distance-Based Reordering

A simple strategy to deal with reordering of words in PBSMT is a distance-based reordering model. According to such a model, each phrase pair probability $\phi(\bar{f}_i \mid \bar{e}_i)$ is associated with a distance-based reordering function:

$$d(\text{start}_i - \text{end}_{i-1} - 1)$$

In such a function, the reordering of a phrase is relative to the previous phrase: start_i is the position of the first word of the source phrase that translates to the *ith* target phrase; end_i is the position of the last word of that source phrase. The reordering distance, computed as $(\text{start}_i - \text{end}_{i-1} - 1)$, is the number of words skipped (forward or backward) when source words are taken out of sequence. For example, if two continuous source phrases are translated in sequence, then $\text{start}_i = \text{end}_{i-1} + 1$, i.e., the position of the first word of phrase i is next to the position of the last word of the previous phrase. In that case, the reordering cost will be zero, i.e., a cost of $d(0)$ will be applied to that phrase. This model therefore penalizes movements of phrases over large distances.

The reordering probability can be estimated from data, although a common practice is to handle it by using an exponentially decaying cost function $d(x) = \alpha^{|x|}$, where α is assigned a value in $[0,1]$ so that d becomes a probability distribution.

3.2.7. Lexicalized Reordering

The distance-based reordering model described above uses a cost that is linear to the reordering distance, i.e., skipping over two words will cost twice as much as skipping over one word, regardless of the actual words reordered. Therefore, such a model penalizes movement in general. As a consequence, unless the language model prefers translations with placement of words in a different order, very little reordering will be done in practice.

An alternative is to use *lexicalized* reordering models with different reordering probabilities for each phrase pair learned from data, in order to take into account the fact that some phrases are reordered more frequently than others. The *Moses* system provides three types of lexicalized reordering (Koehn, 2010a):

- Monotone order (m);
- Swap with previous phrase (s); and
- Discontinuous (d).

These reordering types are used in a reordering model p_0 that predicts an orientation type, m, s, or d, given the phrase pairs in the current translation hypothesis:

$$\text{orientation} \in \{m, s, d\}$$

$$p_0(\text{orientation} \mid \bar{f}, \bar{e})$$

The probability distribution can be learned from data using the word alignment information: whenever a phrase pair is extracted, the orientation type of that specific occurrence is also extracted. The frequencies of each of the three alignment orientation types are then computed for each phrase pair. The probability distribution p_0 can be estimated based on these frequency counts using MLE:

$$p_0(\text{orientation} \mid \bar{f}, \bar{e}) = \frac{count(\text{orientation}, \bar{e}, \bar{f})}{\sum_o count(o, \bar{e}, \bar{f})}$$

where o assumes all the three orientation types.

A number of feature functions based on variations of this lexicalized reordering model can be considered. For example, one can combine the orientation information with:

- Whether the model is conditioned on the source phrase $\bar{f}$ or on both $\bar{f}$ and $\bar{e}$; and
- Whether the ordering is unidirectional or bidirectional: if unidirectional, for each phrase, its ordering with respect to the previous phrase is considered; if bidirectional, the ordering of the next phrase with respect to the current phrase is also modeled.

3.3. Decoding

A *decoder* is the component responsible for finding the best scoring translation among the possibilities given by the log-linear model. The best translation **e** * can be found by maximizing this model, i.e.:

$$\mathbf{e}* = \underset{\mathbf{e}}{\operatorname{argmax}}\, P(\mathbf{e} \mid \mathbf{f})$$

Since there are an exponential number of translation options, the search problem is classified as NP-complete (Knight, 1999), so no efficient algorithm can be used in the general case. In practice, PBSMT systems implement heuristic search methods. The most popular method is a stack-based beam search decoder. In what follows we briefly describe the process of generating a translation through the creation and expansion of translation hypotheses from options in the phrase-table, as well as the basic mechanism of a stack-based beam search algorithm with a few strategies to prune the search space.

3.3.1. Translation Options and Hypotheses Expansion

Given a source sentence, a number of phrase translations available in the phrase table can be applied to translate it. Each applicable phrase translation is called a *translation option*. Each word can be translated individually (phrases of length 1), or by phrases with two or more source words (given the existing phrases in the phrase table), or any combination of these.

For example, consider the translation of the Spanish sentence "*Maria no dio una bofetada a la bruja verde*" into English, assuming some of the phrases available in the phrase table as shown in Table 1, based on the example from Callison-Burch and Koehn (2005). The translation options include translating every Spanish word individually into their corresponding English word(s), using different options for each ambiguous entry (such as "*no*" and "*dio*"), and using the phrases as opposed to single words. A subset of the possible combinations of these translation options is shown in Table 2.

Given the translation options, the search process builds a graph starting with an initial state where no source words *f* have been translated (or covered) and no target words *e* have been generated. New states are created in the graph by extending the target output with a phrasal translation that covers some of the source words not yet translated. At every expansion, the *current cost* of the new state is the cost of the original state multiplied with the feature functions under consideration, for example, translation, distortion, and language model costs of the added phrasal translation. Final states in the search graph are hypotheses that cover all source words. Among these, the hypothesis with the lowest cost (highest probability) is selected as the best translation.

If an exhaustive search was to be performed, then all translation options, in different orders, could be used to build alternative hypotheses. However, in practice a heuristic search is used and the search space is pruned in different ways, as we describe in the following sections.

3.3.2. Hypothesis Recombination

Hypothesis recombination is a strategy for reducing the search space that can be used when a given translation is reached by two or more paths in the search graph. In those cases, the more costly hypothesis can be disregarded and excluded from the search graph. Two hypotheses can be recombined

Table 1. Examples of phrase pairs in a Spanish-English phrase table

Spanish	English
Maria	Mary
no	not
no	did
no	did not
dio	gave
dio	slap
una	a
bofetada	slap
a	to
la	the
bruja	witch
verde	green
dio una bofetada	slap
a la	the
Maria no	Mary did not
no dio una bofetada	did not slap
bruja verde	green witch
a la bruja verde	the green witch
....	....

if they are identical or look similar. Different strategies can be used to define hypothesis similarity, taking into account, for example:

- The source words covered so far;
- The last *n* target words generated;
- The end of the last source phrase covered.

For example, using the translation options in Table 2, there are multiple options to translate "Maria no," including the two following options:

<Maria, Mary> + <no, did not>

<Maria no, Mary did not>

In the example, both hypothesis paths lead to the same state: they cover the same source words, and the same target words are generated as output. If one of these hypotheses is more costly, its path can be safely dropped.

3.3.3. Stack-Based Beam Search Decoding and Pruning Strategies

A common way to organize hypotheses in the search space is by using stacks of hypotheses, which are based on the number of source words translated by the hypotheses. One stack contains all hypotheses that translate one source word; another stack contains all hypotheses that translate two source words in their path, and so on. Figure

Table 2. A subset of combinations of translation options for the Spanish sentence "Maria no dio una bofetada a la bruja verde" into English given the phrase pairs in Table 1

Maria	no	dio	una	bofetada	a	la	bruja	verde
Mary	not	gave	a	slap	to	the	witch	green
Mary	not	slap	a	slap	to	the	witch	green
Mary	did	gave	a	slap	to	the	witch	green
Mary	did	slap	a	slap	to	the	witch	green
Mary	did not	gave	a	slap	to	the	witch	green
Mary	did not	slap	a	slap	to	the	witch	green
Mary did not		gave	a	slap	to	the	witch	green
Mary did not		slap	a	slap	to	the	witch	green
Mary	did not slap				to	the	witch	green
Mary	did not slap				the green witch			

3 shows the representation of stacks of hypotheses considering some of the translation options given in Table 2.

The initial null hypothesis is placed in the stack of hypotheses with zero source words covered. New hypotheses are then generated by using phrasal translations that cover previously untranslated source words. For example, as shown in Figure 3 one can cover initially the first word in the sentence ("*Maria*") or the second word in the sentence ("*no*"), and so on. Each derived hypothesis is placed in a stack based on the number of source words it covers. The decoding algorithm proceeds through these hypothesis stacks, going through each hypothesis in the stacks, deriving new hypotheses for it and placing them into the appropriate stack. For example, in Figure 3 the stack covering three words has different hypotheses translating "Maria no dio": "Mary did not gave" and "Mary not gave." At the end of the decoding process, the best hypothesis from the stack covering all source words is taken as the best translation.

The use of stacks for decoding allows for different pruning strategies. A stack has fixed space, so after a new hypothesis is placed into a stack, some hypotheses might need to be pruned to make space for better hypotheses. The idea

is to keep only a number of hypotheses that are "promising" and remove the worst hypotheses from the stack. This is a judgment or guess at an early stage, hence a pruned hypothesis could in fact be good, but it is only possible to know that at a later state: it is too expensive to compute all paths in the graph until completion to find out the real cost of each hypothesis.

Examples of pruning strategies are *threshold pruning* and *histogram pruning*. Histogram pruning simply keeps a certain number n of hypotheses in each stack (e.g. $n = 1000$). In threshold pruning, a hypothesis is rejected if its score is less than that of the best hypothesis by a factor (e.g., threshold $= 0.001$). The idea of this threshold is to define a *beam* of good hypotheses and prune those hypotheses that fall out of this beam. The beam follows the (presumably) best hypothesis path, but with a certain width to allow the retention of comparable hypotheses, i.e., neighboring hypotheses that are close in score from the best one.

By using stacks, the beam search algorithm also keeps track of a number of alternative good translations. For some applications, besides the actual *best* translation for a given source sentence, it can be helpful to have the second best translation, third best translation, and so on. A list of n best translations, the so-called **n-best list**, can thus be

Figure 3. Stacks of hypotheses in a beam search decoder for translation options in Figure 2

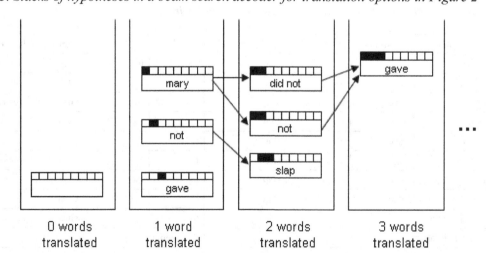

produced. N-best lists can be used, among other applications, to rerank the output of an SMT system as a post-processing step using features that are richer than those internal to the SMT system (Section 6). For example, one could parse all n-best translations and rerank them according to their parse tree score as an attempt to check the grammaticality of the translations.

3.3.3. Future Cost Estimation

The judgment about the cost of a given hypothesis is important not only to select the best translation, but as a criterion for many pruning strategies. If this judgment is solely based on the cost of producing each hypothesis so far, it can bias the pruning to keep the hypotheses that deal with the easy part of the sentence first (lower current cost), discarding at an early stage potentially good hypotheses which start with the hardest parts of the sentence (higher current cost). Therefore, the cost measure for pruning out hypotheses during the search can also take into account the *future cost*. The future cost is an estimate of how hard it is to translate the untranslated part of the source sentence. This, in combination with the current cost, gives more reliable estimates for pruning out bad translations.

Estimating the exact future cost is computationally too expensive, since it would require trying all possible translation options to find the less costly hypotheses, which is the actual search problem that the decoder has to solve in order to find the best translation. One solution is to consider only a subset of feature functions of the SMT model for this estimation. For example, the cost of each translation option can be given based on the translation probability for each translation option in the phrase table, or using the language model score for the generated target word(s) alone. The future cost of a given path can be approximated by combining (for example, summing) the costs of the translation options or spans of multiple translation options that make that path.

3.4. Parameter Tuning

As previously mentioned, log-linear PBSMT models consist of the interpolation of a number of feature functions following a supervised machine learning approach in which a weight is learned for each feature function. The goal of this approach is to estimate such weights using iterative search methods to find the single optimal solution. However, this is a computationally expensive process. In what follows, we describe a common approximation to such a process for estimating the weights of a small set of features, the *Minimum Error-Rate Training* (MERT) algorithm (Och, 2003).

MERT assumes that the best model is the one that produces the smallest overall error with respect to a given error function, i.e., a function that evaluates the quality of the system translation. Therefore, for the training of the parameters of the system it is common to use the same function that will be considered for assessing the final translations. Most evaluation metrics are based on n-gram comparisons between the system translations (hypotheses) and one or more human translations (references). MERT uses a *development set* containing a number of source sentences and their reference translations. The learning process is thus *supervised* because of the use of reference translations. For the standard settings with approximately a dozen feature functions, usually 1-2K source-reference sentence pairs, along with their n-best lists of translations, are sufficient. Over several iterations, MERT optimizes the feature functions weights such as to make the system translations as close as possible to the reference translations according to an evaluation metric such as BLEU (Papineni, et al., 2002) (Section 7).

Formally, given an error function $E(e*, e)$ defining the difference (error) between the hypothesized translation $e*$ and a known good translation e, learning the vector of parameters for all features λ_1^K can be defined as (Lopez, 2008):

$$\lambda_1^K = \underset{\hat{\lambda}_1^K}{\operatorname{argmin}} \sum_{(\mathbf{e},\mathbf{f}) \in C} E(\underset{\mathbf{e}*}{\operatorname{argmax}} \; P_{\hat{\lambda}_1^K}(\mathbf{e}* \mid \mathbf{f}), \mathbf{e})$$

This process can be decomposed in the following major steps:

1. The weights of all features are initialized with random values or uniformly.
2. The log-linear model with such weights is applied to translate all sentences in the development set, producing a list of n-best translations for each input sentence.
3. The error function is computed for all n-best translations with respect to the reference translations. The goal is that translation candidate with the smallest error is ranked as the top translation.
4. The weight of each feature is optimized, one at a time, to minimize the error function, while the weights of all other features are kept fixed. The algorithm iteratively generates values for λ_1^K and tries to improve them by minimizing the error resulting from changing each parameter λ_k while holding the others constant. At the end of this optimization step, the optimized λ_1^K yielding the greatest error reduction is used as input to the next iteration. In practice, heuristics are used to generate values for the parameters, as the space of possible parameter values is too large to be exhaustively searched in a reasonable time even with only a small set of features.
5. This process can be repeated until convergence or a pre-defined number of iterations.

4. INCORPORATING LINGUISTIC INFORMATION IN SMT MODELS

SMT has been originally proposed as an alternative to designing linguistic rules for MT. The word- and phrase-based models described so far do not take any linguistic information into account and for more than a decade the focus was on trying to gather and use efficiently more data to improve such models. Although the quality of such SMT may be considered satisfactory for certain applications, in recent years it has been noticed that it reached a certain level that will be hard to surpass without adding other types of information, as opposed to simply adding more examples of translations. The use of linguistic information has thus become one of the most prominent new research directions in SMT.

Linguistic information can be used at different stages of the SMT model, from modifying the input text so that it can be better translated (pre-processing) or modifying the output text to improve the machine translated segments (post-processing), to different levels of modifications in the SMT formulation so that linguistic information can be used as part of the model.

4.1. Linguistic Information as Pre-Processing

One example of pre-processing strategies is the simplification of morphological features when translating from a morphologically rich language (like French) into a less morphologically rich language (like English). Various morphological features in the source language can be disregarded when translating into the target language. For example, inflections of a given French verb to indicate different person conjugations can be disregarded in translations into English, except for the second person singular. If we take the present tense of the verb "*aimer*," all occurrences of most of its variations in the source side of the parallel corpus (*"aime," "aimes," "aimons," "aimez," "aiment,"* etc.) could be normalized to the verb's infinitive form, "*aimer*," since the translation in English will have the same form in all cases ("*like/love*"). This can significantly reduce data sparsity problems and make the relative frequency counts more reliable. The normalization can be done using the basic form of the word (lemma) or its stem.

Also aiming at reducing data sparsity, linguistic pre-processing can include more complex levels of word segmentation for compound words. Some simple examples of compound words in English are *skyscraper* (sky + scraper), homework (home + work), etc. This is particularly critical for translating from polysynthetic languages, where words can be built by composition using many morphemes. Segmenting the words in the source side of the parallel corpus before learning the translation model can thus be a good strategy. In agglutinative languages like Turkish, the segmentation is somehow trivial, since the morphemes do not change their form when put together. Segmentation of fusional languages like Russian, German, or Polish is a harder problem, since the multiple morphemes composing a word may overlap and therefore the boundaries between morphemes is not always clear. In both cases, the decomposition of complex words and the representation of its individual morphemes decreases data sparsity, since the chances of seeing long compound words is usually much smaller than the chance of seeing a subset of its morphemes in different words. If compounds are split in the target side of the parallel corpus, a post-processing step is necessary to merge the compounds back (Stymne, 2009).

Another example of linguistic pre-processing is the application of transliteration techniques to better translate named entities. Structural information can also be used to change the source language text. Certain language pairs have very different structures, requiring long-distance reordering of words, which is not possible in standard PBSMT. For example, while English is an SVO (Subject-Verb-Object) language, Japanese is an OSV (Object-Subject-Verb) language. Translating from Japanese into English may result in having the English words in the wrong order, particularly for long sentences. To avoid this, the Japanese text can be first parsed and the syntactic constituents reordered following specific rules according to the expected order in English. Simpler cases of

reordering include repositioning of adverbial adjuncts, adjectives and other modifiers. The reordering can be done using different levels of linguistic information, from simple POS tags to clauses, phrases, and even syntactic subtrees. Such rules can also be learned from corpus, as opposed to specified manually, as in Habash (2007) for Arabic-English translation.

4.2. Linguistic Information as Post-Processing

Linguistic information can be used at post-processing stages to either modify the translations or choose among the various possibilities produced by the SMT system available in the n-best list by reranking such options. For example, when translating from a morphologically poor language into a morphologically rich language, post-processing can be used to generate inflections or other form variations, or choose among the variations already generated by the system. The first strategy requires more complex language processing components, such as morphological generators. The second requires the SMT system to produce multiple candidate translations (i.e., n-best lists), the use of simpler language processing components to analyze the candidate translations, such as morphological analyzers, POS-taggers and syntactic parsers, and a procedure to rank the candidate translations based on linguistic information, so that the best translation can be selected.

An example of post-processing analysis consists in checking whether the morphological features of the source text are preserved in the translation. Therefore, morphological analyzers for the source and target languages are necessary, along with word-alignment information. With a morphological analyzer for the target language, agreement (or number, gender, etc.) violations in the translation can be checked. Deeper language processing components, such as parsers, can also be used. For example, a language model trained on syntactic trees can be used to estimate how likely each of the candidate translations are in terms of the syntax of the target language.

For reranking, a basic algorithm simply takes the score of one or more of such language processing components. For example, one could rank the candidate translations according to their syntax-based language model score. More elaborate algorithms may consider multiple linguistic features whose weights are learned from a training set with input texts and their correctly ranked list of candidate translations (Och, et al., 2004).

For examples of other pre- and post-processing strategies to exploit linguistic information in SMT, see Koehn (2010a, Chapter 10). While these strategies allow handling certain linguistic phenomena, they are constrained by the fact that only one (pre-processing) or a limited number (post-processing) of possibilities can be actually exploited. Emerging SMT approaches concentrate on using linguistic information as part of the model, so that a much larger number of translation possibilities can be exploited during the search for the best translation. In the next sections we describe how to incorporate word-level (Section 4.3) and structural information (Section 5) into SMT models.

4.3. Factored Translation Models

A popular way of exploiting linguistic information at the word level is the use of factored translation models in PBSMT approaches (Koehn & Hoang, 2007). Multiple types of word-level information can be used in addition to the standard surface forms, for example, lemmas, POS tags and morphological features. In standard PBSMT, each word form is treated completely independently from other word forms. Very similar words, such as "car" and "cars" are taken as two completely independent words. If both words occur in the training set, the frequency statistics will be computed independently. Moreover, if there are translation examples for "cars," but not for "car," the system will never be able to translate "car." Therefore, it may be useful to consider the lemma

of the word ("car") as the basic translation unit, and then generate the morphological features separately.

The basic idea behind factored translation models is that of representing additional features of the word forms, the so-called *factors*, and translating these factors independently in order to reduce data sparsity, particularly for morphologically rich languages. The translation of word factors can be seen as a sequence of mapping steps. Some steps directly *translate* the source factors into target factors, while others *generate* additional target factors from existing ones, thus requiring only information about the target language. These steps can be implemented in different ways. Taking as example the translation from the French word "*voitures*" into the English word "*cars*," common steps are the following (Koehn, 2010a), where multiple options indicate natural ambiguity of the word:

1. Translate input lemmas into target lemmas: *voiture* → *car, vehicle, carriage, coach, wagon, motorcar*

2. Translate source morphological features and POS tags into target morphological features and POS tags: *NN|Singular|Feminine* → *NN|Singular, NN|Plural*

3. Generate surface forms for the target lemmas based on the morphological features and POS tags: *car|NN|Singular* → *car, car|NN|Plural* → *cars, vehicle|NN|Singular* → *vehicle, vehicle|NN|Plural* → *vehicles, carriage|NN|Singular* → *carriage*, etc.

Once the corpus is pre-processed to consider the additional factors, word-alignment and phrase extraction and scoring can be performed as in standard PBSMT. However, additional model components need to be computed to account for the extra factors. A translation table for each factor can be produced from the word-aligned parallel corpus as in standard phrase tables. The generation models are estimated based on data for the target language only. The factored translation models can therefore be seen as an extension of the standard phrase-based models where additional components are used, which may be defined over phrase pairs (translation models) or over target words (generation models). The weights of such components can be learned using MERT. The decoding process is also performed in the same way as for PBSMT, with the pre-computation of all the translation steps as translation options prior to the beam search process.

5. TREE-BASED SMT

As discussed in the previous sections, one of the main limitations of the PBSMT approach is the fact that it does not allow appropriate handling of long-distance reordering, which is necessary for many language pairs. Although some of the model components account for reordering, over-relaxing their constraints to allow for more reordering to happen will very likely yield disfluent translations. A natural development from phrase-based models is the introduction of structural information in such models.

Early attempts include models that allow gaps in the phrases to deal with multi-word expressions that can be discontinuous in either or both source and target sides (Simard, et al., 2005) and hierarchical models, which formalize the use of structural information using synchronous Context Free Grammars (CFG) (Chiang, 2005). In the next section, we focus on the latter approach, since it also serves as the basis for more advanced models based on syntax (Section 5.2).

5.1. Hierarchical Models

Chiang's (2005) hierarchical phrase-based model converts standard phrases into synchronous context-free grammar rules, i.e., context-free grammar rules (or derivations) that derivate both source and target language simultaneously. Such

rules have the form $X \rightarrow \langle \gamma, \alpha \rangle$, with X a non-terminal, γ strings of non-terminals and source terminals symbols, and α strings of non-terminals and target terminal symbols. Therefore, only one non-terminal symbol can appear on the left-hand side of the rules. An additional constrain is that there is a one-to-one alignment between the source and target non-terminal symbols on the right-hand side of the rules. We note that only one general non-terminal symbol is possible in the rules (here, *X*), since no linguistic information is available to describe such symbols. However, in what follows we use POS and phrase tags to better illustrate the motivating example. For example, consider the rule to derivate an English noun phrase (NP) made up of an adjective (JJ) and a noun (N) NP $\rightarrow$ JJ N and the equivalent rule for the French language NP $\rightarrow$ N JJ. The rule to translate such a noun phrase from English into French could be represented as

$$NP \rightarrow JJ_1 \ N_2 \mid N_2 \ JJ_1$$

where the correspondences between strings are indicated via co-indexed non-terminal symbols.

Word or phrase translations can also be represented as rules containing only terminals (i.e., words), for example:

$$N \rightarrow car \mid voiture$$

or a mixture of terminals and non-terminals, for example:

$$NP \rightarrow the \ JJ_1 car \mid la \ voiture \ JJ_1$$

$$JJ \rightarrow blue \mid bleu$$

In Chiang's approach, translation rules are extracted from the flat phrases induced as discussed in Section 3.1, from a parallel word-aligned corpus. Words or sequences of words in phrases are replaced by variables, which can later be instantiated by other words or phrases (hence the notion of hierarchy). Synchronous context-free grammar rules are therefore constructed by subtraction out of the flat phrase pairs: every phrase pair $(\bar{f}, \bar{e})$ becomes a rule $X \rightarrow \bar{f} \mid \bar{e}$. Additionally, it is possible to generalize phrases into other rules: a phrase pair $(\bar{f}, \bar{e})$ can be subtracted from a rule $X \rightarrow \gamma_1 \bar{f} \gamma_2 \mid \alpha_1 \bar{e} \alpha_2$ to form a new rule $X \rightarrow \gamma_1 X_i \gamma_2 \mid \alpha_1 X_i \alpha_2$, where any other rule (phrase pair) can, in principle, be used in the X_i slots. For example, consider that the following two phrase pairs are extracted as discussed in Section 3.1: (*the blue car is noisy, la voiture bleu est bruyante*) and (*car, voiture*). These phrase pairs would be converted into the following rules:

$X \rightarrow$ *the blue car is noisy* | *la voiture bleu est bruyante*

$X \rightarrow$ *car* | *voiture*

Additionally, a rule with non-terminals would be generated:

$X \rightarrow$ *the blue X_1 is noisy* | *la X_1 bleu est bruyante*

In essence, rules from all existing phrase pairs are constructed and if a phrase pair contains another smaller phrase pair, a new rule X will be constructed where the latter is replaced with a non-terminal symbol. Replacing multiple smaller phrases may result in multiple non-terminals on the right-hand side of the rules. For example, if the phrase (*blue, bleu*) is also available, the following rule can be extracted:

$X \rightarrow$ *the $X_2 X_1$ is noisy* | *la $X_1 X_2$ est bruyante*

To handle the exponential growth of the rule sets and alleviate the computational complexity of the resulting models, a number of restrictions can be imposed to the rule extraction process. These include limiting the number of non-terminals on the right-hand side of the rules, limiting the number of words (terminals) in the rules, not allowing the mixture of terminals and non-terminals on the right-hand side of the rules, etc.

Once the rules are extracted, the scoring of each rule can be done in different ways, generating different features or model components. For example, a feature could be the conditional probability of the right-hand side given the left-hand side of the rule. Overall, some of the components used in hierarchical models are analogous to those used in PBSMT, while others are specific to hierarchical models. Assuming that rules have the format $LHS \rightarrow RHS_f \mid RHS_e$, where LHS stands for *left-hand side*, RHS for *right-hand side*, f and e for source and target languages, respectively, some examples of features that can be computed include:

- Joint rule probability:
  $p(LHS, RHS_f, RHS_e)$
- Bidirectional translation probabilities:
  $p(RHS_f \mid RHS_e, LHS)$ and
  $p(RHS_e \mid RHS_f, LHS)$
- Rule application probability:
  $p(RHS_f, RHS_e \mid LHS)$
- Bidirectional lexical probabilities estimated from word alignment information a: $\prod_{e_i \in RHS_e} p(e_i \mid RHS_f, a)$ and $\prod_{f_i \in RHS_f} p(f_i \mid RHS_e, a)$
- Pre-defined rule penalty, which allows the model to learn preferences for longer or shorter rules
- Pre-defined word penalty, which considers the number of terminals (words) in the rules
- Language model over n-grams of words.

The probability distributions of rules can be estimated using MLE, i.e., counting the relative frequency of the rules, as in the phrase-based models. The lexical probabilities can be estimated using word alignment information about the words in the rules. Language models are usually computed over n-grams of words, although there exists research in exploiting syntactic information for language modeling (Chelba & Jelinek, 2000; Charniak, et al., 2003; Tan, et al., 2011).

Like in PBSMT, the overall score of a given translation is computed as the product of all rule scores that are used to derivate that translation, where the scores are given by the combination of the model components described above using a log-linear model over synchronous derivations. The weights of the model component can be estimated using MERT, as in PBSMT (Section 3.4).

The process of finding the optimal translation is similar to that of finding the best parse tree for an input sentence using a probabilistic context-free grammar parser. Therefore, decoding is performed using a beam search algorithm together with a process to map source derivations into target derivations using *chart parser* (Chiang, 2007). In *chart parsing*, data is organized in a chart structure with chart entries that cover continuous spans of increasing length of this input sentence. Chart entries are added bottom-up, generally first with lexical rules, then rules including non-terminal nodes, until the sentence node (root of the tree) is reached. Similar heuristics as in phrase-based beam search decoding can be used to make the search process more efficient. For example, chart entries are also put into stacks and strategies like histogram pruning or threshold pruning can be applied to reduce the search space. Additionally, if chart entries are equivalent from a search perspective, they can be recombined.

Hierarchical models like the one we just described do not use any linguistic information. They have shown better performance than standard flat phrase-based models for certain language pairs which often require long-distance reordering, such as English-Chinese. Variations of the basic hierarchical approach using linguistic information have also been proposed. In what follows, we describe one of such variations: the syntax-based models.

5.1. Syntax-Based Models

While the definition of hierarchical models does not imply the need for syntactic information, this information can be used to produce linguistically-motivated hierarchical rules. In order to use syntactic information, the parallel corpus needs to be pre-processed to produce a parse tree for each source and/or target sentence. When syntactic information is used in both source and target texts, the resulting approach is called *tree-to-tree syntax-based SMT*. The description that follows is based on the models in Koehn (2010a).

Syntactic information allows different and more informative non-terminals symbols, which constrain the application of the rules according to the grammar of the languages. For example, given the following English and French subtrees:

English: (NP (DT the) (JJ blue) (NN car))

French: (NP (DT la) (NN voiture) (JJ bleu))

a rule for simple noun phrases with reordering of adjectives could be extracted using similar heuristics as in the basic hierarchical models, but now using linguistic information (POS and phrase tags) as part of the rules:

NP → the JJ_1 *car* | la *voiture* JJ_1

Rule extraction in syntax-based SMT follows the same basic constraints as in hierarchical models: (1) rules can have a single non-terminal on the left-hand side, (2) rules need to be consistent with word-alignment, and (3) there needs to be a one-to-one alignment between source and target non-terminal symbols on the right-hand side of the rules. For example, given the sentence pair and its word alignment in Table 3:

English: (S (NP (PRP I)) (VP (VBP have) (NP (JJ black) (NNS eyes))))

French: (S (NP (PRP J')) (VP (VBP ai) (NP (DT les) (NNS yeux) (JJ noir))))

The following rules could be generated, among others:

PRP → J' | I

JJ → noirs | black

NP → les yeux JJ$_1$ | JJ$_1$ eyes

VBP → ai | have

VP → ai NP$_1$ | have NP$_1$

In the examples described so far, the rules only allow a simple representation of non-terminal or terminal symbols on the right-hand side. With such representation, the reordering is limited to the swapping of children nodes directly under a parent. Such limitation requires that the syntactic trees in both languages are isomorphic in terms of child-parent relationships, which is not a realistic requirement for most language pairs. If the syntactic trees of the two languages have significant differences in their structures, such as their number of non-terminal nodes or their depths, standard synchronous context free grammar rules may not be sufficient to represent many syntactic correspondences. For example, given the following trees:

English: (VP (VB take)

(PRT (RP off))

(NP (PRP your) (NNS shoes)))

French: (VP (VB enlevez)

(NP (PRP vos) (NNS chaussures)))

a VP synchronous rule that represents the fact that two English words (*take off*) can be translated as one French word (*enlevez*) and that these words have specific phrase/POS tags cannot be extracted, since this would infringe the constraint that there is a one-to-one mapping of the non-terminal nodes in the right hand side of the rules. To overcome this problem, Zhang et al. (2007) proposed the use of *synchronous tree substitution grammars*, an extension of the synchronous grammar formalism to include not only non-terminal and terminal symbols in the right-hand side of the rules, but also *trees*. For example, the following rule in Box 1 could be extracted for VPs:

The phrase extraction procedure using synchronous tree substitution grammars is the same as with the phrase structure synchronous grammar rules: rules that are consistent with word-alignment are extracted, except that additional structure is introduced. The constraint that only one non-terminal node is allowed on the left-hand side of the rules may require special attention, since the labels of the nodes may be different in both languages, particularly if different parsers are used for each language. In those cases, one solution is to merge the node labels into a single node. Interested readers are referred to Koehn (2010a) for a formal definition of the rule extraction process.

Table 3. Example of French-English word-alignment for CFG rule extraction

	J'	ai	les	yeux	noirs
I	X				
have		X			
black					X
eyes			X	X	

Box 1.

VP →	VB take PRT (RP off) NP$_1$	|	VB enlevez NP$_1$

A number of variations of the syntax-based SMT approaches have been proposed in recent years (Nesson, et al., 2006; Hanneman, et al., 2008; Zhang, et al., 2008) using syntactic information for both source and target languages (*tree-to-tree*), like the example given above. In addition, since syntactic parsers with good enough quality are not available for many languages, other approaches use syntactic information for the source or target language only. Explicitly representing linguistic information can help produce better translations in different ways. If the information is used for the source language, it helps further constraining the application of rules based on deeper linguistic information of that language. If the information is used in the target language, it refines the set of translations that can be generated by assuring that they follow the syntax of the target language.

Models using syntactic information on the source language are commonly called *tree-to-string* models (Quirk, et al., 2005; Huang, et al., 2006; Zhou, et al., 2008; Liu & Gildea, 2008; Haque, et al., 2010), whereas models using syntactic information on the target language are referred to as *string-to-tree* or *syntax-augmented* models (Galley, et al., 2006; Marcu, et al., 2006; Zollmann, et al., 2008). Some approaches which allow multiple parse trees are known as *forest-based SMT* (Mi, et al., 2008; Zhang, et al., 2009). Some of these approaches use different grammar formalisms from the one described in this chapter, as well as different features functions, parameter estimation and decoding strategies. Early approaches use syntactic information in ways that differ considerably from Chiang's (2005) hierarchical SMT approach. For example, Yamada and Knight (2001, 2002) present a generative tree-based model that is trained using the EM algorithm, thus aligning the words in the parallel corpus while extracting syntactic transfer rules. For details and pointers on a number of alternative approaches, please refer to specialized literature such as the proceedings of the several editions of the workshop on *Syntax and Structure in Statistical Translation*.[3] Some variations of hierarchical and syntax-based models are implemented in *Moses* and *Joshua* (Li, et al., 2009), [4] both freely available open source SMT toolkits.

6. DISCRIMINATIVE TRAINING FOR SMT

As previously mentioned, the state of the art phrase-based and hierarchical approaches to SMT formulate the problem of MT as a supervised machine-learning task. They use a few features to represent several aspects that are regarded as relevant to distinguish between good and bad translations. These features are combined using a log-linear model, and their weights are learned using a supervised learning approach during the step of parameter tuning (Section 3.4).

A practical limitation of the discriminative learning framework for parameter tuning described in Section 3.4 is that it can only handle a small number of features due to very large space of possible parameter values that has to be searched. This approach has been extended in two directions to use additional features: discriminative reranking approaches and fully discriminative approaches.

In discriminative reranking, a baseline model generates a list of n-best candidate translations using the standard training procedure with a few features, and then a separate discriminative classifier using additional features is trained to rerank the translations so that the best translation appears as the top candidate (Och, et al., 2004). For example, Shen et al. (2004) use a number of syntactic features, while Specia et al. (2008) exploits word sense disambiguation features at reranking stage. The reranking approach is very simple and efficient; however, its performance is bounded by the performance of the baseline system: if the baseline system is not able to produce the best candidate translation (or a good translation) amongst a list of n candidates, the reranking of these translations may be in vain. Given that there is usually very little variation in the top n translations, even for n as large as 1,000 translations, this is a crucial limitation.

With the fully discriminative approaches, the idea is to use a much larger numbers of features and different learning algorithms. For example, instead of using maximum likelihood estimates for word or phrase probabilities, as suggested by Liang et al. (2006), each word or phrase pair from a phrase table can be represented as a feature function, for example, (*the blue car, la voiture bleu*), whose value will be a binary indicator of whether a candidate translation contains that pair, and whose weight shall indicate how useful that word/phrase pair is. Other examples of features are words or phrases in the target language, for example, (*la voiture bleu*), whose value will be a binary indicator of the presence of the word/phrase in the candidate translation. Linguistic information can also be added, for example, the phrase pairs can be represented by their POS tags, as opposed to the actual words: (*DT JJ NN, DT NN JJ*).

While the translation units (phrases or words) can be extracted from word-alignment using the heuristics as the ones described in Section 3.1, some of the existing works on discriminative training also address the phrase extraction as a machine learning problem by parameterizing the phrase extraction heuristics (Liang, et al., 2006).

The tuning of the feature weights is generally made by directly minimizing a loss function that measures machine translation error, similar to the one described in Section 3.4. Different sentence-level metrics can be used to measure the distance between the reference (correct) translation and the translation produced by the MT system. Following the formulation in Koehn (2010a, p. 274), given a set of input sentences f_i, the reference translation for that input sentence $e_{i,ref}$, the candidate translations $e_{i,j}$ and a parameter setting $\bar{\lambda}$, each candidate translation is assigned a score $score(e_{i,j}, \bar{\lambda})$. The candidate translations are then sorted according to their scores so that the best translation is ranked first. The weights should be learned in a way that the best scoring translation is as close as possible to the reference translation. The learning goal can thus be defined in different ways in terms of the error in the ranking of the candidate translations or directly by considering the scores assigned by the error metric. For example, a likelihood function can be used to maximize the probability mass assigned to the correct translations:

$$Likelihood(\bar{\lambda}) = \prod_i \frac{score(e_i, ref, \bar{\lambda})}{\sum_j score(e_{i,j}, \bar{\lambda})}$$

This process is done iteratively from a certain initialization of $\bar{\lambda}$ so that in each iteration the weights are changed in order to reduce the error. This is usually done using *gradient descent* or *perceptron* optimization algorithms.

Exploiting very large feature sets requires that the tuning is performed using a large parallel corpus, with millions of sentences, since all variations of translation units must be seen during tuning. Issues such as scalability and over-fitting when tuning millions of parameters and sentences are on-going research topics. Examples of approaches that have been proposed include Liang et al. (2006), Bangalore et al. (2007), Kääriäinen (2009), and Venkatapathy and Bangalore (2009).

7. EVALUATION

The ability to automatically assess the performance of SMT systems is an important aspect of the field and has attracted considerable attention in recent years. Most research papers report results in terms of BLEU (Papineni, et al., 2002), although this metric has well-known limitations and a number of alternative metrics are available. In this section we describe BLEU and a few other popular metrics for automatic MT evaluation.

A common element in most automatic MT evaluation metrics is the use of human translations, i.e., the *reference translations*. The intuition behind such metrics is that automatic translations should resemble human translations. In order to measure the level of resemblance, these metrics consider some form of distance, in terms of string matching, between the MT outputs and the reference translations. Single words or phrases can be considered as the matching units. Most of these metrics can be applied when either a single reference or multiple references are available for every sentence in the test set. Since a source sentence can usually have more than one correct translation, the use of multiple references allows avoiding any bias towards one specific human translation. A few metrics can also consider inexact matches, for example, using lemmas instead of word forms, paraphrases, or entailments to compute matches.

7.1. Edit Rate Metrics

Edit or error rate metrics estimate the amount of edits that must be applied to the automatic translation in order to transform it into a reference translation. Common variations of such metrics are WER, PER, and TER/HTER.

Word Error Rate (WER) (Tillmann, et al., 1997; Nießen, et al., 2000) is a measure based on the *Levenshtein distance* (Levenshtein, 1966). It computes the minimum number of substitutions, deletions, and insertions that have to be performed to convert the automatic translation into a reference translation.

$$WER = \frac{\# edits}{\# reference\_words}$$

A word that is translated correctly but in the wrong position will be penalized as a deletion (from the incorrect position) and an insertion (in the correct position). Position-independent Word Error Rate (PER) (Tillmann, et al., 1997), on the other hand, does not penalize reorderings. PER compares the words in the machine and reference translations without taking into account the word order, i.e., the words in the machine and reference translations are considered as unordered bags of words.

A further improvement of the edit rate metrics is Translation Edit Rate (TER) (Snover, et al., 2006). In addition to the standard edit operations (insertions, deletions, and substitutions of single words), TER takes into account *shifts* of word sequences. Different weights can be given to each type of edits. Recent implementations also allow the use of a database of paraphrases for inexact matches (Snover, et al., 2010).

For multiple references, the number of edits is computed with respect to each reference individually, and the one with the fewest number of edits is chosen. In the search process for the minimum number of edits, shifts are prioritized over other edits; a greedy search process tries to find the shifts that maximally reduce the number of insertions, deletions, and substitutions.

Human-targeted Translation Edit Rate (HTER) is a semi-automatic variation of TER in which the references are built as human-corrected versions of the machine translations. This guarantees that the edit rate is measured as the minimum number of edits necessary to transform the system output into a fluent and adequate translation. HTER was found to have a significantly higher correlation with human scores as compared to TER (Snover, et al., 2006).

7.2. Precision, Recall, and F-Measure Metrics

The most commonly used metric for SMT evaluation is BLEU (Bilingual Evaluation Understudy; Papineni, et al., 2002). BLEU focuses on lexical precision, i.e., the proportion of lexical units in the automatic translation, which are covered by reference translations. It computes lexical matching at the n-gram level (from 1 up to some maximum n, usually 4) between the system and the reference translation. BLEU rewards translations whose word choice and word order are similar to the reference.

Let $count_{clipped-match}(\text{n-gram})$ be the count of n-gram matches between a given system output sentence C and the reference translation, where the count of repeated words is *clipped* by the maximum number of occurrences of that word in the reference. Let $count(\text{n-gram})$ be the total of n-grams in the MT system output. BLEU sums up the clipped n-gram matches for all the sentences in the test corpus, normalizing them by the number of candidate n-grams in the machine translated test corpus. For a given n, this results in the precision score, p_n, for the entire corpus:

$$p_n = \frac{\sum\limits_{C \in \{\text{Candidates}\}} \sum\limits_{\text{n-gram} \in C} count_{clipped-match}(\text{n-gram})}{\sum\limits_{C \in \{\text{Candidates}\}} \sum\limits_{\text{n-gram} \in C} count(\text{n-gram})}$$

BLEU averages multiple n-gram precisions, p_n, for n-grams of different sizes. The score p for a given test corpus is the geometric mean of the p_ns, using n-grams up to a length N (usually 4) and positive weights $w_n = N^{-1}$ summing to 1:

$$p = \exp\left(\sum_{n=1}^{N} w_n \log p_n\right)$$

BLEU also uses a brevity penalty BP to avoid giving preference to short translations, since the denominator in each p_n contains the total number of n-grams used in the machine-translated text, as opposed to the reference. The brevity penalty aims at compensating for the lack of a recall component by contrasting the total number of words c in the system translations against the reference length r. If multiple references are used, r is defined by the length of the closest reference to the system output:

$$BP = \begin{cases} 1, & \text{if } c > r \\ e^{(1-r/c)}, & \text{if } c \leq r \end{cases}$$

The final BLEU metric is therefore computed as:

$$BLEU = BP \cdot p$$

BLEU has many well known limitations, including the following: (1) the n-gram matching requires exact word matches, ignoring morphological variations, synonyms, etc.; (2) all matched words are weighed equally, i.e., the matching of a function word will count the same as the matching of a content word; (3) a zero match for a given n-gram, which is common for higher order n-grams, will result in BLEU score equal to zero and the need for smoothing techniques; (4) it does not correlate well with human judgments at sentence level; (5) it does not provide an absolute quality score, but instead a score that is highly dependent on the test corpus, given its n-gram distributions; (6) the brevity penalty does not adequately compensate for the lack of recall. Despite these limitations, BLEU has been shown to correlate well with human evaluation when comparing document level outputs from different SMT systems, or measuring improvements of a given SMT system during its development using the same corpus. Currently, it is the most widely used metric for such purposes.

A number of other MT evaluation metrics have been proposed to overcome the limitations of BLEU. Some of these metrics explicitly address recall by combining lexical precision and recall (F-measure). One of such metrics which is often used nowadays is METEOR: Metric for Evaluation of Translation with Explicit Ordering (Lavie & Agarwal, 2007). This metric includes a fragmentation score, which accounts for word ordering, enhances token matching considering stemming, synonymy and paraphrase lookup and allows tuning in order to weight scoring components to optimize correlation with human judgments at document or sentence level. METEOR is defined as:

$$METEOR = (1 - Pen) \cdot F_{mean}$$

A matching algorithm performs word-to-word alignment between the system output and reference translations. If multiples references are available, the matches are computed against each reference separately and the best match is selected. METEOR allows the unigram matches to be exact word matches, or generalized to stems, synonyms, and paraphrases, if language resources are available. Based on those matches, precision and recall are calculated, resulting in the following F_{mean} metric:

$$F_{mean} = \frac{P \cdot R}{\alpha \cdot P + (1 - \alpha) \cdot R}$$

where: P is the unigram precision, i.e., the fraction of words in the system output that match with words in the reference, and R is the unigram recall, i.e., the fraction of the words in the reference translation that match with words in the system output.

The matching algorithm returns the fragmentation fraction, which is used to compute a discount factor Pen (for 'penalty') as follows. The sequence of matched unigrams between system output and reference translation is split into the fewest (and hence longest) possible chunks, where the matched words in each chunk are adjacent and in identical order in both strings. The number of chunks (ch) and the total number of matching words in all chunks (m) are then used to calculate a fragmentation fraction $frag = ch / m$. The discount factor Pen is then computed as:

$$Pen = \gamma \cdot frag^{\beta}$$

The parameters of METEOR determine the relative weight of precision and recall (α), the discount factor (γ), and the functional relation between the fragmentation and the discount factor (β). These weights can be optimized for better correlation with human judgments on a particular quality aspect (fluency, adequacy, etc.), dataset, language pair, or evaluation unit (system, document, or sentence level) (Lavie & Agarwal, 2007; Agarwal & Lavie, 2008).

MT evaluation is a very active field currently. A number of alternative metrics have been proposed and many of these metrics have shown to correlate better with human evaluation, particularly at the sentence level. Some of these metrics exploit the matching of linguistic information at different levels, as opposed to simple matching at the lexical level. For example, Giménez and Márquez (2010) present a number of variations of linguistic metrics for document and sentence level evaluation. For other recent developments in MT evaluation metrics, the readers are referred to the proceedings of recent MT evaluation campaigns, which now include tracks for meta-evaluation of MT evaluation metrics (Callison-Burch, et al., 2010, 2011). In spite of many criticisms, BLEU and other simple lexical matching metrics continue to be the most commonly used alternative, since they are fast and cheap to compute.

8. STATE OF THE ART AND FURTHER RESEARCH DIRECTIONS

SMT is still a relatively recent research area having achieved considerable success in the past decade. This resulted in a large number of people being interested in research, development, and commercialization of SMT approaches. Research papers on SMT constitute a large percentage of the material published in relevant conferences, such as the annual meetings of the *Association for Computational Linguistics*,[5] as well as in a number of specialized conferences and workshops on MT, such as the conferences organized by the American[6] and European[7] Associations for Machine Translation. The readers are referred to the *MT Archive*[8] for a very comprehensive compilation of papers on all aspects of MT published since 1990.

There has been significant government funding in this field in recent years with a number of projects sponsored particularly by the US *Defense Advanced Research Projects Agency* (DARPA) under programs such as the *Global Autonomous Language Exploitation* (GALE),[9] and the European Commission, including projects such as EuroMatrix,[10] SMART,[11] EuroMatrixPlus,[12] FAUST,[13] LetsMT!,[14] etc. As a consequence, a number of free, open-source systems and related tools have been released, including the previously mentioned *Moses toolkit* for phrase-based, hierarchical and syntax-based SMT and the *Joshua toolkit* for hierarchical and syntax-based SMT.

The state of the art performance in the field varies according to language pair, text genre and domain, training conditions, among other variables. It is not possible to provide absolute numbers reflecting the top SMT systems' performances, since evaluation campaigns focus on comparing different systems and ranking them according to such comparisons, as opposed to providing absolute quality scores. Moreover, for practical reasons the evaluations are always limited to a relatively small test set, on a given text genre and domain. However, from the results of recent

campaigns, it is prevalent that SMT systems or hybrid systems involving SMT are ranked the top systems for virtually all language pairs considered (Callison-Burch, et al., 2010, 2011). For up-to-date results in several settings, interested readers are referred to the main evaluation campaigns in MT:

- WMT, the *Workshop on Statistical Machine Translation*,[15] which has been running for the past six years as an open evaluation campaign to compare MT systems, combinations of systems and evaluation metrics; and
- NIST Open MT Evaluation,[16] which has been running since 2001 and focuses on MT systems funded by the US government.

While the field of SMT continues progressing at a fast pace, there are still opportunities for improvement. Developments in a number of new directions can be mentioned, including the following:

- The use of linguistic knowledge at different levels. Morphological and syntactic knowledge have only proven to be beneficial for certain language pairs and/or experimental settings. For example, word-level factors are very useful for translating into morphologically rich languages. Syntax-based translation models, on the other hand, improve performance for translating between languages, which differ considerably in word ordering, such as English and Chinese. Completely new formulations, as opposed to extensions of existing ones, may be necessary to achieve better performance for other language pairs and settings. Using other types of linguistic information is also an interesting direction, for example, the use of named-entities (Baker, et al., 2010) and semantic roles (Liu & Gildea, 2008, 2010; Wu & Fung, 2009; Aziz, et al., 2011).

- Strategies for combining MT systems to take advantage of their individual strengths. The combination can be done at different levels. At one extreme, MT systems can be considered as black-boxes and a strategy can be defined to select the best translation from multiple MT systems, an instance of *system selection*, for example, using confidence estimation features (Specia, et al., 2010; Hildebrand & Vogel, 2010). These systems may follow the same or different MT paradigms. Particularly with SMT systems, the selection of the best translation can be done considering partial translations, such as phrases, by using word lattices from the decoder's search graph, which is generally called *system combination*, as in He and Toutanova (2009) and Cui et al. (2010). At the other extreme, much tighter integration strategies can be exploited by implementing hybrid systems that combine features of different types of MT paradigms, such as rule-based and example-based MT. Interested readers are referred to Way (2010) for a recent overview of hybrid systems.
- More reliable evaluation metrics. Fast and cheap lexical matching metrics such as BLEU are still the *de facto* automatic metrics for progress evaluation during system development and for system comparison. However, it is now clear that such metrics cannot be used as absolute indicators of the quality of an MT system. Therefore, a number of alternative metrics along with improvements over existing metrics are proposed every year, including metrics that try to mimic human post-editing effort, such as HTER (Section 7.1) and metrics that rely on linguistic annotation (e.g., Giménez & Márquez, 2010). While some of these metrics have achieved satisfactory correlation with human judgments, none of them has yet replaced BLEU as the standard metric for general MT evaluation. Metrics that offer a good balance between the level of linguistic or human annotation required and the correlation achieved, such as METEOR, seem to be the most promising direction.
- Building systems or interfaces that are more suitable to end-users, mainly professional translators. For many years, the interest for SMT was limited to the research community and the usability of the tools developed was not a concern. However, SMT has proven to achieve satisfactory levels of performance for certain tasks and as a consequence has been attracting interest from non-academic users, such as translation service providers and human translators in general. It is thus crucial that the tools are developed in a way that they can be mostly useful and efficient for end-users. Several research directions can be mentioned here, including the integration of SMT and translation memory systems (He, et al., 2010; Koehn & Senellart, 2010), metrics to estimate the quality of machine translations (Specia & Farzindar, 2010), design of post-editing tools (Koehn, 2010b), etc.
- Exploiting contextual information. The use of source context in SMT is limited to a few words in the phrases: in practice 3 or 4 words for phrases extracted from parallel corpora with at least a few hundred thousand sentence pairs, in order to guarantee reliable probability estimates. While in principle longer phrases can be considered if large quantities of parallel data are available, this is not the case for most languages pairs and text domains. This results in a number of problems, particularly due to ambiguity issues. For example, it may not be possible to choose among different translations of a highly ambiguous word without having access to the global

context of the input text. While hierarchical models allow using some contextual information, this only has an effect in terms of reordering. Other attempts have been made in order to explicitly use contextual information. For example, Carpuat and Wu (2007) and Chan et al. (2007) incorporate features for word sense disambiguation models as part of the SMT system, where alternative translations for a given phrase are considered as alternative senses, and the source sentence context is used to choose among them. Specia et al. (2008) use WSD models with dictionary translations as senses and a method to rerank translations in the n-best list according to their lexical choices for ambiguous words. Mirkin et al. (2009) and Aziz et al. (2010) use contextual models on the source and target languages to choose among alternative substitutions for unknown words in SMT. Alternative ways of using contextual information include Stroppa et al. (2007), Giménez and Márquez (2007), Max et al. (2008), Gimpel and Smith (2008), Chiang et al. (2009), and Haque et al. (2010).

- Domain adaption. SMT is known to achieve better translations when large quantities of parallel data are available for the text domain under consideration. When this is not possible, one option is to use data from different domains to build SMT systems. The sub-field of domain adaptation aims at improving the SMT performance in cases when testing data deviate from training data. Existing strategies include adapting models trained on large out-of-domain corpora using small in-domain corpora. Phrase tables can be generated from these different corpora and then interpolated by learning adequate weights for alternative model components using each of these phrase tables. Dynamic adaptation, in which the model can be adapted according to the context of the input text, is also an interesting topic (Foster & Kuhn, 2007). An alternative strategy consists in exploiting large monolingual in-domain corpora, either in the source or in the target language, which is normally much more feasible to obtain than parallel corpora. Monolingual data can be used to train in-domain target language models, or to generate additional synthetic bilingual data, which is then used to adapt the model components through the interpolation of multiple phrase tables (Bertoldi & Federico, 2010).

The readers are referred to the additional reading material for more pointers to these and other research directions.

REFERENCES

Agarwal, A., & Lavie, A. (2008). METEOR, m-BLEU and m-TER: evaluation metrics for high-correlation with human rankings of machine translation output. In *Proceedings of the 3rd Workshop on Statistical Machine Translation*, (pp. 115-118). Columbus, OH: IEEE.

Aziz, W., Dymetman, M., Mirkin, S., Specia, L., Cancedda, N., & Dagan, I. (2010). Learning an expert from human annotations in statistical machine translation: The case of out-of-vocabulary words. In *Proceedings of the 14th Annual Conference of the European Association for Machine Translation*, (pp. 28-35). Saint-Raphael, France: EAMT.

Aziz, W., Rios, M., & Specia, L. (2011). Shallow semantic trees for SMT. In *Proceedings of the Sixth Workshop on Statistical Machine Translation*. Edinburgh, UK: SMT.

Baker, K., Bloodgood, M., Callison-Burch, C., Dorr, B., Miller, S., & Piatko, C. ... Levin, L. (2010). Semantically-informed syntactic machine translation: A tree-grafting approach. In *Proceedings of American Association for Machine Translation*. Denver, CO: AAMT.

Bangalore, S., Haffner, P., & Kanthak, S. (2007). Statistical machine translation through global lexical selection and sentence reconstruction. In *Proceedings of the 45th Annual Meeting of the Association of Computational Linguistics*, (pp. 152-159). Prague, Czech Republic: ACL.

Bertoldi, N., & Federico, M. (2009). Domain adaptation for statistical machine translation with monolingual resources. In *Proceedings of the Fourth Workshop on Statistical Machine Translation*, (pp. 182-189). Athens, Greece: SMT.

Brown, P. F., Cocke, J., Pietra, S. A. D., Pietra, V. J. D., Jelinek, F., & Laferty, J. D. (1990). A statistical approach to machine translation. *Computational Linguistics*, *16*(2), 79–85.

Brown, P. F., Lai, J. C., & Mercer, R. L. (1991). Aligning sentences in parallel corpora. In *Proceedings of the 29th Annual Meeting of the Association for Computational Linguistics*, (pp. 169-176). Berkeley, CA: ACL.

Brown, P. F., Pietra, S. A. D., Pietra, V. J. D., & Mercer, R. L. (1993). The mathematics of statistical machine translation. *Computational Linguistics*, *19*(2), 263–311.

Callison-Burch, C., & Koehn, P. (2005). *Introduction to statistical machine translation*. Paper presented at the 17th European Summer School in Logic, Language and Information. Retrieved from http://www.iccs.informatics.ed.ac.uk/~pkoehn/publications/esslli-slides-day3.pdf

Callison-Burch, C., Koehn, P., Monz, C., Peterson, K., Przybocki, M., & Zaidan, O. (2010). Findings of the 2010 joint workshop on statistical machine translation and metrics for machine translation. In *Proceedings of the Joint Fifth Workshop on Statistical Machine Translation and MetricsMATR*, (pp. 17-53). Uppsala, Sweden: MetricsMATR.

Callison-Burch, C., Koehn, P., Monz, C., & Zaidan, O. (2011). Findings of the 2011 workshop on statistical machine translation. In *Proceedings of the Sixth Workshop on Statistical Machine Translation*, (pp. 22-64). Edinburgh, UK: SMT.

Carpuat, M., & Wu, D. (2007). Improving statistical machine translation using word sense disambiguation. In *Proceedings of the Joint Conference on Empirical Methods in Natural Language Processing and Computational Natural Language Learning*, (pp. 61-72). Prague, Czech Republic: ACL.

Chan, Y. S., Ng, H. T., & Chiang, D. (2007). Word sense disambiguation improves statistical machine translation. In *Proceedings of the 45th Annual Meeting of the Association for Computational Linguistics*, (pp. 33-40). Prague, Czech Republic: ACL.

Charniak, E., Knight, K., & Yamada, K. (2003). Syntax-based language models for statistical machine translation. In *Proceedings of the MT Summit IX Conference*. New Orleans, LA: MT Summit.

Chelba, C., & Jelinek, F. (2000). Structured language modeling. *Computer Speech & Language*, *14*(4), 283–332. doi:10.1006/csla.2000.0147

Chiang, D. (2005). A hierarchical phrase-based model for statistical machine translation. In *Proceedings of the 43rd Annual Meeting of the Association for Computational Linguistics*, (pp. 263-270). Ann Arbor, MI: ACL.

Chiang, D. (2007). Hierarchical phrase-based translation. *Computational Linguistics*, *33*(2), 201–228. doi:10.1162/coli.2007.33.2.201

Chiang, D., Knight, K., & Wang, W. (2009). 11,001 new features for statistical machine translation. In *Proceedings of the Conference of the North American Chapter of the Association for Computational Linguistics*, (pp. 218-226). Boulder, CO: ACL.

Cui, L., Zhang, D., Li, M., Zhou, M., & Zhao, T. (2010). Hybrid decoding: Decoding with partial hypotheses combination over multiple SMT systems. In *Proceedings of the 23rd International Conference on Computational Linguistics*, (pp. 214-222). Beijing, China: ACL.

Dempster, A. P., Laird, N. M., & Rubin, D. B. (1977). Maximum likelihood from incomplete data via the EM algorithm. *Journal of the Royal Statistical Society. Series B. Methodological, 39*(1), 1–38.

Doddington, G. (2002). Automatic evaluation of machine translation quality using n-gram co-occurrence statistics. In *Proceedings of the Human Language Technology Conference*, (pp. 138-145). San Diego, CA: Human Language Technology.

Foster, G., & Kuhn, R. (2007). Mixture-model adaptation for SMT. In *Proceedings of the Second Workshop on Statistical Machine Translation*, (pp. 128-135). Prague, Czech Republic: SMT.

Gale, W. A., & Church, K. W. (1991). A program for aligning sentences in bilingual corpora. In *Proceedings of the 29th Annual Meeting of the Association for Computational Linguistics*, (pp. 177-184). Berkeley, CA: ACL.

Galley, M., Graehl, J., Knight, K., Marcu, D., DeNeefe, S., Wang, W., & Thayer, I. (2006). Scalable inference and training of context-rich syntactic translation models. In *Proceedings of the 21st International Conference on Computational Linguistics and 44th Annual Meeting of the Association for Computational Linguistics*, (pp. 961-968). Sydney, Australia: ACL.

Giménez, J., & Márquez, L. (2007). Context-aware discriminative phrase selection for statistical machine translation. In *Proceedings of the Second Workshop on Statistical Machine Translation*, (pp. 159-166). Prague, Czech Republic: SMT.

Giménez, J., & Márquez, L. (2010). Asiya: An open toolkit for automatic machine translation (meta-) evaluation. *The Prague Bulletin of Mathematical Linguistics, 94*.

Gimpel, K., & Smith, N. A. (2008). Rich source-side context for statistical machine translation. In *Proceedings of the Third Workshop on Statistical Machine Translation*, (pp. 9-17). Columbus, OH: SMT.

Habash, N. (2007). Syntactic preprocessing for statistical machine translation. In *Proceedings of the MT Summit XI*. Copenhagen, Denmark: MT Summit.

Hanneman, G., Huber, E., Agarwal, A., Ambati, V., Parlikar, A., Peterson, E., & Lavie, A. (2008). Statistical transfer systems for French-English and German-English machine translation. In *Proceedings of the Third Workshop on Statistical Machine Translation*, (pp. 163-166). Columbus, OH: SMT.

Haque, R., Naskar, S. K., van den Bosch, A., & Way, A. (2010). Supertags as source language context in hierarchical phrase-based SMT. In *Proceedings of the 9th Conference of the Association for Machine Translation in the Americas (AMTA 2010)*. Denver, CO: AMTA.

He, X., & Toutanova, K. (2009). Joint optimization for machine translation system combination. In *Proceedings of the 2009 Conference on Empirical Methods in Natural Language Processing*, (1202-1211). Singapore: Empirical Methods in Natural Language Processing.

He, Y., Ma, Y., van Genabith, J., & Way, A. (2010). Bridging SMT and TM with translation recommendation. In *Proceedings of the 48th Annual Meeting of the Association for Computational Linguistics*, (pp. 622-630). Uppsala, Sweden: ACL.

Hildebrand, A. S., & Vogel, S. (2010). CMU system combination via hypothesis selection for WMT'10. In *Proceedings of the Joint Fifth Workshop on Statistical Machine Translation and MetricsMATR*, (pp. 307-310). Uppsala, Sweden: MetricsMATR.

Huang, L., Knight, K., & Joshi, A. (2006). Statistical syntax-directed translation with extended domain of locality. In *Proceedings of the 5th Conference of the Association for Machine Translation in the Americas (AMTA)*. Boston, MA: AMTA.

Hutchins, J. (1997). Milestones in machine translation: Part 1: How it all began in 1947 and 1948. *Language Today*, *3*, 22–23.

Kääriäinen, M. (2009). Sinuhe: Statistical machine translation using a globally trained conditional exponential family translation model. In *Proceedings of the Conference on Empirical Methods in Natural Language Processing*, (pp. 1027-1036). Singapore: Empirical Methods in Natural Language Processing.

Knight, K. (1999). Decoding complexity in word-replacement translation models. *Computational Linguistics*, *25*(4), 607–615.

Koehn, P. (2010a). *Statistical machine translation*. Cambridge, UK: Cambridge University Press.

Koehn, P. (2010b). Enabling monolingual translators: Post-editing vs. options. In *Proceedings of the Conference of the North American Chapter of the Association for Computational Linguistics*, (pp. 537-545). Los Angeles, CA: ACL.

Koehn, P., & Hoang, H. (2007). Factored translation models. In *Proceedings of Joint Conference on Empirical Methods in Natural Language Processing and Computational Natural Language Learning*, (pp. 868-876). Prague, Czech Republic: ACL.

Koehn, P., Hoang, H., Birch, A., Callison-Burch, C., Federico, M., & Bertoldi, N. ... Herbst, E. (2007). Moses: Open source toolkit for statistical machine translation. In *Proceedings of the 45th Annual Meeting of the Association for Computer Linguistics*, (pp. 177-180). Prague, Czech Republic: ACL.

Koehn, P., Och, F. J., & Marcu, D. (2003). Statistical phrase-based translation. In *Proceedings of the North American Chapter of the Association for Computational Linguistics on Human Language Technology*, (pp. 48-54). Edmonton, Canada: ACL.

Koehn, P., & Senellart, L. (2010). Convergence of translation memory and statistical machine translation. In *Proceedings of the AMTA-2010 Workshop Bringing MT to the User: MT Research and the Translation Industry*. Denver, CO: AMTA.

Lavie, A., & Agarwal, A. (2007). METEOR: An automatic metric for MT evaluation with high levels of correlation with human judgments. In *Proceedings of the 2nd Workshop on Statistical Machine Translation*, (pp. 228-231). Prague, Czech Republic: SMT.

Levenshtein, V. I. (1966). Binary codes capable of correcting deletions, insertions, and reversals. *Soviet Physics, Doklady*, *10*, 707–710.

Li, Z., Callison-Burch, C., Dyer, C., Ganitkevitch, J., Khudanpur, S., & Schwartz, L. ... Zaidan, O. F. (2009). Demonstration of Joshua: An open source toolkit for parsing-based machine translation. In *Proceedings of the ACL-IJCNLP 2009 Software Demonstrations*, (pp. 25-28). Singapore: ACL-IJCNLP.

Liang, P., Bouchard-Côté, A., Klein, D., & Taskar, B. (2006). An end-to-end discriminative approach to machine translation. In *Proceedings of the Joint Conference on Computational Linguistics and Annual Meeting of the Association for Computational Linguistics*, (pp. 761-768). Sydney, Australia: ACL.

Liu, D., & Gildea, D. (2008). Improved tree-to-string transducer for machine translation. In *Proceedings of the Third Workshop on Statistical Machine Translation*, (pp. 62-69). Columbus, OH: SMT.

Liu, D., & Gildea, D. (2010). Semantic role features for machine translation. In *Proceedings of the 23rd International Conference on Computational Linguistics*, (pp. 716-724). Beijing, China: ACL.

Lopez, A. (2008). Statistical machine translation. *ACM Computing Surveys, 40*(3), 1–49. doi:10.1145/1380584.1380586

Marcu, D., Wang, W., Echihabi, A., & Knight, K. (2006). SPMT: Statistical machine translation with syntactified target language phrases. In *Proceedings of the Conference on Empirical Methods in Natural Language Processing*, (pp. 44-52). Sydney, Australia: ACL.

Marcu, D., & Wong, W. (2002). A phrase-based, joint probability model for statistical machine translation. In *Proceedings of the Conference on Empirical Methods in Natural Language Processing*, (pp. 133-139). Philadelphia, PA: ACL.

Max, A., Makhloufi, R., & Langlais, P. (2008). Explorations in using grammatical dependencies for contextual phrase translation disambiguation. In *Proceedings of the 12th Annual Conference of the European Association for Machine Translation*, (pp. 114-119). Hamburg, Germany: EAMT.

Mi, H., Huang, L., & Liu, Q. (2008). Forest-based translation. In *Proceedings of the 46th Annual Meeting of the Association for Computational Linguistics and the Human Language Technology Conference*, (pp. 192-199). Columbus, OH: ACL.

Mirkin, S., Specia, L., Cancedda, N., Dagan, I., Dymetman, M., & Szpektor, I. (2009). Source-language entailment modeling for translating unknown terms. In *Proceedings of the 47th Annual Meeting of the Association for Computational Linguistics and the 4th International Joint Conference on Natural Language Processing*, (pp. 791-799). Singapore: ACL.

Nesson, R., Shieber, S., & Rush, A. (2006). Induction of probabilistic synchronous tree-insertion grammars for machine translation. In *Proceedings of the 7th Conference of the Association for Machine Translation in the Americas*, (pp. 128-137). Cambridge, MA: AMT.

Nießenn, S., Och, F. J., Leusch, G., & Ney, H. (2000). An evaluation tool for machine translation: Fast evaluation for MT research. In *Proceedings of the 2nd International Conference on Language Resources and Evaluation (LREC)*. Athens, Greece: LREC.

Och, F. J. (2003). Minimum error rate training in statistical machine translation. In *Proceedings of the 41st Annual Meeting on Association for Computational Linguistics*, (pp. 160-167). Sapporo, Japan: ACL.

Och, F. J., Gildea, D., Khudanpur, S., & Sarkar, A. (2004). A smorgasbord of features for statistical machine translation. In *Proceedings of the HLT-NAACL*, (pp. 161-168). Boston, MA: HLT-NAACL.

Och, F. J., & Ney, H. (2003). A systematic comparison of various statistical alignment models. *Computational Linguistics, 29*(1), 19–51. doi:10.1162/089120103321337421

Papineni, K., Roukos, S., Ward, T., & Zhu, W. (2002). BLEU: A method for automatic evaluation of machine translation. In *Proceedings of the 40th Meeting of the Association for Computational Linguistics*, (pp. 311-318). Philadelphia, PA: ACL.

Quirk, C., Menezes, A., & Cherry, C. (2005). Dependency treelet translation: Syntactically informed phrasal SMT. In *Proceedings of the 43rd Annual Meeting of the Association for Computational Linguistics*, (pp. 271-279). Ann Arbor, MI: ACL.

Shannon, C. E. (1949). *A mathematical theory of communication*. Urbana, IL: University of Illinois Press.

Shen, L., Sarkar, A., & Och, F. J. (2004). Discriminative reranking for machine translation. [Boston, MA: HLT-NAACL.]. *Proceedings of the HLT-NAACL, 2004*, 177–184.

Simard, M., Cancedda, N., Cavestro, B., Dymetman, M., Gaussier, E., Goutte, C., & Yamada, K. (2005). Translating with non-contiguous phrases. In *Proceedings of the Joint Conference on Human Language Technology and Empirical Methods in Natural Language Processing*, (pp. 755-762). Vancouver, Canada: ACL.

Snover, M. G., Dorr, B., Schwartz, R., Micciulla, L., & Makhoul, J. (2006). A study of translation edit rate with targeted human annotation. In *Proceedings of the 7th Conference of the Association for Machine Translation in the Americas*, (pp. 223-231). Cambridge, MA: AMTA.

Snover, M. G., Madnani, N., Dorr, B., & Schwartz, R. (2010). TER-plus: Paraphrase, semantic, and alignment enhancements to translation edit rate. *Machine Translation, 23*(2-3), 117–127. doi:10.1007/s10590-009-9062-9

Specia, L., & Farzindar, A. (2010). Estimating machine translation post-editing effort with HTER. In *Proceedings of the AMTA-2010 Workshop Bringing MT to the User: MT Research and the Translation Industry*. Denver, CO: AMTA.

Specia, L., Raj, D., & Turchi, M. (2010). Machine translation evaluation versus quality estimation. *Machine Translation, 24*(1), 39–50. doi:10.1007/s10590-010-9077-2

Specia, L., Sankaran, B., & Nunes, M. G. V. (2008). n-Best reranking for the efficient integration of word sense disambiguation and statistical machine translation. *Lecture Notes in Computer Science, 4919*, 399–410. doi:10.1007/978-3-540-78135-6_34

Stolcke, A. (2002). SRILM - An extensible language modeling toolkit. In *Proceedings of the International Conference on Spoken Language Processing*, (pp. 901-904). Denver, CO: SLP.

Stroppa, N., van den Bosch, A., & Way, A. (2007). Exploiting source similarity for SMT using context-informed features. In *Proceedings of the 11th Conference on Theoretical and Methodological Issues in Machine Translation*, (pp. 231-240). Skövde, Sweden: Theoretical and Methodological Issues in Machine Translation.

Stymne, S. (2009). A comparison of merging strategies for translation of german compounds. In *Proceedings of the Student Research Workshop at EACL 2009*, (pp. 61-69). Athens, Greece: EACL.

Tan, M., Zhou, W., Zheng, L., & Wang, S. (2011). A large scale distributed syntactic, semantic and lexical language model for machine translation. In *Proceedings of the 49th Annual Meeting of the Association for Computational Linguistics*, (pp. 201-210). Portland, OR: ACL.

Tillmann, C., Vogel, S., Ney, H., Zubiaga, A., & Sawaf, H. (1997). Accelerated DP based search for statistical translation. In *Proceedings of the European Conference on Speech Communication and Technology*, (pp. 2667-2670). Rhodes, Greece: Speech Communication and Technology.

Venkatapathy, S., & Bangalore, S. (2009). Discriminative machine translation using global lexical selection. *ACM Transactions on Asian Language Information Processing, 8*(2). doi:10.1145/1526252.1526256

Vogel, S., Ney, H., & Tillmann, C. (1996). HMM-based word alignment in statistical translation. In *Proceedings of COLING 1996: The 16th International Conference on Computational Linguistics*, (pp. 836-841). Copenhagen, Denmark: ICCL.

Way, A. (2010). Machine translation. In Clark, A., Fox, C., & Lappin, S. (Eds.), *The Handbook of Computational Linguistics and Natural Language Processing* (pp. 531–573). Chichester, UK: Wiley Blackwell. doi:10.1002/9781444324044.ch19

Wu, D., & Fung, P. (2009). Semantic roles for SMT: A hybrid two-pass model. In *Proceedings of the Annual Conference of the North American Chapter of the Association for Computational Linguistics*, (pp. 13-16). Boulder, CO: ACL.

Yamada, K., & Knight, K. (2001). A syntax-based statistical translation model. In *Proceedings of the 39th Annual Meeting of the Association for Computational Linguistics*, (pp. 523-530). Toulouse, France: ACL.

Yamada, K., & Knight, K. (2002). A decoder for syntax-based statistical MT. In *Proceedings of the 40th Annual Meeting of the Association for Computational Linguistics*, (pp. 303-310). Philadelphia, PA: ACL.

Zhang, H., Zhang, M., Li, H., Aw, A., & Tan, C. L. (2009). Forest-based tree sequence to string translation model. In *Proceedings of the Joint Conference of the 47th Annual Meeting of the ACL and the 4th International Joint Conference on Natural Language Processing of the AFNLP*, (pp. 172-180). Singapore: ACL.

Zhang, M., Jiang, H., Aw, A., Li, H., Tan, C. L., & Li, S. (2008). A tree sequence alignment-based tree-to-tree translation model. In *Proceedings of the 46th Annual Meeting of the Association for Computational Linguistics and the Human Language Technology Conference*, (pp. 559-567). Columbus, OH: ACL.

Zhang, M., Jiang, H., Aw, A., Sun, J., Li, S., & Tan, C. L. (2007). A tree-to-tree alignment-based model for statistical machine translation. [Copenhagen, Denmark: MT Summit.]. *Proceedings of the MT Summit, XI*, 535–542.

Zhou, B., Xiang, B., Zhu, X., & Gao, Y. (2008). Prior derivation models for formally syntax-based translation using linguistically syntactic parsing and tree kernels. In *Proceedings of the Second Workshop on Syntax and Structure in Statistical Translation (SSST-2)*, (pp. 19-27). Columbus, OH: SSST.

Zollmann, A., Venugopal, A., & Vogel, S. (2008). The CMU syntax-augmented machine translation system: SAMT on Hadoop with n-best alignments. In *Proceedings of the International Workshop on Spoken Language Translation*, (pp. 18-25). Honolulu, HI: SLT.

ADDITIONAL READING

Knight, K. (1999). *A statistical MT tutorial workbook*. Retrieved from http://www.isi.edu/natural-language/mt/wkbk.pdf

Koehn, P. (2010). *Statistical machine translation*. Cambridge, UK: Cambridge University Press.

Lopez, A. (2008). Statistical machine translation. *ACM Computing Surveys*, *40*(3), 1–49. doi:10.1145/1380584.1380586

Specia, L., & Cancedda, N. (Eds.). (2010). Pushing the frontier of statistical machine translation. *Journal of Machine Translation*, *24*(2).

Way, A. (2010). Machine translation. In Clark, A., Fox, C., & Lappin, S. (Eds.), *The Handbook of Computational Linguistics and Natural Language Processing* (pp. 531–573). Chichester, UK: Wiley Blackwell. doi:10.1002/9781444324044.ch19

ENDNOTES

1. http://fjoch.com/GIZA++.html
2. http://www.statmt.org/
3. http://www.cs.ust.hk/~dekai/ssst
4. http://cs.jhu.edu/~ccb/joshua/
5. http://www.aclweb.org/
6. http://www.amtaweb.org/
7. http://www.eamt.org/
8. http://www.mt-archive.info/
9. http://www.darpa.mil/Our_Work/I2O/Programs/Global_Autonomous_Language_Exploitation_%28GALE%29.aspx
10. http://www.euromatrix.net/
11. http://www.smart-project.eu/
12. http://www.euromatrixplus.net/
13. http://www.faust-fp7.eu/faust/
14. http://www.letsmt.eu/
15. http://www.statmt.org/wmt11/
16. http://www.itl.nist.gov/iad/mig//tests/mt/

Chapter 5
A Computational Cognitive Model of Human Translation Processes

Michael Carl
Copenhagen Business School, Denmark

ABSTRACT

Human translation process research analyzes the translation behavior of translators, such as memory and search strategies to solve translation problems, types of units that translators focus on, etc., identifies the temporal (and/or contextual) structure of those activities, and describes inter- and intra-personal variation. Various models have been developed that explain translators' behavior in terms of controlled and uncontrolled workspaces and with micro- and macro-translation strategies. However, only a few attempts have been made to ground and quantify translation process models in empirical user activity data. In order to close this gap, this chapter outlines a computational framework for a cognitive model of human translation. The authors investigate the structure of the translators' keystrokes and gaze data, discuss possibilities for their classification and visualization, and explain how a translation model can be grounded and trained on the empirical data. The insight gained from such a computational translation model not only enlarges our knowledge about human translation processes, but also has the potential to enhance the design of interactive MT systems and help interpret user activity data in human-MT system interaction.

1. INTRODUCTION

In recent years, MT has become widely available, covering many language pairs.[1] Development for new language pairs is being increasingly short (Lewis, 2010) and the quality of the translation product increases based on the available resources and the similarity of the source and target languages.

However, to obtain high quality translations e.g., for dissemination, some kind of human intervention is necessary. In order to ensure the required quality of the translations and simultaneously increase translation production time,

DOI: 10.4018/978-1-4666-2169-5.ch005

numerous technologies exist or are experimentally implemented that ease human-machine interaction. A Machine Translation (MT) system may either work in a batch process as is the case in MT post- or pre-editing (e.g., controlled language translation) or in an interactive modus. In the case of interactive *rule-based MT*, the user interfaces of some MT systems (e.g., Systran, ProMT) allow the translator to extend or modify the lexical databases of the system at translation time; other systems interactively ask for disambiguation information (Boguslavsky, et al., 2005), which may be stored in a 'companion' file for later reuse (Choumane, et al., 2005). Recent implementations of interactive *data-driven MT systems* experiment with translation completion (TransType2, [Macklovitch, 2004]) or translation options (Koehn & Haddow, 2009).

Interactive rule-based MT systems ask for assistance to disambiguate the *source text* analysis by providing linguistic knowledge of the source language, whereas interactive data-driven MT systems ask the translator to disambiguate or chose from the generated *translation proposals*, thereby putting the user into the center of the translation process (Macklovitch, 2004). However, none of the approaches has yet led to a completely satisfactory solution to the issue of human computer interaction for MT.

Inadequate user interfaces, the translators' feeling of competition and misrepresentation, and the lack of knowledge of their needs during translation have until now not led to a wider acceptance of the technology in the professional world. The challenge is not only how to improve machine translation technology itself so that it can adapt interactively to the translators' needs, but also how to communicate, instrumentalize, and personalize the inherent value of MT for the stakeholder. It thus becomes important to study the *human translator*, who is at the center of the work and to understand their cognitive processes that take place during translation.

Current models of human translation processes (Göpferich, 2009; Hönig, 1991) aim at explaining and predicting translation behavior of novice and experienced translators, the types of units that translators focus on, memory and search strategies to solve translation problems, etc., and how these strategies are acquired. This work establishes and interprets in-depth empirically grounded knowledge of human translation processes to understand in detail how humans translate. Insights from empirical translation process research could then be carried over to the design of interactive MT systems, which could help interpret the user activity data in a way that would lead to improved human-machine interaction. Reactive and adaptable user interfaces can then be designed that can anticipate the translators' needs to better support the translation processes.

In this chapter, we analyze and model the behavior of human translators when translating texts from scratch. A basic understanding of the unassisted translation processes is a prerequisite for developing more sophisticated systems. We have collected student and professional translator activity data—gaze and keyboard data—from 24 translation sessions. Each of the translations consists of three phases, which different translators realize to a different degree: an orientation phase, where a translator gets familiar with the text and activates subsets of the mental dictionary; a drafting phase where sequences of words are read and translated in a loop process; and a revision phase, where the translated text is re-read and revised.

This chapter focuses on formalizing and modeling the drafting phase: We fragment gaze and keyboard data into coherent units and analyze the amount of their overlap. Novice translators generally have a larger Source Text (ST) reading effort than experienced translators while experts show less fragmented typing behavior. Cognitive theories explain the reduced effort of expert performance by a higher degree of automatization of the mental processes, and the transformation of declarative knowledge into procedural knowledge (Ericsson, 2000). This transformation makes mental space for the experts' superior analytical, creative, and practical skills, which allows them to produce more fluent translations in shorter time and with lower effort. This chapter shows that experts need a smaller number of production units and are better able to process ST comprehension and Target Text (TT) production in parallel than novices. The chapter describes the underlying translation theories and the translators' user activity data, and develops computational models for an instance of expert performance.

In section 2, we outline current translation process theories. Section 3 describes the translators' user activity data, which we collect from our translation experiments. We introduce translation progression graphs, a visualization method, and discuss the coarse structure of human translation processes. In section 4, we look into more details of the user activity data, their segmentation and classification. We discuss two examples of 'unchallenged' translation and provide indicators, which distinguish students from more experienced translators. Section 5 discusses an example of a difficult translation. The conclusion here is that translators work with a minimal context, and produce revised meaning hypotheses only when needed during text production. Section 6 gives an overview of cognitive architectures. Sections 7 and 8 describes two models of human translation processes, one based on ACT-R (Anderson, 2007) (section 7) and the other a statistical approach (section 8), both of which simulate an instance of unchallenged expert performance.

2. MODELS OF HUMAN TRANSLATION PROCESSES

A distinction can be made between translation product research and translation process research. Whereas translation product research and comparative linguistics analyze the (differ-

ences between the) structure of the source text and their translation, translation process research investigates the cognitive processes of human translation activities.

Lörscher (1992) was one of the first researchers to use thinking aloud, which according to him represents "a useful instrument to formulate hypotheses on mental processes in general and about translation processes in particular." Based on a number of translation experiments, he isolates five basic translator types and a number of complex types which differ with respect to how much the solution of a translation problem is automatized, whether the translator requires search, whether a translation problem is decomposed into smaller parts, and to what extent the translation problems can be verbalized. Lörscher finds that translators translating into their mother tongue use more automatized and less complex linguistic strategies, while translators translating into their second language more likely fragment the translation problems into smaller pieces, using more complex translation strategies.

Lörscher also shows that processing takes place at various levels. Translators process largely in syntactic units at the word, phrase and clause level, but only very little at the sentence level. The higher the translation expertise, the more translators work in bigger units including the discourse level.

Hönig (1991) proposes a translation process model, which makes the distinction between uncontrolled associative translation competence and a controlled translation workspace in which micro- and macro-strategies are stored. The uncontrolled workspace is a necessary condition for the production of translations, which is more developed in expert translators and which is complemented by a controlled workspace. While the uncontrolled workspace activates frames and schemes from long term memory and generates a number of translation options, the controlled workspace is acquired through extensive professional translation activities and serves to choose appropriate translation (sub)strategies. Göpferich (2009) complements this model with translation competence comprising:

1. Psychomotor competence: reading, writing, typing
2. Translation routine activation competence: recall and application of language pair specific transfer operations
3. Tools and research competence: use translation specific conventional and electronic tools
4. Domain competence, such as terminological competence
5. Communicative competence in the two languages: lexical, grammatical, pragmatic knowledge in the languages

Such models describe translators' activities and competences from a high-level perspective. In this chapter, we will look into a bottom-up perspective and ground the investigation in empirical user activity data.

3. ANALYSIS OF TRANSLATORS' ACTIVITY DATA

Within CRITT[2], we have developed a method and a data acquisition software, Translog[3], with which translators' activities (keystrokes and eye-movements) can be recorded. This tool is now the most widely used tool of its kind (Jakobsen, 2006). CRITT has also collected over the past years a substantial amount of translation process data from numerous translation sessions. The analysis of this data has given rise to more grounded translation models and a novel understanding of the underlying human translation processes (Mees & Göpferich, 2009).

As shown in Figure 1, Translog separates the screen into two windows: the source text is shown in the upper window while subjects type a translation into the lower window. Figure 1 also shows the accumulations of gaze fixations (in blue) during the time span in which a translator reads the beginning of the source language sentence "China which has extensive investments in the Sudanese oil industry, maintains close" and begins producing (i.e. typing in) its translation.

A translation session (or parts of it) can be represented in translation progression graphs as in Figures 2, 4, and 5. The notion of *progression graph* was introduced by Perrin (2003) to conceptualize and visualize writing progression. A *translation progression graph* represents the gaze and typing data in time. Translation progression graphs show where pauses and deletions occurred, and how keystrokes and gaze activities were distributed over time. It gives a general picture of how the translation developed, by relating each activity to the ST unit which is being translated.

The translation progression graph in Figure 2 shows a fragment of 700 seconds in which an English ST of 160 words was translated into Danish. The graph shows the distribution of ST fixations on the 160 ST words and the keystrokes by which the TT was produced. Blue circles represent fixations on the ST, black dots TT insertions, and red dots TT deletions. Note that there are longer stretches of time with no gaze activities (i.e. no blue circles). These are likely to be times where the translator watches the keyboard or reads the Target Text (TT). The translation progression graphs show only reading behaviour on the ST, since our software can only register and map gaze movements on the source text window. Due to the fact that translators frequently had to move their eyes from the keyboard or the target window on the bottom of the screen to the top of the screen, where the source text was displayed (see Figure 1), some of the fixations in the source text may be random.

Translation progression graphs are computed by mapping activity data on manually aligned ST ↔ TT units. In Carl and Jakobsen (2010) and Carl (2009), it was shown in detail how keystrokes

Figure 1. The figure shows the number and durations of gaze fixation points accumulated during 10 seconds of translation pause when starting to read the third English sentence in the upper window. At this time, the subject has already translated the beginning of the text into Danish in the lower window.

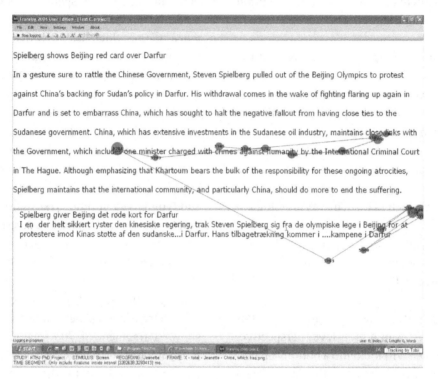

Figure 2. The translation progression graph plots activity data, keystroke, and gaze movements in milliseconds against word positions in the source text. The progression graph shows a separation into orientation, drafting, and revision phases. It also shows that some keystrokes are unaligned while others cannot be mapped on any ST word.

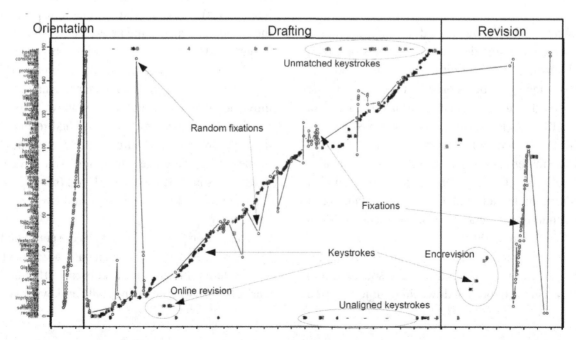

are matched on the aligned units. Here, we just point out that manually aligned units in the product data may be more complex than merely 1-to-1 relation: Figure 3 shows a fragment of a manual alignment of the translation in Figure 5. It contains a discontinuous phrase where the English noun "staff" together with the definite article and a preposition is aligned to the Danish noun "personale." The words "awareness" and "other" are aligned outside the discontinuous phrase, while "hospital" and "det" are unaligned words in the ST and TT, respectively. Buch-Kromann (2003) gives more background on this alignment schema.

Figure 2 shows that some of the TT words are not aligned to any ST word, which leads to *un-aligned* keystrokes.[4] There are also *unmatched* keystrokes, which could not be associated to any of the ST words. If translators revise, insert, and delete long sequences of text and/or reorder passages, it becomes difficult to trace which ST words these activities should be assigned to. In some cases, these keyboard activities remain unmatched.

Figure 2 shows several translation phases: initial orientation, translation drafting, and revision. The graph shows that text revisions can take place during drafting (online revision) or during revision phase (Endrevision).

Human translators are usually trained to produce translations in three phases: *initial orientation, translation drafting* and *translation revision.*

Figure 3. A discontinuous 3-to-1 alignment intermingled with unaligned and single alignments.

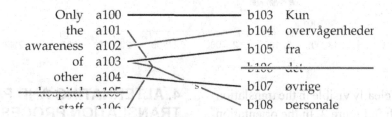

Figure 4. Zooming into a translation progression graph: source text (vertical) and translation activities (horizontal). The graph plots translation activities of 20 seconds (ms. 186.000 to 206.000). It shows a long reading pattern at the onset of the sentence (sec. 186-189) followed by a number of parallel reading and typing activities. The larger hatched boxes represent production units, the smaller boxes are fixation units. Fixation units largely overlap with production units.

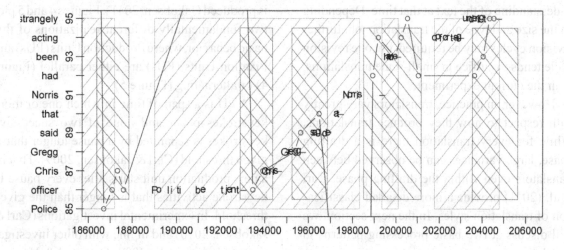

115

Figure 5. This progression graph shows translation activities of 24 seconds, which are the continuation of the translation in Figure 4 for the same translator. Three reading patterns can be observed: one at the onset of the sentence (sec. ca. 214-218), one in the middle of the sentence (secs. 229-232) and a third before the beginning of the second sentence translation (sec. 237-238). This graph shows alternating (serial) fixation units (reading) and and production units (typing activities): a ST sequence is read and then typed. Note also that it shows the production process which leads to the translation in Figure 3. While three English words (a101, a103, a106) in Figure 3 are aligned to one Danish word "personale," the keystrokes in time, which actually lead to the translation only appear once in the translation progression graph, on line 106.

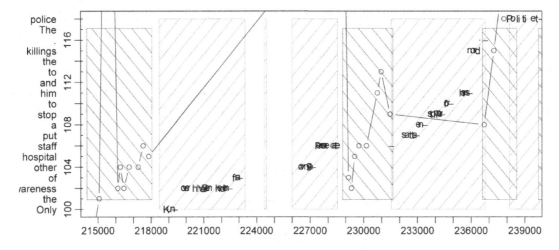

These phases are clearly visible in the translation progression graph in Figure 2. In the orientation phase, the translator gets acquainted with the material, discovers the meaning of the source text, detects difficult terms, and may search for possible translations; in the drafting phase the actual translation is produced; and in the revision phase the draft is checked and revised, based on a better understanding of the text at that time. Depending on the size and type of the translation job, further revision cycles may be required, but one revision cycle tends to suffice in small-scale translations, as in the current experiment.

However, in practice, translators vary greatly with respect to how they produce translations. While for every translation there is a drafting phase, large variances can be observed between translators even within the drafting phase. Carl et al. (2011) provide a more detailed classification of translation styles. In the next section, we will discuss at two basic processing patterns in translation drafting.

4. ALTERNATING AND PARALLEL TRANSLATION PROCESSING

Before a translation can be typed, a translator needs to read the source text passage, which is to be translated. As a basic translation behavior we can thus expect a loop in which a passage of the ST is read and then the corresponding translation is produced (Jakobsen, 2011). Figures 4 and 5 plot two fundamentally different realizations of this basic behavior, where Production Units (PUs) and Fixation Units (FUs) are either parallel (Figure 4) or alternating (Figure 5).

A PU is a span of time in which one or more keystrokes occur and none of two successive keystrokes is separated by a pause longer than a given threshold (Carl & Jakobsen, 2009). That is, a new production unit starts after every pause in keystroke activities that is longer than the given threshold. In experimental investigations (Carl & Jakobsen, 2010) and in line with other investigations (Alves & Vale, 2009; Dragsted & Hansen,

2008) this threshold is generally set at 800 ms to 1000 ms. That is, a lapse of time of more than 800-1000 ms indicates a shift in the translators' mind to another textual unit to be translated.

There is a strong correlation between the number of PUs and the overall translation time. Table 1 shows that student translators produce more and shorter PUs than professional translators, and that the translation time increases if more PUs are produced. In addition, Table 1 shows that professional translators produce longer segments in time and in length, while the speed with which characters are typed is approximately identical for both groups, while Figure 6 shows the relation between translation time and fragmentation of translation production.

In a similar fashion, we fragment the stream of gaze samples into Fixation Units (FUs). An FU is a sequence of two or more ST[5] fixations where the time interval between the end of one fixation and the beginning of the next fixation does not exceed a given time threshold. Since reading is generally less linear than writing, and likely to skip, e.g., function words (Radach, et al., 2004), we also allow long saccades[6] between non-adjacent words in the ST. A FU border occurs either if the translator's gaze leaves the the ST window, or if two successive fixations on the ST are separated by a long gap in time, which exceeds a predefined FU segmentation threshold.

While the eyes of the translator move back and forth between the two windows on the Translog

Table 1. Average PU duration, length, and typing speed for professional and student translators.

	Professionals	Students
av. PU duration in ms	3113	2216
av. PU length in chars	17.61	12.54
av. (PU chars/PU dur.)	5.44	5.70
median (PU chars/PU dur.)	5.61	5.53

Figure 6. The graph shows a strong correlation between the overall translation time (horizontal) and the number of PUs needed to produce the translation (vertical). Students are represented with rectangular symbols; professionals with diamond symbols. An identifying number is given in the rectangular and diamond symbols.

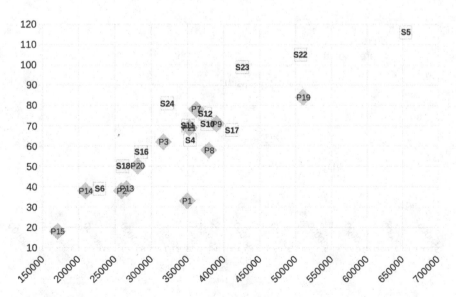

screen, it is possible for the eye-tracker to register stray fixations, which actually do not indicate reading activities. Since an FU should capture a coherent reading activity of the ST, we filter out those random fixations by setting the minimum number of fixations per FU to 2.

FUs and PUs can occur in parallel at the same time when the translator writes a translation while reading a ST fragment (Figure 4), or sequentially, in an alternating fashion as in Figure 5, when the translator either writes or reads.

A parallel segment is defined as an FU during which at least one key is simultaneously pressed, while an alternating segment is defined as an FU during which no keystrokes occur. (Carl & Jakobsen, 2010) found that student and professional translators differ in their degree of parallel reading and writing activity. Figure 7 shows the correlation between translation time and the amount of alternating FUs: more alternating FUs go along with longer total translation time.

Table 2 shows that only a fraction of the overall gaze time is spent on ST reading during translation, 20.3% and 22.9% for professionals and students, respectively. These results approximate the findings of Dragsted (2010), who measured 20% of gaze activities on the ST, and Jensen (2009), who found that "by far the most attention is devoted to the TT."

However, the average duration of the FUs differs with respect to their types (alternating vs. parallel) and with respect to whether they are produced by students or by professional translators: students have longer FUs than professionals (roughly 20%) and alternating FUs are longer than parallel FUs.

While for professional translators half of the FUs overlap with text production (i.e. parallel production), this is only the case for roughly 1/3 of the students' gaze patterns. Notice also that the duration of alternating FUs is slightly longer than the duration of parallel FUs.

Since professionals need only 84% of the students' time to translate the texts, we suspect that the main factor that distinguishes student and professional translators is the latter group's ability to better process ST comprehension and TT production in parallel. The graphs in Figures 6 and 7 put into relation the overall translation time

Figure 7. Translation time (horizontal) and number of alternating FUs (vertical) for students and professional translators. A strong correlation can be seen between the number of alternating gaze segments and translation time. Students tend to produce more alternating activity than professionals.

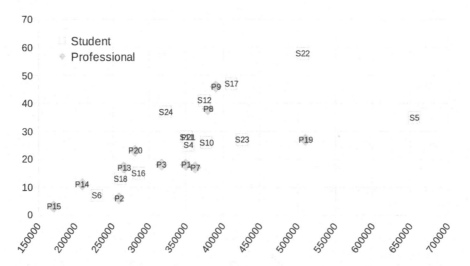

Table 2. Parallel and alternating translation (FU) for professional and student translators: while students and professionals have approximately the same overall number of FUs (first row), professionals show more parallel activities (352 FUs), and students work more in a alternating manner (411 FUs). The average duration of alternating FU is longer than the average duration of a parallel FU.

	Professionals	Students
#FU	652	634
ST reading time %	20.3	22.9
Parallel #FU	352	223
Parallel FU %	53.99	35.17
Parallel average dur.	1073	1428
Alternating #FU	300	411
Alternating FU %	46.01	64.83
Alternating av. dur.	1286	1588

with the number of PUs and alternating FUs for student and professional translators.

According to Sharmin et al. (2008), students struggle more with ST comprehension than professional translators: in many instances, all attention is absorbed by reading and understanding the ST, and thus no TT production can take place at the same time. Skilled professional translators, on the contrary, may already start typing the translation of a passage when still reading/understanding the end of that ST passage. Accordingly, gaze patterns on the ST and typing activities of the TT may overlap and translation production time becomes shorter. A similar observation is also made by Dragsted and Hansen (2008), who finds it hard to distinguish between ST and TT processing.

5. CHALLENGED AND UNCHALLENGED TRANSLATION

While the examples in Figures 4 and 5 show instances of unchallenged translation, where translation production proceeds smoothly in a parallel or in an alternating mode, there are also instances of more challenged and demanding translation

problems. A translation problem is characterized by delayed text production, which comes along with extended reading activities of the translation context and/or deletions, re-insertions, etc. Figure 8 plots an instance of a translation problem, where the translator has increasing reading activity in the source sentence. Already while typing the translation for "technologies" around time stamp 108000, the translator reads ahead until the end of the sentence. She then looks at the beginning ("Incentives must be offered") and then again reads the end of the sentence. The translator writes the relative pronoun "hvilket" (around 112000) which is then 6 seconds later deleted (between timestamps 118000 and 120000). After re-scanning the entire sentence repeatedly, the translator continues with fluent typing at time stamp 129000.

In this process, which lasted about 30 seconds, it is interesting to note how reading and text production interact. Presumably, the lack of a subject in the English clause "and could also help minimise emissions from deforestation" and its sentence final position make the translator think that this is a relative clause of "technologies," despite the fact that English "and" does not translate into a Danish relative pronoun. After producing the

Figure 8. Processing example of a translation problem. The translator needs approximately 30 seconds to solve a translation problem and to continue with smooth typing.

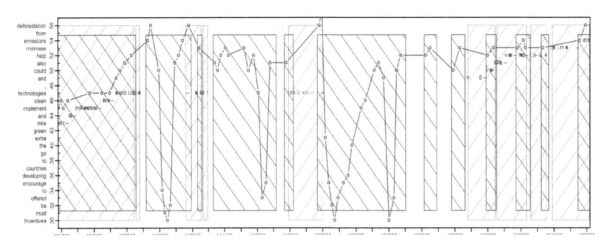

relative pronoun ("hvilket") and after re-scanning the source sentence, the translator realizes that the English clause actually a main clause conjunction (with omitted subject "Incentives"), and not a relative clause of "technologies."

The situation initially triggered a misguided expectation on the part of the translator which had to be sorted out and which required extra reading effort in the ST context. The example shows that there may be only a partial understanding of the source sentence when a translator starts typing its translation, and that more advanced meaning representations are generated "on the fly" when needed, and only to the extent they are necessary to proceed with text production. In reading research, it is well known that the reader constructs an analysis of the sentences' syntactic structure in a highly incremental manner, usually on a word-by-word basis (Staub & Rayner, 2007). Our data show that this might also be the case in translation production.

We distinguish two types of behavior, which are important for computational modeling.

Much of the translation drafting is monotonous:[7] translators look only a few words ahead into the ST from the position, which they are currently translating. Many of the smaller translation problems, such as multi-word translations or local reordering may be solved by this process. The degree of parallel activity depends on experience and typing skills of the translator. A touch typist would show behavior similar to the one in Figure 4 while a translator with less developed typing skills would produce translation patterns as in Figure 5.

At some points, extensive reading behavior can be observed, signaling more serious translation problems. This activity seems to be triggered by a TT production problem rather than an ST comprehension problem. That is, the ST is only understood, and meaning hypotheses are only generated to the degree required to keep producing the translation. If, for whatever reason, TT production cannot go on smoothly and the typing flow is interrupted, a new interpretation needs to be generated. This may lead to re-reading of an ST passage to be verified or reinterpreted, and/ or revision of the produced TT. In these cases, understanding of the ST is mediated through TT production.

Based on these, we will now develop a computational model for the first type of behavior.

6. COMPUTATIONAL COGNITIVE ARCHITECTURES

While there are a large number of computational models to reproduce the human translation product (e.g., rule-based, statistical Machine Translation systems, etc.) there exists, to the author's knowledge no computational model of human translation processes.[8] However, there are computational models of reading (Reichle, et al., 2002; Salvucci, 2001) and computational models of writing (John, 1996). There exist also more generalized approaches to simulate the human mind in general, such as ACT-R (Anderson, 2007) or ICARUS (Langley, et al., 2009). The ACT-R architecture adopts the view that cognition can be characterized as two distinct resources: a declarative resource that serves as a storage memory for factual knowledge and a procedural resource that integrates information and effects new behavior. In addition, there are perceptual modules (motor, visual, auditory, speech) in ACT-R. Cognitive architectures have been applied to model and explain a number of human faculties, such as planning and problem solving, car driving, etc.

More specialized models simulate certain aspects of human capacities. John (1996) suggests an "engineering model" of typing texts which consists of three operators, a perceptual, a cognitive and a motor operator: The perceptual operator perceives a written word and encodes it into a an ordered list of letters, the cognitive operator initiates the characters in the list, and the motor operator executes the typing activity.

"The first three words are perceived with three perceptual operators; the spelling of the first word is retrieved from LTM with the cognitive operator; and the letters of the word, and the space following it, are initiated and executed in turn" (John, 1996, p. 105).

These operators can work simultaneously: while a portion of the text is perceived, another portion that is already encoded can be typed. However, for a word to be typed, it first needs to be encoded and perceived. According to the model, no more than three words are perceived ahead of the word, which is currently being typed. Hence, as the typist looks only 3 words ahead in the text, no complete sentence understanding is required prior to typing. We observe similar behaviour in undisturbed, monotonous translation, as in Figures 1 and 2.

According to John, the perception of a word requires 340 ms, the retrieval and encoding of that word takes 50 ms and typing of each character between 30 and 230 ms, according to the expertise of the typist. Whereas the duration of the perceptual and cognitive operators remains constant; practice in typing increases the typing speed, i.e. inter-keystroke time is reduced.

As is the case for typing (copying), for reading a number of computational models have been developed as well, most importantly the E-Z reader (Reichle, et al., 2002), and the EMMA model (Salvucci, 2001) as an ACT-R implementation of it. The E-Z Reader (Reichle, et al., 2002) provides a theoretical framework for understanding how word identification, visual processing, attention, and oculomotor control jointly determine when and where the eyes move during reading, while EMMA (Salvucci, 2001) is an implementation of E-Z Reader which is applicable more generally than merely to model reading.

EMMA predicts the observable movements of the eyes that correspond to the unobservable shifts of visual attention. Visual attention begins with a command from the cognitive processor to move attention to a given visual object, whereas the visual system drives the eye movements and saccade planning. For instance, a visual object with value '3' represents a memory of the character '3' available via the eyes, not the semantic *three* used in arithmetic. A declarative retrieval is necessary to make that mapping.

EMMA's control flow distinguishes four processes: cognition that drives shifts of attention, vision that shifts attention and encodes objects, eye-movement preparation that prepares an eye movement and eye-movement execution that includes both motor programming and execution. These processes run in parallel. Saccadic programming and eye-movement are, hence, decoupled from the shifts of attention.

Like E-Z Reader and EMMA, the vision module in ACT-R also has two subsystems, a "where" system and a "what" system. The where system finds objects in the environment on the basis of spatial location and visual properties, and the what system identifies and "attends" the object by placing a representation of it in a visual buffer, where "attention" refers to the process of integrating features that allows individual words to be identified. In the next section, we describe an ACT-R implementation

7. AN ACT-R TRANSLATION PROCESS MODEL

We have previously introduced a distinction between *translation processes models* and *translation product models*. While machine translation systems are computational models that simulate the relations between the source and the target texts, a computational model of human translation processes would seek to reproduce the sequence(s) of human translation activity for a given translation. In this and the next section we discuss two translation process models, an ACT-R model and a statistical model.

The ACT-R model consists of 5 production rules (shown below) which run in a loop and which simulate unchallenged expert translation. The loop starts with the rule "locate-word" by searching for the location of the (next) word to fixate and by executing a saccade to that word (the "where" system). The rule "attend-word" then shifts attention to the word looked at and recognizes the fixated visual object. Next, a retrieval operation ("encode-word") encodes the object and maps the

form of the object to a (shallow) semantic representation. This is sufficient for retrieving by the next production rule an associated translation of the ST word. Whereas the rule "translate-word" retrieves the translation from memory, the rule "type-word" serializes the characters of the word and enters them across the keyboard.

- **Locate-word:** find physical location on the screen
- **Attend-word:** shift attention to word
- **Encode-word:** retrieve word from mental dictionary
- **Translate-word:** retrieve associated translation
- **Type-word:** serialize spelling and type word

ACT-R makes it possible to proceduralize the retrieval actions in the two rules "encode-word" and "translate-word" into one production rule by means of a process referred to as "production rule compilation," which could correspond to the behavior observed in expert translators. However, the modelling bottleneck in this ACT-R model is made up of the motor activities and the keying of the characters: within ACT-R, it takes 250 ms to prepare the typing action, 50 ms to initiate the typing action, another 100 ms for the key to be struck, and finally it takes another 150 ms for the finger to return to the home row. In a ten-finger model, each inter-key time may reduce to 200 ms. A plot of the translation progression in a ten-finger model is shown in Figure 9. While the ACT-R translation simulation in Figure 9 is produced in exactly the same lapse of time (20 sec.) as the human one in Figure 4, all keystrokes are equidistant in time, and there is exactly one fixation on each ST word immediately before the translation is produced.

However, in our data we observe that many successive keystrokes are separated by less than 200 ms. Each keystroke-bigram seems to have their own temporal distribution. Figure 10 plots

Figure 9. The translation progression graph shows ACT-R simulation for the translation in Figure 4

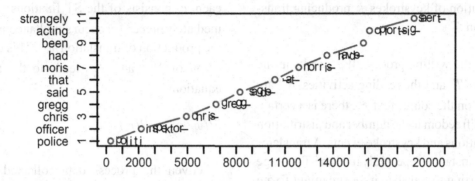

Figure 10. Distribution of time intervals between the 6 most frequent successive keystrokes in Danish

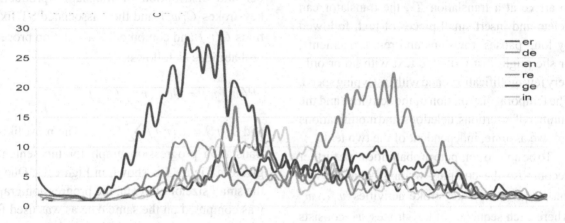

inter-key times for the six most frequent bigrams for Danish. For instance, the sequence "er" is most frequent in our Danish keystroke data and most of these bigrams are produced within a delay of around 60 to 80 ms. That is, the delay between the typing of "e" and the following "r" keystroke is frequently around 60 to 80 ms. The second most frequent keystroke bigram is "de" with a peak production time of around 160 ms, while the less frequent keystroke combination "rt" has a peak around 190 ms.

8. A STATISTICAL TRANSLATION PROCESS MODEL

Since such statistical distributions are difficult to integrate into the ACT-R model, we have also experimented with a statistical translation process

model. While a statistical model of the *translation product* (i.e. a statistical machine translation system) seeks to find the best (or most likely) translation T for given a source text S, a statistical model of the *translation process* would try to maximize the reading behavior R_S and writing behavior W_T for a given translation $S \rightarrow T$. We formalize the translation process model as a joint probability of the observed behaviour in the following way:

$$P(W_T, R_S) = P(W_T \mid R_S) * P(R_S)$$

where:

- $R_S : f_1 \ldots f_n$ represents the temporal distribution of fixations f on the source text S

- $W_T : k_1 \ldots k_m$ represents the temporal distribution of keystrokes k producing translation T

While the writing process W_T results in the translation T and the reading activities R_S are measured on the source text S, there is a certain amount of freedom in the number and distribution of the fixations and keystroke events. A translator might, for instance, repeatedly read an ST passage before starting to translate it, or she might fixate every words just once, as in Figure 9. Similarly, to arrive at a translation T, the translator can delete and insert small pieces of text, followed by long pauses, revisions and re-arrangements, or she might just write the text with no or only very few modifications, and with fast typing speed. The temporal distribution of the activities and the number of insertions, deletions, and modifications are, we assume, independent of the two texts.

To be able to compute probabilities, we further decompose the complex writing behavior W_T into sequences of keystroke activities $w_1 \ldots w_s$ where each sequence of keystrokes w_i consists of inter-key times for the typing activities of the translation of source unit i, [9] and where s is the number of units in S. The gaze activities R_S are decomposed into sets of fixations $r_1 \ldots r_s$ where each r_i consists of the ST fixations which immediately precede or occur simultaneously during the production of translation w_i. This decomposition of W_T and R_S leads to the following equation:

$$P(w_i \mid r_i) * P(r_i)$$

Given the process data collected from 24 translators, we count for each ST unit i the number and distribution of translation-producing keystrokes $C(w_i)$ and their associated ST fixations $C(r_i)$ and compute the translation process probabilities as follows:

$$P(w_i \mid r_i) = C(w_i, r_i) / C(r_i)$$

and $P(r_i) = C(r_i) / \sum C(r_j)$. The most likely translation progression graph for the sentence given in Figure 4 is shown in Figure 11. Due to the small size of our data, the progression graph was computed on the same data as was used for training the probabilities. The graph thus represents an averaged fit of the training data.

Figure 11. This translation progression graph represents the same translation as the one in Figure 4 and Figure 9 and is generated by means of the statistical model

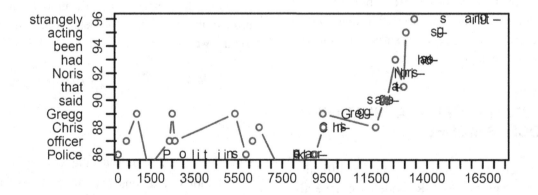

9. DISCUSSION

We compare the three translation progression graphs in Figures 4, 9, and 11. The human translation progression in Figure 4 shows some reading activities before the onset of typing and towards the end of the sentence translation activity. There is less reading activity in the middle of the sentence where some of the ST words are looked at that are currently being translated.

In contrast to this, the ACT-R simulation in Figure 9 has a very regular, static behavior: 200 ms are needed for each inter-key time, and there is exactly one fixation on every source word immediately before it is translated. Even though the distribution of the keystroke events in the ACT-R simulation and in the human translation is quite different, the overall translation time is identical for both translations (20 sec).

The statistical translation process simulation in Figure 11 has a rhythmical keystroke distribution, with longer pauses during sentence initial typing of "Politiinspektor" and shorter interkey times towards the middle of the sentence, when the proper nouns are translated. As in the human translation (Figure 4), there are sentence initial and sentence final reading activities. This might be the reason why the statistical simulation appears closer to the human translation than the ACT-R simulation does, even though the overall translation time is 20% less.

Note, however, that these simulations only account for "undisturbed" translation. As in the E-Z reader, EMMA and for TYPIST, higher-order processes would only intervene when "something is wrong" and a signal would be sent to stop moving forward. As for the eye-movement behavior, we assume that also typing movement needs to be initiated and interrupted by meta-processes.

As discussed in section 2, meta-processes (Göpferich, 2009; Hönig, 1991) guide the human translation process and intervene during translation production. Just as the E-Z reader (Reichle, et al., 2002) assumes word identification to be the forward "driving engine" in reading, we view the monotonous translation production to be the driving engine for translation, by which the translation product emerges and chunks of words are knitted into larger target text units. Only in exceptional cases will we observe more complex patterns as discussed in section 5.

10. CONCLUSION AND OUTLOOK

In this chapter, we describe two models of human translation processes based on a definition of production units, which is in line with word boundaries. In an unchallenged translation situation, source text fixations trigger target text production, with only little look-ahead and a linear word-for-word translation production. Our data show that novice translators proceed in a more disrupted, alternating fashion (Figure 4) than professional translators (Figure 5). The models therefore simulate the more experienced professional translator.

In a previous study (Carl & Jakobsen, 2009), it has been shown that short sequences of keystrokes are typed at a similar speed both by novice and professional translators. This seems to indicate that keystrokes are not individually prepared, initiated and struck, but rather that they are generated as small 'programs' where the preparation triggers a short sequence of keystrokes, irrespective of the translator's expertise.

These small motor programs could be interrupted if a spelling difficulty/uncertainty occurs, if a typo is detected, if a different wording comes to the translator's mind, or if any other doubts occur. Our data show sequences of up to 6 characters, such as "iserne," "ntlige," or "ations" are typed in less than 600 ms, with every inter-keystroke interval less than 150 ms. Note that these typing programs do not always coincide with the spellings of words. More than 27% of these quickly typed sequences start and end in the middle of a word while only 33% start and end at a word boundary (Carl & Jakobsen, 2009).

In the future, we seek to model text production in line with these observed PUs characteristics. In analogy to the reading model, those units could constitute the "driving engine" for translation production where higher-order processes intervene if translation problems occur. The model should then be able to explain and simulate some of the observed regressions, revisions and corrections, and indicate at what moment automated assistance might be helpful for the translator.

REFERENCES

Alves, F., & Vale, D. C. (2009). Probing the unit of translation in time: aspects of the design and development of a web application for storing, annotating and querying translation process data. *Across Language and Cultures, 10*(2), 251–273.

Anderson, J. (2007). *How can the human mind occur in the physical universe?* Oxford, UK: Oxford University Press. doi:10.1093/acprof:o so/9780195324259.001.0001

Boguslavsky, I. M., Iomdin, L. L., Lazursky, A. V., Mityushin, L. G., Sizov, V. G., Kreydlin, L. G., & Berdichevsky, A. S. (2005). Interactive resolution of intrinsic and translational ambiguity in a machine translation system. [Berlin, Germany: Springer-Verlag.]. *Proceedings of CICLing, 2005*, 383–394.

Carl, M. (2009). Triangulating product and process data: Quantifying alignment units with keystroke data. *Copenhagen Studies in Language, 38*, 225–247.

Carl, M., Dragsted, B., & Jakobsen, A. L. (2011). On the systematicity of human translation processes. *Translation Journal, 16*(2). Retrieved from http://translationjournal.net/journal/56taxonomy. htm

Carl, M., & Jakobsen, A. L. (2009). Objectives for a query language for user-activity data. In *Proceedings of the Natural Language Processing and Cognitive Science (NLPCS 2009)*. Milan, Italy: NLPCS.

Carl, M., & Jakobsen, A. L. (2010). Towards statistical modelling of translators' activity data. *International Journal of Speech Technology, 12*(4). Retrieved from http://www.springerlink. com/content/3745875x22883306/

Choumane, A., Blanchon, H., & Roisin, C. (2005). Integrating translation services within a structured editor. In *Proceedings of the 2005 ACM Symposium on Document Engineering*, (pp. 165–167). New York, NY: ACM Press.

Dragsted, B. (2010). Coordination of reading and writing processes in translation. In *Translation and Cognition* (pp. 41–62). Amsterdam, The Netherlands: Benjamins.

Dragsted, B., & Hansen, I. G. (2008). Comprehension and production in translation: A pilot study on segmentation and the coordination of reading and writing processes. *Copenhagen Studies in Language, 36*, 9–12.

Ericsson, K.-A. (2000). Expertise in interpreting: An expert-performance perspective. *Interpreting, 5*(2), 187–220. doi:10.1075/intp.5.2.08eri

Göpferich, S. (2009). Towards a model of translation competence and its acquisition: The longitudinal study TransComp. In Göpferich, S., Jakobsen, A. L., & Mees, I. M. (Eds.), *Behind the Mind: Methods, Models, and Results in Translation Process Research* (pp. 11–37). Copenhagen, Denmark: Samfundslitteratur.

Göpferich, S., Jakobsen, A. L., & Mees, I. M. (Eds.). (2009). *Behind the mind: Methods, models and results in translation process research*. Copenhagen, Denmark: Samfundslitteratur.

Hönig, H. G. (1991). Translation studies: The state of the art, the first James Holmes symposium on translation studies. In *Proceedings of the First James S Holmes Symposium on Translation Studies*, (pp. 77–89). Amsterdam, The Netherlands: James S Holmes.

Jakobsen, A. L. (2006). Research methods in translation - Translog. In Sullivan, K. P. H., & Lindgren, E. (Eds.), *Computer Keystroke Logging and Writing: Methods and Applications* (*Vol. 18*, pp. 95–105). Oxford, UK: Elsevier.

Jakobsen, A. L. (2011). Tracking translators' keystrokes and eye movements with Translog. In Alvstad, C., Hild, A., & Tiselius, E. (Eds.), *Integrative Approaches in Translation Studies* (pp. 37–55). Copenhagen, Denmark: Benjamins.

Jensen, K. (2009). Distribution of attention between source text and target text during translation. In *Proceedings of IATIS*. IATIS.

John, B. E. (1996). Typist: A theory of performance in skilled typing. *Human-Computer Interaction*, *11*(4), 321–355. doi:10.1207/s15327051hci1104_2

Koehn, P., & Haddow, B. (2009). Interactive assistance to human translators using statistical machine translation methods. In *Proceedings of the MT Summit*. MT Summit.

Kromann, M. T. (2003). The Danish dependency treebank and the DTAG treebank tool. In *Proceedings of the 2nd Workshop on Treebanks and Linguistic Theories*. Växjo, Sweden: ACL.

Langley, P., Laird, J., & Rogers, S. (2009). Cognitive architectures: Research issues and challenges. *Cognitive Systems Research*, *10*(2), 141–160. doi:10.1016/j.cogsys.2006.07.004

Lewis, W. D. (2010). Haitian creole: How to build and ship an mt engine from scratch in 4 days, 17 hours, & 30 minutes. In *Proceedings of EAMT*. Berlin, Germany: Springer-Verlag.

Lörscher, W. (1992). Investigating the translation process. *Meta*, *37*(3), 426–439. doi:10.7202/003517ar

Macklovitch, E. (2004). The contribution of end-users to the transtype2 project. In *Proceedings of the 6th Conference of the Association for Machine Translation in the Americas (AMTA-2004)*, (pp. 197–207). Kyoto, Japan: AMTA.

Mees, I. M., & Göpferich, S. (Eds.). (2009). *Methodology, technology and innovation in translation process research* (*Vol. 38*). Copenhagen, Denmark: Samfundslitteratur.

Nagao, M. (1984). A framework of a mechanical translation between Japanese and English by analogy principle. In Elithorn, A., & Banerji, R. (Eds.), *Artificial and Human Intelligence* (pp. 173–180). Amsterdam, The Netherlands: Elsevier.

Perrin, D. (2003). Progression analysis (PA): Investigating writing strategies at the workplace. *Pragmatics*, *35*, 907–921. doi:10.1016/S0378-2166(02)00125-X

Radach, R., Kennedy, A., & Rayner, K. (2004). *Eye movements and information processing during reading*. East Sussex, UK: Psychology Press.

Reichle, E. D., Rayner, K., & Pollatsek, A. (2002). The e-z reader model of eye movement control in reading: Comparisons to other models. *The Behavioral and Brain Sciences*, *26*(4), 445–476l.

Salvucci, D. (2001). An integrated model of eye movements and visual encoding. *Cognitive Systems Research*, *1*, 201–220. doi:10.1016/S1389-0417(00)00015-2

Sharmin, S., Špakov, O., Räihä, K., & Jakobsen, A. L. (2008). Where on the screen do translation students look? *Copenhagen Studies in Language*, *36*, 30–51.

Staub, A., & Rayner, K. (2007). Eye movements and on-line comprehension processes. In *The Oxford Handbook of Psycholinguistics* (pp. 327–342). Oxford, UK: Oxford University Press.

Sullivan, K. P. H., & Lindgren, E. (Eds.). (2006). *Computer keystroke logging and writing: Methods and applications* (*Vol. 18*). Oxford, UK: Elsevier.

ENDNOTES

[1] At the time of writing this chapter, Google translate offers 58 source and target languages, which amounts to more than 3000 different language pairs.

[2] CRITT is the "Center for Research and Innovation in Translation and Translation Technology" at Copenhagen Business School, which aims at building up new knowledge of translation and communication processes and provide a basis for technological innovation in this field.

[3] www.translog.dk

[4] The word "det" in Figure 3 is an example of unaligned TT word. Accordingly, the keystrokes do not occur in the progression graph in Figure 5.

[5] Due to the fact that our software at the time of the experiments could not register fixations and word-mappings in the TT window, we only have fixations, and FUs in the ST.

[6] Saccades occur between fixations, and they are identified by large changes in eye position in an extremely short time span. Saccades during reading often move the eyes about 8 characters, and they normally last around 30 ms. Saccades account for about 10-15 percent of all eye activity in reading, while the remainder 85-90 percent are fixations.

[7] This conclusion is based on our translation material from English into Danish, two relatively close languages with similar word order.

[8] Nagao (1984) proposes to emulate MT systems according to human translation behaviour, and a large number of systems have been inspired by his seminal paper. However, the performance of these systems is usually assessed based on the quality of the translation product, rather than by their proximity to human translation processes.

[9] A source unit is the ST part of an alignment unit, which can consist of one or more ST words. The source unit words may be continuous or discontinuous, but must be aligned to the same TT word(s).

Section 3
Advanced Question Answering System

Chapter 6
Advanced Question–Answering and Discourse Semantics

Patrick Saint-Dizier
IRIT-CNRS, France

ABSTRACT

In this chapter, the authors develop the paradigm of advanced question-answering that includes how-to, why, evaluative, comparative, and opinion questions. They show the different parameters at stake in answer production, involving several aspects of cooperativity. These types of questions require quite a lot of discourse semantics analysis and domain knowledge. The second part of this chapter is devoted to a short presentation of those text semantics aspects relevant to answering questions. The last part of this chapter introduces <TextCoop>, a platform the authors have developed for discourse semantics analysis that they use for answering complex questions, in particular how-to and opinion questions.

INTRODUCTION

Question-answering is not a new area of research. Question answering underwent through three major steps, motivated by major NLP technological progress. The first phase, starting as early as 1961, is characterized by small prototypes, running on very restricted domains and interacting with databases. In this first generation of question answering systems fall, for example, Baseball, LUNAR, QUALM, and STUDENT. A second generation emerged with the ARDA (AQAINT

program) and TREC-QA capable of managing very large volumes of data, working on either open or closed domains, answering factoid or definition questions. A number of commercial products were developed, among which: START at MIT, Askjeeves, AnswerBus, QuASM, and IONAUT. More recently, road maps (Burger, et al., 2001) focus on the needs of deeper modes of language understanding and elaborated reasoning schemas to properly answer questions. Over the last decade, many international question answering contests have been held, such as TREC (Voorhees, 2001), CLEF, and NTCIR. Question answering is investigated over several languages and within a mul-

DOI: 10.4018/978-1-4666-2169-5.ch006

tilingual perspective. Thus far, eleven languages have been tested on monolingual or cross-lingual question answering tasks. A new trend emerges around the notions of multi-media question answering. This will not be further developed here since this is somewhat outside the scope of this chapter. Dialogue for QA and user profiling also become major challenges that make QA more realistic (see dedicated chapter in this volume).

Question-Answering (QA) involves a large diversity of techniques and resources that depend on the type of system to realize (e.g. domain dependent or not) and on a number of requirements. QA can involve shallow techniques to retrieve passages in documents as well as deep, linguistic-based natural language processing techniques. Statistical QA is the major trend (i.e. answer retrieval is based on statistical algorithms), but knowledge-based approaches are now emerging to resolve complex situations. The main issues are: question analysis (type of the expected answer, focus and constraints on the expected answer), answer extraction from various kinds of documents (including analysis of the best match and answer reliability evaluation), and answer formulation (which is often very basic). Besides these three main aspects, let us note: the taking into account the question context, interactive and multimedia QA, and multilingual QA.

Questions are usually categorized according to the type of answer they induce. Various categorizations have been elaborated by Lehnert (1978), Rilo et al. (1994), Hermjakob (2001), and Li et al. (2002). For example, in Lehnert (1978), question categories are, among others: *goal, cause, enablement, verification, instrumental, expectation, judgmental, or quantificational*. These types are highly conceptual and difficult to indentify in questions. The QALC system (Ferret, et al., 2001) introduced 17 types of questions among which *person, organization, quantity, and place*. These are closer to semantic types, which characterize here the semantic type of the expected information. We then observed a proliferation of

typologies: while Lasso (Moldovan, et al., 1999), and Webclopedia (Hermjakob, et al., 2002) postulated respectively 25 and 70 types which are somewhat heterogeneous, some systems use the whole WordNet concept hierarchy, leading to more than 8000 types.

However, a major distinction can be made between questions that basically induce factoid responses, i.e. a short piece of information which can be directly extracted from a text (e.g. dates, costs, names) and questions where the response is a well-formed text portion (or a set of portions), e.g. a procedure to follow to realize something or the causes of an event. Answering these questions requires more complex language and reasoning treatments, possibly radically different approaches and technologies. These types of questions fall into the paradigm of advanced question-answering, not to be confused with complex question answering, which includes, among others, questions composed of several layers such as hypothesis, given data, pre-requisites or sub-questions.

Advanced question answering may also include situations where complex additional treatments are needed before being able to answer the question. It is an area that, for example, deals with those numerous cases found in real situations where (1) there is no direct answer to a question (some form of treatment or revision of the question is needed before being able to produce an answer), (2) there are too many responses (making the answer somewhat confusing), or (3) the response has a complex structure that requires elaborations and planning. Language processing and generation as well as dedicated reasoning procedures, often based on domain knowledge, must often be used to produce accurate and adequate responses.

In this chapter, we first survey the different types of questions, which require advanced language processing treatments and develop the various linguistic resources and treatments they need. Besides the analysis of elementary propositions, sometimes viewed as Elementary Discourse Units (EDU), we develop some aspects of discourse semantics of interest for answering those types of questions. Discourse semantics is still an emerging field of research and development in the area of language processing. It is much more developed in applied linguistic circles (e.g. the study of the various kinds of rhetorical relations), in philosophy (e.g. the study of causality), in theoretical linguistics (e.g. the DRT framework) and in cognitive psychology (e.g. the well-known frames and scripts frameworks). In this chapter, some tools that show interesting properties for our aim, such as Gate or <TextCoop>, are introduced.

ADVANCED QUESTION-ANSWERING

In this section, we first introduce and illustrate the major types of questions advocated above. We then elaborate on how responses can be provided to users. This section basically raises challenges. Advanced question answering is still in an early development stage: directions proposed here are essentially prospective.

Classes of Questions and Related Problems

Some of the main types of questions that fall into the area of what we call advanced question answering are the following:

- *Procedural questions*, where the answer to an 'how-to' question is a well-formed fragment of a procedure (Delpech et al., 08), i.e. a set of organized instructions, pre-requisites, warnings, etc. For example, when one is asking *how to change a mother card,* then an ordered or at least clearly organized set of instructions and recommendations is expected in order to reach this goal (Van der Linden, 1993). Answering how-to questions requires an extensive discourse analysis since procedures show very diverse structures that depend on the domain,

the target audience, etc. Investigations show that they cover quite a large part of the questions asked to online services, they range from Do It Yourself (DIY) to professional applications (such as maintenance), social behavior recommendations, health care, and video game solutions,

- *Causal questions*, are questions of the form 'why P?' (Pechsiri, 2008; Vazquez-Reyes, 2008) where the answer is in general a more or less organized set of events that caused P (Otero, et al., 2004). The difficulty is obviously to identify, in various documents, chains of relevant events leading to P that make the response useful for the user (Woodward, 2003). Once again, an accurate discourse analysis is necessary, in particular to identify events connected by causal relations and their temporal structure.

- *Evaluative and comparative questions*, where the challenge is to understand the terms of a given evaluation or a comparison and then how it can be elaborated (Kearsley, 1976; Lim, et al., 2009). For example, *is X an innovative researcher?* needs subtle semantic elaborations around the semantics of the adjective *innovative* applied to researchers. The criteria used to characterize the semantics of this adjective would be different when applied to other terms, like e.g. *an innovative company.* So far, there is no foundational result in this area, however, some basic results from database querying, adjectival modification analysis (e.g. McNally, et al., 2004), and from generalized quantifiers theory (Barwise, et al., 1981) can be considered as a useful contribution. A contextualized semantics of adjectives is extremely challenging because of its dependence to the properties of the terms they modify. This is however a necessary step to dynamically answer this type of question.

- *Opinion questions,* related to opinion mining (Bing, 2010), opinion questions (Minqing, et al., 2004) require an elaborated form of answer where opinions about a fact, possibly controversial, must often be developed and contrasted, probably via the use of relevant arguments for or against this fact (see TAC 2008, session on opinion QA with a global approach to opinion analysis). This type of question is also very challenging since it may require taking into account arguments and therefore would include the use of techniques for argument mining (Saaba, et al., 2008) and classification following the schemes proposed in Walton et al. (2008), document relevance and strength analysis, and then the identification of the relation (e.g. attack, support, explanation) that an argument has with the fact at stake (Bal, et al., 2010).

We will not address here the problem of question-document matching since it is reported in many papers for factoid questions or questions that have relatively direct answers, via e.g. query reformulation techniques as in, e.g. Pasca (2009) and Ravi (2008). For causal questions, evaluative and opinion questions the needed techniques and formalisms are still an open issue and may involve a lot of deep semantic interpretation and reasoning since it is often necessary to match not words but entire propositions (the queries) with propositions in documents, possibly written in a very different way.

The Art of Providing Cooperative Answers

Most 'real' questions, including factoid questions, may require advanced treatments for various reasons that are developed below. As developed in the famous Grice's maxims (Grice, 1975; Wilson, et al., 1981), a number of principles in the question-answer matching and in the answer

production must be carefully investigated in order to make sure the user's expectations are met and that the user does understand the response correctly. While response retrieval techniques are relatively well developed, answer production is a rather neglected aspect. However, it is clear that users expect to get some form of feedback or context related to the kind of response they get. This is a rather open area whose development is crucial for QA.

One of the first reasons is that there is no direct answer or there are too many answers to a query. For example, if one asks: *Give me a list of hotels in Toulouse with rooms for 9 persons*, there will not be any answer because there is not such a resource (See Benamara, et al., 2004). A cooperative attitude, expected by most users, would be that the system is able to propose alternative solutions, as any travel agent would. A strategy could be to first indicate that the resource does not exist (the diagnosis), so that the user understands the reason of an alternative solution, and then to relax some constraints in the question, e.g. the number of persons per room while keeping active the constraint on the total number of persons. This requires well-tuned reasoning strategies, since the ideal answer would be to propose a group of say, 4 rooms in the same hotel, that allow to accommodate 9 persons.

An opposite case occurs when there are too many answers to a question; a solution is either to restrict the question via a dialogue or to abstract over or categorize those answers and to propose a kind of intentional answer. For example, if asking for the price of regular gas in Paris, instead of getting fares for each gas station in Paris, getting a kind of interval in which most fares are is much more interesting (Moriceau, 2006). Once again, this requires well-tuned, domain dependent knowledge and, in our example, a well-tuned data fusion algorithm. It is even more interesting, taking into account the creation date of the returned Web pages, to indicate if this price has recently increased, is stable or has decreased: *Gaz fares are in general between 1.45 and 1.60 Euros in Paris; They recently increased by about 0.15 Euros.* Finally, such a question probably underlies the search of the cheapest place where to buy gas; in that case, a cooperative response could include a short list of such cheap places in Paris among which the user can choose.

Another situation where reasoning is required occurs when the retrieved answer is not complete, fully relevant, or fully reliable w.r.t. the query. Since users expect fully relevant and comprehensive answers, it is necessary to develop response generation strategies to adequately respond to the user when this is not the case, outlining the response limitations. For example, if the answer comes from a blog or from any kind of personal website, the system should indicate that the answer may not be fully reliable.

Response relevance, in particular accounting for the quality of the matching between the question and the retrieved document is a major component of a response. A typical example is the case where the information retrieved by the system has a coarser grain than the one expected by the user. For example, if the user asks: *Did typhoon A pass over Manilla at night on June 20th?* if the retrieved answer is just: *'Typhoon A affected Manilla on June 20th,'* then the answer must not be just *'yes,'* but it must clearly indicate that the response is only approximate: *Typhoon A passed over Manilla some time on June 20th, may be not at night.* Moreover, if typhoon *A* did not go over Manilla, then a response such as *'no'* would be misleading. A cooperative response must indicate that the question has a false presupposition: *This typhoon did not pass over Manilla but over Taipei.*

A third situation occurs when the question is not sufficiently precise or contains terms, which are not appropriate for document search (e.g. metaphors, technical terms). In that case, the question may have too many answers, no answers or incorrect answers. A strategy is to start a short and well-targeted dialogue aiming at clarifying terms (e.g. making propositions of more appropriate

ones) or at getting missing information. In this latter case, a domain model is certainly necessary, so that the missing information can be induced from a conceptual schema, a script, or equivalent.

As can be noted from these different situations, where some form of accuracy and cooperativity is needed to get appropriate answers, the need of knowledge, dedicated inferences, and accurate question term interpretation is central and very crucial. Lexical inference as well as textual inference are crucial devices that require accurate language resources. These are emerging fields in language processing. Natural language generation is also a central issue (see e.g. Reiter, et al., 1997) with the difficulty of being able to merge the question terms and form with the response terms in order to produce an informative response. Lexical choice as well as sentence micro-planning must be tailored to the question terms and structure.

The necessity of undergoing clarification via dialogue also occurs quite frequently (Kupic, 1993). The landscape of QA widely opens to a large number of ongoing and very challenging research topics in various areas. Cooperativity is most certainly central, and schemas for cooperative strategies need to be developed. A certain level of domain dependency makes the development of such schemas quite challenging (Olney, et al., 2002; Quarteroni, 2008, 2010; Moschitti, et al., 2010).

Answering Questions: Some Semantic and Knowledge Representation Challenges

Besides responding cooperatively, another major challenge in question answering is the production of an appropriate, well-formed, and relevant answer, the *'what to say'* of natural language generation. In the factoid-question framework, the answer is, in general, limited to a portion of a text where the answer has been found. The answer is then simply this text fragment without any other language element. This may be sufficient for factoid questions where the answer does not need any elaboration a priori, but this is not appropriate for the types of questions presented above. Concerning the need of an elaboration, in some applications of factoid questions, an interesting feature is the adjunction of links that allow the user to access the main documents in which the answer was found in order to get more information around the answer he gets.

Answer generation is a complex and crucial task, which has seldom been addressed, in the question-answering community. As in other areas of language processing, most of the language generation aspects have been somewhat neglected; the result is that applications may have a rich question analysis facet but a poor output, possibly leading to misunderstandings. Let us briefly discuss below the issue of answer production for a number of types of questions. We will in particular focus on the semantic and knowledge representation aspects, which are crucial for answer production, while syntactic, planning and lexical choice aspects will not be addressed. These have indeed been relatively accurately investigated in the natural language generation community (see e.g. Reiter, et al., 1997).

Concerning procedural questions, the answer is identified from matching the question with document titles viewed as goals. The answer is not the title but one or more well formed text fragments in procedures that describe the actions to undertake (realized by means of instructions possibly structured by a set of sub-goals). These text fragments are linked to this title by means of a discourse relation, e.g. a goal-plan structure. In the case of multiple candidates (several titles may match the question) several closely related answers can be provided, associated with e.g., navigational tools, in order to let the user choose his/her preferred solution among them (e.g., different ways to make a Margarita pizza). In each case, it is important to note that each procedure, which is provided, must be a comprehensive response. A priori, procedure fusion is excluded because of its complexity and the diversity of viewpoints for each action. However, the actions to be undertaken can be associated with a synthesis of hints and warnings, extracted from the set of response documents, in order to guide and help the user (Fontan, 2008). As can be seen, the discourse articulations needed to produce the answer are not straightforward to identify.

Causal or consequence questions call for answers formed out of sequences of events (e.g. Boguraev, et al., 2005). These events may be interrelated at various degrees; they may also be more or less strongly involved in the causal or consequence chain. Besides the difficulty of matching the question with a statement in a text, identifying the causes it is related to may be complex, consider e.g.: *Why is smoking dangerous? My rice has some yellow leaves, with some small holes at the end of the leaves, what should I do?* The extraction of relevant causes requires a detailed analysis of the questions (prerequisites, hypothesis, conditions, circumstances, etc.) and the taking into account of several forms of entailment (e.g. to deal with implicit information) and how they are linguistically realized (Talmy, 2001). Next, the construction of the answer requires an elaborated and accurate planning of the chains of events that have been identified (most events are caused or entailed by several other events). These events do not have the same importance in the chain, some are central (kernels) while others are peripheral (satellites, such as: elaborations, sub-events, illustrations, etc.). The answer should be able to outline the causal backbone, i.e., the main events and their internal relations as well as their relations with the terms of the question (Khoo, et al., 2000). The level of granularity of the events included in the answer, as well as the explicit vs. implicit character of some of these events needs to be investigated. Furthermore, the answer may be constructed via fusion of causal events from several documents.

Although evaluative and comparative questions have not been the subject of many investigations so far; they nevertheless cover quite a large set of questions (see the TAC conference advocated above). The problematic behind evaluative expressions, deep semantic interpretation, is very complex in terms of the identification of the properties involved in the comparison and domain sensitivity (Ravi, et al., 2008). In some professional domains, the response may involve semantic elements, which go beyond properties usually found in lexicons or ontologies; these may be related to the domain know-how or practices. The challenge is then to be able to indicate in the answer the basis on which the evaluation has been carried out. For instance, in the case of the adjective *innovative* applied to companies, with a question such as: *Is company A innovative?*

The following response does make explicit the evaluation criteria: *Company A is innovative in drug production because it buys a lot of basic technologies and has a large set of customers that buy its know-how*. Obviously, *innovative* applied to researchers would be different. Besides the characterization of properties at stake in an evaluation, comparative and superlative questions require comparing results. The additional challenge is then to help the user perceive on what basis the comparison has been carried out. For example in *Is company A more innovative than company B?* it is necessary to evaluate the different components given above, to produce a synthesis for the user and probably to make a decision based on given criteria.

Answering opinion questions is also very challenging and requires the access to a large variety of knowledge. Given a statement, e.g., *Should I get immunized against H1N1 flu?*, the response can just be *yes* or *no* if the objective is just to sum up the main trend from the documents for or against the vaccine. This is however not very satisfactory because one does not know the reasons (or criteria) behind the *yes* or *no* and cannot therefore apply his preferences on those criteria. This clearly prevents users from referring to their own system of values or priorities. A more

appropriate response would be to propose a set of articulated arguments for or against the statement given in the question, possibly associated with e.g., elaborations and illustrations. Arguments can be more or less strongly marked, by means of a number of linguistic marks such as adverbs. Argument may attack or support each other, as postulated in argumentation theory (Caminada, 2007). Argument being identified, no explicit answer can then be formulated because the final decision depends on the person asking the question: the user's decision depends on the individual weights he associates with each argument. From a natural language perspective, the answer is a set of sorted arguments with redundancy elimination, which can be structured according to argumentation schemes (Walton, 2008) or explanation schemes.

Besides these very challenging and very open answer generation problems, the *what to say* and planning issues of natural language generation (Dale, 2000; McKeown, 1985), answer production, as advocated above, may also need some forms of information fusion or conflation (Moriceau, 2006) to avoid redundancies. This requires quite an extensive domain knowledge base and accurate fusion strategies, possibly demanding uncertainty reasoning as the analysis from questions and documents might yield uncertain results. Automatic linking and fusion of information is becoming an important research topic. Very often, the answer to a question, especially in an advanced question-answering framework, requires information fusion from different sentences, documents, and media (Moriceau, 2006; Marcu, 2000).

In the same range of ideas, offering multiple answers, all equally possible, to a user requires the development of adequate visualization or navigation tools (e.g. the different ways of making a pizza, the different causes of a disease, the different fares of gas in various parts of a city, the different ways of going to an airport from a city center).

Finally, since one of the major challenges is to be cooperative with the user, answer personalization (conceptually and linguistically speaking) is crucial. This includes adequate lexical choice and sentence planning, reference generation as well as managing implicit data and response layout. Explanation production (Pollock, 1974; Keil, 2000; Wright, 2004), when the answer is not direct, is also an important feature; however, explanation production has not been the subject of much investigation so far in computational linguistic circles (Bourse, et al., 2012). It has however been investigated in didactics and psychology with a very different and much more applied perspective, which can nevertheless be considered for answering questions.

To answer complex questions, it may be appropriate not to leave the system elaborate an answer while leaving the user in a relatively passive attitude. One possibility is to view an advanced question answering system as a help for the user, a kind of collaborative tool where the user contributes in several ways, yet to be explored, to the production of the answer. One example is the case of evaluative questions where the system cannot always 'guess' the meaning of modifying expressions. For example, the difference in meaning between *a competitive company* and *a competitive researcher* is characterized in conceptual semantics by the set of properties of a company or of a researcher, which are modified in some way by this adjective. Obviously, these are not the same. If the system has no predefined definition and no means to automatically infer that list of properties, then it may be best to suggest to the user to identify properties (possibly via examples) among a set of properties, and then to memorize the result and its context. Some cases are even almost impossible to answer without such a dialogue, e.g. *Which are the most kid-friendly cities in Asia?*

To conclude, it is clear that a large variety of types of general purpose and domain knowl-edge is required to develop accurate advanced question-answering systems. This is a very challenging situation since domain knowledge representation remains an open issue, in spite of the major progress around domain ontology contents and acquisition and the use of general purpose knowledge bases (e.g. Cyc, accessible at: http://www.cyc.com/cyc/technology/whatiscyc or the SUMO system: http://www.ontologyportal.org/). It is clear that at the moment only domain dependent systems can be developed. Let us note some interesting attemps to capture knowledge from the Web for answering questions (Katz, et al., 2004; Pasca, et al., 2009). This is a rather general situation for applications where natural language processing and reasoning is involved (Harabagiu, et al., 2000; Helbig, 2005). This is not necessarily a strong limitation if portability issues can be addressed. Another argument is that, in professional environments, most queries are related to a precise domain, with precise semantic interpretations, as in e.g. evaluative questions used in business intelligence.

DISCOURSE SEMANTICS FOR ANSWERING QUESTIONS

Discourse analysis is a vast and emerging area in computational linguistics, with many open challenges (see the RTE and TAC workshops for example). Discourse semantics has been widely investigated in linguistics, pragmatics, and psychology, but there is so far a rather limited set of contributions in the area of computational linguistics. The area which is probably the most active in this area is natural language generation where the needs in term of e.g. planning are central for producing correct utterances and texts. We will not develop discourse analysis technology here, but focus on those linguistics elements, which are crucial for answering questions.

Some Parameters of Discourse Analysis

When processing a text a number of strategies can be deployed depending on the target objectives. Let us briefly review here the most relevant parameters worth considering in our framework.

The first parameter is *granularity*, which characterizes the accuracy with which the discourse analysis needs to be carried out. Depending on the linguistic aspects that need to be considered, granularity can be adjusted, allowing the analysis to focus on the most relevant discourse or informational aspects at stake. Zoom effects can then be produced on text fragments. A higher granularity (a more fine-grained analysis) involves more linguistic complexity, higher error risks, and lower analysis performances by a computer.

The second parameter is *density*. It is associated with granularity: given a certain level of granularity, it consists in identifying those conceptual elements that need to be kept (and tagged). Density may also operate on complex conceptual units (e.g. arguments) with the aim of selecting only those elements, which are relevant for the problem at stake. For example, the illocutionary force of arguments could be ignored.

A third parameter is *differentiation*. It allows for the characterization and the representation of the articulation(s) between two or more discourse structures. Several factors need to be considered at this level such as the contiguous-discontinuous character of the discourse units considered.

The Rhetorical Structure (RST)

There is a very large and rich literature on rhetorical structures, where their conceptual roles and functions when understanding a text are investigated. The pragmatic effect(s) and the linguistic structure of these relations are also central issues, which need to be developed to design an accurate and expressive language-processing model of discourse semantics.

The notion of rhetorical structure is a very old notion. It received its contemporary formulation in a foundational article by Mann et al. (1988). The goal of rhetorical structure is to provide an as comprehensive as possible semantic structure to any kind of text, postulated to be composed of a network of discourse units connected by means of rhetorical relations. These relations are essential to establish the coherence of a text and to access to its informational contents. Basically, rhetorical structures establish conceptual relations between minimal discourse units (sometimes called Elementary Discourse Units, EDUs). Mann et al. (1988) introduce a basic set of 23 relations, among which: *justification, elaboration, goal, motivation*, etc. These are far from being comprehensive: we now observe a proliferation of rhetorical relations, up to 200, with more or less clear definitions and possible overlaps. Nevertheless, the initial relations are the most frequent and may be identified in most cases on the basis of linguistic clues, but this is not an inherent property (Saito, et al., 2006).

A rhetorical relation may be established between two discourse segments: the central segment is called the kernel, while the second segment is the satellite. For example, in the case of the reformulation relation, the kernel is the original formulation while the satellite is the reformation. Some relations have kernel to kernel relations or may be multi-nucleus. Rhetorical relations may be embedded.

Rhetorical structures are used in a number of applications, directly or indirectly. Applications include evaluating text coherence, the study of clause combinations and planning more generally in natural language generation (McKeown, 1985), the development of strategies in text summarization and text indexing. A detailed study of the identification of 7 major relations is reported in Kosseim et al. (1994). Within the framework of procedures, for answering how-to questions, Van der Linden (1993) has identified a number of criteria that influence the grammatical form of rhetorical relations. Responding to procedural, causal and opinion questions require the identification of several rhetorical relations, for example the identification of the various argumentation structures are central in opinion questions.

The Causal Structure

To answer *why* questions, it is clear that it is crucial to be able to identify causal structures in texts and, most of the time, causal chains. The notion of causality (e.g. Talmy, 2001) has been very much investigated both from the empirical and formal points of view. This notion overlaps with a number of related phenomena, such as explanation, goal expression, argumentation, and temporal structure. Causal chains, leading to consequences, may be very complex; they may also not follow each other in texts. They may also contain presuppositions and implicit elements and may be associated with conditions, propositional attitudes, etc. Causality has been characterized by means of dedicated connectors: *because, therefore*, etc., which also have a strong argumentative flavor. Causality can also be characterized by verbs of 'consequence' or 'entailment,' such as *provoke, entail, favor, create*, etc. It can also be characterized by a number of metaphorical constructions.

Looking at verbs in more detail, which are the most clear marks of causality, we can distinguish four major types: (1) implicative verbs: *entail, imply, induce, allow*, each of them with a specific connotation, (2) effect verbs, which can induce positive effects: *improve, reinforce, extend, corroborate*, or negative: *deteriorate, weaken, reduce*; also with numerous metaphorical uses, (3) verbs supporting a cause: *contribute, prevent, risk*, etc., and (4) instrument causes constructed from a verb combined with an instrument.

On a conceptual level, the very extensive work realized by Talmy (2001) outlines various types of causal forms and related structures of much interest in question answering, e.g. direct causality, instrumental causality, continuous forms of causality, indirect causality (e.g. facilitation), causative

of resulting event, causative agent with expected result, serial causative chain, co-extension of causative event. The relations between temporal structure and causality are also explored in great depth. Temporal succession or concomitance of events indeed trigger a kind of implicative view of these events. All these factors may have an influence on the way the response is found and on the form of the answer.

Argumentation Structures

A number of texts contain arguments (Walton, et al., 2008) for or against a certain controversial fact; this is in particular the case of news documents, blogs, etc. Arguments care also frequent in procedural and didactic texts, with a more restricted form. An argument applies to a fact or to an event and in general either support or attack it with more or less strength. It often has the 'surface' form of causal structures: '*I like this product because it is cheap.*' Argument analysis is particularly developed in philosophy, didactics, cognitive science, and artificial intelligence. It is emerging in computational linguistics circles, where it is of much interest e.g. for opinion analysis and support. Arguments indeed make explicit why people like, dislike, agree with or disagree with a certain fact or event.

Argument analysis is therefore central for responding to opinion questions. Collecting warnings and advice about a certain task in procedural documents is also of much interest in order to be able to produce hints for users willing to perform a certain task. A question such as: '*How to use a parquetry grinder ?*' expects a set of advice and warnings related to the use of this tool.

Arguments are basically rhetorical structures. Their specific forms make their recognition relatively feasible in a number of types of texts. An example is given below in the next section devoted to <TextCoop>. However, there remain major difficulties for answering opinion questions. For example, given a statement (e.g. '*How *do the Europeans feel about vaccine against H1N1?'*) one difficulty is to identify in various texts those arguments which are indeed related to this statement. Formulations are seldom direct and relatedness metrics must often be used. This usually involves lexical and textual inference, if not domain knowledge. For example, in the case of a response such as: '*Dr. X said that adjuvant of the vaccine may entail some allergy problems.*' it is necessary to know that a vaccine is diluted into an adjuvant and that this adjuvant is also injected into the patient, therefore problems related to the adjuvant entail a negative opinion on the vaccine as a whole.

The Language of Explanation

Explanation and its relations to language is a vast area of investigation (Pollock, 1974; Keil, 2000; Wright, 2004). It is of much interest for producing cooperative answers to questions, adding relevant information to the answer. Explanation covers a subset of rhetorical relations (e.g. elaboration, reformulation, illustration) and serves a specific purpose. Explanation analysis is quite well developed in didactics. In artificial intelligence, it is often centered on the notion of argumentation, negotiation, and planning issues. Two decades ago, explanations were used to produce natural language outputs to make more explicit the proofs realized by experts systems. In that case, language generation was in general carried out from predefined templates associated with each form of proof the expert system could carry out. Quite interesting principles have emerged from this research in terms of planning and granularity of 'explanations.' Explanation analysis and production is an open issue in language processing circles and has been the focus of little attention in spite of its usefulness. Let us note the series of workshops *Exact* that address some useful aspects.

In ergonomy and cognitive science (Pollock, 1974; Wright, 2004), the ability for humans to integrate explanations about a task (possibly via a guidance system) when they perform that task is measured as such and in relation with the document properties (typography, pictures). Finally, explanation is a field, which is investigated in pragmatics (e.g. cooperative principles, dialogue principles) and in philosophy (e.g. rationality and explanation, phenomenology of explanation, causality, etc.) (Keil, et al., 2000). These investigations may motivate and support more applied investigations in language processing circles, however, they turn out to be of little immediate and practical use as they are studied in these areas.

Explanations are in general structured with the aim of reaching a goal (e.g. making sure that someone has all the details to perform a given task or to understand a certain position or attitude). Explanations are often associated with a kind of instructional style, which ranges from injunctive to advice-like forms. Procedures of various kinds (social recommendations, as well as DIY, maintenance procedures, health, didactic texts) form an excellent source of corpus to observe how explanations are constructed, linguistically realized and which communicative goals they serve. Indeed, in procedures, style is often quite straightforward, procedures being essentially oriented towards action: there must be little space for inferences that may lead to misinterpretations, hence the need for explanations.

Explanations occur also in goal-driven but non-procedural contexts, for example, as a means to justify a decision in legal reasoning, or as a way to explain the reasons of an accident in accident reports. Explanation may also be associated with various pragmatic effects (irony, emphasis, dramatization, etc.) for example in political discourse. In each case, explanation has a goal-oriented structure.

Explanation analysis and production is essential in opinion analysis to make more explicit how a certain opinion is supported; it is also essential in question answering when the response, which is produced, is not the direct response: the user must then understand why the response provided is appropriate. Finally, it is central in a number of types of dialogues, clarification situations, and persuasion strategies.

Explanations are related to the notion of *explanation function* that specifies the communicative goals of explanations. Explanation functions are abstract constructs which are realized in language via explanation schemes of various sorts based on rhetorical structures, in particular elaboration, illustration, reformulation, result, contrast, analogy, evidence, encouragement, hint, and evaluation. An important feature of explanation is that it is transcategorial: it includes syntactic and lexical semantics factors, as well as typographic and pragmatic factors.

An example of an extensive explanation structure, in readable form, from didactics, is the following in Box 1, where annotated brackets follow the usual notation of syntactic analysis:

Discourse Frames

Discourse frames are an important issue in question answering. By discourse frames, we mean structures, often placed at the beginning of sections or paragraphs, that introduce various forms of constraints on the validity of the statements contained in that section or paragraph. For example:

In 1969, saving loans were not so much appreciated by ...

In X's PhD dissertation, it is shown that Morgan's law is...

Discourse frames give information related to a certain period or view, which may be different at another period or from another viewpoint. In a number of situations, the constraint on the validity of a discourse segment has scope over a number of informational elements. It is therefore often not contiguous to the information retrieved and requires a contextual analysis to avoid returning out of context or outdated information.

The same situation occurs with propositional attitudes (*think, assume, believe*, etc.), attitudes related to enunciation (*report, confirm, assume,* etc.) and modal attitudes (*possible, probable*) which must be taken into account to evaluate the validity and scope of a statement.

Processing Discourse Structures for Answering Questions

Answering questions can be decomposed into three major steps: question analysis and representation, question-document matching and response production. Question analysis has been widely addressed in the literature and will not be treated here. Response production is not yet very

Box 1.

[procedure [purpose Writing a paper: [elaboration Read light sources, then thorough]]
[assumption/circumstance Assuming you've been given a topic,]
[circumstance When you conduct research], move from light to thorough resources [purpose to make sure you're moving in the right direction].
Begin by doing searches on the Internet about your topic [purpose to familiarize yourself with the basic issues;]
    [temporal-sequence then] move to more thorough research on the Academic Databases;
    [temporal-sequence finally], probe the depths of the issue by burying yourself in the library.
    [warning Make sure that despite beginning on the Internet, you don't simply end there.
        [elaboration A research paper using only Internet sources is a weak paper,
            [consequence which puts you at a disadvantage...]]]
While the Internet should never be your only source of information, [contrast it would be ridiculous not to utilize its vast sources of information.
        [advice You should use the Internet to acquaint yourself with the topic more
            before you dig into more academic texts.]]]

much developed in question answering: we will basically consider the principles given above in section 1 for the future steps. Question-document matching is a complex process where the contents of the question must be made flexible enough so that it can match with different discourse forms that correspond to the response (via paraphrases, lexical inference, partial representations, etc.). This matching process has been investigated in depth for answering factoid questions. For the type of questions discussed here, both question-document matching and response elaboration require a relatively in-depth discourse analysis.

The last part of this chapter introduces <TextCoop>, a platform developed for textual semantics analysis which is used for answering complex questions, in particular 'how-to' and 'opinion' questions. The literature abounds in systems and platforms that can recognize and tag text fragments for the purpose of information retrieval and answering questions. However, the language structures that these platforms can recognize turn out to be relatively limited w.r.t. the needs for answering complex questions. Among several platforms, let us mention the LinguaStream platform, which integrates a large number of processing facilities, and the GATE platform, which is probably the most developed and elaborated one for document analysis. It is involved in a large number of projects over a large number of languages; however, little is said about its application to discourse analysis.

<TextCoop> Objectives and Approach

<TextCoop> is an environment for text semantics analysis. In a first experimental stage, it has been dedicated to procedure processing for testing and evaluation (Delpech, et al., 2008). This includes the recognition of quite a large number of diverse structures: titles, instructions, pre-requisites, warnings, advice, illustrations, etc. Procedures also include a number of forms of explanations.

The major features of <TextCoop> are:

- A formalism specifically designed for discourse structure analysis, based on patterns (implemented by means of rules), that recognizes structures and tags them appropriately, a distinction is made between the pattern and the resulting tagged structure,
- A modular view of the specification of discourse structure patterns, with the identification of potential conflicts or overlaps between patterns,
- A set of resources described in modules: local structure parsers and dedicated lexical resources, and an architecture for linguistic resources use and deployment,
- A constraint-based approach for the management of patterns,
- Linking patterns and strategies to bind annotated structures into larger units, this is in particular crucial to bind kernels and satellites for rhetorical relations,
- The preservation of already existing tags and their structure, in particular when dealing with semi-structured documents,
- An engine, at the moment realized in Prolog with some constraint solving features, based on an extension of Definite Clause Grammars. The use of Prolog allows for easy connections with reasoning mechanisms and advanced forms of knowledge representation.

The formalism of a rule in <TextCoop> is the following:

1. **Left-hand part:** structure identifier (e.g. illustration),
2. **Right-hand part:** a finite sequence of the following symbols:
   - Terminal strings of words or any other kind of element such as html or XML tags, or icons, since typography is taken into account.
   - Non-terminal symbols (with the particular case of pre-terminal symbols

to structure lexical knowledge), these symbols refer to various linguistic or ad hoc structures as observed in corpora.

○ Gaps: which are symbols that stand for a finite sequence of words of no present interest. Gaps allow to skip words, they may include the specification of symbols which must not be skipped. If such a symbol is found before reaching the end of the gap, the gap fails.

○ Insertion points, which indicate where to insert tags related to the recognition of the discourse structure at stake. These may be inserted anywhere in the recognized structure, they may be realized via some computations specified in the insertion point.

Symbols may be specified as being optional, or as having multiple occurrences, as in any regular expressions. Gaps are not allowed to start or end a pattern since their boundaries are not explicit. Finally, although this is possible, it is not recommended to have an optional symbol between two gaps.

As an illustration, consider the following two short examples:

Pattern for advice (tags are given explicitly here for the sake of readability), with the left and right-hand parts of the rule and the resulting tagged expression in Box 2"

The Art of Writing Rules for the Recognition of Discourse Structures

Recognizing discourse structures is in general more difficult than recognizing sentence structures since the complexity and the size in terms of number of words of those structures is much higher. The difficulty is threefold: (1) identifying a structure, in general from a number of triggers (e.g. specialized terms), (2) identifying the boundaries of the structure (from markers or based on well-formedness principles), and (3) binding kernels with appropriate satellites.

Although discourse structure recognition can be realized a priori via learning algorithms from large sets of previously annotated texts, we believe that this approach leads to several forms of imprecision due to the vagueness of discourse structures and their large diversity. We favor in our approach a linguistic analysis from corpora, with a gradual definition of rules and patterns. <TextCoop> has been designed to be an interactive tool: it is possible to update or add rules or patterns and see immediately on a few examples what is recognized and how (which structures are changed and in what way). Therefore, fine-tuning of rules and patterns is relatively straightforward based on a 'see what you get' strategy.

In addition, the <TextCoop> platform includes a number of structured linguistic resources, among which:

- Lexical resources of various kinds: sets of connectors with their type (temporal, causal, concessive, etc.), verbs organized by types (as in WordNet), classes of ad-

Box 2.

Advice → Pronoun, {to be/modal}, {adv}, verb/advice-expression, gap, end-mark.,
    Annotation: <advice> Pronoun, {to be/modal}, <strength ...> {adv}, </strength>
        verb/advice-expression, gap, end-mark </advice>.
as in: *It's better to install a grounding electrode.*
Or *We advise you to use a waterproof box.*

---

verbs (e.g. manner, temporal, etc.). At the moment, resources are available in French and English.

- Local grammars of various kinds, such as the specification of temporal expressions, quantities, instrumental expressions, etc.

These resources come as modules, which can be directly introduced in the rule or pattern specification. They can also be modified, updated, tuned, etc.

<TextCoop> is an open system that allows, via its Java interfaces to introduce a number of add-ons and plug-ins. In terms of performances, on a standard PC, windows XP, an average of 300Mo of input text is processed per hour, with a lexicon and ontology of a few thousand terms and about 25 tagging patterns. Examples are given in Delpech et al. (2008) and Fontan et al. (2008). More details on the uses and performances of the <TextCoop> system will be published shortly (Saint-Dizier, 2011).

5. FUTURE RESEARCH DIRECTIONS AND CONCLUSION

The elements presented here cover a large variety of research challenges related to advanced question answering. We have focused on two areas, which are not so much developed within this framework: developing informative and cooperative answers and using accurate discourse analysis in order to be able to identify well-formed text portions, which are the answer to those questions.

It is clear that these two topics are basically emerging and that they will remain quite challenging for a number of years, in spite of the rapid evolution of the language processing technology. Question-document matching has been much more investigated via a number of competitions. Another open area is the use of knowledge and dedicated

inference patterns to better answer questions, be cooperative or to detect forms of misconceptions, such as false presuppositions.

REFERENCES

Bal, B. K., & Saint-Dizier, P. (2010). Towards building annotated resources for analyzing opinions and argumentation in news editorials. In *Proceedings of LREC*. Malta: ELRA.

Barwise, J., & Cooper, R. (1981). Generalized quantifiers and natural language. *Linguistics and Philosophy*, *4*, 159–219. doi:10.1007/BF00350139

Benamara, F., & Saint-Dizier, P. (2004). Advanced relaxation for cooperative question answering. In Maybury, M. (Ed.), *New Directions in Question Answering*. Cambridge, MA: MIT Press.

Bing, L. (2010). Sentiment Analysis and subjectivity. In *Handbook of Natural Language Processing* (2nd ed.). Boca Raton, FL: CRC Press.

Boguraev, B., & Ando, R. K. (2005). TimeML-Compliant text analysis for temporal reasoning. In *Proceedings of IJCAI 2005*. IJCAI.

Burger, J., et al. (2001). *Issues, tasks and program structures to roadmap research in question & answering (Q&A)*. Retrieved from http://www.inf.ed.ac.uk/teaching/courses/tts/papers/qa_roadmap.pdf

Caminada, M., & Amgoud, L. (2007). On the evaluation of argumentation formalisms. *Artificial Intelligence Journal*, *171*(5-6), 286–310. doi:10.1016/j.artint.2007.02.003

Dale, R., & Reiter, E. (2000). *Building natural language generation systems*. Cambridge, UK: Cambridge University Press.

Delpech, E., & Saint-Dizier, P. (2008). Investigating the structure of procedural texts for answering how-to questions. In *Proceedings of the Language Resources and Evaluation Conference (LREC 2008)*. Marrakech, Morocco: European Language Resources Association (ELRA).

Ferret, O., & Grau, B. (2001). Document selection refinement based on linguistic features for QALC: A question answering system. In *Proceedings of RANLP 2001*. RANLP.

Fontan, L., & Saint-Dizier, P. (2008). Analyzing the explanation structure of procedural texts: Dealing with advices and warnings. In J. Bos (Ed), *International Symposium on Text Semantics (STEP 2008)*. STEP.

Grice, H. (1975). Logic and conversation. In Cole & Morgan (Eds.), *Syntax and Semantics*. New York, NY: Academic Press.

Harabagiu, S. M., Pasca, M., & Maiorano, S. J. (2000). Experiments with open-domain textual question answering. In *Proceedings of COLING-2000*. Saarbruken, Germany: COLING.

Helbig, H. (2005). *Knowledge representation and the semantics of natural language*. Berlin, Germany: Springer-Verlag.

Hermjakob, U. (2001). Parsing and question classification for question answering. In *Proceedings of the Workshop on Question Answering at the Conference ACL-2001*. Toulouse, France: ACL.

Hermjakob, U., Hovy, E., & Chin-Yew, L. (2000). Knowledge-based question answering. In *Proceedings ACL 2002*. ACL.

Katz, B., Felshin, S., Lin, J. J., & Marton, G. (2004). Viewing the web as a virtual database for question answering. M. Maybury (Ed.), *New Directions in Question-Answering*. Cambridge, MA: MIT Press.

Katz, B., Lin, J. J., Stauer, C., & Grimson, W. E. L. (2004). Answering questions about moving objects in videos. In Maybury, M. (Ed.), *New Directions in Question-Answering*. Cambridge, MA: MIT Press.

Kearsley, G. P. (1976). Questions and question asking in verbal discourse: A cross-disciplinary review. *Journal of Psycholinguistic Research*, 12.

Keil, F. C., & Wilson, R. A. (2000). *Explanation and cognition*. Cambridge, MA: Bradford Book.

Khoo, C. S. G., Chan, S., & Niu, Y. (2000). Extracting causal knowledge from a medical database using graphical patterns. In *Proceedings of ACL 2000*. ACL.

Kosseim, L., & Lapalme, G. (2000). Choosing rhetorical structures to plan instructional texts. In *Computational Intelligence*. Boston, MA: Blackwell. doi:10.1111/0824-7935.00118

Kupic, J. (1993). MURAX: A robust linguistic approach for question answering using an online encyclopedia. In *Proceedings of the 16th Annual International ACM SIGIR, Conference on Research and Development in Information Retrieval*, (pp. 181-190). ACM.

Kwok, C., Etzioni, O., & Weld, D. S. (2001). Scaling question answering to the web. *ACM Transactions on Information Systems, 19*(3). Girju, R., & Moldovan, D. I. (2002). Text mining for causal relations. In *Proceedings of FLAIRS Conference*. FLAIRS.

Lehnert, W. (1978). *The process of question answering*. Hillsdale, NJ: Lawrence Erlbaum Associates.

Li, X., & Roth, D. (2002). Learning question classifier. In *Proceedings of 19th International Conference on Computational Linguistics (ACL)*. ACL.

Lim, N., Saint-Dizier, P., & Roxas, R. (2009). Some challenges in the design of comparative and evaluative question answering systems. In *Proceedings of the ACL-KRAQ 2009 Workshop.* Singapore: ACL.

Mann, W., & Thompson, S. (1988). Rhetorical structure theory: Towards a functional theory of text organization. *Text, 8*(3). doi:10.1515/text.1.1988.8.3.243

Marcu, D. (2000). *The theory and practice of discourse parsing and summarization.* Cambridge, MA: MIT Press.

Maybury, M. T. (Ed.). (2004). *New directions in question answering.* Cambridge, MA: MIT Press.

McKeown, K. (1985). *Text generation: Using discourse strategies and focus constraints to generate natural language text.* Cambridge, UK: Cambridge University Press. doi:10.1017/CBO9780511620751

McNally, L., & Boleda, G. (2004). Relational adjectives as properties of kinds. *Empirical Issues in Formal Syntax and Semantics, 5,* 179–196.

Minqing, H., & Bing, L. (2004). Mining and summarizing customer reviews. In *Proceedings of the ACM SIGKDD International Conference on Knowledge Discovery & Data Mining.* Seattle, WA: ACM Press.

Moldovan, D., Harabagiu, S., Pasca, M., Milhalcea, R., & Goodrum, R. ... Rus, V. (1999). LASSO: A tool for surfing the answer net. In *Proceedings of ACL.* ACL.

Moriceau, V. (2006). Generating intelligent numerical answers in a question-answering system. In *Proceedings of the 4th International Natural Language Generation Conference (INLG).* Sydney, Australia: INLG.

Moschitti, A., Morarescu, P., & Harabagiu, S. M. (2003). Open domain information extraction via automatic semantic labeling. In *Proceedings FLAIRS Conference.* FLAIRS.

Moschitti, A., & Quarteroni, S. (2010). Linguistic kernels for answer re-ranking in question answering systems. *Information Processing & Management, 47*(6), 825–842. doi:10.1016/j.ipm.2010.06.002

Olney, A., Person, N., Louwerse, M., & Graesser, A. (2002). I-MINDS: A conversational tutoring environment. In *Proceedings of the ACL-02 Demonstration Session,* (pp. 108-109). Philadelphia, PA: Association for Computational Linguistics.

Otero, J., Caldeira, H., & Gomes, C. J. (2004). The influence of the length of causal chains on question asking and on the comprehensibility of scientific texts. *Journal of Contemporary Educational Psychology, 29*(1). doi:10.1016/S0361-476X(03)00018-3

Pasca, M., & Alfonseca, E. (2009). Web-derived resources for web information retrieval: From conceptual hierarchies to attribute hierarchies. [SIGIR.]. *Proceedings of SIGIR, 2009,* 596–603.

Pechsiri, C., Sroison, P., & Janviriyasopa, U. (2008). Know-why extraction from textual data. In *Proceedings of KRAQ 2008 Workshop.* Manchester, UK: COLING.

Pollock, J. L. (1974). *Knowledge and justification.* Princeton, NJ: Princeton University Press.

Quarteroni, S. (2008). Personalized, interactive question answering on the web. In *Proceedings of KRAQ 2008.* Manchester, UK: COLING.

Quarteroni, S. (2010). Personalized question answering. *Traitement Automatique des Langues, 51*(1).

Ravi, S., & Pasca, M. (2008). Using structured text for large-scale attribute extraction. In *Proceedings of CIKM*. CIKM.

Reiter, E., & Dale, R. (1997). Building applied natural language generation systems. *Journal of Natural Language Engineering, 3*(1). doi:10.1017/S1351324997001502

Rilo, E., & Lehnert, W. (1994). Information extraction as a basis for high-precision text classification. *ACM Transactions on Information Systems, 12*(3), 296–333. doi:10.1145/183422.183428

Saaba, A., & Sawamura, H. (2008). Argument mining using highly structured argument repertoire. In *Proceedings EDM 2008*. Niigata, Japan: EDM.

Saito, M., Yamamoto, K., & Sekine, S. (2006). Using phrasal patterns to identify discourse relations. In *Proceedings ACL 2006*. ACL.

Talmy, L. (2001). *Towards a cognitive semantics*. Cambridge, MA: MIT Press.

Van der Linden, K. (1993). *Speaking of actions choosing rhetorical status and grammatical form in instructional text generation*. (PhD Thesis). University of Colorado. Boulder, CO.

Vasquez-Reyez, S., & Black, W. (2008). Evaluating causal questions for question answering. In *Proceedings ENC 2008*. Mexico City, Mexico: ENC. Shen, D., & Lapata, M. (2007). Using semantic roles to improve question answering. In *Proceedings of EMNLP-CoNLL*. EMNLP-CoNLL.

Voorhees, E. M. (2001). The TREC question answering track *natural language engineering*. Cambridge, UK: Cambridge University Press.

Walton, D., Reed, C., & Macagno, F. (2008). *Argumentation schemes*. Cambridge, UK: Cambridge University Press. doi:10.1017/CBO9780511802034

Wilson, D., & Sperber, D. (1981). On Grice's theory of conversation. In Werth, P. (Ed.), *Conversation and Discourse*. New York, NY: St. Martin's Press.

Woodward, J. (2003). *Making things happen: A theory of causal explanation*. Oxford, UK: Oxford University Press.

Wright, von G. H. (2004). *Explanation and understanding*. Ithaca, NY: Cornell University Press.

ADDITIONAL READING

Appelt, D. E. (1985). *Planning English sentences*. Cambridge, UK: Cambridge University Press. doi:10.1017/CBO9780511624575

Brachman, R., & Levesque, H. (2004). *Knowledge representation and reasoning*. San Francisco, CA: Morgan Kaufman.

Burger, J., Cardie, C., Chaudhri, V., Gaizauskas, R., Harabagiu, S., & Israel, D. … Weishedel, R. (2001). *Issues, tasks and program structures to roadmap research in question answering (QA)*. Retrieved from http://www.inf.ed.ac.uk/teaching/courses/tts/papers/qa_roadmap.pdf

Davis, S. (1991). *Pragmatics: A reader*. Oxford, UK: Oxford University Press.

Helbig, H. (2005). *Knowledge representation and the semantics of natural language*. Berlin, Germany: Springer-Verlag.

Hirschman, L., & Gaizauskas, R. (2001). Natural language question answering: The view from here. *Natural Language Engineering, 7*(4). doi:10.1017/S1351324901002807

Hovy, E. (1988). *Generating natural language under pragmatic constraints*. Hillsdale, NJ: Lawrence Erlbaum.

Lakoff, G. (1987). *Women, fire, and dangerous things: What categories reveal about the mind.* Chicago, IL: University of Chicago Press.

Lenat, D., & Guha, R. V. (1989). *Building large knowledge-based systems.* Reading, MA: Addison-Wesley.

Maybury, M. T. (Ed.). (2004). *New directions in question answering.* Cambridge, MA: MIT Press.

Reiter, E., & Dale, R. (1997). Building applied natural language generation systems. *Journal of Natural Language Engineering, 3*(1). doi:10.1017/S1351324997001502

Schiffrin, D. (1987). *Discourse markers.* Cambridge, UK: Cambridge University Press. doi:10.1017/CBO9780511611841

Searle, J. (1999). *Mind, language and society.* New York, NY: Basic Books.

Voorhees, E. M. (2001). The TREC question answering track *natural language engineering.* Cambridge, UK: Cambridge University Press.

KEY TERMS AND DEFINITIONS

Explanation: Discourse form aiming at clarifying a statement via various means such as illustration, definition, reformulation, or elaboration.

Focus: Indicates, in question answering, the text portion which is the most prominent. Focus is widely used in language analysis with dedicated definitions.

Prolog: Logic-based programming language, first implementation developed in 1972 at Marseille, based on Horn clause logic. Mainly designed for language processing and automatic demonstration. One of the simplest grammar formalism using prolog are Definite Clause Grammars (DCGs).

Rhetorical Relation: Discourse level relation that connects two discourse units.

Chapter 7
Interactive Question Answering

Natalia Konstantinova
University of Wolverhampton, UK

Constantin Orasan
University of Wolverhampton, UK

ABSTRACT

The increasing amount of information available online has led to the development of technologies that help to deal with it. One of them is Interactive Question Answering (IQA), a research field that has emerged at the intersection of question answering and dialogue systems, and which allows users to find the answers to questions in an interactive way. During the answering process, the automatic system can initiate a dialogue with the user in order to clarify missing or ambiguous information, or suggest further topics for discussion. This chapter presents the state-of-the-art in the field of interactive question answering. Given that IQA inherits a lot of features from dialogue systems and question answering, these fields are also briefly presented. Analysis of the existing systems reveals that in general IQA systems rely on a scaled-down version of a dialogue system, sometimes built on top of question answering systems. Evaluation of IQA is also discussed, showing that it combines evaluation techniques from question answering and dialogue systems.

INTRODUCTION

The development of the Internet and its increased availability led to a rapid growth of information available. As a result, modern people suffer from information overload and find it difficult to locate a necessary piece of information when they need it or keep track of what is new on a topic. Research carried out in fields of computational linguistics such as information retrieval, information extraction, automatic summarization or question answering tries to address this problem by proposing methods that can help people deal with this information overload. This chapter presents an overview of the state-of-the-art in Interactive Question Answering (IQA), one of the fields that can help users find a nugget of information when they need it.

Interactive Question Answering (IQA) is a research field that emerged at the intersection of question answering and dialogue systems (see the next two sections for more details about these two fields). IQA inherits from Question Answering (QA) the features that allow users to ask questions

DOI: 10.4018/978-1-4666-2169-5.ch007

in natural language and, where possible, locate the actual answer to the question. The interactive aspect of the field comes from the fact that a dialogue can be initiated with a user in cases where there are too many or too few answers, or there is some ambiguity in the request. The IQA systems also allow users to ask additional questions if the obtained result is not really what they are looking for or in cases where they need more information. For this reason, Webb and Webber (2009) define IQA as a *"process where the user is a continual part of the information loop."*

Despite the wide variations in the ways different IQA systems are implemented, they generally rely on a scaled-down version of a dialogue system or at least on some components from such systems. For this reason, the chapter will start with a description of the characteristics of human dialogues and the basic concepts behind dialogue systems. Given the importance of question answering systems in the context of IQA, a brief introduction to question answering is also included focusing on the concepts used in this chapter. For more details about question answering and the latest advances in the field, the reader is invited to consult (Harabagiu & Moldovan, 2003; Webber & Webb, 2010). The longest part of the chapter is dedicated to what IQA is, including the most important approaches used by the IQA systems, followed by the challenges that need to be faced when such systems are evaluated. The chapter finishes with a description of some large projects, which developed and integrated interactive question answering features. Further readings and links to relevant resources are also provided.

DIALOGUE SYSTEMS

The term *dialogue system* is widely used nowadays to refer to automatic systems involving coherent dialogue with a human interlocutor. The editors of the Journal of Dialogue Systems define a dialogue system as:

A computational device or agent that (a) engages in interaction with other human and/or computer participant(s); (b) uses human language in some form such as speech, text, or sign; and (c) typically engages in such interaction across multiple turns or sentences (http://www.jods.org/).

This definition highlights several important aspects of such systems. A dialogue system always has a user, who interacts with the system for a specific goal such as completing some tasks. The interaction involves a conversation in human language between two or more participants and can take several turns. The fact that human language is used in the interaction differentiates the field from other fields such as database access using computer languages (such as SQL) or interaction between software agents that communicate using XML or some other standard computer formats.

Early versions of dialogue systems were referred to as *chatterbots* or *chatbots* (Mauldin, 1994) indicating their rather simple goal. The initial role of these systems was to fool users into thinking they were communicating with humans in an attempt to replicate the Turing test. However, as the field progressed, the interest in dialogue systems shifted from pure academic research to commercial applications of the technology. Some dialogue systems, referred to as *conversational agents* by some researchers (Lester, Branting, & Mott, 2004; Jurafsky & Martin, 2009), are used by companies in fields such as customer service, helpdesks, website navigation, guided selling and technical support. This is thanks to the fact that they offer a natural way of interacting with a computer, meaning that usually dialogue system users do not need any special training as the systems are easy to use and intuitive.

Characteristics of Human Dialogue

Human-to-human conversation is a difficult activity involving a lot of different processes including understanding of natural language and generation of utterances. When building a dialogue system the following characteristics of human dialogue need to be addressed: *turn-taking* (order in which interlocutors participate in the conversation), *grounding* (mutual background of interlocutors), *conversational structure* (structure of the usual dialogue), and *initiative* (who takes the leading role in the conversation) (Jurafsky & Martin, 2009). All these properties of dialogues are studied by "conversational analysis" (Sacks, Schegloff, & Jefferson, 1974), a research field which lies at the confluence of linguistics and sociology. Each of these aspects is presented in more detail in the reminder of this section.

Turn taking defines the moment the next participant needs to start talking and take their turn. Usually humans can understand easily when their turn to talk is, but for dialogue systems, turn taking can be a problem. The most obvious is to assume that people start talking when silence begins, but studies showed the gap in the turns is extremely small and humans can understand when it is their turn, even before the previous speaker stops talking (Jurafsky & Martin, 2009, p. 814). For this reason, an understanding of "what" is being said is crucial for predicting when the next person needs to talk. Sacks, Schegloff, and Jefferson (1974) state that there are some rules of turn taking, giving clues about who is going to speak next and when. Therefore, despite the challenges of taking into account turn taking in dialogue systems, it is a very important aspect as it determines how natural a system sounds.

Grounding is the second characteristic that should be dealt with when building dialogue systems. In order to have successful communication, people should have some information that they use as a background for interpreting their interlocutor's utterances and intentions. This kind of information is called "common ground" (Stalnaker, 1978). Starting with this common ground, participants incrementally construct a "discourse model" by adding small bits of information to produce a coherent dialogue (Ramsay, 2003). Clark and

Schaefer (1989) study this process and confirm that participants presuppose certain information and in the course of a discourse, they try to add it to the common ground. However, participants in a conversation have their own presuppositions and it is really important to make sure that they understand each other. This is sometimes signaled by interlocutors by the use of phrases such as "I see," "uhuh," or by asking additional questions. All this guarantees that the resulting dialogue is meaningful and no one is lost at some point or left with only partial understanding of the conversation.

Another characteristic of any conversation is its specific structure, i.e. "conversational structure." It involves "what" everyone is meant to say, i.e. content of the turn, and also the roles of each speaker and what information he/she should communicate. Studies showed that people have implicit knowledge of the conversational structure and can easily distinguish between naturally occurring conversations and artificially constructed ones (Goldthwaite, 1997). Humans have prior knowledge about the structure of dialogues and know how to use it for successful communication. In many cases, the structure of conversation is predefined by the situation and dictates the content, e.g. it is common to start a conversation with greetings and not a farewell (Clark & Schaefer, 1989). Therefore, if the aim of the interlocutors is to communicate successfully they should follow all these rules and take into account conversational structure.

Another important characteristic of the dialogue is the notion of initiative, which indicates who has control over the conversation and takes the conversational lead (Walker, et al., 1990). We are usually engaged in "mixed-initiative" dialogues, where the initiative passes back and forth between the discourse participants. However, there are situations when the dialogue can be single-initiative, e.g. interrogation by the police or in a courtroom.

This section has briefly presented the characteristics of human dialogues. They are very important for the development of dialogue systems that sound natural, and therefore should be taken into consideration when IQA systems are being developed.

The Architecture of Dialogue Systems

The first dialogue systems, the chatterbots, had a very simple architecture and relied only on pattern matching and the presence of particular keywords in human utterances to produce an output. The first few turns of a conversation with a chatterbot may seem fine, but usually it quickly degrades into nonsense. For this reason, current dialogue systems rely on more complex processing and have several modules. The structure of dialogue systems varies a lot from one system to another, but Jurafsky and Martin (2009) consider that they usually consist of 5 main components: *speech recognition, natural language understanding, dialogue management, natural language generation* and *speech synthesis*, which interact as shown in Figure 1. Some of them are optional and can be absent in some systems. For example, the speech recognition and speech synthesis modules can be omitted due to the additional challenges they pose, despite offering a more natural way of interacting

with the system. With the exception of speech recognition and speech synthesis modules, each of the other components is briefly discussed in the remainder of this section.

Natural Language Understanding Module

The aim of the Natural Language Understanding (NLU) module is to produce a semantic representation appropriate for a dialogue task. Where a speech recognition module is used, it is usually referred to as *Spoken Language Understanding* (SLU) (Mori, et al., 2008). There are two main approaches for developing such modules, depending on the level of complexity of the dialogue system involved and the available resources: handcrafted and data-driven (Ginzburg & Fernandez, 2010).

In order to work, the NLU module relies on a plethora of information sources including world knowledge, context, and discourse information. Where the input of the NLU module comes from a speech recognizer, additional information, such as prosodic features, is used to improve the processing. For example, a partial name detector maps a partial name to its full variant and the edit region detection algorithm is responsible for tracking

Figure 1. Main components

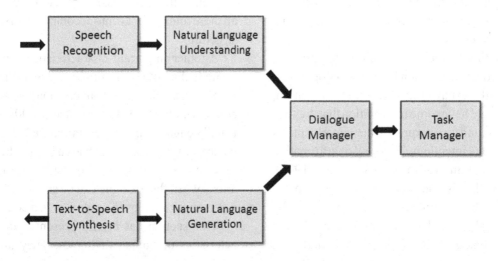

and removing hesitations, repetitions and repair regions. In the CHAT system (Varges, Weng, & Pon-Barry, 2007) several pre-processing components such as edit region detection algorithm, a partial name identifier, a domain-specific shallow semantic parser and a domain-general deep structural parser are included. These modules help the system to deal with irregularities in the spoken input and possible mistakes of the speech recognizer.

Dialogue Management Component

The Dialogue Manager (DM) is one of the most important components of the dialogue system as it *coordinates the activity of several subcomponents in a dialogue system and its main goal is to maintain a representation of the current state of the ongoing dialogue* (Bui, 2006). Traum and Larsson (2003) identify the main tasks of the DM as:

- Updating the dialogue context on the basis of interpreted communication;
- Providing context-dependent expectations for interpretation of observed signals as communicative behavior;
- Interfacing with task/domain processing (e.g., database, planner, execution module, other back-end system), to coordinate dialogue and non-dialogue behavior and reasoning; and
- Deciding what content to express next and when to express it.

They also point out that in many systems some of these functions are delegated to other components of the system.

The dialogue manager has to interpret speech acts, carry out problem-solving actions, formulate responses and in general maintain the system's idea of the state of the discourse (Dale, Moisi, & Somers, 2000). Therefore, the dialogue manager controls the whole architecture and structure of the dialogue and also serves as an interlink between the NLU and NLG components, as it takes information from the former, transforms and passes it to the latter.

Many different ways to classify dialogue managers can be found in the literature. Jurafsky and Martin (2009) consider there are 4 main types of dialogue management architectures: finite-state DM, frame/form based DM, information-state DM and plan-based DM. Bui (2006) combines finite-state and frame-based approaches in one group, and introduces another group—collaborative agent-based approach. Discussion about each of these types is beyond the scope of this chapter, but readers who would like to find out more should consult Jurafsky and Martin (2009), Bui (2006), and Ginzburg and Fernandez (2010).

Natural Language Generation Component

The Natural Language Generation (NLG) component is responsible for automatically creating natural language on the basis of a non-linguistic information representation received. Generally the NLG process consists of three stages: *document planning, microplanning*, and *surface realization* (Reiter & Dale, 2000). Document planning includes content determination (converting the raw system input to the specific kind of data objects) and document structuring/discourse planning (ordering the information to be expressed and determining the structure of the output text). The microplanning stage consists of lexicalization (choosing the right words to express the input information), aggregation (deciding which information to put in one sentence), and referring expression generation. The last stage, surface realization, involves linguistic realization (creating grammatical sentences) and structure realization (converting the output text into some required external format).

In a dialogue system, the input for the NLG module is the output of the dialogue manager. This means the dialogue manager performs the generation tasks of content determination and discourse planning. Thus the responsibility of the NLG module is restricted to the formulation of the system utterances, i.e., the decision of "how to say it." Usually dialogue systems operate in a very restricted domain, so the microplanning stage becomes quite trivial. Therefore, linguistic realization becomes the principal function of the NLG module in terms of dialogue systems and it can be performed relatively easily in a restricted domain. As a result, in many dialogue systems, there is no need for a fully-fledged language generation module and instead a simplified version which relies on predefined templates can be used. The drawback of this approach is that sometimes, the dialogue produced can sound not natural but machine-like. To address this problem, pronouns and paraphrases are used to introduce some variation in the answers from the system.

QUESTION ANSWERING

Question answering is defined as:

An interactive process that encompasses understanding a user's information need, typically expressed in a natural language query; retrieving relevant documents, data, or knowledge from selected sources; extracting, qualifying and prioritizing available answers from these sources; and presenting and explaining responses in an effective manner (Maybury, 2004).

Despite being defined as an interactive process, most of the existing QA systems limit this interaction to giving the user the possibility of asking one question and providing one or several answers without the possibility of any further communication. The existing research has focused mainly on *factoid question answering* where the user asks one question and the answer is a simple fact, which is usually a named entity like a person, organization or location. Systems that answer other types of questions, such as definition questions

(Blair-Goldensohn, et al., 2004), *why* questions (Verberne, et al., 2010), and complex questions (Bilotti & Nyberg, 2006) were also investigated. This section presents only a brief introduction to QA in order to facilitate the understanding of the rest of the article. A comprehensive description of the QA field can be found in Harabagiu and Moldovan (2003) and Webber and Webb (2010).

A standard QA system consists of a pipeline of three modules: *question processor*, *document processor,* and *answer extractor* (Harabagiu & Moldovan, 2003). The role of the question processor is to use various NLP techniques to interpret the question. This interpretation normally involves determining the semantic category of the answer (e.g. person, organization, location, etc.) and extracting sets of keywords from the question in order to produce a list of query terms for the document-processing module. Advanced question processors try to build a more elaborate interpretation of the question, by adding semantic information to these terms and identifying syntactic relations between them. To a certain extent, the question processor performs a similar task to the natural language understanding module of a dialogue system, but usually at a much shallower level.

The document processor indexes the collection of documents from which the answer will be retrieved with information that enables retrieval of paragraphs. Using the output of the question processor, the document processor extracts paragraphs that could answer the user's question. Quite often the processing done at this stage is quite shallow and the only constraints imposed on the paragraphs retrieved are to ensure that they contain all or most of the keywords and at least one word in the same category as the expected answer type (Clarke, et al., 2000). However, there are systems that expand the list of query terms returned by the question processor with semantically related terms (Ittycheriah, et al., 2000) or implement advanced metrics which measure the plausibility of the paragraph containing the answer (Moldovan, et al., 2000).

The answer extraction module takes the paragraphs retrieved by the document processor and locates the actual answer of the question. This is usually achieved using either answer-type pattern extraction or N-gram tiling (Jurafsky & Martin, 2009). The answer-type pattern extraction method relies on handcrafted or automatically extracted patterns to identify the answer to a question. These patterns can be either surface-based or they can rely on syntactic and semantic information extracted by the question processor. The N-gram tiling method uses a large collection of documents such as the Web to extract recurring snippets, which are then scored according to how likely they are to be the answer to the question. For question answering systems that go beyond the factoid QA, the answer extraction stage can require fusing information from several documents in order to generate the answer. From this perspective, this stage is similar to the natural language generation component of dialogue systems. In some cases, an answer validation module is used in order to check the validity of the answer obtained.

The vast majority of the existing QA systems are unidirectional pipelines where each module is run in sequence and the user cannot intervene at all. However, Harabagiu et al. (2000) investigate the use of automatic feedback loops in cases where there are too many or too few answers available to rewrite the input of the document processor. This is similar to what happens in interactive question answering systems where the system asks for clarification from users.

INTERACTIVE QUESTION ANSWERING SYSTEMS

An interactive question answering system is defined as *a QA system that supports at least one exchange between the user and the system, and that allows the user some control over the content that is displayed and the actions that are taken* (Kelly, et al., 2008). However, we argue in this chapter that it is necessary to have more than one exchange in order to consider a QA system interactive. The similarity between dialogue systems and interactive question answering systems is emphasized by the definition given in Lester, Branting, and Mott (2004):

Conversational agents exploit natural language technologies to engage users in text-based information-seeking and task-oriented dialogs for a broad range of applications.

On the basis of these definitions, we argue that any interactive QA system can be considered a dialogue system, but only those dialogue systems that are information-seeking can be regarded as interactive QA systems. This point of view will be used in the remainder of the section to decide which approaches to present. An example of output from the system developed by Varges, Weng, and Pon-Barry (2007) is presented in Table 1. The output in this case is very similar to that of a simple QA system, but the authors argue that in cases where there are more than 10 results, presenting all of them in this format is no longer an option and a dialogue should be initiated to narrow down the

Table 1. Example of an output from Varges, Weng, and Pon-Barry (2007)

User: I want to find an inexpensive Japanese restaurant that takes reservations
Sys: I found 9 inexpensive Japanese restaurants that take reservations
Sys: Here are the first few:
Sys: GINZA JAPANESE RESTAURANT
Sys: OKI SUSHI CAFE
Sys: YONA SUSHI
Sys: Should I continue?

Table 2. Example of conversation with the implementation of Eliza from http://nlp-addiction.com/eliza/

Eliza: Tell me more... Eliza: Hello. My name is Eliza. How may I help you?
User: I wonder where to have dinner tonight. Do you have any suggestion?
Eliza: We were discussing you, not me.
User: Ok, I would like to have Italian food tonight.
Eliza: Can you elaborate on that?
User: I like pizza.
Eliza: Tell me more...

---

request. In contrast, Table 2 presents a conversation of one of the authors with an online version of Eliza, a chatbot that behaves like a Rogerian psychotherapist. As can be seen, the chatbot does not try to answer the questions, but carries out a conversation and therefore cannot be considered an IQA system.

Interactive question answering systems give users the opportunity to ask questions and refine them on the basis of feedback received from the system until they find the answer needed (Webb & Webber, 2009). Some interactive question answering systems also allow follow-up questions when the user wants to obtain more information related to the question or clarify the answer, so that IQA becomes an iterative process (Van Schooten, et al., 2009). For this reason, we can consider interactive question answering systems a step forward from simple question answering systems by offering users a more natural way of finding the information they need. Moreover, given that the sought information is obtained in an iterative manner by asking several simple questions, instead of combining all of them in one complicated question, the IQA systems could be more accurate than usual QA systems. This is due to the fact that IQA systems are less likely to have to deal with ambiguous language constructions such as prepositional phrase attachment or complicated syntactic structures. Moreover, when an IQA system encounters such an ambiguous construction, it can initiate a dialogue to clarify the user request.

As mentioned in the previous section, there are systems that automatically expand or remove some of the query terms used to find potential answers to a question. In a similar manner, one of the most common ways of interacting with IQA systems is by asking users to clarify their questions by rewriting them when the system provides too many answers or too few. From this point of view, interactive question answering should be seen as a mixed-initiative dialogue. This is due to the fact that even though the user is the one who normally asks the questions, it is possible for the computer to take the initiative when it requires clarification.

IQA systems give users the possibility to have a dialogue, which makes them similar to dialogue systems; however, they differ in several ways in this respect. The interaction between IQA systems and human users is more task-oriented and usually involves fewer turns. Also unlike a dialogue system, they usually lack "human" characteristics, so interaction with them seems less natural. IQA is oriented on information seeking, this is why IQA sessions have a clearer structure than dialogue systems, and in most cases, it is obvious whose turn is next. In both information-seeking dialogue systems and IQA systems, the common ground and context can be established by making the system domain-dependent. In this way, both the human participants and the computer can interpret the utterances with respect to that domain and diminish the extent of ambiguities in questions and answers. For example, the QALL-ME project (Sacaleanu, et al., 2008) has developed a prototype of an interactive QA system that works in the domain of tourism. To achieve this, an ontology for tourism was created and used in the answering process. Whenever a question could not be analyzed or answered with respect to the domain ontology, the system concluded that the request was out of domain.

TYPES OF IQA SYSTEMS

The field of interactive question answering is quite new and there are not many systems available. For this reason, the existing systems differ a lot in terms of their structure and the solution used to implement them. In this subsection, we will present the most important strategies used for developing IQA systems.

There are two ways of developing IQA systems: by producing a scaled-down version of an information-seeking dialogue system or by integrating additional functionalities into a standard QA system. These two approaches are presented next. In addition, researchers have also experimented with follow-up questions where the system interacts with users by proposing which questions it can answer next.

IQA as a Problem of Constraint Management

Several systems treat IQA as a problem of constraint management. They identify constraints in the questions and interact with the users when these constraints need to be modified. Usually, most of this processing is done by the dialogue manager.

Qu and Green (2002) developed a module that helps to handle under- or over-constrained requests in terms of the dialogue systems. It uses a Constraint-Based Problem-Solver (CBPS) which enables a dialogue system to 1) incrementally interleave query construction with solution construction, 2) immediately detect under-constrained and over-constrained information requests, and 3) provide cooperative responses when these types of problems are detected. The model was implemented in a prototype system providing airline

flight information, COMIX. This system queries a relational database of airline flight information using a form-based user interface depicted in Figure 1. With the help of this interface, the user specifies an information need by filling in fields on a query form. If there are some ambiguous values, COMIX takes the initiative and displays a clarification dialogue window. After all fields are filled in, the system submits a query. If the request was over-constrained, using information provided by the CBPS, constraints to relax are suggested (see Figure 2).

For the interaction with the user, the system relies on a frame-based dialogue manager, which employs a Constraint-Based Problem-Solver (CBPS), consisting of three subcomponents: *Solution Construction, Solution Evaluation,* and *Solution Modification.* The Solution construction module collects constraints and queries the database to get results, therefore fulfilling the role of answering the question. The Solution Evaluation module is similar to the answer validation used in question answering and evaluates the results to determine whether a satisfactory solution has been found. If it determines that the query is currently over-constrained or under-constrained, the Solution Modification module studies constraints and tries to identify relaxation or restriction candidates, which are presented to the user.

Results of evaluation showed that the CBPS helps to improve the performance in terms of dialogue efficiency and the task success scores for the harder tasks. This was expected given the presence of over-constrained queries in these tasks. The CBPS gave an opportunity to offer cooperative relaxation suggestions to make dialogue more effective.

Varges, Weng, and Pon-Barry (2007) explored the ways in which a dialogue system managed the results of database queries phrased in natural language. Their aim was to find efficient ways of managing a dialogue and providing a sufficient amount of information to users so that they are neither overwhelmed with too much information,

Figure 2. Screenshot

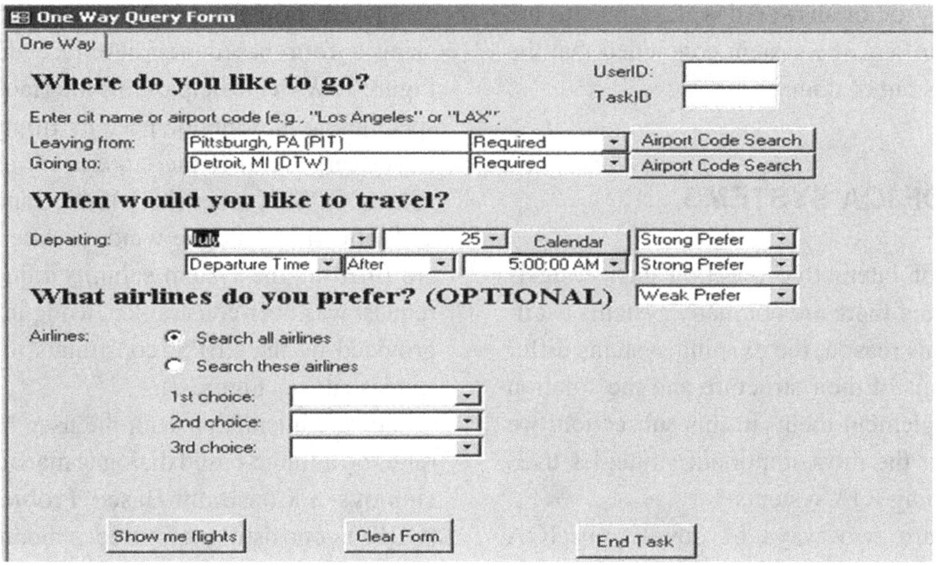

nor left uncertain about some details. The authors describe several systems dealing with restaurant selection, MP3 player operation, and navigation tasks. Their goal is to choose a single item out of a larger set of items and at the same time make the dialogue as natural as possible. The task of interactive question answering is presented in the context of a much larger system that also includes speech language understanding and text to speech generation modules.

The interaction with the user is coordinated by a dialogue manager, which uses a content optimization module and an ontology of constraints. The role of the optimization module is to control the amount of content, resolve ambiguities, and provide recommendations to users. The ontology contains information about three major types of constraints: hierarchical, linear-ordinal and binary. Depending on the type of constraint and number of results returned by the system, different strategies of constraint relaxation are used. Dialogue strategies for dealing with query results are manually built and thresholds are predefined. Table 3 presents some examples extracted from Varges,

Weng, and Pon-Barry (2007) showing different dialogue strategies for dealing with user questions.

Table 3 presents the output of the system when different questions are asked. It also indicates the number of results available (the #*results* column) and whether a modified list of the constraints is available (the *Modified* column). In the first example, the system finds a small number of answers to the question and returns all of them without suggesting any modifications. The system treats the question in example (4) in a similar manner, but does not display all the results because there are too many. Example (2) shows how a simple QA system answers when there is no answer for a question. An answer can be obtained by modifying, automatically or interactively, the constraints of the initial query as shown in example (3). Example (5) shows how an IQA system initiates a dialogue for narrowing the number of answers returned to a user, by clarifying the user request.

The authors perform two evaluations: a general one and a controlled experiment to test the use of a suggestion strategy. General tests show a 94.44% completion rate of the given tasks and

Table 3. Strategies for dealing with user questions

	# results	Modified	System's answer
(1)	Small	No	There are 2 cheap Thai restaurants in Lincoln in my database: Thai Mee Choke and Noodle House.
(2)	0	No	I'm sorry but I found no restaurants on Mayfield Road that serve Mediterranean food
(3)	Small	Yes	I found no cheap Greek restaurants that have a formal dress code but there are 4 inexpensive restaurants that serve other Mediterranean food and have a formal dress code in my database: ...
(4)	Medium	No	I found 9 restaurants with a two star rating and a formal dress code that are open for dinner and serve French food. Here are the first ones: ...
(5)	Large	Yes	I found no [NP-original]. However, there are N [NP-optimized]. Would you like to try searching by [Constraint]?

overall user satisfaction with the system results. Evaluation of the suggestion strategy shows that users prefer to get suggestions only when they have too many matches, but it is not crucial in cases when there are no matches.

Rieser and Lemon (2009) use an approach similar to the previous one and adapt dialogue policies for QA to obtain an IQA system. They work with a domain of in-car and in-home applications and provide examples of dialogues for choosing a song for a playlist. The main focus of their research is how to acquire enough reliable query constraints, how many results to present to a user and when to present them. They try to solve the problem of trade-off between the length of the dialogue (how many questions are asked) and the number of items in the resulting list. Their system learns the best dialogue strategies for interactive question answering, making it possible to choose the most appropriate dialogue move. Evaluation of the system showed significantly better results

for the learned policies compared to hand-coded threshold-based policies. In 93% of the cases, the learned policies outperformed the hand-coded ones. In contrast with the IQA systems presented above, this system is meant to be open domain, trying to answer any question.

Enhanced QA

Magnini, Speranza, and Kumar (2009) rely on an enhanced QA system to develop an IQA system. In contrast to the approaches described in the previous section, they use a traditional QA system as a starting point and suggest ways of interacting with the user in cases of failure. Table 4 presents some examples of interaction with the system.

The authors rely on a special IQA ontology as an addition to the domain ontology. This ontology captures significant aspects of interaction and becomes a basis for analysis of both questions and answers, and is used in modeling dialogue

Table 4. Interactions with the system in case of failure

Question: Where is *Titanic* by Spielberg showing today in Trento?
Answer: I don't know of any movies named *Titanic* directed by Spielberg. *Titanic* by Cameron is showing at Cinema Astra.
Question: Where is *Titanic* by Spielberg showing today in Trento?
Answer: I don't know of any movie *Titanic* directed by Spielberg. Are you interested in *Titanic* by Cameron or in movies by Spielberg?
Question: Where is *Shrek* showing in Trento?
Answer: No theatre is showing the movie *Shrek* today. Are you interested in tomorrow's scheduling?

templates. They analyze a question according to three features: *ExpectedAnswerType* (*EAT*), *Constraints,* and *ContextOfUtterance*. *EAT* is the semantic category associated with the desired answer, *Constraints* help to specify and restrict the information sought as an answer to a question and *ContextOfUtterance* provides additional information to the question such as the time and place where the question was uttered. The ontology also dictates the components of the answers: *CoreInformation* (*CoreInfo*), *Justification*, and *ComplementaryInfo* (*ComplInfo*). *CoreInfo* represents the actual answer to the question, *Justification* gives some contextualization of the answer, and *ComplInfo* is additional non-mandatory information that can be added to any type of answer if considered useful. In cases where a failure is encountered, the reason for this failure is analyzed with the help of the ontology and dialogue templates are then used to create a natural dialogue.

Dornescu and Orasan (2010) show how it is possible to implement interaction in the QALL-ME framework (Sacaleanu, et al., 2008). The QALL-ME framework is an architecture for implementing closed domain QA systems. At the core of the QALL-ME framework, there is a domain ontology and a text entailment engine, which are used, together with other language processing components, to generate procedures to answer questions. In the case of the prototypes developed in the QALL-ME project these answering procedures are in SPARQL, a query language that extracts data from an RDF (Resource Description Framework) database. Dornescu and Orasan (2010) propose a solution, which injects metadata indicating the system's understanding of the question with respect to the underlying domain ontology in the SPARQL queries returned. This metadata contains both information about the expected answer type and the constraints associated with the question. When the system fails to answer a question, it uses the metadata to begin an interaction with the user asking which constraints

to modify. In this respect, the solution proposed by them is similar to the systems presented in the previous section.

Quarteroni and Manandhar (2009) present an IQA system, YourQA, which combines an open-domain QA system with a chatbot. The underlying QA system is open domain and relies on the Web to obtain answers to both factoid and non-factoid questions. For this reason, it can be argued that it is a question answering system enhanced by a dialogue interface. The authors decide to use AIML (Artificial Intelligence Markup Language) to add some interactivity. The system is based on pattern matching, which matches the last user utterance against a range of dialogue patterns and then produces a coherent answer using a list of responses associated with such a pattern. Several evaluations were performed and showed that most users (in the first evaluation – 87.5%, second – 58.3%) prefer the interactive interface of the system instead of the simple QA system.

Follow-Up Questions

Question answering systems that can deal effectively with follow-up questions can also be considered as belonging to the domain of IQA. Van Schooten et al. (2009) tackle the problem of follow-up question classification and discuss challenges that have to be addressed while handling follow-up questions. Using two systems (IMIX and Ritel), they show how this approach can bring interaction to classical QA.

Harabagiu et al. (2005) try to predict the range of questions a user is likely to ask given a context and a topic, in this way producing an interactive system. After asking a question, a user gets not only the answer, but also suggestions for some follow-up questions. This is done by using a special database of "predicted" questions and answers (QUAB). Their IQA system (FERRET) uses the similarity between the user question and questions in QUAB to suggest follow-up questions.

Table 5. Example of follow-up questions from Harabagiu et al. (2005)

(Q1) Where did Egypt inherit its first stockpiles of chemical weapons?
(Q2) Is there evidence that Egypt has dismantled its stockpiles of weapons?
(Q3) Where are Egypt's weapons stockpiles located?
(Q4) Who oversees Egypt's weapons stockpiles?

Users can ignore the suggestion or select one of the proposed questions. The system is evaluated on questions about weapons of mass destruction. The evaluations show that usage of QUAB helps to improve both efficiency and effectiveness of the system and contributes to the rise of user satisfaction. However, it also revealed that the system is still not very accurate. Table 5 presents examples of follow-up questions after a user asks *What weapons are included in Egypt's stockpiles?*

Bernardi and Kirschner (2008), Kirschner and Bernardi (2009), Kirschner et al. (2009), Bernardi, Kirschner, and Ratkovic (2010) study the way answering follow-up questions can benefit from the context. Bernardi and Kirschner (2008) claim that an IQA system can be improved by predicting the focus of the follow-up questions. They study what makes a dialogue coherent, what "things" users focus on and how this focus evolves. Based on these theoretic findings, they train a module to track the focus in dialogues and show that it helps to improve the performance of an IQA system. This research is continued in Kirschner and Bernardi (2009) which studies follow-up questions that are not topic shifts, but rather continuations of the previous topic. The authors identify different relations that are held between follow-up questions and preceding dialogue and show how this model can help to select the correct answer among several answer candidates.

Using the previous results, Kirschner et al. (2009) explore ways the distinction between topic shift and continuations of the previous topic can improve the results of IQA systems. They notice that it is crucial when deciding whether or not to apply context fusion techniques for retrieving the answer. They rely on shallow features such as lexical similarity, distributional similarity, semantic similarity, and action sequence. Even though usage of shallow features gives some promising results, Bernardi, Kirschner, and Ratkovic (2010) enhance their previous model by adding deep features based on discourse structure and centering theory. However, the results showed that these features do not outperform the shallow ones on their own, but a combination of shallow and deep features increases the precision of an interactive question answering system.

EVALUATION

As in many other fields in computational linguistics, evaluation plays an important role in IQA. Despite this, there are no methods that are specific to the field and the only existing options are adaptations of the evaluation methods used in QA and dialogue systems. The main difficulty of designing an evaluation method for IQA comes from the fact that it is rarely possible to predict in advance how an interactive session will evolve. For this reason, it is necessary to have humans involved in the evaluation process, which makes the process slow, expensive, and difficult to replicate. Given that there is no framework for IQA evaluation, this section focuses on the evaluation methods used for QA and dialogues systems applied to IQA systems.

QA evaluations differ depending on whether they evaluate factoid or complex questions (like definition, relationship, and scenario questions). One of the ways is to create a set of "gold standard" questions and answers and see how successfully a system matches this gold standard. This method is not very robust for complex questions where the correct answer can be expressed in many different ways or there can even be several possible answers. In this case human-in-the-loop evaluations (like TREC evaluation competitions) are used, where human assessors are involved in the process. The abovementioned techniques can be used as well for IQA answering to check the correctness of the answers returned to users; however, on their own they do not provide enough information about the quality of an IQA system. For this reason, evaluation methods for dialogue systems are used as well.

The QA-CLEF 2008 evaluation competition tried to simulate a pseudo-interactive QA session by presenting questions grouped into topics (Forner, et al., 2009). Some of these questions contained co-references between each other, and there were also questions which relied on the answer to a previous question. Despite arranging this pseudo-interactive setting, each question was assessed individually, not like in a real interactive session.

Evaluation of dialogue systems is also a tricky task and a lot of different methods of evaluation can be found in the literature. Dale, Moisi, and Somers (2000) suggest using task-based evaluation where quality of a dialogue system is measured in terms of the task completion. The same approach can be found in Jurafsky and Martin (2006) who suggested measuring three different characteristics:

- Completion success (correctness of the solution found using the dialogue system);
- Efficiency cost (how much time was spent on finding a solution, for example, number of turns);
- Quality costs (how well the system works, for example, number of times user had to interrupt the system).

Spitters et al. (2009) address the last characteristic by simply asking people to complete a questionnaire and rank the quality of the system by giving grades. These questions include, for example, a request to evaluate the naturalness of the system in general, but the objectivity of such a method is debatable.

Harabagiu et al. (2005) note that in terms of interactive question answering (and in dialogue systems) dialogue as a whole is usually evaluated in terms of:

- Efficiency, defined as the number of questions that the user must pose to find particular information;
- Effectiveness, defined by the relevance of the answers returned;
- User satisfaction.

Given that questionnaires are used to evaluate dialogue systems, it seems natural to adapt the same strategy for IQA, which will provide an opportunity to evaluate various aspects of the system work.

Dornescu and Orasan (2010) ask human assessors to rank alternative questions generated by the system in cases where the system cannot answer a question. In this way, they try to find out which constraints users prefer to be modified first in order to obtain an answer.

Kelly et al. (2009) describe a first attempt to combine methods from QA and dialogue systems to develop a general framework for IQA evaluation. This framework relies on adaption of the existing technologies or creation of new ones. The authors use three questionnaires (a Cognitive Workload Questionnaire, Task, and System Questionnaires) and adapt them for specific IQA applications. This method provides ways to evaluate systems from different angles, but involves a lot of preliminary manual work and time-consuming labor of human assessors.

As in many other application-oriented fields where complex systems need to be evaluated not only as end-to-end systems, evaluation of IQA systems can be also performed at component level. This entails applying the relevant evaluation methods to each component on its own. However, these evaluation methods are component-specific and are beyond the scope of this chapter.

ADDITIONAL READING

As emphasized throughout this chapter, the boundary between dialogue systems and interactive question answering systems is quite fuzzy. In most cases, a task-oriented dialogue system can be considered an IQA system as well. Therefore, most of the research done for development of dialogue systems in application-oriented projects is also relevant for interactive question answering. This section presents several projects that can give the reader additional insights into the field of IQA. There are several groups that have been developing dialogue systems for a long time and have produced several working applications.

- The Conversational Interaction and Spoken Dialogue Research Group, University of Rochester[1] has completed several projects connected to building various dialogue systems: TRIPS (The Rochester Interactive Planning System), TRAINS, and PLOW (Procedure Learning On the Web). The TRIPS and TRAINS projects developed dialogue interfaces for planning trips. The PLOW project (Allen, et al., 2007) assists humans in teaching machines to perform new tasks using speech and natural language dialogue, which makes learning sessions quicker and more intuitive.
- Spoken Language Systems Group, MIT[2] has also developed several dialogue systems for restricted domains such as City Browser, Mercury, and Jupiter. City Browser (Gruenstein & Seneff, 2007) is an example of a spoken dialogue system, which assists humans in accessing urban information. The Mercury system (Seneff & Polifroni, 2000) provides telephone access to an online flight database and gives the possibility of planning and obtaining the price of itineraries. Jupiter is a conversational system that provides weather forecasts over the phone. All these systems are task-oriented and give users the possibility of refining their requests, and therefore they are relevant to IQA.

Several other already developed systems can be mentioned to give a better overview of the tasks where dialogue systems are involved. The AMITIÉS system (Hardy, et al., 2004) provides a dialogue interface to a financial call-system and deals with tasks such as balance checking and money transfer. The system was trained using large corpora of human-human and human-computer dialogues recorded by call centers. The Carnegie Mellon Communicator system (Rudnicky, et al., 1999) helps users to create complex travel itineraries through a conversational interface. SmartCom (Wahlster, 2003) is a system developed to ease communication between humans and computers using different modalities (such as speech, gestures, facial expression) via 16 different devices. This system opens new possibilities for interaction with computers and other high-tech devices. The CLASSiC (Computational Learning in Adaptive Systems for Spoken Conversation) project (Henderson, et al., 2008) (http://www.classic-project.org/) is an ongoing project which develops a system based "on statistical learning methods with a unified treatment of uncertainty across the entire system." At this stage, CLASSiC's spoken dialogue system is able to interact in natural language and provide information about restaurants in a chosen area.

Other projects in the field of dialogue systems are mostly aimed at development of new technologies, toolkits and other reusable components, for example, TRINDI (http://www.ling.gu.se/projekt/trindi/), SIRIDUS (http://www.ling.gu.se/projekt/siridus/), TALK (http://www.talk-project.org/index.php?id=1436). For example, TALK (Pinkal

& Lemon, 2006) technologies were integrated in a number of applications including multimodal in-car and in-home dialogue systems.

A more advanced type of dialogue system is embodied conversational agents (Cassell, et al., 2000). These systems have a body, which allows them to interact with users using both verbal and nonverbal ways. The development of such systems requires much more than language processing and is beyond the scope of this chapter. Such humanlike conversational agents are often used as financial advisers on the sites of banks, sales agents, or online shops as they allow a more natural interaction.

Other lines of research are also partially related to interactive question answering. Interaction from the point of view of information retrieval was studied by Koenemann and Belkin (1996), Kruschwitz and Al-Bakour (2005), and Nunzio (2008), whereas interaction from the point of view of database inferences was studied by Damerau, Joshi, and Kaplan (1981). Other research is connected to generation of cooperative answers, responses for dialogue systems to deal with successful and unsuccessful database searches (Kruijff-Korbayova & Karagjosova, 2002) and the ways to express tradeoffs of the system results effectively (Demberg & Moore, 2006).

ACKNOWLEDGMENT

We would like to thank Nancy Green and Yan Qu for providing us with a screenshot of their system presented in Figure 2. We would also like to thank Alison Carminke, Iustin Dornescu, and our anonymous reviewers for helping us improve the chapter.

REFERENCES

Bernardi, R., & Kirschner, M. (2008). Context modeling for IQA: The role of tasks and entities. In *Proceedings of Workshop for Knowledge and Reasoning for Answering Questions (KRAQ 2008)*. Manchester, UK: KRAQ.

Bernardi, R., Kirschner, M., & Ratkovic, Z. (2010). Context fusion: The role of discourse structure and centering theory. In *Proceedings of the Seventh Conference on International Language Resources and Evaluation (LREC 2010)*. Valletta, Malta: LREC.

Bilotti, M. W., & Nyberg, E. (2006). Evaluation for scenario question answering systems. In *Proceedings of the International Conference on Language Resources and Evaluation*. LREC.

Blair-Goldensohn, S., McKeown, K., & Schlaikjer, A. (2004). Answering definitional questions: A hybrid approach. In Maybury, M. T. (Ed.), *New Directions in Question Answering* (pp. 47–58). Menlo Park, CA: AAAI Press.

Bui, T. (2006). *Multimodal dialogue management - State of the art. Technical Report*. Enschede, The Netherlands: University of Twente.

Clark, H. H., & Schaefer, E. F. (1989). Contributing to discourse. *Cognitive Science, 13*, 259–294. doi:10.1207/s15516709cog1302_7

Clarke, C., Cormack, G., Kisman, D., & Lynam, T. (2000). Question answering by passage selection. In *Proceedings of 9th Text Retrieval Conference (TREC-9)*. Gaitherburg, MD: TREC.

Dale, R., Moisi, H., & Somers, H. (Eds.). (2000). *Handbook of natural language processing*. Boca Raton, FL: Marcel Dekker, Inc.

Damerau, F. J., Joshi, A. K., & Kaplan, S. J. (1981). A note on the utility of computing inferences in a real data base query environment. *Computational Linguistics, 7*(1), 43–45.

Demberg, V., & Moore, J. D. (2006). Information presentation in spoken dialogue systems. In *Proceedings of the 11th Conference of the European Chapter of the Association for Computational Linguistics*. ACL.

Dornescu, I., & Orasan, C. (2010). Interactive QA using the QALL-ME framework. *International Journal of Computational Linguistics and Applications, 1*(1-2), 233–247.

Forner, P., Peñas, A., Agirre, E., Alegria, I., Forăscu, C., & Moreau, N. … Tjong Kim Sang, E. (2009). Overview of the Clef 2008 multilingual question answering track. *Lecture Notes in Computer Science, 34*, 262-295.

Ginzburg, J., & Fernandez, R. (2010). Computational models of dialogue. In Clark, A., Fox, C., & Lappin, S. (Eds.), *The Handbook of Computational Linguistics and Natural Language Processing* (pp. 429–481). Oxford, UK: Wiley-Blackwell. doi:10.1002/9781444324044.ch16

Goldthwaite, D. (1997). Knowledge of pragmatic conversational structure. *Journal of Psycholinguistic Research, 26*(5), 497–508. doi:10.1023/A:1025071513114

Harabagiu, S., Hickl, A., Lehmann, J., & Moldovan, D. (2005). Experiments with interactive question-answering. In *Proceedings of the 43rd Annual Meeting on Association for Computational Linguistics,* (pp. 205-214). Ann Arbor, MI: ACL.

Harabagiu, S., & Moldovan, D. (2003). Question answering. In Mitkov, R. (Ed.), *The Oxford Handbook of Computational Linguistics* (pp. 560–582). Oxford, UK: Oxford University Press.

Harabagiu, S., Moldovan, D., Pasca, M., Mihalcea, R., Surdeanu, M., & Bunescu, R. … Morarescu, P. (2000). FALCON: Boosting knowledge for answer engines. In *Proceedings of 9th TExt Retrieval Conference (TREC-9)*. Gaitherburg, MD: TREC.

Ittycheriah, A., Franz, M., Zhu, W., & Ratnaparkhi, A. (2000). IBM's statistical question answering system. In *Proceedings of 9th TExt Retrieval Conference (TREC-9)*. Gaitherburg, MD: TREC.

Jurafsky, D., & Martin, J. H. (2009). *Speech and language processing an introduction to natural language processing, computational linguistics, and speech recognition* (2nd ed.). Upper Saddle River, NJ: Prentice-Hall, Inc.

Kelly, D., Kantor, P. B., Morse, E. L., Scholtz, J., & Sun, Y. (2009). Questionnaires for eliciting evaluation data from users of interactive question answering systems. *Natural Language Engineering, 15*(1), 119–141. doi:10.1017/S1351324908004932

Kirschner, M., & Bernardi, R. (2009). Exploring topic continuation follow-up questions using machine learning. In *Proceedings of NAACL HLT 2009: Student Research Workshop*. Boulder, CO: NAACL.

Kirschner, M., Bernardi, R., Baroni, M., & Dinh, L. T. (2009). Analyzing interactive QA dialogues using logistic regression models. In *Proceedings of XIth International Conference of the Italian Association for Artificial Intelligence (AI*IA 2009)*. Reggio Emilia, Italy: AI*IA.

Koenemann, J., & Belkin, N. J. (1996). A case for interaction: a study of interactive information retrieval behavior and effectiveness. In *Proceedings of the SIGCHI Conference on Human Factors in Computing Systems (CHI 1996),* (pp. 205-212). New York, NY: ACM Press.

Kruijff-Korbayova, I., & Karagjosova, E. (2002). Enhancing collaboration with conditional responses in information-seeking dialogues. In *Proceedings of 6th Workshop on the Semantics and Pragmatics of Dialogue*. ACL.

Kruschwitz, U., & Al-Bakour, H. (2005). Users want more sophisticated search assistants: Results of a task-based evaluation. *Journal of the American Society for Information Science and Technology, 56*, 1377–1393. doi:10.1002/asi.20230

Lester, J., Branting, K., & Mott, B. (2004). Conversational agents. In Singh, M. P. (Ed.), *The Practical Handbook of Internet Computing*. London, UK: Chapman & Hall.

Magnini, B., Speranza, M., & Kumar, V. (2009). Towards interactive question answering: An ontology-based approach. In *Proceedings of 2009 IEEE International Conference on Semantic Computing*, (pp. 612 - 617). Los Alamitos, CA: IEEE Computer Society.

Mauldin, M. L. (1994). Chatterbots, tinymuds, and the turing test: Entering the Loebner prize competition. In *Proceedings of the Eleventh National Conference on Artificial Intelligence*. AAAI Press.

Maybury, M. T. (2004). Question answering: An introduction. In Maybury, M. T. (Ed.), *New Directions in Question Answering* (pp. 3–18). Boca Raton, FL: AAAI Press.

Mitkov, R. (Ed.). (2003). *Handbook of computational linguistics*. Oxford, UK: Oxford University Press.

Moldovan, D., Harabagiu, S., Pasca, M., Mihalcea, R., Girju, R., Goodrum, R., & Rus, V. (2000). The structure and performance of an open-domain question answering system. In *Proceedings of ACL 2000*. Hong Kong, China: ACL.

Mori, R. D., Béchet, F., Hakkani-Tr, D., McTear, M., & Riccardi, G. (2008). Spoken language understanding: A survey. *IEEE Signal Processing Magazine, 25*, 50–58. doi:10.1109/MSP.2008.918413

Nunzio, G. M. D. (2008). Interactive undergraduate students: UNIPD at iCLEF 2008. *Lecture Notes in Computer Science, 5706*.

Qu, Y., & Green, N. (2002). A constraint-based approach for cooperative information-seeking dialogue. In *Proceedings of the Second International Natural Language Generation Conference*. ACL.

Quarteroni, S., & Manandhar, S. (2009). Designing an interactive open-domain question answering system. *Natural Language Engineering, 15*, 73–95. doi:10.1017/S1351324908004919

Ramsay, A. (2003). Discourse. In Mitkov, R. (Ed.), *Handbook of Computational Linguistics*. Oxford, UK: Oxford University Press.

Reiter, E., & Dale, R. (2000). *Building natural generation systems*. Cambridge, UK: Cambridge University Press. doi:10.1017/CBO9780511519857

Rieser, V., & Lemon, O. (2009). Does this list contain what you were searching for? Learning adaptive dialogue strategies for interactive question answering. *Natural Language Engineering, 15*(1), 55–72. doi:10.1017/S1351324908004907

Sacaleanu, B., Orasan, C., Spurk, C., Ou, S., Ferrandez, O., Kouylekov, M., & Negri, M. (2008). Entailment-based question answering for structured data. In *Proceedings of Coling 2008: Companion Volume: Posters and Demonstrations*. Manchester, UK: Coling.

Sacks, H., Schegloff, E. A., & Jefferson, G. (1974). A simplest systematics for the organization of turn-taking for conversation. *Language, 50*(4), 696–735. doi:10.2307/412243

Spitters, M., Boni, M. D., Zavrel, J., & Bonnema, R. (2009). Learning effective and engaging strategies for advice-giving human-machine dialogue. *Natural Language Engineering, 15*(3), 355–378. doi:10.1017/S1351324908004956

Stalnaker, R. (1978). Assertion. In Cole, P. (Ed.), *Pragmatics: Syntax and Semantics* (*Vol. 9*, pp. 315–332). New York, NY: Academic Press.

Traum, D., & Larsson, S. (2003). The information state approach to dialogue management. In van Kuppevelt, J., & Smith, R. (Eds.), *Current and New Directions in Discourse and Dialogue* (pp. 325–354). Berlin, Germany: Springer. doi:10.1007/978-94-010-0019-2_15

Van Schooten, B. W., Op Den Akker, R., Rosset, S., Galibert, O., Max, A., & Illouz, G. (2009). Follow-up question handling in the IMIX and Ritel systems: A comparative study. *Natural Language Engineering, 15*(1), 97–118. doi:10.1017/S1351324908004920

Varges, S., Weng, F., & Pon-Barry, H. (2007). Interactive question answering and constraint relaxation in spoken dialogue systems. *Natural Language Engineering, 15*(1), 9–30. doi:10.1017/S1351324908004889

Verberne, S., Boves, L., Oostdijk, N., & Coppen, P. (2010). What is not in the bag of words for why-QA? *Computational Linguistics, 32*(2), 229–245.

Walker, M., Whittaker, S., Laboratories, H. P., & Qz, B. (1990). Mixed initiative in dialogue: An investigation into discourse segmentation. In *Proceedings of the 28th Annual Meeting of the Association for Computational Linguistics*. ACL.

Webb, N., & Webber, B. (2009). Introduction. *Natural Language Engineering, 15*(1), 1–8. doi:10.1017/S1351324908004877

Webber, B., & Webb, N. (2010). Question answering. In Clark, A., Fox, C., & Lappin, S. (Eds.), *The Handbook of Computational Linguistics and Natural Language Processing* (pp. 630–654). Oxford, UK: Wiley-Blackwell. doi:10.1002/9781444324044.ch22

ADDITIONAL READING

Allen, J., Chambers, N., Ferguson, G., Galescu, L., Jung, H., Swift, M., & Taysom, W. (2007). PLOW: A collaborative task learning agent. In *Proceedings of the Twenty-Second Conference on Artificial Intelligence (AAAI-07)*. AAAI.

Cassell, J., Sullivan, J., Prevost, S., & Churchill, E. F. (Eds.). (2000). *Embodied conversational agents*. Cambridge, MA: MIT Press.

Damerau, F. J., Joshi, A. K., & Kaplan, S. J. (1981). A note on the utility of computing inferences in a real data base query environment. In *Computational Linguistics* (pp. 43–45). Cambridge, MA: MIT Press.

Demberg, V., & Moore, J. D. (2006). Information presentation in spoken dialogue systems. In *Proceedings of the 11th Conference of the European Chapter of the Association for Computational Linguistics*. ACL.

Gruenstein, A., & Seneff, S. (2007). Releasing a multimodal dialogue system into the wild: User support mechanisms. In *Proceedings SIGdial Workshop on Discourse and Dialogue*. SIGdial.

Hardy, H., Biermann, A., Inouye, R. B., Mckenzie, A., Strzalkowski, T., & Ursu, C. … Wu, M. (2004). Data-driven strategies for an automated dialogue system. In *Proceedings of the 42nd Annual Meeting of the Association for Computational Linguistics*. ACL.

Henderson, J., Lemon, O., & Georgila, K. (2008). Hybrid reinforcement/supervised learning of dialogue policies from fixed data sets. *Journal of Computational Linguistics, 34*, 487–511. doi:10.1162/coli.2008.07-028-R2-05-82

Koenemann, J., & Belkin, N. J. (1996). A case for interaction: A study of interactive information retrieval behavior and effectiveness. In *Proceedings of the SIGCHI Conference on Human Factors in Computing Systems (CHI 1996)*, (pp. 205-212). ACM Press.

Kruijff-Korbayova, I., & Karagjosova, E. (2002). Enhancing collaboration with conditional responses in information-seeking dialogues. In *Proceedings of 6th Workshop on the Semantics and Pragmatics of Dialogue*. ACL.

Kruschwitz, U., & Al-Bakour, H. (2005). Users want more sophisticated search assistants: Results of a task-based evaluation. *Journal of the American Society for Information Science and Technology, 56*, 1377–1393. doi:10.1002/asi.20230

Nunzio, G. M. D. (2008). Interactive undergraduate students: UNIPD at iCLEF 2008. *Lecture Notes in Computer Science, 5706*.

Pinkal, M., & Lemon, O. (2006). *Talk and look - Tools for ambient linguistic knowledge*. Retrieved from http://www.talk-project.eurice.eu/fileadmin/talk/publications_public/TALK_Publishalbe_final_activity_report.pdf

Rudnicky, A., Thayer, E., Constantinides, P., Tchou, C., Shern, R., & Lenzo, K. … Oh, A. (1999). Creating natural dialogs in the Carnegie Mellon communicator system. In *Proceedings of Eurospeech*, (pp. 1531-1534). Eurospeech.

Seneff, S., & Polifroni, J. (2000). Dialogue management in the mercury flight reservation system. In *Proceedings of Satellite Dialogue Workshop, ANLP-NAACL*. ANLP-NAACL.

Wahlster, W. (2003). SmartKom: Modality fusion for a mobile companion based on semantic web technologies. In *Proceedings of Cyber Assist Consortium Second International Symposium*. Cyber Assist Consortium.

KEY TERMS AND DEFINITIONS

Dialogue System: A computational device or agent that (a) engages in interaction with other human and/or computer participant(s), (b) uses human language in some form such as speech, text, or signs, and (c) typically engages in such interaction across multiple turns or sentences.

Chatterbot: (or **Chatbot**): A type of conversational agent, a computer program designed to simulate an intelligent conversation with one or more human users via auditory or textual methods.

Common Ground: Mutual belief or shared conception among the participants of the conversation.

Constraint: A restriction imposed by a specific model or system (e.g. constraints imposed on the relation between anaphor and the antecedent in an anaphora resolution model; constraints imposed on the participants by a conversational system etc.).

Dialogue Manager: The central component in a spoken dialogue system which is responsible for coordinating the different levels of analysis the system has to perform and controlling the communication between the user and the system. It anchors the user input in context, selects the content of the next system message, and provides predictions about the next user utterance.

Dialogue: Communicative linguistic activity in which at least two speakers or agents participate.

Discourse: An extended sequence of sentences produced by one or more people with the aim of conveying or exchanging information.

Embodied Conversational Agents: An intelligent conversational agent that interacts with the environment through a physical body (usually represented graphically) within that environment.

Grounding: The process of adding to the common ground between agents; the process by which participants in a dialogue gain mutual belief or shared conception.

Initiative: In the dialogue management of spoken dialogue systems, a control mechanism according to which what is or can be expressed in a dialogue at a given time depends on which agent in the dialogue currently holds, or is allowed to hold, the initiative: the user (user initiative), the system (system initiative), or both (mixed or variable initiative).

Interactive Question Answering: Systems that involve users in a continual information loop, giving the possibility to ask questions and refine them on the basis of feedback received from the system until the users find the answer needed.

Natural Language Generation: The automatic generation of natural language texts.

Natural Language Understanding: The automatic understanding of natural language texts.

Question Answering: The process of providing answer(s) to question(s) on large collections of documents, using NLP techniques.

Turn Taking: A basic characteristic in interactions, defining the change of the identity of the speaker from time to time and including the knowledge of who speaks when.

ENDNOTES

1   Conversational Interaction and Spoken Dialogue Research Group, University of Rochester http://www.cs.rochester.edu/research/cisd/.

2   Spoken Language Systems Group, MIT http://groups.csail.mit.edu/sls/sls-blue-noflash.shtml.

Section 4
Multilingual Information Access

Chapter 8
Issues and Challenges in Building Multilingual Information Access Systems

Vasudeva Varma
IIIT Hyderabad, India

Aditya Mogadala
IIIT Hyderabad, India

ABSTRACT

In this chapter, the authors start their discussion highlighting the importance of Cross Lingual and Multilingual Information Retrieval and access research areas. They then discuss the distinction between Cross Language Information Retrieval (CLIR), Multilingual Information Retrieval (MLIR), Cross Language Information Access (CLIA), and Multilingual Information Access (MLIA) research areas. In addition, in further sections, issues and challenges in these areas are outlined, and various approaches, including machine learning-based and knowledge-based approaches to address the multilingual information access, are discussed. The authors describe various subsystems of a MLIA system ranging from query processing to output generation by sharing their experience of building a MLIA system and discuss its architecture. Then evaluation aspects of the MLIA and CLIA systems are discussed at the end of this chapter.

INTRODUCTION

Information Access is the process of making the information available in various documents accessible and usable to the user who have a specific information need. The documents may be of various media, formats, document sources, or even languages. For the current discussion, we shall only focus on text documents, but the models and ideas discussed in this chapter can be extended to other formats such as audio and video documents. Information Retrieval (IR) technologies enable information access by retrieving a set of ranked documents that are likely to be relevant to the information need of the user. However, IR is only a part of the information access puzzle. Role of IR technologies ends once the relevant documents are obtained. After the results are obtained, the

DOI: 10.4018/978-1-4666-2169-5.ch008

user needs to skim through the documents, judge the relevance of these documents, compare them against each other, find out relevant portions of the document that might satisfy their information need, extract elements of the text that provide answers, and perhaps summarize multiple documents or portions of the documents. All this requires possessing and processing of world knowledge. Information Access technologies are expected to provide these functionalities that is more cognitive in nature.

Cross-Language Information Retrieval (CLIR) can be seen as a variation of Information Retrieval that deals with searching and retrieving information written/recorded in a language different from the language of the user's query. Thus, CLIR research mainly deals with the study of IR systems that accept queries (or information needs) in one language and return objects of a different language. These objects could be text documents, passages, images, and audio/video documents.

CLIR can be seen also as a technology that combines both Information Retrieval and Machine Translation (MT). The structure of CLIR system is broken down into categories like Indexing (IR), translation, ranking, and matching. Oard and Dorr (1996) work is perhaps the first attempt to study various approaches and techniques of CLIR in a detailed manner and showed that CLIR is not exactly the combination of IR and MT and somewhere between them. IR focuses on retrieving the relevant documents given a query by a human user and MT aims at producing single accurate target equivalent of a given input text. CLIR's functionality may be a hybrid of both these systems in the sense that the IR engine of CLIR system can take multiple translations produced by a program (as opposed to human user's single query), and the translation system tries to process not so complete input text (for example, just named entities, multiword expressions or simple sentence fragments) and produce multiple target language equivalents focusing less on producing grammatically correct translations.

Cross Language Information Access (CLIA) systems do more than the CLIR systems by further processing the results obtained in the target language. In other words, they are extensions of the CLIR paradigm. Users unfamiliar with the language of documents returned using CLIR are often unable to extract relevant information from these documents. This requires further processing which might include producing a summary of the multiple documents retrieved, translating such summary back to the source or the query language, extracting structured information from the retrieved documents and then producing human consumable information nuggets, and translating the entire or the relevant portions of the document.

Thus, the objective of CLIA is to provide additional post-retrieval processing to enable users to make use of these retrieved documents. This additional processing may take the form of applying techniques such as Machine Translation, Text Summarization, or Information Extraction.

Multi-Language Information Retrieval (MLIR) involves dealing with several target languages as opposed to one specific language. That means, given a query in one language, if the relevant documents are available in several languages, the MLIR system is expected to retrieve them and rank them based on the relevance to the user need. Multi-Language Information Access (MLIA) systems are expected to make the output of CLIR systems accessible to the user in the language of the query.

Evaluating the effectiveness of CLIR, CLIA, MLIR, and MLIA systems is non-trivial. There are two types of evaluations possible in dealing with such systems: user-based evaluation methodology and system-based evaluation methodology.

In user-based methodology, the actual human users are presented with the output of the system, which will be rated by the human user either as relevant or irrelevant (binary feedback). The user can also give more discrete feedback using some rating criteria like using certain rubrics. In some cases, the feedback can be descriptive and informative.

ISSUES AND CHALLENGES

There are different issues and challenges in building any research system. In addition, it should be transparent and flexible. Same thing is applicable in building information access and retrieval systems either it may be CLIR, CLIA, MLIR, or MLIA.

Good system performance is equated with good retrieval effectiveness. It is obvious that this is only one part of the CLIR problem. Cross-language information retrieval is equivalent (in the probabilistic sense) to the assumption of independence between the translation step and the retrieval step (Mayfield & McNamee, 2002). CLIR is primarily dependent on the correctness of query translation. Serious problem in query translation is ambiguity. It is done based on bilingual dictionary or using the corpora or machine translation. Key issues can be limitation in availability of resources. In addition, for effective retrieval translating, the entire document collection is preferred, which can be computationally expensive. Named Entities (NE) are essential components of texts and NE extraction and translation are vital for CLIR (Ananthakrishnan, 2003).

If we look at CLIA systems, they not only perform the tasks of CLIR systems but also help the users to access the relevant information by providing summary and translation of that information. It means CLIA extends CLIR paradigm to incorporate various possible post-retrieval processes to enable users to access information contained in retrieved documents. However, CLIA still faces problem with MT. Fully automatic high quality translation is still not available as MT is in general computationally expensive, and the translation output will usually contain at least stylistic flaws and disambiguation mistakes. These challenges still needed to be addressed to build efficient CLIA systems.

MLIR also contains varied problems as posed by the CLIR and CLIA systems. The MLIR system should be able to retrieve documents across languages. This extension to the classical IR problem is challenging, as significant amount of resources are required (Hull & Grefenstette, 1996) to perform the task. There are several other essential components in MLIR systems, which include multilingual resources, machine translation systems, and multilingual information extraction modules. Multilingual resources include corpora, lexicons, and ontology. Parallel and comparable corpora are important for generating a statistical translation model to overcome the limitations of a manually generated dictionary (Christopher & Wai, 2006). However, in order to obtain experimental results that are both reliable and quantifiable, it is necessary to have test document collection with large numbers of relevance judgments. Complexity in the MLIR systems is because of the language dependent nature of the translation process. There is no guarantee that document similarity scores obtained by translation of the query into several different languages can be compared. Merging of multiple languages into single index also needs to be addressed. The MLIR system must be able to handle the character sets of each language that is supported and also multilingual document collections which may be benefited for some facilities for automatic language recognition (Sibun & Spitz, 1994; Grefenstette, 1995).

A typical MLIA system is a CLIA system extending the MLIR capabilities to several languages and information access technologies. It should not only meet the needs of the application communities but also should provide facilities to investigate many other aspects including not just retrieval but also on other genres which may have their own specific access and retrieval problems. System performance is to be enhanced for wider usability issues that affect the users. Ability to recognize relevant information and refine search results even when documents are written in an unfamiliar language is to be handled by the system. Not just document retrieval, but also targeted information location and extraction are required.

Queries and documents are in different languages in CLIA system, they need to be standardized into a common representation, so that monolingual retrieval techniques can be applied. An MLIA system task is seen as an extension of the CLIA tasks, where queries can be of any language. However, unlike the case of CLIA system, the target collection consists of different language documents. However, an integration of monolingual and cross-language retrieval methods is usually effective to enhance the performance for MLIA system. Building such systems is challenging and require efficient problem solving techniques. There are several subsystems in any MLIA system. We see number of research and engineering issues associated with each of these subsystems starting from user entering a query to display of results.

Subsystems mentioned above can be broadly divided into two stages primarily collecting and indexing the document collections, secondly for query processing, retrieval, ranking, and presentation of information. These two stages can also be named as offline and online processing. The following are the major subsystems of a typical MLIA system.

1. Offline Processing

Offline processing involves pre processing of the document collections. Tasks performed during this stage are generally considered offline because they do not deal with user inputs in analyzing the information. Major tasks that are performed during the offline processing stage are listed below.

a. Indexing.
b. Named Entity Recognition.
c. Multiword Expression Detection in the documents.
d. Information Extraction (domain specific) MLIA systems.

2. Online Processing

Online Processing involves post offline processing tasks that handle user inputs and feedback. Listed below are some of the non-trivial tasks in building efficient MLIA system.

a. Query processing, which includes translation and transliteration, pre-translation query expansion and post translation query refinement and expansion, named entity and multiword expression recognition in query, word sense disambiguation
b. Retrieval
c. Ranking
d. Output generation, which includes snippet generation, snippet translation, and summary generation (query focused multi document summarization and cross language summarization).

We shall discuss the challenges and issues in each of these major subsystems under online and offline processing task below for MLIA system.

OFFLINE PROCESSING

As mentioned above offline processing tasks deal with huge amount of document collections and require proper pruning before proceeding to the results display to the user in MLIA system. We shall see now some of the challenges and issues in performing these offline tasks.

Indexing

Indexing is the major task in offline processing. It needs to characterize the entire collection of text and store this characterization on cache or other storage where retrieval should take minimum time for further use.

Like any (Braschler, et al., 1999; Buckley, et al., 1999) IRsystem, for MLIA, an indexer programs required to build an index database. This index could be an inverted index or some other data structures suitable for IR with some meta-data useful for ranking and presentation of information to the user. Index tokens should be obtained after stop-word removal and stemming. MLIA system also requires indexer module to store information such as the multiple language documents in which the tokens has occurred and frequencies and position of such occurrences in these documents.

For MLIA systems, we need enhanced indexing capabilities to store fielded indices. A fielded index would store the index information per field per document store (Pingali & Varma, 2007). For example, a multi language search engine application may want to provide ability to search a particular portion or meta-data of a document, such as the title of the document or the body text or Web-based fields such as search within a language and a given website. An indexer module should be capable of building data structures, such as term based inverted indices that enable fast retrieval of relevant documents and also enable ranking of these documents. The design of data-structure for index should also be sensitive to transaction aspects such as locking of indices for writes and updatability of index without difficulty.

The indexer program should also be capable of indexing named entities, multi-word expressions and perhaps concepts (as opposed to mere strings of text) to enhance the quality of the retrieval. All these deeper language-processing capabilities will enhance the probability of finding right documents irrespective of the language and the surface form in which the user need is expressed. Below, we will see the major challenges in NE and Multiword Expression (MWE) Recognition in the in multi language documents.

Named Entity Recognition (NER)

NER is an important subtask in many natural language processing problems. The challenge in detection of NEs is that such expressions are hard to analyze using rule based natural language processing techniques because they belong to the open class of expressions, i.e., there is an infinite variety and new expressions are constantly being invented. In addition, the level of ambiguity in NER makes it difficult to attain human performance.

In case of multiple languages scenario NEs often contain or entirely made up of words that are phonetically transliterated or have a common etymological origin across languages, and thus are phonetically similar. Thus, they can be exploited from such weak synchronicity across languages to associate them. Generally, it is the task of identifying and classifying tokens in into a predefined set of classes like Geographic Entity, Affiliation, Organization, Humans, Documents, Equipment and Scientific etc. NER in documents is a vital task and challenging. It plays a major role in retrieval performance.

Multilingual NER should be possible with existing supervised, unsupervised, and semi-supervised methods but each of them has their own limitations. These methods should also provide extension to many new languages and must be easy and fast. If we try to find the person names, they can be recognized in text through a lookup procedure, by analyzing the local lexical context, by looking at part of a sequence of candidate words that is a known name component etc. Some organizations names can be identified by looking at contain organization-specific candidate words. Identification of place names necessarily involves lookup against a gazetteer. But most of these context markers are too weak and ambiguous. As these throws big challenge in building proper gazetteer systems.

In multilingual system, person name detection can pose some more complex problems as the same person can be referred to by different name variants. The main reasons for these variations are: the reuse of name parts to avoid repetition, morphological variants such as the added suffixes, spelling mistakes, adaptation of names to local spelling rules, transliteration differences due to different transliteration rules or different target languages etc. Name variants can be found within the same language documents. The major challenges in identifying place names can be posed by problems in looking up place names in a multilingual gazetteer. Place names are frequently homographic with common words or with person names, presence of a number of exonyms (foreign language equivalences), endonyms (local variants) (Asif, et al., 2008), and historical variants for many place names etc. Application of NER to multilingual document sets helps to find more and more accurate information on each NE.

Multiword Expression (MWE) Detection

MWE is a set of two or more words (i.e. an expression) with non-compositional semantics, i.e. for which the sense of the whole expression cannot be directly or completely inferred from the sense of its individual words. From a textual perspective, the words of a MWE co-occur more often than they would normally do if they were a set of ordinary words co-occurring by chance (Manning & Schütze, 1999). Due to their heterogeneous characteristics, MWEs provide a real challenge.

In MLIA scenario MWE depend on MT also. If MT does not happen properly then the performance of identifying the MWE is affected. MWE's form a core issue and a challenging problem for NLP applications in MLIA because the meaning of the expression is not directly understood from the meaning of words. In this aspect, we observe that compositionality varies between phrases that are highly compositional and those that show a

degree of idiomatic behavior. In extreme cases the meaning of the expression as a whole is utterly unrelated to the component words (Attia, et al., 2010).

Identification of compound noun MWE is helpful for parsing and dictionary based applications like MT and CLIA. As word sequences should be treated as a single unit (Kunchukuttan & Damani, 2008), we see these challenges as categorization problem. There can be a compound nouns which is a noun consisting of more than one free morpheme. Such concepts in open form may be multiword. However, not all compound nouns are MWEs, such expressions needs to be classified accordingly.

Information Extraction (IE) (Domain Specific)

Content analysis/extraction of free-form texts is important for any information operation. It is type of information retrieval whose goal is to automatically extract structured information from unstructured and/or semi-structured machine-readable documents. Automatic extraction of information is necessary from unstructured sources as it plays vital role for querying, organizing, and analyzing data by drawing upon the clean semantics of structured databases and the abundance of unstructured data. This can be realized through Information Extraction.

The IE technology is used for the content extraction mainly NE's and MWEs, which are identified from each sentence and the content of the sentences. The information of interest mentioned earlier is described through domain-specific lexicon rules and patterns called templates. During the IE task these templates are filled with the collected information. These templates can be domain and task specific, i.e. for each new task and domain they must be newly created.

Multilingual information extraction is extraction of information about a specific entity and/or action from documents written in different languages. Adaptation of IE systems to new languages means that we need to adapt the components of IE to new languages. This system also poses problems of language identification, proper machine translation, text alignment and cross language projection and also POS tagging (Philipp, 2004). Also, some other issues like co reference resolution and discourse analysis. Some of the major challenges in employing IE methods are the manual efforts required to create templates to cater to all possible information needs of the users. Another challenge is the sparsely available information in the unstructured text to fill in the structured templates. We can expect limited utility of such methods in a well-defined domain.

For domain specific MLIA systems, like a multilingual search engine for tourism domain, IE methods are used to fill in pre-defined templates with the information available in the given set of documents. Once these templates are filled, the information extracted can be used to process more complex queries like in structured databases.

ONLINE PROCESSING

Tasks like query processing, retrieval, ranking and output generation becomes major chunk of online processing. Each of them has different issues and challenges and needs to be efficiently researched upon. We will dissert each of these areas more profoundly in the below sections.

Query Processing

Query processing is perhaps the most important task in building MLIA systems as the accuracy of the results are directly linked to the accuracy of query transliteration or translation and its representation. The user input in any form shouldbe considered as a query—including the options the user selects and the text string given.

Since we are looking into the MLIA system these queries can be of any language. Identify-

ing the language is an important task; this helps in screening the content to provide better search results in the source language. The goal of MLIA system is not only to bring results from the source language but also from target languages, which requires query translation/transliteration. It requires pre translation query expansion, post translation query expansion and reduction, named entity recognition, multi word expression detection and word sense disambiguation which improve the precision in the results retrieved.

We will see below each of the procedures and techniques helpful in improving query processing.

Transliteration/Translation

Transliteration, the pronunciation-based translation or keyword-based translation from a source language to a desired target language, is important to many multilingual natural languages processing tasks. In addition, success of any MLIA system depends on efficiency of its translation or transliteration of queries. When not carefully handled, the Mean Average Precision (MAP) can reach 50% degradation (Larkey, et al., 2003). Generally these queries may contain MWEs, NEs, or general language terms. The challenge for the system is to identify the type of query terms and decide accordingly whether to translate or transliterate. In addition, mining appropriate transliterations from the top results of the first-pass retrieval should be considered as it achieves enhanced cross lingual performance of the system overall, in addition to enhancing individual performance of more queries (Saravanan, 2010).

There are some drawbacks, which need to be handled if transliteration does not produce the exact spelling variants used in the document collection. An approximate string matching technique is usually required to alleviate this drawback. By doing so, retrieval performance should not be compromised. If inaccurate or confusing transliterations occur in multiple alternative transliterations (Ea-Ee, 2010) appropriate action should be taken.

In addition, if translated or transliterated query is human readable it ensures proper transliteration and ultimately provides good search results.

Pre-Translation Query Expansion

Query expansion extends the query words to include similar concepts to allow for better retrieval. In case of multi lingual information systems, pre-translation expansion adds new query words from the language the query was written in. Expectation is pre translation expansion should greatly improve results (McNamee & Mayfield, 2002). It should also reduce ambiguity and increase recall. It should also involve evaluating a user's input (what words were typed into the search query area) and expanding the query to match additional documents.

Query expansion will typically depend on either dictionary based or corpus based methods. So pre-translation query expansion faces challenges in identifying techniques for finding similar words and synonyms. It also should enumerate all possible morphological forms of words by fixing spelling errors or automatically searching for the corrected form or suggesting it in the results and re-weighting the terms in the original query.

Post-Translation Query Expansion and Reduction

Post-translation, takes the translated query and then extends it by some means. Problems and challenges here can be due to translation. When translating a query, it is not possible to do a reliable exact translation, especially because queries tend to include isolated words and phrases out of context, as well as possibly full clauses or sentences. Any automated translation risks selecting the wrong meaning of the query terms, and therefore the wrong translation. Hence, some better means are required to perform an expansion in which all

meanings of all query terms are generated, properly weighed for base-line and co-occurrence statistics (Frederking, et al., 1997) so that no meaning is lost. This should improve recall results though at some degradation in precision. One reason for this is that the documents themselves serve as filters, since it is unlikely that a single document will hit one sense of each term unless they are coherent sense-choices.

Post-translation query expansion faces some challenges in finding the synonym sets like Word Net, etc., and dictionaries in reformulating the query. Languages with fewer resources need to follow different alternatives for query expansion. It also needs to consider all possible transliterated words for a query for efficient results. Once the query is expanded, it is used for retrieval.

Since queries translated may contain spurious results query reduction techniques also need to be employed. Query reduction should identify unnecessary words by removing words that may detract the retrieval performance. Attributes that identify these words has to be obtained by using decision methods.

Multiword Expression (MWE) Query Detection

Generally, queries need to be understood as MWEs rather than token of words. A MWE is a lexeme made up of a sequence of two or more lexemes that has properties that are not predictable from the properties of the individual lexemes or their normal mode of combination. A MWE can also be a fragment of a sentence, or a complete sentence. The group of lexemes makes up a MWE, which can be continuous or discontinuous. It is not always possible to mark an MWE with parts of speech. This throws an important issue that query needs to be efficiently translated or transliterated not to hinder the results retrieved when dealing MWEs in CLIA environment.

Word Sense Disambiguation (WSD)

Basic research is needed to investigate the relationship between sense ambiguity, disambiguation, and information retrieval. Understanding the influence of ambiguity and disambiguation on a probabilistic IR system is required to improve the retrieval results. Word sense ambiguity is only problematic to an IR system when it is retrieving from very short queries (Sanderson, 1994). In addition, word senses has to resolve to high degree of accuracy.

For MLIA, this creates much more complex problems as it involves understanding the query in multiple languages. To determine the sense of a word, a WSD algorithm typically should understand the context of the ambiguous word, external resources such as machine-readable dictionaries, or a combination of both. Although dictionaries provide useful word sense information and thesauri provide additional information about relationships between words, they lack pragmatic information as unavailability of them in corpora. However, there are major barriers in building a high-performing Word Sense Disambiguation (WSD) system as it includes difficulty of labeling data and predicting fine-grained sense distinctions.

User queries can be diversified into different topics and areas and could mean differently in each of those areas. This creates problem of word disambiguation. Thus, any system that attempts to retrieve good results has to determine the sense of a word from contextual features.

RETRIEVAL

Retrieval is the science of searching information within documents and metadata about those documents. MLIR is a subset of information retrieval, which has the ability to process a query for information in any language. It also searches a collection of objects, including text, images, sound files, etc., and returns the most relevant objects translated if necessary into the user's language.

In many respects, as discussed above, the two fields IR and MLIR share exactly the same goals; as such, well-known IR techniques such as vector space indexing, Latent Semantic Indexing (LSI), similarity functions for matching documents and query processing procedures are equally useful in MLIR. However, MLIR differs from IR in several other significant ways also like translation component. Where in most of the IR has no such requirement since it involves single language. While keeping track of translations across several languages is part of the standard multi lingual information retrieval process.

Choices of translations are also important to get better understanding of how different domains are getting affected due to translation possibilities. Another problem is determining how to filter from all those possible choices and retain the best one. However, the expectation from a good retrieval system is to retain a wider set of possibilities that can later be automatically filtered and used. Thus, the MLIR system has to balance the amount of inaccurate translations (noise) that degrade results against the amount of processing performed to disambiguate the terms and ensure accuracy. Hovy et al. (2001) suggests more than one translation is to be retained and a set of well-chosen possible terms for the best retrieval performance is to be used.

In addition, the task of retrieval from multiple languages can also be considered as clustering problem. Multilingual documents are clustered and then they are retrieved. A multilingual document cluster will contain a set of documents, possibly written in different languages, which are related to the same topic. Aim is to extract important topics that exist in a multilingual document collection. This task differs from information retrieval in which we do not consider specific queries that define the relevant topics, and we have to compare each document with the others in a symmetric way. This task also differs from text categorization because the topics identified by the clustering phase are not predefined, and a document can be assigned to more than one cluster.

RANKING

Searching a large database with documents makes us realize that there are not enough documents one could ever assimilate. However, there are more relevant documents that one could ever assimilate. If only we could reduce or eliminate redundancy, we would have a much more manageable subset of relevant documents that nonetheless span the information space. This requires proper ranking of documents to get the most relevant documents displayed first. Thus, ranking provides the most relevant documents for a user query.

Ranking is a challenging problem in MLIA scenario. Integrating the results from heterogeneous resources is one of the major issues in MLIR. In many cases, relevant documents will be found predominantly in a collection containing a particular language (non-uniform distribution).It is more difficult to compare the relative relevance of documents in disparate languages than to rank documents in a single language. Merging result lists of individual languages is common approach, but needs to follow different approaches of merging (Lin & Chen, 2004). Generally, in monolingual retrieval scenario relevancy scores should be maintained from different settings and are to be normalized so that it is comparable for final combination and ranking. Such approaches do not directly incorporate features that are relevant to multiple language information retrieval; hence do not work well for multilingual. In addition, there is little research to adapt the state-of-the-art ranking algorithms for MLIR systems.

Ranking for MLIR is the task of ranking documents of different languages solely based on their relevancy to the query, irrespective of the query language. For this, we need to understand the relevance scores of different retrieval settings

for different languages and also ranking function. There is need to exploit the correlations among documents, and induce the joint relevance probability for all the documents. It means we should generate probabilistic models of relevance for the documents. Using this method, the relevant documents of one language can be leveraged to improve the relevance estimation for documents of different languages.

For personalization and better results more processing to be done by re-ranking the top results received. This needs to employ different heuristics or machine learning approaches like learning to rank etc to provide better results in multilingual information access systems.

OUTPUT GENERATION

Output generation depends on different parameters. It is understood that the way user queries are handled also make difference in the information displayed. Output generated contains different features for the user-entered queries. These features contain information summarized in a document as snippet or information extracted from multiple format documents. Content from multiple documents is extracted either by query focused or multiple language documents summarization.

We shall discuss various forms of the output present inside MLIA systems and also the challenges and issues below. It is emphasized that output generation is the key differentiator between MLIR and MLIA systems.

Snippet Generation

Snippets give the searcher a sneak preview of the document contents. They are short fragments of text extracted from the document content (or its metadata). A snippet can range from a fragment of a sentence to a paragraph. They may be static that always show the first 50 words of the document or the content of its description metadata, or a description taken from a directory. However, it does not make any sense to show the static snippets as the user queries change and query-biased snippet generation urges the requirement.

Challenge in a query-biased snippet is that it should be selectively extracted on the basis of its relation to the searcher's query. In addition, the addition of informative snippets to search results should substantially increase their value to searchers. Accurate snippets always allow the searcher to make good decisions about which results are worth accessing and which can be ignored. In the best case, snippets may obviate the need to open any documents by directly providing the answer to the searcher's real information need. These requirements pose challenge to generate text, preferably containing query terms, that summarizes that document.

In MLIA Systems issue is to choose best possible solution as one can either search the query in source language documents and then translate the output to target language or translate the source language documents to target language and search the MT output, or search both and combine the outputs. But approaches that are languages independent are always needed (DilekHakkani-Tür, et al., 2010).

Snippet Translation

Snippet Translation depends on the MT abilities. If the MT occurs properly then the results retrieval will improve in precision and recall. However, MT itself is challenge as it depends on dictionary-based services. To overcome these challenges and to improve the efficiency of retrieval different techniques can be used like sentence aligned parallel corpus (Toth, et al., 2008), parallel NE list for creation of the phrase translation probability tables.

In addition, some other techniques like forwarding snippet to the decoder and letting it to translate the output. Problem can be with HTML page that also needs to be processed by decoding or translation. For this MOSES phrase-based decoder[1]can be used as it gives language model. So efficiency now depends on the language model that is generated.

Summarization

Summarization is a task where summary of a text is produced from one or more texts, that convey important information in the original text(s), and is no longer than half of the original text(s) and usually significantly less than that. There are different challenges of summarization that require summaries from a single document or multiple documents and expected to preserve important information in concise manner.

An efficient extraction procedure is required for identifying important sections of the text and producing them verbatim. Summarization can be observed from two different modes one is extractive summarization and other is abstractive summarization. Extractive summarization is mainly concerned with what the summary content should be, usually relying solely on extraction of sentences, abstractive summarization puts strong emphasis on the form, aiming to produce a grammatical summary; this usually requires advanced language generation techniques.

In a paradigm more tuned to IR, one can also consider topic-driven summarization, which assumes that the summary content depends on the preference of the user and can be accessed via a query, making the summary focused on a particular topic. In cross language scenario more depth in understanding the summarization procedures is required, mainly in query focused multi document summarization and Cross lingual multi document summarization

Let us understand the challenges in both of them separately.

Query Focused Summarization

Query-focused summarization mainly used to extract the content from multiple documents. These is based on extraction summarization techniques and involve ranking of textual units, usually sentences, using some scoring mechanism and picking the top scoring units and concatenating them in a certain order to generate the summary.

The key requirement here is to get multiple relevant documents summary using querying question. In standard multi document summarization (without a query), we have to get relevant documents for some user need. Similarly, in the case of a Web-search application, an underlying IR engine will retrieve multiple relevant documents for a given query.

To achieve query-sensitivity within the context in cross language scenarios, we need to examine word distributions towards the query by calculating distribution sensitive features. Finding this distribution in a document set is done by extracting features from a sentence. Query containing these words will have larger feature values.

Cross Lingual Multi Document Summarization

Cross language query focused summarization could play a vital role in multilingual information access, as a bridge between CLIR and machine translation. Cross-language document summarization is the task of producing a summary in one language for a document set in a different language. Cross lingual multi-document summarization is an automatic procedure aimed at extracting information from multiple texts written about the same topic. Resulting summary report allows individual users to quickly familiarize themselves with information contained in a large cluster of documents.

Cross language multi-document summarization task has turned out to be much more complex than summarizing a single monolingual document, even a very large one. This difficulty arises because of limitation of resources in translation and also in understanding the context and theme within a large set of documents for foreign languages. A good summarization technology aims to combine the main themes with completeness, readability, and conciseness. An expectation from an ideal multi document summarization system is that it should not simply shorten the source texts but should present information organized around the key aspects to represent a wider diversity of views on the topic. When such quality is achieved, an automatic multi-document summary is perceived more like an overview of a given topic. The latter implies that such text compilations should also meet other basic requirements for an overview text compiled by a human.

There are many issues in doing cross language multi document summarization, as it requires best machine translation services. If translation efficiency is low, it affects the results in their quality of the cross-language summary both in readability and in its content. This task is very important in the field of multilingual information access. Multiple document summarizations require not only translation but also ranking of the sentences to choose the essence of documents.

In this section, we have discussed key challenges in building various subsystems of the MLIA systems mainly categorized into online and offline processing. We now shall look at general approaches to building the MLIA and CLIA systems.

GENERAL APPROACHES

General approaches used in building a MLIA system will be discussed in this section. Acquisition and representation of translation knowledge plays a central role in the process. There are different general approaches in developing a multiple language information system. Below we will discuss two major approaches, namely: Knowledge-Based Approaches and Machine Learning Approaches.

Knowledge-Based Approaches

Knowledge based systems use knowledge from the existing ontology, thesauri, lexicons etc. Knowledge is used for translation or finding the relationships between the terms in the text either in query or documents. Some of the approaches are listed down.

Dictionary-Based Approach

In dictionary based approaches ontology are generally used for representation of concepts and relationships. Thesaurus is used as a resource containing lists of words grouped based on the similarity of meaning. In cross lingual scenario bilingual lexicons are used as specialized resources that help in translating a token in source language into a token of target language. These resources are typically built for machine consumption. In addition, bilingual dictionaries are similar to bilingual lexicons but they are built for mainly for human consumption but also employed in machine translation. By far the most commonly used query translation approach is to replace each query term with appropriate translations that are automatically extracted from an online bilingual dictionary.

Also due to steadily increasing Internet, commercial dictionaries in multiple languages had considerable increase. For example Collins COBUILD English Language Dictionary[2] and its series in major European languages, Leo Online Dictionary[3], Oxford Advanced Learner's Dictionary[4] of Current English, Webster's New Collegiate Dictionary[5]. Electronic monolingual and bilingual dictionaries build a solid platform for developing multilingual applications. Using dictionary-based techniques queries will be translated into a language in which a document may be found. However, this technique some-

times achieves unsatisfactory results because of ambiguities. Many words do not have only one translation and the alternate translations have very different meanings. Moreover, the scope of a dictionary is limited. It lacks in particular a technical and topical terminology, which is very crucial for a correct translation. Nevertheless, this technique can be used for implementing simple dictionary-based multi lingual application or can be combined with other approaches to overcome the above-mentioned drawbacks.

Dictionary-based approach for some tasks like query translation has achieved an effectiveness of 40-60% in comparison with monolingual retrieval (Ballesteros & Croft, 1996; Hull & Grefenstette, 1996).

Corpus-Based Technique

Corpus-based technique considered promising compared to dictionary-based approach. It analyzes large collections of corpora and automatically extracts the information needed on which the translation will be based. Corpora are collections of information in electronic form to support e.g. spelling and grammar checkers, and hyphenation routines (lexicographer, word extractor or parser, glossary tools). A few examples of mono, bi-lingual and multilingual corpora are brown Corpus[6], Hansard[7], and United Nation documents (Eisele & Chen, 2010), respectively. WordNet[8] is used as synonym set to increase the query space for improving recall. Similar work has been done for multiple languages as in EuroWordNet[9] to improve the multilingual lingual systems. Some of the other systems are ACQUILEX[10], Hindi WordNet[11] etc.

Collections may contain parallel and/or comparable corpora. A parallel corpus is a collection that may contain documents and their translations. A comparable corpus is a document collection in which documents are aligned based on the similarity between the topics. Document alignment deals with documents that cover similar stories, events, etc. For instance, the newspapers are often describing political, social, economical events and other stories in different languages. These high-quality parallel corpora can be used as efficient input for evaluating cross-language techniques.

An automatic thesaurus construction has been done based on a collection of comparable multilingual documents (Sheridan & Ballerini, 1996).Other experiments on English, French and German have been presented in (Wechsler & Schäuble, 1998) using the document alignment in this work was based on indicators, such as proper nouns, numbers, dates, etc. There is also alignment based on term similarity. This allows mapping text between those documents in different languages.

Although these methods works better to certain extent, there are still constraints in getting efficient retrieval and precision values.

Indexing by Latent Semantic Analysis

Latent Semantic Indexing (LSI) analysis is based on singular-value decomposition (Scott, et al., 1990) considering the term-document matrix terms and documents that are very close will be ordered according to their degree of "semantic" neighborhood. The result of LSI analysis is a reduced model that describes the similarity between term-term, document-document, and term-document relationship.

Previous approaches mentioned like dictionary based and corpus based has the ambiguity of terms and their dependency leads to poor results. LSI approach in multilingual information retrieval allows user to retrieve documents by concept and meaning and not only by pattern matching. If the query words have not been matched, this does not mean that no document is relevant. In contrast, there are many relevant documents that, however, do not contain the query term word by word. This is the problem of synonymy. The documents do not contain all possible terms that all users will

submit. Using thesauri to overcome this issue remains ineffective, since expanding query to un-suitable terms decreases the precision drastically.

LSI applied to cross-language text retrieval (Davis & Dunning, 1995) on the TREC collection achieved approximately 75% of the average preci-sion in comparison to the monolingual system on the same material (Davis & Ogden, 1997). Results reported in TREC-5 showed that the use of only dictionary-based query expansion yields approx. 50% of the average precision in comparison to results of the multilingual system. This degrada-tion can be explained by the ambiguity of term translation using dictionaries.

This technique has been used for multilingual filtering experiments (Oard, 1996) and encourag-ing results have been achieved. The representation of documents by LSI is "economical" through eliminating redundancy. It reduces the dimension-ality of document representation as well. However, updating (adding new terms and documents) in representation matrices is time-consuming.

Latent Semantic Co-Indexing

Latent semantic co-indexing is an extension of Latent Semantic Indexing (LSI) a vector space information retrieval method based on factor analysis, which has demonstrated improved per-formance over the original vector space technique used in Salton SMART (Deerwester, et al., 1990) system.

Still there are several problems with knowl-edge-based approaches in multilingual scenario.

- Untranslatable keywords because the words are not in the dictionary. One of the reasons is that natural languages evolve and new words are not added to diction-aries on a regular basis. Other categories of words that are not generally found in dictionaries are compound words, proper names, spelling variants and special terms.

- Inflected word forms also pose problems. If the source language words appear in inflected form, they cannot be easily translated, because they do not match the words as entered in the dictionary. A common way to deal with this problem is stemming - to remove prefixes and suffixes from the word forms so as to find a common root or stem of different forms. One of the drawbacks of stemming is that different head forms may be conflated to the same form. Some languages have a high frequency of compounds

Machine Learning-Based Approaches

The aim of machine learning is to infer automatically a model for some domain on the basis of the given data from the domain, thus a system learning syntactic rules would be supplied with a set of phrase structure rules to be used for training. The learning algorithms can be of two types: unsupervised and supervised. An unsupervised algorithm has to induce a model capable of generalizing to new data it has not been given before, and does this purely from the data. A supervised algorithm is trained on a set of correct answers to the learning data, so that the induced model would result in more accurate decisions.

Machine learning is largely founded on the stochastic research paradigm rooted in the development of character recognition, spelling correction, machine translation, classifying text, extracting relationships from the text, learning to rank in multi lingual data access scenario. All of these methods require training data to develop models based on features and extract the similar results from the testing data. An essential probabilistic framework employs the Bayes Rule and the noisy

channel model (Kozerenko, 2004) which plays an important role in many problems.

For example, learning a good ranking function plays a key role for many applications including the task of information retrieval. While there are a few rank learning methods available, most of them need to explicitly model the relations between every pair of relevant and irrelevant documents, and thus result in an expensive training process for large collections. A considerable progress of Natural Language Processing (NLP) techniques based on machine learning has also been observed to improve information retrieval and access. Let us see below some of these approaches below based on machine learning.

Machine Translation

The appearance of large parallel texts corpora promoted the statistical methods of NLP, which augment the scheme of the principal existing approaches to machine translation design—direct translation, transfer, and interlingua-based methods. A statistical machine translation was first introduced by Brown et al. (1990, 1993).

A model for machine translation based on an aligned text corpus is example-based machine translation, which means that the example-based (Nagao, 1984; Sato, 1992) translation employs the closest match in aligned corpora as a template for translation. The existing computational resources provided for today's MT systems allow accumulating and recalling previously corrected translations (Translation Memory and Example-Based Machine Translation) (Sumita & Iida, 1991; Brown, 1996).

The evidence of the latest research and development projects shows that machine-learning methods alone are unlikely to yield the finely tuned language processing decisions. However, the use of combined techniques brings the increase of "meaningful" performance of language processing systems in different aspects; thus, it was exhibited in Segalovich (2003) that introduction of linguistic parse rules into the multilingual search engine considerably enforces the precision of search results.

Thus, it is understood that models are generated using different rules for modeling syntactic structures of two languages simultaneously to perform the translation. These models are run on the testing data to remove different levels of disambiguation as the parsing processes in order to generate a translation with high quality. It is possible to say that at the present moment the systems solely based on translation memory are giving way to the systems which comprise several complementary techniques: though the systems based on the principles of Translation memory produce understandable translations, they still lack grammatical accuracy.

Probabilistic Tagging

Tagging the words in corpora helps to understand the context of the word in more appropriate manner. It helps in understand the context of the query and improves the retrieval results. Therefore, for any MLIA system, tagging plays prominent role. Different stochastic taggers have been developed over the time; the idea shared by all stochastic taggers consists in choosing the most likely tag for a given word. One of the most popular probabilistic taggers is the Hidden Markov Model. An approach to machine learning based on rules and stochastic tagging is known as the Transformation-Based Learning (TBL). TBL is a supervised learning technique, and employs a pre-tagged training corpus.

Multilingual Lexicon

Limited data resources can be exploited by machine learning approaches for multilingual lexicon generations. Acquiring a lexicon from a corpus of sentences labeled with representations of their meaning is an important problem. Learning algorithms are required to perform fairly well on this task and obtain superior performance in lexicon acquisition system on a corpus. Methods should extend to a variety of natural languages and has to be multilingual. Also it has to be successfully integrated to build a complete MLIA system. WOLFIE (Word Learning from Interpreted Examples [Thompson & Mooney, 1999]) and CHILL (Zelle & Mooney, 1996) were some systems developed to produce multilingual lexicons.

CHILL learns to parse sentences into semantic representations. It uses inductive logic programming and takes an input sentence. It treats parser induction as a problem of learning rules to control the actions of a shift-reduce parser. WOLFIE acquires a semantic lexicon from a corpus of sentences paired with semantic representations. The lexicon learnt consists of words paired with meaning representations.

There is some effort done using machine-learning approaches building lexicons for south Asian languages. Most of the south Asian languages in spite of belonging to various families have a lot of similarity (Emeneau, 1956). Work on identifying cognates (Singh & Surana, 2007) across south Asian languages based on unified computational model of scripts (Singh & Surana, 2007a) that have previously used for solving several practical problems like spell checking, text normalization, improving information retrieval etc. In addition, it is understood that different languages corpus data can be learnt with different feature vectors and values are extracted for generating lexicons will differ.

Terminology Extraction

The goal of terminology extraction is to automatically extract relevant terms from a given corpus. Typically, approaches to automatic term extraction make use of linguistic processors to extract terminological candidates. Terminological entries are then filtered from the candidate list using statistical and machine learning methods. From an information retrieval point of view, terms are any words that together can describe the semantics of a document.

Computational terminology extraction methods usually fall into one of three camps. Either the method is based on linguistic properties, statistical properties, or a mix of these two. An example of a term extraction method using linguistic properties would annotate text using a POS-tagger, then extract token sequences that follow common POS patterns for terms. A statistical method would calculate the inverse document frequency of a word and use this metric and a threshold to extract terms.

Ripper (Cohen, 1995) is used as rule induction learning algorithm to perform learning that produces good performance by combining both and linguistic and statistical approach (Vivaldi, et al., 2001).

Word Alignment

Word alignment techniques are used in transliteration of the text. There are different word alignment techniques which use models generated using techniques such as Conditional Random Fields (CRF) (Lafferty, 2001) or Markov models.

Cross-Lingual Text Classification

Classification can be done using machine-learning approaches like SVM (Support Vector Machine)[12]. The features used in SVM based text chunking process contains different scores, which are used for classification.

Many issues still exist and machine learning provides a lending hand in solving the problems in information retrieval. In addition, it is improving efficiency to build state of art systems.

AN APPROACH FOR BUILDING MLIA SYSTEM

Building MLIA systems require solving issues and challenges mentioned in earlier sections. It also should have robust architecture and design to provide best results. In doing so, we may use some of the general approaches mentioned above.

There are several multilingual access systems built earlier, like SPIRIT (Syntactic and Probabilistic System for Indexing and Retrieving Textual Information) created by CEA (Commissariat à L'Energieatomique, French Atomic Center). It uses EMIR project[13] (European Multilingual Information Retrieval) and provides a user with multiple languageslike English, French, German, and Russian search capability. EuroSpider[14] is another such system developed at the Swiss Federal Institute of Technology, which is based on thesaurus-based query expansion approach performed over a collection of comparable multilingual documents. The MULINEX project[15] is another one that aims at providing an efficient management component of multilingual online information. This project is coordinated by DFKI (Deutsches Forschungszentrum für Künstliche Intelligenz GmbH) in Saarbrucken, Germany. Project translated search queries and summaries of Web documents to enable the user to make use of multilingual information. CANAL/LS[16] (Catalogue with Multilingual Natural Language Access /Linguistic Server) is a project supported within the framework of the LIBRARIES program to allow a user to search in multilingual online catalogs supported by European Union and coordinated by TEXTEC Software[17] in Germany. For evaluation existing tools (e.g. machine translation, grammar parser and checker) and corpora (such as terminological databases, thesauri and electronic dictionaries) TRANSLIB[18] project is started which is coordinated by the KNOWLEDGE S.A Company in Greece. It supports three languages mainly English, Greek, and Spanish. There are some other systems like TITAN(Total Information

Traverse Agent) developed at Information and Communication Systems Laboratories in Japan that support Japanese people searching the Internet resources and TWENTYONE for multilingual and multimedia documents and supports Dutch, French, and German.

In this section, we describe our experience of building a multi-lingual information access system by explaining our system's architecture and its features followed by the evaluation metrics. Difference of this system with existing MLIA systems is that developed system provides information access across Indian languages mainly Telugu, Hindi, and English.

System Architecture

MLIA system we present below is divided into different levels and modules. These levels consist of Crawling stage, indexing stage, query processing and searching, and ranking stages. We segregate each stage and explain the sub steps that were addressed at each level.

Crawling

A Crawler is a program, which browses the World Wide Web or the given document collection in a methodical automated manner and creates a copy of all the visited pages for later processing. In the MLIA system, we have a focused crawler (Chakrabarti, 1999) that looks for pages that fit a particular description. The pages belonging to certain selected topics, or satisfying certain criteria, are indexed and maintained. The crawler is guided by a classifier to recognize the relevance of the pages crawled.

In this system we have specified domains, which crawls only 'Tourism' and 'Health' domains and also classifies the Indian languages. For classification, machine-learning methods using SVM are used.

Indexing

An indexer module should be capable of building data structures, which enable fast retrieval of relevant documents and also enable ranking of these documents. The design of data structure for index should also be sensitive to transaction aspects such as locking of indices for writes, updatability of index without difficulty etc.

Indexing is the heart of an Information Retrieval system. Data structures such as term based inverted indices (Zobel, 2003) have proved to be very effective for IR using vector space retrieval models(Frakes & Baeza-Yates, 1992). However when functional aspects of such models were tested, it was soon felt that better relevance models were required to more accurately compute the relevance of a document towards a query.

It was shown that language-modeling approaches in monolingual IR (Ponte & Croft, 1998) tasks improve the quality of search results in comparison with TFIDF algorithm. The disadvantage of language modeling approaches when used in monolingual IR task as suggested is that they would require both the inverted index (term-to-document) and the forward index (document-to-term) to be able to compute the rank of document for a given query. This calls for an additional space and computation overhead when compared to inverted index models. Such a cost may be acceptable if the quality of search results is significantly improved.

In a Cross-lingual IR task using a bilingual dictionary along with term co-occurrence statistics and language modeling approach (Pingali, et al., 2007) helps improve the functional IR performance. An augmented index model is used for fast retrieval while having the benefits of language modeling in a MLIR task. This model is capable of retrieval and ranking with or without query expansion techniques using term collocation statistics of the indexed corpus (Pingali & Varma, 2007).

Some of the sub tasks involved in performing the multi language indexing is listed below.

Language / Encoding Identifier

As we are building system for Indian languages that have multiple encodings in each language needs to be addressed. Good number of language encodings is in usage on Internet and other document repositories. Especially in Indian language document repositories, these document collections are available in a set of national and international standards for Indian language character set encodings, while a number of publishers use proprietary non-standard encodings. For example, Telugu language has some proprietary fonts like Hemalatah, Tikkana, Vaartha, Karthika, etc. In order to be able to index such content, it is very important to identify the language and such encodings to achieve a better recall in retrieval by having much broader coverage. For language identification a set of statistical and non-statistical (rule-based) techniques can be used to identify the language of a document with a certain precision. Script based recognition for Unicode character sets works to an extent, but still ambiguities might exist. We use a set of heuristic based techniques using fonts and character ranges to recognize character encodings such as UTF-8, ISCII, or other proprietary encodings from HTML and PDF documents (Pingali, 2006).

Encoding Converter

Character encodings are identified for a particular document or a particular piece of text within a document, such content needs to be converted into a standard encoding so that it can be indexed. Unless all the character encodings of a single language are converted into a single encoding, it will not be possible to compare strings and match queries for retrieval. Therefore, an automatic encoding converter is essential to enable information access. Again similar to language identification, a set of heuristic based, or statistical methods can be used to convert content of one encoding into another. For example, one could come up with a mapping table of various glyphs or glyph sequences of one encoding into another that can be then used to automatically convert one character encoding into another. Since Indian languages are syllabic in nature most of these are rarely one to one glyph mappings and end up being one too many or many to one.

Stop-Word Remover

A lexicon containing Hindi and English stop words (Fox, 1990) is used to remove stop words before indexing. These words can be generated using the maximum frequency words in a corpus.

Lucene for Indexing

Indexing mechanism is required to support such a MLIA system. The main purpose of the indexer is to create indexing units and index tables. Index units consist of content words, Multi words and Named Entities. In the UNL system, the index units are UNL expressions and UWs. The Indexer requires Stemmed words (output of Stemmer / Language Analyzer), Multi Word Expression Lists (output of MWE Engine), and Named Entities (output of the NER Engine) as input.

For this purpose, we should use a traditional inverted index concept and it can be extended for this task. Lucene[19] inverted index mechanism works good for this and modifying it to suits our need. An inverted index is an inside-out arrangement of documents in which terms take center stage. Each term points to a list of documents that contain it. On the contrary, in a forward index, documents take the center stage, and each document refers to a list of terms it contains. Lucene uses an inverted index as its index structure while a forward index facility can be optionally created. Here both inverted and forward index are used as core index.

The fundamental concepts in Lucene are index, segments, document, field and term. An index contains a sequence of segments, which contain documents. Each document is a sequence of fields. A field is a named sequence of terms and a term is a string. Each segment index maintains Field names, Stored Field values, Term dictionary, Term Frequency data, and Term Proximity data, Normalization factors, Term Vectors, Deleted documents.

Main index files in Lucene contain file structures like Segments file, Fields information file, Text information file, Frequency file, Position file, which are used for index storage. In this system three new additional meta-index files are created, namely a collocation file to store co-occurrence frequencies of two terms, a query translation file to store weighted term-based translations between languages and a modified text information file to provide pointers to the first two meta-index files (Pingali & Varma, 2007). The text information file mentioned in the core Lucene index model is overridden to accommodate MLIR functions such as stemming and query translation. Term structure is modified to include the Suffix Length to determine the length of the suffix that needs to be stemmed. Storing the suffix as part of the term data structure instead of actually indexing the conflated variants allows the MLIR system to be able to search with or without stemming at the same time.

Query Processing

Query processing is important step in improving recall and precision of any system. In case of MLIA systems this takes at most importance as query can be of any language. Query pre-processing needs to be done to improve efficiency in retrieval. In this MLIA system, query processing module uses n-gram based translation of query words using bi-lingual lexicons. Identification of named entities is done by Named Entity Recognizers. If translation is not possible transliteration of the identified named entities is been carried out. In addition, a Boolean query-scoring sub-module used to weigh Boolean queries to generate the output of the query-processing module.

Lets us see below briefly some of the query processing steps performed in building this MLIA system for Telugu, Hindi and English.

Removal of Stop Words

List of stop words for Telugu and Hindi using a document set has been calculated with document frequency (the number of documents a word has figured in) for various terms from the given Telugu and Hindi documents and picked those terms with high document frequency as potential stop words. This list was then manually cleaned to obtain the final list of Telugu and Hindi stop words are prepared which is used to remove stop words from the query before translation or transliteration.

Shallow Stemming

Telugu is a highly agglutinative language, and in some cases, a whole phrase or a sentence from English could be translated into a single word in Telugu. Complexities such as these demand a very good lemmatization module to process Telugu. However the existing lemmatization modules do not have a comprehensive list of words, and hence we used some shallow rules (Pingali, Jagarlamudi, & Varma, 2006) which can remove some common prefixes and suffixes. Some of the very common prefixes and suffixes are removed from a given Telugu word. These prefixes and suffixes were picked from the lexicon that was built from Telugu document corpus and choosing words that share common prefixes and suffixes with high frequency. This list was then manually pruned to come up with an optimal list of prefixes and suffixes. A given word is stemmed from these prefixes and suffixes recursively until a stem is obtained.

Named Entities Identification

Named Entity Recognition is the task of identifying and classifying all proper nouns in a document as person names, organization names, location names, date and time expressions, and miscellaneous. Identification of named entities or Out Of Vocabulary words (OOVs) in the given query is very critical in deciding the words to be transliterated. Such a binary classification is of much help rather than recognizing the class of the named entities.

Previous work (Cucerzan & Yarowsky, 1999) was done using the complete words as features that suffer from a low recall problem. Character n-gram-based approach (Klein, 2003) using generative models, was experimented on English language and it proved to be useful over the word based models. This technique was applied on Indian Languages as well with inclusion of Conditional Random Fields (CRFs) (Wallach, 2004) with two Indian languages Telugu and Hindi (Shishtla, et al., 2008). The character n-gram-based models showed considerable improvement over the word based models.

Other techniques like using Stanford Named Entity Recognizer can be used to identify the named entities in English present in the queries. For Hindi and Telugu queries above mentioned method is used for identifying named entities in the queries and been passed to the transliteration module for transliteration.

Query Translation using Lexicons

Resources containing English-Hindi[20] and English-Telugu cross language dictionaries[21] were primarily used in English to Indian language query translation. Available English-Hindi dictionary was conveniently formatted for machine processing; however, the English-Telugu dictionary was a digitized version of a human readable dictionary. In order to convert the human readable dictionary to machine processing form, a set of regular expressions were used (Pingali & Varma, 2006). Similar approaches were previously tried to convert human readable dictionaries into a form easily processed by machines (Mayfield & McNamee, 2002). Set of standard high frequency suffixes both from the queries and dictionaries beforehand. The set of prefixes we used for Hindi are similar to those mentioned in Larkey (2003).

However, there are some problems like a set of multiple English meanings for a given query terms can be obtained for a given Indian language term. Many of the terms may not be found in the bilingual lexicon since the term is a proper name or a word from a foreign language or a valid Indian language word, which just did not occur in the dictionary. In some of the cases dictionary lookup for a term might also fail because of improper stemming or suffix removal. Indian languages are agglutinative languages[22]; especially Telugu is highly agglutinative which would demand a good stemming algorithm. However, due to lack of availability of such a resource we used suffix removal technique (Pingali & Varma, 2006) with a set of high frequency suffixes mainly for lookup failure cases where the word was a proper name.

Transliteration

Transliteration task is considered to be non-trivial as its output decides the quality of the results retrieved in MLIA systems. Transliteration module is build on a grapheme based model (Jong-Hoon, et al., 2006b) in which transliteration equivalents were identified by mapping the source language names to their equivalents in a target language index, instead of generating them.

The basic principle is to compress the source word into its minimal form and align it across an indexed list of target language words to arrive at the top n-equivalents based on the modified edit distance. Mapping based model ensures accuracy and fastness. To speed up the process of arriving at the right match in the target index, Compressed Word Format (CWFs) of the target named entities and indexing the CWFs along with their actual forms is done. When any new query word arrives for transliteration CWF form is to be generated and is to be compared with the CWF of the source query word with the CWFs of the target language. Entries in the index of the matching entries with modified Levenshtein distance equal to zero will be returned.

Query Scoring

Query scoring helps to rank the retrieved results. Once the source language queries were translated and transliterated, the resultant target language keywords is to be used for constructing Boolean queries using the OR operator. Different scores for the words originated from the different parts of the source topic are to be used. Order of weights is decided for the different words found at different places of the document. These weights are assigned in the descending order starting from more weight to the least. The weight assigned to target language words originated from the title section of the source topic are given highest weight followed by the weight assigned to target language words originated from the description section of the source topic and then the least weight assigned to target language words originated from the narration section of the source topic. If a particular keyword occurs in multiple sections of the query, it has to be given greater score compared to the other keywords accordingly. Hence, cumulative weight for each word to be calculated based on the number of occurrences (Ballesteros, 1997). Other important keywords like years, numbers, are also given higher weight factors. The translated query word in the Boolean query and the scoring weight are associated and the final query output for a given source language query from the system would be of the formed.

Snippet Generation

Snippet is a short summary of each document retrieved by the MLIA system for a user query. To retrieve the content of the retrieved document from search engine query words are given to the MLIA system. If a snippet is human readable which consists of a title and a short summary relevant to the query then it can be though that snippet has been effectively generated.

In our system, the query words will be highlighted in the snippet produced and then forwarded to the snippet Translation module. Indian language Web documents sometimes contain the META description in English which reduces readability and efficient in fetching the actual Indian language content. If this META description content is not available then the system generates the snippet. Extracted snippet is considered efficient if the sentence extraction has language specific sentence boundary delimiter task. For this title extracted using the title tags obtained from the HTML source file or from the document files is checked for accuracy. This process will receive as its input the output of the title and text Content Extraction process.

This extracted text content is then scanned for complete sentences using the sentence delimiter. Each complete sentence will be checked for the presence of the query words in question. Sentences are ranked based on the number of query words, key words and domain ontology words present in the sentence. The generated short summary or snippet contains the context (five to ten words depending on the number of query words) of the highlighted query words subject to a predetermined length of the snippet. If no complete sentences are identified, the menu list on the Web page will be listed as the snippet of the Web page.

Searching and Ranking

Probabilistic retrieval algorithm BM25 (Robertson & Zaragoza, 2009) is used for multi lingual

Figure 1. MLIA architecture diagram

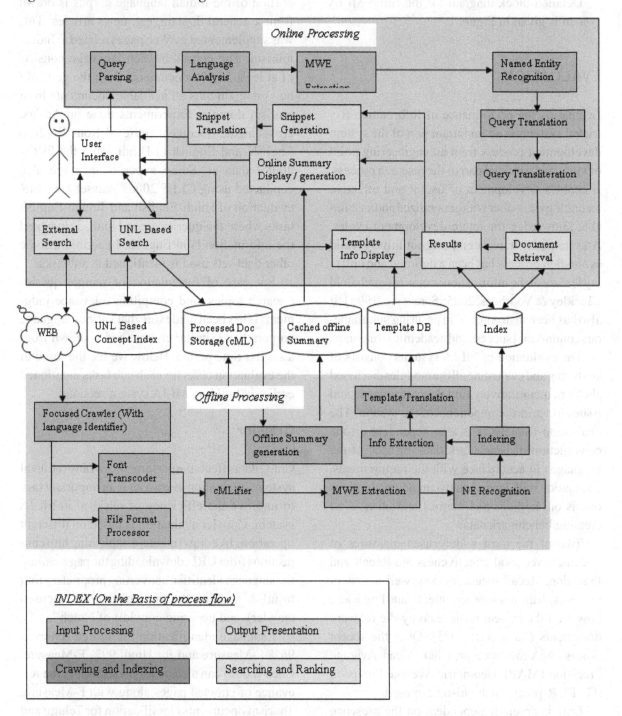

information retrieval. It is a ranking function used to rank matching documents according to their relevance to a given search query. It uses bag-of-words approach for retrieval function that ranks a set of documents based on the query terms appearing in each document, regardless of the inter-relationship between the query terms within a document. It is not a single function, but actually a whole family of scoring functions, with slightly different components and parameters.

Detailed block diagram for the entire MLIA system is given in Figure 1.

EVALUATION

Evaluating the performance of Information Retrieval systems is an important part of the system development process from an engineering point of view, and a crucial part of the research process. It enables development of useful and effective technology, together with generalized and sustainable knowledge for future development cycles. A systematic, transparent, and intuitively valid evaluation process has been a defining and unifying feature of the information access research field (Buckley & Voorhees, 2005; Saracevic, 1995). It also has been instrumental in ensuring simultaneous commercial success and academic stringency.

The evaluation of MLIA systems consists of analyzing and evaluating all the modules discussed above to quantitatively find the performance and issues in various components of the system. The evaluation framework is also dependent on the construction of benchmark data for each of the languages in accordance with the requirements. Evaluation will depend on two major evaluations one is on methods and metrics and other is on creating benchmark data.

Two of the most widely used measures of document retrieval effectiveness are Recall and Precision. Recall measures how well a system retrieves all the relevant documents; and Precision, how well the system retrieves only the relevant documents (Saracevic, 1975). Over the recent time some other measures like Mean Average Precision (MAP), Geometric Average Precision (GAP), R-precision are also been used.

Data is crucially dependent on the presence of appropriate corpora in each language. In keeping with the standards with kind of corpora used at international IR/IE evaluation forum such as TREC, CLEF, NTCIR, MUC, etc, a sizeable portion of the Indian language corpus is drawn from a general domain, e.g. news articles. This was supplemented by Web pages related to Indian tourism. The corpus in each language consists of at least 50,000 documents from the general / news domain plus all available documents from tourism domain. Experiments done on Ad-hoc cross-lingual document retrieval from Hindi to English, and English to Hindi using the FIRE-2008[23] dataset. Some experiments were also conducted using CLEF 2006[24] dataset for CLIR evaluation of Hindi-English and Telugu-English tasks where the queries are in Hindi, Telugu and the information is in English. In addition, some other data sets used is mentioned in subtasks.

For ease of formulation of sample queries / search topics, and compiling relevance judgments is has been made sure that various language corpora have similar content and is drawn from a similar time period. Below we see the some of the evaluation tasks for each sub tasks mentioned earlier in building MLIA system sections.

Crawler

Crawl data affects the performance of any retrieval system. Evaluation of crawler is an important task to improve the efficiency of retrieval in MLIA system. Crawler evaluation is based on different operations like crawl queue, establishing http connections from URL, downloading the page, calling the language identifier, converting proprietary font to utf-8, fetching the topic of interest (focused crawler), and updating crawldB of Nutch[25].

Language identification for Telugu achieved 96% F-Measure and for Hindi 99% F-Measure. Chen (2005) can also be used to compute the relevance of crawled pages along with F-Measure. Tourism documents classification for Telugu and Hindi languages are done using SVM Light[26] that attained 83.5% precision for Telugu and 66% precision for Hindi.

Stemmer / Morphological Analyzer, MWE, and NER

Stemmer/morphological analysers are used in identifying the root words. Extracted root words are used in searching. The stems and their positions make up the long index list. The short index will comprise of the important terms from the title, heading, as well as anchor text of incoming links. Telugu and Hindi stemmer has achieved 96% precision measure.

MWEs in the query words based on pre-created lists of MWE expressions checked for effectiveness as during the offline processing, indexing MWEs are identified in the words of the documents and populated into field of the index. In the case of query word, the word will be tagged as an MWE and list contains about 8846 entries.

In the offline processing, we check for NER engine, which extracts NE's from the crawled documents and NER tags. The NER engine is integrated with the indexer. The tagged text becomes input to the IE module. Before extraction of NE's from existing corpus training of data provided for NERSSEAL[27] competition is used. The corpus in total consisted of 64026 tokens out of which 10894 were NEs. Corpus is divided into training and testing sets. The training set consisted of 46068 tokens out of which 8485 were NEs. The testing set consisted of 17951 tokens out of which 2407 were NEs. The tag set as mentioned in the release, was based on AUKBC's ENAMEX, TIMEX, and NAMEX has the following tags: NEP (Person), NED (Designation), NEO (Organization), NEA (Abbreviation), NEB (Brand), NETP (Title-Person), NETO (Title-Object), NEL (Location), NETI (Time), NEN (Number), NEM (Measure), and NETE (Terms). A word window 6 words at a time having Parts Of Speech (POS), suffix, and prefix gave F-Measure 44.91% for Hindi (Shishtla, et al., 2008). Another approach using n-grams has been performed which attained F-Measure of

44.57% for Hindi if n=4 and 49.62% for Telugu if n=3 (Shishtla, et al., 2008).

Retrieval Effectiveness

To find the effectiveness of the information retrieval we have to evaluate by different methods either by certain predefined parameters or by human judgment. A set of certain search topics / queries in different languages need to be queried, for each query a list of top-ranked 100 documents retrieved by the MLIA system in response to that query in the corpus those are relevant to that query is analyzed.

For the results retrieved Recall, precision at various cutoffs, interpolated average precision, and average non-interpolated precision can be calculated. Of these metrics, we used relevant documents retrieved, Mean Average Precision (MAP), binary preference (b-pref) and precision for first 10 results (P10) (Pingali, et al., 2007). After running the results, it has been found that the Hindi English CLIR performs reasonably. Also from P@10, it has been observed that systems using Boolean AND operator with appropriate boosting of metadata results in better ranking. However, it resulted in lower recall.

It is also observed that system is able to retrieve more relevant documents when queries are combined using Boolean OR operator. The monolingual query expansion applied to Hindi-English and Telugu-English CLIR tasks improved recall however for English it dint improve much. However, in the case of CLIR, we found there call to increase a lot since query expansion increases the probability of translating a source language keyword into target language even when the keyword is not found in the bilingual lexicon.

Information Extraction

The Information Extraction engine runs as a background process that extracts the pertinent information from text into pre-defined templates. Information Extraction requires the presence of Information Extraction templates. These templates are domain specific for example in the tourism domain the following templates are being used like Travel, Accommodation, Food, and Places of Tourist Interest. These templates contains the extracted information is sent to the template driven translation engine for translating the extracted information to the source language. To evaluate the efficiency of the data extraction and the quality of data filled into the template system and the relevance of the data is been measured. Relevance is also measured by metrics mentioned earlier in the previous sections. Also for IE some preprocessing steps are involved like POS tagging, NP Chunking, and a shallow parsing, which has been measured by earlier mentioned evaluation metrics for cross language documents.

Snippet Translation

Snippet translation is been carried from the query language Telugu to English and Hindi snippets generated by the snippet generation module. Generated Snippet in English or Hindi after snippet translation is been evaluated by the results retrieved and also the accuracy of the snippet which is been translated. We used user based evaluation metrics by manually evaluating the effectiveness of the machine translation.

Summary Generation

For the evaluation of the performance of the summarization system, DUC 2005[28] data set is been used. Each topic has either 4 (for 30 topics) or 9 (for the rest of 20 topics) model summaries that were written by humans, for the evaluation of peer summaries. For automatic scores calculation and evaluation metrics ROUGE (Lin, 2004) is extended to ROUGE-SU4 (Pingali, 2006), F-measure scores attained by the system is 0.11323, which is 30% improvement above the English

monolingual baseline and our system is currently about 45% less than an average human summary.

Summary Translation

Single document query specific summary translation is carried out for English and Hindi Web pages for translating the summaries generated by the summary generation module into the query language. This achieved 60% precision as observed by human evaluators.

SUMMARY

We have described the key differences between the CLIR, MLIR, CLIA, and MLIA systems depending on the languages considered and their outputs. If the system handles information between pair of languages they are called cross language systems, while handling more than that they are termed multi lingual systems. If the output of a system consists of ranked set of retrieved documents then it is a retrieval system, but if the output generated is further processed for easier consumption and presented in the language of the query, it can be called as an information access system.

All these multilingual information access systems essentially benefit from the Information Retrieval technologies, which enable information access by retrieving a set of ranked documents that are likely to be relevant to the information. However, the role of IR technologies ends once the relevant documents are obtained. However, there are other problems when dealing with CLIR systems. They require query translation/translation, NE identification, results ranking, which have dependencies on lexicons having good coverage, bilingual dictionaries, and parallel corpora for efficient information retrieval. In this chapter, we have presented major challenges in building MLIA systems. In addition, we described two major approaches to building the MLIA systems, namely, knowledge based and machine learning approaches. We have used both of these approaches in building a large-scale MLIA system that deals with English and two other Indian languages, Telugu and Hindi.

For MLIA system, user evaluation is also plays very important role to understand the quality of performance of the system. Evaluation helps in quantitatively understanding the relevance of the results, compare them against each other, and find out relevant portions of the document that might satisfy their information need. Extracting exact elements of the text that provide answers and perhaps summarize multiple documents or portions of the documents also enhances user experience.

ACKNOWLEDGMENT

We acknowledge the funding we have received from Ministry of Communication and Information Technology (MCIT), Government of India. Working with various members of the Cross Language Information Access (CLIA) consortium helped us directly and indirectly in writing this chapter.

REFERENCES

Ananthakrishnan, R. (2003). State of the art in cross-lingual information retrieval. *Vivek Journal, 15*(2).

Asif, E., Rejwanul, H., & Sivaji, B. (2008). Named entity recognition in Bengali: A conditional random field approach. In *Proceedings of the 3rd International Joint Conference on Natural Language Processing (IJCNLP-2008)*, (pp. 589-594). Hyderabad, India: IJCNLP.

Attia, M., Toral, A., Tounsi, L., Pecina, P., & Genabith, J. (2010). Automatic extraction of arabic multiword expressions. In *Proceedings of the COLING 2010, Workshop on Multiword Expressions: From Theory to Applications (MWE 2010)*. Beijing, China: COLING.

Ballesteros, L., & Croft, W. B. (1996). Dictionary methods for cross-lingual information retrieval. In *Proceedings of the 7th International DEXA Conference on Database and Expert Systems,* (pp. 791-801). DEXA.

Ballesteros, L., & Croft, W. B. (1997). Phrasal translation and query expansion techniques for cross-language information retrieval. In *Proceedings of the 20th Annual International ACM Conference on Research and Development in Information Retrieval*, (pp. 84-91). Philadelphia, PA: ACM Press.

Braschler, M., Wechsler, M., Mateev, B., Mittendorf, E., & Schauble, P. (1999). SPIDER retrieval system. In *Proceedings of TREC7*. TREC.

Brown, P. F., Cocke, J., Della Pietra, S. A., Della Pietra, V. J., Jelinek, F., & Lafferty, J. (1990). A statistical approach to machine translation. *Computational Linguistics, 16*, 79–85.

Brown, P. F., Della Pietra, S. A., & Mercer, R. L. (1993). The mathematics of statistical machine translation: Parameter estimation. *Computational Linguistics, 19*(2), 263–311.

Brown, R. D. (1996). Example-based machine translation in the Pangloss system. [Copenhagen, Denmark: COLING.]. *Proceedings of COLING, 1996*, 169–174.

Buckley, C., Mitra, M., Walz, J., & Cardie, C. (1999). SMART high precision. In Voorhees, E., & Harman, D. (Eds.), *TREC7. NIST.*

Buckley, C., & Voorhees, E. M. (2005). Retrieval system evaluation. In *TREC: Experiment and Evaluation in Information Retrieval*. Cambridge, MA: MIT Press.

Chakrabarti, S., Dom, B., & van den Berg, M. (1999). Focused crawling: A new approach for topic-specific resource discovery. In *Proceedings of the 8th World Wide Web Conference*, (pp. 545-562). Amsterdam, The Netherlands: Elsevier Science.

Chen, Z., Ma, J., Lei, J., Yuan, B., Lian, L., & Song, L. (2009). A cross-language focused crawling algorithm based on multiple relevance prediction strategies. *Computers & Mathematics with Applications (Oxford, England)*, *57*(6), 1057–1072. doi:10.1016/j.camwa.2008.09.021

Cohen, W. (1995). Fast effective rule induction. In *Proceedings of the 12th International Conference on Machine Learning*, (pp. 115-123). IEEE.

Cucerzan, S., & Yarowsky, D. (1999). Language independent named entity recognition combining morphological and contextual evidence. In *Proceedings of the Joint SIGDAT Conference on Empirical Methods in Natural Language Processing and Very Large Corpora*, (pp. 90-99). SIGDAT.

Davis, M. W., & Dunning, T. E. (1995). A TREC evaluation of query translation methods for multilingual text retrieval. In Harman, D. K. (Ed.), *TREC-4. NIST.*

Davis, M. W., & Ogden, W. C. (1997). Implementing cross-language text retrieval system for large-scale text collection on the world wide web. In *Proceedings of the AAAI Symposium on Cross-language Text and Speech Retrieval*. American for Artificial Intelligence.

Deerwester, S. S., Dumais, S. T., Furnas, G. W., Landauer, T. K., & Harshman, R. (1999). Indexing by latent semantic analysis. *Journal of the American Society for Information Science American Society for Information Science*, *41*(6).

Eisele, A., & Chen, Y. (2010). *MultiUN: A multilingual corpus from United Nations documents.* In *Proceedings of the Seventh International Conference on Language Resources and Evaluation*, (pp. 2868-2872). Valletta, Malta: LREC.

Emeneau, M. B. (1956). India as linguistic area. *Linguistics*, *32*, 3–16.

Fox, C. (1990). A stop list for general text. *SIGIR Forum, 24*(1-2), 19–21.

Frakes, W., & Baeza-Yates, R. (1992). *Information retrieval: Data structures & algorithms.* Englewood Cliffs, NJ: Prentice Hall.

Frederking, R., Mitamura, T., Nyberg, E., & Carbonell, J. (1997). Translingual information access. In *Proceedings of the AAAI Spring Symposium on Cross-Language Text and Speech Retrieval*. Stanford, CA: AAAI.

Grefenstette, G. (1995). Comparing two language identification schemes. In *Proceedings of JADT*. JADT.

Hakkani-Tür, D., Tur, G., Levit, M., Gillick, D., Singla, A., & Yaman, S. (2010). Statistical sentence extraction for multilingual information distillation. In Olive, McCary, Dietrich, & Christianson (Eds.), *Handbook of Natural Language Processing and Machine Translation: DARPA Global Autonomous Language Exploitation (GALE) Program*. Berlin, Germany: Springer.

Hovy, E., Ide, N., Frederking, R., Mariani, J., & Zampolli, A. (2001). Multilingual information management: Current levels and future abilities. In *Linguistica Computazionale (Vol. 14-15)*. Pisa, Italy: Istituti Editoriali e Poligrafici Internazionali.

Hull, D. A., & Grefenstette, G. (1996). Experiments in multilingual information retrieval. In *Proceedings of the 19th Annual International ACM SIGIR Conference on Research and Development in Information Retrieval*. ACM Press.

Hull, D. A., & Grefenstette, G. (1996). *Querying across languages: A dictionary-based approach to multilingual information retrieval.* Paper presented at SIGIR 1996. Zurich, Switzerland.

Jan, E.-E., Lin, S.-H., & Chen, B. (2010). Transliteration retrieval model for cross lingual information retrieval. *Lecture Notes in Computer Science, 6458,* 183–192. doi:10.1007/978-3-642-17187-1_17

Jong-Hoon, Key-Sun, Choi, & Isahara, H. (2006b). A machine transliteration model based on correspondence between graphemes and phonemes. *ACM Transactions on Asian Language Processing, 5*(3), 185–208.

Klein, D., Smarr, J., Nguyen, H., & Manning, C. (2003). Named entity recognition with character-level models. In *Proceedings of the Seventh Conference on Natural Language Learning at HLT-NAACL 2003,* (Vol 4). NAACL.

Kozerenko, E. (2004). *Multilingual systems: Grammar acquisition by machine learning.* Moscow, Russia: Institute for Informatics Problems of the Russian Academy of Sciences.

Kunchukuttan, A., & Damani, O. P. (2008). A system for compound nouns multiword expression extraction for Hindi. In *Proceedings of 6th International Conference on Natural Language Processing (ICON 2008).* Pune, India: ICON.

Lafferty, J., McCallum, A., & Pereira, F. (2001). Conditional random fields: Probabilistic models for segmenting and labeling sequence data. In *Proceedings of ICML 2001,* (pp. 282-289). ICML.

Larkey, L., Abdul Jaleel, N., & Connell, M. (2003). *What's in a name? Proper names in Arabic cross language information retrieval. CIIR Technical Report, IR-278.* Amherst, MA: University of Amherst.

Leah, S. L., Connell, M. E., & Abduljaleel, N. (2003). Hindi CLIR in thirty days. *ACM Transactions on Asian Language Information Processing, 2*(2), 130–142. doi:10.1145/974740.974746

Lin, C. Y. (2004). ROUGE: A package for automatic evaluation of summaries. In *Proceedings of Workshop on Text Summarization.* Barcelona, Spain: ACL.

Lin, W. C., & Chen, H. H. (2004). Merging multilingual information retrieval results based on prediction of retrieval effectiveness. In *Proceedings of the Fourth NTCIR Workshop Meeting: Cross-Lingual Information Retrieval Task.* NTCIR.

Manning, C. D., & Schütze, H. (1999). *Foundations of statistical natural language processing.* Cambridge, MA: MIT Press.

Mayfield, J., & McNamee, P. (2002). Converting on-line bilingual dictionaries from human readable to machine-readable form. In *Proceedings of the 25th Annual International ACM SIGIR Conference on Research and Development in Information Retrieval,* (pp. 405-406). New York, NY: ACM Press.

Mayfield, J., & McNamee, P. (2002). *Three principles to guide CLIR research.* In Proceedings of a workshop at SIGIR-2002. Tampere, Finland.

McNamee, P., & Mayfield, J. (2002). Comparing cross-language query expansion techniques by degrading translation resources. In *Proceedings of the 25th Annual International ACM SIGIR Conference on Research and Development in Information Retrieval,* (pp. 159–166). ACM Press.

Nagao, M. (1984). A framework of a mechanical translation between Japanese and English by analogy principle. In *Artificial and Human Intelligence* (pp. 173–180). Edinburgh, UK: North-Holland.

Oard, D. &Dorr, B. (1996). *A survey of multilingual text retrieval*. Technical Report UMIACS-TR-96-19. College Park, MD: University of Maryland.

Oard, D. W. (1996). *Adaptive vector space text filtering for monolingual and cross-language applications*. (Ph.D. Thesis). University of Maryland. College Park, MD.

Philipp, M. (2004). *Multilingual information extraction*. (Master's Thesis). University of Helsinki. Helsinki, Finland.

Pingali, P., Jagarlamudi, J., & Varma, V. (2006). *A dictionary based approach with query expansion to cross language query based multi-document summarization: Experiments in Telugu English*. Paper presented at the National Workshop on Artificial Intelligence. Mumbai, India.

Pingali, P., Jagarlamudi, J., & Varma, V. (2006). Webkhoj: Indian language ir from multiple character encodings. In *Proceedings of the 15ᵗʰ International Conference on World Wide Web*, (pp. 801-809). Edinburgh, UK: ACM Press.

Pingali, P., Kula, K. T., & Varma, V. (2007). Hindi, Telugu, Oromo, English CLIR evaluation. *Evaluation of Multilingual and Multi-Modal Information Retrieval, 4730*.

Pingali, P., Tune, K. K., & Varma, V. (2006). *Hindi, Telugu, Oromo, English CLIR evaluation*. Paper presented at the CLEF 2006. New York, NY.

Pingali, P., & Varma, V. (2006). *Hindi and Telugu to English cross language information retrieval*. Barcelona, Spain: Working Notes of Cross Language Evaluation Forum Workshop.

Pingali, P., & Varma, V. (2007). Multilingual indexing support for CLIR using language modeling. *Bulletin of the IEEE Computer Society Technical Committee on Data Engineering, 30*(1), 70–85.

Ponte, J., & Croft, W. B. (1998). A language modeling approach to information retrieval. In *Proceedings of the 1998 SIGIR Conference on Research and Development in Information Retrieval*, (pp. 275-281). SIGIR.

Robertson, S., & Zaragoza, H. (2009). Probabilistic relevance framework: BM25 and beyond. *Foundations and Trends in Information Retrieval, 3*(4), 333–389. doi:10.1561/1500000019

Sanderson, M. (1994). Word sense disambiguation and information retrieval. In *Proceedings of the 17th Annual International ACM SIGIR Conference on Research and Development in Information Retrieval*, (pp. 142-151). Dublin, Ireland: ACM Press.

Saracevic, T. (1975). Relevance: A review of and a framework for thinking on the notion in information science. *Journal of the American Society for Information Science and Technology, 26*(6), 321–343. doi:10.1002/asi.4630260604

Saracevic, T. (1995). Evaluation of evaluation in information retrieval. In *Proceedings of the 18th Annual international ACM SIGIR Conference on Research and Development in information Retrieval*, (pp. 138-146). Seattle, WA: ACM Press.

Saravanan, K., Udupa, R., & Kumaran, A. (2010). Cross lingual information retrieval system enhanced with transliteration generation and mining. In *Proceedings of Forum for Information Retrieval Evaluation (FIRE-2010) Workshop*. Kolkata, India: FIRE.

Sato, S. (1992). CTM: An example-based translation aid system. [COLING.]. *Proceedings of COLING, 14*, 1259–1263.

Scott, C. D., Deerwester, Dumais, S. T., Landauer, T. K., Furnas, G. W., & Harshman, R. A. (1990). Indexing by latent semantic analysis. *Journal of the American Society for Information Science American Society for Information Science, 41*(6), 391–407. doi:10.1002/(SICI)1097-4571(199009)41:6<391::AID-ASI1>3.0.CO;2-9

Segalovich, I. V. (2003). A fast morphological algorithm with unknown word guessing induced by a dictionary for a web search engine. In *Proceedings of the International Conference on Machine Learning, Models, Technologies and Applications,* (pp. 273-280). Las Vegas, NV: CSREA Press.

Sheridan, P., & Ballerini, J. P. (1996). Experiments in multilingual information retrieval using the SPIDER system. In *Proceedings of the 19th ACM SIGIR Conference on Research and Development in Information Retrieval,* (pp. 58–64). ACM Press.

Shishtla, P. M., Pingali, P., & Varma, V. (2008a). A character n-gram based approach for improved recall in Indian language NER. In *Proceedings of IJCNLP-08 Workshop on Named Entity Recognition for South and South East Asian Languages,* (pp. 67-74). Hyderabad, India: IJCNLP.

Shishtla, P. M., Pingali, P., & Varma, V. (2008b). Experiments in Telugu NER: A conditional random field approach. In *Proceedings of IJCNLP-08 Workshop on Named Entity Recognition for South and South East Asian Languages,* (pp. 105-110). Hyderabad, India: IJCNLP.

Sibun, P., & Spitz, A. (1994). Language determination: Natural language processing from scanned document images. In *Proceedings of Applied Natural Language Processing* (pp. 15–21). Stuttgart, Germany: ACL.

Singh, A. K., & Surana, H. (2007). Study of cognates among south Asian languages for the purpose of building lexical resources. In *Proceedings of National Seminar on Creation of Lexical Resources for Indian Language Computing and Processing.* ACL.

Singh, A. K., & Surana, H. (2007). *There can be depth in the surface: A unified computational model of scripts and its applications.* Unpublished.

Sumita, E., & Iida, H. (1991). Experiments and prospects of example-based machine translation. [Berkeley, CA: ACL.]. *Proceedings of, ACL-91,* 185–192.

Thompson, C. A., & Mooney, R. J. (1999). Automatic construction of semantic lexicons for learning natural language interfaces. In *Proceedings of the Sixteenth National Conference on Artificial Intelligence (AAAI 1999),* (pp. 487-493). Orlando, FL: AAAI.

Toth, K., Farkas, R., & Kocsor, A. (2008). Sentence alignment of Hungarian English parallel corpora using a hybrid algorithm. *Acta Cybern, 18*(3), 463–478.

Vivaldi, J., Màrquez, L., & Rodríguez, H. (2001). Improving term extraction by system combination using boosting. In *Proceedings of the 12th European Conference on Machine Learning (ECML),* (pp. 515–526). ECML.

Wallach, H. M. (2004). *Conditional random fields: An introduction.* Technical Report MS-CIS-04-21. Philadelphia, PA: University of Pennsylvania.

Wechsler, M., & Schäuble, P. (1998). Multilingual information retrieval based on document alignment techniques. In *Proceedings of the Second European Conference on Research and Advanced Technology for Digital Libraries ECDL 1998.* Crete, Greece: ECDL.

Yang, C. C., & Lam, W. (2006). Introduction to the special topic section on multilingual information systems. *Journal of the American Society for Information Science and Technology, 57*(5), 629–631. doi:10.1002/asi.20325

Zelle, J., & Mooney, R. (1996). Comparative results on using inductive logic programming for corpus-based parser construction. In *Symbolic, Connectionist, and Statistical Approaches to Learning for Natural Language Processing.* Berlin, Germany: Springer Verlag. doi:10.1007/3-540-60925-3_59

Zobel, J., Moffat, A., & Ramamohanarao, K. (1998). Inverted files versus signature files for text indexing. *ACM Transactions on Database Systems, 23*(4), 453–490. doi:10.1145/296854.277632

ENDNOTES

[1] http://www.statmt.org/moses/

[2] http://www.collinslanguage.com/shop/english-cobuild.aspx

[3] http://dict.leo.org/ende?lang=de&lp=ende

[4] http://www.oxfordadvancedlearnersdictionary.com/

[5] http://www.merriam-webster.com/

[6] http://nora.hd.uib.no/corpora.html

[7] http://www.ldc.upenn.edu/Catalog/CatalogEntry.jsp?catalogId=LDC95T20

[8] http://wordnet.princeton.edu/

[9] http://nlp.shef.ac.uk/eurowordnet/euro-wordnet.html

[10] http://www.cl.cam.ac.uk/Research/NL/acquilex

[11] http://www.cfilt.iitb.ac.in/wordnet/webhwn/

[12] http://www.support-vector-machines.org/

[13] http://www-uk.research.ec.org/esp-syn/text/5312.html

[14] http://www.eurospider.ch/

[15] http://www.dfki.de/lt/projects/mulinex

[16] http://saarland.sz-sb.de:2222/canal/can1.htm

[17] http://www.textec.de

[18] http://peterpan.uc3m.es/proyectos/translib/HomePage.htm

[19] http://lucene.apache.org/java/docs/index.html

[20] http://www.shabdkosh.com/archives/content/shabdanjali_-_english_hindi_dictionary/

[21] http://ltrc.iiit.net/onlineServices/

[22] http://en.wikipedia.org/wiki/Agglutinative_language

[23] http://www.isical.ac.in/~clia/ [24] http://www.clef-campaign.org

[25] http://nutch.apache.org/

[26] http://svmlight.joachims.org/

[27] http://ltrc.iiit.ac.in/ner-ssea-08/index.cgi?topic=5

[28] http://duc.nist.gov/duc2005/

Chapter 9
Multilingual Information Access

Víctor Peinado
ETSI Informática, Spain

Álvaro Rodrigo
ETSI Informática, Spain

Fernando López-Ostenero
ETSI Informática, Spain

ABSTRACT

In spite of the fact that English is the dominant language of the Web, as the usage of the Internet spreads all over the world, the number of users who do not speak English as a mother tongue is continuously growing. Language barriers become a key obstacle to the full exploitation of the available information, and cross-language search is one of the major challenges Web search companies are currently facing. When performing multilingual information searches, there are two important challenges to be solved: a) how to find information written in a foreign language and b) how to use the information we found.

This chapter focuses on Multilingual Information Access (MLIA), a multidisciplinary area that aims to solve accessing, querying, and retrieving information from heterogeneous information sources expressed in different languages. Current Information Retrieval technology, combined with Natural Language Processing tools allows building systems able to efficiently retrieve relevant information and, to some extent, to provide concrete answers to questions expressed in natural language. Besides, when linguistic resources and translation tools are available, cross-language information systems can assist to find information in multiple languages. Nevertheless, little is still known about how to properly assist people to find and use information expressed in unknown languages. Approaches proved as useful for automatic systems seem not to match with real user's needs.

1. INTRODUCTION

Since the second half of the 20th century, English is the lingua franca for business, science, and cultural interchange. It is still the dominant language of Web content, but the number of Web users who do not speak English as first language is continuously growing. Today's global world and the ever-growing digital universe require to effectively and efficiently interact with information across languages boundaries and multiple media, such as text, speech, images and video. Indeed, it is one of the major challenges Web

DOI: 10.4018/978-1-4666-2169-5.ch009

Figure 1. Search trends for the query "translate"

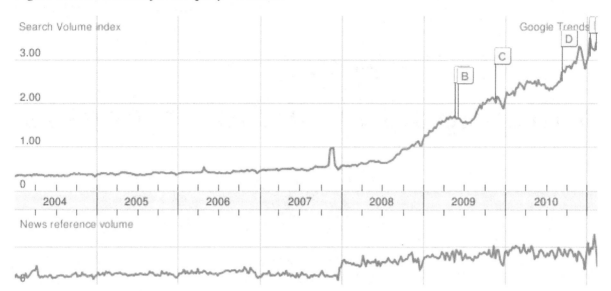

search companies are currently facing (Spector, 2009), as a result of the growing interest from Web users, as Figure 1 shows.

Multilingual Information Access (MLIA) integrates tools, technologies, and resources[1] from other disciplines as Natural Language Processing (NLP) and Information Retrieval (IR) to allow accessing, querying, and retrieving information from collections of documents in any language. Indeed, an ideal MLIA system, in the broadest sense, should help people find and understand (or interpret) the information they seek, regardless the linguistic skills of the user and the language(s) in which queries and information sources are expressed. MLIA always involves Cross-Language Information Retrieval (CLIR), i.e., how to access documents written in anyone of a range of different languages.

However, in spite of the growing interest on MLIA technology, few operational systems exist. Salton, in the late 1960s, was the pioneer trying to address the CLIR problem. By using a manually-built thesaurus between German and English, he reported similar results compared to monolingual IR (Salton, 1969). Later on, from 1996, CLIR became a true research field when

conferences and evaluation initiatives such as SIGIR[2], TREC[3], NTCIR[4], FIRE[5], and, above all, CLEF[6]—the major evaluation campaign mainly focused on the multilingual aspects of the information access—started to encourage innovation and experimentation by creating resources and methodologies and setting robust evaluation frameworks. However, developing MLIA systems still remain a complex task.

The remainder of this chapter is as follows. In Section 2, we present the idea of an Information Retrieval system supporting MLIA, breaking up the three different stages a Cross-Language Information Retrieval system is made of, namely: 1) processing and indexing the document collection; 2) translation and techniques to overcome the language gap; and 3) matching queries and documents. In addition, further details about the difficulties and problems to solve when dealing with multiple languages are provided. Then, Section 3 focuses on Question Answering, a more sophisticated form of IR systems, along with the most successful cross-lingual approaches reported in the field. The experiences described so far are based on automatic MLIA systems and batch experiments, but in Section 4, we introduce the user's perspective with the difficulties associated to conduct and evaluate user-centered experiments: the most relevant results on interactive TREC and CLEF, along with an introduction on user-generated search logs analysis are presented. Lastly, in Section 5, we draw some final conclusions.

2. INFORMATION RETRIEVAL SUPPORTING MLIA

Information Retrieval (IR) in its classical form (van Rijsbergen, 1979) is understood as the automatic process which, from an spontaneous ad hoc query by a user denoting an information need and a collection of documents, delivers a list of search results ordered according to their relevance. Thus, an ideal IR system should retrieve every relevant document satisfying the user's information need—obtaining a perfect *recall*—and only those documents being truly relevant—achieving a complete *precision*.

This classical model (see Figure 2), known as monolingual IR, assumes that both queries

and information sources are written in the same language. This is still the case of most of the web search engines available today that are able to retrieve only documents expressed in the same language of the user's query.

On the other hand, Cross-Language Information Retrieval (CLIR) is understood as the IR process in which queries in a given language are used to find documents written in another. As will be shown below, this task addresses the same steps found in monolingual information retrieval: processing queries, filtering, selecting, and ranking documents. However, it also requires some kind of translation, and, consequently, other issues resulted from the multilingual nature of the collection of documents arise: handling different character encodings, language identification, indexing documents in multiple languages, merging different rankings of retrieved documents, etc.

2.1. Structure of a CLIR System

In this section, we will detail the most successful techniques and approaches reported in the literature (with special emphasis on the works

Figure 2. Classical architecture of a monolingual information retrieval system

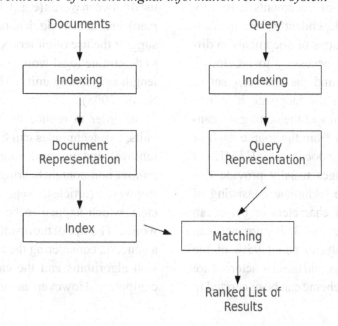

presented at CLEF) for each stage of a Cross Language Information Retrieval system.

The structure of a CLIR system can be broken up into three main stages, namely:

1. **Indexing:** Documents and queries are converted to an internal representation suitable to calculate distances between them during the matching phase.
2. **Translation:** CLIR always implies some kind of translation to save the language gap, either query translation, document translation or both.
3. **Matching:** The system computes scores for each document with respect to the query and ranks the retrieved documents accordingly.

2.2. Preprocessing and Indexing Documents in Multiple Languages

Indexing consists of storing the text documents in a database in order to efficiently search over large volumes of data. Different index structures might be used, but the most popular one is the inverted file (Baeza-Yates & Ribeiro-Neto, 1999), which allows rapid identification of which documents contain specific terms.

Building the index of documents is usually carried out offline, independently from queries. When handling collections of documents in different languages, it is necessary to previously identify the language and the character set of each document. When the language in which the document is written and the coding set cannot be inferred directly from the source itself or from the metadata of the document—HTML and XML mark-up languages usually provide this information—a simple technique consisting of counting sequences of characters or bytes can be performed over the text. This approach can yield to accurate results in about 95% of the cases. Once the language and the character set are known, the encoding scheme can be concerted to a standard representation (typically Unicode) in order to avoid inconsistencies and to cover also non-Roman languages.

Before building the index, documents need to be split into smaller units. Thus, the next step is to identify the specific words or terms to be included in the inverted file by performing some kind of segmentation or tokenization. The easiest approach to produce a valid stream of tokens from text documents written in western languages is to segment into words and treat as a single token everything located between two whitespaces (spaces, newline, tabulator, etc.) or punctuation characters (comma, semicolon, question mark, parenthesis, etc.). However, this option is not always good and, especially in an MLIA application, more sophisticated processing is usually required to be able to properly identify and translate—if necessary—named entities or multiword expressions such as New York City, Dr. Christian Shepard or Yahoo! Answers.

In addition, while the use of whitespaces is straightforward to determine word boundaries in languages such as English or French, this is not the case in languages where compounding is a frequent mechanism to form new words (e.g., German or Finnish) or where no spaces at all are used between words (e.g., Chinese, Japanese, Korean). Previous works dealing with these problems suggest the use of either dictionaries or lexicons to determine legal words or ngrams of different length as indexing units (Abdou & Savoy, 2006; Savoy, 2005).

In order to reduce the number of indexing units, two techniques can be applied: stopwords removal and normalization. Most IR systems remove non-content bearing tokens, the so-called stopwords (articles, prepositions, conjunctions, etc.), which happen to be the highest frequent words.[7] The size of the resulting index is no longer a concern, considering the advances in compression algorithms and the capabilities of current computers. However, in order to minimize the effects of mistranslation of very common words, stopwords deletion is still a common technique in CLIR systems.

Once stopwords have been removed, the simplest type of normalization of the remaining content words consists of reducing them to their stem form by removing prefixes, suffixes, and inflection. The most famous stemmer was developed by Porter (1980) but other language-specific tools have been reported for English (Lovins, 1968; Dawson, 1974), French (Savoy, 1999), Spanish (Figuerola, et al., 2002), Arabic (Abu-Salem, et al., 1999), Dutch (Kraaij & Pohlmann, 1994), Greek (Kalamboukis, 1995), Indic inflexional languages such as Bengali, Hindi, and Marathi (Paik & Parui, 2008), and even Latin (Schinke, et al., 1996). Most of these tools work by following a simple set of pre-defined language-specific rules to remove any morphological marks. Unfortunately, this operational behavior often leads to artificial truncated representation of words and—what is even worse in terms of retrieval effectiveness—overstemming (two different words are assigned the same stem) and understemming (two forms of the same words are assigned two different stems). For those languages lacking extensive linguistic resources, other proposals have been tested, such as clustering-based techniques to discover equivalent root words and morphological variants (Majumder, et al., 2007; Loponen, et al., 2010). Surprisingly, even though the initial intuition recommends reducing the amount of morphological information in the index, empirical results indicate that stemming do not produce actual relevant improvements in IR effectiveness (Manning & Schüzte, 2002, p. 132).

Alternatively, a more sophisticated approach known as lemmatization is recommended. It consists of performing morphological analysis on the text to reduce words to their lemmas or lexical forms, as they would appear in a dictionary. This task, unlike stemming, is more complex because it requires linguistic knowledge in order to, e.g., identify correctly irregular forms.

Finally, it is worth to mention that there are a variety of additional techniques that can be used in order to enrich the index and broaden the search. The most common approaches consist of detecting phrases, recognizing named entities or incorporating synonyms or hyponyms, etc.

2.3. Translation

The most distinctive aspect of any MLIA setting is that some form of translation will eventually be needed in order to bridge the language gap between the query and the collection of documents. There are three main difficulties a CLIR system has to be able to address (Grefenstette, 1998): How can a term written in a given language be expressed in another one? How to choose the most appropriate translation, among a set of candidate translations? and How to assign different weights to possible translations so that they indicate their quality or importance in a given context?

2.3.1. Translation Approaches

In any MLIA application, translation remains the key challenge. The language barrier can be overtaken by implementing four different strategies, all of which have some advantages and drawbacks:

- Query translation: the information need is translated in query time into the language(s) of the target documents.
- Document translation: the documents are translated at indexing time into the language(s) of the queries.
- Both query and documents are translated into a third language or interlingua.
- No translation is performed, retrieval is based on cognates or sub-word matching.

The first criterion to choose one option over the others is the number of language pairs involved and the availability and quality of the translation resources. Query translation (see Figure 3) is the

Figure 3. Architecture of a cross-language information retrieval system with query translation

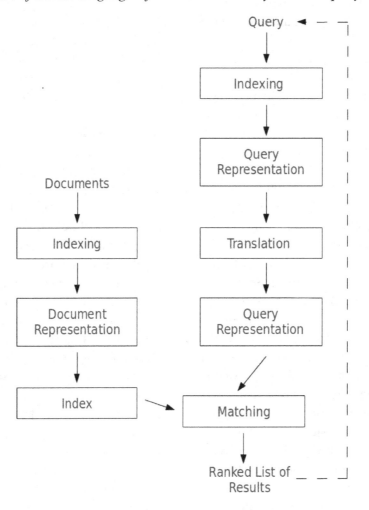

simplest and preferable choice when dealing with multiple target languages or when the cost of translating the entire document collection is too high. However, resources for every potential pair of query/document languages are required and translation at query time for a number of languages can penalize the system performance. In addition, CLIR based on query translation implies retrieving a separate list of results ordered by relevance for each target language, which causes new problems, such as merging and re-ranking the results.

On the other hand, document translation (see Figure 4) solves the problem of merging different rankings, but translating all documents in multiple languages is a very cost operation both in terms of computational time and storage.

The third option—translating queries and documents into a carefully chosen third language (see Figure 5)—has been shown to be preferable to a direct translation, when reliable and quality resources for the language pair considered do not exist (Chen & Gey, 2004).

Finally, some authors have tested the viability of not using explicit translation but the identification of cognates[8] or sub-string matches. These experiments assume that cognate terms have the same meaning and can translate one another, which is not always the case. Some interesting works have tested this approach by correcting the spelling in languages with enough vocabulary overlap as French and English (Buckley, et al., 2000) or taking advantage of the usage of Chinese-origin

Figure 4. Architecture of a cross-language information retrieval system with document translation

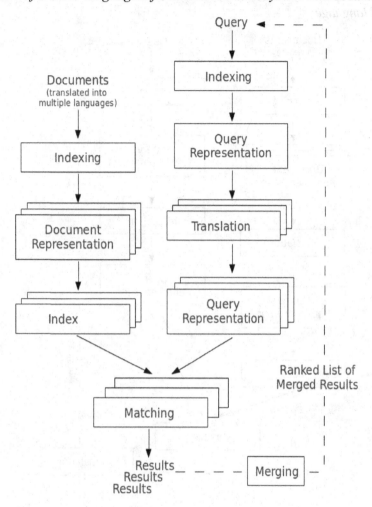

Kanji characters when searching Chinese topics on Japanese documents (Gey, 2005), respectively.

2.3.2. Translation Tools

In any case, regardless the translation approach chosen, three different types of translation tools can be used, namely:

- Machine Translation.
- Knowledge-based resources: thesauri and dictionaries.
- Parallel and comparable corpora.

Machine Translation (MT) seems the most evident solution to bridge the language gap in any MLIA scenario; however, it is not always the best solution for CLIR. The key idea behind MT is that a system with no a priori knowledge about a given language can learn how to recognize and replicate patterns of language use by computing statistical data (translation probabilities) from a large collection of texts. Thus, an ideal MT system aims to produce a unique reliable and human-readable translated version of an input text source. As Oard (2009) claims, among all the advances in CLIR, translation probabilities have had the biggest effect. However, to provide good translations, MT systems perform complex

Figure 5. Architecture of a cross-language information retrieval system translating documents and queries into a third language

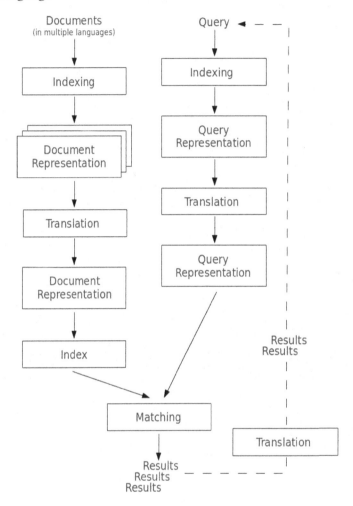

statistical and linguistic analyses, which are not essential to support matching documents and queries across languages. In addition, in spite of the advances in MT technology, translating entire collections of documents is still expensive and generating document translation in a number of different languages is unfeasible. Therefore, MT-based approaches have mainly focused on query translation. To make things worse, queries are usually made of simple sequences of keywords without syntactic structure, and word-sense disambiguation techniques cannot be properly applied without enough context.

On the other hand, among the most common knowledge-based resources employed in CLIR, we can mention thesauri and dictionaries. A thesaurus is a controlled vocabulary containing domain-specific terminology where relationships between concepts such as synonymy, hyponymy, hyperonymy are made explicit. Multilingual thesauri, which can be understood as individual controlled vocabularies allowing mappings between equivalent concepts across languages, have been tested in CLIR tasks with acceptable performance since the beginning (Salton, 1969; Pevzner, 1972). Under this approach, there is no place for ambiguity, since a pre-defined set of terms—included in the thesaurus—are carefully chosen to index and search. However, the main problem is that the task of assigning unambiguous terms to each document has traditionally been carried out by human experts, and this is expensive. In addition, thesauri are generally costly to build and maintain so in recent years its usage has been dropped in favor of free text searching and other resources.

Machine Readable Dictionaries (MRD) have been extensively used as translation resources (Pirkola, et al., 2001). Even though the simplest dictionary-based word by word query translation can achieve an acceptable outcome, it has been shown that word by word translation can drop effectiveness about 40% - 60% with respect to the monolingual retrieval (Ballesteros & Croft, 1996; Hull & Grefenstette, 1996). On the other hand, Ballesteros and Croft (1996) have been able to outperform a commercial MT system using carefully chosen dictionaries. In general, the drawbacks of dictionary-based translations are several, namely:

1. Dictionaries do not contain inflected forms of words, so a previous normalization process (via stemming or lemmatization) is required before translation.
2. General purpose dictionaries try to maximize their coverage but do not usually contain specialized terms for a given domain. Terms with no entry in the dictionary—known as Out-Of-Vocabulary words (OOVs)—remain untranslated and are claimed to be responsible for about 23% of the effectiveness lost (Peters & Sheridan, 2001).
3. Dictionary-based translation does not solve the problem of ambiguity, and choosing the most appropriate translation among all the possibilities remains a difficult task. When translating with dictionaries, polysemous words are usually replaced with all their possible translations. This kind of 'expansion' technique can work in some contexts,

but in most cases, it will contribute to generate noisy queries and retrieve irrelevant documents.

4. It is difficult to correctly identify and translate multiword expressions or idioms. Word by word translation of these expressions also increases the noise in the query.

A variety of works have tested different techniques to solve or at least alleviate these problems. Davis (1997) proposed to use the grammatical category of the query words in order to choose the most appropriate translation among the candidates, increasing the precision as much as 37% with regard to previous experiments. Ballesteros and Croft (1997) tried to improve their translation effectiveness with the aid of dictionaries of multiword expressions (sequences of nouns or pairs of adjectives and noun). They were able to improve their search precision as much as 150%. Unfortunately, this type of dictionaries is uncommon. In other successful work, Pirkola (1998) studied the effects of applying different translation techniques.

The third approach that has been successfully applied to CLIR is by using corpus-based techniques. First of all, we call parallel corpora two sets of documents written in two different languages, where one document from the first set is a direct translation—at different levels of alignment: e.g., sentences or paragraphs—of another document in the second set. In these cases, statistical methods are applied over vast collections of documents in order to extract translation probabilities, which are eventually used to build translation resources. Unfortunately, parallel corpora are not plentiful, but different authors have proposed automatic methods for building parallel corpora by, e.g., searching pairs of web pages likely to be translation of each other (Resnik, 1998; Chen & Nie, 2000). When parallel corpora are not an option, statistical analyses over monolingual corpora have been used to extract translation probabilities to, in this case, complement a bilingual dictionary (Chen & Gey, 2001). Finally, a last less expensive choice consists of using comparable corpora, i.e., two domain-specific large sets of documents, which, in spite of not being translation equivalent, are likely to share vocabulary, genre, and register. The classical example of comparable corpora is the news collections available at evaluation campaigns such as TREC and CLEF. Another successful experience of applying comparable corpora in CLIR tasks consists of building the so-called similarity thesauri (Sheridan & Ballerini, 1996) which, unlike classical thesauri, are automatically built from the relationships of thematic proximity among vocabulary found in a collection of texts. By taking advantage of the query expansion, this kind of resources can enhanced the searching process both in monolingual (Qiu, 1995) and multilingual environments (Sheridan, et al., 1997; Braschler & Schäuble, 2001).

2.4. Matching Queries and Documents

Early IR applications consisted of boolean systems, where the query was expressed as a combination of Boolean operators. In this type of systems there is no inherent notion of document ranking, and the result of the search process retrieves a list of relevant documents (the documents satisfy the Boolean query) presented in no particular order. On the other hand, in modern IR systems, a retrieval function is used to measure the similarity between a query and a document. Under this paradigm, we obtain an ordered list of documents according to their similarities with respect to the initial query.

A typical retrieval function combines values such as Term Frequency (TF)—the number of occurrences of a term in a given document—and Inverse Document Frequency (IDF)—the proportion of documents containing the given term in the whole collection—to calculate the weights of the vocabulary included in the index. Notice that while TF promotes those terms occurring frequently in

a single document, and IDF penalizes those terms appearing frequently across the entire document collection, the combination of both helps to locate the most representative terms.

One of the most successful approaches is the Vector Space Model (VSM), introduced by Salton et al. (1975). Documents and queries are represented by a vector of terms and retrieval function measures the similarity between the query and document vectors. Thus, a typical retrieval function consists of measuring the cosine of the angle between the two vectors. Some authors have been able to outperform the results of a classical VSM with the pivoted normalization method (Singhal, et al., 1996): terms' weights are normalized by applying a correction factor calculated from the length of the documents.

The probabilistic model, proposed by Maron and Kuhns (1960), is based on the probabilistic ranking principle (Robertson, 1977). Documents are ranked by decreasing probability of their relevance with respect to the query. Since true probabilities are not available, probabilistic IR systems actually try to estimate them. Different assumptions on the estimation of these probabilities will produce different probabilistic models. A typical probabilistic retrieval function is the Okapi BM25 (Robertson, et al., 1999), which is widely used directly or with some variations, such as divergence from randomness (Amati & van Rijsbergen, 2002).

Other approaches try to infer a language model for each document and rank them according to the probability of producing the query according to that model (Ponte & Croft, 1998). The Dirichlet prior retrieval method (Zhai & Lafferty, 2001) has been shown as one of the best performing language modeling approaches.

All these matching processes require query and documents to be written in the same language. From the analysis of the research works presented during the last TREC (Harman, 2005) and CLEF (Braschler, et al., 2009) campaigns, it has been shown that in order to address effective multilingual retrieval, a good monolingual matching in all languages to be covered is a must. During the years, it is been shown that no specific development is required and the most used weighting schema has been Okapi/BM25 and subtle variations of it. In addition, different language models, divergence from randomness or pivoted normalization method have been tested.

3. MULTILINGUAL QUESTION ANSWERING

After the general introduction on Information Retrieval systems supporting MLIA introduced in the previous section, now we are focusing on a more specific information access task: Question Answering.

3.1. Question Answering

Question Answering (QA) is a sophisticated form of Information Retrieval (IR). Unlike classical IR, in which a ranking of relevant documents is retrieved, QA systems are expected to retrieve, for a given query expressed as a natural language statement or question, one (or several) correct answer(s). In this section, we will review some of the attempts reported in the literature to tackle the development of QA systems able to handle the retrieval of answers in multiple languages and even able to retrieve answers in the user's language, regardless the language of the source.

A QA system receives a question expressed in natural language and return small snippets of text, which contain an answer to the input question, instead of the list of documents returned by classical IR systems such as Web search engines (Voorhees & Tice, 1999). Thus, QA systems can be seen as IR systems able to return more precise answers. Furthermore, the query asked to QA systems is usually a natural language question, while in IR it is used a string made of keywords.

In some way, the QA field is related with both Information Retrieval and Information Extraction (IE). The relation with IR arises from the fact that a QA system must be able to search in a collection of documents for finding one containing a correct answer. On the other hand, a QA system must be able to extract an exact answer to a question by recognizing, maybe, relations among words or entities, what is a common task in IE. We can distinguish two different types of systems involving the usage of multiple languages (Aceves-Pérez, et al., 2008):

- Cross-lingual systems, where questions are expressed in a language different from the one of the document collection.
- Multilingual systems, where the search is performed over collections of documents expressed in different languages. Ideally, a perfect multilingual QA system should be capable of providing answers regardless the language of the question.

Despite the different types of QA systems, in this section we will only focus on the definition of QA system provided in evaluations such as TREC, CLEF, and NTCIR, i.e. automatic QA systems searching for answers over collections of free text, with no interaction from the user. Besides, these evaluations have tested mainly fact-based questions, where it is not necessary to apply a deep level of analysis and inference for finding answers.

3.2. Architecture of a QA System

QA architectures are typically designed as a pipeline of different modules with the aim to separate and discard the pieces of text unlikely to an answer while focusing on candidate texts likely to contain a correct answer. With this purpose in mind, quick methods for performing a pre-selection of candidate texts are used at the beginning of the pipeline, while modules able to perform a deeper analysis are applied afterwards in order to locate and extract the exact answer (Hovy, et al., 2001; Moldovan, et al., 2000; Prager, et al., 2000). The main modules of a QA system are shown in Figure 6.

3.2.1. Question Analysis

Question analysis represents one of the most important stages of a QA system since the information obtained at this step will be used by the subsequent modules. Thus, this phase has a very important role in the final performance of a system. The information obtained by this module can be mainly divided in two types:

Figure 6. Classical architecture of a QA system

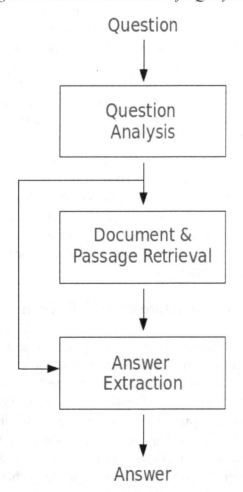

1. Information useful for retrieving relevant documents and passages from the target collection.
2. Information helpful for extracting the final answer from relevant passages.

In order to obtain such information, several processes can be applied. The most common approaches reported in the literature are, to name a few:

- **Detection of the Expected Answer Type (EAT):** it is useful to know what kind of answer is going to be searched for. With this purpose, the question is classified in a predefined taxonomy (Hirschman & Gaizauskas, 2001). The methods applied for this classification range from the most simples ones based on simple heuristics over the interrogative term (who, what, where, when, etc.), to more complex methods that rely on a deeper analysis and larger taxonomies (Li & Roth, 2002).

- **Detection of question focus:** the expected answer type is sometimes too generic and it does not give enough information. In these situations, the question focus gives more precise information about the answer type. The focus is a word or a sequence of words that define the question and can be used to disambiguate it. For instance, given the question 'In what year was Gandhi born?' the focus would be 'year.' The focus is usually close to the interrogative term (what, when, etc.) and it rarely appears in the documents that contain the answer. Thus, this focus is not usually added to the keywords list used to feed the information retrieval system.

- **Extraction of keywords:** the IR engine is fed with an input query which is usually made of a set of keywords from the question. An easy solution to build the query is to remove stopwords and question focus and take all the query terms. Other more complex systems expand the query by adding synonyms and hyperonyms (Hovy, et al., 2001).

3.2.2. Document and Paragraph Selection

This is a typical IR module where the query is built using keywords extracted from the previous module, with the possibility of expanding the query with synonyms. The final answer will be extracted only over the documents returned by this module. It is possible to perform a new retrieval over the selected documents with the objective of selecting fragments of text shorter than documents, commonly referred as passages.

3.2.3. Answer Extraction

The goal of this module is to extract an exact answer from the candidate texts returned by the previous step. The level of analysis applied depends on the expected answer type. Some common techniques use the recognition of named entities, while others rely on the extraction of answers from syntactic trees.

3.3. Multilingual QA

A multilingual QA system can be seen as a set of monolingual QA systems, where two additional tasks must be tackled:

1. Translating questions into different languages; and,
2. Combining the results retrieved by different monolingual systems.

As in any other MLIA task, a multilingual QA system may also choose to translate the document collection instead of the question. However, this option has been—to our concerned—discarded,

due to the difficulty of translating whole document collections and the high computational cost associated.

3.3.1. Translating Questions

As in any other information access system involving multiple languages, cross-lingual QA systems eventually need to add a translation module to its classical monolingual architecture. Notice that this step does not only consist of translating a question term by term. A more consistent translation of the whole question in natural language with a reasonable quality is required. Hence, the quality of this translation represents a key factor of the overall performance of a multilingual system.

There have been different proposals for addressing the translation of questions. The easiest approach consists of using a Machine Translation (MT) system able to cover the pair of languages considered (Jijkoun, et al., 2004; Martinez-Gonzalez, et al., 2009). However, this option is too sensitive to errors when dealing with short texts such as the input questions. Tanev et al. (2005) proposed to translate term by term the keywords of the question. In order to select the most appropriate translation for each term, the authors selected the combination of keywords' translations with the highest co-occurrence in an English corpus. However, since they did not translate the whole question, specific modules for analyzing the question (e.g., detection of expected answer type, detection of focus, etc.) were developed in each target language.

Another option also tested in multilingual QA consists of translating the questions into an interlingua. In Laurent et al. (2005) English was successfully used as a pivot language. As mentioned in Section 2.1.2, this is a solution typically used when translating resources are not available for the pair of languages taken into account.

Other approaches tried to obtain a better translation by combining different ones, under the assumption that the more frequent a possible translation appears, the more likely this translation is a correct one. Sutcliffe et al. (2006) created a translated question from two different automatic translations and a dictionary. All the translations were performed at phrase level. Whenever a possible translation was found in the dictionary, the other two MT translations were ignored, since the former resource was assumed to have higher precision. Otherwise, the two automatic translations were combined.

On the other hand, Aceves-Perez et al. (2007) chose the best translation from a set of candidates ones by evaluating its fluency based on its pertinence to a predefined language model. The evaluation was performed measuring the pertinence of each translation to the n-gram model of the target document collection. Thus, the document collection was used to evaluate the quality of each translation.

Finally, another way of evaluating question translations worth to be mentioned consists of measuring the quality of the translated question according to its linguistic analysis, assuming that the more complete the linguistic analysis was, the more useful its outcome was for the following modules of the QA system (Neumann & Sacaleanu, 2006).

3.3.2. Combining Results in Different Languages

Along with query translation, MLIA systems require at some point of their architecture the merging of results generated in different languages. The two most common approaches are the combination at passage level and the combination at answer level. Both approaches usually need some kind of translation of texts to a common language.

When the combination is performed at passage level, the retrieval of paragraphs in each language is performed in parallel as it is shown in Figure 7. These lists of paragraphs are merged into a single list and the extraction of answers is made over

the paragraphs contained in that list. The issue here is that most of the common merging strategies need to receive all the passages expressed in the same language. Therefore, the different lists of paragraphs must be translated into the same language in order to begin this merging process. Thus, the final list contains paragraphs expressed in the same language, and a typical monolingual answer extraction module can be applied. Notice, anyway, that the problem of accumulating errors during the translation may arise again.

An alternative approach proposes to perform the merging at the answer level, as it is shown in Figure 8. In this case, each monolingual system works independently of the others and then, the different list of candidate answers are merged into a single one.

Among the most common merging strategies, we can mention round robin and raw score value. When using round robin, the results (either paragraphs or answers) from different monolingual systems are merged according to their ranking in each list. More specifically, the final list is built taking one result in turn from each list, alternating them. This method assumes that the relevant information across languages is distributed homogeneously, which is not always the case. Then, when applying raw score values, the final list of results is sorted by the original confidence score given by each monolingual system. This strategy assumes that the scores given in the different languages are comparable. Hence, this is a good option when the monolingual systems applied in each language are the same or have similar features.

Finally, the 2stepRSV method is another merging strategy proposed by Martinez-Santiago et al. (2006). This method consists of two different processes. In the first step, a multilingual collection made of the relevant passages retrieved from each collection is created. Moreover, a vocabulary containing the original question and its translations is also created. This multilingual collection is indexed taking into account only those terms

Figure 7. Architecture of a QA system based on passage merging

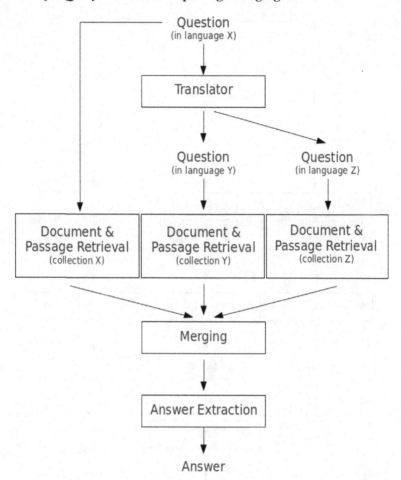

appearing in this vocabulary. Then, in the second step, a query using the terms from the vocabulary is generated and launched to search the index. The ranking retrieved by this search process is the final ranking used by the answer extraction module.

3.4. Evaluation of a QA System

The main evaluations of QA systems have been conducted during TREC, CLEF, and NTCIR campaigns. While TREC has focused only on the evaluation of monolingual English systems, CLEF proposed from 2003 the evaluation of both monolingual and cross-lingual systems in several European languages. As far as NTCIR

is concerned, there have also been monolingual and cross-lingual QA evaluations over Asian languages.

Several measures have been proposed for evaluating QA systems, considering different aspects such as: the number of answers allowed per question, the self-confidence of a system in its responses and the amount of relevant information given in an answer, to name a few.

Regarding the evaluation of multilingual systems, most of them have been evaluated only in a cross-lingual scenario, i.e., the questions were expressed in a language different than the target collection. These evaluations have been conducted at the same time that the monolingual ones, using

Figure 8. Architecture of a QA system based on answer merging

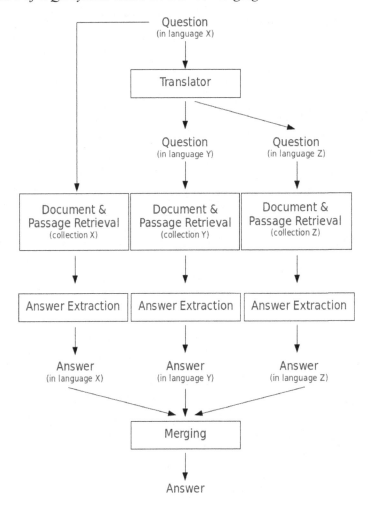

the same set of questions and collections than monolingual systems. However, there is still a big difference in performance when comparing monolingual results against cross-lingual ones. This observation is clearly shown in Forner et al. (2008), where the results of monolingual and cross-language systems at CLEF from 2003 to 2008 are compared. It can be seen that the best monolingual system was able to answer correctly almost 70% of questions, while the best cross-lingual system answered correctly 50% of questions. Again, translation remains the key challenge.

4. INTERACTIVE INFORMATION RETRIEVAL: THE USER'S PERSPECTIVE

So far, we have only dealt with automatic information access systems. Ultimately any information access system is designed to provide useful information to people.

4.1. Interactive Information Retrieval

Searching for information is an eminently interactive process involving a real user trying to solve an information need by using an Information Retrieval (IR) system. Unfortunately, designing and conducting interactive IR experiments is complex and costly, their validity is limited (statistically significant differences are difficult to find) and they are hard to evaluate and reproduce (performance is greatly influenced by searchers as well as by topics and systems). Thus, while the development and evaluation of automatic IR have been extensively studied, little is known about the user-oriented perspective, either in monolingual (Dumais & Belkin, 2005; Hersh, 2006) or cross-language (Braschler, et al., 2009) environments.

How do subjects behave when they search for information in unknown languages? Do their effectiveness vary according to their linguistic competence? Do users' behavior and perceptions match? Such questions are far from being answered, even though in recent years different evaluation campaigns have been organized in order to fulfill this need. In the following sections, we are summarizing some of the most important experiences reported to date at the evaluation campaigns organized by TREC and CLEF on interactive information access.

4.2. The Interactive Track at TREC

TREC has been studying users and their interaction with IR systems since its beginning (Over, 2001). The interactive track was formally established from TREC-3 to TREC-11 (Dumais & Belkin, 2005) even though other interactive analyses were conducted in the framework of other tracks (e.g., in TREC-12). During the life of the track, a wide range of issues has been addressed: from different presentation and visualization techniques to evaluation of search processes and effectiveness. However, the first difficulties arose soon: comparing interactive systems posed major challenges and the basic TREC structure did not seem suitable to the interactive environment. Unlike in batch search considered in other tracks, overall performance is highly influenced by expertise and skills of the

searchers (Egan, 1988; Bhavnani, 2001). Therefore, experiments needed to be carefully designed in order to minimize the effects of topic, system, and searcher (Largergren & Over, 1998).

During the first campaigns (TREC-3 and TREC-4), interactive systems were compared to automatic systems by re-using documents and queries from the ad hoc retrieval and routing tasks. Later, it was shown the difficulty to evaluate and capture users' performance (the number of relevant documents retrieved was not a good indicator) so in TREC-5 and TREC-6 an experimental framework for comparing systems, topics, and searchers was developed. In addition, the interactive track moved towards a question answering approach and notions such as qualitative and quantitative analyses on searcher characteristics, user satisfaction, and search process were included in the studies. Later, in TREC-7, TREC-8, and TREC-9, the track dropped the interest on cross-systems comparison and allowed participants to focus on the effects of their experimental manipulation, regardless the searcher and topic effects. Finally, TREC-10 and TREC-11 proposed a more realistic environment of Web-based searches. See Dumais and Belkin (2005) for a complete overview of the studies presented at TREC.

The history of the interactive track at TREC can be summarized as the progressive evolution of a methodology for conducting interactive IR experiments. One of the most valuable results has been the standardization of tasks, queries, corpora and data collections, and the development of a methodology. Along with an evaluation framework (Hersh, 2006), a number of other standardized procedures have been undertaken: experiment design, common data collection, and questionnaires to collect users' feedback, to name a few. In addition, as will be shown in the following section, these experiences have inspired other research initiatives.

4.3. The Interactive Track at CLEF (iCLEF)

CLEF is the European counterpart of TREC for cross-language information access evaluation. Since 2001, iCLEF[9] has focused on the study and evaluation of the search capabilities from a user-inclusive viewpoint and in a multilingual environment. Thus, the central research question has always been related to how to assist users when searching information written in a language they cannot understand, rather than which algorithm can find better information written in languages different from the query language. During the last eight years, iCLEF dealt with two main aspects of the interactive Information Access: 1) document selection and results explorations; and 2) query formulation, refinement and translation. Both aspects have been addressed for different information access tasks (document retrieval, question answering and image retrieval), from various methodological perspectives (hypothesis-driven and observational studies), and for different users' profiles (different language skills of the user with respect to the target language).

In its first editions (Oard & Gonzalo, 2002; Oard, et al., 2004; Gonzalo & Oard, 2003; Oard & Gonzalo, 2004; Gonzalo & Oard, 2005; Gonzalo, et al., 2006) iCLEF organization used to propose MLIA tasks on news collections (a standard for text retrieval experiments) and a hypothesis-driven experiment. Participants typically designed two cross-language search interfaces (a reference and a contrastive system), recruited and trained as many users as possible and run a number of search sessions. The sessions were conducted with a prescribed combination of topic/user/system in order to minimize topic and user effects. Then, the aim was to improve the outcome of the search process in terms of the classic notion of relevance and to study the system effects, which should eventually confirm or discard the initial hypothesis.

However, this experimental setting leads to major limitations: user populations tend to be small, the cost of recruiting and training suitable users, and the effort of scheduling and monitoring search sessions are very high, to name a few. So, in 2006 (Karlgren, et al., 2007), in order to explore users' behavior in a more realistic cross-language scenario, iCLEF moved away from newswire documents to a multilingual large-scale user-generated image collection: Flickr.[10] And more recently, iCLEF08 and iCLEF09 tracks (Gonzalo, et al., 2009, 2010) were defined as a search log analysis problem, focusing on the shared analysis of a medium/large search log generated by a single search interface provided by the iCLEF organizers. Therefore, participants have studied a search log generated by heterogeneous groups of users playing online with a multilingual text-based image retrieval interface called FlickLing. Upon registration in the search interface (where they were asked to specify their language profile), users were proposed a classical known-item retrieval task. The subjects were shown a raw (without annotations or descriptions) target image. The search interface allowed them to submit monolingual and/or multilingual queries to Flickr's public image database without time limits. The more images the users found, the better score they obtained for them and their team. This iCLEF search log is a valuable resource created on purpose to address the open questions mentioned at the beginning of this section.

4.4. Search Log Analysis in Interactive Information Retrieval

Search logs are one of the most useful resources to be analyzed when evaluating interactive IR experiments. They provide detailed information on users' interactions and they are a key resource to understand users' behavior when using information access systems. Adapting the definition of transaction log found in Jansen (2006), a search log file is an electronic record of interactions that have occurred during the searching episode between an information access system and users searching for information on that system. These log file typically include a unique user identifier, a timestamp, and the query string launched. Richer logs may also contain further information about the ranking of results retrieved and the documents clicked, if any.

In spite of their usefulness, search log files publicly available are few, usually outdated, and too small (containing less than 3 million queries from a few hundred thousand users). The first analyses on query logs were conducted from the late 1990s by Jansen, Spink, and their group on logs collected and released by commercial search engines such as Excite (Jansen, et al., 1998; Wolfram, et al., 2001; Spink, et al., 2001; Jansen & Spink, 2000; Spink, et al., 2002a), AlltheWeb (Spink, et al., 2002b), or AltaVista (Jansen, et al., 2005). More recently, in 2006, AOL released a much bigger log file (Pass, et al., 2006) containing about 30 million queries from over 650,000 users, which, unfortunately, became notorious when some privacy flaws were exposed by the media. As more services exist and more users interact with them, log file analysis becomes a thriving research field applied to different domains: web data mining (Kolari & Joshi, 2004; Baeza-Yates, 2007), digital libraries (Cooper, 2001), search behavior (Mat-Hassan & Levene, 2001; Jansen & Spink, 2005), Web search evaluation and optimization (Liu, et al., 2007; Joachims, 2002), adaptive systems and personalization (Eirinaki & Vazirgiannis, 2003; Brusilovsky, et al., 2007), and business intelligence (Srivastava & Cooley, 2003).

Finally, it is worth to mention LogCLEF[11], the track organized from 2009 within the framework of CLEF Labs devoted to improve search systems by exploring log files and analyzing queries as an expression of users' behavior.

5. CONCLUSION

As the number of Internet users grows and more people have access and tools to generate Web contents—as the world gets flatter and smaller, as Thomas L. Friedman claims in his book *The World is Flat*—more people who do not speak English as their first language enter the global playing field. The language gap is the first barrier to the full exploitation of the available information and Multilingual Information Access (MLIA) technology can facilitate accessing, querying, and retrieving information from multiple sources and across languages.

Along this chapter, we have described the stages a general Cross-Language Information Retrieval (CLIR) system features, and we have also focused on a specific IR problem, Question Answering, in the multilingual scenario. In both cases, translation is the key challenge. When the appropriate (in terms of quality and quantity) linguistic resources, dictionaries, corpora, and tools are available, when we can count on reliable translation probabilities, it has been shown that a CLIR system can obtain reasonable good performance, compared to its monolingual counterparts.

Unfortunately, the advances achieved in automatic IR systems have not been proved successful with real users. While searching for information is an eminently interactive process, little is still known about how to properly assist people to find and use information expressed in unknown languages. In spite of the effort to standardize methodologies drawn from evaluation campaigns such as TREC, CLEF, NTCIR, and FIRE, and from their participants, many questions remain open.

REFERENCES

Abdou, S., & Savoy, J. (2006). Statistical and comparative evaluation of various indexing and search models. *Information Retrieval Technology*. Retrieved from http://doc.rero.ch/lm.php ?url=1000,43,4,20100208172751-SI/Abdou_ Samir_-_Statistical_and_Comparative_Evaluation_of_Various_20100208.pdf

Abu-Salem, H., Al-Omari, M., & Evens, M. (1999). Stemming methodologies over individual queries words for an Arabian information retrieval system. *Journal of the American Society for Information Science and Technology, 50*, 524–529. doi:10.1002/(SICI)1097-4571(1999)50:6<524::AID-ASI7>3.0.CO;2-M

Aceves-Pérez, R., Montes-y-Gómez, M., & Villaseñor-Pineda, L. (2007). Enhancing cross-language question answering by combining multiple question translations. In *Proceedings of the 8th International Conference in Computational Linguistics and Intelligent Text Processing (CICLing-2007)*, (pp. 485-493). CICLing.

Aceves-Pérez, R., Montes-y-Gómez, M., Villaseñor-Pineda, L., & Ureña-López, L. A. (2008). Two approaches for multilingual question answering: Merging passages vs. merging answers. *International Journal of Computational Linguistics and Chinese Language Processing, 13*(1).

Amati, G., & van Rijsbergen, C. J. (2002). Probabilistic models of information retrieval based on measuring the divergence from randomness. *ACM Transactions on Information Systems, 20*(4), 357–389. doi:10.1145/582415.582416

Baeza-Yates, R., & Ribeiro-Neto, B. (1999). *Modern information retrieval*. Reading, MA: Addison Wesley.

Baeza-Yates, R., & Tiberi, A. (2007). Extacting semantic relation from query logs. In *Proceedings of the 13th International Conference on Knowledge Discovery and Data Mining (SIGKDD 2007)*. SIGKDD.

Ballesteros, L., & Croft, W. B. (1996). Dictionary methods for cross-lingual information retrieval. In *Proceedings of the Database and Expert Systems Applications*, (pp. 791-801). DEXA.

Ballesteros, L., & Croft, W. B. (1997). Phrasal translation and query expansion techniques for cross-language information retrieval. *Research and Development in Information Retrieval*. Retrieved from http://www.mtholyoke.edu/~lballest/Pubs/sigir97_ir104.pdf

Bhavnani, S. K. (2001). Important cognitive components of domain-specific search knowledge. In E. M. Voorhees & D. K. Harman (Eds.), *The Tenth Text Retrieval Conference (TREC 2001)*, (pp. 571–578). Washington, DC: NIST.

Braschler, M., Gonzalo, J., Peinado, V., & López-Ostenero, F. (2009). *Best practices in system-oriented and user-oriented multilingual information access (d3.3). Technical Report: TrebleCLEF Project: FP7 IST ICT-1-4-1*. TrebleCLEF Project.

Braschler, M., & Schäuble, P. (2001). Experiments with the Eurospider retrieval system for CLEF 2000. *Lecture Notes in Computer Science, 2069*.

Brusilovsky, P., Kobsa, A., & Nejdl, W. (2007). Data mining for personalization. *Lecture Notes in Computer Science, 4321*, 90–135. doi:10.1007/978-3-540-72079-9

Buckley, C., Mitra, M., Walz, J., & Cardie, C. (2000). Using clustering and superconcepts within SMART: TREC 6. *Information Processing & Management, 36*(1), 109–131. doi:10.1016/S0306-4573(99)00047-3

Chen, A., & Gey, F. C. (2001). Translation term weighting and combining translation resources in cross-language retrieval. In *Proceedings of the 10th Text Retrieval Conference (TREC10)*. Gaithersburg, MD: National Institute of Standards and Technology (NIST).

Chen, A., & Gey, F. C. (2004). Combining query translation and document translation in cross-language retrieval. *Lecture Notes in Computer Science, 3237*.

Chen, J., & Nie, J.-Y. (2000). Parallel web text mining for cross-language IR. In *Proceedings of RIAO 2000: Content-Based Multimedia Information Access*, (Vol. 1), (pp. 62-78). RIAO.

Cooper, M. D. (2001). Usage patterns of a web-based library catalog. *Journal of the American Society for Information Science and Technology, 52*(2), 137–148. doi:10.1002/1097-4571(2000)9999:9999<::AID-ASI1547>3.0.CO;2-E

Davis, M. (1997). New experiments in cross-language text retrieval at NMSU's computing research lab. In *Proceedings of the 5th Text Retrieval Conference (TREC5)*, (pp. 447-454). Gaithersburg, MD: National Institute of Standards and Technology (NIST).

Dawson, J. (1974). Suffix removal and word conflation. *Bulletin of the Association for Literacy and Linguistic Computing, 2*, 33–46.

Dumais, S. T., & Belkin, N. J. (2005). The TREC interactive tracks: Putting the user into search. In Vorhees, E. M., & Harman, D. K. (Eds.), *TREC: Experiment and Evaluation in Information Retrieval* (pp. 123–152). Cambridge, MA: MIT Press.

Egan, D. (1998). Individual differences in human-computer interaction. In *Handbook of Human-Computer Interaction* (pp. 543–568). Oxford, UK: North Holland.

Eirinaki, M., & Vazirgiannis, M. (2003). web mining for web personalization. *ACM Transactions on Internet Technology, 3*(1), 1–27. doi:10.1145/643477.643478

Figuerola, C., Gómez, R., Zazo, A., & Alonso Berrocal, J. L. (2002). Spanish monolingual track: The impact of stemming on retrieval. *Lecture Notes in Computer Science, 2406*, 253–261. doi:10.1007/3-540-45691-0_23

Forner, P., Peñas, A., Agirre, E., Alegria, I., Moreau, N., & Osenova, P. … Rocha, P. (2008). Overview of the CLEF 2008 multilingual question answering track. *Lecture Notes in Computer Science, 5706*, 262-295.

Gey, F. C. (2005). How similar are Chinese and Japanese for cross-language information retrieval. In *Proceedings of the Fifth NTCIR Workshop Meeting on Evaluation of Information Access Technologies: Information Retrieval, Question Answering and Cross-Lingual Information Access*. NTCIR.

Gonzalo, J., Clough, P., & Karlgren, J. (2009). Overview of iCLEF 2008: Search log analysis for multilingual image retrieval. *Lecture Notes in Computer Science, 5706*.

Gonzalo, J., & Oard, D. (2003). The CLEF 2002 interactive track. *Lecture Notes in Computer Science, 2785*, 372–382. doi:10.1007/978-3-540-45237-9_33

Gonzalo, J., & Oard, D. (2005). iCLEF 2004 track overview: Pilot experiments in interactive cross-language question answering. *Lecture Notes in Computer Science, 3491*.

Gonzalo, J., Peinado, V., Clough, P., & Karlgren, J. (2010). Overview of iCLEF 2009: Exploring search behaviour in a multilingual folksonomy environment. *Lecture Notes in Computer Science, 6242*, 13–20. doi:10.1007/978-3-642-15751-6_2

Grefenstette, G. (1998). *The problem of cross-language information retrieval*. Dordrecht, The Netherlands: Kluwer Academic Publishers. doi:10.1007/978-1-4615-5661-9

Harman, D. K. (2005). Beyond English. In Vorhees, E. M., & Harman, D. K. (Eds.), *TREC: Experiment and Evaluation in Information Retrieval* (pp. 153–181). Cambridge, MA: MIT Press.

Hersh, W. (2006). Evaluating interactive question answering. In Ide, N., Véronis, J., Baayen, H., Church, K. W., Klavans, J., & Barnard, D. T. (Eds.), *Advances in Open Domain Question Answering* (pp. 431–455). Berlin, Germany: Springer.

Hirschman, L., & Gaizauskas, R. (2001). Natural language question answering: The view from here. *Natural Language Engineering, 7*(4), 275–300. doi:10.1017/S1351324901002807

Hovy, E., Gerber, L., Hermjakob, H., Junk, M., & Lin, C.-Y. (2001). Question answering in Webclopedia. In *Proceedings of the 9th Text REtrieval Conference*, (pp. 655-664). TREC.

Hull, D. A., & Grefenstette, G. (1996). Querying across languages: A dictionary-based approach to multilingual information retrieval. In *Proceedings of the 19th International Conference on Research and Development in Information Retrieval*, (pp. 49-57). ACL.

Jansen, B. J. (2006). Search log analysis: What it is, what's been done, how to do it. *Library & Information Science Research, 28*, 407–432. doi:10.1016/j.lisr.2006.06.005

Jansen, B. J., & Spink, A. (2000). Methodological approach in discovering user search patterns through Web log analysis. *Bulletin of the American Society for Information Science, 27*, 15–17. doi:10.1002/bult.185

Jansen, B. J., & Spink, A. (2005). How are we searching the world wide web? An analysis of nine search engine transaction logs. *Information Processing & Management, 42*(1), 248–563. doi:10.1016/j.ipm.2004.10.007

Jansen, B. J., Spink, A., Bateman, J., & Saracevic, T. (1998). Real life information retrieval: A study of user queries on the Web. *ACM SIGIR Special Interest Group on Information Retrieval, 32*(1), 5–17.

Jansen, B. J., Spink, A., & Pedersen, J. (2005). A temporal comparison of AltaVista web searching. *Journal of the American Society for Information Science and Technology, 56*, 559–570. doi:10.1002/asi.20145

Jijkoun, V., Mishne, G., de Rijke, M., Schlobach, S., Ahn, D., & Muller, K. (2004). *The University of Amsterdam at QA@CLEF 2004*. Working Notes of the Cross-Language Evaluation Forum (CLEF 2004). New York, NY.

Joachims, T. (2002). Optimizing search engines using clickthrough data. In *Proceedings of the 8th ACM SIGKDD International Conference on Knowledge Discovery and Data Mining*, (pp. 133-142). ACM Press.

Kalamboukis, T. Z. (1995). Suffix stripping with modern Greek. *Program, 29*, 313–321. doi:10.1108/eb047204

Karlgren, J., Gonzalo, J., & Clough, P. (2007). iCLEF 2006 overview: Searching the Flickr www photo-sharing repository. *Lecture Notes in Computer Science, 4730*, 186–194. doi:10.1007/978-3-540-74999-8_27

Kolari, P., & Joshi, A. (2004). Web mining: Research and practice. *Computing in Science & Engineering, 6*(4), 49–53. doi:10.1109/MCSE.2004.23

Kraaij, W., & Pohlmann, R. (1994). Porter's stemming algorithm for Dutch. In Noordman, L., & de Vroomen, E. (Eds.), *Informatiewetenschap*. STINFON.

Largergren, E., & Over, P. (1998). Comparing interactive information retrieval systems across sites: The TREC-6 interactive track matrix experiment. In *Proceedings of the 21st Annual International ACM SIGIR Conference*, (pp. 164-172). ACM Press.

Laurent, D., Séguela, P., & Nègre, S. (2005). *Cross lingual question answering using QRISTAL for CLEF 2005*. Working Notes of the Cross-Language Evaluation Forum (CLEF 2005). New York, NY.

Li, X., & Roth, D. (2002). Learning question classifiers. In *Proceedings 19th International Conference on Computational Linguistics*. ACL.

Liu, Y., Fu, Y., Zhang, M., Ma, S., & Ru, L. (2007). Automatic search engine performance evaluation with click-through data analysis. In *Proceedings of the 16th International Conference on World Wide Web*, (pp. 1133-1134). WWW.

Loponen, A., Paik, J., & Jarvelin, K. (2010). *UTA stemming and lemmatization experiments in the Bengali ad hoc track at FIRE 2010*. Working Notes of the Forum for Information Retrieval Evaluation (FIRE 2010). New York, NY.

Lovins, J. B. (1968). Development of a stemming algorithm. *Mechanical Translation and Computational Linguistics, 11*, 22–31.

Majumder, P., Mitra, M., Parui, S. K., Kole, G., Mitra, P., & Datta, K. (2007). YASS: Yet another suffix stripper. *ACM Transactions on Information Systems, 25*(4).

Manning, C. D., & Schüzte, H. (2002). *Foundation of statistical natural language processing*. Cambridge, MA: The MIT Press.

Maron, M. E., & Kuhns, J. L. (1960). On relevance, probabilistic indexing and information retrieval. *Journal of the ACM, 7*, 216–244. doi:10.1145/321033.321035

Martínez-González, A., de Pablo-Sánchez, C., Polo-Bayo, C., Vicente-Díez, M. T., Martínez Fernández, P., & Martínez-Fernández, J. L. (2009). Lecture Notes in Computer Science: *Vol. 5706. The MIRACLE team at the CLEF 2008 multilingual question answering track* (pp. 409–420). Springer. doi:10.1007/978-3-642-04447-2_48

Martínez-Santiago, F., Ureña-López, L. A., & Martín-Valdivia, M. (2006). A merging strategy proposal: The 2-step retrieval status value method. *Information Retrieval, 9*(1), 71–93. doi:10.1007/s10791-005-5722-4

Mat-Hassan, M., & Levene, M. (2001). Associating search and navigation behavior through log analysis. *Journal of the American Society for Information Science and Technology, 56*(9), 913–934. doi:10.1002/asi.20185

Moldovan, D., Harabagiu, S., Pasca, M., Mihalcea, R., Girju, R., Goodrum, R., & Rus, V. (2000). The structure and performance of an open-domain question answering system. In *Proceedings of the 39th Annual Meeting of the Association for Computational Linguistics*, (pp. 563–570). ACL.

Moreau, N. (2009). *Best practices in language resources for multilingual information access (d5.2). Technical Report: TrebleCLEF Project: FP7 IST ICT-1-4-1*. TrebleCLEF Project.

Neumann, G., & Sacaleanu, B. (2006). Lecture Notes in Computer Science: *Vol. 40. Experiments of cross-linguality and question-type driven strategy selection for open-domain QA* (pp. 429–438). Springer. doi:10.1007/11878773_48

Oard, D. W. (2009). Multilingual information access. In *Encyclopedia of Library and Information Sciences*. New York, NY: Taylor & Francis.

Oard, D. W., & Gonzalo, J. (2002). The CLEF 2001 interactive track. *Lecture Notes in Computer Science, 2406*, 353–439. doi:10.1007/3-540-45691-0_30

Oard, D. W., & Gonzalo, J. (2004). The CLEF 2003 interactive track. *Lecture Notes in Computer Science, 3237*, 425–434. doi:10.1007/978-3-540-30222-3_41

Oard, D. W., Gonzalo, J., Sanderson, M., López-Ostenero, F., & Wang, J. (2004). Interactive cross-language document selection. *Information Retrieval*, *7*(1-2), 205–228. doi:10.1023/B:INRT.0000009446.22036.e3

Over, P. (2001). The TREC interactive track: An annotated bibliography. *Information Processing & Management*, *37*(3), 369–382. doi:10.1016/S0306-4573(00)00053-4

Paik, J. H., & Parui, S. K. (2008). *A simple stemmer for inflectional languages*. Working Notes of the Forum for Information Retrieval Evaluation (FIRE 2008). New York, NY.

Pass, G., Chowdhury, A., & Torgeson, C. (2006). A picture of search. In *Proceedings of the 1st International Conference on Scalable Information Systems*. IEEE.

Peters, C., & Sheridan, P. (2001). Multilingual information access. In *Lectures on Information Retrieval* (pp. 51–80). Berlin, Germany: Springer. doi:10.1007/3-540-45368-7_3

Pevzner, B. R. (1972). Comparative evaluation of the operation of the Russian and English variants of the pusto-nepusto-2 system. *Automatic Documentation and Mathematical Linguistics*, *6*(2), 71–74.

Pirkola, A. (1998). The effects of query structure and dictionary setups in dictionary-based cross-language information retrieval. In *Proceedings of SIGIR 1998, 21st ACM International Conference on Research and Development in Information Retrieval*, (pp. 55-63). ACM Press.

Pirkola, A., Hedlund, T., Keskustalo, H., & Järvelin, K. (2001). Dictionary-based cross-language information retrieval: Problems, methods, and research findings. *Information Retrieval*, *4*(3), 209–230. doi:10.1023/A:1011994105352

Ponte, J. M., & Croft, B. W. (1998). A language modeling approach to information retrieval. In *Proceedings of the 21st Annual International ACM SIGIR Conference on Research and Development in Information Retrieval*, (pp. 275-281). ACM Press.

Porter, M. F. (1980). An algorithm for suffix stripping. *Program*, *14*, 130–137. doi:10.1108/eb046814

Prager, J., Brown, R., Coden, A., & Radev, D. R. (2000). Question-answering by predictive annotation. In *Proceedings of the 23rd SIGIR Conference*, (pp. 184–191). SIGIR.

Qiu, Y. (1995). Automatic query expansion based on a similarity Thesaurus. (PhD Thesis). Swiss Federal Institute of Technology. Geneva, Switzerland.

Resnik, P. (1998). Parallel strands: A preliminary investigation into mining the web for bilingual text. *Lecture Notes in Computer Science*, *1529*, 72–82. doi:10.1007/3-540-49478-2_7

Robertson, S. E. (1977). The probabilistic ranking principle in IR. *The Journal of Documentation*, *33*, 294–304. doi:10.1108/eb026647

Robertson, S. E., Walker, S., & Beaulieu, M. (1999). Okapi at TREC–7: Automatic ad hoc, filtering, VLC and filtering tracks. In *Proceedings of the 7th Text REtrieval Conference (TREC-7)*, (pp. 253-264). TREC.

Salton, G. (1969). Automatic processing of foreign language documents. In Proceedings *of the 1969 Conference on Computational Linguistics*, (pp. 1-28). ACL.

Salton, G., Wong, A., & Yang, C. S. (1975). A vector space model for information retrieval. *Communications of the ACM*, *18*(11), 613–620. doi:10.1145/361219.361220

Savoy, J. (1999). A stemming procedure and stopword list for general french corpora. *Journal of the American Society for Information Science American Society for Information Science, 50,* 944–952. doi:10.1002/(SICI)1097-4571(1999)50:10<944::AID-ASI9>3.0.CO;2-Q

Savoy, J. (2005). Comparative study of monolingual and multilingual search models for use with Asian languages. *ACM Transactions on Asian Language Information Processing, 4*(2), 163–189. doi:10.1145/1105696.1105701

Schinke, R., Robertson, A., Willet, P., & Greengrass, M. (1996). A stemming algorithm for Latin text databases. *The Journal of Documentation, 52,* 172–187. doi:10.1108/eb026966

Sheridan, P., & Ballerini, J. P. (1996). Experiments in multilingual information retrieval using the SPIDER system. In *Proceedings of the 19th Annual International ACM SIGIR Conference on Research and Development in Information Retrieval,* (pp. 58-65). ACM Press.

Sheridan, P., Braschler, M., & Schäuble, P. (1997). Cross-language information retrieval in a multilingual legal domain. In *Proceedings of the Research and Advanced Technology for Digital Libraries,* (pp. 253–268). Springer.

Singhal, A., Buckley, C., & Mitra, M. (1996). Pivoted document length normalization. In *Proceedings of ACM SIGIR 1996,* (pp. 21-29). ACM Press.

Spector, A. Z. (2009). *The continuing metamorphosis of the web.* Paper presented at the World Wide Web Conference (WWW 2009). New York, NY.

Spink, A., Jansen, B. J., Wolfram, D., & Saracevic, T. (2002a). From e-sex to e-commerce: Web search changes. *Computer, 35*(3), 107–109. doi:10.1109/2.989940

Spink, A., Ozmutlu, S., Ozmutlu, H. C., & Jansen, B. J. (2002b). US versus European web searching trends. *ACM SIGIR Forum, 36*(2), 32-38.

Spink, A., Wolfram, D., Jansen, B. J., & Saracevic, T. (2001). Searching the web: The public and their queries. *Journal of the American Society for Information Science and Technology, 52*(3), 226–234. doi:10.1002/1097-4571(2000)9999:9999<::AID-ASI1591>3.0.CO;2-R

Srivastava, J., & Cooley, R. (2003). Web business intelligence: Mining the web for actionable knowledge. *INFORMS Journal on Computing, 15*(2), 191–207. doi:10.1287/ijoc.15.2.191.14447

Sutcliffe, R., Mulcahy, M., Gabbay, I., O'Gorman, A., White, K., & Slatter, D. (2006). Cross-language French-English question answering using the DLT system at CLEF 2005. *Lecture Notes in Computer Science, 4022.*

Tanev, H., Negri, M., Magnini, B., & Kouylekov, M. (2005). The DIOGENE question answering system at CLEF-2004. *Lecture Notes in Computer Science, 3491,* 435–445. doi:10.1007/11519645_43

van Rijsbergen, C. J. (1979). *Information retrieval* (2nd ed.). London, UK: Butterworths.

Voorhees, E. M., & Tice, D. M. (1999). The TREC-8 question answering track evaluation. In *Proceedings of the Text Retrieval Conference TREC-8,* (pp. 83-105). TREC.

Wolfram, D., Spink, A., Jansen, B. J., & Saracevic, T. (2001). Vox populi: The public searching of the Web. *Journal of the American Society for Information Science and Technology, 52*(12), 1073–1074. doi:10.1002/asi.1157

Zhai, C., & Laffery, J. (2001). A study of smoothing methods for language models applied to ad hoc information retrieval. [SIGIR.]. *Proceedings of SIGIR, 2001,* 334–342.

KEY TERMS AND DEFINITIONS

Cross-Language Information Retrieval: Information retrieval process in which queries in a given language are used to find documents expressed in another.

Indexing: Storing text documents in a database in order to efficiently search over large volumes of data.

Information Retrieval: Automatic process which, from an spontaneous ad hoc query by a user denoting an information need and a collection of documents, delivers a list of search results ordered according to their relevance.

Lemmatization: Normalization process consisting of performing a morphological analysis on the text to reduce words to their lemmas or lexical forms, as they would appear in a dictionary.

Log File: Electronic record of interactions occurred during a searching episode between an information access system and users.

Named Entities Recognition: Process performed over text to properly identify pieces of information such as proper names (denoting people, organizations, geographic locations) collocations, multiword expressions or dates which require more complex processing and, in an MLIA scenario, careful translating.

Stemming: Normalization process consisting of removing prefixes, suffixes and inflection to reduce words to their stem forms or roots.

Stopwords: Words presumably lacking of lexical meaning (grammatical particles, function words, conjunctions) and other common terms which, unlike content-bearing words, are usually filtered out in order to reduce the size of the index.

Thesaurus: A controlled vocabulary containing domain-specific terminology where relationships between concepts are explicitly established.

Tokenization: Segmentation process performed over a stream of text in order to identify the single tokens or terms which are to be included in a subsequent indexing step.

ENDNOTES

1. For a comprehensive and updated catalog of NLP tools and linguistic resources suitable to be integrated in an MLIA system, see the survey by Moreau (2009).
2. Special Interest Group on Information Retrieval: http://www.sigir.org
3. Text REtrieval Conference: http://trec.nist.gov
4. NTCIR; Evaluation of Information Access Technologies: http://research.nii.ac.jp/ntcir
5. Forum for Information Retrieval Evaluation: http://www.isical.ac.in/~clia/
6. Cross-Language Evaluation Forum: http://www.clef-campaign.org
7. Following Zipf's law, frequency counts of words are very uneven: very few words are used extremely often in a text, while most words occur rarely.
8. In this context, we call cognates those words from different languages sharing a common etymological origin, as in: night (English), Nacht (German), nuit (French), nit (Catalan), noche (Spanish), noite (Portuguese), notte (Italian).
9. See http://nlp.uned.es/iCLEF.
10. Flickr (see http://www.flickr.com) is an online community for sharing and embedding video and images. As of September 2010, it claims to host more than 5 billion photographs. See http://blog.flickr.net/en/2010/00/19/5000000000/.
11. See http://www.uni-hildesheim.de/logclef.

Section 5
Digital Content Management

Chapter 10
Mining User–Generated Content for Social Research and Other Applications

Rafael E. Banchs
Institute for Infocomm Research, Singapore

Carlos G. Rodríguez Penagos
Barcelona Media Innovation Centre, Spain

ABSTRACT

User-generated content is currently becoming a valuable means for sensing and measuring real world variables and parameters that are of interest to several actors in the society: politicians, government departments, security agencies, marketing researchers, service providers, etc. In response to this new scenario, large research efforts are being invested in the so-called "social media" phenomenon by a wide spectrum of institutions and organizations around the world, with many different objectives and a diverse scope of fields and disciplines. As a consequence, new technologies and applications are currently emerging on the grounds of human participation, interaction, and behavior on the Internet.

The main objective of this chapter is to present a general overview of the most relevant applications of text mining and natural language processing technologies evolving and emerging around the Web 2.0 phenomenon (such as automatic categorization, document summarization, question answering, dialogue management, opinion mining, sentiment analysis, outlier identification, misbehavior detection, and social estimation and forecasting) along with the main challenges and new research opportunities that are directly and indirectly derived from them.

INTRODUCTION

Internet has changed human communications in several different ways, but perhaps one of the most prominent changes has come hand-in-hand with the so-called Web 2.0. Within the scenario of these second generation of Web technologies, information is generated, delivered and consumed by "end" users of traditional mass media communication: the general public. According to this view, and as several Web 2.0 applications currently demonstrate,[1] the ability to broadcast has become available, theoretically, to almost everybody. This constitutes one major milestone

DOI: 10.4018/978-1-4666-2169-5.ch010

since the introduction of mass media communication experimented by our modern information society, with deep repercussions in culture, sociology and economics (Ala-Mutka, et al., 2009). Consequently, traditional technologies are evolving and new technologies and applications are emerging from, and for, the Web 2.0. Some examples of these are opinion mining (Funk, et al., 2008), sentiment analysis (Pang & Lee, 2008), question answering (Chali, 2009), user profiling (Kontostathis, et al., 2009), recommender systems (Ricci & Werthner, 2006), behavioral marketing (Berkman, 2008), and social forecasting (Durant & Smith, 2007), among others.

One of the most important issues regarding the Web 2.0 phenomenon is that most of the user interactions, as well as generated contents, involve human language; so the Web 2.0 era demands natural language processing technologies more than ever. Main types of user-generated text range from formal journalistic and/or biographic contents, such as in the case of blogs; to shorter and more informal contents, such as discussion forums and consumer reviews, opinions and recommendations; and, in the micro-blog extreme, to very short messages known as "tweets." All these impose particular requirements of speed and efficiency on traditional natural language applications, as well as accuracy, scalability and robustness requirements that are difficult to tackle with current available technologies. Additionally, when considering natural language processing techniques, new communication styles, and varieties of language usage must be taken into account too. The extended use of non-standard practices such as emoticons (character sequences denoting emotions or gestures) and chatspeak (special spelling and terminology associated with informal social media exchanges), as well as their corresponding context-dependent protocols, are generating new communication and language "standards" that have to be tackled by analysis applications focused on user-generated content.

At this moment, it is still not possible to fully foresee the implications and consequences of massive user-generated content analysis in terms of both scientific and commercial exploitation. This is mainly because of the complex and multidimensional nature of the Web 2.0 phenomenon itself. Indeed, practical experience demonstrates that, although many Web 2.0 websites have been growing at a very fast pace during the last few years, only few of them have actually been able to develop successful business models from their corresponding virtual communities. Nevertheless, what it is actually possible to foresee are some trends emerging from this new framework of human interaction and communication. The main objective of this chapter is to present a general overview of the most relevant applications of text mining and natural language processing technologies currently emerging around the Web 2.0 phenomenon, along with the main challenges and new research opportunities that are derived from them.

The chapter is structured as follows. First, a background section providing the main definitions and general discussions on social media and user-generated content analysis is presented. This section covers some fundamental issues regarding the Web 2.0, social media, and natural language processing technologies, which should provide necessary background for the following sections. Second, a section on technical challenges is presented. This section presents the main issues and challenges related to processing user-generated content in the context of the Web 2.0, namely: encoding, chatspeak, emoticons, ungrammaticality, normalization, co-referencing, spamming, multilingualism, communication structure, and user roles. An important point in the discussion is deciding how much natural language processing is warranted for each task, and when the emerging regularities in vast amounts of data allow for the use of language-independent statistical methods.

Next, a section on applications related to user-generated content analysis is presented. In each case, reference to relevant studies reported in the literature are provided and the main specific open research problems are described. These applications include: automatic categorization, document summarization, question answering, dialogue systems, opinion mining and sentiment analysis, outlier identification and misbehavior detection, and social estimation and forecasting. Then, we present a section on future trends and research opportunities. This section presents our vision about the most important future trends related to processing and analysis of user-generated content in the context of the Web 2.0. Additionally, the most relevant research opportunities which are derived from the presented applications and future trends are also described.

Lastly, we discuss ethical and legal issues concerning privacy and proprietary rights that arise when processing and using user-generated content. Finally, some conclusions are presented along with a list of complementary recommended reading.

Background

Although the origin of the term Web 2.0 is not clear, it became popular in 2004, when the first Web 2.0 conference was held in San Francisco, California (O'Reilly & Battelle, 2004). With that name, the idea that the Web had become a platform for interaction, beyond a former paradigm of publishing content for others to consume, was highlighted. Indeed, the term Web 2.0 refers to a new generation of interactive websites and applications where users can upload and edit the content. Technically speaking, this concept does not represent any technological advancement by itself. Since the introduction of distributed systems, important efforts have been devoted to provide system users with friendly and easy-to-use interfaces for searching, handling, and editing contents in a collaborative way. Such an objective has been central in the development of standard applications such as Content Management

Systems (CMS) and Media Asset Management Systems (MAMS). The natural extension of these principles to the Internet is what we call Web 2.0. However, there are two fundamental factors that make it markedly different from conventional collaborative systems: the universality and freedom offered by Internet.[2]

Contrary to conventional collaborative applications, Internet-based ones provide the general public with a valuable resource for searching and sharing information and content at their own pace and on their own terms. These have encouraged the use of such resources for personal and social activities in addition to their use in professional or technical settings. In addition to information search, shopping was, for instance, one of the first non-technical activities the general public was engaged in the Internet (Weisman, 2000). These technologies provided the basis for more comprehensive marketing strategies in which user interactions could be exploited to improve both sales rates and user satisfaction. The use of feedback from Internet customers became a valuable resource for target segmentation and on-line advertisement campaigns (Jarvenpaa & Todd, 1996). This feedback can be either direct, such as ratings or explicit valuations on products, or indirect, as in the traces left in log-files when interacting with the system. Techniques such as collaborative filtering exploit this kind of information to associate customers with similar needs and wants, which further allow to generate recommendations that are more suitable for them (Su & Khoshgoftaar, 2009). In addition, experience has shown that there is always an important number of customers who are willing to provide direct feedback in a more comprehensive way in the form of product reviews, opinions and comments.

In addition to shopping, the scope and amount of social activity have increased in the Internet in the form of blogs, forums, and networking applications such as Facebook, MySpace, or LinkedIn, just to mention a few. Nowadays, the general public can register and participate actively in a lot of different applications to search, share, manage and edit information and content. In this new sort of applications, users are not passive consumers anymore; they have become the producers and receptors of content and information. In this sense, the term social media has been adopted to describe the complex and heterogeneous set of Web 2.0 applications people are using for sharing user-generated content (Kaplan & Haenlein, 2010). From people's interactions in social media, a network of relationships or connections can be derived, and this constitutes what is commonly referred to as the social network underneath the given application (Freeman, 2004; Knoke & Yang, 2008). The interactions used for deriving these networks can be either extracted from direct connections among people, such as the list of friends explicitly defined by each user, or inferred from indirect relationships among them, such as the list of users that comment on, visit to, or explicitly link some other user's contents.

It is true that much of the data generated and consumed by users in social media and other Web 2.0 applications is non-textual in nature, and much of the registered interactions are available as navigation-logs. Nevertheless, it is also true that a significant part of the content and social interaction in the context of the Web 2.0 occurs in the form of natural language. In this sense, natural language processing and text mining techniques have become a fundamental necessity for Web 2.0 analysis. In addition to the challenges and restrictions imposed by the particular nature of user-generated content, most of which will be described in detail in the following sections, specific necessities and requirements imposed by new emerging Web 2.0 applications are providing an unprecedented scenario for the development of new methods and technologies for the analysis of textual contents and natural language.

Although still very far from the goal of unrestricted and domain-independent understanding, natural language processing, both for generation and for interpretation, has come a long way from its humble beginnings in the mid-twentieth century. Nowadays, at least some sort of basic and robust human language technologies are present in most systems that need to interact with people, as for example, orthography and grammar correctors, document classifiers, adaptive user interfaces, recommender systems, basic dialogue systems for e-commerce, etc. Language technologies are finally coming of age, as illustrated in surveys (Varile, et al., 1997), reference books (Manning & Schütze, 2000; Jurafsky & Martin, 2000), and active domain conferences and journals (such as the ones from the Association for Computational Linguistics).

Finally, there is a sociological dimension that cannot be ignored (DiMaggio, et al., 2001). The Web 2.0 is about people and people's interactions. This simple fact has created a lot of excitement among the scientific, political and commercial communities, not just because of its implications with regard to how to understand, exploit and capitalize human participation and interactions in this new medium (Surowiecki, 2005), but also on how to use this highly measurable environment to better understand the real word phenomena (Haase, et al., 2002; Qualman, 2009). Indeed, the so called virtual world can be regarded as a projection of real life into a virtual space where humans behave like humans that just have a new medium for communicating with and relating to each other. The simultaneous anonymity and ubiquity of presence allowed by online networking may help us define ourselves as individuals and as a society in ways that, although certainly available before, were not as fundamental to the fabric of everyday life (Ramakrishnan & Tomkins, 2007). Creating an online identity in the new digital ecosystem might become a defining fact of human culture in years to come (Madden, et al., 2007).

MAIN TECHNICAL CHALLENGES

There are important technical challenges that make the problem of processing user-generated content different from conventional text mining and natural language processing. This section discusses the most relevant of these challenges: encoding, chatspeak, emoticons, ungrammaticality, normalization, co-referencing, spamming, multilingualism, communication structure, and user roles.

Encoding

Anyone who has ever worked with Web 2.0 textual content in a language other than English knows that text encoding constitutes a nagging but non-trivial issue. This is mainly due to the existence of multiple encoding schemes even for the same language. Most of the text encoding problems observed when working with user-generated online texts can be classified into two categories: wrong character encoding and corrupted html or XML character entities.

Although the general issue of encoding detection and conversion has been dealt with exhaustively,[3] the text encoding problem described here is a bit different in nature. When a user copies a fragment of text from one editor and pastes it into another editor with a different encoding setting, a composite encoding is generated. As this process can be repeated several times over different fragments of the original text, an automatic procedure for decomposing composite codes is not a trivial problem. Some basic encoding detection algorithms use lists or distributions of byte sequences that allow for identifying a specific encoding. As user-generated content can mix different encodings in the same text, this approach is insufficient, or would result in the correct identification of only a segment of the document. Other more sophisticated methods are available, including a composite one used by Mozilla browsers (Li & Momoi, 2001), but we might need to provide further heuristics to filter and convert them into a unified scheme. Dealing with composite or non-standard encodings is important since natural language processing applications can be sensitive to them.

Chatspeak

Chatspeak is the term used to describe the abbreviated text writing style originally adopted by young people in SMS messaging (Crystal, 2008). Although chatspeak style communication was originally restricted to SMS and some online chat applications, more recently, Twitter has boosted its relative weight within the Web 2.0. Chatspeak is actually a general category where many different styles and modalities can be identified. Among these styles, two main categories can be mentioned here: phonetic-based and acronym-based. In the first case, phonetic similarities between characters and syllables are exploited to compress word spellings; typical examples include the use of "u" for "you," "c" for "see," "r" for "are," "2" for "to," "4" for "for," "w8" for "wait," and so on. In the second case, acronyms are used to represent commonly used words and expressions; typical examples include the famous "LOL" (Laughing Out Loud) and the less popular "BTW" (By The Way), which can also refer to "between."

Although some rule-based methods and dictionaries can help to cope with the problem of chatspeak, converting chatspeak into a normalized and readable text is not always an easy task since, in many cases, conventional forms can be either ambiguous (e.g., "BTW") or constantly evolving into more complex and context-dependent expressions that convey not only meanings but also non-verbal communication elements such as emotions and expressiveness. Another viable approach is to renounce to conversion into a canonical form, and treat chatspeak as a dialect or a genre, with its own specificities and vocabularies. Although this approach is more theoretically sound, it would mean having training and development corpus, for all the processing tools, that are identical or very similar to chatspeak, and this is a very effort-intensive and impractical proposition (Dey & Haque, 2009).

Emoticons

Information in human communications is also transmitted by means of paralinguistic elements that complement verbal communication (Segerstrale & Molnar, 1997). In formal writing, this information is traditionally not registered but, in some specific cases, annotations can be used to provide limited information about these non-verbal elements through the pragmatic component of language (Levinson, 1983), i.e., the purely contextual aspects of meaning. However, most textual contents in the Web 2.0 are far from being formal written communication. In some senses, user-generated content is closer to spoken language than to written one. An emoticon can be as simple as the traditional happy face ":-)" or as complex as an actual artwork piece created by means of keyboard characters and symbols. The term *emoticon* comes from the combination of the words "emotion" and "icon," and they can be considered to be the equivalents of paralinguistic elements (gestures, actions, etc.) in verbal communications.

In a broader sense, emoticons are to be considered much more than graphical signatures used in textual communications. Indeed, any kind of formatting or style used with the intention of conveying paralinguistic information about the author's attitudes or intended message can be considered an emoticon. According to this, two main categories of emoticons can be distinguished: explicit emoticons, such as happy faces and similar symbols; and implicit emoticons, such as the use of uppercase, colors or any other resources to emphasize or nuance textual contents. A common example of this latter case would be the use of expressions such as "gooooooaaaaaallll" or "looooong" to furnish a given word with additional paralinguistic information.

Although seemingly straightforward to interpret by a human, machine interpretation is more complex because it might involve extra-linguistic information not available to the algorithms (for instance, why a "wink" using a semicolon resembles a closing eye). Several works have addressed emoticon usage in the Web 2.0 (Walther & D'Addario, 2001; Gajadhar & Green, 2003; Yuasa, et al., 2006; Derks, et al., 2007; Provine, et al., 2007), as it constitutes a very important research area for understanding and interpreting sentiments in user-generated content.

Ungrammaticality

Formal literacy is not one of the characteristics of the Web 2.0 society, and might not be needed since its main defining trait is expediency, not precision or correctness as in other more technical or formal domains. In fact, most of user-generated texts are informal in nature and they are very far from being grammatically correct. This is also true for spoken language, and it is not surprising that "net speak" can be considered as being in between written and spoken, everyday discourse, where there are redundancies, continuous corrections, hesitations, inconsistencies; but where nevertheless end communication is as certain as in the less dynamic and interactive written channels.

Such fluidity and heterogeneity represent an important challenge to conventional natural language processing methods, which usually have been designed and tuned to work with edited textual content that make proper use of grammar and vocabulary. This is one of the reasons why statistical methods have become so popular in user-generated content analysis, as they are much more robust than conventional rule-based methods when dealing with informal style texts (Foster & Vogel, 2004; Burek & Gerdemann, 2009; Mithun & Kossein, 2009).

In any case, we must keep in mind that the success of statistical methods is mainly due to the availability of large volumes of data with enough quality, a condition that is not necessarily always met in user-generated content analysis scenarios. According to this, an important point when designing systems that exploit user-generated content is to decide how much of natural language processing is warranted for each task, and when the assumed regularities in vast amounts of data allow for language-independent statistical methods.

Normalization

Each of the problems previously described represents a specific issue that makes user-generated text analysis different from conventional textual content analysis. Each of these specific problems imposes some particular restrictions to the direct application of conventional processing techniques and algorithms. On the one hand, as we have mentioned earlier, one possible solution is to adapt current state-of-the-art technologies to be able to deal with the new characteristics of Web 2.0 user-generated content, tackling it in its own terms. On the other hand, there is the possibility of designing and implementing algorithms able to transform user-generated texts into "normalized" textual content that can be processed and analyzed by current state-of-the-art technologies. This last alternative is referred to as normalization.

In addition to dealing with all the problems previously described: text encoding, chatspeak, emoticons, and ungrammaticality, normalization must also address the important problems of sentence boundary detection, capitalized word disambiguation and abbreviation identification (Mikheev, 2000), as well as the classical problems of identifying and correcting misspellings and typos (Kukich, 1992). In our view of the problem, neither current technology adaptation nor normalization as isolated strategies constitutes the most appropriate road to follow, since the problems to be addressed are too varied for a unified approach (for instance, with user names and spam intrusion in text, no spelling dictionary will ever be close to enough). Both solutions should be considered as complementary and must be approached in a coordinated manner, depending on the specific objective and tools at hand. Translating, for instance, emoticons into "proper" text words might make some of their specific nuances and context invisible, and any normalization can potentially lead to an erroneous or unwarranted interpretation.

Another potential danger is over-correction, since some of the algorithms rely on common word dictionaries that are not exhaustive or might be outdated, and a new word, brand or expression might be transformed systematically into something completely different to what was intended (e.g., correcting "BTW" for another similar word using a minimum edit distance algorithm would result in "BOW," for instance). Here, again, a principled combination of rule-based and stochastic techniques go a long way ensuring good precision while retaining a commensurate coverage for free-form online text (Dey & Haque, 2009; Thewald, et al., 2010).

Co-Referencing

A very important problem in natural language processing is co-reference and anaphora resolution. It is about identifying what are the persons, objects and entities the discourse refers to. This implies knowing, for example, that "General Motors," "they," and "the giant car maker" all refer to the same entity throughout a given text. In this sense, the problem is not exclusive to user-generated content analysis and is relevant to information extraction and retrieval technologies in general. However, it acquires significant relevance in the case of the Web 2.0, since anaphoric references might constitute a greater proportion than explicit mentions in informal text, and (as in spoken discourse) ambiguity might be pervasive, but manageable nonetheless.

A large amount of user-generated text in the Web is constituted by comments, descriptions, opinions, and comparisons about services, products, or even other people. In such a scenario, co-referencing techniques play a very important role in precisely determining targets and sources of a given opinion or comment. A large body of literature (Hobbs, 1978; Reinhart, 1983; Lappin & Leass, 1994; Ng & Cardie, 2002; Barss, 2003; Markert & Nissim, 2005; Ponzetto & Poesio, 2009) is available on the general problems of co-referencing and anaphora resolution, and more recently other studies (Jackson & Moulinier, 2007; Jijkoun, et al., 2008) have focused on its application to user-generated content analysis.

Spamming

A non-negligible proportion of texts in the Web 2.0 belongs to the category of spam. Although several different definitions of spam can be found, the term mainly refers to unsolicited textual content that is typically generated, posted, or distributed in an automatic manner (Ham, 2004). Most of the spam in the Web 2.0 is generated with marketing and promotional objectives in mind. However, there have been also cases of malicious spamming with the exclusive objective of collapsing resources and/or slowing down communication systems.

Filtering spam and separating it from genuine, relevant content is a challenge for text mining and natural language processing applications in the Web 2.0. This is mainly because spamming is so frequent that, in some cases, data statistics can be significantly altered because of its presence. A large body of literature about the problem of spamming has been published during the last few years. Similarly, several commercial applications for filtering spam have become available, especially for the case of e-mail based applications (Cormack, 2007).

Interestingly, both spammers and application developers have turned to techniques from natural language processing in a continuing and escalating war. When spam filters were trained to only allow through documents which resembled human-generated text (by requiring it to contain certain words that are always present in human-generated text, like prepositions, articles, etc.), a

new generation of spam incorporating pseudo-text generated from frequent n-grams appeared, which, even though made no sense to human readers, was robust enough to fool some of the implemented filters.

Multilingualism

Another important issue regarding the Web 2.0 and the Web in general is multilingualism. Few years ago, most of the Web contents were produced in English. Nowadays, as the use of the Web has become immensely popular, Web content is produced and published in a large amount of different languages (Danet & Herring, 2007). Although most statistics about percentages of online language usage are unreliable, a UNESCO-sponsored study provides some relevant figures (Pimienta, et al., 2009).

Recent advances in machine translation, including both rule-based and statistical approaches, have allowed for developing online translation systems able to provide automatic translations of textual contents in the Web with some reasonable quality (Ney, 2005). However, again, the quality of automatic translation results severely depends on variables such as input text quality, domain, and vocabulary. Despite recent advances, machine translation technologies are still far from being reliable for many applications and, in particular, the nature of Web 2.0's user-generated texts imposes several important challenges to current state-of-the-art machine translation systems.

Two other important issues regarding multilingualism are: the distinction between language-dependent versus language-independent technologies, and the development of language-specific resources and tools, with particular regard to minority languages (Sagot, 2005, 2007; Dandapat, et al., 2007; Gambäck, et al., 2009; Sagot & Walther, 2010; Walther & Sagot, 2010). Finally, another issue, which is commonly encountered in both user-generated content and spontaneous speech, is the problem of code switching, which consists in the use of terms in different languages in the same sentence or utterance (Joshi, 1982).

Structure and Roles

Two final important issues that are relevant to the Web 2.0 are the problems of inferring communication structure and user roles from online communications. Although most Web 2.0 sites support nested communication structures such as the "threads" commonly arising in discussion forums and online debates, there are some sites where such structure support is not available. In these latter cases, users generally adopt standard procedures for artificially providing structure to communication. A typical example is the case of using quotes in replying to posts in linearly structured sequences of comments. In these situations, a user replying to a post (that is located several comments before) starts her/his own post by partially, or completely, quoting the post she/he intends to respond to. Inferring structure from this kind of communication requires the capability of identifying repeated texts, as well as possible co-references to other users, in order to reconstruct the corresponding threaded structure from purely textual information.

In the case of dialogue roles, an important problem in online discussion analysis is the identification of user roles and impersonation. Different from meaning and intentions, in this case, the main focus of the analysis is the identification of the specific roles played by the different participants: leaders, followers, lurkers, etc. This kind of analysis is fundamentally important for identifying who are the most influential users in a virtual community, as well as for ranking discussions and forums (Mishne & Glance, 2006a; Sakurai & Orihara, 2006; Zhang, et al., 2007; Singla & Richardson, 2008; Kaltenbrunner, et al., 2009; Garcia, et al., 2009).

APPLICATIONS RELATED TO USER-GENERATED CONTENT ANALYSIS

This section presents a selected set of applications related to user-generated content analysis in the context of the Web 2.0. In each case, references to some relevant studies reported in the literature are provided and related research problems are described. The applications described within this section are:

- *Automatic Categorization*, which deals with processing large volumes of user-generated content to automatically extract categories.
- *Document Summarization*, which deals with extracting the most relevant information within a given document or group of documents.
- *Question Answering*, which deals with the problem of extracting, validating and rating, from a large collection of user-generated content, possible answers to specific questions formulated in natural language by other users.
- *Dialogue Systems*, which deals with the problem of automatically handling and mediating human-computer communication at the pragmatic level.
- *Opinion Mining and Sentiment Analysis*, which deals with the problem of analyzing consumers' reviews and comments in discussion forums for extracting relevant information for marketing research and business intelligence.
- *Outlier Identification and Misbehavior Detection*, which deals with a variety of problems related to the identification of users that are engaged in misleading practices or criminal activity.
- *Social Estimation and Forecasting*, which deals with the problem of estimating and

predicting real world variables (such as presidential approval rate, or specific marketing campaign success) by means of what the general public is saying online.

Automatic Categorization

In the same way that documents and texts in the traditional Web, digital libraries and other document repositories are categorized and organized for ease of access, textual information in the Web 2.0 must also be provided with structure.

In addition to system predefined categories, user-generated content search and management can benefit considerably from user-defined categories, as well as from automatically generated categories. In the first case, it is the users themselves that are in charge of classifying the content that they have generated into either user-defined, or system predefined categories previously specified by the application's administrators. A common modality of this kind of user-based classification scheme is known as a "folksonomy," which is often also referred to as collaborative tagging or social classification (Peters, 2009). This scheme is based on tagging, i.e. users assigning tags to contents in a collaborative manner. In this way, contents in the collection are represented as vectors of tags, and similarities among different contents can be computed by means of a distance metric in a vector space. This procedure has demonstrated to be very effective and efficient, as it can be used to categorize not only textual contents, but also non-textual media (Lamere, 2008). In consequence, several social media applications such as Youtube, Freesound, and Flickr, just to name a few, have adopted tagging mechanisms for allowing collaborative categorization of user-generated content.

In the second case, unsupervised clustering and classification techniques are used to identify the fundamental categories emerging from the structure of the data collection. From these emerging categories, the most relevant terms can be automatically extracted, which could serve as tags to represent the cluster as well as to provide some hints of the semantic categories involved in the cluster. "Hot topics," which are relevant themes or topics that most of the people are commenting about at a given moment in time, can be derived from this kind of analysis (Bengel, et al., 2004; Zheng & Li, 2009; Cataldi, et al., 2010). Similarly, the time evolution of such "hot topics" can be tracked and evaluated (Bun & Ishizuka, 2006; Zhu, et al., 2008). The problem of automatically identifying "hot topics" and following their temporal evolution is closely related to the problem of topic detection and tracking in the contexts of news and press (Allan, et al., 1998).

Document Summarization

Another important task of special interest when searching for information on large volumes of user-generated text is the problem of summarization. This problem can be considered at two different levels: document level and cluster level (Mani, 2001).

In case of document summarization, the most relevant information contained in a given document or unit of content (post, comment, opinion, etc.) is to be extracted. This problem has been extensively studied by researchers (Jing, et al., 1998; Conroy & O'Leary, 2001; Zajic, et al., 2002; Halteren & Teufel, 2003). Two main different approaches to the problem of document summarization can be distinguished: extractive and abstractive. While extractive methods rely on the same principles used for relevant term identification in order to identify the most relevant and informative sentences within the given document (Brandon, et al., 1995; Goldstein, et al., 1999), abstractive methods depends on paraphrasing and generation techniques in order to produce the summaries (Witbrock & Mittal, 1999).

In the second case, summarization at the cluster or sub-collection level is considered. In this case, summarization must take into account a group of contents that are related to each other in a semantic sense: they cover the same topic, similar semantic categories, or some closely related concepts (Radev, et al., 2000; Lin & Hovy, 2002). Most of the time, the superposition principle can be used to deal with the problem of cluster summarization, i.e. the summary of a document set is computed as the summary of the summaries of individuals documents in the set. Summarization at the sub-collection level is of great importance in some business intelligence and decision support applications as huge collections of user-generated content can be quickly overviewed by means of a very small set of summaries (McKeown, et al., 2005).

Question Answering

Different from current information retrieval systems, which use keyword-based queries and return a ranked list of documents, the ideal information retrieval application should allow users to place a query in the form of a question (or information request) in natural language, and receive as a result the most accurate answer the available document collection allows to produce. This is what is referred to as question answering (Voorhees & Tice, 2000; Hirschman & Gaizauskas, 2001; Mollá & Vicedo, 2007). A large amount of effort have been invested in this problem, and several proof-of-concept systems are currently available (Ittycheriah, et al., 2001; Ferres, et al., 2004; Garcia, et al., 2006; Hickl, et al., 2007; Kaisser, 2008). However, these current state-of-the-art systems are able to offer a fair performance only when limited domains and controlled scenarios are considered.

In order to generalize from available data and being able to generate answers that are not explicitly stated in the document set, a measure of inference is needed. This is why textual entailment has lately been considered as a central technology for question answering (Lin & Pantel, 2001; Harabagiu & Hickl, 2006; Celikyilmaz & Thint, 2008). Textual entailment refers to the process whereby the truth of one piece of text depends

or can be derived logically from the meaning of another; a task that humans can do with little effort but is enormously difficult for machine understanding. Statistical inference approaches have recently been used in the implementation of textual entailment engines (Androutsopoulos & Malakasiotis, 2010).

In the context of the Web 2.0, question answering represents an interesting application that has been explored in a very limited way. Nevertheless, some interesting alternatives to the problem of question answering have been successfully implemented in the social media context relying on human-based collaborative approaches. One clear example of this is Yahoo! Answers. This application allows users to post specific questions, as well as to answer questions that have been posted by other users. After a question has received several answers, the user who posted the question can indicate which answer he considers to be the most appropriate. Notice then that a collection of user-generated content constructed in such a way, allows for a conventional query search system to approximate a question answering system; i.e. given a question formulated in natural language, the search engine can retrieve a list of similar questions along with their corresponding answers. Additionally, a collection of these characteristics constitutes an excellent dataset for research and experimentation (Adamic, et al., 2008; Harper, et al., 2008; Wang, et al., 2009, 2010; Kao, et al., 2010).

Some important peculiarities can be identified for question answering applications in the context of Web 2.0 user-generated content. Probably, the most interesting one has to do with the possibility of finding two or more contradictory or incompatible answers to a given question. On one hand, this leads to the problem of estimating the reliability of the informative source (Magnini, et al., 2002; Metzger, 2007; Banerjee & Han, 2009), as this would provide the necessary means for identifying possible sources of errors and discarding erroneous or unreliable information. On the other hand, different opinions on the same issue can be either contradictory or incompatible and still constitute valid answers to the given question. In this sense, the system must be able to identify contents of opinionated nature (more on this after the next subsection).

Dialogue Management Systems

Another important application, closely related to question answering, is automatic dialogue management. Similar to question answering, a large body of literature can be found around the topic of dialogue management systems (Lambert & Carberry, 1992; Smith & Hipp, 1995; Maier, et al., 1996; Levin, et al., 2000; Van Kuppevelt & Smith, 2003). Several experimental experiences with dialogue robots have been reported (Zhao, 2006; Bohus, et al., 2007; Wallis, 2010), as well as some other systems that are currently operating in the Web, like the avatar-driven system implemented in IKEA websites to aid product search (Loquendo, 2007) and the popularly known Cleverbot system.[4]

However, despite these interesting advances, current state-of-the-art in dialogue management systems is still far from passing the Turing test (a test proposed by the English mathematician Alan Turing, in 1950, regarding the possibility of a computer fooling an interlocutor into thinking it is a human). Again, similar to the case of question answering technologies, available dialogue systems are able to offer a reasonable performance only on limited domains and under controlled conditions. Originally, dialogue management systems were "programmed" on finite state automata, but such an approach imposed a lot of restrictions on the design phase as the complexity of the dialogue systems increased (McTear, 1998). More recent approaches rely on goal-oriented approximations, in which a system must accomplish a set of goals and there is much more freedom in the dialogue flow (Wei & Rudnicky, 2000; Lee, et al., 2006; Young, et al., 2007).

Although not a popular option yet, the incursion of dialogue management systems into the Web 2.0 is just a matter of time. From our point of view, it is possible that most of the information search to be conducted over the Web in the near future will be carried mainly over user-generated content, and the search protocol and interface will be heavily based on interactive interfaces, including question answering and dialogue management applications.

Opinion Mining and Sentiment Analysis

Often used interchangeably, opinion mining and sentiment analysis are terms that refer to very similar tasks, although they come from different research traditions and each defends the appropriateness of their designation, which focus on the different aspects (polarity, emotions, etc.) of how people express their attitudes and opinions. We refer interested readers to Pang and Lee (2008) since a full discussion on finer distinctions between these two topics is beyond the scope of this section. The main general objective of this group of related technologies is to extract relevant information about people's opinions in relation to some topic, product, or service. Most of the time, opinion mining applications are used to mine user-generated content that is collected from websites in which explicit opinions or comments are requested from users. This task is of special interest to marketing and customer management departments that need direct feedback from the public.

Technically speaking, opinion mining involves at least three specific subtasks: subjectivity identification, polarity detection and intensity estimation (Pang & Lee, 2008). In the case of subjectivity detection, the main objective is to differentiate factual statements from opinionated contents. This problem is generally approached as a binary classification problem in which a given segment of text must be tagged either as "objective" or as "subjective," which happens to be a very complex and ambiguous task. Subjectivity analysis has been a subject of study long before the Web 2.0 era, and several approaches have been proposed and evaluated (Wiebe, et al., 1999; Hatzivassiloglou & Wiebe, 2000; Wiebe, et al., 2004).

In the case of polarity detection, the objective is to determine the orientation of a given opinionated content. Although two different orientations are possible: "positive" and "negative," it is also common and useful to incorporate the notion of "neutral" opinionated content (Koppel & Schler, 2006). In a simplistic approach, the problem of polarity detection can be approximated as a binary classification problem, which can be implemented by means of either supervised (Pang, et al., 2002; Esuli & Sebastiani, 2006a) or unsupervised (Turney, 2002; Zhou & Chaovalit, 2008) techniques. Inclusion of a neutral category transforms the polarity estimation problem into a three-category classification problem. In the case of intensity estimation, the objective is to assign a specific value on a discrete intensity scale to a content that have been already categorized as positive or negative. In such a discrete-polarity representation, which ranges, for example, from "very negative" in one extreme to "very positive" in the other extreme, the aforementioned "neutral" class can be naturally defined to be at the center of the scale. It has to be noted here that, in contrast to some other straightforward tasks in natural language processing, where human annotators present a consistent and high inter-annotator agreement, polarity and intensity annotations generally exhibit a considerable low agreement among individual annotators. This poses special challenges for the evaluation of the systems that attempt to tackle the problem.

More complex representations combine the notions of subjectivity and polarity in a two-dimensional space where each textual content can be mapped into a triangle which vertices are represented by the pure categories of "positive," "negative" and "factual" (Esuli & Sebastiani, 2006b). The conventional formulation of the opinion-mining problem as the cascade combination of subjectivity identification and polarity

detection assumes that polarity detection is to be conducted only over textual contents of subjective nature. However, the recent introduction of the notion of polar facts (Toprak, et al., 2010) and contextual polarity (Wilson, et al., 2009) has changed this conception adding more complexity to the problem.

From a practical point of view, two main categories of opinion mining applications can be distinguished: target-oriented and sector-oriented. The first case includes those applications where opinions about a specific target are to be identified (Morinaga, et al., 2002; Kim & Hovy, 2006). In this type of applications, problems such as co-reference resolution, negation identification and polarity detection at the sentence and sub-sentence level are of great importance. The second case includes those applications where different attributes and their corresponding descriptors are to be extracted for a given sector or family of products (Hu & Liu, 2004; Popescu & Etzioni, 2005). In this case, statistical methods applied to large volumes of data, at either sentence or comment level, are required to extract major trends in an aggregated form. In this second type of data-driven approach, opinion-mining applications have significantly benefited from the availability of large volumes of annotated data. Generally, in many of the websites where consumer's opinions are collected, the users are requested to provide numerical ratings along with their textual inputs. This kind of data constitutes a valuable resource for the implementation of opinion mining application based on supervised learning methods.

The second and closely related task under consideration in this section is sentiment analysis, which, in a broader sense, aims at determining the sentimental and emotional load that a given user-generated content may convey (Alm, et al., 2005; Mishne, 2005; Sood & Vasserman, 2009). Although several different types of sentiments have been proposed, the most commonly used ones can be reduced to a few emotional dimensions: happiness, sadness, anger, and neutral. In this case, the degree of prevalence of each emotional dimension within a given textual content is to be estimated. Some useful resources such as the online lexicon of general inquirer (Stone, et al., 1966) and the ANEW list (Bradley & Lang, 1999), are commonly used for performing sentiment analysis in textual contents.

Some other interesting problems within the scope of sentiment analysis include humor analysis and detection (Mihalcea & Pulman, 2007; Reyes & Rosso, 2009), personality analysis and classification (Nowson, 2006; Oberlander & Nowson, 2006), and socio-demographic analysis (Schler, et al., 2006).

Outlier Identification and Misbehavior Detection

As it also happens in the real world, the Web 2.0 has become a scenario for improper, or even criminal, activity. In several cases of abuse, initial contact between the aggressor and the victim has been reported to occur in social media. Under the notion of outlier identification and misbehavior detection, we are including a large variety of problems related to the identification of users that are engaged in improper activities that range from slightly misleading practices to actual criminal activity. Within this variety of problems, we will focus here on the following: off-topic posting, harassment, identity supplantation, and plagiarism.

Off-topic posting constitutes, in the majority of the cases, a minor form of misbehavior. This occurs when a certain user in a discussion forum, or community, continuously posts information that is not related to the central topic of the forum. This form of misbehavior is actually related to the problem of spam (Ham, 2004), which is used to massively promote or advertise certain products or services. Most of the time, posts of this type are not generated by actual human users but by automatic generated accounts or "bots" (Web robots). This kind of misbehavior can be detected by

means of conventional spam filtering techniques (Kolari, et al., 2006; Jindal & Liu, 2007; Wanas, et al., 2009).

Harassment constitutes another common, but more dangerous, form of misbehavior. More specifically, harassment refers to those cases in which some users perform disturbing actions against others in a continuous and systematic manner. It can be as simple as a continuous insistence for being accepted or recommended for a particular action in a social media application, or it can be as serious as bullying (Hinduja & Patchin, 2008). In any case, the nature of harassment in Web 2.0 interactions can be so diverse that the problem of harassment detection by automatic means can be very difficult in practice (Kontostathis, et al., 2009; Yin, et al., 2009; Kontostathis, et al., 2010). In response to both problems of off-topic posting and harassment, several social media have implemented moderation schemes that allow the same users of the system to report, or even disable, other users who engage in misbehavior practices (Lampe & Resnick, 2004).

Identity supplantation refers to situations in which one person disguises his or her identity in order to deceive other users and gain their confidence. This is probably one of the more dangerous forms of misbehavior, which, if not detected on time, can be the first step for further criminal activity as several cases of reported abuses have demonstrated (Kontostathis, et al., 2010). Most common identity supplantation practices include providing incorrect contact information such as name, age, gender, and location. Text mining and classification techniques have been proven to be useful for characterizing different roles of social media participants (Fisher, et al., 2006), as well as identifying outliers in age and gender distributions among social media participants (Costa-Jussà, et al., 2010). These results can help to identify suspicious people on whom to focus investigations when looking for possible misbehaving users on the Web.

Finally, plagiarism detection deals with the problem of identifying plagiarized copyrighted material within textual contents distributed through the Web. Two different types of plagiarism detection tasks must be distinguished: external and intrinsic (Potthast, et al., 2009). In the first case, the source material being plagiarized is available, and the problem of plagiarism detection focuses on comparing suspicious text segments against the available material to determine if plagiarism has occurred or not (Hoad & Zobel, 2003). In the second case, the source material is not available, and the possible plagiarized segment of text within the suspicious material must be identified by means of a style-coherence analysis among the different sections of the suspicious material (Eissen, et al., 2007). An interesting variant of the plagiarism detection problem includes the notion of cross-language plagiarism. In this case, a plagiarized segment of text from a copyrighted material that was originally in a different language must be identified (Potthast, et al., 2010).

Social Estimation and Forecasting

In only few years, Web 2.0 applications have turned the Web into an appropriate environment for social scientists to conduct social research. In contrast with conventional sociological and anthropological observation and experimentation methods, the Web 2.0 offers an environment where observer's interference can be significantly reduced. Similarly, analysis and evaluation of user-generated content can, in some cases, replace expensive questionnaire-based techniques and avoid the typical problems of response biases such as acquiescence bias and social desirability bias (Furnham, 1986).

Initial effervescence on social media research mainly focused its attention on explaining and understanding human behavior and interactions in the social media space, as well as the social media phenomenon itself. However, more recent research work is starting to focus on the impact the social media phenomenon can have on the real world, as well as how social media activity and interactions can be used as proxies to explain, or even predict, human activity and interactions in the real world (Gruhl, et al., 2005; Mishne & Glance, 2006b; Durant & Smith, 2007; Chen, 2008). According to this, social estimation and social forecasting can be defined as social research work that is conducted with the objective of estimating or predicting human activity in the real world by observing human interactions and communications in the virtual world.

A more recent study showed how postings in twitter can be actually used to predict box office revenues for movies by means of very simple models (Asur & Huberman, 2010). In a similar way, another study showed how the emotional contents on Usenet's political forums can be used to estimate and predict presidential approval rates (Gonzalez-Bailon, et al., 2010). Another interesting example was the use of Google trends data related to Web searches on medications for reporting flu spreads across the United States in advance to official reports generated by government institutions (Ginsberg, et al., 2009). As these particular experiences reveal, massive trends in social media can be regarded as powerful indicators of what people are currently valuing and approving. Such information can be useful for predicting real world outcomes in the near future, as well as adopting appropriate feedback mechanisms for improving public policies and services.

As more and more organizations, institutions and agencies are recognizing the importance of what people are saying and doing in social media, several social media monitoring and tracking systems and services are starting to proliferate.[5] This constitutes definitively an important change in the way public opinion is formed and delivered to different actors in the society. As the volume of user-generated content explodes as more users are engaged in social media applications, text mining and natural language processing applications are becoming fundamentally important for better exploiting and capitalizing new opportunities in both the real and the virtual world.

FUTURE TRENDS AND RESEARCH OPPORTUNITIES

As follows from what was stated in previous sections, the Web 2.0 has opened a window of opportunities for many actors in the society, among them, research communities in different fields that play a role in the fundamental evolution of technologies applied to society's dynamics. In particular, as the amount of user-generated textual content increases rapidly, researches in the fields of text mining and natural language processing have a lot of work to do in the near future in order to satisfy the necessities and demands imposed by commercial, political, and social players within the scope of the Web 2.0.

It is actually very difficult to foresee future trends for a phenomenon that in only few years has intruded so abruptly into the modern information society. However, it is possible to observe certain signs that seem to be showing the road ahead for the next few years. Based on these signs, and with the help of some basic thought exercises, we can figure out some of the possible future trends that could be considered important in the years to come:

- **Semantics:** The recent development of markup, ontology-oriented languages such as OWL (Web Ontology Language) and RDF (Resource Description Framework) are providing the grounds for what is announced to be the Web 3.0, or the "Semantic Web." In such scenario, the Web should become readable for computers and artificial agents in general. Some important efforts in this direction include the linked open data project[6] (Auer, et al., 2007). Although it is not clear at all whether the "Semantic

Web" will become a reality or not in the years to come, the preponderant role of text mining and natural language technologies in such scenario is clear, as user-generated content must be annotated and indexed according to Semantic Web standards. After the times of data processing and information analysis applications, it comes the era of "knowledge management" applications, in which semantics plays a fundamental role.

- **Active Learning:** As labeling data is expensive and unlabeled data is abundant, data mining and natural language processing technologies can be substantially benefited by using active learning strategies. Active learning refers to an interactive machine learning modality in which the system is able to request information from the user and use it for improving its performance. In this way, both text mining and natural language processing systems would be able to learn from user-generated content.

- **Multilingualism:** As the volume of contents in languages other than English is increasing faster than the volume of English contents, efforts on generating resources and tools for dealing with languages other than English will continue. Several different issues must be considered: a clear distinction between language-dependent and language-independent technologies must be made, the development of resources and tools for minority languages constitutes a challenging and important problem, and machine translation and cross-language search technologies should adapt to tackle the main restrictions imposed by user-generated content.

- **Efficiency:** As ubiquity becomes one of the major characteristic of the Web 2.0, major requirements such as portability and readiness impose important constraints on

Web 2.0 technologies. On one hand, from the service provider side, data processing algorithms are required to handle huge volumes of data while maintaining acceptable rates of performance quality and execution time. On the other hand, from the user side, portable devices impose very important restrictions on memory usage and computing capacity for algorithms at the user-application level.

- **Interfacing:** The problems of human-computer interaction and computer-mediated human interaction have been a complex subject of study since computers appeared more than half a century ago. In recent years, however, the state-of-the-art in technologies such as question answering, dialogue generation, automatic speech recognition, text to speech conversion, machine translation, and eye and body tracking, just to mention a few, have been evolving and improving. All these "interfacing" technologies are preparing the grounds for a new generation of applications which will provide a more natural and human-like means for interaction and communication. Although this represents a trend that is much more general in scope, the Web 2.0 will certainly benefit from these "interfacing" technologies, especially if portable (or even "wearable") computing ever becomes truly ubiquitous.

- **Sensing:** As already stated in previous sections, the fact that the Web 2.0 has allowed common users to become actual content providers is somehow changing the way political, cultural, and socio-economical variables, as well as public opinion in general, are generated, measured, and evaluated. Sensing, interpreted here as monitoring and tracking of individuals and collectivities, is one of the major and most important byproducts of the Web 2.0. The notions of collective wisdom and collaborative gen-

eration and aggregation of information, knowledge, and opinion have converted the Web 2.0 in an actual image of the real word society, where interactions, contents, and social activity are more easily measurable and analyzable.

- **Privacy and Intellectual Property:** This is perhaps the area where the most prominent and relevant changes are to be observed in the years to come. From our point of view, the current conceptions of what is private and what is public, as well as the conception of intellectual property, are not compatible with some of the paradigms emerging from the Web 2.0. Indeed, we think that preserving our traditional definitions of privacy and intellectual property in this new model of information society without compromising our current conception of liberty does not seem to be possible.

ETHICAL AND LEGAL ISSUES

Although certainly not relevant from the technical point of view, ethical and legal issues concerning privacy and proprietary rights constitute a very important matter when conducting user-generated content analysis and research. Indeed, it is almost impossible to debate with colleagues or friends about the Web 2.0 and the Web in general without ending up with a discussion about ethical or legal implications. Although most technical papers and research presentations omit this topic on the basis that it constitutes a practical issue, which is not relevant to the scientific community, we consider it to be important enough to merit a section in a chapter about user-generated content analysis. The objective of this section is just to call the readers' attention on the fact that there are actually some ethical and legal issues to consider when dealing with user-generated content analysis.[7]

One of the major implications of general public becoming content providers has to do with copyright. From a naïve perspective, and as it might be supposed under logical assumptions, it could be thought that the copyright of a given user-generated content belongs to the user who created that content. This is not necessarily true as recent controversies involving major social media websites have demonstrated (Light, et al., 2008; Walters, 2009). A few common misunderstandings about user-generated content, and other publicly available materials in general, include believing that those materials can be freely and unlimitedly used and shared because one or more of the following reasons: (1) they are user-generated content, (2) they are freely accessible through a public website or link, (3) they can be downloaded for free, (4) they are distributed under a creative commons license, or (5) they are going to be used to conduct research or any other non-profitable activity.

Another major implication of the Web 2.0 phenomenon has to do with privacy. An interesting debate on this new means for human interaction and communication has been raised over a possible redefinition of the classical concepts of public and private spheres (Poster, 2001; Youngs, 2009). Similar to the case of proprietary rights, logical assumptions on the issues of what is public or private in the context of Internet are not enough for a holistic definition and understanding of this complex problem. Probably, this constitutes one of the more obscure issues in the incipient legal framework currently regulating human activity in the cyberspace. For instance, one of the most commonly unanswered (or ambiguously answered) questions about privacy issues in the Internet is the one regarding the legality of crawling (Cleland, 2008). From a pragmatic point of view, attempting to answer this question based on the observation of what actually happens in practice leads to an interesting paradox: while most websites are very restrictive on what they allow to be crawled (at least as they make it explicit in their *robots.txt* page), most websites also include hidden metadata and link structures specifically designed to improve

their ranking on search engine results. Although access restriction by means of usernames and passwords seems to provide a clear separation between the public and private spheres in the Web, the truth is that privacy is not guaranteed in the digital world (Barbaro & Zeller, 2006).

As legal issues regarding proprietary rights and privacy in the context of the Web 2.0 are far from being solved, some prudence and care must be exercised when collecting, handling, and analyzing user-generated content. Not surprisingly, most of this exercise can be adequately oriented by some basic and universal ethical principles. As in any other context where human interaction occurs, respect and cordiality must guide all procedures and steps. We recommend some simple guidelines here to follow when working with user-generated content extracted from the Web:

- Before crawling any website, always check its *robots.txt* page to see what can be crawled and what cannot be crawled within the website; then, proceed accordingly. Crawling applications know how to interpret and obey such file-specified site guidelines.
- Never obtain data or contents that are only accessible after any validation procedure such as login with a username and password, or captcha systems, without securing first rights from the intellectual property owners.
- If you are going to conduct an exhaustive and continuous vertical crawling, it is better to contact the system administrator to request permission.
- Always anonymize collected data as much as possible. Sometimes, this is actually a very complex problem as personal information is not only conveyed by metadata but also explicitly mentioned in the content. Sometimes just the mention of a "Ms. Arnold" can make obvious which specific individual in the world the reference is be-

ing made to, or what he/she is searching online, as American Online was reminded some years ago when releasing data for research purposes that was supposedly "anonymized" (Barbaro & Zeller, 2006).

- Do not make collected data available in a public manner. Sometimes it is very important to share data with other researches to compare results or engage in cooperation activities, but privacy safeguards should be implemented and respected. Therefore, when data is to be shared always anonymize it and pass it in private form.

- Do not publish or distribute any content that may be offensive or harmful to other people's reputation, values, or beliefs.

- Request your collaborators and colleagues to follow ethical principles when handling and conducting research with user-generated content and public data.

CONCLUSION

We have presented a general overview of the main technological challenges, areas of research, and applications related to the problem of user-generated content analysis in the context of the Web 2.0. First, the main definitions and general discussions on social media and user-generated content analysis were presented, covering some fundamental topics regarding the Web 2.0, social media and natural language processing technologies. Then, the main technical challenges of dealing with user-generated content were presented and discussed, namely: encoding, chatspeak, emoticons, ungrammaticality, normalization, co-referencing, spamming, multilingualism, communication structure, and user roles. Afterwards, seven applications that we consider fundamental for user-generated content analysis were described: automatic categorization, document summarization, question answering, dialogue management, opinion mining and sentiment analysis, outlier identification and

misbehavior detection, and social estimation and forecasting. Finally, we presented our vision about the most important future trends, and discussed the ethical and legal issues concerning privacy and proprietary rights that are relevant to user-generated content analysis and research.

As derived from most of the discussions presented in this chapter, some of the technological problems and challenges related to content analysis in the Web 2.0 are not exclusive of this topic. Some of them, indeed, have been around for many years and there is a vast amount of literature covering them. Nevertheless, the specificities of the Web 2.0 scenario (e.g., huge amounts of data) and the main characteristics of user-generated content (e.g. low signal-to-noise ratios) impose some new challenges and constraints to these traditional problems. The availability of large amounts of data, in some cases, combined with the constantly increasing computing capabilities, has offered an excellent condition for statistical methods to proliferate. However, from our point of view, no amount of language processing or statistical analysis alone will be able to attain what both of them can do in synergistic collaboration. Each approach has its strengths and weaknesses, and the best approach is to combine them.

In this sense, the diverse challenges of processing user-generated content mean that a unified approach that can encompass and address all at once is unlikely. Very short "tweets" microblogs can be very different in form and content from lengthy consumer-driven product reviews, or from blogs that achieve almost newspaper edited quality. Irregular capitalization will have a higher impact on named entity recognition than in other processing tasks. An ideal compromise is to employ hybrid approaches that profit from the individual strengths of specific techniques while minimizing their inevitable weaknesses. As noisy text implies having to deal with artificially large vocabularies, statistical analysis can help expand and fine-tune handcrafted correction dictionaries. In order to deal with resource sparseness in developing natural language processing capabilities for noisy text, either crowdsourcing (e.g., Amazon Mechanical Turk) or bootstrapping (e.g. existing product reviews with self-assessed numerical ratings) can be explored (Kittur, et al., 2008).

Both text mining and natural language processing disciplines have benefited from the continuous growth of online digital textual content; and, in return, they have empowered new applications to cope with the problems posed by the immense amount of available information. In any case, the Web has added a new dimension to human communications in which language continues to play a fundamental role. Text mining and natural language processing technologies should be there for helping humans to better understand humans.

But we also believe that one of the most important consequences of increased individual digital connectivity and communication in our society is that the putative distinction between a "real" and a "virtual" world, is becoming less and less important, more irrelevant, since increasingly we are doing more things and living our lives through online interaction and computer processing. More than just our informational needs or our communal activities are involved therein: our own identities, both as projected toward others and as understood by ourselves, are being mediated through digital means. We, ourselves, are becoming in more ways than one, a 2.0 version of ourselves.

ACKNOWLEDGMENT

The authors want to thank their corresponding institutions, the Institute for Infocomm Research and Barcelona Media Innovation Centre, for their support and permission to publish this work. They are also very grateful to the reviewers and the editors for their valuable feedback and suggestions that certainly helped improving the original version of the manuscript.

REFERENCES

Adamic, L. A., Zhang, J., Bakshy, E., & Ackerman, M. S. (2008). Knowledge sharing and yahoo answers: Everyone knows something. In *Proceeding of the 17th International Conference on World Wide Web (WWW 2008),* (pp. 665-674). Beijing, China: WWW.

Ala-Mutka, K., Broster, D., Cachia, R., Centeno, C., Feijoo, C., & Hache, A. … Valverde, J. (2009). *The impact of social computing on the EU information society and economy.* JRC Scientific and Technical Reports: EUR 24063 EN – 2009. Geneva, Switzerland: European Commission.

Allan, J., Carbonell, J., Doddington, G., Yamron, J., & Yang, Y. (1998). Topic detection and tracking pilot study: Final report. In *Proceedings of DARPA Broadcast News Transcription Understanding Workshop,* (pp. 194-218). DARPA.

Alm, C. O., Roth, D., & Sproat, R. (2005). Emotions from text: machine learning for text-based emotion prediction. In *Proceedings of the conference on Human Language Technology and Empirical Methods in Natural Language Processing,* (pp. 579-586). ACL.

Androutsopoulos, I., & Malakasiotis, P. (2010). A survey of paraphrasing and textual entailment methods. *Journal of Artificial Intelligence Research, 38,* 135-187. Retrieved September 24, 2010, from http://arxiv.org/abs/0912.3747

Asur, S., & Huberman, B. A. (2010). *Predicting the future with social media.* Ithaca, NY: Cornell University Library. Retrieved September 27, 2010, from http://arxiv.org/abs/1003.5699

Auer, S., Bizer, C., Kobilarov, G., Lehmann, J., Cyganiak, R., & Ives, Z. (2007). DBpedia: A nucleus for a web of open data. In *Proceedings of the 6th International Semantic Web and 2nd Asian Conference on Asian Semantic Web Conference,* (pp. 722-735). Busan, Korea: IEEE.

Banerjee, P., & Han, H. (2009). Answer credibility: A language modeling approach to answer validation. In *Proceedings of Human Language Technologies, Annual Conference of the North American Chapter of the Association for Computational Linguistics,* (pp. 157-160). Boulder, CO: ACL.

Barbaro, M., & Zeller, T. (2006). A face is exposed for AOL searcher no. 4417749. *New York Times*. Retrieved January 28, 2011, from http://www.nytimes.com/2006/08/09/technology/09aol.html

Barss, A. (2003). *Anaphora: A reference guide.* Malden, MA: Blackwell Publishing Ltd.

Bengel, J., Gauch, S., Mittur, E., & Vijayaraghavan, R. (2004). Chattrack: Chat room topic detection using classification. In *Proceedings of the 2nd Symposium on Intelligence and Security Informatics,* (pp. 266-277). Tucson, Arizona: IEEE.

Berkman, R. I. (2008). *The art of strategic listening: Finding market intelligence through blogs and other social media.* New York, NY: Paramount Market Publishing.

Bohus, D., Raux, A., Harris, T. K., Eskenazi, M., & Rudnicky, A. I. (2007). Olympus: An open-source framework for conversational spoken language interface research. In *Proceedings of the NAACL-HLT Workshop on Bridging the Gap: Academic and Industrial Research in Dialog Technologies,* (pp. 32-39). Rochester, NY: NAACL.

Bradley, M. M., & Lang, P. J. (1999). *Affective norms for English words (ANEW): Stimuli, instruction manual, and affective ratings.* Technical Report C-1. Gainesville, FL: University of Florida.

Brandon, R., Mitze, K., & Rau, L. (1995). Automatic condensation of electronic publications by sentence selection. *Information Processing & Management, 31*(5), 675–685. doi:10.1016/0306-4573(95)00052-I

Breiger, R. (2005). Introduction to special issue: Ethical dilemmas in social network research. *Social Networks, 27*(2), 89–93. doi:10.1016/j.socnet.2005.01.002

Bun, K. K., & Ishizuka, M. (2006). Emerging topic tracking system in WWW. *Knowledge-Based Systems, 19*(3), 164–171. doi:10.1016/j.knosys.2005.11.008

Burek, G., & Gerdemann, D. (2009). Maximal phrases based analysis for prototyping online discussion forums postings. In *Proceedings of the Workshop on Adaptation of Language Resources and Technology to New Domains,* (pp. 12-18). Borovets, Bulgaria: ACL.

Cataldi, M., Di Caro, L., & Schifanella, C. (2010). Emerging topic detection on Twitter based on temporal and social terms evaluation. In *Proceedings of the Tenth International Workshop on Multimedia Data Mining, KDD,* (pp. 1-10). Washington, DC: KDD.

Celikyilmaz, A., & Thint, M. (2008). Semantic approach to text entailment for question answering - New domain for uncertainty modeling. In *Proceedings of the 7th IEEE International Conference on Cognitive Informatics (ICCI 2008),* (pp. 481-487). Stanford, CA: IEEE Press.

Chali, Y. (2009). Question answering using question classification and document tagging. *Applied Artificial Intelligence, 23*(6), 500–521. doi:10.1080/08839510903078093

Chen, H. (2008). Sentiment and affect analysis of dark web forums: Measuring radicalization on the internet. In J. Hajic & Y. Matsumoto (Eds.), *IEEE International Conference on Intelligence and Security Informatics,* (pp. 104-109). Taipei, Taiwan: IEEE Press.

Cleland, S. (2008). *The blind eye to privacy law arbitrage by Google – Broadly threatens respect for privacy*. Testimony before the House Energy & Commerce Subcommittee on Internet Hearing. Retrieved September 16, 2010, from http://www. netcompetition.org/Written_Testimony_House_ Privacy_071707.pdf

Conroy, J., & O'leary, D. P. (2001). *Text summarization via hidden Markov models and pivoted QR matrix decomposition*. Technical Report CS-TR-4221. College Park, MD: University of Maryland.

Cormack, G. V. (2007). Email spam filtering: A systematic review. *Foundations and Trends in Information Retrieval, 1*(4), 335–455. doi:10.1561/1500000006

Costa-Jussà, M. R., Banchs, R. E., & Codina, J. (2010). Where are you from? Tell me HOW you write and I will tell you WHO you are. In *Proceedings of the International Conference on Agents and Artificial Intelligence ICAART,* (pp. 406-410). Valencia, Spain: ICAART.

Crystal, D. (2008). *Txtng: The Gr8 Db8*. Oxford, UK: Oxford University Press.

Dandapat, S., Sarkar, S., & Basu, A. (2007). Automatic part-of-speech tagging for Bengali: An approach for morphologically rich languages in a poor resource scenario. In *Proceedings of the 45th Annual Meeting of the Association for Computational Linguistics Companion Volume Proceedings of the Demo and Poster Sessions,* (pp. 221–224). Prague, Czech Republic: ACL.

Danet, B., & Herring, S. C. (Eds.). (2007). *The multilingual internet: Language, culture, and communication online*. Oxford, UK: Oxford University Press.

Derks, D., Bos, A. E., & Von Grumbkow, J. (2007). Emoticons and social interaction on the Internet: The importance of social context. *Computers in Human Behavior, 23*(1), 842–849. doi:10.1016/j. chb.2004.11.013

Dey, L., & Haque, S. K. (2009). Opinion mining from noisy text data. *International Journal on Document Analysis and Recognition, 12*(3), 205–226. doi:10.1007/s10032-009-0090-z

DiMaggio, P., Hargittai, E., Newman, W. R., & Robinson, J. P. (2001). Social implications of the Internet. *Annual Review of Sociology, 27*, 307–336. doi:10.1146/annurev.soc.27.1.307

Durant, K. T., & Smith, M. D. (2007). Predicting the political sentiment of web log posts using supervised machine learning techniques coupled with feature selection. In *Proceedings of Advances in Web Mining and Web Usage Analysis* (pp. 187–206). Heidelberg, Germany: Springer. doi:10.1007/978-3-540-77485-3_11

Eissen, S. M., Stein, B., & Kulig, M. (2007). Plagiarism detection without reference collections. In Decker, R., & Lenz, H. J. (Eds.), *Advances in Data Analysis* (pp. 359–366). Berlin, Germany: Springer. doi:10.1007/978-3-540-70981-7_40

Esuli, A., & Sebastiani, F. (2006a). Determining term subjectivity and term orientation for opinion mining. In *Proceedings of EACL-06, 11th Conference of the European Chapter of the Association for Computational Linguistics,* (pp. 193-200). Trento, Italy: ACL.

Esuli, A., & Sebastiani, F. (2006b). Sentiwordnet: A publicly available lexical resource for opinion mining. In *Proceedings of the 5th Conference on Language Resources and Evaluation,* (pp. 417-422). ACL.

Ferres, D., Kanaan, S., Gonzalez, E., Ageno, A., Rodriguez, H., Surdeanu, M., & Turmo, J. (2004). TALP-QA system at TREC 2004: Structural and hierarchical relaxing of semantic constraints. In *Proceedings of the 13th Text REtrieval Conference (TREC 2004)*. TREC.

Fisher, D., Smith, M., & Welser, H. (2006). You are who you talk to: Detecting roles in usenet newsgroups. In *Proceedings of the 39th Hawaii International Conference on System Sciences,* (pp. 59-68). Kauai, HI: IEEE.

Floridi, L. (2010). *The Cambridge handbook of information and computer ethics*. Cambridge, UK: Cambridge University Press. doi:10.1017/CBO9780511845239

Foster, J., & Vogel, C. (2004). Parsing ill-formed text using an error grammar. *Artificial Intelligence Review, 21*(3-4), 269–291. doi:10.1023/B:AIRE.0000036259.68818.1e

Freeman, L. C. (2004). *The development of social network analysis*. Vancouver, Canada: Empirical Press.

Funk, A., Li, Y., Saggion, H., Bontcheva, K., & Leibold, C. (2008). Opinion analysis for business intelligence applications. In *Proceedings of the First International Workshop on Ontology-Supported Business Intelligence,* (pp. 1-9). IEEE.

Furnham, A. (1986). Response bias, social desirability and dissimulation. *Personality and Individual Differences, 7*(3), 385–400. doi:10.1016/0191-8869(86)90014-0

Gajadhar, J., & Green, J. (2003). *An analysis of nonverbal communication in an online chat group*. Working Paper. Retrieved September 16, 2010, from http://www.openpolytechnic.ac.nz/static/pdf/research/res_wp203gajadharj1.pdf

Gambäck, B., Olsson, F., Argaw, A. A., & Asker, L. (2009). Methods for Amharic part-of-speech tagging. In *Proceedings of the First Workshop on Language Technologies for African Languages,* (pp. 104–111). Morristown, NJ: ACL.

Garcia, A. C., Standlee, A. I., Bechkoff, J., & Cui, Y. (2009). Ethnographic approaches to the internet and computer-mediated communication. *Journal of Contemporary Ethnography, 38*(1), 52–84. doi:10.1177/0891241607310839

Garcia, V. L., Motta, E., & Uren, V. (2006). AquaLog: An ontology-driven question answering system to interface the semantic web. In *Proceedings of the 2006 Conference of the North American Chapter of the Association for Computational Linguistics on Human Language Technology,* (pp. 269-272). New York, NY: ACL.

Ginsberg, J., Mohebbi, M. H., Patel, R. S., Brammer, L., Smolinski, M. S., & Brilliant, L. (2009). Detecting influenza epidemics using search engine query data. *Nature, 457,* 1012–1014. doi:10.1038/nature07634

Goldstein, J., Kantrowitz, M., Mittal, V. O., & Carbonell, J. (1999). Summarizing text documents: Sentence selection and evaluation metrics. In *Proceedings of the 22nd Annual International ACM SIGIR Conference on Research and Development in Information Retrieval,* (pp. 121-128). Berkeley, CA: SIGIR.

Gonzalez-Bailon, S., Banchs, R. E., & Kaltenbrunner, A. (2010). *Emotional reactions and the pulse of public opinion: Measuring the impact f political events on the sentiment of online discussions*. Cornell University Library. Retrieved September 27, 2010, from http://arxiv.org/abs/ 1009.4019

Gruhl, D., Guha, R., Kumar, R., Novak, J., & Tomkins, A. (2005). The predictive power of online chatter. In *Proceedings of the SIGKDD Conference on Knowledge Discovery and Data Mining,* (pp. 78-87). SIGKDD.

Haase, A. Q., Wellman, B., Witte, J., & Hampton, K. (2002). Capitalizing on the Internet: social contact, civic engagement, and sense of community. In Wellman, B., & Haythornthwaite, C. (Eds.), *The Internet and Everyday Life*. Oxford, UK: Blackwell. doi:10.1002/9780470774298.ch10

Halteren, H., & Teufel, S. (2003). Examining the consensus between human summaries: Initial experiments with factoid analysis. In *Proceedings of the HLT-NAACL on Text Summarization Workshop,* (pp. 57-64). NAACL.

Ham, R. (2004). *Spamming: Exploring dimensions of internet misuse*. Queensland, Australia: Griffith University.

Harabagiu, S., & Hickl, A. (2006). Methods for using textual entailment in open-domain question answering. In *Proceedings of the 21st International Conference on Computational Linguistics and 44th Annual Meeting of the ACL,* (pp. 905-912). Sydney, Australia: ACL.

Harper, F. M., Raban, D., Rafaeli, S., & Konstan, J. A. (2008). Predictors of answer quality in online Q&A sites. In *Proceeding of the Twenty-Sixth Annual SIGCHI Conference on Human Factors in Computing Systems (CHI 2008),* (pp. 865-874). Florence, Italy: SIGCHI.

Hatzivassiloglou, V., & Wiebe, J. (2000). Effects of adjective orientation and gradability on sentence subjectivity. In *Proceedings of the International Conference on Computational Linguistics (COLING),* (pp. 299-305). Saarbrücken, Germany: COLING.

Hickl, A., Roberts, K., Rink, B., Bensley, J., Jungen, T., Shi, Y., & Williams, J. (2007). Question answering with LCC's Chaucer-2 at TREC 2007. In *Proceedings of the 2007 Text Retrieval Conference (TREC 2007)*. Gaithersburg, MD: TREC.

Hinduja, S., & Patchin, J. W. (2008). Cyberbullying: An exploratory analysis of factors related to offending and victimization. *Deviant Behavior, 29*(2), 129–156. doi:10.1080/01639620701457816

Hirschman, L., & Gaizauskas, R. (2001). Natural language question answering: The view from here. *Natural Language Engineering, 7*(4), 275–300. doi:10.1017/S1351324901002807

Hoad, T. C., & Zobel, J. (2003). Methods for identifying versioned and plagiarised documents. *American Society for Information Science and Technology, 54*(3), 203–215. doi:10.1002/asi.10170

Hobbs, J. R. (1978). Resolving pronoun references. *Lingua, 44*, 311–338. doi:10.1016/0024-3841(78)90006-2

Hu, M., & Liu, B. (2004). Mining and summarizing customer reviews. In *Proceedings of the ACM SIGKDD International Conference on Knowledge Discovery & Data Mining,* (pp. 168-177). Seattle, WA: ACM Press.

Ittycheriah, A., Franz, M., Zhu, W. J., & Ratnaparkhi, A. (2001). IBM's statistical question answering system. In *Proceedings 9th Text Retrieval Conference (TREC-9)*. TREC.

Jackson, P., & Moulinier, I. (2007). *Natural language processing for online applications: Text retrieval, extraction and categorization*. New York, NY: John Benjamins Publishing Company.

Jarvenpaa, S. L., & Todd, P. A. (1996). Consumer reactions to electronic shopping on the world wide web. *International Journal of Electronic Commerce, 1*(2), 59–88.

Jijkoun, V., Khalid, M. A., Marx, M., & de Rijke, M. (2008). Named entity normalization in user generated content. In *Proceedings of SIGIR 2008 – Workshop on Analytics for Noisy Unstructured Text Data,* (pp. 23-30). SIGIR.

Jindal, N., & Liu, B. (2007). Review spam detection. In *Proceedings of the 16th International Conference on the World Wide Web,* (pp. 1189-1190). Banff, Canada: WWW.

Jing, H., Barzilay, R., McKeown, K., & Elhadad, M. (1998). Summarization evaluation methods: Experiments and analysis. In *Proceedings of the AAAI Symposium on Intelligent Summarization,* (pp. 60-68). AAAI.

Joshi, A. K. (1982). Processing of sentences with intra-sentential code-switching. In *Proceedings of the 9th Conference on Computational Linguistics,* (pp. 145-150). Praha, Czechoslovakia: ACL.

Jurafsky, D., & Martin, J. (2000). *Speech and language processing: An introduction to natural language processing, computational linguistics and speech recognition.* Upper Saddle River, NJ: Prentice Hall.

Kaisser, M. (2008). The QuALiM question answering demo: Supplementing answers with paragraphs drawn from Wikipedia. In *Proceedings of the ACL-08: HLT Demo Session,* (pp. 32-35). Columbus, OH: ACL.

Kaltenbrunner, A., Bondia, E., & Banchs, R. E. (2009). Analyzing and ranking the Spanish speaking MySpace community by their contributions in forums. In *Proceedings of the 18th International Conference on World Wide Web.* Madrid, Spain: WWW.

Kao, W. C., Liu, D. R., & Wang, S. W. (2010). Expert finding in question-answering websites: A novel hybrid approach. In *Proceedings of the 2010 ACM Symposium on Applied Computing (SAC 2010),* (pp. 867-871). Sierre, Switzerland: ACM Press.

Kaplan, A. M., & Haenlein, M. (2010). Users of the world, unite! The challenges and opportunities of social media. *Business Horizons, 53*(1), 59–68. doi:10.1016/j.bushor.2009.09.003

Kim, S. M., & Hovy, E. (2006). Automatic identification of pro and con reasons in online reviews. In *Proceedings of the COLING/ACL 2006,* (pp. 483-490). ACL.

Kittur, A., Chi, E. H., & Suh, B. (2008). Crowdsourcing user studies with mechanical turk. In *Proceedings of the 26th Annual SIGCHI Conference on Human Factors in Computing Systems,* (pp. 453-456). SIGCHI.

Knoke, D., & Yang, S. (2008). *Social network analysis.* Thousand Oaks, CA: Sage Publications, Inc.

Kolari, P., Java, A., Finin, T., Oates, T., & Joshi, A. (2006). Detecting spam blogs: A machine learning approach. In *Proceedings of the 21st National Conference on Artificial Intelligence (AAAI).* AAAI.

Kontostathis, A., Edwards, L., & Leatherman, A. (2009). ChatCoder: Toward the tracking and categorization of internet predators. In *Proceedings of the 7th Text Mining Workshop,* (pp. 1-7). ACL.

Kontostathis, A., Edwards, L., & Leatherman, A. (2010). Text mining and cybercrime. In M. W. Berry & J. Kogan (Eds.), *Text Mining: Applications and Theory.* Chichester, UK: John Wiley & Sons. Retrieved from http://onlinelibrary.wiley.com/doi/10.1002/9780470689646.ch8/summary

Koppel, M., & Schler, J. (2006). The importance of neutral examples in learning sentiment. *Computational Intelligence, 22*(2), 100–109. doi:10.1111/j.1467-8640.2006.00276.x

Kukich, K. (1992). Techniques for automatically correcting words in text. *ACM Computing Surveys, 24*(4), 377–439. doi:10.1145/146370.146380

Lambert, L., & Carberry, S. (1992). Modeling negotiation subdialogues. In *Proceedings of the 30th Annual Meeting of the Association for Computational Linguistics,* (pp. 193-200). Morristown, NJ: ACL.

Lamere, P. (2008). Social tagging and music information retrieval. *Journal of New Music Research*, *37*(2), 101–114. doi:10.1080/09298210802479284

Lampe, C., & Resnick, P. (2004). Slash(dot) and burn: Distributed moderation in a large online conversation space. In *Proceedings of SIGCHI Conference on Human Factors in Computing Systems CHI 2004*, (pp. 543-550). Vienna, Austria: SIGCHI.

Lappin, S., & Leass, H. J. (1994). An algorithm for pronominal anaphora resolution. *Computational Linguistics*, *20*(4), 535–561.

Lee, C., Jung, S., & Jeong, M. (2006). Chat and goal-oriented dialog together: A unified exmple-based architecture for multi-domain dialog management. In *Proceedings of the IEEE Spoken Language Technology Workshop*, (pp. 194-197). Palm Beach, FL: IEEE Press.

Levin, E., Pieraccini, R., & Eckert, W. (2000). A stochastic model of human-machine interaction for learning dialog strategies. *IEEE Transactions on Speech and Audio Processing*, *8*(1), 11–23. doi:10.1109/89.817450

Levinson, S. C. (1983). *Pragmatics*. Cambridge, UK: Cambridge University Press.

Li, S., & Momoi, K. (2001). A composite approach to language/encoding detection. In *Proceedings of the 19th International Unicode Conference*. San José, CA: IEEE.

Light, B., McGrath, K., & Griffiths, M. (2008). More than just friends? Facebook, disclosive ethics and the morality of technology. In *Proceedings of ICIS 2008*, (p. 193). ICIS.

Lin, C. Y., & Hovy, E. (2002). From single to multi-document summarization: A prototype system and its evaluation. In *Proceedings of the ACL*, (pp. 457-464). ACL.

Lin, D., & Pantel, P. (2001). Discovery of inference rules for question-answering. *Natural Language Engineering*, *7*(4), 343–360. doi:10.1017/S1351324901002765

Loquendo. (2007). *Loquendo and artificial solutions announce integration of their technologies into IKEA online assistant*. Retrieved September 24, 2010, from http://www.loquendo.com/en/news/news_loquendo_ikea.htm

Madden, M., Fox, S., Smith, A., & Vitak, J. (2007). *Digital footprints: Online identity management and search in the age of transparency*. Pew Internet & American Life Project. Retrieved February 15, 2011, from http://pewresearch.org/pubs/663/digital-footprints

Magnini, B., Negri, M., Prevete, R., & Tanev, H. (2002). Is it the right answer? Exploiting web redundancy for answer validation. In *Proceedings of the Annual Meeting of the Association for Computational Lingustistics*, (pp. 425-432). Philadelphia, PA: ACL.

Maier, E., Mast, M., & LuperFoy, S. (Eds.). (1996). *Dialogue processing in spoken language systems: ECAI 1996 Workshop*. Heidelberg, Germany: Springer-Verlag.

Mani, I. (2001). *Automatic summarization*. Amsterdam, The Netherlands: John Benjamins Publishing Co.

Markert, K., & Nissim, M. (2005). Comparing knowledge sources for nominal anaphora resolution. *Computational Linguistics*, *31*(3), 367–402. doi:10.1162/089120105774321064

McKeown, K., Passonneau, R. J., Elson, D. K., Nenkova, A., & Hirschberg, J. (2005). Do summaries help? A task-based evaluation of multi-document summarization. In *Proceedings of SIGIR*, (pp. 15-19). Salvador, Brazil: SIGIR.

McTear, M. (1998). Modelling spoken dialogues with state transition diagrams: Experiences with the CSLU toolkit. In *Proceedings of the 5th International Conference on Spoken Language Processing,* (pp. 1223-1226). Sydney, Australia: ACL.

Metzger, M. J. (2007). Making sense of credibility on the web: Models for evaluating online information and recommendations for future research. *Journal of the American Society for Information Science and Technology, 58*(13), 2078–2091. doi:10.1002/asi.20672

Mihalcea, R., & Pulman, S. (2007). Characterizing humour: An exploration of features in humorous texts. In *Proceedings of the 8th International Conference on Computational Linguistics and Intelligent Text Processing, CICLing 2007,* (pp. 337-347). Springer.

Mikheev, A. (2000). Document centered approach to text normalization. In *Proceedings of the 23rd Annual International ACM SIGIR Conference on Research and Development in Information Retrieval,* (pp. 136-143). Athens, Greece: ACM Press.

Mishne, G. (2005). Experiments with mood classification in blog posts. In *Proceedings of the 1st Workshop on Stylistic Analysis of Text for Information Access.* ACL.

Mishne, G., & Glance, N. (2006a). Leave a reply: An analysis of weblog comments. In *Proceedings of the 3rd Annual Workshop on the Weblogging Ecosystem.* Edinburgh, UK: ACL.

Mishne, G., & Glance, N. (2006b). Predicting movie sales from blogger sentiment. In *Proceedings of the AAAI 2006 Spring Symposium on Computational Approaches to Analysing Weblogs.* Palo Alto, CA: AAAI.

Mithun, S., & Kossein, L. (2009). Summarizing blog entries versus news texts. In *Proceedings of the Workshop on Events in Emerging Text Types,* (pp. 1-8). Borovets, Bulgaria: ACL.

Mollá, D., & Vicedo, J. L. (2007). Question answering in restricted domains: An overview. *Computational Linguistics, 33*(1), 41–61. doi:10.1162/coli.2007.33.1.41

Morinaga, S., Yamanishi, K., Tateishi, K., & Fukushima, T. (2002). Mining product reputations on the web. In *Proceedings of the 8th ACM SIGKDD International Conference on Knowledge Discovery and Data Mining,* (pp. 341-349). ACM Press.

Ney, H. (2005). One decade of statistical machine translation: 1996-2005. In *Proceedings of the 10th MT Summit,* (pp. i12-i17). Phuket, Thailand: MT Summit.

Ng, V., & Cardie, C. (2002). Improving machine learning approaches to coreference resolution. In *Proceedings of the 40th Annual Meeting of the Association for Computational Linguistics,* (pp. 104-111). ACL.

Nowson, S. (2006). *The language of weblogs: A study of genre and individual differences.* (PhD Thesis). University of Edinburgh. Edinburgh, UK.

O'Reilly, T., & Battelle, J. (2004). Opening welcome: The state of the internet industry. *Web 2.0 Conference.* San Francisco, CA: Web 2.0. Retrieved September 14, 2010, from http://conferences.oreillynet.com/presentations/web2con/intro_tim_john.ppt

Oberlander, J., & Nowson, S. (2006). Whose thumb is it anyway? Classifying author personality from weblog text. In *Proceedings of the COLING/ACL,* (pp.627-634). Sydney, Australia: ACL.

Pang, B., & Lee, L. (2008). Opinion mining and sentiment analysis. *Foundations and Trends in Information Retrieval, 2*(1-2), 1–135. doi:10.1561/1500000011

Pang, B., Lee, L., & Vaithyanathan, S. (2002). Thumbs up? Sentiment classification using machine learning techniques. In *Proceedings of the ACL-02 Conference on Empirical Methods in Natural Language Processing,* (pp. 79-86). ACL.

Peters, I. (2009). *Folksonomies: Indexing and retrieval in web 2.0.* Berlin, Germany: De Gruyter. doi:10.1515/9783598441851

Pimienta, D., Prado, D., & Blanco, Á. (2009). *Twelve years of measuring linguistic diversity in the Internet: Balance and perspectives.* Paris, France: UNESCO. Retrieved February 15, 2011, from http://portal.unesco.org/ci/en/ev.php-URL_ID=29594&URL_DO=DO_TOPIC&URL_SEC-TION=201.html

Ponzetto, S. P., & Poesio, M. (2009). State-of-the-art NLP approaches to coreference resolution: Theory and practical recipes. In *Proceedings of the ACL-IJCNLP 2009,* (p. 6). Suntec, Singapore: ACL.

Popescu, A. M., & Etzioni, O. (2005). Extracting product features and opinions from reviews. In *Proceedings of the Conference on Human Language Technology and Empirical Methods in Natural Language Processing,* (pp. 339-346). ACL.

Poster, M. (2001). Cyberdemocracy: Internet and the public sphere. *Reading Digital Culture.* Retrieved from http://www.hnet.uci.edu/mposter/writings/democ.html

Potthast, M., Barron-Cedeno, A., Stein, B., & Rosso, P. (2010). Cross-language plagiarism detection. *Language Resources and Evaluation, 45*(1), 45–62. doi:10.1007/s10579-009-9114-z

Potthast, M., Stein, B., Eiselt, A., Barron-Cedeno, A., & Rosso, P. (2009). Overview of the 1st international competition on plagiarism detection. In B. Stein, P. Rosso, E. Stamatatos, M. Koppel, & E. Agirre (Eds.), *Proceedings of SEPLN 2009 Workshop on Uncovering Plagiarism, Authorship and Social Software Misuse,* (pp. 1-9). San Sebastian, Spain: SEPLN.

Provine, R. R., Spencer, R. J., & Mandell, D. L. (2007). Emotional expression online: Emoticons punctuate website text messages. *Journal of Language and Social Psychology, 26*(3), 299. doi:10.1177/0261927X06303481

Qualman, E. (2009). *Socialnomics: How social media transforms the way we live and do business.* New York, NY: John Wiley and Sons.

Radev, D. R., Jing, H., & Budzikowska, M. (2000). Centroid-based summarization of multiple documents: Sentence extraction, utility-based evaluation, and user studies. In *Proceedings of the NAACL-ANLP Workshop on Automatic Summarization,* (pp. 21-30). Seattle, WA: NAACL.

Ramakrishnan, R., & Tomkins, A. (2007). Toward a peopleweb. *Computer, 40*(8), 63–72. doi:10.1109/MC.2007.294

Reinhart, T. (1983). *Anaphora and semantic interpretation.* New York, NY: Taylor & Francis.

Reyes, A., & Rosso, P. (2009). Linking humour to blogs analysis: Affective traits in posts. In *Proceedings of the First International Workshop on Opinion Mining and Sentiment Analysis.* ACL.

Ricci, F., & Werthner, H. (2006). Introduction to the special issue: Recommender systems. *International Journal of Electronic Commerce, 11*(2), 5–9. doi:10.2753/JEC1086-4415110200

Sagot, B. (2005). Automatic acquisition of a Slovak lexicon from a raw corpus. In *Lecture Notes in Artificial Intelligence, 3658,* 156–163.

Sagot, B. (2007). Building a morphosyntactic lexicon and a pre-syntactic processing chain for Polish. In *Proceedings of the 3rd Language & Technology Conference,* (pp. 423–427). Poznan, Poland: ACL.

Sagot, B., & Walther, G. (2010). A morphological lexicon for the Persian language. In *Proceedings of the 7th Language Resources and Evaluation Conference, (LREC 2010)*, (pp. 300-303). Valetta, Malta: LREC.

Sakurai, S., & Orihara, R. (2006). Discovery of important threads from bulletin board sites. *International Journal of Information Technology and Intelligent Computing, 1*(1), 217–228.

Schler, J., Koppel, M., Argamon, S., & Pennebaker, J. W. (2006). Effects of age and gender on blogging. In *Proceedings of 2006 AAAI Spring Symposium on Computational Approaches for Analyzing Weblogs*. AAAI.

Segerstrale, U., & Molnar, P. (Eds.). (1997). *Nonverbal communication: Where nature meets culture*. Mahwah, NJ: Lawrence Erlbaum Associates.

Singla, P., & Richardson, M. (2008). Yes, there is a correlation: From social networks to personal behaviour on the web. In *Proceeding of the 17th International Conference on World Wide Web*, (pp. 655–664). Beijing, China: WWW.

Smith, R. W., & Hipp, D. R. (1995). *Spoken natural language dialog systems: A practical approach*. Oxford, UK: Oxford University Press.

Sood, S. O., & Vasserman, L. (2009). Esse: Exploring mood on the web. In *Proceedings of International Conference on Weblogs and Social Media*. Seattle, WA: ACL.

Stone, P. J., Dunphy, D. C., Smith, M. S., & Ogilvie, D. M. (1966). *The general inquirer: A computer approach to content analysis*. Cambridge, MA: The MIT Press.

Su, X., & Khoshgoftaar, T. M. (2009). A survey of collaborative filtering techniques. *Advances in Artificial Intelligence, 2009*(421425), 19 pages. doi:10.1155/2009/421425

Surowiecki, J. (2005). *The wisdom of crowds*. New York, NY: Knopf Doubleday Publishing Group.

Thelwall, M., Buckley, K., Paltoglou, G., Cai, D., & Kappas, A. (2010). Sentiment in short strength detection informal text. *Journal of the American Society for Information Science and Technology, 61*(2), 2544–2558. doi:10.1002/asi.21416

Toprak, C., Jakob, N., & Gurevych, I. (2010). Sentence and expression level annotation of opinions in user generated discourse. In *Proceedings of the 48th Annual Meeting of the Association for Computational Linguistics*, (pp. 575-584). Uppsala, Sweden: Association for Computational Linguistics.

Turney, P. (2002). Thumbs up or thumbs down? Semantic orientation applied to unsupervised classification of reviews. In *Proceedings of ACL-02, 40th Annual Meeting of the Association for Computational Linguistics*, (pp. 417-424). Philadelphia, PA: ACL.

Van Kuppevelt, J., & Smith, R. W. (Eds.). (2003). *Current and new directions in discourse and dialogue*. Dordrecht, The Netherlands: Kluwer Academic Publishers. doi:10.1007/978-94-010-0019-2

Varile, G., Cole, R., & Zampolli, A. (1997). *Survey of the state of the art in human language technology*. Cambridge, UK: Cambridge University Press.

Voorhees, E. M., & Tice, D. M. (2000). The TREC-8 question answering track evaluation. In E. M. Voorhees & D. K. Harman (Eds.), *Proceedings of the Eighth Text REtrieval Conference*, (pp. 83-105). TREC.

Wallis, P. (2010). A robot in the kitchen. In *Proceedings of the ACL Workshop on Companionable Dialogue Systems*, (pp. 25-30). Uppsala, Sweden: ACL.

Walters, C. (2009). Facebook's new terms of service: "We can do anything we want with your content. Forever". *The Consumerist*. Retrieved September 15, 2010, from http://consumerist. com/2009/02/facebooks-new-terms-of-service-we-can-do-anything-we-want-with-your-content-forever.html

Walther, G., & Sagot, B. (2010). Developing a large-scale lexicon for a less-resourced language: General methodology and preliminary experiments on Sorani Kurdish. In *Proceedings of the 7th Workshop on Creation and use of Basic Lexical Resources for Less-Resourced Languages, (LREC 2010)*. Valetta, Malta: LREC.

Walther, J. B., & D'Addario, K. P. (2001). The impacts of emoticons on message interpretation in computer-mediated communication. *Social Science Computer Review*, *19*, 323–345. doi:10.1177/089443930101900307

Wanas, N., Magdy, A., & Ashour, H. (2009). Using automatic keyword extraction to detect off-topic posts in online discussion boards. In *Proceedings of the First International Workshop on Content Analysis in the Web 2.0*. Madrid, Spain: ACL.

Wang, K., Ming, Z. Y., & Chua, T. S. (2009). A syntactic tree matching approach to finding similar questions in community-based QA services. In *Proceedings of the 32nd international ACM SIGIR Conference on Research and Development in Information Retrieval, (SIGIR 2009)*, (pp. 187-194). Boston, MA: ACM.

Wang, K., Ming, Z. Y., Hu, X., & Chua, T. S. (2010). Segmentation of multi-sentence questions: Towards effective question retrieval in QA services. In *Proceeding of the 33rd International ACM SIGIR Conference on Research and Development in Information Retrieval, (SIGIR 2010)*, (pp. 387-394). Geneva, Switzerland: ACM.

Wei, X., & Rudnicky, A. (2000). Task-based management using an agenda. In *Proceedings of ANLP/NAACL Workshop on Conversational Systems*, (pp. 42-47). ACM.

Weisman, J. (2000, August 22). The making of e-commerce: 10 key moments. *E-Commerce Times*. Retrieved September 15, 2010, from http://www.ecommercetimes.com/story/4085. html?wlc=1284530145

Wiebe, J. M., Bruce, R. F., & O'Hara, T. P. (1999). Development and use of a gold standard data set for subjectivity classifications. [College Park, MD: ACL.]. *Proceedings of, ACL-99*, 246–253.

Wiebe, J. M., Wilson, T., Bruce, R., Bell, M., & Martin, M. (2004). Learning subjective language. *Computational Linguistics*, *30*, 277–308. doi:10.1162/0891201041850885

Wilson, T., Wiebe, J., & Hoffmann, P. (2009). Recognizing contextual polarity: An exploration of features for phrase-level sentiment analysis. *Computational Linguistics*, *35*(5), 399–433. doi:10.1162/coli.08-012-R1-06-90

Witbrock, M. J., & Mittal, V. O. (1999). Ultra-summarization (poster abstract): A statistical approach to generating highly condensed non-extractive summaries. In *Proceedings of the 22nd Annual International ACM SIGIR Conference on Research and Development in Information Retrieval*, (pp. 315-316). Berkeley, CA: ACM.

Yin, D., Xue, Z., Hong, L., Davison, B., Kontostathis, A., & Edwards, L. (2009). Detection of harassment on web 2.0. In *Proceedings of the First International Workshop on Content Analysis in the Web 2.0*. Madrid, Spain: ACL.

Young, S., Schatzmann, J., Weilhammer, K., & Ye, H. (2007). The hidden information state approach to dialog management. In *Proceedings of Human Language Technologies: The Annual Conference of the North American Chapter of the Association for Computational Linguistics*, (pp. 27-28). ACL.

Youngs, G. (2009). Blogging and globalization: The blurring of the public/private spheres. *Aslib Proceedings, 61*(2), 127–138. doi:10.1108/00012530910946884

Yuasa, M., Saito, K., & Mukawa, N. (2006). Emoticons convey emotions without cognition of faces: An fMRI study. *In Proceedings of CHI 2006 Extended Abstracts on Human Factors in Computing Systems,* (pp. 1565-1570). Montréal, Canada: CHI.

Zajic, D., Dorr, B., & Schwartz, R. (2002). Automatic headline generation for newspaper stories. In *Proceedings of the ACL Workshop on Automatic Summarization and Document Understanding Conference,* (pp. 78-85). ACL.

Zhang, J., Ackerman, M. S., & Adamic, L. (2007). Expertise networks in online communities: Structure and algorithms. In *Proceedings of the 16th International Conference on World Wide Web,* (pp. 221–230). New York, NY: WWW.

Zhao, S. (2006). Humanoid social robots as a medium of communication. *New Media & Society, 8*(3), 401–419. doi:10.1177/1461444806061951

Zheng, D., & Li, F. (2009). Hot topic detection on BBS using aging theory. *Lecture Notes in Computer Science, 5854,* 129–138. doi:10.1007/978-3-642-05250-7_14

Zhou, L., & Chaovalit, P. (2008). Ontology-supported polarity mining. *Journal of the American Society for Information Science and Technology, 69,* 98–110. doi:10.1002/asi.20735

Zhu, M., Hu, W., & Wu, O. (2008). Topic detection and tracking for threaded discussion communities. In *Proceedings of the International Conference on Web Intelligence and Intelligent Agent Technology,* (pp. 77-83). ACM.

ADDITIONAL READING

Agarwal, N., Liu, H., Tang, L., & Yu, P. S. (2008). Identifying the influential bloggers in a community. In *Proceedings of the International Conference on Web Search and Web Data Mining,* (pp. 207-218). Stanford, CA: ACM.

Birdsall, W. F. (2007). Web 2.0 as a social movement. *Webology, 4*(2). Retrieved September 24, 2010, from http://webology.ir/2007/v4n2/a40.html

Callison-Burch, C., & Dredze, M. (2010). Paper. In *Proceedings of the NAACL HLT 2010 Workshop on Creating Speech and Language Data with Amazon's Mechanical Turk.* Los Angeles, CA: NAACL.

Codina, J., Kaltenbrunner, A., Grivolla, J., Banchs, R., & Baeza-Yates, R. (2009). Paper. In *Proceedings of the First International Workshop on Content Analysis in Web 2.0.* Madrid, Spain. Retrieved October 6, 2010, from http://www2009.eprints.org/255/

Floridi, L. (2010). *The Cambridge handbook of information and computer ethics.* Cambridge, UK: Cambridge University Press. doi:10.1017/CBO9780511845239

Glance, N., Hurst, M., Nigam, K., Siegler, M., Stockton, R., & Tomokiyo, T. (2005). Analyzing online discussion for marketing intelligence. In *Proceedings of the 14th International Conference on the World Wide Web,* (pp. 1172-1173). Chiba, Japan: WWW.

Jiang, M., & Yu, B. (Eds.). (2009). Paper. In *Proceeding of the 1st International CIKM Workshop on Topic-Sentiment Analysis for Mass Opinion.* New York, NY: ACM.

Jurafsky, D., & Martin, J. H. (2000). *Speech and language processing: An introduction to natural language processing, computational linguistics and speech recognition*. Upper Saddle River, NJ: Prentice Hall.

Manning, D., & Schütze, H. (2000). *Foundations of statistical natural language processing*. Cambridge, MA: MIT Press.

Pang, B., & Lee, L. (2008). Opinion mining and sentiment analysis. *Foundations and Trends in Information Retrieval*, *2*(1-2), 1–135. doi:10.1561/1500000011

Pekar, V. (2008). Discovery of event entailment knowledge from text corpora. *Computer Speech & Language*, *22*(1), 1–16. doi:10.1016/j.csl.2007.05.001

Rodriguez, C., Banchs, R., Codina, J., & Grivolla, J. (2010). COMETA: Semantic exploration of customer reviews to extract valuable information for business intelligence. *Barcelona Media Innovation Centre Technical Reports*. Barcelona, Spain. Retrieved July 12, 2011, from http://comunicacio.barcelonamedia.org/technical_reports/BM2010_01.pdf

Stein, B., Rosso, P., Stamatatos, E., Koppel, M., & Agirre, E. (Eds.). (2009). Paper. In *Proceedings of the SEPLN 2009 Workshop on Uncovering Plagiarism, Authorship and Social Software Misuse*. San Sebastian, Spain: SEPLN. Retrieved October 6, 2010, from http://sunsite.informatik.rwth-aachen.de/Publications/CEUR-WS/Vol-502/

KEY TERMS AND DEFINITIONS

Automatic Categorization: Processing large volumes of content to automatically extract categories.

Dialogue System: Application that is able to follow and plan a structured verbal or written communication with humans.

Document Summarization: Distilling the most relevant information from a text or group of texts.

Misbehavior Detection: Identifying inappropriate and/or offensive conducts from users in a given social media environment.

Opinion Mining: Analyzing consumers' reviews and comments in discussion forums for extracting relevant information for marketing research and business intelligence.

Outlier Identification: Detecting and classifying users that do not behave as regular users do.

Question Answering: Extracting, validating and rating from a large collection of data possible answers to a question posed in natural language format.

Sentiment Analysis: Detecting and classifying the emotional load in language communications.

Social Estimation and Forecasting: Estimating and predicting real world variables and trends by means of what general public is saying online.

Social Media: User centered Web 2.0 applications that people use for sharing user-generated content.

User Generated Content: Any kind of online data (text, audio, video, images, etc.) that has been generated by users.

Web 2.0: Refers to the new generation of interactive websites and online applications where users can upload and edit the content.

ENDNOTES

[1]   As, for instance, Wikipedia (http://www.wikipedia.org/), Twitter (http://twitter.com/), YouTube (http://www.youtube.com/), and Facebook (http://www.facebook.com/), just to mention a few.

[2]   The International Federation of Library Associations (IFLA) Internet Manifesto (2002) states that "unhindered access to information is essential to freedom, equality, global understanding and peace."

3 All major text-editing systems provide useful resources and documentation on how to deal with text in a multilingual context. See, for instance: *MULE* (http://www.xemacs.org/Documentation/21.5/html/lispref_64.html) and *MLang* (http://msdn.microsoft.com/en-us/library/aa767865(v=VS.85).aspx).

4 IKEA's avatar-driven Help Center is available at http://193.108.42.79/ikea-us/cgi-bin/ikea-us.cgi, and Cleverbot is available at http://www.cleverbot.com/.

5 Just to mention a few, the following social media monitoring and tracking systems can be pointed as representative examples: Web-MetricsGuru (http://www.webmetricsguru.com), BuzzNumbers (http://www.buzznumbershq.com/), GNIP (http://www.gnip.com), trendpedia (http://www.trendpedia.com/), trackur (http://www.trackur.com/).

6 The linked open data project is available at http://linkeddata.org/.

7 It is beyond the scope of this chapter to solve, clarify, or provide any final recommendation on the issues related to ethical and legal implications of collecting, handling, and analyzing user-generated content. For a more comprehensive review on this topic, refer to Breiger (2005) and Floridi (2010).

APPENDIX

Recent Conferences and Events Addressing User-Generated Content Analysis Related Problems

As already said, the Web 2.0 has opened a window for a wide variety of research opportunities, most of which have been already identified by major research communities and organizations. We have already discussed a selected sample of evolving and emerging technologies as well as the most relevant technical problems related to them along the chapter. In the specific cases of text mining and natural language processing applications, a large number of conferences and workshops are being organized around some of the specific problems we have mentioned, as well as other important research problems that have been identified within the Web 2.0 and the Web in general. Some of these events organize shared tasks and evaluation campaigns providing an excellent environment for academic cooperation and collaboration. Here, we list some relevant events in these areas:

- **Web 2.0 Summit:** The first edition of this event, which was previously referred to as Web 2.0 conference, was held in San Francisco, California, in 2004. Since then, it has been held on a yearly basis also in San Francisco. This event is co-organized by O'Reilly Media, Inc. and MediaLive International and, although its scope is more commercial-oriented than scientific, it constitutes a reference forum about the Web 2.0. More information about the Web 2.0 Summit is available at http://www.web2summit.com/web2010

- **World Wide Web Conference:** The first edition of this conference was held in Geneva in 1994. Since then, it has been held on a yearly basis rotating its venue among Europe, Asia and America. This conference is organized by the International World Wide Web Conferences Steering Committee and endorsed by the World Wide Web Consortium. Its scope includes both academic and commercial content. Although it is a discussion forum for the Web and the Internet in general, in recent years major research problems and topics related to the Web 2.0 have been covered by the conference program. More information on the several World Wide Web conference editions can be found at http://www.iw3c2.org/conferences

- **ICWSM – International AAAI Conference on Weblogs and Social Media:** The first edition of this conference was held in Boulder, Colorado, in 2007. It was derived from a series of Workshops on the Weblogging Ecosystem and the Spring Symposium on Computational Approaches to Analyzing Weblogs. Since then, it has been held on a yearly basis. This conference is sponsored by the Association for the Advancement of Artificial Intelligence. More information about this conference is available at http://www.icwsm.org

- **UCMedia – International ICST Conference on User Centric Media:** The first edition of this conference was held in Venice in 2009. The main objective of this new forum of discussion is to understand the changes the "media landscape" is experimenting. It is organized by the Institute for Computer Sciences, Social Informatics and Telecommunications Engineering. More information about this conference is available at http://www.usercentricmedia.org

- **TSA 2009 – First International CIKM Workshop on Topic-Sentiment Analysis for Mass Opinion Measurement:** This workshop was collocated with the 18th ACM International Conference on Information and Knowledge Management. It aimed at bringing together both computer and social science researches around the issues related to sentiment analysis. It covered topics such as opinion retrieval and categorization, and sentiment analysis related applications. More information is available at http://sites.google.com/site/tsa2009workshop/

- **CAW 2.0 – First International Workshop on Content Analysis for the Web 2.0:** This workshop was collocated with the 18th International World Wide Web Conference (2009). It focused on three specific problems related to user generated content analysis: text normalization, sentiment analysis and opinion mining, and misbehavior detection. Shared tasks and evaluations were conducted for each problem under consideration. More information is available at http://caw2.barcelonamedia.org/

- **SMUC 2010:** The Second International Workshop on Search and Mining User generated Content was collocated with the 19th ACM International Conference on Information and Knowledge Management. It covered four main areas of interest: mining social media, opinion mining and sentiment analysis, search in social media, and other social intelligent systems. More information is available at http://labs.brainsins.com/events/smuc2010/

- **OMBI 2010:** The First International Workshop on Opinion Mining for Business Intelligence was collocated with The 2010 IEEE/WIC/ACM International Conferences on Web Intelligence and Intelligent Agent Technology. It aimed at fostering the communication among the different actors involved in the Web 2.0. It included a diverse variety of topics such as opinion retrieval and summarization, sentiment analysis, economic implications of user generated content and scalability and efficiency of technologies. More information is available at http://www.yorku.ca/xhyu/OMBI10/

- **NAACL 2010 Workshop on Creating Speech and Language Data with Amazon's Mechanical Turk:** This workshop was collocated with the 11th Annual Conference of the North American Chapter of the Association for Computational Linguistics. Its main objective was to explore the possibilities offered by crowdsourcing platforms such as Amazon's Mechanical Turk for creating resources for natural language applications. More information can be had from http://sites.google.com/site/amtworkshop2010/home

- **PAN 2010 LAB:** The 4th International Workshop on Uncovering Plagiarism, Authorship, and Social Software Misuse was collocated with the Conference on Multilingual and Multimodal Information Access Evaluation. Its main focus is plagiarism detection in both monolingual and cross-language scenarios. The workshop organizes an evaluation campaign in which both external and intrinsic plagiarism detection tasks are evaluated. More information is available at http://pan.webis.de/

Chapter 11
NLP and Digital Library Management

Lyne Da Sylva
University of Montreal, Canada

ABSTRACT

The field of study of Natural Language Processing (NLP) has developed over the past 50 years or so, producing an array of now mature technology, such as automatic morphological analysis, word sense disambiguation, parsing, anaphora resolution, natural language generation, named entity recognition, etc. The proliferation of large digital collections (evolving into Digital Libraries) and the emerging economic value of information demand efficient solutions for managing the information which is available, but which is not always easy to find. This chapter presents the requirements for handling documents in digital libraries and explains how existing NLP technology can be used to facilitate the task of document management.

INTRODUCTION

The field of study of Natural Language Processing (NLP) has developed and ripened in the past 50 years or so, from the first machine translation and information retrieval applications to the present. These two areas of research have been far-reaching and pervasive. In the process of resolving issues of understanding natural language, for both translation and retrieval, many sub-areas of NLP have emerged: automatic morphological analysis, word sense disambiguation, parsing, anaphora resolution, natural language generation, named entity recognition, etc.

DOI: 10.4018/978-1-4666-2169-5.ch011

In today's research in NLP, attention has shifted from machine translation over to different versions of Information Retrieval (IR) applications. The increasing availability of large collections of digital documents has spurred interest in devising useful technology to handle these. Specifically, the notion of "digital libraries" (Adams, 1995; Fox, et al., 1995; Arms, 2000) has emerged, with specific architecture and functionality. This is an area where many mature NLP applications can be brought into play. It is an area mostly associated with IR, which has traditionally used little NLP and yet produced efficient tools; methods needed to include more sophisticated, NLP-based approaches were, up to recently, beyond the reach of IR systems. But digital libraries are much more than simply IR.

This chapter has the following three objectives: (1) to describe the issues relating to the task of managing a digital library; (2) to explore various NLP applications which can be applied to the task; (3) to identify new research problems related to these issues.

BACKGROUND: DIGITAL LIBRARIES, DOCUMENT MANAGEMENT, AND NLP

Digital Libraries

Digital collections existed long before the advent of the Web and the coinage of the term "digital library." NetLib (http://www.netlib.org/), created in 1985, contains a collection of freely available software, documents, and databases of interest to the numerical, scientific computing, and other communities. The Perseus project (http://www.perseus.tufts.edu/hopper/) was created in 1985 to host a collection of resources on Ancient Greece: documents, images of artefacts, maps and the like, all linked together to allow a better understanding of Ancient Greek texts. Cornell University's e-prints archive (http://arxiv.org/), formerly the Los Alamos E-print Archive, dates from 1991. It contains prepublications in the field of physics and related disciplines. These are but a few examples among many. They were, however, isolated initiatives, suffering from minimal interfaces providing access to resources over less than efficient networks. Improvements in interface design and in network configurations, the advent of the WWW and increasing publication of materials on the Web led naturally to the creation of communities of users wishing to share and publish resources – and of technology to support it.

From a computer science perspective, digital libraries are an extension of network technologies, databases and search engines. From an information science viewpoint however, digital libraries are institutions and not machines; they are a logical extension of traditional libraries, whose mission is to acquire, organise and disseminate information. They also mean other things to other groups: a new outlet for content providers, publishers, museums, and commercial vendors; a democratization tool for governments; a new service channel for educators. In addition, from the viewpoint of NLP they represent a new opportunity, a new area of application in which to deploy existing technology, perfect it and invent more.

Definitions for what constitutes a digital library are many, and reflect the fact that work on digital libraries stems from a number of different fields, including computer science and information science of course. Relevant literature on new research is to be found in topical conference proceedings: the European Conference on Digital Libraries (ECDL), the Joint (ACM-IEEE) Conference on Digital Libraries, the International Conference of Asian Digital Libraries, the International Conference on Digital Libraries and the new Theory and Practice of Digital Libraries (formerly ECDL). It also is present in library association conferences and pre-existing conferences of information scientists, publishers, abstracting and indexing services, and online database providers (Bearman, 2008).

An early definition, still cited today, comes from Borgman (2000, p. 42), in which a digital library is as follows:

... A set of electronic resources and associated technical capabilities for creating, searching, and using information. In this sense they are an extension and enhancement of information storage and retrieval systems that manipulate digital data in any medium (text, images, sounds; static or dynamic images) and exist in distributed networks. The content of digital libraries includes data, metadata that describe various aspects of the data (e.g. representation, creator, owner, reproduction rights), and metadata that consist of links or relationships to other data or metadata, whether internal or external to the digital library.

Digital libraries may also be viewed according to the so-called 5S model comprising Streams, Structures, Spaces, Scenarios, and Societies (Gonçalves, et al., 2004). As a digital library may mean different things to different people, it may be useful to draw on the model proposed by the DELOS Digital Library Reference Model (Candela, et al., 2007), which separates levels of application. A Digital Library may be defined as follows:

An organisation, which might be virtual, that comprehensively collects, manages and preserves for the long term rich digital content, and offers to its user communities specialised functionality on the content, of measurable quality and according to codified policies (Candela, et al., 2007, p. 17).

According to this, a Digital Library is an abstract entity, with the specific purpose of catering to a community of users. We focus on three crucial entities in the DELOS model: (1) collections of digital resources, (2) users who access these resources, and (3) intermediaries that provide functionality for accessing them. The quality requirements and policy issues will not be addressed here. The aim of this chapter is to explore the NLP applications, which may be included in a DL to provide useful functionality to its users. The resources we will mainly be concerned with are those expressed in natural language: text documents are the prime example, but audio recordings, scanned text, descriptions of images or video, and the like are also relevant. The users are understood to be human (and not machine agents). The functionalities we are primarily interested in are those that facilitate document access and retrieval by users (as opposed to long-term preservation, for example). The goal of ensuring access to documents involves the task of document management: describing, organizing, and storing them in such a way that their retrieval is facilitated. Which type of functionality is possible and desirable for document management (and ultimate retrieval) is described in the next section.

Different types of digital libraries exist (see for instance Bearman, 2008). A digital library may be thematic, containing resources linked to a particular theme or discipline. Alternatively, it may be genre- or format-based, such as libraries of images or video. Mission- and audience-oriented digital libraries are viewed as a service, such as digital libraries supporting distance education instruction, or digital libraries for children. Another type is institutional repositories, which contain publications and resources of various kinds emanating from a particular institution; many universities have such institutional repositories.

Given this definition, the World Wide Web is not a digital library, lacking a focused community of users, a curator and a central service provider. Nonetheless, many research efforts applied to the Web as a whole can be fruitfully applied to a digital library context.

Some notable digital libraries include: the National Science Digital Library (NSDL) in the United States; Europeana, the ambitious library of Europe's documented cultural materials currently featuring more than 15 million works of art, books, music, and film; the Gutenberg Project, the first collection of free electronic books; the ERIC (Education Resources Information Centre) collection; the Internet Public Library; the Hathi Trust (a partnership of major research institutions and libraries in the United States); and the National Library of Australia.

Document Management

The metaphor chosen to describe collections of digital content has been the library, not only because of the fact it houses a collection of documents, but also because its aim is that of the traditional library: to allow its users to access its contents (a set of digital resources) efficiently. It follows naturally that the desired functionality from a digital library can be inspired by its traditional counterpart.

Document management as performed in a traditional library setting (as described in Lancaster, 2003, for example) involves a series of steps. First, from an initial potentially infinite source of resources (the Web, for example), a selection is made by the library's managers to retain a certain type or a certain number of resources, hereafter referred to as documents, to make up the library's collection. On the representational axis, these documents need to be represented by a formal description, including title or name, author or creator, source, location, format, etc., i.e. with descriptive metadata. The descriptions are then inserted in a local organisational system: a catalogue; they may have additional metadata attached to them, such as index terms or classification codes, a short summary or description (semantic metadata). On the physical axis, the documents (or their representation) are stored (or accessible via hyperlinks). Finally, functionality is provided to the user for searching or accessing these documents: a search engine,

a browsable index or classification scheme, etc., which provide access to the descriptions and/or the documents. In addition, the library, or rather its agents, can disseminate information (such as new acquisitions) to its users. The steps are thus: document selection and acquisition, description, classification, indexing and abstracting, storage, and distribution or presentation to users.

In the digital realm, this so-called "document chain" is a closed one, as users are very often document creators themselves. In addition, with today's facilities for document annotation and tagging, the user may even provide descriptions of various kinds, thus taking an even more important role in the chain, which may not be best described as a chain at all. This is represented schematically in Figure 1, where blocks contain the documents and users and the annotated arrows represent the processes, where NLP technology can be deployed.

Document management has experienced major changes with the spread of personal comput-

Figure 1. Document processing chain or cycle

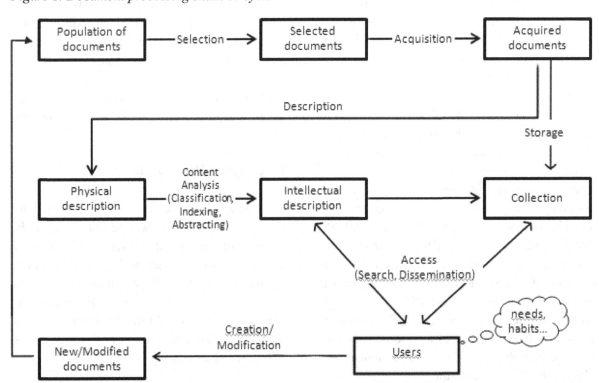

ers, the development of the Internet and the proliferation of digital text collections. Many operations are done on or by computers, even in a traditional setting. In the context of a digital library, all these operations are of course performed on digital content, which opens a host of possibilities for NLP. In addition, the growing number and size of digital libraries demand management efforts that are time-efficient and consistent, which is what computational methods can offer.

The basic requirements for a digital document management system include the following: a repository of documents (able to handle multimedia content); a system providing access points to documents (i.e. indexing terms); optionally, surrogate representations of documents (e.g. as summaries, especially for non-textual items); retrieval tools (e.g. a search interface); a browsing facility; distribution tools (to disseminate information to existing or new users). The latter is optional but may offer a definite economic advantage.

A Note on Metadata

From a Library and Information Science (LIS) perspective, metadata corresponds to cataloguing information; that is, the description of a resource by (mainly) its physical or "external" attributes: title, author, publication or creation date, format, length (page numbers for texts, minutes for video and audio), etc. From a computer science perspective, an early definition:

Metadata is data associated with objects which relieves their potential users of having to have full advance knowledge of their existence or characteristics. It supports a variety of operations. A user could be either a program or a person (Dempsey & Heery, 1998).

Until the middle of the 1990s, the term was used by the data management and systems design communities with a narrower interpretation, relative to a set of standards (Gilliland-Swetland,

2000). Today, its meaning extends to normalized descriptions of resources, digital or other (catalogues, indexes, archival search tools, museum documentation, etc.).

The Dublin Core metadata scheme (http://dublincore.org/documents/dces/), although intended to describe any online resource, contains much of the basic information that librarians recognize as cataloguing information. Its fifteen elements are: contributor, coverage, creator, date, description, format, identifier, language, publisher, relation, rights, source, subject, title and type. The subject and description metadata element correspond to indexing and summarization. Supplying values for these elements requires more than a perusal of superficial document properties, but rather a relatively thorough examination and description of the resource's topic, focus, and content.

Metadata comes in two flavours: terse elements encased in a highly structured container, such as author names and dates of various kinds; or unstructured, perhaps lengthy content, such as summaries. The latter may not always be easily apprehended and may require sophisticated NLP technology to analyse it or indeed to produce it. The former is sometimes straightforward and taken from a controlled vocabulary (for instance, language can be expressed using the ISO 639 standard). However, in the case of person's names (authors, creators and the like), predictable variations on names may make the process more difficult.

In addition, metadata can be wrong. Automatic checking of the accuracy of the metadata can be a useful application in and of itself. The Google Books collection might join the ranks of digital libraries, were it not for its unreliable metadata and its lack of "added-value" functionalities (see a critical review namely in Nunberg, 2009).

NLP and Document Management

The role that NLP can play in document management was realized early on (e.g. Masterman, et al., 1958; Sparck Jones, 1967), particularly for document retrieval. The interest is growing (see for example Ambroziak & Woods, 1998; Strzalkowski, 1999; Voorhees, 1999; Perez-Carballo & Strzalkowski, 2000; Oard, et al., 2001; Todiraşcu & Rousselot, 2001; Ruch, 2003; Radev & Lapata, 2008; Kastner, 2009). There are important links to be made with the semantic Web, aimed at improving retrieval based on semantic grounds rather than on the presence of character strings in documents. See for instance the International Conference on Digital Libraries and the Semantic Web (http://www.icsd-conference.org/). A new development, with the advent of powerful players like Google and the like, is that there are very important stakes involved, due to the growing economic value of digital information.

Practically all NLP applications are relevant and potentially useful in a digital library setting. In particular, methods for information retrieval are an integral part of search engines, and as such are incorporated in virtually any digital library along with all supporting technologies such as word-sense disambiguation, etc.

Here are the basic characteristics of digital libraries and how they may influence the method of deployment of NLP approaches:

- Large collections of texts: sentence-based processing is of limited use if not coupled with other types. Semantic processing, lexical as well as textual, is of utmost importance; discourse analysis is also useful, especially for summarization.
- Digital material comprising text as well as image, sound and multimedia documents: the resources come in different formats, but the metadata associated with them is homogeneous—and text based.
- A variety of genres: digital libraries' text documents are not restricted to newswire nor to scientific articles, which have received special treatment in the recent his-

tory of NLP (for TREC, DUC, and TAC conferences, among others); the NLP technology deployed in digital libraries must be adaptable to different settings, different types of documents, with different structural properties.

- Existence of multilingual collections: resources and technologies for various languages are needed to give access to these.
- Substantial links among documents: a digital library's collection usually houses material, which is thematically linked, or linked in some other special way. This is what justifies and allows the classification of resources. In published research articles, these links enable the study of various types of relationships between sets of documents, i.e. bibliometrics, or the statistical analysis of published literature. This may use citation analysis (the study of citation patterns and citation ancestry for a given document). A common application of this LIS field is to study the impact of a particular paper (how many publications cite it?), of a group of authors (from a given research laboratory, for instance) or of a given field. For digital libraries, it can allow broadened search (searching for papers on a topic and the papers that each original paper cite, for example). Within thematic-based collections, this means that the documents may address the same topic in subtly different ways, which imply that indexing and retrieval must make finer distinctions among related topics.
- Reliance on metadata to describe the resources: a tendency to embrace normalized schemes and encodings for metadata cohabits with user-defined and user-supplied, locally relevant metadata of various types. The creation of the metadata can be a focus for NLP, as can be operations of classification on resulting metadata.

A mandate or mission for the collection and a community of users with fairly specific needs, habits and search behaviour (as opposed to the heterogeneous Web): this defines the requirements for a given digital library. Note that this does not exclude the degenerate example of personal collections of digital images or music, where the target community is a single user. But the mandate can focus the processing by constraining it. One important difference between the Web as a whole and a digital library is that of "community": a digital library is designed by and for a community, which determines the contents of the collection (via discriminating criteria for the inclusion of documents) and the services that are to be provided. The latter notion of "services" is indeed crucial in the definition of what a digital library is, in the information science community. A digital library cannot be a mere gathering of documents with minimal functionality.

These characteristics constrain and shape features of the NLP applications that are needed and useful.

Previous work has addressed particular features of digital libraries and has applied NLP in various implementations, especially in information retrieval. Also, data mining (Cohen, 2006) and text mining (Witten, et al., 2003; Sanderson & Watry, 2007) tools are used to extraction information from text documents in order to perform tasks such as classification, metadata extraction and the like (Li, et al., 2010). A collection which draws much attention is Wikipedia (Kanhabua & Nørvåg, 2010; Popescu & Grefenstette, 2010).

After 15 years or so of work on digital libraries, and in the face of a wide array of mature NLP technology, a comprehensive overview of how the two can be brought together is timely.

OVERVIEW OF NLP TOOLS IN DOCUMENT MANAGEMENT

This section sketches the spectrum of NLP applications for document management, grouped according to four aspects:

- Resource acquisition (including creation, representation and storage)
- Content processing
- Getting users in touch with documents
- Knowledge organisation tools

Resource Acquisition

This aspect covers issues dealing with the acquisition of resources and the related questions of the representation of document files, which are sensitive to language.

A library's collection is never final; it is continually augmented by newly acquired material. Which material is added is determined by library policy, based on a number of criteria. Leaving economic matters aside, the criteria may include the following:

- **Topic:** E.g. ornithology for a bird-watching club documentation center; business-related literature for a financial institution's library;
- **Genre:** Biographies or novels for a public library; conference proceedings for a university or research library; personal correspondence for an archival library; movies for a cinema school's library;
- **Intended Audience:** Picture books for a preschool library; junior dictionaries for a school library;
- **Author:** For government libraries;

Documents can be added to a digital collection by downloading, creation, digitization, transformation (from one format to another), etc.

Acquiring Documents

In some cases, the acquisition of new documents to be added to a digital library can be automated using NLP tools. This is especially true when the selection criteria involve topic: a profile can be defined which expresses the selection criteria for the digital library, as features of the documents; new documents' contents can compared to the profile and processed by an automatic classification algorithm. Joorabchi and Mahdi (2008) describe an implementation of such functionality for a national repository for course syllabi (see also references therein). A very similar task is also performed by so-called "information-filtering systems" (see among others Belkin & Croft, 1992; Hanani, et al., 2001), which intervene between an automated retrieval system and a user, to restrict the number of documents retrieved.

In addition, it is sometimes necessary to transform non-textual documents into textual documents, by NLP means: optical character recognition (see Mello & Lins, 1999, for a comparative study of OCR tools and their performance level), handwriting recognition (Plamondon & Srihari, 2000) for certain historical archives, transcription of audio materials, machine translation, extraction of text from HTML or PDF formats, etc. An additional step of checking for spelling, grammar and style of documents can be performed, when they are acquired by these types of transformations, and thus quite error-prone.

Determination of Proper Processing Tools

Tools, which will be used to process the documents, for example term extractors, part-of-speech taggers, summarizers, etc., are language-sensitive: German texts for instance require different tools than Chinese texts. It is a reasonable assumption in today's understanding of digital libraries that they are intended to be multilingual. To optimize the overall functioning of the library management

system, it is desirable to include in the system functionalities for the automatic identification of language and encoding. Such systems have been developed in the past 15 years, based on character *n*-gram profiles. Řehůřek and Kolkus (2009) provide an up-to-date presentation in the context of the Web.

Document Description

To represent and store documents in a digital library, it is necessary to produce some sort of record by which they are accessed. This corresponds to a traditional library's bibliographic entry, or a metadata record (i.e. descriptive metadata). This record is typically produced explicitly, either hand coded or automatically produced by extracting metadata from the resource. No semantics is involved and usually very little NLP technology. However, the normalisation of author names and titles is a reasonable objective, and would require NLP tools similar to those for the normalisation of named entities (see for instance Andréani & Lebarbé, 2010). See also Kanhabua and Nørvåg (2008) on automatic means of determining a timestamp for documents that lack one. In addition, one can imagine including here the results of automatic identification of document language and encoding, or of date formats.

The descriptive or "physical" metadata described above is often not sufficient, or not ideal, for retrieval by a library's users. Additional metadata can be produced automatically by content processing.

Content Processing

Content processing is a major part of the document management endeavour. It consists in producing enhanced metadata descriptions, in order to facilitate document retrieval by users, in addition to the retrieval capabilities provided by full-text searching. Resulting metadata is to be included in the digital library's knowledge organisation system. Content processing implies performing an analysis of the linguistic and/or conceptual contents of the text documents, and produces appropriate representations for these documents (such as indexing terms, summaries, classification codes, etc.). Content processing thus covers the traditional tasks of classifying, indexing, and summarizing documents. Classifying implies grouping together documents on similar topics, and usually makes use of a classification scheme (such as the Dewey Decimal Classification or the Universal Decimal Classification, etc.); its analog in the digital world would be the hierarchical presentations of directories. Indexing (which may be interpreted differently by different communities) involves here the description of documents with a short list of terms or keywords representing the main topics discussed in the document. Summarization yields a shortened form of documents in a (usually) narrative style.

These content processing tasks are tackled by three basic NLP technologies. First comes the triplet of automatic classification, categorization and clustering (Yang, 1999; Boutella, et al., 2004; Tsoumakas & Katakis, 2007). An overview of techniques for automatic text classification is presented in Sebastiani (2002). Toms and McCay-Peet (2009) discuss the relevance for this topic for digital libraries, in that it may enable serendipitous discovery such as is possible when browsing a physical library's shelf, and may enhance focused search. This is the reasoning, of course, behind approaches, which cluster a search engine's results. Classification using an established bibliographic-type classification (such as Dewey) has been gaining attention: Vizine-Goetz (1996), Thompson et al. (1997), Jenkins et al. (1998), Prabowo et al. (2002), Hodge et al. (2003), Golub (2006). Wang (2009) notes the challenges posed to state-of-the-art text categorization technologies by library classification systems, such as the Dewey classification, with its deep hierarchy, data sparseness, and skewed distribution; they offer reasons why classification

is desirable in the context of growing digital collections and describe previous approaches before offering their machine-learning solution to the problem. On clustering, see, for instance Aas and Eikvil (1999), Steinbach et al. (2000), and Grira et al. (2006), for general presentations. Yoo (2006) performs a comprehensive comparison study of various document-clustering approaches on MEDLINE and also applies a domain ontology such as MeSH to document clustering; this is done in order to investigate if the ontology improves clustering quality for MEDLINE articles. Chengzi and Dan (2008) introduce a new approach for building a topical digital library, using concept extraction and document clustering; thus clustering here is used for collection creation. Note that automatic classification can also be applied to search results, as variants in the presentation (see for instance Palmer, et al., 2001).

The second content processing task is indexing; it is implemented by search and retrieval methods. All forms of information retrieval (Van Rijsbergen, 1979; Perez-Carballo & Strzalkowski, 2000; Sparck-Jones, 2007, to name only a few), and the related topics of automatic annotation (essentially a synonym for automatic indexing) and metadata extraction (e.g. Edvardsen, et al., 2009; Ciravegna, et al., 2004; Kelly, 2004; Péter, 2004) are highly relevant to digital libraries; see also Rasmussen (2004) on information retrieval challenges for digital libraries. Examples of applications for indexing include the following. Krapivin et al. (2010) add NLP techniques to machine learning (Support Vector Machines [SVM], Local SVM, Random Forests) to improve the extraction of keyphrases from scientific documents; the digital library to which they apply their algorithm consists of ACM papers from the Computer Science domain. Tahmasebi et al. (2010) study word sense discrimination on a historical document collection to improve understanding and accessibility of this particular digital archive. For search and retrieval: Batjargal et al. (2010) use a translation dictionary to enable retrieval of ancient historical documents written in traditional Mongolian using a query in modern Mongolian; Gou et al. (2010) use a combination of tf-idf measures and social networks (of the user community) to improve ranking algorithms for retrieval. Finally, recommender-type systems (Hwang, et al., 2003; Krottmaier, 2002; Faensen, et al., 2001; Huang, et al., 2002; Smeaton & Callan, 2005; Avancini, et al., 2007) and user-preference based ranking (Manolopoulos & Sidiropoulos, 2005; Mutschke, 2003) can also bring much-appreciated functionality to the search facilities of digital libraries. For recommender systems, the underlying technology can be document classification, i.e. determining whether a new document belongs to the (theoretical, virtual) class of "documents interesting to this user." Note however that Bearman (2008, p. 242) remarks that no recent studies have examined user satisfaction with different methods of ranking.

The third content processing task, automatic summarization, tries to replicate and improve on human summarization of documents. Sparck Jones (2007) presents an overview of present-day summarization technology; Kan and Klavans (2002) use librarian's techniques to produce summaries for information retrieval; Ou et al. (2009) describe summarization in the context of a digital library. Jaidka et al (2010) perform multi-document summarization of research papers based on techniques drawn from human summarization behaviour and guided by discourse analysis. Wan et al. (2009) use properties of scholarly articles, namely citations. They construct a summary for a cited text, which is focused on the context: sentences from the cited document are extracted based on elements from the citation context.

Within a digital library framework, content processing (specifically: indexing, summarizing and classifying documents) enables the system to add information to the basic bibliographic entries containing metadata such as a document's title, author, date of creation, URL, format, etc. The result of content processing adds indexing keywords or classification codes, i.e. additional access points which should enable easier retrieval, or summaries which make it easier to ascertain the document's relevance to the user's needs.

Getting Users in Touch with Documents

This aspect deals with the *raison d'être* of libraries: access to documents by users, either by their own initiative (retrieval) or by the information system's ability to broadcast news out to a community of users.

Document/Information Retrieval

In a traditional library setting, actual document retrieval is often preceded by a "reference interview," where a librarian tries to ascertain the exact information needs of the user and thus to develop a successful search strategy which will include online search as well as searches in other sources. In a digital library world, this initial phase is non-existent. Users refine their search strategy themselves, gradually, as a reaction to the responses of the system and to what they discover about the contents of the collection. In addition, certain features of the digital library system have been designed to simulate the broadening or sophistication of the search that a librarian would perform. Thus, document retrieval in a digital setting is reducible to so-called "information retrieval." This is probably the best-researched field in document management. The presentation here will only aim to underline the array of NLP technology used (this is also addressed by Mustafa el Hadi, 2004).

Search engines minimally tackle basic issues of matching terms or concepts between queries and documents. More specifically, the match is performed between a query and a previously compiled index of terms and expressions extracted from the document collection (see Indexing, above). The query may also undergo the same processing as documents did during the indexing phase, i.e.

stemming or lemmatization, disambiguation, etc. Search engines of all types perform this daily.

Query expansion refers to the process of adding terms to a query, to broaden a search for example, or on the contrary to further specify one of the query terms; this, incidentally, would be done naturally by a librarian devising a search strategy. This may be achieved by using a thesaurus to capture synonyms to add to the query (thus adding words like "building" to a query containing "construction," to capture related items). Alternatively, more general terms can be added, such as adding "material" to a query containing "concrete" and "plaster," to capture other types of building materials. Finally, more specific terms can be added: "lark" or "finch" could be added to a query containing "bird," in case some documents mention only specific breeds. This can be performed if the system contains an appropriate thesaurus. Additional semantic processing may be required, to determine which strategy should be taken for a given query. See Song et al. (2006) for an application of query expansion to digital libraries.

A multilingual document base can present a challenge to document retrieval: the user's query may not contain words used to index the documents, because they are in a different language. Cross-Linguistic Information Retrieval (CLIR) relies on translation dictionaries, or other translation technology, to bridge the gap between users' queries and documents. See for instance Nie (2010) for a presentation of the field, and Oard (1997) for an early recognition of its relevance to digital libraries.

A librarian would verify that the information supplied to a user does indeed answer his or her needs, by asking whether the supplied documents are deemed relevant by the user. In a digital information retrieval setting, so-called relevance feedback is an automated version of this exchange. It can be used to improve search results by using additional knowledge sources. The most basic type of relevance feedback relies on a user's judgment of relevance of selected documents. These judgments are used to issue a new query, which includes terms extracted from the relevant documents. Simple co-occurrence statistics on words or terms can be used, but there is also an opportunity for more elaborate semantic processing to be performed in ascertaining the relevance of documents for a given user in a specific community.

Broadcasting Documents to Users

It is customary for an information service such as a library to issue bulletins to its users, informing them of new material or special events, when appropriate. This can be done through mailing lists, billboards, etc. The equivalent in the digital world is straightforward. What is novel here, however, is that bulletins can be tailored to individual user profiles. Specifically, new documents can be analysed (indexed, classified, or summarised) and compared to a user profile consisting of user-supplied or system-supplied keywords; in the event of a match, users can be notified of these new documents through appropriate messaging technology (e-mail, RSS feed, etc.). Such a system is described in Morales del Castillo et al. (2009) while Gu et al. (2008) present a similar functionality to support learning.

Answering Users' Questions

A major part of every librarian's day involves answering questions for users. Some modern versions of such a reference service employ chat rooms and the like ("Ask-a-librarian" services), with a human librarian accessible over the Internet. An even more modern take on the idea is to use a question answering system, such as in Mittal et al. (2005) or Bloehdorn et al. (2007).

The task of relating users to documents is obviously at the core of a library's mission and of digital libraries' functionalities. NLP tools can assist in various ways, as has been illustrated so far. We now turn to an aspect, which transcends document management tasks.

Knowledge Organisation Tools

We refer here to linguistic resources used in the text management and processing tasks described above. The one that is most specific to document management is the thesaurus (other knowledge organisation tools relevant for digital libraries are presented in Soergel, 2009).

Properties of Thesauri

Note that the term "thesaurus" means slightly different things to information professionals (librarians) and computer scientists, or to language educators for that matter. Loosely speaking, a thesaurus is some kind of synonym dictionary; in reality, it is much more. It encodes not only synonymous terms but also hierarchical relationships (i.e. which terms are broader and narrower than a given term) and other types of semantic relationships, depending on the resource. Specifically, the "thesaurus" most used in NLP applications, WordNet, is not a thesaurus by LIS standards.

The LIS version of the thesaurus (defined by international standards ISO 2788 and ISO 5064) adopts a stricter definition of thesaural relationships. These are restricted to only three types: (1) hierarchy (broader/narrower terms or generic/specific terms, otherwise known as hypernym/hyponym terms); (2) synonymy (semantic equivalents which may include spelling variants, shortened forms, etc.); and (3) the so-called associative relationship, relating terms that are neither synonyms nor in a hypernym/hyponym relation, yet are related semantically. Thesaural relations exclude (almost all) partitive (part-whole) relationships and others, which are routinely introduced in ontologies.

An innovation of the WordNet thesaurus is the declaration of *synsets*, i.e. sets of words based on their meanings, which are deemed synonymous and have an equal status in the system. In a traditional thesaurus, when synonyms are identified, one term is promoted to the rank of descriptor (or "preferred term," an indexing candidate), and its synonyms are relegated to non-descriptors or non-preferred terms, not used in indexing. Only descriptors may entertain hierarchical or associative relationships with other terms. Potentially ambiguous descriptors (such as river *banks* and financial *banks*) are disambiguated not through their meaning, but through explicit descriptor modification. All descriptors in a thesaurus are formally or graphically different: thus, a thesaurus would differentiate explicitly "river bank" and "financial bank," or the modified terms "bank (boundary)" and "bank (financial institution)." In addition, synonyms need not be true semantic synonyms, but merely recognized as sufficiently synonymous in a given (indexing and retrieval) context. For instance, "bow" and "arrow" can be declared synonyms in a thesaurus used to describe a collection where so few documents mention either that they are best handled together.

The associative relationship is more vague (and is seen as problematic by automatic semantic processing approaches) but is deemed easier to understand and use by humans in the context of indexing and subsequent searching.

Uses of Thesauri in Digital Libraries

The content management tasks (automatic indexing, classification and summarization) can greatly benefit from knowledge sources such as thesauri, which encode semantic relationships among words and terms. The two most basic of these are the synonymy relation and the hypernym/hyponym relation. The two can be used to improve on content processing, such as indexing with more general or more specific terms, and bringing together synonymous expressions to enhance indexing or to allow generalizations in summarizing.

Automatic Construction of Thesauri

Attempts have been made to create thesauri by automatic means, to overcome the problem of the scarcity of appropriate resources. General language thesauri (such as WordNet and the like) offer a wide coverage, but have serious limitations in specialized domains. Specialized thesauri have the opposite flaw (often too narrow in scope), and are in addition fairly rare, often not available for a given specialized domain. To circumvent these problems, the automatic construction of a thesaurus is an endeavour that has been attempted by several researchers (see for instance Auger & Barrière, 2008 and others). The linguistic challenge lies in the automatic identification of semantic relations of synonymy, hypernymy/hyponymy, and other "essential" semantic relationships, which may be difficult to characterize exhaustively. All of these present serious challenges. This research area is close to that of ontology learning and population from text.

Meusel et al. (2010) present a method for extending an existing thesaurus using a mixture of machine learning and NLP; they test their method on MeSH and WordNet. Eckert et al. (2010) use human expert feedback on the relatedness and relative generality of terms to construct dynamically changing concept hierarchies; although not using NLP methods, their work is relevant among other things to suggest novel ways of automating parts of it. However, Arms and Arms (2004) suggest that in heterogeneous collections, controlled vocabularies and shared ontologies are unachievable; accordingly, they recommend brute force, full-text indexing (Bearman, 2008, p. 240).

Summary

Tools for the acquisition, description, and dissemination of resources are basic requirements of a digital library system and may rely on knowledge organisation resources. Many language-related issues must be addressed for the management of a digital library, and it can indeed benefit from natural language processing tools.

A CLOSER LOOK AT SOME CHALLENGES FOR DIGITAL LIBRARY MANAGEMENT

The previous wide-ranging exposé has identified numerous possibilities for NLP applications in the context of digital library management. The rest of this chapter focuses on certain specific challenges met by digital libraries.

Named Entity Recognition and Resolution

It is useful and often necessary to be able to determine when two similar variants of a named entity in fact designate the same one: John Smith, J. Smith, Pres. Smith, John Smith Jr., etc. Organisation names can also vary: Acme Deliveries vs. Acme Deliveries Inc; IBM vs. International Business Machines; The John Hopkins University vs. John Hopkins; etc. This problem is compounded when names come from a foreign country, possibly through transliteration from a foreign language. This has long been recognized in library cataloguing and is the focus of sections in the Anglo-American Cataloguing Rules handbook (Joint Steering Committee for Revision of AACR, 2002). In the domain of scholarly publications, names of institutions, universities, research laboratories, etc. can manifest different variants. This presents a problem when one wants to identify named entities emanating from different sources: different publications, different libraries, in bibliographies from different documents, sometimes dictated by bibliographic styles. It is a problem for a number of endeavours and is indeed a topic of many research papers related to digital libraries.

When creating metadata on authors or creators, it is desirable to ascertain a person's name in a non-ambiguous manner. Feitelson (2004), Hong et al. (2004), Wu et al. (2004), and Bainbridge et al. (2011) study the problem of name variants in digital libraries.

In citation analysis, it is also crucial to distinguish people with similar names while allowing variants for the name of each person. Fereira et al. (2010) discuss the problems encountered in such a task and propose a disambiguation method for a given name based on a two-step method: clustering citation records based on the similarity of co-author names, followed by unsupervised disambiguation. Treeratpituk and Giles (2009) use random forests (a machine learning classification algorithm) to perform the disambiguation task in academic publications. Pereira et al. (2009) use information available on the Web (curricula vitae and Web pages containing publications of the ambiguous authors) and a hierarchical clustering method that groups citations in the same document together, to disambiguate similar names and detect variants. Sugiyama and Kan (2010) tackle the task of recommending new articles to researchers based on their past works, by comparing the cited works in each. In addition, citation analysis is used as a retrieval method by Péter (2004); He et al. (2004) use citation-based retrieval rather than subject retrieval to search scholarly publications.

In another context, Haruechaiyasak and Damrongrat (2010) apply textual analysis to identify persons appearing in photographs in news articles; for this purpose, named entity recognition and disambiguation is necessary.

Not all named entities designate persons, organisations or even geographical entities (see, on the latter, Freire, et al., 2011); in biomedical and chemical literature, proteins, diseases, chemical, genes, etc. are entities which must be identified in the text. They exhibit various peculiarities, which make them difficult to spot consistently (Tönnies, et al., 2010). Kanhabua and Nørvåg (2010) propose methods to identify variants of named entities describing time or events and present an evaluation based on TREC collections.

One can envision coupling citation analysis and content analysis (described in the previous section) to perform multidimensional classification of sets of documents, in which case again

the question of recognizing variants of a named entity is essential. The ability to do so may enable a system to bridge across different digital libraries.

Tools to Assist OCR

Some challenges arise due to the digitization process of certain types of documents: namely, historical documents and so-called retrospective collections of modern digital media. Access to these is hampered by the poor quality of the OCR text. Tahmasebi et al. (2010) investigate the effects of OCR errors on word sense discrimination results on historical documents; evaluations are performed on The Times newspaper archive, with documents dating from 1785 to 1985. Allen et al. (2010) tackle the task of identifying sections and regular features of historical newspapers in order to improve the automatic classification of articles; the ultimate goal is to provide improved search services for these documents.

Search and Retrieval

Improved search strategies are needed. Methods which favour precision (eliminating irrelevant items) are especially sought, as we see the development of topical digital libraries—where distinctions between documents can be finer-grained than on the Web as a whole (Bethard, 2009). On the other hand, to enhance recall, the integration of lexical resources such as thesauri and ontologies should be useful.

The context of a digital—namely, the knowledge that one may have of its users—should enable improved evaluation of the effectiveness of search technology. The evaluation can be done not in a general way, but in a manner specific to the community being serviced by the digital library. It has been suggested that useful metadata is not necessarily linked to content, but that contextual metadata, describing groups that share work processes and workflow process models, are more useful than content descriptors in some instances

(Klas, Fuhr, & Schaefer, 2004). This however is not derived from the source document and thus NLP techniques will have limited impact on this topic.

Question-answering systems can act the part of a librarian, and provide answers to questions rather than documents containing the answers (Bloehdorn, 2007; Vakkari & Taneli, 2009).

A related area of research consists in reconciling controlled vocabulary and natural language tagging (see for instance Seki, et al., 2010): the advantages of the controlled vocabulary may be counterbalanced by those of tagging. Controlled vocabularies offer disambiguation of homonyms/homographs, grouping of synonym terms, which result in higher inter-indexer consistency and higher recall, whereas tagging manifests closeness to the vocabulary of the users, quick adaptation to neologisms, both resulting in higher precision and in some cases higher recall. Applying to natural language tags the same type of processing as that used in automatic thesaurus construction (thus bringing it automatically closer to a controlled vocabulary) could help harness the power of each type.

Retrieval of Non-Textual Documents

One interesting aspect of digital libraries is that they bring together three formerly quite distinct disciplines, i.e. libraries, archives and museums. Digital resources in digital libraries are not limited to textual documents, nor to digital objects, but can include images, video, sound, and digital renderings of three-dimensional physical objects. The extraction of information from the text surrounding images can support automatic indexing of these images (see for instance Haruechaiyasak & Damrongrat, 2010), and the same can be applied to video, audio, or multimedia resources (Da Sylva & Turner, 2005).

Genre-Based Processing

Genre-based processing (i.e. that which takes into account the genre or type of a document and

can adjust accordingly) is an important issue that can be tackled by NLP means. For example, in automatic summarization, Saggion and Lapalme (2000) take advantage of the predictable structure of scientific articles to focus on certain sections from which to extract sentences which will appear in the final extract. Chieze et al. (2010) take a similar approach to handle specific types of legal documents (court judgement renderings, and intellectual property and tax law texts). The latter are examples of single-genre processing. To allow for processing of more than one genre would improve on existing, "off-the-shelf" technology that is geared towards a single genre.

FUTURE RESEARCH DIRECTIONS

One aspect which is less well researched is the access to sub-document structures: how can the system help the user in targeting more precisely the information within a document? This relates to certain applications of XML retrieval (see for instance Smadhi, 2003). Various technologies can provide reading aids for digital documents, enabling a quicker perusal of document contents to ascertain relevance or to enable faster information gathering. Traditionally, this type of information search was enabled by back-of-the-book indexes. Full-text searching may have rendered some aspects of book indexing obsolete, but it can still be a useful tool as a browsable snapshot of the document's contents and as an indicator of the relationships among topics in a document. Work on automatic back-of-the-book indexing has been extremely scarce in the past few decades, although it was experimented with early on (Artandi, 1963; Earl, 1970; Salton, 1988). See however Da Sylva (2004), Da Sylva and Doll (2005), and Nazarenko and El Mekki (2005) for more recent implementations. Owen et al. (2010) explore ways to improve cursory navigation in a document collection; their proposed methods include what they call "semantic" rendering, in which the document display is altered depending on scroll speed. This type of aid to navigation and information evaluation could be explored further to include some types of document summarization or indexing. Melucci (2004) describes the design and the implementation of a tool that generates networks of links within and across hyper-textbooks through a completely automatic and unsupervised procedure; this supports access to information encapsulated in textbooks.

An ongoing concern is that of providing more than the traditional library was capable of: using computer technology in general and NLP in particular to provide functionality, which was impossible in the traditional setting. This includes things such as multi-document or query-based summarizing, which can be produced at will based on varying parameters (as opposed to human-produced summaries, created once and used for every type of query or need).

Other concerns for digital libraries that are not *a priori* the concerns of NLP, but which are ubiquitous and can impact application of technologies: the legal aspects linked to intellectual property for documents included in digital libraries; information-seeking behaviour; processing in distributed architectures (sometimes involving different systems); long-term preservation of digital materials. The latter two aspects may be lessened by adopting recognized, open standards.

Long-term preservation in particular is a serious question, given the non-perennial nature of computer media (including CDs, hard drives, etc.). A traditional library's print collections will last for hundreds of years, but our digital files may not. As mentioned in the DELOS Reference model, preservation may also be viewed as interoperability over time (Candela, et al., 2007, p. 57): ensuring that the digital files of today can still be read and understood correctly in the future. How NLP can contribute to the solution to this problem remains to be seen.

CONCLUSION

The digital library setting represents an interesting opportunity for computational linguistics: it can use many new applications with great potential (notably, a great financial or economic potential, given the new economic value of information). Current focus on very large digital libraries may test the robustness of seemingly mature NLP technology.

In the past, syntax has played a large role in NLP development, notably in symbolic approaches to machine translation, where systems were developed with translation rules from one language's syntactic constructions to another. So far, syntax has played a very small part in NLP for document management (see however Spagnola & Lagoze, 2011). Research must now focus on computational semantics: lexical, phrasal, and sentential semantics, and in even higher-level units. Indeed, text linguistics or discourse analysis will drive new research, especially for summarization and certain approaches to classification. In the long term, the ultimate challenge will be to model more than merely the linguistic dimensions of digital library management, adding also cognitive, communicational, pragmatic, social, or semiotic dimensions, etc. These can appeal to cognitive science and artificial intelligence in general; but even in the linguistic dimensions, challenges abound.

REFERENCES

Aas, K., & Eikvil, L. (1999). *Text categorisation: A survey*. Technical Report. Norwegian Computing Center. Retrieved October 7, 2010, from http://citeseerx.ist.psu.edu/viewdoc/summary?doi=10.1.1.41.2236

Adam, N. R. (Ed.). (1995). Digital libraries: Research and technology advances. In *Proceedings of the ADL 1995 Forum*. McLean, VA: Springer.

Allen, R. B., & Hall, C. (2010). Automated processing of digitized historical newspapers beyond the article level: Finding sections and regular features. [ICADL.]. *Proceedings of ICADL, 2010*, 91–101.

Ambroziak, J., & Woods, W. A. (1998). Natural language technology in precision content retrieval. In *Proceedings of the International Conference on Natural Language Processing and Industrial Applications (NLP+IA 1998)*. Moncton, Canada: NLP. Retrieved October 7, 2010 from http://citeseerx.ist.psu.edu/viewdoc/summary?doi=10.1.1.21.9236

Andréani, V., & Lebarbé, T. (2010). Named entity normalization for termino-ontological resource design: Mixing approaches for optimality. In *Proceedings of 10th International Conference Journées d'Analyse Statistique des Données Textuelles*, (pp. 163-172). ACL.

Arms, W. Y. (2000). *Digital libraries*. Cambridge, MA: MIT Press.

Arms, W. Y., & Arms, C. R. (2004). Mixed content and mixed metadata: Information discovery in a messy world. In Hillmann, D., & Westbrooks, E. (Eds.), *Metadata in Practice* (pp. 223–237). Chicago, IL: American Library Association.

Artandi, S. (1963). *Book indexing by computer*. New Brunswick, NJ: S.S. Artandi.

Auger, A., & Barrière, C. (2008). Pattern based approaches to semantic relation extraction: A state-of-the-art. *Terminology, 14*(1), 1–19. doi:10.1075/term.14.1.02aug

Avancini, H., Candela, L., & Straccia, U. (2007). Recommenders in a personalized, collaborative digital library environment. *Journal of Intelligent Information Systems, 28*(3), 253–283. doi:10.1007/s10844-006-0010-3

Bainbridge, D., Twidale, M. V., & Nichols, D. M. (2011). That's 'é', not 'þ'?' or '□': A user-driven context-aware approach to erroneous metadata in digital libraries. In *Proceedings of JCDL 2011*. Ottawa, Canada: JCDL.

Batjargal, B., Khaltarkhuu, G., Kimura, F., & Maeda, A. (2010). Ancient-to-modern information retrieval for digital collections of traditional Mongolian script. [ICADL.]. *Proceedings of ICADL, 2010*, 25–28.

Bearman, D. (2008). Digital libraries. *Annual Review of Information Science & Technology, 41*(1), 223–272. doi:10.1002/aris.2007.1440410112

Belkin, N., & Croft, B. (1992). Information filtering and information retrieval: Two sides of the same coin? *Communications of the ACM, 35*(12), 29–38. doi:10.1145/138859.138861

Bethard, S., Ghosh, S., Martin, J. H., & Sumner, T. (2009). Topic model methods for automatically identifying out-of-scope resources. In *Proceedings of JCDL 2009: 9th ACM/IEEE-CS Joint Conference on Digital Libraries*, (pp. 19-28). Austin, TX: ACM/IEEE.

Bloehdorn, S., Cimiano, P., Duke, A., Haase, P., Heizmann, J., Thurlow, I., & Völker, J. (2007). Ontology-based question answering for digital libraries. *Lecture Notes in Computer Science, 4675*, 14–25. doi:10.1007/978-3-540-74851-9_2

Borgman, C. L. (2000). *From Gutenberg to the global information infrastructure: Access to information in the networked world*. Cambridge, MA: The MIT Press.

Boutella, M. R., Luob, J., Shena, X., & Brown, C. M. (2004). Learning multi-label scene classification. *Pattern Recognition, 37*, 1757–1771. doi:10.1016/j.patcog.2004.03.009

Chieze, E., Farzindar, A., & Lapalme, G. (2010). An automatic system for summarization and information extraction of legal information. *Lecture Notes in Computer Science, 6036*, 216–234. doi:10.1007/978-3-642-12837-0_12

Ciravegna, F., Chapman, S., Dingli, A., & Wilks, Y. (2004). Learning to harvest information for the semantic web. In *Proceedings of the 1st European Semantic Web Symposium*, (pp. 312-326). IEEE.

Cohen, D. J. (2006). From Babel to knowledge: Data mining large digital collections. *D-Lib Magazine, 12*(3).

Da Sylva, L. (2004). A document browsing tool based on book indexes. In *Proceedings of Computational Linguistics in the North East (CliNE 2004)* (pp. 45–52). Montreal, Canada: CliNE.

Da Sylva, L., & Doll, F. (2005). A document browsing tool: Using lexical classes to convey information. In *Proceedings of the Advances in Artificial Intelligence: 18th Conference of the Canadian Society for Computational Studies of Intelligence, Canadian AI 2005*, (pp. 307-318). New York, NY: Springer-Verlag.

Da Sylva, L., & Turner, J. M. (2005). Using ancillary text to index web-based multimedia objects. *Literary and Linguistic Computing, 21*(2), 219–228. doi:10.1093/llc/fql018

de Mello, C. A. B., & Rafael, D. L. (1999). A comparative study on OCR tools. In *Proceedings of Vision Interface 1999*, (pp. 224-232). Trois-Rivières, Canada: ACL. Retrieved October 7, 2010, from http://citeseerx.ist.psu.edu/viewdoc/summary?doi=10.1.1.12.2361

Dempsey, L., & Heery, R. (1998). Metadata: A current view of practice and issues. *The Journal of Documentation, 54*(2), 145–172. doi:10.1108/EUM0000000007164

Earl, L. L. (1970). Experiments in automatic extraction and indexing. *Information Storage and Retrieval, 6*, 313–334. doi:10.1016/0020-0271(70)90025-2

Eckert, K., Niepert, M., Niemann, C., Buckner, C., Allen, C., & Stuckenschmidt, H. (2010). Crowdsourcing the assembly of concept hierarchies. In *Proceedings of JCDL 2010, 10th ACM/IEEE-CS Joint Conference on Digital Libraries,* (pp. 139-148). Surfer's Paradise, Australia: ACM/IEEE.

Edvardsen, L. F. H., Sølvberg, I. T., Aalberg, T., & Trætteberg, H. (2009). Automatically generating high quality metadata by analyzing the document code of common file types. In *Proceedings of JCDL2009: 9th ACM/IEEE-CS Joint Conference on Digital Libraries,* (pp. 29-38). Austin, TX: ACM/IEEE.

Faensen, D., Faultstich, L., Schweppe, H., Schweppe, H., Hinze, A., & Steidinger, A. (2001). Hermes: A notification service for digital libraries. In *Proceedings of the 1st ACM/IEEE-CS Joint Conference on Digital Libraries (JCDL 2001)*. ACM/IEEE.

Feitelson, D. G. (2004). On identifying name equivalences in digital libraries. *Information Research, 9*(4).

Ferreira, A., Veloso, A., Goncalves, M., & Laender, A. (2010). Effective self-training author name disambiguation in scholarly digital libraries. In *Proceedings of JCDL 2010, 10th ACM/IEEE-CS Joint Conference on Digital Librarie,s* (pp. 39-48). Surfer's Paradise, Australia: ACM/IEEE.

Fox, E. A., Akscyn, R. M., Furuta, R., & Leggett, J. J. (1995). Digital libraries. *Communications of the ACM, 38*(4), 23–28. doi:10.1145/205323.205325

Freire, N., Borbinha, J., Calado, P., & Martins, B. (2011). Metadata geoparsing system for place name recognition and resolution in metadata records. In *Proceedings of JCDL 2011*. Ottawa, Canada: JCDL.

Gilliland-Swetland, A. M. (2000). Setting the stage. In Baca, M. (Ed.), *Introduction to Metadata: Pathways to Digital Information*. Los Angeles, CA: Getty Information Institute.

Golub, K. (2006). Automated subject classification of textual web documents. *The Journal of Documentation*, *62*(3), 350–371. doi:10.1108/00220410610666501

Gonçalves, M. A., Fox, E. A., Watson, L. T., & Kipp, N. A. (2004). Streams, structures, spaces, scenarios, societies (5S): A formal model for digital libraries. *ACM Transactions on Information Systems*, *22*(2), 270–312.

Gou, L., Chen, H.-H., Kim, J.-H., Zhang, X. L., & Giles, C. L. (2010). Social network document ranking. In *Proceedings of JCDL2010, 10th ACM/IEEE-CS Joint Conference on Digital Libraries*, (pp. 313-322). Surfer's Paradise, Australia: ACM/IEEE.

Grira, N., Crucianu, M., & Boujemaa, N. (2006). Unsupervised and semi-supervised clustering: A brief survey. In S. Boughorbel, (Ed.), *A Review of Machine Learning Techniques for Processing Multimedia Content*. Retrieved October 7, 2010 from http://www-rocq.inria.fr/~crucianu/src/BriefSurveyClustering.pdf

Gu, Q., de la Chica, S., Ahmad, F., Khan, H., Sumner, T., Martin, J. H., & Butcher, K. (2008). Personalizing the selection of digital library resources to support intentional learning. *Lecture Notes in Computer Science*, *5173*, 244–255. doi:10.1007/978-3-540-87599-4_25

Hanani, U., Shapira, B., & Shoval, P. (2001). Information filtering: Overview of issues, research and systems. *User Modeling and User-Adapted Interaction*, *11*, 203–259. doi:10.1023/A:1011196000674

Haruechaiyasak, C., & Damrongrat, C. (2010). Identifying persons in news article images based on textual analysis. [ICADL.]. *Proceedings of ICADL*, *2010*, 216–225.

He, Y., Hui, S. C., & Fong, A. C. M. (2003). Citation-based retrieval for scholarly publications. *IEEE Intelligent Systems*, *18*(2), 58–65. doi:10.1109/MIS.2003.1193658

Hodge, G. M., Zeng, M. L., & Soergel, D. (2003). Building a meaningful web: From traditional knowledge organization systems to new semantic tools. In *Proceedings of the 3rd ACM/IEEE-CS Joint Conference on Digital Libraries*, (p. 417). Houston, TX: ACM/IEEE.

Hong, Y., On, B.-W., & Lee, D. (2004). System support for name authority control problem in digital libraries: OpenDBLP approach. In *Proceedings of the 8th European Conference on Digital Libraries*, (pp. 134-144). ACL.

Huang, Z., Chung, W., Ong, T. H., & Chen, H. (2002). A graph-based recommender system for digital library. In *Proceedings of the 2nd ACM/IEEE-CS Joint Conference on Digital Libraries*. ACM/IEEE.

Hwang, S. Y., Hsiung, W. C., & Yang, W. S. (2003). A prototype WWW literature recommendation system for digital libraries. *Online Information Review*, *27*, 169–182. doi:10.1108/14684520310481436

ISO. (1985). *ISO 5964 documentation -- Guidelines for the establishment and development of multilingual thesauri*. Geneva, Switzerland: ISO.

ISO. (1986). *ISO 2788 documentation – Guidelines for the establishment and development of monolingual thesauri*. Geneva, Switzerland: ISO.

Jaidka, K., Khoo, C., & Na, J.-C. (2010). Imitating human literature review writing: An approach to multi-document summarization. [ICADL.]. *Proceedings of ICADL, 2010*, 116–119.

Jenkins, C., Jackson, M., Burden, P., & Wallis, J. (1998). Automatic classification of web resources using java and Dewey decimal classification. *Computer Networks and ISDN Systems Archive, 30*(1-7), 646-648.

Joint Steering Committee for Revision of AACR. (2002). *Anglo-American cataloguing rules* (2nd ed.). Ottawa, Canada: Canadian Library Association.

Joorabchi, A., & Mahdi, A. E. (2008). Development of a national syllabus repository for higher education in Ireland. *Lecture Notes in Computer Science, 5173*, 197–208. doi:10.1007/978-3-540-87599-4_20

Joorabchi, A., & Mahdi, A. E. (2009). Leveraging the legacy of conventional libraries for organizing digital libraries. In *Proceedings of the 13th European Conference, ECDL 2009*, (pp. 3-14). Corfu, Greece: ECDL.

Kan, M.-Y., & Klavans, J. L. (2002). Using librarian techniques in automatic text summarization for information retrieval. In *Proceedings of JCDL 2002*. Portland, OR: JCDL.

Kanhabua, N., & Nørvåg, K. (2008). Improving temporal language models for determining time of non-timestamped documents. *Lecture Notes in Computer Science, 5173*, 358–370. doi:10.1007/978-3-540-87599-4_37

Kanhabua, N., & Nørvåg, K. (2010). Exploiting time-based synonyms in searching document archives. In *Proceedings of JCDL2010, 10th ACM/IEEE-CS Joint Conference on Digital Libraries*, (pp. 79-88). Surfer's Paradise, Australia: ACM/IEEE.

Kastner, I. (2009, December). Developments in information retrieval: Part 1. *Library + Information Update*, 17-19.

Kelly, B. (2004). Interoperable digital library programmes? We must have Q&A! In *Proceedings of the 8th European Conference on Digital Libraries*, (pp. 80-85). ECDL.

Krapivin, M., Autayeu, A., Marchese, M., Blanzieri, E., & Segata, N. (2010). Keyphrases extraction from scientific documents: Improving machine learning approaches with natural language processing. [ICADL.]. *Proceedings of, ICADL2010*, 102–111.

Krottmaier, H. (2002). Automatic references: Active support for scientists in digital libraries. In *Proceedings of the 5th International Conference on Asian Digital Libraries*, (pp. 254-255). ACL.

Lancaster, F. W. (2003). *Indexing and abstracting in theory and practice* (3rd ed.). Champaign, IL: University of Illinois Press.

Li, N., Zhu, L., Mitra, P., & Giles, C. L. (2010). oreChem ChemxSeer: A semantic digital library. In *Proceedings of JCDL2010, 10th ACM/IEEE-CS Joint Conference on Digital Libraries*, (pp. 245-254). Surfer's Paradise, Australia: ACM/IEEE.

Manolopoulos, Y., & Sidiropoulos, A. (2005). A new perspective to automatically rank scientific conferences using digital libraries. *Information Processing & Management, 41*, 289–312. doi:10.1016/j.ipm.2003.09.002

Mas, C.-P., Fuhr, N., & Schaefer, A. (2004). Evaluating strategic support for information access in the DAFFODIL system. In *Proceedings of the 8th European Conference on Digital Libraries*, (pp. 476-487). ECDL.

Masterman, M., Needham, R. M., & Sparck Jones, K. (1958). The analogy between mechanical translation and library retrieval. In *Proceedings of the International Conference on Scientific Information,* (vol 2), (pp. 917-935). Washington, DC: National Academy of Sciences.

Melucci, M. (2004). Making digital libraries effective: Automatic generation of links for similarity search across hyper-textbooks. *Journal of the American Society for Information Science and Technology, 55,* 414–430. doi:10.1002/asi.10390

Meusel, R., Niepert, M., Eckert, K., & Stuckenschmidt, H. (2010). Thesaurus extension using web search engines. [ICADL.]. *Proceedings of ICADL, 2010,* 198–207.

Mittal, A., Gupta, S., Kumar, P., & Kashyap, S. (2005). A fully automatic question-answering system for intelligent search in e-learning documents. *International Journal on E-Learning, 4*(1), 149–166.

Morales del Castillo, J. M., Pedraza-Jimenez, A., Ruiz, A. A., Peis, E., & Herrera-Viedma, E. (2009). A semantic model of selective dissemination of information for digital libraries. *Information Technology and Libraries, 28*(1), 21–30.

Mustafa el Hadi, W. (2004). Human language technology and its role in information access and management. *Cataloging & Classification Quarterly, 37*(1/2), 131–151.

Mutschke, P. (2003). Mining networks and central entities in digital libraries: A graph theoretic approach applied to co-author networks. *Lecture Notes in Computer Science, 2810,* 155–166. doi:10.1007/978-3-540-45231-7_15

Nazarenko, A., & Ait El Mekki, T. (2005). Building back-of-the-book indexes. *Terminology, 11*(1), 199–224. doi:10.1075/term.11.1.09naz

Nie, J.-Y. (2010). *Cross-language information retrieval.* San Francisco, CA: Morgan & Claypool Publishers.

Nunberg, G. (2009, August 31). Google's book search: A disaster for scholars. *The Chronicle of Higher Education.* Retrieved from http://chronicle.com/article/Googles-Book-Search-A/48245/

Oard, D. W. (1997). Serving users in many languages: Cross-language information retrieval. *D-Lib Magazine.* Retrieved from http://www.dlib.org/dlib/december97/oard/12oard.html

Oard, D. W., et al. (2001). Multilingual information retrieval. In E. Hovy, N. Ide, R. Frederking, J. Marian, & A. Zampolli (Eds.), *Multilingual Information Management: Current Levels and Future Abilities.* Retrieved from http://www.cs.cmu.edu/~ref/mlim/

Ou, S., Khoo, C. S. G., & Goh, D. H.-L. (2009). Automatic text summarization in digital libraries. In Theng, Y.-L., Foo, S., Goh, D., & Na, J.-C. (Eds.), *Handbook of Research on Digital Libraries: Design, Development, and Impact* (pp. 159–172). Hershey, PA: IGI Global. doi:10.4018/978-1-59904-879-6.ch016

Owen, T., Buchanan, G., Eslambolchilar, P., & Loizides, F. (2010). Supporting early document navigation with semantic zooming. [ICADL.]. *Proceedings of ICADL, 2010,* 168–178.

Palmer, C. R., Pesenti, J., Valdes-Perez, R. E., Christel, M. G., Hauptmann, A. G., Ng, D., & Wactlar, H. D. (2001). Demonstration of hierarchical document clustering of digital library retrieval results. In *Proceedings of JCDL 2001,* (p. 415). Roanoke, VA: JCDL.

Pereira, D. A., Ribeiro-Neto, B., Ziviani, N., Laender, A. H. F., Gonçalves, M. A., & Ferreira, A. A. (2010). Using web information for author name disambiguation. In *Proceedings of JCDL 2009: 9th ACM/IEEE-CS Joint Conference on Digital Libraries,* (pp. 49-58). Austin, TX: ACM/IEEE.

Perez-Carballo, J., & Strzalkowski, T. (2000). Natural language information retrieval: Progress report. *Information Processing & Management*, *36*(1), 155–178. doi:10.1016/S0306-4573(99)00049-7

Péter, J. (2004). Link-enabled cited references. *Online Information Review*, *28*, 306–311. doi:10.1108/14684520410553804

Plamondon, R., & Srihari, S. N. (2000). On-line and off-line handwriting recognition: A comprehensive survey. *IEEE Transactions on Pattern Analysis and Machine Intelligence*, *22*(1), 63–84. doi:10.1109/34.824821

Popescu, A., & Grefenstette, G. (2010). Spatiotemporal mapping of Wikipedia concepts. In *Proceedings of JCDL 2010, 10th ACM/IEEE-CS Joint Conference on Digital Libraries*, (pp. 129-138). Surfer's Paradise, Australia: ACM/IEEE.

Pouliquen, B., Steinberger, R., & Ignat, C. (2003). Automatic annotation of multilingual text collections with a conceptual thesaurus. In *Proceedings of Ontologies and Information Extraction: Workshop at EUROLAN 2003: The Semantic Web and Language Technology – Its Potential and Practicalities*. Bucharest, Romania: EUROLAN.

Prabowo, R., Jackson, M., Burden, P., & Knoell, H.-D. (2002). Ontology-based automatic classification for web pages: Design, implementation and evaluation. In *Proceedings of the Third International Conference on Web Information Systems Engineering, WISE 2002*, (pp. 182 – 191). WISE.

Rasmussen, E. (2004). Information retrieval challenges for digital libraries. *Lecture Notes in Computer Science*, 3334.

Řehůřek, R., & Kolkus, M. (2009). Language identification on the web: Extending the dictionary method. *Lecture Notes in Computer Science*, *5449*, 357–368. doi:10.1007/978-3-642-00382-0_29

Ruch, P. (2003). *Applying natural language processing to information retrieval in clinical records and biomedical texts*. (Ph.D. Thesis). Imprimerie des Hôpitaux Universitaires de Genève. Geneva, Switzerland.

Saggion, H., & Lapalme, G. (2000). Concept identification and presentation in the context of technical text summarization. In *Proceedings of the Workshop on Automatic Abstracting, NAACL-ANLP 2000*. Seattle, WA: NAACL.

Salton, G. (1988). Syntactic approaches to automatic book indexing. In *Proceedings of the 26th Annual Meeting on Association for Computational Linguistics*, (pp. 204-210). Buffalo, NY: ACL.

Sanderson, R., & Watry, P. (2007). Integrating data and text mining processes for digital library applications. In *Proceedings of the 7th ACM/IEEE-CS Joint Conference on Digital Libraries*, (pp. 73-79). ACM/IEEE.

Sebastiani, F. (2002). Machine learning in automated text categorization. *ACM Computing Surveys*, *34*(1), 1–47. doi:10.1145/505282.505283

Seki, K., Qin, H., & Uehara, K. (2010). Impact and prospect of social bookmarks for bibliographic information retrieval. In *Proceedings of JCDL 2010, 10th ACM/IEEE-CS Joint Conference on Digital Libraries*, (pp. 357-360). Surfer's Paradise, Australia: ACM/IEEE.

Smadhi, S. (2003). System of information retrieval in XML documents. In Becker, S. A. (Ed.), *Effective Databases for Text & Document Management* (pp. 1–11). Hershey, PA: IGI Global. doi:10.4018/978-1-93177-747-6.ch001

Smeaton, A. F., & Callan, J. (2005). Personalisation and recommender systems in digital libraries. *International Journal on Digital Libraries*, *5*(4), 299–308. doi:10.1007/s00799-004-0100-1

Soergel, D. (2009). Digital libraries and knowledge organization. In Kruk, S. R., & McDaniel, B. (Eds.), *Semantic Digital Libraries* (pp. 3–39). Berlin, Germany: Springer. doi:10.1007/978-3-540-85434-0_2

Song, M., Song, I. Y., Allen, R. B., & Obradovic, Z. (2006). Keyphrase extraction-based query expansion in digital libraries. In *Proceedings of the 6th ACM/IEEE-CS Joint Conference on Digital Libraries,* (pp. 202-209). Chapel Hill, NC: ACM/IEEE.

Spagnola, S., & Lagoze, C. (2011). Word order matters: Measuring topic coherence with lexical argument structure. In *Proceedings of JCDL 2011.* Ottawa, Canada: JCDL.

Sparck Jones, K. (1967). Current work on automatic classification for information retrieval. *T.A. Informations, 2,* 92–96.

Sparck Jones, K. (2007). Automatic summarising: The state of the art. *Information Processing & Management, 43*(6), 1449–1481. doi:10.1016/j.ipm.2007.03.009

Steinbach, M., Karypis, G., & Kumar, V. (2000). A comparison of document clustering techniques. In *Proceedings of the KDD Workshop on Text Mining.* Retrieved October 7, 2010 from http://glaros.dtc.umn.edu/gkhome/node/157

Strzalkowski, T. (Ed.). (1999). *Natural language information retrieval.* Dordrecht, The Netherlands: Kluwer Academic Publishers.

Sugiyama, K., & Kan, M.-Y. (2010). Scholarly paper recommendation via user's recent research interests. In *Proceedings of JCDL 2010, 10th ACM/IEEE-CS Joint Conference on Digital Libraries,* (pp. 29-38). Surfer's Paradise, Australia: ACM/IEEE.

Tahmasebi, N., Niklas, K., Theuerkauf, T., & Risse, T. (2010). Using word sense discrimination on historic document collection. In *Proceedings of JCDL2010, 10th ACM/IEEE-CS Joint Conference on Digital Libraries,* (pp. 89-98). Surfer's Paradise, Australia: ACM/IEEE.

Thompson, R., Shafer, K., & Vizine-Goetz, D. (1997). Evaluating Dewey concepts as a knowledge base for automatic subject assignment. In *Proceedings of the Second ACM International Conference on Digital Libraries,* (pp. 37-46). Philadelphia, PA: ACM.

Todirascu, A., & Rousselot, F. (2001). Ontologies for information retrieval. [TALN.]. *Proceedings of TALN, 2001,* 305–314.

Toms, E., & McCay-Peet, L. (2009). Chance encounters in the digital library. In M. Agosti et al. (Eds.), *Research and Advanced Technology for Digital Libraries, 13th European Conference, ECDL 2009,* (pp. 192-202). Corfu, Greece: ECDL.

Tönnies, S., Köhncke, B., Koepler, O., & Balke, W.-T. (2010). Exposing the hidden web for chemical digital libraries. In *Proceedings of JCDL2010, 10th ACM/IEEE-CS Joint Conference on Digital Libraries,* (pp. 235-244). Surfer's Paradise, Australia: ACM/IEEE.

Treeratpituk, P., & Giles, C. L. (2010). Disambiguating authors in academic publications using random forests. In *Proceedings of JCDL2009: 9th ACM/IEEE-CS Joint Conference on Digital Libraries,* (pp. 39-48). Austin, TX: ACM/IEEE.

Tsoumakas, G., & Katakis, I. (2007). Multi-label classification: An overview. *International Journal of Data Warehousing and Mining, 3*(3), 1–13. doi:10.4018/jdwm.2007070101

Vakkari, P., & Taneli, M. (2009). Comparing Google to ask-a-librarian service for answering factual and topical questions. In M. Agosti, et al. (Eds.), *Research and Advanced Technology for Digital Libraries, 13th European Conference, ECDL 2009*, (pp. 352-363). Corfu, Greece: ECDL.

Van Rijsbergen, C. J. (1979). *Information retrieval.* Newton, MA: Butterworth-Heinemann.

Vizine-Goetz, D. (1996). Using library classification schemes for internet resources. *OCLC Internet Cataloging Project Colloquium.* Retrieved October 8, 2010, from http://webdoc.sub.gwdg.de/ebook/aw/oclc/man/colloq/v-g.htm

Voorhees, E. M. (1999). Natural language processing and information retrieval. In Pazienza, M. T. (Ed.), *Information Extraction: Towards Scalable, Adaptable Systems* (pp. 32–48). Berlin, Germany: Springer-Verlag.

Wang, J. (2009). An extensive study on automated Dewey decimal classification. *Journal of the American Society for Information Science and Technology, 60*(11), 2269–2286. doi:10.1002/asi.21147

Witten, I. H., Don, K. J., Dewsnip, M., & Tablan, V. (2003). Textmining in a digital library. *International Journal on Digital Libraries, 5*, 1–4.

Wu, P. H.-J., Na, J.-C., & Khoo, C. S. G. (2004). NLP versus IR approaches to fuzzy name searching in digital libraries. In *Proceedings of the 8th European Conference on Digital Libraries*, (pp. 145-156). ECDL.

Yang, Y. (1999). An evaluation of statistical approaches to text categorization. *Information Retrieval, 1*(1-2), 69–90. doi:10.1023/A:1009982220290

Yoo, I. (2006). A comprehensive comparison study of document clustering for a biomedical digital library MEDLINE. In *Proceedings of the 6th ACM/IEEE-CS Joint Conference on Digital Libraries*, (pp. 220-229). Chapel Hill, NC: ACM/IEEE.

ADDITIONAL READING

Agosti, M., Borbinha, J., Kapidakis, S., Papatheodorou, C., & Tsakonas, G. (2009). Lecture Notes in Computer Science: *Vol. 5714. Paper.*

Andrews, J., & Law, D. G. (Eds.). (2004). *Digital libraries: Policy, planning, and practice.* Aldershot, UK: Ashgate.

Archer, D. W., Delcambre, L. M. L., Corubolo, F., Cassel, L., Price, S., & Murthy, U. ... McCall, J. (2008). Superimposed information architecture for digital libraries. *Lecture Notes in Computer Science, 5173*, 88-99.

Bontcheva, K., Maynard, D., Cunningham, H., & Saggion, H. (2002). Using human language technology for automatic annotation and indexing of digital library content. In *Proceedings of ECDL 2002: European Conference on Research and Advanced Technology for Digital Libraries*, (vol 2458), (pp. 613-625). Rome, Italy: Springer-Verlag.

Buchanan, G., Masoodian, M., & Cunningham, S. J. (Eds.). (2008). Paper. In *Proceedings of the 11th International Conference on Asian Digital Libraries, ICADL 2008.* Bali, Indonesia: Springer-Verlag.

Chengzhi, Z., & Dan, W. (2008). Concept extraction and clustering for topic digital library construction. In *Proceedings of the IEEE/WIC/ACM International Conference on Web Intelligence and Intelligent Agent Technology*, (pp. 299-302). IEEE/WIC/ACM.

(2008). In Christensen-Dalsgaard, B., Castelli, D., Jurik, B. A., & Lippincott, J. (Eds.). Lecture Notes in Computer Science: *Vol. 5173. Paper.*

Ferro, N. (2009). Annotation search: The FAST way. *Lecture Notes in Computer Science, 5714.*

Golub, K. (2006). Using controlled vocabularies in automated subject classification of textual web pages, in the context of browsing. *TCDL Bulletin, 2*(2). Retrieved October 8, 2010 from http://www.ieee-tcdl.org/Bulletin/v2n2/golub/golub.html

(2007). InKovács, L., Fuhr, N., & Meghini, C. (Eds.). Lecture Notes in Computer Science: *Vol. 4675. Research and advanced technology for digital libraries.* doi:10.1007/978-3-540-74851-9

Lagoze, C., Payette, S., Shin, E., & Wilper, C. (2006). Fedora: An architecture for complex objects and their relationships. *International Journal on Digital Libraries, 6*(2), 124–138. doi:10.1007/s00799-005-0130-3

Mitchell, S. (2006). Machine assistance in collection building: New tools, research, issues, and reflections. *Information Technology and Libraries, 25*(4), 190–216.

Rydberg-Cox, J. A. (2006). *Digital libraries and the challenges of digital humanities.* Oxford, UK: Chandos Publishing. doi:10.1533/9781780630816

Shiri, A., & Molberg, K. (2005). Interfaces to knowledge organization systems in Canadian digital library collections. *Online Information Review, 29*(6), 604–620. doi:10.1108/14684520510638061

Soergel, D. (2002). A framework for digital library research. *DLIB Magazine, 8*(12). Retrieved October 8, 2010 from http://www.dlib.org/dlib/december02/soergel/12soergel.html

Tedd, L. A., & Large, A. (2005). *Digital libraries: Principles and practice in a global environment.* Berlin, Germany: K.G. Saur.

Tuominen, K., Talja, S., & Savolainen, R. (2003). Multiperspective digital libraries: The implications of constructionism for the development of digital libraries. *Journal of the American Society for Information Science and Technology, 54,* 561–569. doi:10.1002/asi.10243

Witten, I. H., Bainbridge, D., & Boddie, S. J. (2001). Greenstone: Open-source digital library software with end-user collection building. *Online Information Review, 25*(5), 288–298. doi:10.1108/14684520110410490

KEY TERMS AND DEFINITIONS

Abstracting (or Summarization): The operation by which the subject contents of a document are expressed by a short, narrative-style text.

Classification: A system of organising library materials (books, periodicals, audiovisual materials, etc.) according to their subject. Also the process of attributing a class (or a call number) to a given information resource.

Citation Analysis: The study of the frequency and patterns of citations to other works in articles and books.

Classification Scheme: A descriptive system used for grouping together works on similar subjects. *See also* Classification.

Collection (or Document Collection): Set of documents selected and housed by a given information service for a specific user community.

Content Processing: The set of operations performed on documents to describe their subject contents. This includes classification, indexing and abstracting (or summarization). The result is semantic metadata.

Controlled Vocabulary: A carefully selected set of terms from a natural language, used to describe or index a document collection. It applies formal restrictions (singular number only, for example) as well as semantic restrictions (homonym disambiguation, grouping of synonyms, etc.). The vocabulary may include compound terms not usually found in language, such as "World War II – history."

Document Description: A step of document management consisting of supplying descriptive metadata for a given resource.

Document Management: A series of operations relevant to the use of a document collection: creation, selection, acquisition, description, content processing, organisation, storage, and retrieval of documents.

Indexing: Analysing the content of a document and assigning to it a small set of terms to represent its main topics; the terms are usually taken from a controlled vocabulary.

Information Retrieval: The area of study concerned with searching for documents, for information within documents, and for metadata about documents.

Metadata: Information about the subject contents of a resource (semantic metadata), such as keywords, or about its physical or external characteristics (descriptive metadata), such as author, date of publication or format.

Named Entity: A natural language expression referring to a single entity in the world, such as persons' names, organisations, geographical locations, timestamps, or other.

Thesaurus: A type of controlled language that makes explicit certain types of semantic relations among terms, namely hierarchy (hypernym-hyponym relation), equivalence (synonymy), and associative relations (covering various other semantic relations).

Section 6
Speech Processing

Chapter 12
Speechreading using Modified Visual Feature Vectors

Preety Singh
Malaviya National Institute of Technology, India

Vijay Laxmi
Malaviya National Institute of Technology, India

M. S. Gaur
Malaviya National Institute of Technology, India

ABSTRACT

Audio-Visual Speech Recognition (AVSR) is an emerging technology that helps in improved machine perception of speech by taking into account the bimodality of human speech. Automated speech is inspired from the fact that human beings subconsciously use visual cues to interpret speech. This chapter surveys the techniques for audio-visual speech recognition. Through this survey, the authors discuss the steps involved in a robust mechanism for perception of speech for human-computer interaction. The main emphasis is on visual speech recognition taking only the visual cues into account. Previous research has shown that visual-only speech recognition systems pose many challenges. The authors present a speech recognition system where only the visual modality is used for recognition of the spoken word. Significant features are extracted from lip images. These features are used to build n-gram feature vectors. Classification of speech using these modified feature vectors results in improved accuracy of the spoken word.

INTRODUCTION

Automatic Speech Recognition (ASR) technology allows a computer to recognize words that a person speaks. ASR systems have been shown to give word recognition rates of 98-99% in controlled

DOI: 10.4018/978-1-4666-2169-5.ch012

environments where there is a single speaker, a microphone in close proximity and minimal background noise. In real-life, ideal situations like these are not feasible and the automatic speech recognition techniques show a marked degradation in performance. Psycholinguistic research has shown that speech perception is improved by visual cues (Dodd & Campbell, 1987). While the auditory signal degrades as the Signal-to-Noise Ratio (SNR) decreases, the visual signal is not affected by it. By incorporating a visual input along with the audio signal, there is significant improvement in the noise robustness of speech recognition. This is referred to as *Audio-Visual Speech Recognition* (AVSR). This can improve the intelligibility of speech in a multi-speaker environment or in a noisy background. In cases when an accented speech or a foreign language is to be understood, it is easy to identify the linguistic message if it is accompanied by visual cues (Sumby & Pollack, 1954).

The production and perception of human speech is bimodal in nature. It has also been shown that addition of visual information is equivalent to about 12 dB gain in SNR (Chen, 2001). Though visual information might not prove to be very beneficial for a small vocabulary set, it plays an important role for a large vocabulary or in presence of noise. Visual cues help in localization of the audio source. They supplement the audio signal by providing speech segmental information and also supply important information about the position of articulators (Potamianos, Neti, Gravier, Garg, & Senior, 2003).

Though humans have an inherent ability to lip-read, it is difficult to train computers in the same manner. Interpretation of speech by man is improved because of his knowledge of the context of the conversation and facial movements. People having hearing disabilities rely heavily on lip-reading and the movement of eyebrows, cheeks, and chin aids their comprehension of speech. While observation of these articulatory gestures comes naturally to man and helps him to abstract visual cues to identify speech, machines have not been able to perform similarly. Lip-reading systems usually take sequence of lip images as visual input but lip segmentation itself is a challenging task. Lot of research has been done in the field of visual speech recognition. However, the accuracy achieved has been around 40% only (Matthews, Cootes, Bangham, Cox, & Harvey, 2002).

Production of sound involves speech articulators, some of which may be visible (lips, tongue, and teeth) and some may not (velum, vocal cord, nasal tract, etc.). Various speech articulators affect the speech that is produced. Visible articulators, participating in the modulation of sound wave are known as *primary indicators* for visual speech and are most important. Image sequences of speech show that the tongue and teeth are partially visible and their individual extraction is not always feasible. The cheeks, chin, and nose are used as *secondary indicators*. The linguistic message can be decoded by observation of some of the articulatory movements that produce the acoustic signal. This can improve auditory speech perception. The place of articulators can help in distinguishing between ambiguous sounds, for example, /p/ (a bilabial) and /k/ (a velar), /b/ (a bilabial) and /d/ (an alveolar), /m/ (a bilabial) and /n/ (an alveolar). These three pairs are frequent cause of acoustic confusion for humans unless aided by visual input or contextual information.

The distinctive sounds produced are known as *phonemes* and the specific shape of the mouth while producing this sound is called *viseme*. For the English alphabet, the ARPABET table (Shoup, 1980), consisting of 48 phonemes is generally used for classification though there is no standard viseme table. These phonemes and visemes are in context of human perception and not computer perception of speech.

This chapter is organized as follows: Section 2 describes the various steps involved in the processing of the audio and visual cues for better recognition. Section 3 focuses on speech processing using audio signal only. Section 4 concentrates on the various steps involved in visual signal processing, including face detection, lip segmentation and extraction of lip features. Section 5 discusses the recognition methods usually employed for classification of these two signals. Section 6 is devoted to the fusion of the audio and visual streams. Section 7 gives a brief discussion on some of the available audio-visual databases.

Section 8 describes our proposed methodology for a visual speech recognition system. Finally, Section 9 concludes the chapter by mentioning the factors affecting the performance of lip-reading.

AUDIO AND VISUAL SIGNAL PROCESSING

The existing AVSR systems are developed in restricted environments with minimal noise, single speaker and controlled illumination. These systems are then tested for noise by decreasing the SNR (Movellan & Mineiro, 1998). Different types of noise signals are added and it is expected that a robust system will perform well in adverse conditions. A typical AVSR system consists of the following:

- Audio signal processing system
- Visual signal processing system
- Application of learning and recognition methods
- Integration of audio and visual channels

Compared to audio-only speech recognition systems, there are a number of challenges associated with AVSR systems. Apart from having an audio front-end system, a visual front-end system is also required for acquisition of visual cues (refer Figure 1). This requires robust face detection, segmentation of the mouth region and tracking of the lip contour. Informative features are extracted from both the audio and video signals. Identification of a minimal feature set is a challenging task. The fusion of the audio and visual streams should be such that the classifiers and recognition methods applied should result in bettering the performance of an ASR. Accuracy and reliability at each step is required for correct recognition and an enhanced performance of the AVSR system.

AUDIO FRONT-END

Speech recognition involves two main tasks: feature extraction and feature matching. The first task consists of converting the speech waveform to a different kind of representation for further processing. The extracted information is known as the feature vector. Conversion of the audio speech into the feature vector is done by the audio front-end module. The extracted feature vector is matched against an acoustic model. The output of the model with the maximum score is considered as the recognized word.

Audio signal is time varying. It is always better to characterize the speech signal with a short-term spectral analysis since its characteristics are more or less the same over a short period (10 to 25 ms). It is observed that the feature vector extracted during this interval corresponds to a single phoneme. Any word in the English language can be constructed using a concatenation of the available 48 phonemes.

The methods frequently used for extracting feature vector are: (a) Mel-Frequency Cepstrum Coefficient (MFCC) and (b) Linear Predictive Coding (LPC). The structure of a person's vocal tract is a distinguishable physical property, which can be reflected in the speech spectrum. The LPC and MFCC coefficients are commonly used to represent the speech spectrum. The LPC is used for representing the spectrum of speech in a compressed form. It is a useful method for encoding good quality speech at a low bit rate. The MFCCs are derived from a cepstral representation of the audio clip. The normal cepstrum have linearly spaced frequency bands on the mel scale whereas they are equally spaced in the mel-frequency cepstrum which approximates the human auditory response more closely. The extracted feature vector from the front end is given as an input to the acoustic model for mapping the feature vector to a symbol. The acoustic models generally used are Gaussian Mixture Model (GMM) and Vector Quantization (VQ)-Code Book.

Figure 1. An audio-visual speech recognition process

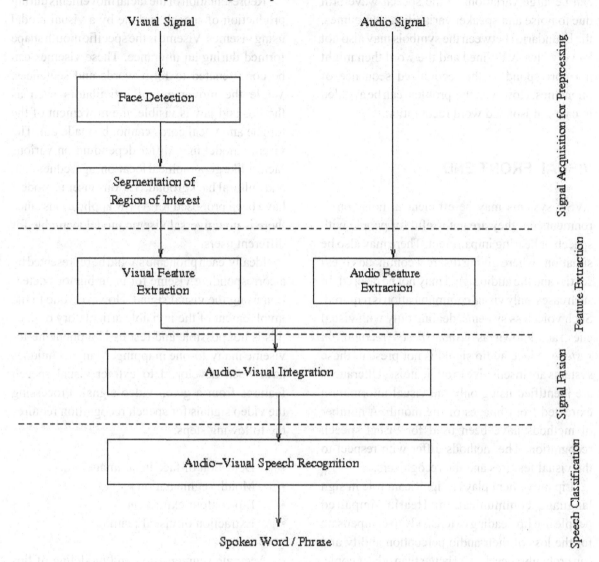

Speech recognition methods include dynamic programming, neural networks and hidden Markov models. When HMMs are used for this purpose, a unique HMM is associated with each phoneme. Each phoneme can be represented by three states: start, middle and end state. The feature vectors are mapped to a symbol using the acoustic model and each state of the HMM corresponds to a feature vector symbol.

Each phoneme is represented by a HMM. These phonemes are linked together to represent the chosen vocabulary set. During recognition, this linked network is searched for finding the given occurrence of the spoken word. Each word (sequence of phonemes) in the vocabulary will have a distinct HMM. Any spoken word is compared with all the HMM models and the HMM with the maximum score gives the recognized word.

The task of recognition is very challenging. Many words might have the same phoneme sequence. In such cases, the language structure has to be considered which uses context information to choose the correct recognized word to resemble the given grammar construct. Furthermore, there can be large variations in the speech waveform due to noise and speaker variability. Sometimes, the boundaries between the symbols may also not be very clearly defined and the word then might not correspond to the recognized sequence of phonemes. However, this problem can be avoided in cases of isolated word recognition.

VISUAL FRONT END

AVSR systems may be efficient in noisy environments but they are not useful for people with speech or hearing impairment. There may also be situations where giving discreet commands is essential and the audio signal may not be desired. In such cases, only visual communication is required. Such voiceless systems, dealing only with visual cues, are known as *visual speech recognition systems*. Since audio signal is not present, these systems are insensitive to audio noise. Utterances are identified using only the visual information extracted from images of the mouth. A number of methods have been used for visual speech recognition. The methods differ with respect to the visual features and the recognizers.

Lip movement plays a significant role in sign language communication. Hearing-impaired people use lip-reading extensively to compensate for the loss of their audio perception ability and can probably speech-read better than other people. People adept in lip-reading can identify speech by looking at the motion of the visible articulators of the speaker along with lexical, syntactic, semantic and pragmatic information (Chen, 2001). The visual signal helps to focus attention of the listener and is useful in pinpointing the speaker in a multi-speaker environment. It is also beneficial when background noise is present. When the listener lacks familiarity with the speech (as might be the case while listening to a foreign language or accented speech), the visual channel aids in comprehension (Potamianos, et al., 2003).

Representation of the facial movements during production of speech is done by a visual model using visemes. Viseme is the specific mouth shape formed during an utterance. These visemes can be concatenated to form words and sentences. While the movement of articulators such as the lips and jaw is visible, the movement of the tongue and vocal cords cannot be made out. The viseme model may differ depending on various factors like geographical location, age, education, and cultural background. Various viseme models have been proposed for AVSR applications since there is no universal viseme model available for different users.

Ideally, each phoneme should be represented by a corresponding viseme for unambiguous detection using the visual signal. However, due to the involvement of the invisible articulatory organs, this is not possible and results in a phoneme-to-viseme many-to-one mapping. Many techniques have been developed to extract visual speech features from a given video signal. Processing the video signals for speech recognition requires the following steps:

- Detection of face in an image
- Mouth segmentation
- Lip contour extraction
- Extraction of visual features

Accurate segmentation and modeling of lips and feature extraction are important tasks and affect the quality of the speechreading system since its accuracy depends heavily on the reliability of the extracted visual features.

Detection of Face

The AVSR system should be able to detect the face in a cluttered image and identify the boundary of the face. However, face detection is not a very easy task because of changes in pose (frontal, profile), facial expression, lighting conditions, occlusion, and orientation (up right, rotated). The methods normally used for face detection include traditional techniques like thresholding, colour segmentation, edge detection, and template matching or a statistical approach using neural networks or Hidden Markov Models (HMM).

Colour

Using colour for face detection has proven to be an effective method as skin colour does not show much difference between individuals or people belonging to different races (Yang & Waibel, 1996). Several studies have shown that for people of different ethnic background, the difference in their skin colour lies in the intensity and not in chrominance. The simplest method to build a model using skin colour is to define pixels using the chrominance values of the red and blue components, i.e. the C_r and C_b values from samples of skin colour pixels and then defining thresholds for values of C_r and C_b. If a pixel value lies within this range, then it is said to have skin tone. However, skin colour models are not very effective where there are changes in illumination conditions.

Skin colour can be modelled using Gaussian density functions and a mixture of Gaussians. The latter can be used because the colour histogram for the skin of people of different races does not form a unimodal but a multimodal distribution. Chen (2001) modelled the face using a Gaussian mixture model (GMM) with two Gaussian functions for the face region taking into account the face and the hair colour. The Expectation Maximization (EM) algorithm (Dempster, Laird, & Rubin, 1977) was then used to parameterize the GMM. A single Gaussian function was used for the background.

Facial Features

Facial features can also be used to detect faces. These techniques use global features like colour, size and shape to locate faces and then work on detailed features like hair, eyebrows, nose and mouth.

Pixels belonging to the skin region are grouped together using clustering algorithms or connected component analysis. An elliptical or oval shape is used to define a face. Local features are then applied for verification. Colour segmentation can also be done in HSV (Hue-Saturation-Value) space to locate the skin regions. Connected components are determined and each connected component that can be approximated by an ellipse is selected as a face and verified by local features. Clustering techniques can also be applied to detect faces. A small window is passed over all portions of the image and it is checked whether a face exists in that sub-image or not.

Templates

Templates are also applied for face detection. Generally, a standard face pattern is parameterized by a function. For a given image, the correlation values with the defined template are computed for the face contour and the face features like eyes, nose, and mouth. Detection of face depends upon the match in the correlation values. However, this method does not work for variations in scale, shape and pose.

Deformable templates can also be used to track the face. The facial features can be described by parameterized templates (Yuille, 1991). An energy function defines a link between edges, peaks and valleys in the input image to corresponding parameters in the template. By minimizing the energy function of the parameters, the best fit of the model can be determined.

Kwon and Lobo (1994) have described a system based on snakes (Kass, Witkin, & Terropoulos, 1988) and templates (Hallinan, Cohen, & Yuille, 1989). First, the image is convolved with a blurring filter. The edges are then enhanced using a morphological operator. Small curve segments are eliminated using a modified *n*-pixel snake, where *n* is very small. Each face is approximated by an ellipse. A dominant ellipse can be determined by applying Hough transform on the remaining snakelets. The ellipses have a set of four parameters describing them. For each ellipse the detailed features can be found using a method similar to deformable templates. If there is a significant match between the detected features and the features on the face template, then a face is detected.

Appearance-Based

In appearance-based methods, statistical analysis and machine learning techniques are used to determine face and non-face images. Distribution models or discriminant functions are used for face detection. Appearance based methods can be defined using a probabilistic approach also. An image or feature vector is taken as a random variable and characterized as face or non-face depending upon the class-conditional density functions. These can be classified using Bayesian classification or maximum likelihood.

Another approach is to find a discriminant function between face and non-face classes. Image patterns are projected to a lower dimensional space and a discriminant function is formed. Recently, Support Vector Machines (SVM) have come up as alternative techniques. These project the image patterns to a higher dimensional space and form a decision surface between face and non-face.

Locating the Region of Interest

The *Region Of Interest* (ROI) is generally the mouth region which has to be located once the face has been detected in the image. The ROI can also include the jaw and the cheeks. It can also be a three dimensional rectangle containing adjacent ROIs for dynamic speech information. Techniques for analyzing mouth shapes are often based on edge extraction or colour segmentation plus deformable templates. Graf, Cosatto, and Potamianos (1997) use a combination of shape and texture analysis, colour segmentation and motion information to first locate the whole face. Then each individual facial feature is analyzed. The pixel-based method uses the information around the lip region. Even though the accurate lip contour is not obtained but this method gives density information of tooth and tongue. The model based method extracts the lip contour and uses some features. This gives more accurate recognition results.

The mouth can also be located by using triangulation with eyes or nose. The approach used by Chen (2001) to model the face is applied for lip tracking also by modeling the lip region using a GMM with three Gaussian functions (for the three different colours of the tongue, teeth, and the mouth interior). The non-lip region is modelled by a simple Gaussian function.

A system developed by Saitoh and Konishi (2006) uses video and thermal images for lip reading. Lip detection is done by video sequences and the image thermal density gives the surface temperature. Since images are not synchronized, time and spatial synchronization methods are applied. Lip regions are detected from both images. Then, an eigenimage waveform is computed and DP matching is applied.

Colour

Many research studies have shown that colour is an important factor in face analysis. Prior studies have revealed that human skin colour belonging to different races falls in a compact region in colour spaces. Different colour spaces include RGB, HSV, YC_rC_b, YIQ, and CIELAB. Determining the shape of the mouth using colour is usually very difficult since there is little difference between the lip colour and the surrounding skin. To overcome this problem, the mouth area is divided into segments and a lip-clustering algorithm determines the shape of the lips. The interior of the mouth is also analysed using intensity cross-sections. This provides information about the visibility of teeth and tongue.

Lip search can be based on transforming an image to a linear combination of red, green and blue chrominance components of the RGB colour space. Sadeghi, Kittler, and Messer (2002) described a Gaussian mixture model of the RGB values of the pixels for lip detection. Model parameters are selected using a modified version of predictive validation technique. Dargham and Chekima (2006) developed a new method called maximum intensity normalization where the intensity of the colour image is first normalized. The skin regions are determined by histogram thresholding the C_{rb} and C_{rg} chrominance components. The skin regions are then segmented into lip and non-lip regions. A similar technique can also be applied using fuzzy clustering for extraction of lip contour.

Thresholding in the HSV space is also used to segment lips from the face. However, hue is generally very noisy as low values of hue lie close to high values and this hinders the accuracy of segmentation. In addition, for certain speakers, the hue values of the skin and lip region are almost similar and it is difficult to segment them using thresholding.

Edge Content

Finding an area with high edge-content in the lower half of the face region can also be used to find the mouth. Hybrid edges can be combined with colour and intensity information, for detecting the mouth region. To make the model more flexible, a cubic polynomial is used instead of parabolas introduced by Yuille (1991).

Edge detection can be done using the gradient or Laplacian method. The gradient method detects edges by taking into account the maxima and minima in the first derivative of the image. Roberts, Sobel and Prewitt operators come under this category. The Laplacian method, on the other hand, detects edges by looking for zero crossings in the second derivative of the image. The Marr-Hildreth algorithm uses the Laplacian method.

Learning-Based Methods

A Radial Basis Function Neural Network (RBF NN) mouth tracking system has been proposed by Hui, Seng, and Tse (2004). The conventional approach of finding the mouth centre using a linear Kalman filter is replaced by RBF NN. The approach combines the universal approximation property and straightforward computation of neural networks along with parallel processing to develop a fast mouth tracking system.

Active Contour Models

The movement of the lips is also important for machine lip-reading. Active contour models (Kass, Witkin, & Terropoulos, 1988) and work well on static images of the mouth. Some researchers have used optical flow to study lip movement which processes the result of snakes in the previous frame and the optical flow between the previous frame and the target frame. For a fast and precise extraction of lip shape from a series of images, the modified sampled active contour model (Sugahara, Shinchi, Kishino, & Konishi, 2000) is presented which is operated by forces that act on the contour points. From the coordinate of these contour points, new parameters for recognition are obtained and recognized by a 4-state HMM.

Extraction of Lip Features

Accuracy and consistency are two important aspects while extracting lip features. Useful features extracted from the lips are sent to recognition methods for speech recognition. The features usually extracted from the lip region are usually, the general mouth shape, the lip corner pair, width, and the height of the lips. Dynamic features and inter-frame motion may also be extracted. These features are generally taken from the lip area or obtained from the histogram of the image. If the profile view of the lip is being considered, lip protrusion might also be an important feature parameter.

Sometimes the dimensionality of the extracted features might be too large for statistical modeling. Many transforms can be applied to reduce the dimensionality but at the same time preserving the speechreading information. Some of the commonly used transforms are the discrete cosine transform (Ahmed, Natarajan, & Rao, 1974), discrete wavelet transform (Mallat, 1999), principal component analysis (Jolliffe, 1986), Hadamard and Haar transform (Rao, Narasimhan, & Revuluri, 1975), and Linear Discriminant Analysis (Fisher, 1936).

Principal Component Analysis (PCA) is a useful statistical technique that is applied for image compression and finding patterns in data of high dimension. From the given multi-dimensional data, eigenvectors and eigenvalues are calculated for the covariance matrix. The eigenvalues, placed highest to lowest (ev_1, ev_2...ev_n), give the principal components in order of significance. The lower order components can be ignored and will not cause much loss of data if their values are small. The new feature space will then be along the eigenvectors of the top m components. These are multiplied with the original data set to get the new data. The transformed data is expressed in terms of the patterns between the original data. The greatest variance by any projection of data is represented by the first principal component.

The *Discrete Cosine Transform* (DCT) converts a signal into its elementary frequency components. It is widely used in image compression. It is similar to Discrete Fourier Transform and transforms a image from the spatial domain to the frequency domain. This helps separate the image into parts of differing importance with respect to the image's visual quality. Each element of the transformed list is the dot product of the input list and a n x n orthogonal matrix whose rows are the basis vectors. Higher frequencies are often small enough to be neglected with little visible distortion.

Many techniques exist for mouth feature extraction. Early research worked on gray images and obtained the lip corner from the histogram.

Edge detecting operators like Prewitt and Sobel are used for enhancement of the image and obtaining the lip edges. However, this method does not work effectively for bearded speakers. This led to working in colour spaces like RGB and HSV. Application of pixel-based techniques (Movellan & Mineiro, 1998) causes minimal alteration in the original image.

The visual features that are extracted from mouth images for identification of speech can be broadly classified into two main categories (Luettin & Thacker, 1997):

- **Top-down approach (shape based):** Features are estimated from model parameters
- **Bottom-up approach (intensity based):** Features are estimated from the image itself

The shape-based features use the geometric shape of the mouth and lips and are represented by a small number of parameters. Examples of this are Active Shape Models (ASM) (Cootes, Taylor, Cooper, & Graham, 1995) which fit a statistical shape model of the lip to the images. This approach is more resistant to image noise and camera angle but do not contain information of other speech articulators. The Active Appearance Models (AAM) are an extension to the ASM since they combine the shape model with the grey levels in the mouth region. Other model-based techniques are active contours and deformable templates. Using this approach for feature extraction however, leads to loss of information due to the data reduction involved.

Intensity based features are derived directly from the intensity values of the pixels of the mouth area. These features can represent visual data in and around the mouth cavity. Here, accurate modelling of the lips is not required. Intensity-based features have a much higher dimensionality and require dimension reduction techniques leading to computational disadvantage. In addition, normalization because of lighting, translation, and other factors is more difficult compared to the shape-based approach.

In Rockwell and Chan (2001), feature extraction is done by combining the two types of features. The largest elliptical connected region with expected hue values is identified as the lip region and tracking is done based on locations of steepest gradient in the image using optimal combination of all RGB components. The geometric-base features, including the width and height of lips and their temporal derivatives are estimated. The pixel-based features are defined by the vertical intensity profile of a subset of pixels delimited by the tracked boundary of the lips. This set of pixels varies as the lip boundary changes during speech. The vertical profile is mapped to a feature vector. Both the shape-based and pixel-based features are then combined. It has been shown that the centre profile contains information about the appearance and spatial relationship of the teeth and tongue which leads to higher recognition accuracy. This hybrid approach of combining both the features and using their normalized values for classification showed improved results.

In Matthews, Cootes, Bangham, Cox, and Harvey (2002), the top-down and bottom-up approach have both been used. The top-down approach uses an Active Shape Model (ASM) to trace the lip contour, determined using Point Distribution Model (PDM). Points in this space are directly used as features. The grey-level values are taken from a shape-normalized image. The addition of both the models shows considerable improvement in lip-reading performance. They also present a new bottom-up approach of applying a non-linear scale-space image transform to a domain where the scale, amplitude and position information are separated. This gives a method of extracting visual features, which are invariant to these factors. The visual features are recognized using the Hidden Markov Model classifier.

Yau, Kumar, and Arjunan (2006) use two different non-acoustic modalities for identification of visual speech. Consonants are easier to see

and are much easier to identify using visual data. Absolute values of Zernike moments are used as visual features as these are invariant to rotational changes. Surface Electromyogram (SEMG) determines the movement of select facial muscles as facial muscles are less discernible during vowel articulation. Both features are classified using a multilayer perceptron artificial neural network.

In Gordan, Kotropoulos, and Pitas (2002), the classification of mouth shapes to viseme classes has been done using Support Vector Machines. The temporal sequences of visemes are used to build visual word models, which can be implemented by Viterbi lattices with each node generating the emission probability of a viseme at a certain time instant.

The vector-quantized image of the mouth can be used as a feature vector. Gravier, Potamianos, and Neti (2002) combined the audio and visual features to form a joint feature vector. Similarly, Chen (2001) has cascaded the sixteenth order LPC coefficients of the audio features and the visual features with proper weights to create a joint audio-visual feature vector. The optimal weighting depends upon the SNR of the audio signal. For a higher SNR, audio features are given more weightage and for a lower SNR acoustic signal, visual features are given more weightage. The size of the feature vectors can be reduced by Principal Component Analysis (PCA) or Singular Valued Decomposition (SVD). Reduction in vector size is especially beneficial while training neural networks.

Yashwanth, Mahendrakar, and David (2004) have presented an AVSR system using Coupled Hidden Markov Model (CHMM) model for fusion of audio and video modalities. The extraction of audio features of the input speech was done using Mel Frequency Cepstral Coefficients (MFCC). The face was detected by the Haar face detector. Linear Discriminant Analysis was then done to assign the pixels in the mouth region to the lip and face classes. The CHMM parameters were then estimated with the help of the Expectation

Maximization (EM) algorithm. PCA was applied to map the gray level pixels into a 32 dimensional feature space. The resulting vector of size 32 was standardized using Feature Mean Normalization (FMN).

Recently, a lip contour extraction system based on manifold has been developed by Yaling and Minghui (2008). It works on a colour image and gets the lip contour directly. The system takes into consideration that the mouth area has high edge content and the change in lip contour is bigger than in other area. Another inner contour based lip moving feature extraction method (Chen, Deng, Wang, & Huang, 2006) combines the lip area extraction in chromatic colour space with lip contour extraction using Laplacian of Gaussian operator. Three quadratic curves are used to represent the upper and lower inner lip contour which reduces the feature vector. The parameters are then computed using the nearest-neighbour interpolation algorithm. A recent technique (Saitoh, Morishita, & Konishi, 2008) describes a lip reading method by first applying the Active Appearance Model (AAM) to simultaneously extract the outer and inner lip contour. Five regions—external lip, internal lip, lip, intraoral, and tooth—are then described and features obtained from all of them. A new trajectory feature is introduced which is a time change of n features expressed as an n-dimensional trajectory of the lip motion. HMM is utilized for recognition. For an *n*-dimensional trajectory matching, *n*-dimensional Dynamic Programming (DP) matching is done.

Lip region extraction can also be done using active contour models like snakes and Active Shape Models (ASM). However, if the initial position is far from the edge of the lips, active contours might lead to inaccurate results. Dupont and Luettin (2000) used the active shape model to extract lip features. He also compared the static images with features having time varying information also. The templates can also be generalized for rotation and asymmetry by minimizing their energy function (Chen, 2001). Active shape

models have a limitation when there is not much difference between lip colour and the colour of the face or when the lip edges are not very clear.

Deformable templates are used to extract structural information. The shape of the template depends on the object to be located. While snakes work on a closed contour, deformable templates model the outer contour of the mouth by two intersecting parabolas.

RECOGNITION METHODS

Recognition refers to the pattern matching algorithms applied for recognition of the phonemes and visemes. The feature vectors extracted from the audio and visual cues are sent to classifiers for recognition. Some early automatic speech recognition systems were based on Dynamic Time Warping (DTW). This algorithm measures the similarities between two sequences which may vary in time or speed. However, in recent research, Hidden Markov Model (HMM) and Neural Networks (NN) are two popular recognition methods.

Hidden Markov Models are statistical models that can generate speech (sequences of spectral or cepstral vectors) using a number of states for each model. The state transition probabilities are the parameters of the models. The means, variances, and mixture weights characterize the state output distributions. HMMs are inherently rate invariant and very useful in speaker independent ASR systems. In addition, large amount of visual data can be processed using HMMs because it can be trained for recognition using efficient algorithms. However, HMMs are fairly complex and require a large amount of training data to optimize the model parameters.

Neural networks have the advantage of their ability to generalize from large training sets and not make any data assumptions. The only disadvantage of using NNs is their slow trainability and variance due to rate. Recognition methods often influence the type of integration methods that will be used. Recent research has also shown good results with a Support Vector Machine (SVM) classifier. This is a discrimination-based statistical algorithm. It tries to minimize an upper bound on the generalization error. Due to its good ability to generalize, it shows good performance in speech recognition tasks.

The first audio-visual system was developed by Petajan, Bischoff, Bodoff, and Brooke (1988). In this, the mouth image was thresholded into black and white. This binary image was analyzed to derive mouth open area, perimeter, height, and width. These parameters were sent for recognition. First speech was processed by an acoustic recognizer and then, these recognized words were sent to the visual recognizer. In further research, they used the binary mouth images themselves as visual features instead of deriving features from them. These images were classified using clustering algorithms and the sequence of images was compared using dynamic time warping. This system was later used by Goldschen (1993). He used the features from binary images and their time-derivatives and fed them to a HMM based recognition system. He showed in his study that time derivative information about the lips i.e. the lip movements, as compared to lip positions give better recognition results.

Recently, a new method by Lv, Jiang, Zhao, and Hou (2007) describes a multi-stream asynchrony Dynamic Bayesian Network models for Audio-Visual Speech Recognition (AVSR). The results demonstrate that the asynchrony description between audio and visual stream is important for AVSR system and the proposed model has the best performance for the task of continuous Audio-Visual (AV) speech recognition.

Potamianos et al. (2003) have used the joint feature vectors of the audio and visual features to train an HMM based recognizer. Chen (2001) has built an HMM with five states, each having an observation probability distribution modelled as a mixture of three Gaussian functions. For each word to be recognized the likelihood of each model is calculated and the model with the highest likelihood is selected. The HMM is trained for each word based on the joint audio-visual feature vectors with clean speech data and tested with noisy speech data.

Yuhas, Goldstein, and Sejnowski (1989) converted the gray scale image of the mouth region to be used as a feature vector. He then trained the neural network to recognize the acoustic signal based on images of the mouth. This estimated spectrum was combined with the measured spectrum and fed to another recognition system. Time-Delayed Neural Networks (TDNNs) are recognition systems that also take into account the temporal variations of the mouth features. Stork and Hennecke (1996) used TDNNs for recognition and used both the early and late integration methods for the audio and video signals. They also found that late integration produced slightly better results than an early integration strategy.

INTEGRATION OF AUDIO AND VISUAL SIGNALS

Audio and video signals can be integrated using the Direct Identification (DI) technique, also known as *Early Integration* or by Separate Identification (SI) technique, referred to as *Late Integration*. The main difference is basically in the timing of integration and the representations used.

Early Integration

In the early integration method, both the audio and visual data are combined at an early stage and the combined feature vector is fed into the recognition system. A single classifier is trained on the concatenated vector of audio and visual features. The recognition engine decides the important features. The signals are processed by a bimodal classifier and a phoneme is selected.

Late Integration

In late integration technique, the audio and video signals are processed separately and their individual feature vectors are then combined and sent to the recognition system. Parallel identification processes are used to identify the signal in each modality. A hypothesized phoneme is then produced from the fused signal. One possibility while using late integration could be where the audio and visual signals are processed by separate NNs produce two feature vectors, which can be fed into another NN, which will integrate them. If HMMs are being used, then the resulting log-likelihoods are combined to produce the final result. This method poses some difficulties. If the accuracy of the result of the fused signals is less than the accuracy of both the individual systems, then fusion of the two signals may lead to catastrophic fusion (Movellan & Mineiro, 1998). Research has also been done to give weightage to one signal when the other signal is not very strong. It is desirable that the stream exponents (weights) be independent of the utterance-level or frame-level. This can be done by obtaining an estimate of the local environment conditions using signal-based approaches like the audio SNR or voicing index. In addition, statistical indicators can be used to capture the reliability of each stream at a local frame level.

It has been shown recently that an AVSR system based on late integration can also be improved by enhancing the performance of the three parts composing the system (Lee & Park, 2008). The performance of the visual subsystem is improved by using the stochastic optimization method for the HMM as the speech recognizer. A new method considers the joint distribution of frames by the Gaussian Mixture Model (GMM) enabling the HMMs to capture the dynamic characteristics of speech. The acoustic and the visual subsystems are effectively integrated by using trainable neural networks which can automatically determine appropriate integration weights.

A new system (Koiwa, Nakadai, & Imura, 2007) proposes a new AVSR system based on two approaches. One is audio-visual integration based on missing feature theory to cope with missing or unreliable audio and visual features for recognition. Second is a biologically-inspired approach, that is, phoneme and viseme grouping based on coarse-to-fine recognition. This visual feature vector is fused with the audio feature vector as a 29-dimensional audio-visual feature vector and sent to Audio-Visual Missing Feature Mask Generation and Coarse Speech Recognizer. An AV missing feature mask is used to cover unreliable features in an AV feature vector, and it has 29 mask values corresponding to the AV features. Thus, it consists of two kinds of masks: audio missing feature mask and visual missing feature mask. These masks are independently estimated.

AUDIO-VISUAL DATABASE

Typically, an audio-visual database for a speech recognition system should contain samples of all speech sounds of the target language. It should also include the dialects and foreign accents. It is desirable to have a large vocabulary set. The subjects should cover both the genders—male and female, of different ages and educational levels. The microphone settings should be varied, ranging from head-mounted, distant to mobile phones. Various noise signals can be added to the speech signal, also incorporating simultaneous speaker situations. The video sequences should cover different facial expressions, cases of bearded and spectacled subjects, with varying illumination conditions and poses.

Though many speechreading systems have been developed in recent times, it has been difficult to compare them, as they have not been tested on a common audio-visual database. In contrast to the audio-only corpora, very few databases are available for AVSR. This is because audio-visual corpora face additional challenges of database collection and storage. The common tasks generally include recognition of letters, isolated words, closed-set sentences, digits etc. Most of these datasets suffer from a few shortcomings as they have been developed with limited resources. They contain small number of subjects, have small duration, and generally have a small vocabulary set.

Some datasets commonly used are IBM-LVCSR, AV-TIMIT, XM2VTS, CUAVE, Tulips, etc. The *IBM-LVCSR* corpus is suitable for Large Vocabulary Continuous Speech Recognition (LVCSR) tasks which is the ultimate goal of speech recognition. It is produced by IBM but not commercially available. It contains speech samples from 290 subjects. The *CUAVE* database from the Clemson University is freely available for all universities to use. It contains isolated/continuous digits spoken by 37 speakers. *AV-TIMIT* has continuous sentences of 223 speakers. *XM2VTS* is a continuous digit database of 295 subjects. *Tulips* contains isolated digits spoken by 12 subjects.

PROPOSED LIP READING SYSTEM

In our lip reading system, we outline a speech recognition system based on visual cues only. As stated earlier, this requires extraction of visual features from image sequences of speech. We have primarily focused on lip movement. The steps involved for classification of speech using features derived from lip images are as follows:

- Lip segmentation.
- Contour detection.
- Location of key points on lip boundary.
- Feature extraction.
- Determination of significant features.
- Classification of the spoken word using the visual feature vector.

The proposed system (refer Figure 2) presents a model-based outer lip contour detection algorithm which uses thresholding and edge information to segment the lips (Singh, Laxmi, Gupta, & Gaur, 2010). The movement of the lips is characterized using key points on the contour and six independent cubic curves defining the lip boundary. Geometrical parameters are extracted from the contour. Temporal derivatives of these parameters are also taken into account. The coefficients of the cubic curves are also taken as part of the feature vector. Significant features are determined and used to build *n*-gram models. These new feature vectors are used for classification of speech.

Lip Contour Detection

For extraction of parameters from the lip region, the lip area is to be located and the lip boundary is to be obtained. Lip segmentation is not an easy

Figure 2. Proposed lip model

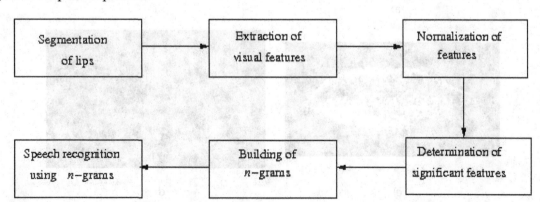

task as skin and lip colours are not easily distinguishable in RGB space. As lip segmentation is not our primary objective, we have applied blue colour on lips while recording our database. This gives us better segmentation of lips in the HSV space. Our approach is as follows:

- The RGB image is converted into the HSV space, as shown in Figure 3. Hue has good discriminative power and has well-separated values for the skin and the lips. Segmentation of the lips from the skin is done using thresholding techniques.
- The segmented image is subjected to morphological operations like erosion and dilation using appropriate structuring elements.
- Edge detection is now applied to the image. We have used Sobel operator as it is fast and has smoothing along the edge direction, which avoids noisy edges.
- Connectivity analysis is done after applying edge detection methods. It is seen that

after the application of suitable morphological operations, the largest connected component will give the outer contour of the lips.

- From the extracted outer boundary of the lips, six key points are detected which give important information about the lip shape. Six independent cubic curves are constructed using these key points.

Key Points Detection and Feature Extraction

The visual features extracted from the contour should best convey the information regarding the shape of the lip during movement. For this purpose, we define the lip boundary using key points and curves. Eveno, Caplier, and Coulon (2004) have proposed a flexible lip model made of cubic curves. This method is modified in Alizadeh, Boostani, and Asadpour (2008) by using four cubic curves. We have defined the lip boundary by means of six cubic curves $C_1, C_2, ..., C_6$.

Figure 3. Extraction of lip contour a) RGB image, b) HSV image, c) segmented lips, d) lip contour

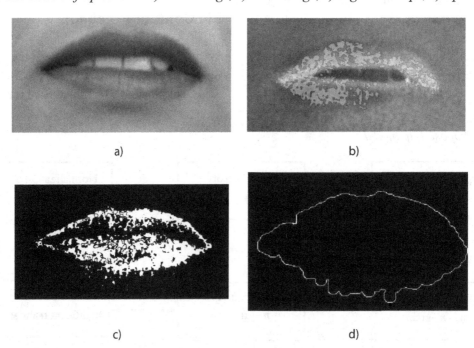

a)

b)

c)

d)

Figure 4. Extracted visual parameters

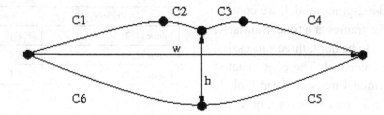

Key points and cubic curves
C1..C6 are cubic curves
h = total height of lips
w = total width of lips

- On the extracted outer contour of the lip, we detect six key points giving important information about the lip shape. The key points are shown in Figure 4.
- The key points are the two corners of the lip, the bottom-most point of the lower lip and three points on the arch of the top lip.
- These key points are used to construct six independent cubic curves.
- The total height and width of the lip is extracted from the contour. Their ratio and temporal derivatives are also taken as features.
- The lip contour is modelled using six cubic curves, each represented by four coefficients. These coefficients are also included in the feature vector. The extracted visual parameters are shown in Figure 4.
- The complete set of the visual feature vector consists of the width of the lip (w), its height (h), ratio of height to width ($\alpha = h/w$), temporal derivatives of width (dw) and height (dh) and the coefficients of the six cubic curves. This results in a feature vector of 29 parameters for each frame.

Building *n*-Gram Models

n-grams are sequences of substrings with length *n*. Their usage is prevalent in the area of pattern recognition (Li, Wang, Stolfo, & Herzog, 2005). Motivated by their success in other fields, we propose the same approach for building *n*-grams using the extracted visual features.

- The obtained feature vector contains actual values of the parameters. This data is normalized speaker-wise by dividing all values of a particular parameter with the largest value in that set. Different combinations of the normalized features are classified using multiple classifiers in WEKA to narrow down to significant features. These significant features are used for building *n*-gram models.
- In our approach, we have concatenated the frames using a sliding-window, where, each frame is associated with the next few frames of the speech utterance as explained below. The new feature vectors so formed are used for recognition.

Let a speech utterance contain *f* number of frames. A feature vector is obtained from each frame. Let each frame *i* be associated with feature vector $[V_i]$. For a complete set of *f* frames for a particular utterance, we have a set of feature vectors, $[V_1][V_2]...[V_f]$.

Consider the following example. Let there be 8 frames in a speech sample. The feature vectors for these frames are: $[V_1]$, $[V_2]$, $[V_3]$, $[V_4]$, $[V_5]$, $[V_6]$, $[V_7]$, $[V_8]$. To build a 2-gram model, we concatenate two successive frames at a time. Similarly, if a 3-gram model is to be built, three successive frames will be concatenated. The concatenated frames for a 2-gram model are as shown in Table 1.

Similarly, for the 3-gram model, the new feature vectors will be $[V_1V_2V_3]$, $[V_2V_3V_4]$, $[V_3V_4V_5]$, $[V_4V_5V_6]$, $[V_5V_6V_7]$, $[V_6V_7V_8]$.

- A normalized combination of significant features from each frame is used to build 1-gram to 8-gram models for each speech sample.

Classification of Spoken Word

Two sets of experiments are performed for classification of speech using the *n*-gram feature vector. HMMs have proved invaluable in speech recognition. Considering this as a typical pattern recognition problem, classification is also done by using different data mining algorithms.

- The feature vectors formed with the *n*-gram models are used for training the Hidden Markov Model. This is done with the HTK Toolkit (HTK Toolkit homepage). The trained model is then tested with the training set.
- Each *n*-gram model, built with the normalized top features, is also used for classification of speech, using data mining algorithms available in WEKA (University of Waikato homepage), a data mining tool widely used by researchers.

EXPERIMENTAL SETUP AND RESULT ANALYSIS

Speech samples of twelve speakers were collected. Ten speakers were female and two were male (one with moustache). The preliminary

Table 1. 2-gram model frames

Frames	New Feature Vector
Frame (1, 2)	$[V_1V_2]$
Frame (2, 3)	$[V_2V_3]$
Frame (7, 8)	$[V_7V_8]$

vocabulary consists of three digits—*zero, one,* and *two*. Each digit is uttered three times by each speaker. Speakers began and end the utterance with the mouth in the closed position. Recording was done under moderate illumination and the focus of the camera was on the lower part of the speaker's face. A total of 108 samples were collected. The framing of the videos was done at 30 frames/second. From each frame, obtained from the speech samples, lip contour parameters were derived. The 29 parameters extracted from the lip boundary form a feature vector for each image frame.

The raw data was then normalized for each speaker. Using the normalized data, different combinations of features were tested using the WEKA toolkit. These are Multilayer Perceptron, Random Forest and IB1. The combination of the features $[C_5 C_6 h w \alpha \, dh \, dw]$ gives best recognition results. It is also observed that there is very little loss of efficiency if the curve coefficients are not considered. To reduce space and computational efforts, the significant features are narrowed down to $[h w \alpha \, dh \, dw]$. This gives us a final feature vector containing $5n$ features compared to the $29n$ feature vector for any *n*-gram model. These features are used to build *n*-gram models for each utterance. We built eight models with $n = \{1, 2, ..., 8\}$.

Each *n*-gram model was tested using the classifiers. The new feature vectors from all frames of an utterance were fed as an input to the same classifiers. For testing purpose, the 10-fold cross validation method was employed since the dataset is not very large. This creates subsets of the supplied dataset. At each test time, it uses all but one subset for training and tests with the remaining subset.

In the second set of experiments, the *n*-gram models were classified with a 3-state, left-to-right Hidden Markov Model using the HTK toolkit. Out of the 108 speech datasets available, 81 speech samples (from 9 subjects) are used for training and 27 samples (from 3 subjects) are used for testing.

Evaluation Metrics

The results were analyzed using the parameters True Positive Rate (TPR), False Positive Rate (FPR), and Precision (P).

- *True Positives (TP)* is the number of correctly identified speech samples of a particular word.
- *False Positives (FP)* is positively classified speech samples, which are not actually true.
- *True Negatives (TN)* is speech samples, which are correctly classified as belonging to another class.
- *False Negatives (FN)* is speech samples falsely classified as belonging to another class.
- *Precision (P)* is also known as the Positive Predictive Value (PPV). It is the ratio of True Positives to the total number of samples classified as belonging to a particular class (sum of TP and FP).
- *True Positive Rate (TPR)* is the ratio of True Positives and the total number of samples belonging to that particular class (sum of TP and FN).
- *False Positive Rate (FPR)* is the ratio of False Positives and the total number of speech samples belonging to another class (sum of FP and TN).

Results and Analysis

A speaker-independent lip-reading system, based on *n*-gram modeling of visual features is trained

and tested for speech recognition. Five normalized significant features are used to build *n*-gram models and used for speech classification.

Data Mining Algorithms

The *n*-gram models are tested with three classifiers. The best results are obtained with Multilayer Perceptron (MLP) classifier since it takes advantage of any redundancy in the training set and to detect patterns in a complex dataset. First three columns of Table 1 show the results for the classifiers: Random Forest, Multilayer Perceptron and IB1, for $n = \{1, 2,..., 8\}$. The columns give the values of the parameters *TPR*, *FPR* and *P*. As can be seen, for the 8 - gram model, the Multilayer Perceptron classifier gives a classification accuracy of 74.92% with a *FPR* value of 0.13. It is seen that there is a gradual improvement in the recognition accuracy as the value of *n* goes on increasing.

Hidden Markov Model

The *n*-gram models formed from the normalized feature vectors of each speech utterance are used to train a 3-state HMM. The results of classification using the HMM are shown in Table 2. As can be seen, the efficiency of recognition with HMM improves as the value of *n* increases.

In Matthews et al. (2002), continuous hidden Markov models have been used for classification of letters *A-Z*. The best accuracy reported for visual-only recognition is 44.6%. In Yau et al. (2006), nine viseme based consonants have been recognized using artificial neural network and an accuracy of 84.7% has been mentioned. This system was trained and tested for a single speaker. Alizadeh et al. (2008) report a minimum word error rate of 44.88% when testing on continuously pronounced French digits from *zero* to *nine* using HMM. In Da Silveira, Facon, and Borges (2003), the average success rate reported is 35% while classifying ten digits in Brazilian Portuguese

Table 2. Speech recognition results with 1-8 gram models. Values are for classifiers—random forest, MLP, IB1, and HMM.

	Random Forest			MLP			IB1			HMM
n	TPR	FPR	P(%)	TPR	FPR	P(%)	TPR	FPR	P(%)	Accuracy(%)
1	0.60	0.20	60.00	0.55	0.23	54.93	0.61	0.19	60.59	25.92
2	0.59	0.21	59.26	0.59	0.21	59.92	0.61	0.19	60.84	45.00
3	0.62	0.19	61.84	0.64	0.18	64.06	0.61	0.20	60.46	59.25
4	0.62	0.19	62.31	0.65	0.18	65.12	0.61	0.20	60.47	62.67
5	0.63	0.19	63.29	0.67	0.17	67.08	0.62	0.19	61.61	62.67
6	0.66	0.18	66.05	0.69	0.16	68.87	0.62	0.19	61.95	62.96
7	0.67	0.17	67.01	0.72	0.14	72.00	0.65	0.18	64.95	70.37
8	0.68	0.17	68.26	0.75	0.13	74.92	0.67	0.17	66.73	74.07

using four lip distances as features. Recent literature (Matthews, et al., 2002) indicates that for a small vocabulary, single speaker and controlled conditions, positive classification figures of 40% are the highest. Our proposed *n*-gram model shows encouraging and comparable results even when the training dataset is not very large.

FACTORS AFFECTING PERFORMANCE

The performance of AVSR systems is usually specified by their accuracy and speed. The accuracy is given by the Word Error Rate (WER) while the speed is measured in terms of real time factor. Recognition systems which claim 98%-99% accuracy are often based on performance of the system in optimal conditions which include a noise-free environment and the testing data matching the training data.

System performance can be affected by many factors. The quality of the captured audio and visual data varies over time. Noise bursts, face occlusion or other viewing conditions play an important role and may change the reliability of a particular modality. Poor lighting can make it difficult to detect the shape of the mouth region. It may also affect judgement about the other visible speech articulators. The distance between

the speaker and the listener is also an important factor. As the distance increases, important visual cues may not be very clear and defined. The viewing angle can also affect lip-reading. It has been shown by Neely (1956), that a frontal view of the speaker gives better results than using a profile view or a view from any other angle. Lack of training can also be a hindrance. Co-articulation, which is the process by which one sound affects the production of neighbouring sounds, can also affect the quality of lip-reading. According to this study by Berger (1972), the place of articulation may not be fixed, but may depend on context. He suggests that the tongue may be in different positions for the /r/ sound in `art' and `arc.' This would affect the visibility of the tongue and thus recognition accuracy.

Detection of lip movement can help to increase the performance of speech recognition systems. The lip location is extracted from the image in different frames and a combination of lip features from these frames is fed into the classifier. The varying nature of the speech signal can be characterized by using temporal derivatives of feature by feature differences between successive frames. It is a better idea to use differences between every *k* frame as neighbouring frames might carry similar information and subtracting them would result in the loss of significant information.

Though the tongue is an important part of human speech production, it's position is generally not taken into account during visual speech recognition due to the problems associated with tracking this invisible articulator. Some phonemes, for example, /d/ and /k/, are not easy to distinguish by lip shapes alone as the movement of the tongue plays an important part in it. If a geometric and kinematic model can describe the movement of the tongue, then it would lead to improved visual speech recognition. However, the tongue is a complex and flexible organ with highly articulated and irregular motions.

SUMMARY

This chapter discussed in brief the basic methods used in audio-visual speech recognition. Our modified visual feature speech recognition system gives encouraging results with a small database. Improved results using the n-gram model motivate us to find an optimal value of n. We would like to increase the size of the dataset and incorporate other visual features to check the efficiency of this model.

Much progress has been done in the past few years but these have worked well only in controlled environments. Applicability in real-world scenario involving multiple speakers, background noise, and changes in speaker position is still not very clearly defined in the present research domain. Optimum techniques that may yield improved results are yet to be explored. In addition, developing techniques for pose and illumination invariant feature extraction is an open challenge for researchers for Human Computer Interaction. Certain key issues to be used in the design are still under investigation. The practicality of combining both audio and visual signals for speech perception is emerging as a challenging area as extraction of visual cues places an increased demand on the cost, storage, and computer processing and this needs better understanding of the underlying models and parameters. Real-time speech recognition on a large vocabulary set of a large number of speakers is another open issue. Research in these areas will result in a robust system for human-computer interaction.

ACKNOWLEDGMENT

The authors are grateful to the Department of Science and Technology, Government of India, for supporting this project.

REFERENCES

Ahmed, N., Natarajan, T., & Rao, K. R. (1974). Discrete cosine transform. *IEEE Transactions on Computers*, *23*(1), 90–93. doi:10.1109/T-C.1974.223784

Alizadeh, S., Boostani, R., & Asadpour, V. (2008). Lip feature extraction and reduction for HMM-based visual speech recognition systems. In *Proceedings of the 9th International Conference on Signal Processing (ICSP 2008)*, (pp. 561-564). ICSP.

Berger, K. W. (1972). *Speechreading*. Baltimore, MD: National Educational Press.

Chen, T. (2001). Audiovisual speech processing. *IEEE Signal Processing Magazine*, *18*(1), 9–21. doi:10.1109/79.911195

Chen, Q. C., Deng, G. H., Wang, X. L., & Huang, H. J. (2006). An inner contour based lip moving feature extraction method for Chinese speech. In *Proceedings of the International Conference on Machine Learning and Cybernetics*, (pp. 3859-3864). IEEE.

Cootes, T. F., Taylor, C. J., Cooper, D. H., & Graham, J. (1995). Active shape models - Their training and application. *Computer Vision and Image Understanding*, *61*, 38–59. doi:10.1006/cviu.1995.1004

Da Silveira, L. G., Facon, J., & Borges, D. L. (2003). Visual speech recognition: A solution from feature extraction to words classification. In *Proceedings of the 16th Brazilian Symposium on Computer Graphics and Image Processing (SIBGRAPI 2003)*, (pp. 399-405). Sao Carlos, Brazil: IEEE Computer Society.

Dargham, J. A., & Chekima, A. (2006). Lip detection in the normalised RGB colour scheme. In *Proceedings of the 2nd Conference on Information and Communication Technologies (ICTTA 2006)*, (vol 1), (pp. 1546-1551). ICTTA.

Dempster, A. P., Laird, N. M., & Rubin, D. B. (1977). Maximum likelihood from incomplete data via the EM algorithm. *Journal of the Royal Statistical Society. Series B. Methodological*, *39*(1), 1–22.

Dodd, B., & Campbell, R. (1987). *Hearing by eye: The psychology of lip-reading*. Hillsdale, NJ: Lawrence Erlbaum Associates.

Dupont, S., & Luettin, J. (2000). Audio-visual speech modeling for continuous speech recognition. *IEEE Transactions on Multimedia*, *2*(3), 141–151. doi:10.1109/6046.865479

Eveno, N., Caplier, A., & Coulon, P. Y. (2004). Accurate and quasi-automatic lip tracking. *IEEE Transaction on Circuits and Video Technology*, *14*(5), 706–715. doi:10.1109/TC-SVT.2004.826754

Fisher, R. (1936). The use of multiple measurements in taxonomic problems. *Annals of Eugenics*, *7*, 179–188. doi:10.1111/j.1469-1809.1936.tb02137.x

Goldschen, A. J. (1993). *Continuous automatic speech recognition by lipreading*. Washington, DC: George Washington University.

Gordan, M., Kotropoulos, C., & Pitas, I. (2002). A support vector machine-based dynamic network for visual speech recognition applications. *EURASIP Journal on Applied Signal Processing*, *11*, 1248–1259. doi:10.1155/S1110865702207039

Graf, H. P., Cosatto, E., & Potamianos, M. (1997). Robust recognition of faces and facial features with a multi-modal system. In *Proceedings of the International Conference on Systems Man and Cybernetics*, (pp. 2034-2039). IEEE Press.

Gravier, G., Potamianos, G., & Neti, C. (2002). Asynchrony modeling for audio-visual speech recognition. In *Proceedings of the Second International Conference on Human Language Technology Research*. San Diego, CA: Morgan Kaufmann Publishers Inc.

Hallinan, P. W., Cohen, D. S., & Yuille, A. L. (1989). Feature extraction from faces using deformable templates. In *Proceedings of the Computer Vision and Pattern Recognition*, (pp. 104-109). IEEE.

Toolkit, H. T. K. (2012). *HTK hidden Markov model toolkit home page*. Retrieved from http://htk.eng.cam.ac.uk/

Hui, L. E., Seng, K. P., & Tse, K. M. (2004). RBF neural network mouth tracking for audio-visual speech recognition system. In *Proceedings of the IEEE Region 10 Conference (TENCON 2004)*, (pp. 84-87). IEEE Press.

Koiwa, T., Nakadai, K., & Imura, J. (2007). Coarse speech recognition by audio-visual integration based on missing feature theory. In *Proceedings of the IEEE/RSJ International Conference on Intelligent Robots and Systems (IROS 2007)*, (pp. 1751-1756). IEEE.

Jolliffe, I. (1986). *Principle component analysis*. Berlin, Germany: Springer-Verlag.

Kass, M., Witkin, A., & Terropoulos, D. (1988). Snakes: Active contour models. *International Journal of Computer Vision, 1*, 321–331. doi:10.1007/BF00133570

Kwon, Y. H., & Lobo, N. da V. (1994). Face detection using templates. *ICPR-A, 94*, 764-767.

Lee, J. S., & Park, C. H. (2008). Robust audio-visual speech recognition based on late integration. *MultMed, 10*(5), 767–779.

Li, W. J., Wang, K., Stolfo, S. J., & Herzog, B. (2005). Fileprints: Identifying file types by n--gram analysis. In *Proceedings of the 2005 IEEE Workshop on Information Assurance,* (pp. 64-71). West Point, NY: IEEE Press.

Luettin, J., & Thacker, N. A. (1997). Speechreading using probabilistic models. *Computer Vision and Image Understanding, 65*(2), 163–178. doi:10.1006/cviu.1996.0570

Lv, G., Jiang, D., Zhao, R., & Hou, Y. (2007). Multi-stream asynchrony modeling for audio-visual speech recognition. In *Proceedings of the Ninth IEEE International Symposium on Multimedia (ISM),* (pp. 37-44). IEEE Press.

Mallat, S. G. (1999). *A wavelet tour of signal processing.* New York, NY: Academic Press.

Matthews, I., Cootes, T. F., Bangham, J. A., Cox, S., & Harvey, R. (2002). Extraction of visual features for lipreading. *IEEE Transactions on Pattern Analysis and Machine Intelligence, 24*(2), 198–213. doi:10.1109/34.982900

Movellan, J., & Mineiro, P. (1998). Robust sensor fusion: Analysis and application to audio visual speech recognition. *Machine Learning, 32*(2), 85–100. doi:10.1023/A:1007468413059

Neely, K. (1956). Effect of visual factors on the intelligibility of speech. *The Journal of the Acoustical Society of America, 28*(6), 1275–1277. doi:10.1121/1.1908620

Open Source Machine Learning Software Weka. (2012). *University of Waikato.* Retrieved from http://www.cs.waikato.ac.nz/ml/weka

Petajan, E., Bischoff, B., Bodoff, D., & Brooke, N. M. (1988). An improved automatic lipreading system to enhance speech recognition. In *Proceedings of the SIGCHI Conference on Human Factors in Computing Systems (CHI 1988).* Washington, DC: ACM Press.

Potamianos, G., Neti, C., Gravier, G., Garg, A., & Senior, A. W. (2003). Recent advances in the automatic recognition of audiovisual speech. *Proceedings of the IEEE, 91*(9), 1306–1326. doi:10.1109/JPROC.2003.817150

Rao, K. R., Narasimhan, M. A., & Revuluri, K. (1975). Image data processing by Hadamard-Haar transform. *IEEE Transactions on Computers, 24*(9), 888–896. doi:10.1109/T-C.1975.224334

Rockwell, M. C., & Chan, M. T. (2001). HMM-based audio-visual speech recognition integrating geometric- and appearance-based visual features. In *Proceedings of the IEEE Workshop on Multimedia Signal Processing,* (pp. 9-14). IEEE Press.

Sadeghi, M., Kittler, J., & Messer, K. (2002). Modelling and segmentation of lip area in face images. *Vision. Image and Signal Processing, 149*(3), 179–184. doi:10.1049/ip-vis:20020378

Saitoh, T., & Konishi, R. (2006). Lip reading using video and thermal images. In *Proceedings of the International Joint Conference (SICE-ICASE, 2006),* (pp. 5011-5015). SICE-ICASE.

Saitoh, T., Morishita, K., & Konishi, R. (2008). Analysis of efficient lip reading method for various languages. In *Proceedings of the International Conference on Pattern Recognition,* (pp. 1-4). IEEE.

Shoup, J. E. (1980). Phonological aspects of speech recognition. In *Trends in Speech Recognition* (pp. 125–138). Englewood Cliffs, NJ: Prentice-Hall.

Singh, P., Laxmi, V., Gupta, D., & Gaur, M. S. (2010). Lipreading using n–gram feature vector. *Advances in Soft Computing, 85*, 81–88. doi:10.1007/978-3-642-16626-6_9

Stork, D. G., & Hennecke, M. E. (1996). Speechreading: An overview of image processing, feature extraction, sensory integration and pattern recognition techniques. In *Proceedings of the 2nd International Conference on Automatic Face and Gesture Recognition,* (pp. 16-26). IEEE.

Sugahara, K., Shinchi, T., Kishino, M., & Konishi, R. (2000). Real time realization of lip reading system on the personal computer. *Proceedings of ICSP, 36*(12), 1145–1151.

Sumby, W. H., & Pollack, I. (1954). Visual contribution to speech intelligibility in noise. *The Journal of the Acoustical Society of America, 26*(2), 212–215. doi:10.1121/1.1907309

Yaling, L., & Minghui, D. (2008). Lip contour extraction based on manifold. In *Proceedings of the International Conference on MultiMedia and Information Technology,* (pp. 229-232). Los Alamitos, CA: IEEE Computer Society.

Yang, J., & Waibel, A. (1996). A real-time face tracker. In *Proceedings 3rd IEEE Workshop on Applications of Computer Vision (WACV 1996),* (pp. 142-147). IEEE Press.

Yashwanth, H., Mahendrakar, H., & David, S. (2004). Automatic speech recognition using audio visual cues. In *Proceedings of the IEEE India Annual Conference (INDICON 2004),* (pp. 166-169). IEEE Press.

Yau, W. C., Kumar, D. K., & Arjunan, S. P. (2006). Voiceless speech recognition using dynamic visual speech features. In *Proceedings of the HCSNet Workshop on Use of Vision in Human-Computer Interaction (VisHCI 2006),* (pp. 93-101). Canberra, Australia: VisHCI.

Yuhas, B. P., Goldstein, M. H. Jr, & Sejnowski, T. J. (1989). Integration of acoustic and visual speech signals using neural networks. *IEEE Communications Magazine, 27*(11), 65–71. doi:10.1109/35.41402

Yuille, A. L. (1991). Deformable templates for face recognition. *CogNeuro, 3*(1), 59–70.

ADDITIONAL READING

Ganapathiraju, A., Hamaker, J., & Picone, J. (2000). Hybrid SVM/HMM architectures for speech recognition. In *Proceedings of Neural Information Processing Systems (NIPS).* NIPS.

Gray, M., Movellan, J., & Sejnowski, T. (2000). *Dynamic features for visual speechreading: A systematic comparision.* Advances in Neural Information Processing Systems Cambridge, MA: MIT Press.

Levinson, S. E., Rabiner, L. R., & Sondhi, M. M. (1983). An introduction to the application of the theory of probabilistic functions of a Markov process to automatic speech recognition. *The Bell System Technical Journal, 62*(4), 1035–1074.

Leymarie, F. F., & Levine, M. D. (1993). Tracking deformable objects in the plane using an active contour model. *Pattern Analysis and Machine Intelligence, 15*(6), 617–634. doi:10.1109/34.216733

Liew, A., Leung, S. H., & Lau, W. H. (2002). Lip contour extraction from colour images using a deformable model. *Pattern Recognition, 35*(12), 2949–2962. doi:10.1016/S0031-3203(01)00231-X

Lucey, P., Martin, T., & Sridharan, S. (2004). Confusability of phonemes grouped according to their viseme classes in noisy environments. In *Proceedings of the 10th Australian International Conference on Speech Science & Technology.* IEEE.

Luettin, J., & Thacker, N. A. (1997). Speechreading using probabilistic models. *Computer Vision and Image Understanding, 65*(2), 163–178. doi:10.1006/cviu.1996.0570

Nilsson, M., Nordberg, J., & Claesson, I. (2007). Face detection using local SMQT features and split up SNoW classifier. In *Proceedings of the IEEE International Conference on Acoustics, Speech, and Signal Processing (ICASSP).* IEEE Press.

Robert-Ribes, J., Piquemal, M., Schwartz, J. L., & Escudier, P. (1996). Exploiting sensor fusion architectures and stimuli complementarity in AV speech recognition. In Stork & Hennecke (Eds.), *Speechreading by Man and Machine: Models, Systems and Applications,* (pp. 193-210). Philadelphia, PA: Springer.

Samil, A., & Iyengar, P. A. (1995). Human face detection using silhouettes. *Pattern Recognition and Artificial Intelligence, 9,* 845–867. doi:10.1142/S0218001495000353

Yang, M. H., Kriegman, D. J., & Ahuja, N. (2002). Detecting faces in images: A survey. *IEEE Transactions on Pattern Analysis and Machine Intelligence, 24*(1), 34–58. doi:10.1109/34.982883

KEY TERMS AND DEFINITIONS

Connected Components: This is a set of connected pixels that share a common property. It is used to detect connected regions.

Dynamic Programming: A method of solving complex optimization problems by breaking them down into smaller and simpler sub-problems.

Edge Detection: Determining sharp changes in image brightness. Edge detection filters out useless information while preserving important properties of the image. It can be performed using the gradient or Laplacian method.

Feature Vector: It is an n-dimensional vector containing numerical values and representing any object. It is important in pattern recognition and machine learning.

Hidden Markov Model: A statistical model where the system is assumed to be a Markov process with a set of finite unobserved states each associated with a probability distribution. These are especially useful in temporal pattern recognition problems.

Neural Network: A system of data structures and programs imitating the working of the human brain by creating connections between processing elements.

n-Gram: Sequences of substrings with length n. Commonly used in pattern recognition tasks.

Phoneme: The smallest unit of sound which can help distinguish between utterances.

Viseme: The specific shape of the mouth while uttering a phoneme.

Compilation of References

Aas, K., & Eikvil, L. (1999). *Text categorisation: A survey*. Technical Report. Norwegian Computing Center. Retrieved October 7, 2010, from http://citeseerx.ist.psu.edu/viewdoc/summary?doi=10.1.1.41.2236

Abdou, S., & Savoy, J. (2006). Statistical and comparative evaluation of various indexing and search models. *Information Retrieval Technology*. Retrieved from http://doc.rero.ch/lm.php?url=1000,43,4,20100208172751-SI/Abdou_Samir_-_Statistical_and_Comparative_Evaluation_of_Various_20100208.pdf

Abney, S. (1996). Part-of-speech tagging and partial parsing. In Young, S., & Bloothooft, G. (Eds.), *Corpus-Based Methods in Language and Speech Processing* (pp. 118–136). Dordrecht, The Netherlands: Kluwer Academic Publishers.

Abu-Salem, H., Al-Omari, M., & Evens, M. (1999). Stemming methodologies over individual queries words for an Arabian information retrieval system. *Journal of the American Society for Information Science and Technology*, *50*, 524–529. doi:10.1002/(SICI)1097-4571(1999)50:6<524::AID-ASI7>3.0.CO;2-M

Aceves-Pérez, R., Montes-y-Gómez, M., & Villaseñor-Pineda, L. (2007). Enhancing cross-language question answering by combining multiple question translations. In *Proceedings of the 8th International Conference in Computational Linguistics and Intelligent Text Processing (CICLing-2007)*, (pp. 485-493). CICLing.

Aceves-Pérez, R., Montes-y-Gómez, M., Villaseñor-Pineda, L., & Ureña-López, L. A. (2008). Two approaches for multilingual question answering: Merging passages vs. merging answers. *International Journal of Computational Linguistics and Chinese Language Processing*, *13*(1).

Adam, N. R. (Ed.). (1995). Digital libraries: Research and technology advances. In *Proceedings of the ADL 1995 Forum*. McLean, VA: Springer.

Adamic, L. A., Zhang, J., Bakshy, E., & Ackerman, M. S. (2008). Knowledge sharing and yahoo answers: Everyone knows something. In *Proceeding of the 17th International Conference on World Wide Web (WWW 2008)*, (pp. 665-674). Beijing, China: WWW.

Afonso, S. (2006). *Árvores deitadas: Descrição do formato e das opções de análise na floresta sintá(c)tica*. Retrieved from http://www.linguateca.pt/documentos/Afonso2006ArvoresDeitadas.pdf

Agarwal, A., & Lavie, A. (2008). METEOR, m-BLEU and m-TER: evaluation metrics for high-correlation with human rankings of machine translation output. In *Proceedings of the 3rd Workshop on Statistical Machine Translation*, (pp. 115-118). Columbus, OH: IEEE.

Agirre, E., & Rigau, G. (1996). Word sense disambiguation using conceptual density. In *Proceedings of the 16th International Conference on Computational Linguistics (COLING)*. COLING.

Agirre, E., & Soroa, A. (2007). Semeval-2007 task 02: Evaluating word sense induction and discrimination systems. In *Proceedings of the Fourth International Workshop on Semantic Evaluations (SemEval 2007)*, (pp. 7–12). Prague, Czech Republic: SemEval.

Agirre, E., & Soroa, A. (2009). Personalizing pagerank for word sense disambiguation. In *Proceedings of the 12th Conference of the European Chapter of the Association for Computational Linguistics*, (pp. 33–41). Morristown, NJ: EACL.

Agirre, E., Aldezabal, I., & Pociello, E. (2006). Lexicalization and multiword expressions in the Basque WordNet. In *Proceedings of Third International WordNet Conference*. Jeju Island, Korea: WordNet.

Agirre, E., Ansa, O., & Martinez, D. (2001). Enriching wordnet concepts with topic signatures. In *Proceedings of the NAACL Workshop on WordNet and Other Lexical Resources: Applications, Extensions and Customizations*. NAACL.

Agirre, E., de Lacalle, O. L., & Soroa, A. (2009). Knowledge-based WSD on specific domains: Performing better than generic supervised WSD. In *Proceedings of IJCAI*. IJCAI.

Agirre, E., de Lacalle, O. L., Fellbaum, C., Marchetti, A., Toral, A., & Vossen, P. (2009). Semeval-2010 task 17: All-words word sense disambiguation on a specific domain. In *Proceedings of the Workshop on Semantic Evaluations: Recent Achievements and Future Directions*, (pp. 123–128). Morristown, NJ: Semantic Evaluations.

Agirre, E., Martínez, D., de Lacalle, O. L., & Soroa, A. (2006). Two graph-based algorithms for state-of-the-art WSD. In *Proceedings of the 2006 Conference on Empirical Methods in Natural Language Processing, EMNLP 2006*, (pp. 585–593). Stroudsburg, PA: EMNLP.

Ahmed, N., Natarajan, T., & Rao, K. R. (1974). Discrete cosine transform. *IEEE Transactions on Computers, 23*(1), 90–93. doi:10.1109/T-C.1974.223784

Ala-Mutka, K., Broster, D., Cachia, R., Centeno, C., Feijoo, C., & Hache, A. ... Valverde, J. (2009). *The impact of social computing on the EU information society and economy*. JRC Scientific and Technical Reports: EUR 24063 EN – 2009. Geneva, Switzerland: European Commission.

Alegria, I., Ansa, O., Xabier, A., Ezeiza, N., Gojenola, K., & Urizar, R. (2004). Representation and treatment of multiword expressions in Basque. In *Proceedings of the ACL Workshop on Multiword Expressions*, (pp. 48–55). Barcelona, Spain: ACL.

Alizadeh, S., Boostani, R., & Asadpour, V. (2008). Lip feature extraction and reduction for HMM-based visual speech recognition systems. In *Proceedings of the 9th International Conference on Signal Processing (ICSP 2008)*, (pp. 561-564). ICSP.

Allan, J., Carbonell, J., Doddington, G., Yamron, J., & Yang, Y. (1998). Topic detection and tracking pilot study: Final report. In *Proceedings of DARPA Broadcast News Transcription Understanding Workshop*, (pp. 194-218). DARPA.

Allen, R. B., & Hall, C. (2010). Automated processing of digitized historical newspapers beyond the article level: Finding sections and regular features. [ICADL.]. *Proceedings of ICADL, 2010*, 91–101.

Alm, C. O., Roth, D., & Sproat, R. (2005). Emotions from text: machine learning for text-based emotion prediction. In *Proceedings of the conference on Human Language Technology and Empirical Methods in Natural Language Processing*, (pp. 579-586). ACL.

Alonso Ramos, M., Rambow, O., & Wanner, L. (2008). Using semantically annotated corpora to build collocation resources. In *Proceedings of the International Language Resources and Evaluation Conference (LREC)*, (pp. 1154–1158). Marrakesh, Morocco: LREC.

Aluísio, S. M., Pelizzoni, J. M., Marchi, A. R., Oliveira, L. H., Manenti, R., & Marquiafável, V. (2003). An account of the challenge of tagging a reference corpus of Brazilian Portuguese. *Lecture Notes in Computer Science, 2721*, 110–117. doi:10.1007/3-540-45011-4_17

Alves, F., & Vale, D. C. (2009). Probing the unit of translation in time: aspects of the design and development of a web application for storing, annotating and querying translation process data. *Across Language and Cultures, 10*(2), 251–273.

Amati, G., & van Rijsbergen, C. J. (2002). Probabilistic models of information retrieval based on measuring the divergence from randomness. *ACM Transactions on Information Systems, 20*(4), 357–389. doi:10.1145/582415.582416

Ambroziak, J., & Woods, W. A. (1998). Natural language technology in precision content retrieval. In *Proceedings of the International Conference on Natural Language Processing and Industrial Applications (NLP+IA 1998)*. Moncton, Canada: NLP. Retrieved October 7, 2010 from http://citeseerx.ist.psu.edu/viewdoc/summary?doi=10.1.1.21.9236

Ananthakrishnan, R. (2003). State of the art in cross-lingual information retrieval. *Vivek Journal, 15*(2).

Anderson, J. (2007). *How can the human mind occur in the physical universe?* Oxford, UK: Oxford University Press. doi:10.1093/acprof:oso/9780195324259.001.0001

Andréani, V., & Lebarbé, T. (2010). Named entity normalization for termino-ontological resource design: Mixing approaches for optimality. In *Proceedings of 10th International Conference Journées d'Analyse Statistique des Données Textuelles*, (pp. 163-172). ACL.

Androutsopoulos, I., & Malakasiotis, P. (2010). A survey of paraphrasing and textual entailment methods. *Journal of Artificial Intelligence Research, 38*, 135-187. Retrieved September 24, 2010, from http://arxiv.org/abs/0912.3747

Apidianaki, M. (2008). Translation-oriented word sense induction based on parallel corpora. In *Proceedings of LREC*. LREC.

Arms, W. Y. (2000). *Digital libraries*. Cambridge, MA: MIT Press.

Arms, W. Y., & Arms, C. R. (2004). Mixed content and mixed metadata: Information discovery in a messy world. In Hillmann, D., & Westbrooks, E. (Eds.), *Metadata in Practice* (pp. 223–237). Chicago, IL: American Library Association.

Artandi, S. (1963). *Book indexing by computer*. New Brunswick, NJ: S.S. Artandi.

Asif, E., Rejwanul, H., & Sivaji, B. (2008). Named entity recognition in Bengali: A conditional random field approach. In *Proceedings of the 3rd International Joint Conference on Natural Language Processing (IJCNLP-2008)*, (pp. 589-594). Hyderabad, India: IJCNLP.

Asur, S., & Huberman, B. A. (2010). *Predicting the future with social media*. Ithaca, NY: Cornell University Library. Retrieved September 27, 2010, from http://arxiv.org/abs/1003.5699

Attia, M., Toral, A., Tounsi, L., Pecina, P., & Genabith, J. (2010). Automatic extraction of arabic multiword expressions. In *Proceedings of the COLING 2010, Workshop on Multiword Expressions: From Theory to Applications (MWE 2010)*. Beijing, China: COLING.

Auer, S., Bizer, C., Kobilarov, G., Lehmann, J., Cyganiak, R., & Ives, Z. (2007). DBpedia: A nucleus for a web of open data. In *Proceedings of the 6th International Semantic Web and 2nd Asian Conference on Asian Semantic Web Conference*, (pp. 722-735). Busan, Korea: IEEE.

Auger, A., & Barrière, C. (2008). Pattern based approaches to semantic relation extraction: A state-of-the-art. *Terminology, 14*(1), 1–19. doi:10.1075/term.14.1.02aug

Avancini, H., Candela, L., & Straccia, U. (2007). Recommenders in a personalized, collaborative digital library environment. *Journal of Intelligent Information Systems, 28*(3), 253–283. doi:10.1007/s10844-006-0010-3

Aziz, W., Dymetman, M., Mirkin, S., Specia, L., Cancedda, N., & Dagan, I. (2010). Learning an expert from human annotations in statistical machine translation: The case of out-of-vocabulary words. In *Proceedings of the 14th Annual Conference of the European Association for Machine Translation*, (pp. 28-35). Saint-Raphael, France: EAMT.

Aziz, W., Rios, M., & Specia, L. (2011). Shallow semantic trees for SMT. In *Proceedings of the Sixth Workshop on Statistical Machine Translation*. Edinburgh, UK: SMT.

Baeza-Yates, R., & Tiberi, A. (2007). Extacting semantic relation from query logs. In *Proceedings of the 13th International Conference on Knowledge Discovery and Data Mining (SIGKDD 2007)*. SIGKDD.

Baeza-Yates, R., & Ribeiro-Neto, B. (1999). *Modern information retrieval*. Reading, MA: Addison Wesley.

Bainbridge, D., Twidale, M. V., & Nichols, D. M. (2011). That's 'é', not 'þ' '?' or '☐': A user-driven context-aware approach to erroneous metadata in digital libraries. In *Proceedings of JCDL 2011*. Ottawa, Canada: JCDL.

Baker, K., Bloodgood, M., Callison-Burch, C., Dorr, B., Miller, S., & Piatko, C. … Levin, L. (2010). Semantically-informed syntactic machine translation: A tree-grafting approach. In *Proceedings of American Association for Machine Translation*. Denver, CO: AAMT.

Bal, B. K., & Saint-Dizier, P. (2010). Towards building annotated resources for analyzing opinions and argumentation in news editorials. In *Proceedings of LREC*. Malta: ELRA.

Balamurali, A. R., Joshi, A., & Bhattacharyya, P. (2011). Harnessing wordnet senses for supervised sentiment classification. In *Proceedings of the 2011 Conference on Empirical Methods in Natural Language Processing*, (pp. 1081–1091). Edinburgh, UK: Empirical Methods in Natural Language Processing.

Baldwin, T., & Bond, F. (2002). Multiword expressions: Some problems for Japanese NLP. In *Proceedings of the 8th Annual Meeting of the Association for Natural Language Processing*, (pp. 379–382). Keihanna, Japan: Natural Language Processing.

Baldwin, T., & Villavicencio, A. (2002). Extracting the unextractable: A case study on verbparticles. In *Proceedings of the Sixth Conference on Computational Natural Language Learning (CoNLL 2002)*, (pp. 99–105). CoNLL.

Ballesteros, L., & Croft, W. B. (1996). Dictionary methods for cross-lingual information retrieval. In *Proceedings of the 7th International DEXA Conference on Database and Expert Systems*, (pp. 791-801). DEXA.

Ballesteros, L., & Croft, W. B. (1997). Phrasal translation and query expansion techniques for cross-language information retrieval. In *Proceedings of the 20th Annual International ACM Conference on Research and Development in Information Retrieval*, (pp. 84-91). Philadelphia, PA: ACM Press.

Banerjee, P., & Han, H. (2009). Answer credibility: A language modeling approach to answer validation. In *Proceedings of Human Language Technologies, Annual Conference of the North American Chapter of the Association for Computational Linguistics*, (pp. 157-160). Boulder, CO: ACL.

Banerjee, S., & Pedersen, T. (2002). An adapted lesk algorithm for word sense disambiguation using wordnet. In *Proceedings of the Third International Conference on Computational Linguistics and Intelligent Text Processing*, (pp. 136–145). London, UK: CICling.

Banerjee, S., & Pedersen, T. (2003). Extended gloss overlaps as a measure of semantic relatedness. In *Proceedings of the 18th International Joint Conference on Artificial Intelligence*, (pp. 805–810). San Francisco, CA: IEEE.

Bangalore, S., Haffner, P., & Kanthak, S. (2007). Statistical machine translation through global lexical selection and sentence reconstruction. In *Proceedings of the 45th Annual Meeting of the Association of Computational Linguistics*, (pp. 152-159). Prague, Czech Republic: ACL.

Banko, M., & Moore, R. C. (2004). Part of speech tagging in context. In *Proceedings of the 20th International Conference on Computational Linguistics*, (pp. 556-561). ACL.

Barbaro, M., & Zeller, T. (2006). A face is exposed for AOL searcher no. 4417749. *New York Times*. Retrieved January 28, 2011, from http://www.nytimes.com/2006/08/09/technology/09aol.html

Barss, A. (2003). *Anaphora: A reference guide*. Malden, MA: Blackwell Publishing Ltd.

Barwise, J., & Cooper, R. (1981). Generalized quantifiers and natural language. *Linguistics and Philosophy*, *4*, 159–219. doi:10.1007/BF00350139

Batjargal, B., Khaltarkhuu, G., Kimura, F., & Maeda, A. (2010). Ancient-to-modern information retrieval for digital collections of traditional Mongolian script. [ICADL.]. *Proceedings of ICADL*, *2010*, 25–28.

Bearman, D. (2008). Digital libraries. *Annual Review of Information Science & Technology*, *41*(1), 223–272. doi:10.1002/aris.2007.1440410112

Belkin, N., & Croft, B. (1992). Information filtering and information retrieval: Two sides of the same coin? *Communications of the ACM*, *35*(12), 29–38. doi:10.1145/138859.138861

Benamara, F., & Saint-Dizier, P. (2004). Advanced relaxation for cooperative question answering. In Maybury, M. (Ed.), *New Directions in Question Answering*. Cambridge, MA: MIT Press.

Bengel, J., Gauch, S., Mittur, E., & Vijayaraghavan, R. (2004). Chattrack: Chat room topic detection using classification. In *Proceedings of the 2nd Symposium on Intelligence and Security Informatics*, (pp. 266-277). Tucson, Arizona: IEEE.

Benson, M., Benson, E., & Ilson, R. (1986). *The BBI combinatory dictionary of English*. Amsterdam, The Netherlands: John Benjamins.

Bentivogli, L., & Pianta, E. (2005). Exploiting parallel texts in the creation of multilingual semantically annotated resources: The multisemcor corpus. *Natural Language Engineering*, *11*, 247–261. doi:10.1017/S1351324905003839

Berber Sardinha, T. (2004). *Lingüística de corpus*. Barueri, Spain: Manole.

Berger, K. W. (1972). *Speechreading*. Baltimore, MD: National Educational Press.

Berkman, R. I. (2008). *The art of strategic listening: Finding market intelligence through blogs and other social media*. New York, NY: Paramount Market Publishing.

Bernardi, R., & Kirschner, M. (2008). Context modeling for IQA: The role of tasks and entities. In *Proceedings of Workshop for Knowledge and Reasoning for Answering Questions (KRAQ 2008)*. Manchester, UK: KRAQ.

Bernardi, R., Kirschner, M., & Ratkovic, Z. (2010). Context fusion: The role of discourse structure and centering theory. In *Proceedings of the Seventh Conference on International Language Resources and Evaluation (LREC 2010)*. Valletta, Malta: LREC.

Bertoldi, N., & Federico, M. (2009). Domain adaptation for statistical machine translation with monolingual resources. In *Proceedings of the Fourth Workshop on Statistical Machine Translation*, (pp. 182-189). Athens, Greece: SMT.

Bethard, S., Ghosh, S., Martin, J. H., & Sumner, T. (2009). Topic model methods for automatically identifying out-of-scope resources. In *Proceedings of JCDL 2009: 9th ACM/IEEE-CS Joint Conference on Digital Libraries*, (pp. 19-28). Austin, TX: ACM/IEEE.

Bhavnani, S. K. (2001). Important cognitive components of domain-specific search knowledge. In E. M. Voorhees & D. K. Harman (Eds.), *The Tenth Text Retrieval Conference (TREC 2001)*, (pp. 571–578). Washington, DC: NIST.

Bick, E. (2000). *The parsing system palavras – Automatic grammatical analysis of Portuguese in a constraint grammar framework*. Aarhus, Denmark: Aarhus University Press. Retrieved from http://beta.visl.sdu.dk/pdf/PLP20-amilo.ps.pdf

Bickel, S., Brückner, M., & Scheffer, T. (2007). Discriminative learning for differing training and test distributions. In *Proceedings of the 24th Annual International Conference on Machine Learning*, (pp. 81-88). IEEE.

Bilotti, M. W., & Nyberg, E. (2006). Evaluation for scenario question answering systems. In *Proceedings of the International Conference on Language Resources and Evaluation*. LREC.

Bing, L. (2010). Sentiment Analysis and subjectivity. In *Handbook of Natural Language Processing* (2nd ed.). Boca Raton, FL: CRC Press.

Blair-Goldensohn, S., McKeown, K., & Schlaikjer, A. (2004). Answering definitional questions: A hybrid approach. In Maybury, M. T. (Ed.), *New Directions in Question Answering* (pp. 47–58). Menlo Park, CA: AAAI Press.

Blitzer, J. (2007). *Domain adaptation of natural language processing systems*. Retrieved from http://john.blitzer.com/papers/adaptationthesis.pdf

Blitzer, J., McDonald, R., & Pereira, F. (2006). Domain adaptation with structural correspondence learning. In *Proceedings of the 2006 Conference on Empirical Methods in Natural Language Processing*, (pp. 120-128). ACL.

Bloehdorn, S., Cimiano, P., Duke, A., Haase, P., Heizmann, J., Thurlow, I., & Völker, J. (2007). Ontology-based question answering for digital libraries. *Lecture Notes in Computer Science*, *4675*, 14–25. doi:10.1007/978-3-540-74851-9_2

Boguraev, B., & Ando, R. K. (2005). TimeML-Compliant text analysis for temporal reasoning. In *Proceedings of IJCAI 2005*. IJCAI.

Boguslavsky, I. M., Iomdin, L. L., Lazursky, A. V., Mityushin, L. G., Sizov, V. G., Kreydlin, L. G., & Berdichevsky, A. S. (2005). Interactive resolution of intrinsic and translational ambiguity in a machine translation system. [Berlin, Germany: Springer-Verlag.]. *Proceedings of CICLing*, *2005*, 383–394.

Bohus, D., Raux, A., Harris, T. K., Eskenazi, M., & Rudnicky, A. I. (2007). Olympus: An open-source framework for conversational spoken language interface research. In *Proceedings of the NAACL-HLT Workshop on Bridging the Gap: Academic and Industrial Research in Dialog Technologies*, (pp. 32-39). Rochester, NY: NAACL.

Borgman, C. L. (2000). *From Gutenberg to the global information infrastructure: Access to information in the networked world*. Cambridge, MA: The MIT Press.

Boser, B. E., Guyon, I. M., & Vapnik, V. N. (1992). A training algorithm for optimal margin classifiers. In *Proceedings of the Fifth Annual Workshop on Computational Learning Theory, COLT 1992*, (pp. 144–152). New York, NY: COLT.

Boutella, M. R., Luob, J., Shena, X., & Brown, C. M. (2004). Learning multi-label scene classification. *Pattern Recognition, 37*, 1757–1771. doi:10.1016/j.patcog.2004.03.009

Boyd-Graber, J., Fellbaum, C., Osherson, D., & Schapire, R. (2006). Adding dense, weighted connections to Word-Net. In *Proceedings of the Third International WordNet Conference*. Brno, Czech Republic: Masaryk University.

Bradley, M. M., & Lang, P. J. (1999). *Affective norms for English words (ANEW): Stimuli, instruction manual, and affective ratings*. Technical Report C-1. Gainesville, FL: University of Florida.

Brandon, R., Mitze, K., & Rau, L. (1995). Automatic condensation of electronic publications by sentence selection. *Information Processing & Management, 31*(5), 675–685. doi:10.1016/0306-4573(95)00052-I

Brants, T. (2000). TnT – A statistical part-of-speech tagger. In *Proceedings of the Sixth Applied Natural Language Processing Conference*, (pp. 224-231). ACL.

Braschler, M., Wechsler, M., Mateev, B., Mittendorf, E., & Schauble, P. (1999). SPIDER retrieval system. In *Proceedings of TREC7*. TREC.

Braschler, M., Gonzalo, J., Peinado, V., & López-Ostenero, F. (2009). *Best practices in system-oriented and user-oriented multilingual information access (d3.3). Technical Report: TrebleCLEF Project: FP7 IST ICT-1-4-1*. TrebleCLEF Project.

Braschler, M., & Schäuble, P. (2001). Experiments with the Eurospider retrieval system for CLEF 2000. *Lecture Notes in Computer Science, 2069*.

Breiger, R. (2005). Introduction to special issue: Ethical dilemmas in social network research. *Social Networks, 27*(2), 89–93. doi:10.1016/j.socnet.2005.01.002

Brill, E. (1995). Transformation-based error-driven learning of natural language: A case study in part-of-speech tagging. *Computational Linguistics, 21*(4), 543–565.

Brin, S., & Page, L. (1998). The anatomy of a large-scale hypertextual web search engine. In *Proceedings of the Seventh International Conference on World Wide Web 7, WWW7*, (pp. 107–117). Amsterdam, The Netherlands: WWW.

Brown, P. F., Lai, J. C., & Mercer, R. L. (1991). Aligning sentences in parallel corpora. In *Proceedings of the 29th Annual Meeting of the Association for Computational Linguistics*, (pp. 169-176). Berkeley, CA: ACL.

Brown, P. F., Cocke, J., Della Pietra, S. A., Della Pietra, V. J., Jelinek, F., & Lafferty, J. (1990). A statistical approach to machine translation. *Computational Linguistics, 16*, 79–85.

Brown, P. F., Della Pietra, S. A., & Mercer, R. L. (1993). The mathematics of statistical machine translation: Parameter estimation. *Computational Linguistics, 19*(2), 263–311.

Brown, R. D. (1996). Example-based machine translation in the Pangloss system. [Copenhagen, Denmark: COLING.]. *Proceedings of COLING, 1996*, 169–174.

Brusilovsky, P., Kobsa, A., & Nejdl, W. (2007). Data mining for personalization. *Lecture Notes in Computer Science, 4321*, 90–135. doi:10.1007/978-3-540-72079-9

Buckley, C., Mitra, M., Walz, J., & Cardie, C. (1999). SMART high precision. In Voorhees, E., & Harman, D. (Eds.), *TREC7. NIST*.

Buckley, C., Mitra, M., Walz, J., & Cardie, C. (2000). Using clustering and superconcepts within SMART: TREC 6. *Information Processing & Management, 36*(1), 109–131. doi:10.1016/S0306-4573(99)00047-3

Buckley, C., & Voorhees, E. M. (2005). Retrieval system evaluation. In *TREC: Experiment and Evaluation in Information Retrieval*. Cambridge, MA: MIT Press.

Bui, T. (2006). *Multimodal dialogue management - State of the art. Technical Report*. Enschede, The Netherlands: University of Twente.

Bun, K. K., & Ishizuka, M. (2006). Emerging topic tracking system in WWW. *Knowledge-Based Systems, 19*(3), 164–171. doi:10.1016/j.knosys.2005.11.008

Burek, G., & Gerdemann, D. (2009). Maximal phrases based analysis for prototyping online discussion forums postings. In *Proceedings of the Workshop on Adaptation of Language Resources and Technology to New Domains,* (pp. 12-18). Borovets, Bulgaria: ACL.

Burger, J., et al. (2001). *Issues, tasks and program structures to roadmap research in question & answering (Q&A).* Retrieved from http://www.inf.ed.ac.uk/teaching/courses/tts/papers/qa_roadmap.pdf

Butt, M. (2003). The light verb jungle. *Workshop on Multi-Verb Constructions.* Retrieved from http://ling.sprachwiss.uni-konstanz.de/pages/home/butt/main/papers/harvard-work.pdf

Callison-Burch, C., & Koehn, P. (2005). *Introduction to statistical machine translation.* Paper presented at the 17th European Summer School in Logic, Language and Information. Retrieved from http://www.iccs.informatics.ed.ac.uk/~pkoehn/publications/esslli-slides-day3.pdf

Callison-Burch, C., Koehn, P., Monz, C., & Zaidan, O. (2011). Findings of the 2011 workshop on statistical machine translation. In *Proceedings of the Sixth Workshop on Statistical Machine Translation,* (pp. 22-64). Edinburgh, UK: SMT.

Callison-Burch, C., Koehn, P., Monz, C., Peterson, K., Przybocki, M., & Zaidan, O. (2010). Findings of the 2010 joint workshop on statistical machine translation and metrics for machine translation. In *Proceedings of the Joint Fifth Workshop on Statistical Machine Translation and MetricsMATR,* (pp. 17-53). Uppsala, Sweden: MetricsMATR.

Calzolari, N., Fillmore, C., Grishman, R., Ide, N., Lenci, A., MacLeod, C., & Zampolli, A. (2002). Towards best practice for multiword expressions in computational lexicons. In *Proceedings of the Third International Conference on Language Resources and Evaluation (LREC 2002),* (pp. 1934–1940). Las Palmas, Spain: LREC.

Calzolari, N., McNaught, J., & Zampolli, A. (1996). *EAGLES final report: EAGLES editors' introduction.* Pisa, Italy: EAGLES.

Calzolari, N. (2004). Computational lexicons and corpora: Complementary components in human language technology. In van Sterkenburg, P. (Ed.), *Linguistics Today – Facing a Greater Challenge* (pp. 89–108). Amsterdam, The Netherlands: John Benjamins.

Calzolari, N., Zampolli, A., & Lenci, A. (2002). Towards a standard for a multilingual lexical entry: The EAGLES/ISLE initiative. *Lecture Notes in Computer Science, 2276,* 264–279. doi:10.1007/3-540-45715-1_25

Caminada, M., & Amgoud, L. (2007). On the evaluation of argumentation formalisms. *Artificial Intelligence Journal, 171*(5-6), 286–310. doi:10.1016/j.artint.2007.02.003

Carl, M., & Jakobsen, A. L. (2009). Objectives for a query language for user-activity data. In *Proceedings of the Natural Language Processing and Cognitive Science (NLPCS 2009).* Milan, Italy: NLPCS.

Carl, M., Dragsted, B., & Jakobsen, A. L. (2011). On the systematicity of human translation processes. *Translation Journal, 16*(2). Retrieved from http://translationjournal.net/journal/56taxonomy.htm

Carl, M. (2009). Triangulating product and process data: Quantifying alignment units with keystroke data. *Copenhagen Studies in Language, 38,* 225–247.

Carl, M., & Jakobsen, A. L. (2010). Towards statistical modelling of translators' activity data. *International Journal of Speech Technology, 12*(4). Retrieved from http://www.springerlink.com/content/3745875x22883306/

Carpuat, M., & Wu, D. (2007). Improving statistical machine translation using word sense disambiguation. In *Proceedings of EMNLP-CoNLL.* EMNLP.

Cataldi, M., Di Caro, L., & Schifanella, C. (2010). Emerging topic detection on Twitter based on temporal and social terms evaluation. In *Proceedings of the Tenth International Workshop on Multimedia Data Mining, KDD,* (pp. 1-10). Washington, DC: KDD.

Celikyilmaz, A., & Thint, M. (2008). Semantic approach to text entailment for question answering - New domain for uncertainty modeling. In *Proceedings of the 7th IEEE International Conference on Cognitive Informatics (ICCI 2008),* (pp. 481-487). Stanford, CA: IEEE Press.

Chakrabarti, S., Dom, B., & van den Berg, M. (1999). Focused crawling: A new approach for topic-specific resource discovery. In *Proceedings of the 8th World Wide Web Conference,* (pp. 545-562). Amsterdam, The Netherlands: Elsevier Science.

Chakraborty, T., Das, D., & Bandyopadhyay, S. (2011). Semantic clustering: An attempt to identify multiword expressions in Bengali. In *Proceedings of the Workshop on Multiword Expressions: From Parsing and Generation to the Real World (MWE 2011),* (pp. 8-13). Portland, OR: MWE.

Chali, Y. (2009). Question answering using question classification and document tagging. *Applied Artificial Intelligence, 23*(6), 500–521. doi:10.1080/08839510903078093

Chan, Y. S., & Ng, H. T. (2005). Word sense disambiguation with distribution estimation. In *Proceedings of the 19th International Joint Conference on Artificial Intelligence,* (pp. 1010-1015). IEEE.

Chan, Y. S., Ng, H. T., & Chiang, D. (2007). Word sense disambiguation improves statistical machine translation. In *Proceedings of the 45th Annual Meeting of the Association for Computational Linguistics,* (pp. 33-40). Prague, Czech Republic: ACL.

Chapman, R. (1977). *Roget's international thesaurus* (4th ed.). New York, NY: Thomas Y. Crowell Company.

Charniak, E., Knight, K., & Yamada, K. (2003). Syntax-based language models for statistical machine translation. In *Proceedings of the MT Summit IX Conference.* New Orleans, LA: MT Summit.

Chelba, C., & Acero, A. (2006). Adaptation of maximum entropy capitalizer: Little data can help a lot. *Computer Speech & Language, 20*(4), 382–399. doi:10.1016/j.csl.2005.05.005

Chelba, C., & Jelinek, F. (2000). Structured language modeling. *Computer Speech & Language, 14*(4), 283–332. doi:10.1006/csla.2000.0147

Chen, A., & Gey, F. C. (2001). Translation term weighting and combining translation resources in cross-language retrieval. In *Proceedings of the 10th Text Retrieval Conference (TREC10).* Gaithersburg, MD: National Institute of Standards and Technology (NIST).

Chen, H. (2008). Sentiment and affect analysis of dark web forums: Measuring radicalization on the internet. In J. Hajic & Y. Matsumoto (Eds.), *IEEE International Conference on Intelligence and Security Informatics,* (pp. 104-109). Taipei, Taiwan: IEEE Press.

Chen, J., & Nie, J.-Y. (2000). Parallel web text mining for cross-language IR. In *Proceedings of RIAO 2000: Content-Based Multimedia Information Access,* (Vol. 1), (pp. 62-78). RIAO.

Chen, Q. C., Deng, G. H., Wang, X. L., & Huang, H. J. (2006). An inner contour based lip moving feature extraction method for Chinese speech. In *Proceedings of the International Conference on Machine Learning and Cybernetics,* (pp. 3859-3864). IEEE.

Chen, A., & Gey, F. C. (2004). Combining query translation and document translation in cross-language retrieval. *Lecture Notes in Computer Science, 3237.*

Chen, T. (2001). Audiovisual speech processing. *IEEE Signal Processing Magazine, 18*(1), 9–21. doi:10.1109/79.911195

Chen, Z., Ma, J., Lei, J., Yuan, B., Lian, L., & Song, L. (2009). A cross-language focused crawling algorithm based on multiple relevance prediction strategies. *Computers & Mathematics with Applications (Oxford, England), 57*(6), 1057–1072. doi:10.1016/j.camwa.2008.09.021

Chiang, D. (2005). A hierarchical phrase-based model for statistical machine translation. In *Proceedings of the 43rd Annual Meeting of the Association for Computational Linguistics,* (pp. 263-270). Ann Arbor, MI: ACL.

Chiang, D., Knight, K., & Wang, W. (2009). 11,001 new features for statistical machine translation. In *Proceedings of the Conference of the North American Chapter of the Association for Computational Linguistics,* (pp. 218-226). Boulder, CO: ACL.

Chiang, D. (2007). Hierarchical phrase-based translation. *Computational Linguistics, 33*(2), 201–228. doi:10.1162/coli.2007.33.2.201

Chieze, E., Farzindar, A., & Lapalme, G. (2010). An automatic system for summarization and information extraction of legal information. *Lecture Notes in Computer Science, 6036,* 216–234. doi:10.1007/978-3-642-12837-0_12

Chikara, H. (2004). *A computational treatment of V-V vompounds in Japanese*. (Ph.D. Dissertation). Kobe Shoin Graduate School of Letters. Kobe, Japan.

Choumane, A., Blanchon, H., & Roisin, C. (2005). Integrating translation services within a structured editor. In *Proceedings of the 2005 ACM Symposium on Document Engineering*, (pp. 165–167). New York, NY: ACM Press.

Church, K. W. (1988). A stochastic parts program and noun phrase parser for unrestricted text. In *Proceedings of the Second Conference on Applied Natural Language Processing*, (pp. 136-143). ACL.

Church, K. W., & Gale, W. A. (1991). Concordances for parallel text. In *Proceedings of the Seventh Annual Conference of the UW Centre for the New OED and Text Research*, (pp. 40–62). UW Centre.

Church, K. W., & Hanks, P. (1990). Word association norms, mutual information and lexicography. *Proceedings of 27th Association for Computational Linguistics*, *16*(1), 22–29.

Ciravegna, F., Chapman, S., Dingli, A., & Wilks, Y. (2004). Learning to harvest information for the semantic web. In *Proceedings of the 1st European Semantic Web Symposium*, (pp. 312-326). IEEE.

Clarke, C., Cormack, G., Kisman, D., & Lynam, T. (2000). Question answering by passage selection. In *Proceedings of 9th Text Retrieval Conference (TREC-9)*. Gaitherburg, MD: TREC.

Clark, H. H., & Schaefer, E. F. (1989). Contributing to discourse. *Cognitive Science*, *13*, 259–294. doi:10.1207/s15516709cog1302_7

Cleland, S. (2008). *The blind eye to privacy law arbitrage by Google – Broadly threatens respect for privacy*. Testimony before the House Energy & Commerce Subcommittee on Internet Hearing. Retrieved September 16, 2010, from http://www.netcompetition.org/Written_Testimony_House_Privacy_071707.pdf

Cohen, W. (1995). Fast effective rule induction. In *Proceedings of the 12th International Conference on Machine Learning*, (pp. 115-123). IEEE.

Cohen, D. J. (2006). From Babel to knowledge: Data mining large digital collections. *D-Lib Magazine*, *12*(3).

Conroy, J., & O'leary, D. P. (2001). *Text summarization via hidden Markov models and pivoted QR matrix decomposition*. Technical Report CS-TR-4221. College Park, MD: University of Maryland.

Cook, P., Fazly, A., & Stevenson, S. (2008). The VNC-Tokens dataset. In *Proceedings of the LREC Workshop on Towards a Shared Task for Multiword Expressions (MWE 2008)*. Marrakech, Morocco: LREC.

Cooper, M. D. (2001). Usage patterns of a web-based library catalog. *Journal of the American Society for Information Science and Technology*, *52*(2), 137–148. doi:10.1002/1097-4571(2000)9999:9999<::AID-ASI1547>3.0.CO;2-E

Cootes, T. F., Taylor, C. J., Cooper, D. H., & Graham, J. (1995). Active shape models - Their training and application. *Computer Vision and Image Understanding*, *61*, 38–59. doi:10.1006/cviu.1995.1004

Cormack, G. V. (2007). Email spam filtering: A systematic review. *Foundations and Trends in Information Retrieval*, *1*(4), 335–455. doi:10.1561/1500000006

Costa-Jussà, M. R., Banchs, R. E., & Codina, J. (2010). Where are you from? Tell me HOW you write and I will tell you WHO you are. In *Proceedings of the International Conference on Agents and Artificial Intelligence ICAART*, (pp. 406-410). Valencia, Spain: ICAART.

Crystal, D. (2008). *Txtng: The Gr8 Db8*. Oxford, UK: Oxford University Press.

Cucerzan, S., & Yarowsky, D. (1999). Language independent named entity recognition combining morphological and contextual evidence. In *Proceedings of the Joint SIGDAT Conference on Empirical Methods in Natural Language Processing and Very Large Corpora*, (pp. 90-99). SIGDAT.

Cui, L., Zhang, D., Li, M., Zhou, M., & Zhao, T. (2010). Hybrid decoding: Decoding with partial hypotheses combination over multiple SMT systems. In *Proceedings of the 23rd International Conference on Computational Linguistics*, (pp. 214-222). Beijing, China: ACL.

Da Silveira, L. G., Facon, J., & Borges, D. L. (2003). Visual speech recognition: A solution from feature extraction to words classification. In *Proceedings of the 16th Brazilian Symposium on Computer Graphics and Image Processing (SIBGRAPI 2003)*, (pp. 399-405). Sao Carlos, Brazil: IEEE Computer Society.

Da Sylva, L., & Doll, F. (2005). A document browsing tool: Using lexical classes to convey information. In *Proceedings of the Advances in Artificial Intelligence: 18th Conference of the Canadian Society for Computational Studies of Intelligence, Canadian AI 2005*, (pp. 307-318). New York, NY: Springer-Verlag.

Da Sylva, L. (2004). A document browsing tool based on book indexes. In *Proceedings of Computational Linguistics in the North East (CLiNE 2004)* (pp. 45–52). Montreal, Canada: CLiNE.

Da Sylva, L., & Turner, J. M. (2005). Using ancillary text to index web-based multimedia objects. *Literary and Linguistic Computing, 21*(2), 219–228. doi:10.1093/llc/fql018

Dagan, I., & Itai, A. (1994). Word sense disambiguation using a second language monolingual corpus. *Computational Linguistics, 20*, 563–596.

Dai, W., Xue, G., Yang, Q., & Yu, Y. (2007). Transferring naive Bayes classifiers for text classification. In *Proceedings of the 22nd AAAI Conference on Artificial Intelligence*, (pp. 540-545). AAAI.

Dale, R., Moisi, H., & Somers, H. (Eds.). (2000). *Handbook of natural language processing*. Boca Raton, FL: Marcel Dekker, Inc.

Dale, R., & Reiter, E. (2000). *Building natural language generation systems*. Cambridge, UK: Cambridge University Press.

Damerau, F. J., Joshi, A. K., & Kaplan, S. J. (1981). A note on the utility of computing inferences in a real data base query environment. *Computational Linguistics, 7*(1), 43–45.

Dandapat, S., Sarkar, S., & Basu, A. (2007). Automatic part-of-speech tagging for Bengali: An approach for morphologically rich languages in a poor resource scenario. In *Proceedings of the 45th Annual Meeting of the Association for Computational Linguistics Companion Volume Proceedings of the Demo and Poster Sessions*, (pp. 221–224). Prague, Czech Republic: ACL.

Danet, B., & Herring, S. C. (Eds.). (2007). *The multilingual internet: Language, culture, and communication online*. Oxford, UK: Oxford University Press.

Dargham, J. A., & Chekima, A. (2006). Lip detection in the normalised RGB colour scheme. In *Proceedings of the 2nd Conference on Information and Communication Technologies (ICTTA 2006)*, (vol 1), (pp. 1546-1551). ICTTA.

Daumé, H., III, Deoskar, T., McClosky, D., & Plank, B. (2010). *ACL 2010 workshop on domain adaptation for natural language processing (DANLP)*. Retrieved from http://sites.google.com/site/danlp2010/call-for-papers

Daumé, H., III. (2007). Frustratingly easy domain adaptation. In *Proceedings of the 45th Annual Meeting of the Association for Computational Linguistics*, (pp. 256–263). ACL. Retrieved from http://www.aclweb.org/anthology-new/P/P07/P07-1033.pdf

Daumé, H. III, & Marcu, D. (2006). Domain adaptation for statistical classifiers. *Journal of Artificial Intelligence Research, 26*(1), 101–126.

Davis, M. (1997). New experiments in cross-language text retrieval at NMSU's computing research lab. In *Proceedings of the 5th Text Retrieval Conference (TREC5)*, (pp. 447-454). Gaithersburg, MD: National Institute of Standards and Technology (NIST).

Davis, M. W., & Ogden, W. C. (1997). Implementing cross-language text retrieval system for large-scale text collection on the world wide web. In *Proceedings of the AAAI Symposium on Cross-language Text and Speech Retrieval*. American for Artificial Intelligence.

Davis, M. W., & Dunning, T. E. (1995). A TREC evaluation of query translation methods for multi-lingual text retrieval. In Harman, D. K. (Ed.), *TREC-4. NIST*.

Dawson, J. (1974). Suffix removal and word conflation. *Bulletin of the Association for Literacy and Linguistic Computing, 2*, 33–46.

de Mello, C. A. B., & Rafael, D. L. (1999). A comparative study on OCR tools. In *Proceedings of Vision Interface 1999*, (pp. 224-232). Trois-Rivières, Canada: ACL. Retrieved October 7, 2010, from http://citeseerx.ist.psu.edu/viewdoc/summary?doi=10.1.1.12.2361

Deerwester, S. S., Dumais, S. T., Furnas, G. W., Landauer, T. K., & Harshman, R. (1999). Indexing by latent semantic analysis. *Journal of the American Society for Information Science American Society for Information Science, 41*(6).

Deksne, D., Skadiņš, R., & Skadiņa, I. (2008). Dictionary of multiword expressions for translation into highly inflected languages. In N. Calzolari, K. Choukri, B. Maegaard, J. Mariani, J. Odjik, S. Piperidis, & D. Tapias (Eds.), *Proceedings of Proceedings of the Sixth International Language Resources and Evaluation (LREC 2008)*. Marrakech, Morocco: European Language Resources Association (ELRA).

Delpech, E., & Saint-Dizier, P. (2008). Investigating the structure of procedural texts for answering how-to questions. In *Proceedings of the Language Resources and Evaluation Conference (LREC 2008)*. Marrakech, Morocco: European Language Resources Association (ELRA).

Demberg, V., & Moore, J. D. (2006). Information presentation in spoken dialogue systems. In *Proceedings of the 11th Conference of the European Chapter of the Association for Computational Linguistics*. ACL.

Dempsey, L., & Heery, R. (1998). Metadata: A current view of practice and issues. *The Journal of Documentation, 54*(2), 145–172. doi:10.1108/EUM0000000007164

Dempster, A. P., Laird, N. M., & Rubin, D. B. (1977). Maximum likelihood from incomplete data via the EM algorithm. *Journal of the Royal Statistical Society. Series B. Methodological, 39*(1), 1–38.

Derks, D., Bos, A. E., & Von Grumbkow, J. (2007). Emoticons and social interaction on the Internet: The importance of social context. *Computers in Human Behavior, 23*(1), 842–849. doi:10.1016/j.chb.2004.11.013

Dey, L., & Haque, S. K. (2009). Opinion mining from noisy text data. *International Journal on Document Analysis and Recognition, 12*(3), 205–226. doi:10.1007/s10032-009-0090-z

Diab, M. T., & Bhutada, P. (2009). Verb noun construction MWE token supervised classification. In *Proceedings of the Workshop on Multiword Expressions: Identification, Interpretation, Disambiguation and Applications, (ACL-JICNLP 2009)*, (pp. 17–22). Singapore: ACL-JICNLP.

Diab, M., & Resnik, P. (2002). An unsupervised method for word sense tagging using parallel corpora. In *Proceedings of the 40th Annual Meeting on Association for Computational Linguistics, ACL 2002*, (pp. 255–262). Morristown, NJ: ACL.

Diaconescu, S. (2004). Multiword expression translation using generative dependency grammar. In *Proceedings of ESTAL 2004 – España for Natural Language Processing*. Alicante, Spain: ESTAL.

DiMaggio, P., Hargittai, E., Newman, W. R., & Robinson, J. P. (2001). Social implications of the Internet. *Annual Review of Sociology, 27*, 307–336. doi:10.1146/annurev.soc.27.1.307

Dodd, B., & Campbell, R. (1987). *Hearing by eye: The psychology of lip-reading*. Hillsdale, NJ: Lawrence Erlbaum Associates.

Doddington, G. (2002). Automatic evaluation of machine translation quality using n-gram co-occurrence statistics. In *Proceedings of the Human Language Technology Conference*, (pp. 138-145). San Diego, CA: Human Language Technology.

Dornescu, I., & Orasan, C. (2010). Interactive QA using the QALL-ME framework. *International Journal of Computational Linguistics and Applications, 1*(1-2), 233–247.

dos Santos, C. N., Milidiú, R. L., & Rentería, R. (2008). Portuguese part-of-speech tagging using entropy guided transformation learning. *Lecture Notes in Computer Science, 5190*, 143–152. doi:10.1007/978-3-540-85980-2_15

Dragsted, B. (2010). Coordination of reading and writing processes in translation. In *Translation and Cognition* (pp. 41–62). Amsterdam, The Netherlands: Benjamins.

Dragsted, B., & Hansen, I. G. (2008). Comprehension and production in translation: A pilot study on segmentation and the coordination of reading and writing processes. *Copenhagen Studies in Language, 36*, 9–12.

Dumais, S. T., & Belkin, N. J. (2005). The TREC interactive tracks: Putting the user into search. In Vorhees, E. M., & Harman, D. K. (Eds.), *TREC: Experiment and Evaluation in Information Retrieval* (pp. 123–152). Cambridge, MA: MIT Press.

Dupont, S., & Luettin, J. (2000). Audio-visual speech modeling for continuous speech recognition. *IEEE Transactions on Multimedia, 2*(3), 141–151. doi:10.1109/6046.865479

Durant, K. T., & Smith, M. D. (2007). Predicting the political sentiment of web log posts using supervised machine learning techniques coupled with feature selection. In *Proceedings of Advances in Web Mining and Web Usage Analysis* (pp. 187–206). Heidelberg, Germany: Springer. doi:10.1007/978-3-540-77485-3_11

Earl, L. L. (1970). Experiments in automatic extraction and indexing. *Information Storage and Retrieval, 6,* 313–334. doi:10.1016/0020-0271(70)90025-2

Eckert, K., Niepert, M., Niemann, C., Buckner, C., Allen, C., & Stuckenschmidt, H. (2010). Crowdsourcing the assembly of concept hierarchies. In *Proceedings of JCDL 2010, 10th ACM/IEEE-CS Joint Conference on Digital Libraries,* (pp. 139-148). Surfer's Paradise, Australia: ACM/IEEE.

Edvardsen, L. F. H., Sølvberg, I. T., Aalberg, T., & Trætteberg, H. (2009). Automatically generating high quality metadata by analyzing the document code of common file types. In *Proceedings of JCDL2009: 9th ACM/IEEE-CS Joint Conference on Digital Libraries,* (pp. 29-38). Austin, TX: ACM/IEEE.

Egan, D. (1998). Individual differences in human-computer interaction. In *Handbook of Human-Computer Interaction* (pp. 543–568). Oxford, UK: North Holland.

Eirinaki, M., & Vazirgiannis, M. (2003). web mining for web personalization. *ACM Transactions on Internet Technology, 3*(1), 1–27. doi:10.1145/643477.643478

Eisele, A., & Chen, Y. (2010). *MultiUN: A multilingual corpus from United Nations documents.* In *Proceedings of the Seventh International Conference on Language Resources and Evaluation,* (pp. 2868-2872). Valletta, Malta: LREC.

Eissen, S. M., Stein, B., & Kulig, M. (2007). Plagiarism detection without reference collections. In Decker, R., & Lenz, H. J. (Eds.), *Advances in Data Analysis* (pp. 359–366). Berlin, Germany: Springer. doi:10.1007/978-3-540-70981-7_40

Ekbal, A., Haque, R., & Bandyopadhyay, S. (2007). Bengali part of speech tagging using conditional random field. In *Proceedings of the 7th International Symposium of Natural Language Processing,* (pp. 131-136). ACL.

Emeneau, M. B. (1956). India as linguistic area. *Linguistics, 32,* 3–16.

Ericsson, K.-A. (2000). Expertise in interpreting: An expert-performance perspective. *Interpreting, 5*(2), 187–220. doi:10.1075/intp.5.2.08eri

Escudero, G., Màrquez, L., & Rigau, G. (2000a). An empirical study of the domain dependence of supervised word sense disambiguation systems. In *Proceedings of the 2000 Joint SIGDAT Conference on Empirical Methods in Natural Language Processing and Very Large Corpora,* (pp. 172–180). Morristown, NJ: SIGDAT.

Escudero, G., Màrquez, L., & Rigau, G. (2000b). Naive bayes and exemplar-based approaches to word sense disambiguation revisited. In *Proceedings of ECAI,* (pp. 421–425). ECAI.

Esuli, A., & Sebastiani, F. (2006a). Determining term subjectivity and term orientation for opinion mining. In *Proceedings of EACL-06, 11th Conference of the European Chapter of the Association for Computational Linguistics,* (pp. 193-200). Trento, Italy: ACL.

Esuli, A., & Sebastiani, F. (2006b). Sentiwordnet: A publicly available lexical resource for opinion mining. In *Proceedings of the 5th Conference on Language Resources and Evaluation,* (pp. 417-422). ACL.

Eveno, N., Caplier, A., & Coulon, P. Y. (2004). Accurate and quasi-automatic lip tracking. *IEEE Transaction on Circuits and Video Technology, 14*(5), 706–715. doi:10.1109/TCSVT.2004.826754

Evert, S. (2005). *The statistics of word cooccurrences: Word pairs and collocations.* (Ph.D. Thesis). University of Stuttgart. Stuttgart, Germany.

Evert, S., & Krenn, B. (2001). Methods for the qualitative evaluation of lexical association measures. In *Proceedings of the 39th Annual Meeting on Association for Computational Linguistics,* (pp. 188–195). ACL.

Faensen, D., Faultstich, L., Schweppe, H., Schweppe, H., Hinze, A., & Steidinger, A. (2001). Hermes: A notification service for digital libraries. In *Proceedings of the 1ˢᵗ ACM/IEEE-CS Joint Conference on Digital Libraries (JCDL 2001)*. ACM/IEEE.

Fazly, A., & Stevenson, S. (2007). Distinguishing subtypes of multiword expressions using linguistically motivated statistical measures. In N. Grégoire, S. Evert, & B. Krenn (Eds.), *Proceedings of the ACL 2007 Workshop on a Broader Perspective on Multiword Expressions,* (pp. 9–16). Prague, Czech Republic: ACL.

Feitelson, D. G. (2004). On identifying name equivalences in digital libraries. *Information Research, 9*(4).

Fellbaum, C. (1998). *WordNet: An electronic lexical database*. WordNet.

Fellbaum, C. (Ed.). (1998). *WordNet: An electronic lexical database*. Cambridge, MA: MIT Press.

Fernández-Amorós, D. (2009). *Word sense disambiguation using English-Spanish aligned phrases over comparable corpora*. In *Proceedings of CoRR*. CoRR.

Ferreira, A., Veloso, A., Goncalves, M., & Laender, A. (2010). Effective self-training author name disambiguation in scholarly digital libraries. In *Proceedings of JCDL 2010, 10ᵗʰ ACM/IEEE-CS Joint Conference on Digital Librarie,s* (pp. 39-48). Surfer's Paradise, Australia: ACM/IEEE.

Ferres, D., Kanaan, S., Gonzalez, E., Ageno, A., Rodriguez, H., Surdeanu, M., & Turmo, J. (2004). TALP-QA system at TREC 2004: Structural and hierarchical relaxing of semantic constraints. In *Proceedings of the 13th Text REtrieval Conference (TREC 2004)*. TREC.

Ferret, O., & Grau, B. (2001). Document selection refinement based on linguistic features for QALC: A question answering system. In *Proceedings of RANLP 2001*. RANLP.

Figuerola, C., Gómez, R., Zazo, A., & Alonso Berrocal, J. L. (2002). Spanish monolingual track: The impact of stemming on retrieval. *Lecture Notes in Computer Science, 2406*, 253–261. doi:10.1007/3-540-45691-0_23

Fillmore, C. J., & Baker, C. F. (2001). Frame semantics for text understanding. In *Proceedings of WordNet and Other Lexical Resources Workshop*. Pittsburgh, PA: NAACL.

Finger, M. (2000). Técnicas de otimização da precisão empregadas no etiquetador Tycho Brahe. In Nunes, M. G. V. (Ed.), *Anais do V Encontro para o Processamento Computacional da Língua Portuguesa Escrita e Falada* (pp. 141–154). Atibaia, Spain: ICMC/USP.

Fisher, D., Smith, M., & Welser, H. (2006). You are who you talk to: Detecting roles in usenet newsgroups. In *Proceedings of the 39th Hawaii International Conference on System Sciences,* (pp. 59-68). Kauai, HI: IEEE.

Fisher, R. (1936). The use of multiple measurements in taxonomic problems. *Annals of Eugenics, 7*, 179–188. doi:10.1111/j.1469-1809.1936.tb02137.x

Floridi, L. (2010). *The Cambridge handbook of information and computer ethics*. Cambridge, UK: Cambridge University Press. doi:10.1017/CBO9780511845239

Fontan, L., & Saint-Dizier, P. (2008). Analyzing the explanation structure of procedural texts: Dealing with advices and warnings. In J. Bos (Ed), *International Symposium on Text Semantics (STEP 2008)*. STEP.

Forner, P., Peñas, A., Agirre, E., Alegria, I., Forăscu, C., & Moreau, N. … Tjong Kim Sang, E. (2009). Overview of the Clef 2008 multilingual question answering track. *Lecture Notes in Computer Science, 34*, 262-295.

Foster, G., & Kuhn, R. (2007). Mixture-model adaptation for SMT. In *Proceedings of the Second Workshop on Statistical Machine Translation*, (pp. 128-135). Prague, Czech Republic: SMT.

Foster, J., & Vogel, C. (2004). Parsing ill-formed text using an error grammar. *Artificial Intelligence Review, 21*(3-4), 269–291. doi:10.1023/B:AIRE.0000036259.68818.1e

Fox, C. (1990). A stop list for general text. *SIGIR Forum, 24*(1-2), 19–21.

Fox, E. A., Akscyn, R. M., Furuta, R., & Leggett, J. J. (1995). Digital libraries. *Communications of the ACM, 38*(4), 23–28. doi:10.1145/205323.205325

Frakes, W., & Baeza-Yates, R. (1992). *Information retrieval: Data structures & algorithms*. Englewood Cliffs, NJ: Prentice Hall.

Frederking, R., Mitamura, T., Nyberg, E., & Carbonell, J. (1997). Translingual information access. In *Proceedings of the AAAI Spring Symposium on Cross-Language Text and Speech Retrieval*. Stanford, CA: AAAI.

Freeman, L. C. (2004). *The development of social network analysis*. Vancouver, Canada: Empirical Press.

Freire, N., Borbinha, J., Calado, P., & Martins, B. (2011). Metadata geoparsing system for place name recognition and resolution in metadata records. In *Proceedings of JCDL 2011*. Ottawa, Canada: JCDL.

Freund, Y., & Schapire, R. E. (1999). A short introduction to boosting. In *Proceedings of the Sixteenth International Joint Conference on Artificial Intelligence*, (pp. 1401–1406). IEEE.

Funk, A., Li, Y., Saggion, H., Bontcheva, K., & Leibold, C. (2008). Opinion analysis for business intelligence applications. In *Proceedings of the First International Workshop on Ontology-Supported Business Intelligence*, (pp. 1-9). IEEE.

Furnham, A. (1986). Response bias, social desirability and dissimulation. *Personality and Individual Differences*, *7*(3), 385–400. doi:10.1016/0191-8869(86)90014-0

Gajadhar, J., & Green, J. (2003). *An analysis of nonverbal communication in an online chat group*. Working Paper. Retrieved September 16, 2010, from http://www.openpolytechnic.ac.nz/static/pdf/research/res_wp203gajadharj1.pdf

Gale, W. A., & Church, K. W. (1991). A program for aligning sentences in bilingual corpora. In *Proceedings of the 29th Annual Meeting of the Association for Computational Linguistics*, (pp. 177-184). Berkeley, CA: ACL.

Gale, W., Church, K., & Yarowsky, D. (1993). A method for disambiguating word senses in a large corpus. *Computers and the Humanities*. Retrieved from http://nlp.cs.swarthmore.edu/~richardw/papers/gale1993-method.pdf

Galley, M., Graehl, J., Knight, K., Marcu, D., DeNeefe, S., Wang, W., & Thayer, I. (2006). Scalable inference and training of context-rich syntactic translation models. In *Proceedings of the 21st International Conference on Computational Linguistics and 44th Annual Meeting of the Association for Computational Linguistics*, (pp. 961-968). Sydney, Australia: ACL.

Gambäck, B., Olsson, F., Argaw, A. A., & Asker, L. (2009). Methods for Amharic part-of-speech tagging. In *Proceedings of the First Workshop on Language Technologies for African Languages*, (pp. 104–111). Morristown, NJ: ACL.

Garcia, V. L., Motta, E., & Uren, V. (2006). AquaLog: An ontology-driven question answering system to interface the semantic web. In *Proceedings of the 2006 Conference of the North American Chapter of the Association for Computational Linguistics on Human Language Technology*, (pp. 269-272). New York, NY: ACL.

Garcia, A. C., Standlee, A. I., Bechkoff, J., & Cui, Y. (2009). Ethnographic approaches to the internet and computer-mediated communication. *Journal of Contemporary Ethnography*, *38*(1), 52–84. doi:10.1177/0891241607310839

Gelbukh. (2012). *Spanish verb-noun lexical functions*. Retrieved from http://www.Gelbukh.com/lexical-functions

Gey, F. C. (2005). How similar are Chinese and Japanese for cross-language information retrieval. In *Proceedings of the Fifth NTCIR Workshop Meeting on Evaluation of Information Access Technologies: Information Retrieval, Question Answering and Cross-Lingual Information Access*. NTCIR.

Gilliland-Swetland, A. M. (2000). Setting the stage. In Baca, M. (Ed.), *Introduction to Metadata: Pathways to Digital Information*. Los Angeles, CA: Getty Information Institute.

Giménez, J., & Márquez, L. (2007). Context-aware discriminative phrase selection for statistical machine translation. In *Proceedings of the Second Workshop on Statistical Machine Translation*, (pp. 159-166). Prague, Czech Republic: SMT.

Giménez, J., & Márquez, L. (2010). Asiya: An open toolkit for automatic machine translation (meta-) evaluation. *The Prague Bulletin of Mathematical Linguistics, 94*.

Gimpel, K., & Smith, N. A. (2008). Rich source-side context for statistical machine translation. In *Proceedings of the Third Workshop on Statistical Machine Translation*, (pp. 9-17). Columbus, OH: SMT.

Ginsberg, J., Mohebbi, M. H., Patel, R. S., Brammer, L., Smolinski, M. S., & Brilliant, L. (2009). Detecting influenza epidemics using search engine query data. *Nature*, *457*, 1012–1014. doi:10.1038/nature07634

Ginzburg, J., & Fernandez, R. (2010). Computational models of dialogue. In Clark, A., Fox, C., & Lappin, S. (Eds.), *The Handbook of Computational Linguistics and Natural Language Processing* (pp. 429–481). Oxford, UK: Wiley-Blackwell. doi:10.1002/9781444324044.ch16

Goldschen, A. J. (1993). *Continuous automatic speech recognition by lipreading*. Washington, DC: George Washington University.

Goldstein, J., Kantrowitz, M., Mittal, V. O., & Carbonell, J. (1999). Summarizing text documents: Sentence selection and evaluation metrics. In *Proceedings of the 22nd Annual International ACM SIGIR Conference on Research and Development in Information Retrieval*, (pp. 121-128). Berkeley, CA: SIGIR.

Goldthwaite, D. (1997). Knowledge of pragmatic conversational structure. *Journal of Psycholinguistic Research, 26*(5), 497–508. doi:10.1023/A:1025071513114

Golub, K. (2006). Automated subject classification of textual web documents. *The Journal of Documentation, 62*(3), 350–371. doi:10.1108/00220410610666501

Gonçalves, M. A., Fox, E. A., Watson, L. T., & Kipp, N. A. (2004). Streams, structures, spaces, scenarios, societies (5S): A formal model for digital libraries. *ACM Transactions on Information Systems, 22*(2), 270–312.

Gonzalez-Bailon, S., Banchs, R. E., & Kaltenbrunner, A. (2010). *Emotional reactions and the pulse of public opinion: Measuring the impact f political events on the sentiment of online discussions*. Cornell University Library. Retrieved September 27, 2010, from http://arxiv.org/abs/ 1009.4019

Gonzalo, J., Clough, P., & Karlgren, J. (2009). Overview of iCLEF 2008: Search log analysis for multilingual image retrieval. *Lecture Notes in Computer Science, 5706.*

Gonzalo, J., & Oard, D. (2003). The CLEF 2002 interactive track. *Lecture Notes in Computer Science, 2785*, 372–382. doi:10.1007/978-3-540-45237-9_33

Gonzalo, J., & Oard, D. (2005). iCLEF 2004 track overview: Pilot experiments in interactive cross-language question answering. *Lecture Notes in Computer Science, 3491.*

Gonzalo, J., Peinado, V., Clough, P., & Karlgren, J. (2010). Overview of iCLEF 2009: Exploring search behaviour in a multilingual folksonomy environment. *Lecture Notes in Computer Science, 6242*, 13–20. doi:10.1007/978-3-642-15751-6_2

Göpferich, S. (2009). Towards a model of translation competence and its acquisition: The longitudinal study TransComp. In Göpferich, S., Jakobsen, A. L., & Mees, I. M. (Eds.), *Behind the Mind: Methods, Models, and Results in Translation Process Research* (pp. 11–37). Copenhagen, Denmark: Samfundslitteratur.

Göpferich, S., Jakobsen, A. L., & Mees, I. M. (Eds.). (2009). *Behind the mind: Methods, models and results in translation process research*. Copenhagen, Denmark: Samfundslitteratur.

Gordan, M., Kotropoulos, C., & Pitas, I. (2002). A support vector machine-based dynamic network for visual speech recognition applications. *EURASIP Journal on Applied Signal Processing, 11*, 1248–1259. doi:10.1155/S1110865702207039

Gou, L., Chen, H.-H., Kim, J.-H., Zhang, X. L., & Giles, C. L. (2010). Social network document ranking. In *Proceedings of JCDL2010, 10th ACM/IEEE-CS Joint Conference on Digital Libraries*, (pp. 313-322). Surfer's Paradise, Australia: ACM/IEEE.

Graf, H. P., Cosatto, E., & Potamianos, M. (1997). Robust recognition of faces and facial features with a multi-modal system. In *Proceedings of the International Conference on Systems Man and Cybernetics*, (pp. 2034-2039). IEEE Press.

Gravier, G., Potamianos, G., & Neti, C. (2002). Asynchrony modeling for audio-visual speech recognition. In *Proceedings of the Second International Conference on Human Language Technology Research*. San Diego, CA: Morgan Kaufmann Publishers Inc.

Greene, B. B., & Rubin, G. M. (1971). *Automatic grammatical tagging of English. Technical Report*. Providence, RI: Brown University.

Grefenstette, G. (1995). Comparing two language identification schemes. In *Proceedings of JADT*. JADT.

Grefenstette, G. (1998). *The problem of cross-language information retrieval*. Dordrecht, The Netherlands: Kluwer Academic Publishers. doi:10.1007/978-1-4615-5661-9

Grégoire, N. (2007). Design and implementation of a lexicon of Dutch multiword expressions. In N. Grégoire, S. Evert, & B. Krenn (Eds.), *Proceedings of the ACL 2007 Workshop on a Broader Perspective on Multiword Expressions,* (pp. 17–24). Prague, Czech Republic: ACL.

Grice, H. (1975). Logic and conversation. In Cole & Morgan (Eds.), *Syntax and Semantics.* New York, NY: Academic Press.

Grira, N., Crucianu, M., & Boujemaa, N. (2006). Unsupervised and semi-supervised clustering: A brief survey. In S. Boughorbel, (Ed.), *A Review of Machine Learning Techniques for Processing Multimedia Content.* Retrieved October 7, 2010 from http://www-rocq.inria.fr/~crucianu/src/BriefSurveyClustering.pdf

Gruhl, D., Guha, R., Kumar, R., Novak, J., & Tomkins, A. (2005). The predictive power of online chatter. In *Proceedings of the SIGKDD Conference on Knowledge Discovery and Data Mining,* (pp. 78-87). SIGKDD.

Gu, Q., de la Chica, S., Ahmad, F., Khan, H., Sumner, T., Martin, J. H., & Butcher, K. (2008). Personalizing the selection of digital library resources to support intentional learning. *Lecture Notes in Computer Science, 5173,* 244–255. doi:10.1007/978-3-540-87599-4_25

Gurrutxaga, A., & Alegria, I. (2011). Automatic extraction of NV expressions in Basque: Basic issues on cooccurrence techniques. In *Proceedings of the Workshop on Multiword Expressions: From Parsing and Generation to the Real World,* (pp. 2-7). Portland, OR: Association for Computational Linguistics.

Haase, A. Q., Wellman, B., Witte, J., & Hampton, K. (2002). Capitalizing on the Internet: social contact, civic engagement, and sense of community. In Wellman, B., & Haythornthwaite, C. (Eds.), *The Internet and Everyday Life.* Oxford, UK: Blackwell. doi:10.1002/9780470774298.ch10

Habash, N. (2007). Syntactic preprocessing for statistical machine translation. In *Proceedings of the MT Summit XI.* Copenhagen, Denmark: MT Summit.

Hakkani-Tür, D., Tur, G., Levit, M., Gillick, D., Singla, A., & Yaman, S. (2010). Statistical sentence extraction for multilingual information distillation. In Olive, McCary, Dietrich, & Christianson (Eds.), *Handbook of Natural Language Processing and Machine Translation: DARPA Global Autonomous Language Exploitation (GALE) Program.* Berlin, Germany: Springer.

Hallinan, P. W., Cohen, D. S., & Yuille, A. L. (1989). Feature extraction from faces using deformable templates. In *Proceedings of the Computer Vision and Pattern Recognition,* (pp. 104-109). IEEE.

Hall, M., Frank, E., Holmes, G., Pfahringer, B., Reutemann, P., & Witten, I. H. (2009). The WEKA data mining software: An update. *SIGKDD Explorations, 11*(1), 10–18. doi:10.1145/1656274.1656278

Halteren, H., & Teufel, S. (2003). Examining the consensus between human summaries: Initial experiments with factoid analysis. In *Proceedings of the HLT-NAACL on Text Summarization Workshop,* (pp. 57-64). NAACL.

Ham, R. (2004). *Spamming: Exploring dimensions of internet misuse.* Queensland, Australia: Griffith University.

Hanani, U., Shapira, B., & Shoval, P. (2001). Information filtering: Overview of issues, research and systems. *User Modeling and User-Adapted Interaction, 11,* 203–259. doi:10.1023/A:1011196000674

Hanneman, G., Huber, E., Agarwal, A., Ambati, V., Parlikar, A., Peterson, E., & Lavie, A. (2008). Statistical transfer systems for French-English and German-English machine translation. In *Proceedings of the Third Workshop on Statistical Machine Translation,* (pp. 163-166). Columbus, OH: SMT.

Haque, R., Naskar, S. K., van den Bosch, A., & Way, A. (2010). Supertags as source language context in hierarchical phrase-based SMT. In *Proceedings of the 9th Conference of the Association for Machine Translation in the Americas (AMTA 2010).* Denver, CO: AMTA.

Harabagiu, S. M., Pasca, M., & Maiorano, S. J. (2000). Experiments with open-domain textual question answering. In *Proceedings of COLING-2000.* Saarbruken, Germany: COLING.

Harabagiu, S., & Hickl, A. (2006). Methods for using textual entailment in open-domain question answering. In *Proceedings of the 21st International Conference on Computational Linguistics and 44th Annual Meeting of the ACL*, (pp. 905-912). Sydney, Australia: ACL.

Harabagiu, S., Hickl, A., Lehmann, J., & Moldovan, D. (2005). Experiments with interactive question-answering. In *Proceedings of the 43rd Annual Meeting on Association for Computational Linguistics*, (pp. 205-214). Ann Arbor, MI: ACL.

Harabagiu, S., Moldovan, D., Pasca, M., Mihalcea, R., Surdeanu, M., & Bunescu, R. ... Morarescu, P. (2000). FALCON: Boosting knowledge for answer engines. In *Proceedings of 9ᵗʰ TExt Retrieval Conference (TREC-9)*. Gaitherburg, MD: TREC.

Harabagiu, S., & Moldovan, D. (2003). Question answering. In Mitkov, R. (Ed.), *The Oxford Handbook of Computational Linguistics* (pp. 560–582). Oxford, UK: Oxford University Press.

Harman, D. (2005). Beyond English. In Voorhees, E. M., & Harman, D. (Eds.), *TREC: Experiment and Evaluation in Information Retrieval* (pp. 153–181). Cambridge, MA: MIT Press.

Harman, D. K. (2005). Beyond English. In Vorhees, E. M., & Harman, D. K. (Eds.), *TREC: Experiment and Evaluation in Information Retrieval* (pp. 153–181). Cambridge, MA: MIT Press.

Harper, F. M., Raban, D., Rafaeli, S., & Konstan, J. A. (2008). Predictors of answer quality in online Q&A sites. In *Proceeding of the Twenty-Sixth Annual SIGCHI Conference on Human Factors in Computing Systems (CHI 2008)*, (pp. 865-874). Florence, Italy: SIGCHI.

Haruechaiyasak, C., & Damrongrat, C. (2010). Identifying persons in news article images based on textual analysis. [ICADL.]. *Proceedings of ICADL, 2010*, 216–225.

Hatzivassiloglou, V., & Wiebe, J. (2000). Effects of adjective orientation and gradability on sentence subjectivity. In *Proceedings of the International Conference on Computational Linguistics (COLING)*, (pp. 299-305). Saarbrücken, Germany: COLING.

Hazelbeck, G., & Saito, H. (2010). A hybrid approach for functional expression identification in a Japanese reading assistant. In *Proceedings of the Workshop on Multiword Expressions: From Theory to Applications (MWE 2010)*, (pp. 80-83). Beijing, China: MWE.

He, X., & Toutanova, K. (2009). Joint optimization for machine translation system combination. In *Proceedings of the 2009 Conference on Empirical Methods in Natural Language Processing*, (1202-1211). Singapore: Empirical Methods in Natural Language Processing.

He, Y., Ma, Y., van Genabith, J., & Way, A. (2010). Bridging SMT and TM with translation recommendation. In *Proceedings of the 48th Annual Meeting of the Association for Computational Linguistics*, (pp. 622-630). Uppsala, Sweden: ACL.

Heikkilä, J. (1995). A TWOL-based lexicon and feature system for English. In Karlsson, F., Voutilainen, A., Heikkilä, J., & Anttila, A. (Eds.), *Constraint Grammar: A Language-Independent System for Parsing Unrestricted Text* (pp. 103–131). Berlin, Germany: Mouton de Gruyter. doi:10.1515/9783110882629.103

Helbig, H. (2005). *Knowledge representation and the semantics of natural language*. Berlin, Germany: Springer-Verlag.

Hermjakob, U. (2001). Parsing and question classification for question answering. In *Proceedings of the Workshop on Question Answering at the Conference ACL-2001*. Toulouse, France: ACL.

Hermjakob, U., Hovy, E., & Chin-Yew, L. (2000). Knowledge-based question answering. In *Proceedings ACL 2002*. ACL.

Hersh, W. (2006). Evaluating interactive question answering. In Ide, N., Véronis, J., Baayen, H., Church, K. W., Klavans, J., & Barnard, D. T. (Eds.), *Advances in Open Domain Question Answering* (pp. 431–455). Berlin, Germany: Springer.

He, Y., Hui, S. C., & Fong, A. C. M. (2003). Citation-based retrieval for scholarly publications. *IEEE Intelligent Systems, 18*(2), 58–65. doi:10.1109/MIS.2003.1193658

Hickl, A., Roberts, K., Rink, B., Bensley, J., Jungen, T., Shi, Y., & Williams, J. (2007). Question answering with LCC's Chaucer-2 at TREC 2007. In *Proceedings of the 2007 Text Retrieval Conference (TREC 2007)*. Gaithersburg, MD: TREC.

Hildebrand, A. S., & Vogel, S. (2010). CMU system combination via hypothesis selection for WMT'10. In *Proceedings of the Joint Fifth Workshop on Statistical Machine Translation and MetricsMATR*, (pp. 307-310). Uppsala, Sweden: MetricsMATR.

Hinduja, S., & Patchin, J. W. (2008). Cyberbullying: An exploratory analysis of factors related to offending and victimization. *Deviant Behavior*, 29(2), 129–156. doi:10.1080/01639620701457816

Hirschman, L., & Gaizauskas, R. (2001). Natural language question answering: The view from here. *Natural Language Engineering*, 7(4), 275–300. doi:10.1017/S1351324901002807

Hirst, G., & St-Ogne, D. (1998). *Combining local context and WordNet similarity for word sense identification*. Cambridge, MA: MIT Press.

Hoad, T. C., & Zobel, J. (2003). Methods for identifying versioned and plagiarised documents. *American Society for Information Science and Technology*, 54(3), 203–215. doi:10.1002/asi.10170

Hobbs, J. R. (1978). Resolving pronoun references. *Lingua*, 44, 311–338. doi:10.1016/0024-3841(78)90006-2

Hodge, G. M., Zeng, M. L., & Soergel, D. (2003). Building a meaningful web: From traditional knowledge organization systems to new semantic tools. In *Proceedings of the 3rd ACM/IEEE-CS Joint Conference on Digital Libraries*, (p. 417). Houston, TX: ACM/IEEE.

Hong, Y., On, B.-W., & Lee, D. (2004). System support for name authority control problem in digital libraries: OpenDBLP approach. In *Proceedings of the 8th European Conference on Digital Libraries*, (pp. 134-144). ACL.

Hönig, H. G. (1991). Translation studies: The state of the art, the first James Holmes symposium on translation studies. In *Proceedings of the First James S Holmes Symposium on Translation Studies*, (pp. 77–89). Amsterdam, The Netherlands: James S Holmes.

Hopfield, J. J. (1982). Neural networks and physical systems with emergent collective computational abilities. *Proceedings of the National Academy of Sciences of the United States of America*, 79(8), 2554–2558. doi:10.1073/pnas.79.8.2554

Hore, C., Asahara, M., & Matsumoto, Y. (2005). Automatic extraction of fixed multiword expressions. *Lecture Notes in Computer Science*, 3651, 565–575. doi:10.1007/11562214_50

Hovy, E., Gerber, L., Hermjakob, H., Junk, M., & Lin, C.-Y. (2001). Question answering in Webclopedia. In *Proceedings of the 9th Text REtrieval Conference*, (pp. 655-664). TREC.

Hovy, E., Ide, N., Frederking, R., Mariani, J., & Zampolli, A. (2001). Multilingual information management: Current levels and future abilities. In *Linguistica Computazionale* (*Vol. 14-15*). Pisa, Italy: Istituti Editoriali e Poligrafici Internazionali.

Hu, M., & Liu, B. (2004). Mining and summarizing customer reviews. In *Proceedings of the ACM SIGKDD International Conference on Knowledge Discovery & Data Mining*, (pp. 168-177). Seattle, WA: ACM Press.

Huang, F., & Yates, A. (2010). *Exploring representation-learning approaches to domain adaptation*. Retrieved from http://www.cis.temple.edu/~yates/papers/2010-danlp-lvlms-for-domain-adaptation.pdf

Huang, L., Knight, K., & Joshi, A. (2006). Statistical syntax-directed translation with extended domain of locality. In *Proceedings of the 5th Conference of the Association for Machine Translation in the Americas (AMTA)*. Boston, MA: AMTA.

Huang, Z., Chung, W., Ong, T. H., & Chen, H. (2002). A graph-based recommender system for digital library. In *Proceedings of the 2nd ACM/IEEE-CS Joint Conference on Digital Libraries*. ACM/IEEE.

Hui, L. E., Seng, K. P., & Tse, K. M. (2004). RBF neural network mouth tracking for audio-visual speech recognition system. In *Proceedings of the IEEE Region 10 Conference (TENCON 2004)*, (pp. 84-87). IEEE Press.

Hull, D. A., & Grefenstette, G. (1996). Experiments in multilingual information retrieval. In *Proceedings of the 19th Annual International ACM SIGIR Conference on Research and Development in Information Retrieval*. ACM Press.

Hull, D. A., & Grefenstette, G. (1996). Querying across languages: A dictionary-based approach to multilingual information retrieval. In *Proceedings of the 19th International Conference on Research and Development in Information Retrieval*, (pp. 49-57). ACL.

Hull, D. A., & Grefenstette, G. (1996). *Querying across languages: A dictionary-based approach to multilingual information retrieval*. Paper presented at SIGIR 1996. Zurich, Switzerland.

Hutchins, J. (1997). Milestones in machine translation: Part 1: How it all began in 1947 and 1948. *Language Today, 3*, 22–23.

Hwang, S. Y., Hsiung, W. C., & Yang, W. S. (2003). A prototype WWW literature recommendation system for digital libraries. *Online Information Review, 27*, 169–182. doi:10.1108/14684520310481436

Ide, N., Erjavec, T., & Tufi, D. (2001). Automatic sense tagging using parallel corpora. In *Proceedings of the 6th Natural Language Processing Pacific Rim Symposium*, (pp. 212–219). Pacific Rim.

Ide, N., & Véronis, J. (1998). Introduction to the special issue on word sense disambiguation: The state of the art. *Computational Linguistics, 24*(1), 1–40.

ISO. (1985). *ISO 5964 documentation -- Guidelines for the establishment and development of multilingual thesauri*. Geneva, Switzerland: ISO.

ISO. (1986). *ISO 2788 documentation – Guidelines for the establishment and development of monolingual thesauri*. Geneva, Switzerland: ISO.

Ittycheriah, A., Franz, M., Zhu, W. J., & Ratnaparkhi, A. (2001). IBM's statistical question answering system. In *Proceedings 9th Text Retrieval Conference (TREC-9)*. TREC.

Jackendoff, R. (1990). *Semantic structures*. Cambridge, MA: The MIT Press.

Jackson, P., & Moulinier, I. (2007). *Natural language processing for online applications: Text retrieval, extraction and categorization*. New York, NY: John Benjamins Publishing Company.

Jaidka, K., Khoo, C., & Na, J.-C. (2010). Imitating human literature review writing: An approach to multi-document summarization. [ICADL.]. *Proceedings of ICADL, 2010*, 116–119.

Jakobsen, A. L. (2006). Research methods in translation - Translog. In Sullivan, K. P. H., & Lindgren, E. (Eds.), *Computer Keystroke Logging and Writing: Methods and Applications* (*Vol. 18*, pp. 95–105). Oxford, UK: Elsevier.

Jakobsen, A. L. (2011). Tracking translators' keystrokes and eye movements with Translog. In Alvstad, C., Hild, A., & Tiselius, E. (Eds.), *Integrative Approaches in Translation Studies* (pp. 37–55). Copenhagen, Denmark: Benjamins.

Jan, E.-E., Lin, S.-H., & Chen, B. (2010). Transliteration retrieval model for cross lingual information retrieval. *Lecture Notes in Computer Science, 6458*, 183–192. doi:10.1007/978-3-642-17187-1_17

Jansen, B. J. (2006). Search log analysis: What it is, what's been done, how to do it. *Library & Information Science Research, 28*, 407–432. doi:10.1016/j.lisr.2006.06.005

Jansen, B. J., & Spink, A. (2000). Methodological approach in discovering user search patterns through Web log analysis. *Bulletin of the American Society for Information Science, 27*, 15–17. doi:10.1002/bult.185

Jansen, B. J., & Spink, A. (2005). How are we searching the world wide web? An analysis of nine search engine transaction logs. *Information Processing & Management, 42*(1), 248–563. doi:10.1016/j.ipm.2004.10.007

Jansen, B. J., Spink, A., Bateman, J., & Saracevic, T. (1998). Real life information retrieval: A study of user queries on the Web. *ACM SIGIR Special Interest Group on Information Retrieval, 32*(1), 5–17.

Jansen, B. J., Spink, A., & Pedersen, J. (2005). A temporal comparison of AltaVista web searching. *Journal of the American Society for Information Science and Technology, 56*, 559–570. doi:10.1002/asi.20145

Jarvenpaa, S. L., & Todd, P. A. (1996). Consumer reactions to electronic shopping on the world wide web. *International Journal of Electronic Commerce, 1*(2), 59–88.

Jenkins, C., Jackson, M., Burden, P., & Wallis, J. (1998). Automatic classification of web resources using java and Dewey decimal classification. *Computer Networks and ISDN Systems Archive, 30*(1-7), 646-648.

Jensen, K. (2009). Distribution of attention between source text and target text during translation. In *Proceedings of IATIS*. IATIS.

Jiang, J. (2008). *Domain adaptation in natural language processing*. Retrieved from http://hdl.handle.net/2142/10870

Jiang, J. J., & Conrath, D. W. (1997). Semantic similarity based on corpus statistics and lexical taxonomy. In *Proceedings of the International Conference on Research in Computational Linguistics*, (pp. 19–33). Research and Computational Linguistics.

Jiang, J., & Zhai, C. (2007). Instance weighting for domain adaptation in NLP. In *Proceedings of the 45th Annual Meeting of the Association for Computational Linguistics*, (pp. 254–261). ACL. Retrieved from http://www.aclweb.org/anthology/P/P07/P07-1034.pdf

Jijkoun, V., Khalid, M. A., Marx, M., & de Rijke, M. (2008). Named entity normalization in user generated content. In *Proceedings of SIGIR 2008 – Workshop on Analytics for Noisy Unstructured Text Data*, (pp. 23-30). SIGIR.

Jijkoun, V., Mishne, G., de Rijke, M., Schlobach, S., Ahn, D., & Muller, K. (2004). *The University of Amsterdam at QA@CLEF 2004*. Working Notes of the Cross-Language Evaluation Forum (CLEF 2004). New York, NY.

Jindal, N., & Liu, B. (2007). Review spam detection. In *Proceedings of the 16th International Conference on the World Wide Web*, (pp. 1189-1190). Banff, Canada: WWW.

Jing, H., Barzilay, R., McKeown, K., & Elhadad, M. (1998). Summarization evaluation methods: Experiments and analysis. In *Proceedings of the AAAI Symposium on Intelligent Summarization*, (pp. 60-68). AAAI.

Joachims, T. (2002). Optimizing search engines using clickthrough data. In *Proceedings of the 8th ACM SIGKDD International Conference on Knowledge Discovery and Data Mining*, (pp. 133-142). ACM Press.

John, B. E. (1996). Typist: A theory of performance in skilled typing. *Human-Computer Interaction, 11*(4), 321–355. doi:10.1207/s15327051hci1104_2

Joint Steering Committee for Revision of AACR. (2002). *Anglo-American cataloguing rules* (2nd ed.). Ottawa, Canada: Canadian Library Association.

Jolliffe, I. (1986). *Principle component analysis*. Berlin, Germany: Springer-Verlag.

Jong-Hoon, Key-Sun, Choi, & Isahara, H. (2006b). A machine transliteration model based on correspondence between graphemes and phonemes. *ACM Transactions on Asian Language Processing, 5*(3), 185–208.

Joorabchi, A., & Mahdi, A. E. (2009). Leveraging the legacy of conventional libraries for organizing digital libraries. In *Proceedings of the 13th European Conference, ECDL 2009*, (pp. 3-14). Corfu, Greece: ECDL.

Joorabchi, A., & Mahdi, A. E. (2008). Development of a national syllabus repository for higher education in Ireland. *Lecture Notes in Computer Science, 5173*, 197–208. doi:10.1007/978-3-540-87599-4_20

Joshi, A. K. (1982). Processing of sentences with intra-sentential code-switching. In *Proceedings of the 9th Conference on Computational Linguistics*, (pp. 145-150). Praha, Czechoslovakia: ACL.

Jurafsky, D., & Martin, J. (2000). *Speech and language processing: An introduction to natural language processing, computational linguistics and speech recognition*. Upper Saddle River, NJ: Prentice Hall.

Jurafsky, D., & Martin, J. H. (2009). *Speech and language processing an introduction to natural language processing, computational linguistics, and speech recognition* (2nd ed.). Upper Saddle River, NJ: Prentice-Hall, Inc.

Kääriäinen, M. (2009). Sinuhe: Statistical machine translation using a globally trained conditional exponential family translation model. In *Proceedings of the Conference on Empirical Methods in Natural Language Processing*, (pp. 1027-1036). Singapore: Empirical Methods in Natural Language Processing.

Kaisser, M. (2008). The QuALiM question answering demo: Supplementing answers with paragraphs drawn from Wikipedia. In *Proceedings of the ACL-08: HLT Demo Session*, (pp. 32-35). Columbus, OH: ACL.

Kaji, H., & Morimoto, Y. (2002). Unsupervised word sense disambiguation using bilingual comparable corpora. In *Proceedings of the 19th International Conference on Computational Linguistics, COLING 2002*, (vol 1), (pp. 1–7). Stroudsburg, PA: COLING.

Kalamboukis, T. Z. (1995). Suffix stripping with modern Greek. *Program, 29*, 313–321. doi:10.1108/eb047204

Kaltenbrunner, A., Bondia, E., & Banchs, R. E. (2009). Analyzing and ranking the Spanish speaking MySpace community by their contributions in forums. In *Proceedings of the 18ᵗʰ International Conference on World Wide Web*. Madrid, Spain: WWW.

Kan, M.-Y., & Klavans, J. L. (2002). Using librarian techniques in automatic text summarization for information retrieval. In *Proceedings of JCDL 2002*. Portland, OR: JCDL.

Kanhabua, N., & Nørvåg, K. (2010). Exploiting time-based synonyms in searching document archives. In *Proceedings of JCDL2010, 10ᵗʰ ACM/IEEE-CS Joint Conference on Digital Libraries*, (pp. 79-88). Surfer's Paradise, Australia: ACM/IEEE.

Kanhabua, N., & Nørvåg, K. (2008). Improving temporal language models for determining time of non-timestamped documents. *Lecture Notes in Computer Science, 5173*, 358–370. doi:10.1007/978-3-540-87599-4_37

Kao, W. C., Liu, D. R., & Wang, S. W. (2010). Expert finding in question-answering websites: A novel hybrid approach. In *Proceedings of the 2010 ACM Symposium on Applied Computing (SAC 2010)*, (pp. 867-871). Sierre, Switzerland: ACM Press.

Kaplan, A. M., & Haenlein, M. (2010). Users of the world, unite! The challenges and opportunities of social media. *Business Horizons, 53*(1), 59–68. doi:10.1016/j.bushor.2009.09.003

Karlgren, J., Gonzalo, J., & Clough, P. (2007). iCLEF 2006 overview: Searching the Flickr www photo-sharing repository. *Lecture Notes in Computer Science, 4730*, 186–194. doi:10.1007/978-3-540-74999-8_27

Karlsson, F., Voutilainen, A., Heikkilä, J., & Anttila, A. (1995). *Constraint grammar: A language-independent system for parsing unrestricted text*. Berlin, Germany: Mouton de Gruyter. doi:10.1515/9783110882629

Kass, M., Witkin, A., & Terropoulos, D. (1988). Snakes: Active contour models. *International Journal of Computer Vision, 1*, 321–331. doi:10.1007/BF00133570

Kastner, I. (2009, December). Developments in information retrieval: Part 1. *Library + Information Update*, 17-19.

Katz, B., Felshin, S., Lin, J. J., & Marton, G. (2004). Viewing the web as a virtual database for question answering. M. Maybury (Ed.), *New Directions in Question-Answering*. Cambridge, MA: MIT Press.

Katz, B., Lin, J. J., Stauer, C., & Grimson, W. E. L. (2004). Answering questions about moving objects in videos. In Maybury, M. (Ed.), *New Directions in Question-Answering*. Cambridge, MA: MIT Press.

Kearsley, G. P. (1976). Questions and question asking in verbal discourse: A cross-disciplinary review. *Journal of Psycholinguistic Research*, 12.

Keil, F. C., & Wilson, R. A. (2000). *Explanation and cognition*. Cambridge, MA: Bradford Book.

Kelly, B. (2004). Interoperable digital library programmes? We must have Q&A! In *Proceedings of the 8th European Conference on Digital Libraries*, (pp. 80-85). ECDL.

Kelly, D., Kantor, P. B., Morse, E. L., Scholtz, J., & Sun, Y. (2009). Questionnaires for eliciting evaluation data from users of interactive question answering systems. *Natural Language Engineering, 15*(1), 119–141. doi:10.1017/S1351324908004932

Kempe, A. (1993). *A probabilistic tagger and an analysis of tagging errors*. Stuttgart, Germany: Research Report, Institut für Maschinelle Sprachverarbeitung. Universität Stuttgart.

Khapra, M., Shah, S., Kedia, P., & Bhattacharyya, P. (2010). Domain-specific word sense disambiguation combining corpus based and wordnet based parameters. In *Proceedings of the 5th International Conference on Global Wordnet*. WordNet.

Khoo, C. S. G., Chan, S., & Niu, Y. (2000). Extracting causal knowledge from a medical database using graphical patterns. In *Proceedings of ACL 2000*. ACL.

Kilgarriff, A., Rychly, P., Smrz, P., & Tugwell, D. (2004). The sketch engine. In *Proceedings of EURALEX*, (pp. 105–116). Lorient, France: EURALEX.

Kim, S. M., & Hovy, E. (2006). Automatic identification of pro and con reasons in online reviews. In *Proceedings of the COLING/ACL 2006*, (pp. 483-490). ACL.

Kim, S. N., & Kan, M.-Y. (2009). Re-examining automatic keyphrase extraction approaches in scientific articles. In *Proceedings of the 2009 Workshop on Multiword Expressions, ACL-IJCNLP 2009*, (pp. 9–16). Singapore: ACL and AFNLP.

Kinoshita, J., Salvador, L. N., & Menezes, C. E. D. (2007). CoGrOO - An OpenOffice grammar checker. In *Proceedings of the Seventh International Conference on Intelligent Systems Design and Applications*, (pp. 525-530). Washington, DC: IEEE Computer Society.

Kirschner, M., & Bernardi, R. (2009). Exploring topic continuation follow-up questions using machine learning. In *Proceedings of NAACL HLT 2009: Student Research Workshop*. Boulder, CO: NAACL.

Kirschner, M., Bernardi, R., Baroni, M., & Dinh, L. T. (2009). Analyzing interactive QA dialogues using logistic regression models. In *Proceedings of XIth International Conference of the Italian Association for Artificial Intelligence (AI*IA 2009)*. Reggio Emilia, Italy: AI*IA.

Kittur, A., Chi, E. H., & Suh, B. (2008). Crowdsourcing user studies with mechanical turk. In *Proceedings of the 26th Annual SIGCHI Conference on Human Factors in Computing Systems*, (pp. 453-456). SIGCHI.

Klapaftis, I. P., & Manandhar, S. (2008). Word sense induction using graphs of collocations. In *Proceeding of the 2008 Conference on ECAI 2008: 18th European Conference on Artificial Intelligence*, (pp. 298–302). Amsterdam, The Netherlands: ECAI.

Klein, D., & Manning, C. D. (2003). Accurate unlexicalized parsing. In *Proceedings of the 41st Annual Meeting of the Association of Computational Linguistics*, (pp. 423–430). ACL.

Klein, D., Smarr, J., Nguyen, H., & Manning, C. (2003). Named entity recognition with character-level models. In *Proceedings of the Seventh Conference on Natural Language Learning at HLT-NAACL 2003*, (Vol 4). NAACL.

Klein, D., Toutanova, K., Ilhan, H. T., Kamvar, S. D., & Manning, C. D. (2002). Combining heterogeneous classifiers for word-sense disambiguation. In *Proceedings of the ACL-02 Workshop on Word Sense Disambiguation: Recent Successes and Future Directions, WSD 2002*, (vol 8), (pp. 74–80). Stroudsburg, PA: WSD.

Klein, S., & Simmons, R. F. (1963). A computational approach to grammatical coding of English words. *Journal of the ACM, 10*(3), 334–347. doi:10.1145/321172.321180

Knight, K. (1999). Decoding complexity in word-replacement translation models. *Computational Linguistics, 25*(4), 607–615.

Knoke, D., & Yang, S. (2008). *Social network analysis*. Thousand Oaks, CA: Sage Publications, Inc.

Koehn, P. (2010b). Enabling monolingual translators: Post-editing vs. options. In *Proceedings of the Conference of the North American Chapter of the Association for Computational Linguistics*, (pp. 537-545). Los Angeles, CA: ACL.

Koehn, P., & Haddow, B. (2009). Interactive assistance to human translators using statistical machine translation methods. In *Proceedings of the MT Summit*. MT Summit.

Koehn, P., & Hoang, H. (2007). Factored translation models. In *Proceedings of Joint Conference on Empirical Methods in Natural Language Processing and Computational Natural Language Learning*, (pp. 868-876). Prague, Czech Republic: ACL.

Koehn, P., & Senellart, L. (2010). Convergence of translation memory and statistical machine translation. In *Proceedings of the AMTA-2010 Workshop Bringing MT to the User: MT Research and the Translation Industry*. Denver, CO: AMTA.

Koehn, P., Hoang, H., Birch, A., Callison-Burch, C., Federico, M., & Bertoldi, N. ... Herbst, E. (2007). Moses: Open source toolkit for statistical machine translation. In *Proceedings of the 45th Annual Meeting of the Association for Computer Linguistics*, (pp. 177-180). Prague, Czech Republic: ACL.

Koehn, P., Och, F. J., & Marcu, D. (2003). Statistical phrase-based translation. In *Proceedings of the North American Chapter of the Association for Computational Linguistics on Human Language Technology*, (pp. 48-54). Edmonton, Canada: ACL.

Koehn, P. (2010a). *Statistical machine translation*. Cambridge, UK: Cambridge University Press.

Koeling, R., McCarthy, D., & Carroll, J. (2005). Domain-specific sense distributions and predominant sense acquisition. In *Proceedings of the Conference on Human Language Technology and Empirical Methods in Natural Language Processing*, (pp. 419–426). Morristown, NJ: HLT.

Koenemann, J., & Belkin, N. J. (1996). A case for interaction: a study of interactive information retrieval behavior and effectiveness. In *Proceedings of the SIGCHI Conference on Human Factors in Computing Systems (CHI 1996)*, (pp. 205-212). New York, NY: ACM Press.

Koiwa, T., Nakadai, K., & Imura, J. (2007). Coarse speech recognition by audio-visual integration based on missing feature theory. In *Proceedings of the IEEE/RSJ International Conference on Intelligent Robots and Systems (IROS 2007)*, (pp. 1751-1756). IEEE.

Kolari, P., Java, A., Finin, T., Oates, T., & Joshi, A. (2006). Detecting spam blogs: A machine learning approach. In *Proceedings of the 21st National Conference on Artificial Intelligence (AAAI)*. AAAI.

Kolari, P., & Joshi, A. (2004). Web mining: Research and practice. *Computing in Science & Engineering, 6*(4), 49–53. doi:10.1109/MCSE.2004.23

Kontostathis, A., Edwards, L., & Leatherman, A. (2009). ChatCoder: Toward the tracking and categorization of internet predators. In *Proceedings of the 7th Text Mining Workshop*, (pp. 1-7). ACL.

Kontostathis, A., Edwards, L., & Leatherman, A. (2010). Text mining and cybercrime. In M. W. Berry & J. Kogan (Eds.), *Text Mining: Applications and Theory*. Chichester, UK: John Wiley & Sons. Retrieved from http://onlinelibrary.wiley.com/doi/10.1002/9780470689646.ch8/summary

Koppel, M., & Schler, J. (2006). The importance of neutral examples in learning sentiment. *Computational Intelligence, 22*(2), 100–109. doi:10.1111/j.1467-8640.2006.00276.x

Kornai, A. (2008). *Mathematical linguistics*. London, UK: Springer-Verlag Limited. doi:10.1007/978-1-84628-986-6

Kosseim, L., & Lapalme, G. (2000). Choosing rhetorical structures to plan instructional texts. In *Computational Intelligence*. Boston, MA: Blackwell. doi:10.1111/0824-7935.00118

Kozerenko, E. (2004). *Multilingual systems: Grammar acquisition by machine learning*. Moscow, Russia: Institute for Informatics Problems of the Russian Academy of Sciences.

Kraaij, W., & Pohlmann, R. (1994). Porter's stemming algorithm for Dutch. In Noordman, L., & de Vroomen, E. (Eds.), *Informatiewetenschap*. STINFON.

Krapivin, M., Autayeu, A., Marchese, M., Blanzieri, E., & Segata, N. (2010). Keyphrases extraction from scientific documents: Improving machine learning approaches with natural language processing. [ICADL.]. *Proceedings of, ICADL2010*, 102–111.

Kromann, M. T. (2003). The Danish dependency treebank and the DTAG treebank tool. In *Proceedings of the 2nd Workshop on Treebanks and Linguistic Theories*. Växjo, Sweden: ACL.

Krottmaier, H. (2002). Automatic references: Active support for scientists in digital libraries. In *Proceedings of the 5th International Conference on Asian Digital Libraries*, (pp. 254-255). ACL.

Kruijff-Korbayova, I., & Karagjosova, E. (2002). Enhancing collaboration with conditional responses in information-seeking dialogues. In *Proceedings of 6th Workshop on the Semantics and Pragmatics of Dialogue*. ACL.

Kruschwitz, U., & Al-Bakour, H. (2005). Users want more sophisticated search assistants: Results of a task-based evaluation. *Journal of the American Society for Information Science and Technology, 56*, 1377–1393. doi:10.1002/asi.20230

Kukich, K. (1992). Techniques for automatically correcting words in text. *ACM Computing Surveys, 24*(4), 377–439. doi:10.1145/146370.146380

Kunchukuttan, A., & Damani, O. P. (2008). A system for compound nouns multiword expression extraction for Hindi. In *Proceedings of 6th International Conference on Natural Language Processing (ICON 2008)*. Pune, India: ICON.

Kupic, J. (1993). MURAX: A robust linguistic approach for question answering using an on-line encyclopedia. In *Proceedings of the 16th Annual International ACM SIGIR, Conference on Research and Development in Information Retrieval*, (pp. 181-190). ACM.

Kwok, C., Etzioni, O., & Weld, D. S. (2001). Scaling question answering to the web. *ACM Transactions on Information Systems, 19*(3). Girju, R., & Moldovan, D. I. (2002). Text mining for causal relations. In *Proceedings of FLAIRS Conference*. FLAIRS.

Kwon, Y. H., & Lobo, N. da V. (1994). Face detection using templates. *ICPR-A, 94*, 764-767.

Lácio-Web. (2007). Lácio-Web manuals. In *Compilação de Córpus do Português do Brasil e Implementação de Ferramentas Para Análises Lingüísticas*. Retrieved July 02, 2007, from http://www.nilc.icmc.usp.br/lacioweb/english/manuais.htm

Lafferty, J., McCallum, A., & Pereira, F. (2001). Conditional random fields: Probabilistic models for segmenting and labeling sequence data. In *Proceedings of ICML 2001*, (pp. 282-289). ICML.

Lager, T. (1999). The μ-TBL system: Logic programming tools for transformation-based learning. In *Proceedings of the 3rd International Workshop on Computational Natural Language Learning*, (pp. 33-42). Retrieved from http://acl.ldc.upenn.edu/W/W99/W99-0705.pdf

Lambert, L., & Carberry, S. (1992). Modeling negotiation subdialogues. In *Proceedings of the 30th Annual Meeting of the Association for Computational Linguistics*, (pp. 193-200). Morristown, NJ: ACL.

Lamere, P. (2008). Social tagging and music information retrieval. *Journal of New Music Research, 37*(2), 101–114. doi:10.1080/09298210802479284

Lampe, C., & Resnick, P. (2004). Slash(dot) and burn: Distributed moderation in a large online conversation space. In *Proceedings of SIGCHI Conference on Human Factors in Computing Systems CHI 2004*, (pp. 543-550). Vienna, Austria: SIGCHI.

Lancaster, F. W. (2003). *Indexing and abstracting in theory and practice* (3rd ed.). Champaign, IL: University of Illinois Press.

Langley, P., Laird, J., & Rogers, S. (2009). Cognitive architectures: Research issues and challenges. *Cognitive Systems Research, 10*(2), 141–160. doi:10.1016/j.cogsys.2006.07.004

Lappin, S., & Leass, H. J. (1994). An algorithm for pronominal anaphora resolution. *Computational Linguistics, 20*(4), 535–561.

Largergren, E., & Over, P. (1998). Comparing interactive information retrieval systems across sites: The TREC-6 interactive track matrix experiment. In *Proceedings of the 21st Annual International ACM SIGIR Conference*, (pp. 164-172). ACM Press.

Larkey, L., Abdul Jaleel, N., & Connell, M. (2003). *What's in a name? Proper names in Arabic cross language information retrieval. CIIR Technical Report, IR-278*. Amherst, MA: University of Amherst.

Laurent, D., Séguela, P., & Nègre, S. (2005). *Cross lingual question answering using QRISTAL for CLEF 2005*. Working Notes of the Cross-Language Evaluation Forum (CLEF 2005). New York, NY.

Lavie, A., & Agarwal, A. (2007). METEOR: An automatic metric for MT evaluation with high levels of correlation with human judgments. In *Proceedings of the 2nd Workshop on Statistical Machine Translation*, (pp. 228-231). Prague, Czech Republic: SMT.

Leacock, C., & Chodorow, M. (1998). *Combining local context and WordNet similarity for word sense identification*. Cambridge, MA: MIT Press.

Leah, S. L., Connell, M. E., & Abduljaleel, N. (2003). Hindi CLIR in thirty days. *ACM Transactions on Asian Language Information Processing, 2*(2), 130–142. doi:10.1145/974740.974746

Lee, C., Jung, S., & Jeong, M. (2006). Chat and goal-oriented dialog together: A unified exmple-based architecture for multi-domain dialog management. In *Proceedings of the IEEE Spoken Language Technology Workshop*, (pp. 194-197). Palm Beach, FL: IEEE Press.

Lee, K. Y., Ng, H. T., & Chia, T. K. (2004). Supervised word sense disambiguation with support vector machines and multiple knowledge sources. In *Proceedings of Senseval-3: Third International Workshop on the Evaluation of Systems for the Semantic Analysis of Text*, (pp. 137–140). Senseval.

Lee, J. S., & Park, C. H. (2008). Robust audio-visual speech recognition based on late integration. *MultMed, 10*(5), 767–779.

Lehnert, W. (1978). *The process of question answering.* Hillsdale, NJ: Lawrence Erlbaum Associates.

Lemnitzer, L., Wunsch, H., & Gupta, P. (2008). Enriching germanet with verb-noun relations - A case study of lexical acquisition. In *Proceedings of the 6th International Language Resources and Evaluation.* ACL.

Lenci, A., Bel, N., Busa, F., Calzolari, N., Gola, E., & Monachini, M. (2000). SIMPLE: A general framework for the development of multilingual lexicons. *International Journal of Lexicography, 13*(4), 249–263. doi:10.1093/ijl/13.4.249

Lesk, M. (1986). Automatic sense disambiguation using machine readable dictionaries: How to tell a pine cone from an ice cream cone. In *Proceedings of the 5th Annual International Conference on Systems Documentation.* Systems Documentation.

Lester, J., Branting, K., & Mott, B. (2004). Conversational agents. In Singh, M. P. (Ed.), *The Practical Handbook of Internet Computing.* London, UK: Chapman & Hall.

Levenshtein, V. I. (1966). Binary codes capable of correcting deletions, insertions, and reversals. *Soviet Physics, Doklady, 10,* 707–710.

Levin, E., Pieraccini, R., & Eckert, W. (2000). A stochastic model of human-machine interaction for learning dialog strategies. *IEEE Transactions on Speech and Audio Processing, 8*(1), 11–23. doi:10.1109/89.817450

Levinson, S. C. (1983). *Pragmatics.* Cambridge, UK: Cambridge University Press.

Lewis, W. D. (2010). Haitian creole: How to build and ship an mt engine from scratch in 4 days, 17 hours, & 30 minutes. In *Proceedings of EAMT.* Berlin, Germany: Springer-Verlag.

Li, N., Zhu, L., Mitra, P., & Giles, C. L. (2010). oreChem ChemxSeer: A semantic digital library. In *Proceedings of JCDL2010, 10th ACM/IEEE-CS Joint Conference on Digital Libraries,* (pp. 245-254). Surfer's Paradise, Australia: ACM/IEEE.

Li, S., & Momoi, K. (2001). A composite approach to language/encoding detection. In *Proceedings of the 19th International Unicode Conference.* San José, CA: IEEE.

Li, W. J., Wang, K., Stolfo, S. J., & Herzog, B. (2005). Fileprints: Identifying file types by n--gram analysis. In *Proceedings of the 2005 IEEE Workshop on Information Assurance,* (pp. 64-71). West Point, NY: IEEE Press.

Li, X., & Roth, D. (2002). Learning question classifier. In *Proceedings of 19th International Conference on Computational Linguistics (ACL).* ACL.

Li, Z., Callison-Burch, C., Dyer, C., Ganitkevitch, J., Khudanpur, S., & Schwartz, L. … Zaidan, O. F. (2009). Demonstration of Joshua: An open source toolkit for parsing-based machine translation. In *Proceedings of the ACL-IJCNLP 2009 Software Demonstrations,* (pp. 25-28). Singapore: ACL-IJCNLP.

Liang, P., Bouchard-Côté, A., Klein, D., & Taskar, B. (2006). An end-to-end discriminative approach to machine translation. In *Proceedings of the Joint Conference on Computational Linguistics and Annual Meeting of the Association for Computational Linguistics,* (pp. 761-768). Sydney, Australia: ACL.

Light, B., McGrath, K., & Griffiths, M. (2008). More than just friends? Facebook, disclosive ethics and the morality of technology. In *Proceedings of ICIS 2008,* (p. 193). ICIS.

Li, H., & Li, C. (2004). Word translation disambiguation using bilingual bootstrapping. *Computational Linguistics, 30,* 1–22. doi:10.1162/089120104773633367

Lim, N., Saint-Dizier, P., & Roxas, R. (2009). Some challenges in the design of comparative and evaluative question answering systems. In *Proceedings of the ACL-KRAQ 2009 Workshop.* Singapore: ACL.

Lin, C. Y. (2004). ROUGE: A package for automatic evaluation of summaries. In *Proceedings of Workshop on Text Summarization.* Barcelona, Spain: ACL.

Lin, C. Y., & Hovy, E. (2002). From single to multi-document summarization: A prototype system and its evaluation. In *Proceedings of the ACL,* (pp. 457-464). ACL.

Lin, D. K. (1997). Using syntactic dependency as local context to resolve word sense ambiguity. In *Proceedings of the 35th Annual Meeting of the Association for Computational Linguistics (ACL),* (pp. 64–71). ACL.

Lin, D. K. (1998). Automatic retrieval and clustering of similar words. In *Proceedings of the 17th International Conference on Computational Linguistics*, (pp. 768–774). Morristown, NJ: ACL.

Lin, W. C., & Chen, H. H. (2004). Merging multilingual information retrieval results based on prediction of retrieval effectiveness. In *Proceedings of the Fourth NTCIR Workshop Meeting: Cross-Lingual Information Retrieval Task*. NTCIR.

Lin, D., & Pantel, P. (2001). Discovery of inference rules for question-answering. *Natural Language Engineering*, 7(4), 343–360. doi:10.1017/S1351324901002765

Linguateca. (2007). CETENFolha. In *Linguateca*. Retrieved February 12, 2007, from http://www.linguateca.pt/CETENFolha/

Linguateca. (2009). Material que compõe a Floresta Sintá(c)tica. In *Linguateca*. Retrieved February 12, 2009, from http://www.linguateca.pt/Floresta/material.html

Liu, D., & Gildea, D. (2008). Improved tree-to-string transducer for machine translation. In *Proceedings of the Third Workshop on Statistical Machine Translation*, (pp. 62-69). Columbus, OH: SMT.

Liu, D., & Gildea, D. (2010). Semantic role features for machine translation. In *Proceedings of the 23rd International Conference on Computational Linguistics*, (pp. 716-724). Beijing, China: ACL.

Liu, Y., Fu, Y., Zhang, M., Ma, S., & Ru, L. (2007). Automatic search engine performance evaluation with click-through data analysis. In *Proceedings of the 16th International Conference on World Wide Web*, (pp. 1133-1134). WWW.

Lopez, A. (2008). Statistical machine translation. *ACM Computing Surveys*, 40(3), 1–49. doi:10.1145/1380584.1380586

Loponen, A., Paik, J., & Jarvelin, K. (2010). *UTA stemming and lemmatization experiments in the Bengali ad hoc track at FIRE 2010*. Working Notes of the Forum for Information Retrieval Evaluation (FIRE 2010). New York, NY.

Loquendo. (2007). *Loquendo and artificial solutions announce integration of their technologies into IKEA online assistant*. Retrieved September 24, 2010, from http://www.loquendo.com/en/news/news_loquendo_ikea.htm

Lörscher, W. (1992). Investigating the translation process. *Meta*, 37(3), 426–439. doi:10.7202/003517ar

Lovins, J. B. (1968). Development of a stemming algorithm. *Mechanical Translation and Computational Linguistics*, 11, 22–31.

Luettin, J., & Thacker, N. A. (1997). Speechreading using probabilistic models. *Computer Vision and Image Understanding*, 65(2), 163–178. doi:10.1006/cviu.1996.0570

Lv, G., Jiang, D., Zhao, R., & Hou, Y. (2007). Multi-stream asynchrony modeling for audio-visual speech recognition. In *Proceedings of the Ninth IEEE International Symposium on Multimedia (ISM)*, (pp. 37-44). IEEE Press.

Macklovitch, E. (2004). The contribution of end-users to the transtype2 project. In *Proceedings of the 6th Conference of the Association for Machine Translation in the Americas (AMTA-2004)*, (pp. 197–207). Kyoto, Japan: AMTA.

Madden, M., Fox, S., Smith, A., & Vitak, J. (2007). *Digital footprints: Online identity management and search in the age of transparency*. Pew Internet & American Life Project. Retrieved February 15, 2011, from http://pewresearch.org/pubs/663/digital-footprints

Magnini, B., Negri, M., Prevete, R., & Tanev, H. (2002). Is it the right answer? Exploiting web redundancy for answer validation. In *Proceedings of the Annual Meeting of the Association for Computational Lingustistics*, (pp. 425-432). Philadelphia, PA: ACL.

Magnini, B., Speranza, M., & Kumar, V. (2009). Towards interactive question answering: An ontology-based approach. In *Proceedings of 2009 IEEE International Conference on Semantic Computing*, (pp. 612 - 617). Los Alamitos, CA: IEEE Computer Society.

Magnini, B., Strapparava, C., Pezzulo, G., & Gliozzo, A. (2002). The role of domain information in word sense disambiguation. *Natural Language Engineering*, 8(4), 359–373. doi:10.1017/S1351324902003029

Maier, E., Mast, M., & LuperFoy, S. (Eds.). (1996). *Dialogue processing in spoken language systems: ECAI 1996 Workshop.* Heidelberg, Germany: Springer-Verlag.

Majumder, P., Mitra, M., Parui, S. K., Kole, G., Mitra, P., & Datta, K. (2007). YASS: Yet another suffix stripper. *ACM Transactions on Information Systems, 25*(4).

Mallat, S. G. (1999). *A wavelet tour of signal processing.* New York, NY: Academic Press.

Manandhar, S., & Klapaftis, I. P. (2009). Semeval-2010 task 14: Evaluation setting for word sense induction & disambiguation systems. In *Proceedings of the Workshop on Semantic Evaluations: Recent Achievements and Future Directions, DEW 2009,* (pp. 117–122). Stroudsburg, PA: DEW.

Mani, I. (2001). *Automatic summarization.* Amsterdam, The Netherlands: John Benjamins Publishing Co.

Manning, C. D., & Schüzte, H. (2002). *Foundation of statistical natural language processing.* Cambridge, MA: The MIT Press.

Mann, W., & Thompson, S. (1988). Rhetorical structure theory: Towards a functional theory of text organization. *Text, 8*(3). doi:10.1515/text.1.1988.8.3.243

Manolopoulos, Y., & Sidiropoulos, A. (2005). A new perspective to automatically rank scientific conferences using digital libraries. *Information Processing & Management, 41,* 289–312. doi:10.1016/j.ipm.2003.09.002

Marcu, D., & Wong, W. (2002). A phrase-based, joint probability model for statistical machine translation. In *Proceedings of the Conference on Empirical Methods in Natural Language Processing,* (pp. 133-139). Philadelphia, PA: ACL.

Marcu, D., Wang, W., Echihabi, A., & Knight, K. (2006). SPMT: Statistical machine translation with syntactified target language phrases. In *Proceedings of the Conference on Empirical Methods in Natural Language Processing,* (pp. 44-52). Sydney, Australia: ACL.

Marcu, D. (2000). *The theory and practice of discourse parsing and summarization.* Cambridge, MA: MIT Press.

Markert, K., & Nissim, M. (2005). Comparing knowledge sources for nominal anaphora resolution. *Computational Linguistics, 31*(3), 367–402. doi:10.1162/089120105774321064

Maron, M. E., & Kuhns, J. L. (1960). On relevance, probabilistic indexing and information retrieval. *Journal of the ACM, 7,* 216–244. doi:10.1145/321033.321035

Martínez-González, A., de Pablo-Sánchez, C., Polo-Bayo, C., Vicente-Díez, M. T., Martínez Fernández, P., & Martínez-Fernández, J. L. (2009). Lecture Notes in Computer Science: *Vol. 5706. The MIRACLE team at the CLEF 2008 multilingual question answering track* (pp. 409–420). Springer. doi:10.1007/978-3-642-04447-2_48

Martínez-Santiago, F., Ureña-López, L. A., & Martín-Valdivia, M. (2006). A merging strategy proposal: The 2-step retrieval status value method. *Information Retrieval, 9*(1), 71–93. doi:10.1007/s10791-005-5722-4

Mas, C.-P., Fuhr, N., & Schaefer, A. (2004). Evaluating strategic support for information access in the DAFFODIL system. In *Proceedings of the 8th European Conference on Digital Libraries,* (pp. 476-487). ECDL.

Masterman, M., Needham, R. M., & Sparck Jones, K. (1958). The analogy between mechanical translation and library retrieval. In *Proceedings of the International Conference on Scientific Information,* (vol 2), (pp. 917-935). Washington, DC: National Academy of Sciences.

Mat-Hassan, M., & Levene, M. (2001). Associating search and navigation behavior through log analysis. *Journal of the American Society for Information Science and Technology, 56*(9), 913–934. doi:10.1002/asi.20185

Matthews, I., Cootes, T. F., Bangham, J. A., Cox, S., & Harvey, R. (2002). Extraction of visual features for lipreading. *IEEE Transactions on Pattern Analysis and Machine Intelligence, 24*(2), 198–213. doi:10.1109/34.982900

Mauldin, M. L. (1994). Chatterbots, tinymuds, and the turing test: Entering the Loebner prize competition. In *Proceedings of the Eleventh National Conference on Artificial Intelligence.* AAAI Press.

Max, A., Makhloufi, R., & Langlais, P. (2008). Explorations in using grammatical dependencies for contextual phrase translation disambiguation. In *Proceedings of the 12th Annual Conference of the European Association for Machine Translation*, (pp. 114-119). Hamburg, Germany: EAMT.

Maybury, M. T. (2004). Question answering: An introduction. In Maybury, M. T. (Ed.), *New Directions in Question Answering* (pp. 3–18). Boca Raton, FL: AAAI Press.

Maybury, M. T. (Ed.). (2004). *New directions in question answering*. Cambridge, MA: MIT Press.

Mayfield, J., & McNamee, P. (2002). Converting on-line bilingual dictionaries from human readable to machine-readable form. In *Proceedings of the 25th Annual International ACM SIGIR Conference on Research and Development in Information Retrieval*, (pp. 405-406). New York, NY: ACM Press.

Mayfield, J., & McNamee, P. (2002). *Three principles to guide CLIR research*.In Proceedings of a workshop at SIGIR-2002. Tampere, Finland.

McCarthy, D., Koeling, R., Weeds, J., & Carroll, J. (2004). Finding predominant word senses in untagged text. In *Proceedings of the 42nd Annual Meeting on Association for Computational Linguistics*, (p. 279). Morristown, NJ: ACL.

McCarthy, D., Koeling, R., Weeds, J., & Carroll, J. (2007). Unsupervised acquisition of predominant word senses. *Computational Linguistics*, *33*(4), 553–590. doi:10.1162/coli.2007.33.4.553

McKeown, K., Passonneau, R. J., Elson, D. K., Nenkova, A., & Hirschberg, J. (2005). Do summaries help? A task-based evaluation of multi-document summarization. In *Proceedings of SIGIR*, (pp. 15-19). Salvador, Brazil: SIGIR.

McKeown, K. (1985). *Text generation: Using discourse strategies and focus constraints to generate natural language text*. Cambridge, UK: Cambridge University Press. doi:10.1017/CBO9780511620751

McNally, L., & Boleda, G. (2004). Relational adjectives as properties of kinds. *Empirical Issues in Formal Syntax and Semantics*, *5*, 179–196.

McNamee, P., & Mayfield, J. (2002). Comparing cross-language query expansion techniques by degrading translation resources. In *Proceedings of the 25th Annual International ACM SIGIR Conference on Research and Development in Information Retrieval*, (pp. 159–166). ACM Press.

McTear, M. (1998). Modelling spoken dialogues with state transition diagrams: Experiences with the CSLU toolkit. In *Proceedings of the 5th International Conference on Spoken Language Processing*, (pp. 1223-1226). Sydney, Australia: ACL.

Mees, I. M., & Göpferich, S. (Eds.). (2009). *Methodology, technology and innovation in translation process research* (*Vol. 38*). Copenhagen, Denmark: Samfundslitteratur.

Mel'čuk, I. (1996). Lexical functions: A tool for the description of lexical relations in a lexicon. In Wanner, L. (Ed.), *Lexical Functions in Lexicography and Natural Language Processing* (pp. 37–102). Amsterdam, The Netherlands: Johm Benjamins.

Melucci, M. (2004). Making digital libraries effective: Automatic generation of links for similarity search across hyper-textbooks. *Journal of the American Society for Information Science and Technology*, *55*, 414–430. doi:10.1002/asi.10390

Metzger, M. J. (2007). Making sense of credibility on the web: Models for evaluating online information and recommendations for future research. *Journal of the American Society for Information Science and Technology*, *58*(13), 2078–2091. doi:10.1002/asi.20672

Meusel, R., Niepert, M., Eckert, K., & Stuckenschmidt, H. (2010). Thesaurus extension using web search engines. [ICADL.]. *Proceedings of ICADL*, *2010*, 198–207.

Mi, H., Huang, L., & Liu, Q. (2008). Forest-based translation. In *Proceedings of the 46th Annual Meeting of the Association for Computational Linguistics and the Human Language Technology Conference*, (pp. 192-199). Columbus, OH: ACL.

Mihalcea, R. (2005). Large vocabulary unsupervised word sense disambiguation with graph-based algorithms for sequence data labeling. In *Proceedings of the Joint Human Language Technology and Empirical Methods in Natural Language Processing Conference (HLT/EMNLP)*, (pp. 411–418). HLT/EMNLP.

Mihalcea, R. F. (2002). Bootstrapping large sense tagged corpora. In *Proceedings of the 3rd International Conference on Language Resources and Evaluations (LREC)*, Las Palmas, Spain: LREC.

Mihalcea, R., & Pulman, S. (2007). Characterizing humour: An exploration of features in humorous texts. In *Proceedings of the 8th International Conference on Computational Linguistics and Intelligent Text Processing, CICLing 2007*, (pp. 337-347). Springer.

Mikheev, A. (2000). Document centered approach to text normalization. In *Proceedings of the 23rd Annual International ACM SIGIR Conference on Research and Development in Information Retrieval*, (pp. 136-143). Athens, Greece: ACM Press.

Miller, G. A., Leacock, C., Tengi, R., & Bunker, R. T. (1993). A semantic concordance. In *Proceedings of the Workshop on Human Language Technology*, (pp. 303–308). Morristown, NJ: HLT.

Minqing, H., & Bing, L. (2004). Mining and summarizing customer reviews. In *Proceedings of the ACM SIGKDD International Conference on Knowledge Discovery & Data Mining*. Seattle, WA: ACM Press.

Mirkin, S., Specia, L., Cancedda, N., Dagan, I., Dymetman, M., & Szpektor, I. (2009). Source-language entailment modeling for translating unknown terms. In *Proceedings of the 47th Annual Meeting of the Association for Computational Linguistics and the 4th International Joint Conference on Natural Language Processing*, (pp. 791-799). Singapore: ACL.

Mishne, G. (2005). Experiments with mood classification in blog posts. In *Proceedings of the 1st Workshop on Stylistic Analysis of Text for Information Access*. ACL.

Mishne, G., & Glance, N. (2006a). Leave a reply: An analysis of weblog comments. In *Proceedings of the 3rd Annual Workshop on the Weblogging Ecosystem*. Edinburgh, UK: ACL.

Mishne, G., & Glance, N. (2006b). Predicting movie sales from blogger sentiment. In *Proceedings of the AAAI 2006 Spring Symposium on Computational Approaches to Analysing Weblogs*. Palo Alto, CA: AAAI.

Mithun, S., & Kossein, L. (2009). Summarizing blog entries versus news texts. In *Proceedings of the Workshop on Events in Emerging Text Types*, (pp. 1-8). Borovets, Bulgaria: ACL.

Mitkov, R. (Ed.). (2003). *Handbook of computational linguistics*. Oxford, UK: Oxford University Press.

Mittal, A., Gupta, S., Kumar, P., & Kashyap, S. (2005). A fully automatic question-answering system for intelligent search in e-learning documents. *International Journal on E-Learning*, *4*(1), 149–166.

Mohanty, R., Bhattacharyya, P., Pande, P., Kalele, S., Khapra, M., & Sharma, A. (2008). Synset based multilingual dictionary: Insights, applications and challenges. In *Proceedings of the Global Wordnet Conference*. Wordnet.

Moldovan, D., Harabagiu, S., Pasca, M., Mihalcea, R., Girju, R., Goodrum, R., & Rus, V. (2000). The structure and performance of an open-domain question answering system. In *Proceedings of ACL 2000*. Hong Kong, China: ACL.

Moldovan, D., Harabagiu, S., Pasca, M., Milhalcea, R., & Goodrum, R. … Rus, V. (1999). LASSO: A tool for surfing the answer net. In *Proceedings of ACL*. ACL.

Mollá, D., & Vicedo, J. L. (2007). Question answering in restricted domains: An overview. *Computational Linguistics*, *33*(1), 41–61. doi:10.1162/coli.2007.33.1.41

Morales del Castillo, J. M., Pedraza-Jimenez, A., Ruiz, A. A., Peis, E., & Herrera-Viedma, E. (2009). A semantic model of selective dissemination of information for digital libraries. *Information Technology and Libraries*, *28*(1), 21–30.

Moreau, N. (2009). *Best practices in language resources for multilingual information access (d5.2). Technical Report: TrebleCLEF Project: FP7 IST ICT-1-4-1*. TrebleCLEF Project.

Moriceau, V. (2006). Generating intelligent numerical answers in a question-answering system. In *Proceedings of the 4th International Natural Language Generation Conference (INLG)*. Sydney, Australia: INLG.

Morinaga, S., Yamanishi, K., Tateishi, K., & Fukushima, T. (2002). Mining product reputations on the web. In *Proceedings of the 8th ACM SIGKDD International Conference on Knowledge Discovery and Data Mining*, (pp. 341-349). ACM Press.

Mori, R. D., Béchet, F., Hakkani-Tr, D., McTear, M., & Riccardi, G. (2008). Spoken language understanding: A survey. *IEEE Signal Processing Magazine, 25*, 50–58. doi:10.1109/MSP.2008.918413

Moschitti, A., Morarescu, P., & Harabagiu, S. M. (2003). Open domain information extraction via automatic semantic labeling. In *Proceedings FLAIRS Conference*. FLAIRS.

Moschitti, A., & Quarteroni, S. (2010). Linguistic kernels for answer re-ranking in question answering systems. *Information Processing & Management, 47*(6), 825–842. doi:10.1016/j.ipm.2010.06.002

Movellan, J., & Mineiro, P. (1998). Robust sensor fusion: Analysis and application to audio visual speech recognition. *Machine Learning, 32*(2), 85–100. doi:10.1023/A:1007468413059

Mustafa el Hadi, W. (2004). Human language technology and its role in information access and management. *Cataloging & Classification Quarterly, 37*(1/2), 131–151.

Mutschke, P. (2003). Mining networks and central entities in digital libraries: A graph theoretic approach applied to co-author networks. *Lecture Notes in Computer Science, 2810*, 155–166. doi:10.1007/978-3-540-45231-7_15

Nagao, M. (1984). A framework of a mechanical translation between Japanese and English by analogy principle. In *Artificial and Human Intelligence* (pp. 173–180). Edinburgh, UK: North-Holland.

Nagao, M. (1984). A framework of a mechanical translation between Japanese and English by analogy principle. In Elithorn, A., & Banerji, R. (Eds.), *Artificial and Human Intelligence* (pp. 173–180). Amsterdam, The Netherlands: Elsevier.

Narayan, D., Chakrabarti, D., Pande, P., & Bhattacharyya, P. (2002). An experience in building the indo wordnet - A wordnet for Hindi. In *Proceedings of the First International Conference on Global WordNet*. WordNet.

Navarro, B., Civit, M., Martí, A. M., Marcos, R., & Fernández, B. (2003). Syntactic, semantic and pragmatic annotation in Cast3LB. In *Proceedings of SProLaC*, (pp. 59–68). SProLaC.

Navigli, R., & Velardi, P. (2005). Structural semantic interconnections: A knowledge-based approach to word sense disambiguation. *IEEE Transactions on Pattern Analysis and Machine Intelligence, 27*(7), 1075–1086. doi:10.1109/TPAMI.2005.149

Nazarenko, A., & Ait El Mekki, T. (2005). Building back-of-the-book indexes. *Terminology, 11*(1), 199–224. doi:10.1075/term.11.1.09naz

Neely, K. (1956). Effect of visual factors on the intelligibility of speech. *The Journal of the Acoustical Society of America, 28*(6), 1275–1277. doi:10.1121/1.1908620

Nesson, R., Shieber, S., & Rush, A. (2006). Induction of probabilistic synchronous tree-insertion grammars for machine translation. In *Proceedings of the 7th Conference of the Association for Machine Translation in the Americas*, (pp. 128-137). Cambridge, MA: AMT.

Neumann, G., & Sacaleanu, B. (2006). Lecture Notes in Computer Science: *Vol. 40. Experiments of cross-linguality and question-type driven strategy selection for open-domain QA* (pp. 429–438). Springer. doi:10.1007/11878773_48

Ney, H. (2005). One decade of statistical machine translation: 1996-2005. In *Proceedings of the 10th MT Summit*, (pp. i12-i17). Phuket, Thailand: MT Summit.

Ng, H. T., & Lee, H. B. (1996). Integrating multiple knowledge sources to disambiguate word sense: an exemplar-based approach. In *Proceedings of the 34th Annual Meeting on Association for Computational Linguistics*, (pp. 40–47). Morristown, NJ: ACL.

Ng, H. T., Wang, B., & Chan, Y. S. (2003). Exploiting parallel texts for word sense disambiguation: An empirical study. In *Proceedings of the 41st Annual Meeting on Association for Computational Linguistics, ACL 2003*, (vol 1), (pp. 455–462). Morristown, NJ: ACL.

Ng, V., & Cardie, C. (2002). Improving machine learning approaches to coreference resolution. In *Proceedings of the 40th Annual Meeting of the Association for Computational Linguistics*, (pp. 104-111). ACL.

Ngai, G., & Florian, R. (2001). Transformation-based learning in the fast lane. In *Proceedings of the Second Conference of the North American Chapter of the Association for Computational Linguistics*, (pp. 40-47). ACL.

Nie, J.-Y. (2010). *Cross-language information retrieval*. San Francisco, CA: Morgan & Claypool Publishers.

Nießenn, S., Och, F. J., Leusch, G., & Ney, H. (2000). An evaluation tool for machine translation: Fast evaluation for MT research. In *Proceedings of the 2nd International Conference on Language Resources and Evaluation (LREC)*. Athens, Greece: LREC.

Ning, H., Yang, H., & Li, Z. (2007). A method integrating rule and HMM for Chinese part-of_speech tagging. In *Proceedings of the 2nd IEEE Conference on Industrial Electronics and Applications*, (pp. 723-725). IEEE Press.

Nowson, S. (2006). *The language of weblogs: A study of genre and individual differences*. (PhD Thesis). University of Edinburgh. Edinburgh, UK.

Nugues, P. M. (2006). *An introduction to language processing with Perl and Prolog: An outline of theories, implementation, and application with special consideration of English, French, and German*. Heidelberg, Germany: Springer.

Nunberg, G. (2009, August 31). Google's book search: A disaster for scholars. *The Chronicle of Higher Education*. Retrieved from http://chronicle.com/article/Googles-Book-Search-A/48245/

Nunzio, G. M. D. (2008). Interactive undergraduate students: UNIPD at iCLEF 2008. *Lecture Notes in Computer Science*, 5706.

Oard, D. &Dorr, B. (1996). *A survey of multilingual text retrieval*. Technical Report UMIACS-TR-96-19. College Park, MD: University of Maryland.

Oard, D. W. (1996). *Adaptive vector space text filtering for monolingual and cross-language applications*. (Ph.D. Thesis). University of Maryland. College Park, MD.

Oard, D. W. (1997). Serving users in many languages: Cross-language information retrieval. *D-Lib Magazine*. Retrieved from http://www.dlib.org/dlib/december97/oard/12oard.html

Oard, D. W., et al. (2001). Multilingual information retrieval. In E. Hovy, N. Ide, R. Frederking, J. Marian, & A. Zampolli (Eds.), *Multilingual Information Management: Current Levels and Future Abilities*. Retrieved from http://www.cs.cmu.edu/~ref/mlim/

Oard, D. W. (2009). Multilingual information access. In *Encyclopedia of Library and Information Sciences*. New York, NY: Taylor & Francis.

Oard, D. W., & Gonzalo, J. (2004). The CLEF 2003 interactive track. *Lecture Notes in Computer Science*, *3237*, 425–434. doi:10.1007/978-3-540-30222-3_41

Oard, D. W., Gonzalo, J., Sanderson, M., López-Ostenero, F., & Wang, J. (2004). Interactive cross-language document selection. *Information Retrieval*, *7*(1-2), 205–228. doi:10.1023/B:INRT.0000009446.22036.e3

Oberlander, J., & Nowson, S. (2006). Whose thumb is it anyway? Classifying author personality from weblog text. In *Proceedings of the COLING/ACL*, (pp.627-634). Sydney, Australia: ACL.

Och, F. J. (2003). Minimum error rate training in statistical machine translation. In *Proceedings of the 41st Annual Meeting on Association for Computational Linguistics*, (pp. 160-167). Sapporo, Japan: ACL.

Och, F. J., Gildea, D., Khudanpur, S., & Sarkar, A. (2004). A smorgasbord of features for statistical machine translation. In *Proceedings of the HLT-NAACL*, (pp. 161-168). Boston, MA: HLT-NAACL.

Och, F. J., & Ney, H. (2003). A systematic comparison of various statistical alignment models. *Computational Linguistics*, *29*(1), 19–51. doi:10.1162/089120103321337421

Olney, A., Person, N., Louwerse, M., & Graesser, A. (2002). I-MINDS: A conversational tutoring environment. In *Proceedings of the ACL-02 Demonstration Session*, (pp. 108-109). Philadelphia, PA: Association for Computational Linguistics.

Open Source Machine Learning Software Weka. (2012). *University of Waikato*. Retrieved from http://www.cs.waikato.ac.nz/ml/weka

O'Reilly, T., & Battelle, J. (2004). Opening welcome: The state of the internet industry. *Web 2.0 Conference*. San Francisco, CA: Web 2.0. Retrieved September 14, 2010, from http://conferences.oreillynet.com/presentations/web2con/intro_tim_john.ppt

Otero, J., Caldeira, H., & Gomes, C. J. (2004). The influence of the length of causal chains on question asking and on the comprehensibility of scientific texts. *Journal of Contemporary Educational Psychology, 29*(1). doi:10.1016/S0361-476X(03)00018-3

Ou, S., Khoo, C. S. G., & Goh, D. H.-L. (2009). Automatic text summarization in digital libraries. In Theng, Y.-L., Foo, S., Goh, D., & Na, J.-C. (Eds.), *Handbook of Research on Digital Libraries: Design, Development, and Impact* (pp. 159–172). Hershey, PA: IGI Global. doi:10.4018/978-1-59904-879-6.ch016

Over, P. (2001). The TREC interactive track: An annotated bibliography. *Information Processing & Management, 37*(3), 369–382. doi:10.1016/S0306-4573(00)00053-4

Owen, T., Buchanan, G., Eslambolchilar, P., & Loizides, F. (2010). Supporting early document navigation with semantic zooming. [ICADL.]. *Proceedings of ICADL, 2010*, 168–178.

Paik, J. H., & Parui, S. K. (2008). *A simple stemmer for inflectional languages*. Working Notes of the Forum for Information Retrieval Evaluation (FIRE 2008). New York, NY.

Palmer, C. R., Pesenti, J., Valdes-Perez, R. E., Christel, M. G., Hauptmann, A. G., Ng, D., & Wactlar, H. D. (2001). Demonstration of hierarchical document clustering of digital library retrieval results. In *Proceedings of JCDL 2001,* (p. 415). Roanoke, VA: JCDL.

Pang, B., Lee, L., & Vaithyanathan, S. (2002). Thumbs up? Sentiment classification using machine learning techniques. In *Proceedings of the ACL-02 Conference on Empirical Methods in Natural Language Processing,* (pp. 79-86). ACL.

Pang, B., & Lee, L. (2008). Opinion mining and sentiment analysis. *Foundations and Trends in Information Retrieval, 2*(1-2), 1–135. doi:10.1561/1500000011

Papineni, K., Roukos, S., Ward, T., & Zhu, W. (2002). BLEU: A method for automatic evaluation of machine translation. In *Proceedings of the 40th Meeting of the Association for Computational Linguistics,* (pp. 311-318). Philadelphia, PA: ACL.

Pasca, M., & Alfonseca, E. (2009). Web-derived resources for web information retrieval: From conceptual hierarchies to attribute hierarchies. [SIGIR.]. *Proceedings of SIGIR, 2009*, 596–603.

Pass, G., Chowdhury, A., & Torgeson, C. (2006). A picture of search. In *Proceedings of the 1st International Conference on Scalable Information Systems*. IEEE.

Patwardhan, S., & Pedersen, T. (2003). *The CPAN Word-Net: Similarity package*. Retrieved from http://search.cpan.org/sid/wordnet-similarity/

Pechsiri, C., Sroison, P., & Janviriyasopa, U. (2008). Know-why extraction from textual data. In *Proceedings of KRAQ 2008 Workshop*. Manchester, UK: COLING.

Pecina, P., & Schlesinger, P. (2006). Combining association measures for collocation extraction. In *Proceedings of the 21th International Conference on Computational Linguistics and 44th Annual Meeting of the Association for Computational Linguistics (COLING/ACL 2006),* (pp. 651–658). COLING/ACL.

Pedersen, T., Banerjee, S., & Patwardhan, S. (2005). *Maximizing semantic relatedness to perform word sense disambiguation. Research Report UMSI 2005/25*. Minneapolis, MN: University of Minnesota Supercomputing Institute.

Pereira, D. A., Ribeiro-Neto, B., Ziviani, N., Laender, A. H. F., Gonçalves, M. A., & Ferreira, A. A. (2010). Using web information for author name disambiguation. In *Proceedings of JCDL 2009: 9th ACM/IEEE-CS Joint Conference on Digital Libraries,* (pp. 49-58). Austin, TX: ACM/IEEE.

Perez-Carballo, J., & Strzalkowski, T. (2000). Natural language information retrieval: Progress report. *Information Processing & Management, 36*(1), 155–178. doi:10.1016/S0306-4573(99)00049-7

Perrin, D. (2003). Progression analysis (PA): Investigating writing strategies at the workplace. *Pragmatics, 35*, 907–921. doi:10.1016/S0378-2166(02)00125-X

Petajan, E., Bischoff, B., Bodoff, D., & Brooke, N. M. (1988). An improved automatic lipreading system to enhance speech recognition. In *Proceedings of the SIGCHI Conference on Human Factors in Computing Systems (CHI 1988)*. Washington, DC: ACM Press.

Péter, J. (2004). Link-enabled cited references. *Online Information Review, 28*, 306–311. doi:10.1108/14684520410553804

Peters, C., & Sheridan, P. (2001). Multilingual information access. In *Lectures on Information Retrieval* (pp. 51–80). Berlin, Germany: Springer. doi:10.1007/3-540-45368-7_3

Peters, I. (2009). *Folksonomies: Indexing and retrieval in web 2.0*. Berlin, Germany: De Gruyter. doi:10.1515/9783598441851

Pevzner, B. R. (1972). Comparative evaluation of the operation of the Russian and English variants of the pusto-nepusto-2 system. *Automatic Documentation and Mathematical Linguistics, 6*(2), 71–74.

Philipp, M. (2004). *Multilingual information extraction*. (Master's Thesis). University of Helsinki. Helsinki, Finland.

Piao, S. L., Sun, G., Rayson, P., & Yuan, Q. (2006). Automatic extraction of Chinese multiword expressions with a statistical tool. In *Proceedings of the Workshop on Multi-Word-Expressions in a Multilingual Context held in Conjunction with the 11th Conference of the European Chapter of the Association for Computational Linguistics (EACL 2006)*, (pp. 17–24). Trento, Italy: EACL.

Pimienta, D., Prado, D., & Blanco, Á. (2009). *Twelve years of measuring linguistic diversity in the Internet: Balance and perspectives*. Paris, France: UNESCO. Retrieved February 15, 2011, from http://portal.unesco.org/ci/en/ev.php-URL_ID=29594&URL_DO=DO_TOPIC&URL_SECTION=201.html

Pingali, P., Jagarlamudi, J., & Varma, V. (2006). *A dictionary based approach with query expansion to cross language query based multi-document summarization: Experiments in Telugu English*. Paper presented at the National Workshop on Artificial Intelligence. Mumbai, India.

Pingali, P., Jagarlamudi, J., & Varma, V. (2006). Webkhoj: Indian language ir from multiple character encodings. In *Proceedings of the 15ᵗʰ International Conference on World Wide Web*, (pp. 801-809). Edinburgh, UK: ACM Press.

Pingali, P., & Varma, V. (2006). *Hindi and Telugu to English cross language information retrieval*. Barcelona, Spain: Working Notes of Cross Language Evaluation Forum Workshop.

Pingali, P., & Varma, V. (2007). Multilingual indexing support for CLIR using language modeling. *Bulletin of the IEEE Computer Society Technical Committee on Data Engineering, 30*(1), 70–85.

Pirkola, A. (1998). The effects of query structure and dictionary setups in dictionary-based cross-language information retrieval. In *Proceedings of SIGIR 1998, 21st ACM International Conference on Research and Development in Information Retrieval*, (pp. 55-63). ACM Press.

Pirkola, A., Hedlund, T., Keskustalo, H., & Järvelin, K. (2001). Dictionary-based cross-language information retrieval: Problems, methods, and research findings. *Information Retrieval, 4*(3), 209–230. doi:10.1023/A:1011994105352

Plamondon, R., & Srihari, S. N. (2000). On-line and off-line handwriting recognition: A comprehensive survey. *IEEE Transactions on Pattern Analysis and Machine Intelligence, 22*(1), 63–84. doi:10.1109/34.824821

Pollock, J. L. (1974). *Knowledge and justification*. Princeton, NJ: Princeton University Press.

Ponte, J. M., & Croft, B. W. (1998). A language modeling approach to information retrieval. In *Proceedings of the 21st Annual International ACM SIGIR Conference on Research and Development in Information Retrieval*, (pp. 275-281). ACM Press.

Ponte, J., & Croft, W. B. (1998). A language modeling approach to information retrieval. In *Proceedings of the 1998 SIGIR Conference on Research and Development in Information Retrieval*, (pp. 275-281). SIGIR.

Ponzetto, S. P., & Poesio, M. (2009). State-of-the-art NLP approaches to coreference resolution: Theory and practical recipes. In *Proceedings of the ACL-IJCNLP 2009*, (p. 6). Suntec, Singapore: ACL.

Popescu, A. M., & Etzioni, O. (2005). Extracting product features and opinions from reviews. In *Proceedings of the Conference on Human Language Technology and Empirical Methods in Natural Language Processing,* (pp. 339-346). ACL.

Popescu, A., & Grefenstette, G. (2010). Spatiotemporal mapping of Wikipedia concepts. In *Proceedings of JCDL 2010, 10th ACM/IEEE-CS Joint Conference on Digital Libraries,* (pp. 129-138). Surfer's Paradise, Australia: ACM/IEEE.

Porter, M. F. (1980). An algorithm for suffix stripping. *Program, 14,* 130–137. doi:10.1108/eb046814

Poster, M. (2001). Cyberdemocracy: Internet and the public sphere. *Reading Digital Culture*. Retrieved from http://www.hnet.uci.edu/mposter/writings/democ.html

Potamianos, G., Neti, C., Gravier, G., Garg, A., & Senior, A. W. (2003). Recent advances in the automatic recognition of audiovisual speech. *Proceedings of the IEEE, 91*(9), 1306–1326. doi:10.1109/JPROC.2003.817150

Potthast, M., Stein, B., Eiselt, A., Barron-Cedeno, A., & Rosso, P. (2009). Overview of the 1st international competition on plagiarism detection. In B. Stein, P. Rosso, E. Stamatatos, M. Koppel, & E. Agirre (Eds.), *Proceedings of SEPLN 2009 Workshop on Uncovering Plagiarism, Authorship and Social Software Misuse,* (pp. 1-9). San Sebastian, Spain: SEPLN.

Potthast, M., Barron-Cedeno, A., Stein, B., & Rosso, P. (2010). Cross-language plagiarism detection. *Language Resources and Evaluation, 45*(1), 45–62. doi:10.1007/s10579-009-9114-z

Pouliquen, B., Steinberger, R., & Ignat, C. (2003). Automatic annotation of multilingual text collections with a conceptual thesaurus. In *Proceedings of Ontologies and Information Extraction: Workshop at EUROLAN 2003: The Semantic Web and Language Technology – Its Potential and Practicalities*. Bucharest, Romania: EUROLAN.

Prabowo, R., Jackson, M., Burden, P., & Knoell, H.-D. (2002). Ontology-based automatic classification for web pages: Design, implementation and evaluation. In *Proceedings of the Third International Conference on Web Information Systems Engineering, WISE 2002,* (pp. 182 – 191). WISE.

Prager, J., Brown, R., Coden, A., & Radev, D. R. (2000). Question-answering by predictive annotation. In *Proceedings of the 23rd SIGIR Conference,* (pp. 184–191). SIGIR.

Provine, R. R., Spencer, R. J., & Mandell, D. L. (2007). Emotional expression online: Emoticons punctuate website text messages. *Journal of Language and Social Psychology, 26*(3), 299. doi:10.1177/0261927X06303481

Pustejovsky, J. (1995). *The generative lexicon*. Cambridge, MA: The MIT Press.

Qiu, Y. (1995). Automatic query expansion based on a similarity Thesaurus. (PhD Thesis). Swiss Federal Institute of Technology. Geneva, Switzerland.

Qu, Y., & Green, N. (2002). A constraint-based approach for cooperative information-seeking dialogue. In *Proceedings of the Second International Natural Language Generation Conference*. ACL.

Qualman, E. (2009). *Socialnomics: How social media transforms the way we live and do business*. New York, NY: John Wiley and Sons.

Quarteroni, S. (2008). Personalized, interactive question answering on the web. In *Proceedings of KRAQ 2008*. Manchester, UK: COLING.

Quarteroni, S. (2010). Personalized question answering. *Traitement Automatique des Langues, 51*(1).

Quarteroni, S., & Manandhar, S. (2009). Designing an interactive open-domain question answering system. *Natural Language Engineering, 15,* 73–95. doi:10.1017/S1351324908004919

Quirk, C., Menezes, A., & Cherry, C. (2005). Dependency treelet translation: Syntactically informed phrasal SMT. In *Proceedings of the 43rd Annual Meeting of the Association for Computational Linguistics,* (pp. 271-279). Ann Arbor, MI: ACL.

Radach, R., Kennedy, A., & Rayner, K. (2004). *Eye movements and information processing during reading*. East Sussex, UK: Psychology Press.

Radev, D. R., Jing, H., & Budzikowska, M. (2000). Centroid-based summarization of multiple documents: Sentence extraction, utility-based evaluation, and user studies. In *Proceedings of the NAACL-ANLP Workshop on Automatic Summarization,* (pp. 21-30). Seattle, WA: NAACL.

Ramakrishnan, R., & Tomkins, A. (2007). Toward a peopleweb. *Computer, 40*(8), 63–72. doi:10.1109/MC.2007.294

Ramisch, C., Villavicencio, A., Moura, L., & Idiart, M. (2008). Picking them up and figuring them out: Verb-particle constructions, noise and idiomaticity. In A. Clark & K. Toutanova (Eds.), *Proceedings of the Twelfth Conference on Natural Language Learning (CoNLL 2008),* (pp. 49–56). Manchester, UK: Association for Computational Linguistics.

Ramsay, A. (2003). Discourse. In Mitkov, R. (Ed.), *Handbook of Computational Linguistics*. Oxford, UK: Oxford University Press.

Rao, K. R., Narasimhan, M. A., & Revuluri, K. (1975). Image data processing by Hadamard-Haar transform. *IEEE Transactions on Computers, 24*(9), 888–896. doi:10.1109/T-C.1975.224334

Rasmussen, E. (2004). Information retrieval challenges for digital libraries. *Lecture Notes in Computer Science, 3334*.

Ratnaparkhi, A. (1996). A maximum entropy model for part-of-speech tagging. In *Proceedings of the Conference on Empirical Methods in Natural Language,* (pp. 133-142). ACL. Retrieved from http://acl.ldc.upenn.edu/W/W96/W96-0213.pdf

Ravi, S., & Pasca, M. (2008). Using structured text for large-scale attribute extraction. In *Proceedings of CIKM*. CIKM.

Řehůřek, R., & Kolkus, M. (2009). Language identification on the web: Extending the dictionary method. *Lecture Notes in Computer Science, 5449*, 357–368. doi:10.1007/978-3-642-00382-0_29

Reichle, E. D., Rayner, K., & Pollatsek, A. (2002). The e-z reader model of eye movement control in reading: Comparisons to other models. *The Behavioral and Brain Sciences, 26*(4), 445–476l.

Reinhart, T. (1983). *Anaphora and semantic interpretation*. New York, NY: Taylor & Francis.

Reiter, E., & Dale, R. (1997). Building applied natural language generation systems. *Journal of Natural Language Engineering, 3*(1). doi:10.1017/S1351324997001502

Reiter, E., & Dale, R. (2000). *Building natural generation systems*. Cambridge, UK: Cambridge University Press. doi:10.1017/CBO9780511519857

Resnik, P. (1995). Using information content to evaluate semantic similarity in a taxonomy. In *Proceedings of the 14th International Joint Conference on Artificial Intelligence,* (vol 1), (pp. 448–453). San Francisco, CA: IEEE.

Resnik, P. (1998). Parallel strands: A preliminary investigation into mining the web for bilingual text. *Lecture Notes in Computer Science, 1529*, 72–82. doi:10.1007/3-540-49478-2_7

Resnik, P., & Yarowsky, D. (1999). Distinguishing systems and distinguishing senses: New evaluation methods for word sense disambiguation. *Natural Language Engineering, 5*, 113–133. doi:10.1017/S1351324999002211

Reyes, A., & Rosso, P. (2009). Linking humour to blogs analysis: Affective traits in posts. In *Proceedings of the First International Workshop on Opinion Mining and Sentiment Analysis*. ACL.

Ricci, F., & Werthner, H. (2006). Introduction to the special issue: Recommender systems. *International Journal of Electronic Commerce, 11*(2), 5–9. doi:10.2753/JEC1086-4415110200

Rieser, V., & Lemon, O. (2009). Does this list contain what you were searching for? Learning adaptive dialogue strategies for interactive question answering. *Natural Language Engineering, 15*(1), 55–72. doi:10.1017/S1351324908004907

Rilo, E., & Lehnert, W. (1994). Information extraction as a basis for high-precision text classification. *ACM Transactions on Information Systems, 12*(3), 296–333. doi:10.1145/183422.183428

Ringger, E., McClanahan, P., Haertel, R., Busby, G., Carmen, M., & Carroll, J..... Lonsdale, D. (2007). Active learning for part-of-speech tagging: Accelerating corpus annotation. In *Proceedings of the Linguistic Annotation Workshop,* (pp. 101–108). Retrieved from http://www.aclweb.org/anthology-new/W/W07/W07-1516.pdf

Robertson, S. E., Walker, S., & Beaulieu, M. (1999). Okapi at TREC–7: Automatic ad hoc, filtering, VLC and filtering tracks. In *Proceedings of the 7th Text REtrieval Conference (TREC-7),* (pp. 253-264). TREC.

Robertson, S. E. (1977). The probabilistic ranking principle in IR. *The Journal of Documentation, 33,* 294–304. doi:10.1108/eb026647

Robertson, S., & Zaragoza, H. (2009). Probabilistic relevance framework: BM25 and beyond. *Foundations and Trends in Information Retrieval, 3*(4), 333–389. doi:10.1561/1500000019

Rockwell, M. C., & Chan, M. T. (2001). HMM-based audio-visual speech recognition integrating geometric- and appearance-based visual features. In *Proceedings of the IEEE Workshop on Multimedia Signal Processing,* (pp. 9-14). IEEE Press.

Ruch, P. (2003). *Applying natural language processing to information retrieval in clinical records and biomedical texts.* (Ph.D. Thesis). Imprimerie des Hôpitaux Universitaires de Genève. Geneva, Switzerland.

Ruppenhofer, J., Ellsworth, M., Petruck, M., Johnson, C. R., & Scheffczyk, J. (2006). *FrameNet II: Extended theory and practice.* Retrieved from http://framenet.icsi.berkeley.edu/book/book.pdf.ICSI

Saaba, A., & Sawamura, H. (2008). Argument mining using highly structured argument repertoire. In *Proceedings EDM 2008.* Niigata, Japan: EDM.

Sacaleanu, B., Orasan, C., Spurk, C., Ou, S., Ferrandez, O., Kouylekov, M., & Negri, M. (2008). Entailment-based question answering for structured data. In *Proceedings of Coling 2008: Companion Volume: Posters and Demonstrations.* Manchester, UK: Coling.

Sacks, H., Schegloff, E. A., & Jefferson, G. (1974). A simplest systematics for the organization of turn-taking for conversation. *Language, 50*(4), 696–735. doi:10.2307/412243

Sadeghi, M., Kittler, J., & Messer, K. (2002). Modelling and segmentation of lip area in face images. *Vision. Image and Signal Processing, 149*(3), 179–184. doi:10.1049/ip-vis:20020378

Sag, I., Baldwin, T., Bond, F., Copestake, A., & Flickinger, D. (2002). Multiword expressions: A pain in the neck for NLP. In *Proceedings of the 3rd International Conference on Intelligent Text Processing and Computational Linguistics (CICLing-2002),* (pp. 1–15). Mexico City, Mexico: CICLing.

Saggion, H., & Lapalme, G. (2000). Concept identification and presentation in the context of technical text summarization. In *Proceedings of the Workshop on Automatic Abstracting, NAACL-ANLP 2000.* Seattle, WA: NAACL.

Sagot, B. (2005). Automatic acquisition of a Slovak lexicon from a raw corpus. In *Lecture Notes in Artificial Intelligence, 3658,* 156–163.

Sagot, B. (2007). Building a morphosyntactic lexicon and a pre-syntactic processing chain for Polish. In *Proceedings of the 3rd Language & Technology Conference,* (pp. 423–427). Poznan, Poland: ACL.

Sagot, B., & Walther, G. (2010). A morphological lexicon for the Persian language. In *Proceedings of the 7th Language Resources and Evaluation Conference, (LREC 2010),* (pp. 300-303). Valetta, Malta: LREC.

Saito, M., Yamamoto, K., & Sekine, S. (2006). Using phrasal patterns to identify discourse relations. In *Proceedings ACL 2006.* ACL.

Saitoh, T., & Konishi, R. (2006). Lip reading using video and thermal images. In *Proceedings of the International Joint Conference (SICE-ICASE, 2006),* (pp. 5011-5015). SICE-ICASE.

Saitoh, T., Morishita, K., & Konishi, R. (2008). Analysis of efficient lip reading method for various languages. In *Proceedings of the International Conference on Pattern Recognition,* (pp. 1-4). IEEE.

Sakurai, S., & Orihara, R. (2006). Discovery of important threads from bulletin board sites. *International Journal of Information Technology and Intelligent Computing, 1*(1), 217–228.

Salton, G. (1969). Automatic processing of foreign language documents. In Proceedings *of the 1969 Conference on Computational Linguistics*, (pp. 1-28). ACL.

Salton, G. (1988). Syntactic approaches to automatic book indexing. In *Proceedings of the 26th Annual Meeting on Association for Computational Linguistics,* (pp. 204-210). Buffalo, NY: ACL.

Salton, G., Wong, A., & Yang, C. S. (1975). A vector space model for information retrieval. *Communications of the ACM, 18*(11), 613–620. doi:10.1145/361219.361220

Salvucci, D. (2001). An integrated model of eye movements and visual encoding. *Cognitive Systems Research, 1*, 201–220. doi:10.1016/S1389-0417(00)00015-2

Sanderson, M. (1994). Word sense disambiguation and information retrieval. In *Proceedings of the 17th Annual International ACM SIGIR Conference on Research and Development in Information Retrieval,* (pp. 142-151). Dublin, Ireland: ACM Press.

Sanderson, R., & Watry, P. (2007). Integrating data and text mining processes for digital library applications. In *Proceedings of the 7th ACM/IEEE-CS Joint Conference on Digital Libraries,* (pp. 73-79). ACM/IEEE.

Saracevic, T. (1995). Evaluation of evaluation in information retrieval. In *Proceedings of the 18th Annual international ACM SIGIR Conference on Research and Development in information Retrieval,* (pp. 138-146). Seattle, WA: ACM Press.

Saracevic, T. (1975). Relevance: A review of and a framework for thinking on the notion in information science. *Journal of the American Society for Information Science and Technology, 26*(6), 321–343. doi:10.1002/asi.4630260604

Saravanan, K., Udupa, R., & Kumaran, A. (2010). Cross lingual information retrieval system enhanced with transliteration generation and mining. In *Proceedings of Forum for Information Retrieval Evaluation (FIRE-2010) Workshop.* Kolkata, India: FIRE.

Sato, S. (1992). CTM: An example-based translation aid system. [COLING.]. *Proceedings of COLING, 14*, 1259–1263.

Savoy, J. (1999). A stemming procedure and stopword list for general french corpora. *Journal of the American Society for Information Science American Society for Information Science, 50*, 944–952. doi:10.1002/(SICI)1097-4571(1999)50:10<944::AID-ASI9>3.0.CO;2-Q

Savoy, J. (2005). Comparative study of monolingual and multilingual search models for use with Asian languages. *ACM Transactions on Asian Language Information Processing, 4*(2), 163–189. doi:10.1145/1105696.1105701

Schinke, R., Robertson, A., Willet, P., & Greengrass, M. (1996). A stemming algorithm for Latin text databases. *The Journal of Documentation, 52*, 172–187. doi:10.1108/eb026966

Schler, J., Koppel, M., Argamon, S., & Pennebaker, J. W. (2006). Effects of age and gender on blogging. In *Proceedings of 2006 AAAI Spring Symposium on Computational Approaches for Analyzing Weblogs.* AAAI.

Schmid, H. (1994). Probabilistic part-of-speech tagging using decision trees. In *Proceedings of the International Conference on New Methods in Language Processing,* (pp. 44-49). ACL.

Schmid, H. (1995). Improvements in part-of-speech tagging with an application to German. In *Proceedings of the EACL SIGDAT Workshop,* (pp. 47-55). EACL.

Scott, C. D., Deerwester, Dumais, S. T., Landauer, T. K., Furnas, G. W., & Harshman, R. A. (1990). Indexing by latent semantic analysis. *Journal of the American Society for Information Science American Society for Information Science, 41*(6), 391–407. doi:10.1002/(SICI)1097-4571(199009)41:6<391::AID-ASI1>3.0.CO;2-9

Sebastiani, F. (2002). Machine learning in automated text categorization. *ACM Computing Surveys, 34*(1), 1–47. doi:10.1145/505282.505283

Segalovich, I. V. (2003). A fast morphological algorithm with unknown word guessing induced by a dictionary for a web search engine. In *Proceedings of the International Conference on Machine Learning, Models, Technologies and Applications,* (pp. 273-280). Las Vegas, NV: CSREA Press.

Segerstrale, U., & Molnar, P. (Eds.). (1997). *Nonverbal communication: Where nature meets culture.* Mahwah, NJ: Lawrence Erlbaum Associates.

Seki, K., Qin, H., & Uehara, K. (2010). Impact and prospect of social bookmarks for bibliographic information retrieval. In *Proceedings of JCDL 2010, 10ᵗʰ ACM/IEEE-CS Joint Conference on Digital Libraries*, (pp. 357-360). Surfer's Paradise, Australia: ACM/IEEE.

Shannon, C. E. (1949). *A mathematical theory of communication*. Urbana, IL: University of Illinois Press.

Sharmin, S., Špakov, O., Räihä, K., & Jakobsen, A. L. (2008). Where on the screen do translation students look? *Copenhagen Studies in Language, 36*, 30–51.

Shen, L., Sarkar, A., & Och, F. J. (2004). Discriminative reranking for machine translation. [Boston, MA: HLT-NAACL.]. *Proceedings of the HLT-NAACL, 2004*, 177–184.

Sheridan, P., & Ballerini, J. P. (1996). Experiments in multilingual information retrieval using the SPIDER system. In *Proceedings of the 19th ACM SIGIR Conference on Research and Development in Information Retrieval*, (pp. 58–64). ACM Press.

Sheridan, P., Braschler, M., & Schäuble, P. (1997). Cross-language information retrieval in a multilingual legal domain. In *Proceedings of the Research and Advanced Technology for Digital Libraries*, (pp. 253–268). Springer.

Shishtla, P. M., Pingali, P., & Varma, V. (2008a). A character n-gram based approach for improved recall in Indian language NER. In *Proceedings of IJCNLP-08 Workshop on Named Entity Recognition for South and South East Asian Languages*, (pp. 67-74). Hyderabad, India: IJCNLP.

Shishtla, P. M., Pingali, P., & Varma, V. (2008b). Experiments in Telugu NER: A conditional random field approach. In *Proceedings of IJCNLP-08 Workshop on Named Entity Recognition for South and South East Asian Languages*, (pp. 105-110). Hyderabad, India: IJCNLP.

Shoup, J. E. (1980). Phonological aspects of speech recognition. In *Trends in Speech Recognition* (pp. 125–138). Englewood Cliffs, NJ: Prentice-Hall.

Sibun, P., & Spitz, A. (1994). Language determination: Natural language processing from scanned document images. In *Proceedings of Applied Natural Language Processing* (pp. 15–21). Stuttgart, Germany: ACL.

Sidorov, G. (1996). Lemmatization in automatized system for compilation of personal style dictionaries of literature writers. In *Word of Dostoyevsky* (pp. 266–300). Moscow, Russia: Russian Academy of Sciences.

Simard, M., Cancedda, N., Cavestro, B., Dymetman, M., Gaussier, E., Goutte, C., & Yamada, K. (2005). Translating with non-contiguous phrases. In *Proceedings of the Joint Conference on Human Language Technology and Empirical Methods in Natural Language Processing*, (pp. 755-762). Vancouver, Canada: ACL.

Singh, A. K., & Surana, H. (2007). Study of cognates among south Asian languages for the purpose of building lexical resources. In *Proceedings of National Seminar on Creation of Lexical Resources for Indian Language Computing and Processing*. ACL.

Singh, A. K., & Surana, H. (2007). *There can be depth in the surface: A unified computational model of scripts and its applications*. Unpublished.

Singhal, A., Buckley, C., & Mitra, M. (1996). Pivoted document length normalization. In *Proceedings of ACM SIGIR 1996*, (pp. 21-29). ACM Press.

Singh, P., Laxmi, V., Gupta, D., & Gaur, M. S. (2010). Lipreading using n–gram feature vector. *Advances in Soft Computing, 85*, 81–88. doi:10.1007/978-3-642-16626-6_9

Singla, P., & Richardson, M. (2008). Yes, there is a correlation: From social networks to personal behaviour on the web. In *Proceeding of the 17ᵗʰ International Conference on World Wide Web*, (pp. 655–664). Beijing, China: WWW.

Smadhi, S. (2003). System of information retrieval in XML documents. In Becker, S. A. (Ed.), *Effective Databases for Text & Document Management* (pp. 1–11). Hershey, PA: IGI Global. doi:10.4018/978-1-93177-747-6.ch001

Smadja, F. (1993). Retrieving collocations from text: Xtract. *Computational Linguistics, 19*, 143–177.

Smeaton, A. F., & Callan, J. (2005). Personalisation and recommender systems in digital libraries. *International Journal on Digital Libraries, 5*(4), 299–308. doi:10.1007/s00799-004-0100-1

Smith, R. W., & Hipp, D. R. (1995). *Spoken natural language dialog systems: A practical approach*. Oxford, UK: Oxford University Press.

Snover, M. G., Dorr, B., Schwartz, R., Micciulla, L., & Makhoul, J. (2006). A study of translation edit rate with targeted human annotation. In *Proceedings of the 7th Conference of the Association for Machine Translation in the Americas*, (pp. 223-231). Cambridge, MA: AMTA.

Snover, M. G., Madnani, N., Dorr, B., & Schwartz, R. (2010). TER-plus: Paraphrase, semantic, and alignment enhancements to translation edit rate. *Machine Translation, 23*(2-3), 117–127. doi:10.1007/s10590-009-9062-9

Snyder, B., & Palmer, M. (2004). The English all-words task. In R. Mihalcea & P. Edmonds (Eds.), *Senseval-3: Third International Workshop on the Evaluation of Systems for the Semantic Analysis of Text*, (pp. 41–43). Barcelona, Spain: Senseval.

Soergel, D. (2009). Digital libraries and knowledge organization. In Kruk, S. R., & McDaniel, B. (Eds.), *Semantic Digital Libraries* (pp. 3–39). Berlin, Germany: Springer. doi:10.1007/978-3-540-85434-0_2

Song, M., Song, I. Y., Allen, R. B., & Obradovic, Z. (2006). Keyphrase extraction-based query expansion in digital libraries. In *Proceedings of the 6th ACM/IEEE-CS Joint Conference on Digital Libraries,* (pp. 202-209). Chapel Hill, NC: ACM/IEEE.

Sood, S. O., & Vasserman, L. (2009). Esse: Exploring mood on the web. In *Proceedings of International Conference on Weblogs and Social Media*. Seattle, WA: ACL.

Spagnola, S., & Lagoze, C. (2011). Word order matters: Measuring topic coherence with lexical argument structure. In *Proceedings of JCDL 2011*. Ottawa, Canada: JCDL.

Spanish WordNet. (2012). *Website.* Retrieved from http://www.lsi.upc.edu/~nlp/web/index.php?Itemid=57&id=31&option=com_content&task=view

Sparck Jones, K. (1967). Current work on automatic classification for information retrieval. *T.A. Informations, 2*, 92–96.

Sparck Jones, K. (2007). Automatic summarising: The state of the art. *Information Processing & Management, 43*(6), 1449–1481. doi:10.1016/j.ipm.2007.03.009

Specia, L., & Farzindar, A. (2010). Estimating machine translation post-editing effort with HTER. In *Proceedings of the AMTA-2010 Workshop Bringing MT to the User: MT Research and the Translation Industry*. Denver, CO: AMTA.

Specia, L., Raj, D., & Turchi, M. (2010). Machine translation evaluation versus quality estimation. *Machine Translation, 24*(1), 39–50. doi:10.1007/s10590-010-9077-2

Specia, L., Sankaran, B., & Nunes, M. G. V. (2008). n-Best reranking for the efficient integration of word sense disambiguation and statistical machine translation. *Lecture Notes in Computer Science, 4919*, 399–410. doi:10.1007/978-3-540-78135-6_34

Spector, A. Z. (2009). *The continuing metamorphosis of the web*. Paper presented at the World Wide Web Conference (WWW 2009). New York, NY.

Spink, A., Ozmutlu, S., Ozmutlu, H. C., & Jansen, B. J. (2002b). US versus European web searching trends. *ACM SIGIR Forum, 36*(2), 32-38.

Spink, A., Jansen, B. J., Wolfram, D., & Saracevic, T. (2002a). From e-sex to e-commerce: Web search changes. *Computer, 35*(3), 107–109. doi:10.1109/2.989940

Spink, A., Wolfram, D., Jansen, B. J., & Saracevic, T. (2001). Searching the web: The public and their queries. *Journal of the American Society for Information Science and Technology, 52*(3), 226–234. doi:10.1002/1097-4571(2000)9999:9999<::AID-ASI1591>3.0.CO;2-R

Spitters, M., Boni, M. D., Zavrel, J., & Bonnema, R. (2009). Learning effective and engaging strategies for advice-giving human-machine dialogue. *Natural Language Engineering, 15*(3), 355–378. doi:10.1017/S1351324908004956

Srivastava, J., & Cooley, R. (2003). Web business intelligence: Mining the web for actionable knowledge. *INFORMS Journal on Computing, 15*(2), 191–207. doi:10.1287/ijoc.15.2.191.14447

Stalnaker, R. (1978). Assertion. In Cole, P. (Ed.), *Pragmatics: Syntax and Semantics* (*Vol. 9*, pp. 315–332). New York, NY: Academic Press.

Staub, A., & Rayner, K. (2007). Eye movements and on-line comprehension processes. In *The Oxford Handbook of Psycholinguistics* (pp. 327–342). Oxford, UK: Oxford University Press.

Steinbach, M., Karypis, G., & Kumar, V. (2000). A comparison of document clustering techniques. In *Proceedings of the KDD Workshop on Text Mining*. Retrieved October 7, 2010 from http://glaros.dtc.umn.edu/gkhome/node/157

Stolcke, A. (2002). SRILM - An extensible language modeling toolkit. In *Proceedings of the International Conference on Spoken Language Processing*, (pp. 901-904). Denver, CO: SLP.

Stone, P. J., Dunphy, D. C., Smith, M. S., & Ogilvie, D. M. (1966). *The general inquirer: A computer approach to content analysis*. Cambridge, MA: The MIT Press.

Stork, D. G., & Hennecke, M. E. (1996). Speechreading: An overview of image processing, feature extraction, sensory integration and pattern recognition techniques. In *Proceedings of the 2nd International Conference on Automatic Face and Gesture Recognition*, (pp. 16-26). IEEE.

Stroppa, N., van den Bosch, A., & Way, A. (2007). Exploiting source similarity for SMT using context-informed features. In *Proceedings of the 11th Conference on Theoretical and Methodological Issues in Machine Translation*, (pp. 231-240). Skövde, Sweden: Theoretical and Methodological Issues in Machine Translation.

Strzalkowski, T. (Ed.). (1999). *Natural language information retrieval*. Dordrecht, The Netherlands: Kluwer Academic Publishers.

Stymne, S. (2009). A comparison of merging strategies for translation of german compounds. In *Proceedings of the Student Research Workshop at EACL 2009*, (pp. 61-69). Athens, Greece: EACL.

Su, X., & Khoshgoftaar, T. M. (2009). A survey of collaborative filtering techniques. *Advances in Artificial Intelligence, 2009*(421425), 19 pages. doi:10.1155/2009/421425

Sugahara, K., Shinchi, T., Kishino, M., & Konishi, R. (2000). Real time realization of lip reading system on the personal computer. *Proceedings of ICSP, 36*(12), 1145–1151.

Sugiyama, K., & Kan, M.-Y. (2010). Scholarly paper recommendation via user's recent research interests. In *Proceedings of JCDL 2010, 10ʰ ACM/IEEE-CS Joint Conference on Digital Libraries*, (pp. 29-38). Surfer's Paradise, Australia: ACM/IEEE.

Sullivan, K. P. H., & Lindgren, E. (Eds.). (2006). *Computer keystroke logging and writing: Methods and applications* (*Vol. 18*). Oxford, UK: Elsevier.

Sumby, W. H., & Pollack, I. (1954). Visual contribution to speech intelligibility in noise. *The Journal of the Acoustical Society of America, 26*(2), 212–215. doi:10.1121/1.1907309

Sumita, E., & Iida, H. (1991). Experiments and prospects of example-based machine translation. [Berkeley, CA: ACL.]. *Proceedings of, ACL-91*, 185–192.

Surowiecki, J. (2005). *The wisdom of crowds*. New York, NY: Knopf Doubleday Publishing Group.

Sutcliffe, R., Mulcahy, M., Gabbay, I., O'Gorman, A., White, K., & Slatter, D. (2006). Cross-language French-English question answering using the DLT system at CLEF 2005. *Lecture Notes in Computer Science, 4022*.

Tahmasebi, N., Niklas, K., Theuerkauf, T., & Risse, T. (2010). Using word sense discrimination on historic document collection. In *Proceedings of JCDL 2010, 10ʰ ACM/IEEE-CS Joint Conference on Digital Libraries*, (pp. 89-98). Surfer's Paradise, Australia: ACM/IEEE.

Talmy, L. (2001). *Towards a cognitive semantics*. Cambridge, MA: MIT Press.

Tan, M., Zhou, W., Zheng, L., & Wang, S. (2011). A large scale distributed syntactic, semantic and lexical language model for machine translation. In *Proceedings of the 49th Annual Meeting of the Association for Computational Linguistics*, (pp. 201-210). Portland, OR: ACL.

Tan, Y. F., Kan, M.-Y., & Cui, H. (2006). Extending corpus-based identification of light verb constructions using a supervised learning framework. In *Proceedings of the EACL Workshop on Multi-Word Expressions in a Multilingual Contexts*, (pp. 49–56). Trento, Italy: Association for Computational Linguistics.

Tanev, H., Negri, M., Magnini, B., & Kouylekov, M. (2005). The DIOGENE question answering system at CLEF-2004. *Lecture Notes in Computer Science, 3491,* 435–445. doi:10.1007/11519645_43

Thelwall, M., Buckley, K., Paltoglou, G., Cai, D., & Kappas, A. (2010). Sentiment in short strength detection informal text. *Journal of the American Society for Information Science and Technology, 61*(2), 2544–2558. doi:10.1002/asi.21416

Thompson, C. A., & Mooney, R. J. (1999). Automatic construction of semantic lexicons for learning natural language interfaces. In *Proceedings of the Sixteenth National Conference on Artificial Intelligence (AAAI 1999),* (pp. 487-493). Orlando, FL: AAAI.

Thompson, R., Shafer, K., & Vizine-Goetz, D. (1997). Evaluating Dewey concepts as a knowledge base for automatic subject assignment. In *Proceedings of the Second ACM International Conference on Digital Libraries,* (pp. 37-46). Philadelphia, PA: ACM.

Tillmann, C., Vogel, S., Ney, H., Zubiaga, A., & Sawaf, H. (1997). Accelerated DP based search for statistical translation. In *Proceedings of the European Conference on Speech Communication and Technology,* (pp. 2667-2670). Rhodes, Greece: Speech Communication and Technology.

Todirașcu, A., & Rousselot, F. (2001). Ontologies for information retrieval. [TALN.]. *Proceedings of TALN, 2001,* 305–314.

Toms, E., & McCay-Peet, L. (2009). Chance encounters in the digital library. In M. Agosti et al. (Eds.), *Research and Advanced Technology for Digital Libraries, 13th European Conference, ECDL 2009,* (pp. 192-202). Corfu, Greece: ECDL.

Tönnies, S., Köhncke, B., Koepler, O., & Balke, W.-T. (2010). Exposing the hidden web for chemical digital libraries. In *Proceedings of JCDL2010, 10ᵗʰ ACM/IEEE-CS Joint Conference on Digital Libraries,* (pp. 235-244). Surfer's Paradise, Australia: ACM/IEEE.

Toolkit, H. T. K. (2012). *HTK hidden Markov model toolkit home page.* Retrieved from http://htk.eng.cam.ac.uk/

Toprak, C., Jakob, N., & Gurevych, I. (2010). Sentence and expression level annotation of opinions in user generated discourse. In *Proceedings of the 48th Annual Meeting of the Association for Computational Linguistics,* (pp. 575-584). Uppsala, Sweden: Association for Computational Linguistics.

Toth, K., Farkas, R., & Kocsor, A. (2008). Sentence alignment of Hungarian English parallel corpora using a hybrid algorithm. *Acta Cybern, 18*(3), 463–478.

Toutanova, K., Klein, D., Manning, C. D., & Singer, Y. (2003). Feature-rich part-of-speech tagging with a cyclic dependency network. In *Proceedings of the 2003 Conference of the North American Chapter of the Association for Computational Linguistics on Human Language Technology,* (vol 1), (pp. 173-180). ACL.

Traum, D., & Larsson, S. (2003). The information state approach to dialogue management. In van Kuppevelt, J., & Smith, R. (Eds.), *Current and New Directions in Discourse and Dialogue* (pp. 325–354). Berlin, Germany: Springer. doi:10.1007/978-94-010-0019-2_15

Treeratpituk, P., & Giles, C. L. (2010). Disambiguating authors in academic publications using random forests. In *Proceedings of JCDL2009: 9ᵗʰ ACM/IEEE-CS Joint Conference on Digital Libraries,* (pp. 39-48). Austin, TX: ACM/IEEE.

Tsoumakas, G., & Katakis, I. (2007). Multi-label classification: An overview. *International Journal of Data Warehousing and Mining, 3*(3), 1–13. doi:10.4018/jdwm.2007070101

Tsujii Laboratory. (2010). Domain adaptation of part-of-speech taggers. In *Research on Advanced Natural Language Processing and Text Mining: aNT.* Retrieved June 30, 2010, from http://www-tsujii.is.s.u-tokyo.ac.jp/aNT/domain-pos.html

Tufi, D., Ion, R., & Ide, N. (2004). Fine-grained word sense disambiguation based on parallel corpora, word alignment, word clustering and aligned wordnets. In *Proceedings of the 20th International Conference on Computational Linguistics, COLING 2004.* Stroudsburg, PA: COLING.

Turney, P. (2002). Thumbs up or thumbs down? Semantic orientation applied to unsupervised classification of reviews. In *Proceedings of ACL-02, 40th Annual Meeting of the Association for Computational Linguistics*, (pp. 417-424). Philadelphia, PA: ACL.

Umansky-Pesin, S., Reichart, R., & Rappoport, A. (2010). A multi-domain web-based algorithm for POS tagging of unknown words. In *Proceedings of the 23rd International Conference on Computational Linguistics*, (pp. 1274-1282). ACL. Retrieved from http://www.aclweb.org/anthology/C10-2146.

Vakkari, P., & Taneli, M. (2009). Comparing Google to ask-a-librarian service for answering factual and topical questions. In M. Agosti, et al. (Eds.), *Research and Advanced Technology for Digital Libraries, 13th European Conference, ECDL 2009*, (pp. 352-363). Corfu, Greece: ECDL.

Van der Linden, K. (1993). *Speaking of actions choosing rhetorical status and grammatical form in instructional text generation.* (PhD Thesis). University of Colorado. Boulder, CO.

Van Kuppevelt, J., & Smith, R. W. (Eds.). (2003). *Current and new directions in discourse and dialogue.* Dordrecht, The Netherlands: Kluwer Academic Publishers. doi:10.1007/978-94-010-0019-2

van Rijsbergen, C. J. (1979). *Information retrieval* (2nd ed.). London, UK: Butterworths.

Van Schooten, B. W., Op Den Akker, R., Rosset, S., Galibert, O., Max, A., & Illouz, G. (2009). Follow-up question handling in the IMIX and Ritel systems: A comparative study. *Natural Language Engineering, 15*(1), 97–118. doi:10.1017/S1351324908004920

Van, A., Hendrickx, I., & Van Den Bosch, A. (2002). Dutch word sense disambiguation: Data and preliminary results. In *Proceedings of Senseval-2, Second International Workshop on Evaluating Word Sense Disambiguation Systems*, (pp. 13–16). Senseval.

Varges, S., Weng, F., & Pon-Barry, H. (2007). Interactive question answering and constraint relaxation in spoken dialogue systems. *Natural Language Engineering, 15*(1), 9–30. doi:10.1017/S1351324908004889

Varile, G., Cole, R., & Zampolli, A. (1997). *Survey of the state of the art in human language technology.* Cambridge, UK: Cambridge University Press.

Vasquez-Reyez, S., & Black, W. (2008). Evaluating causal questions for question answering. In *Proceedings ENC 2008.* Mexico City, Mexico: ENC. Shen, D., & Lapata, M. (2007). Using semantic roles to improve question answering. In *Proceedings of EMNLP-CoNLL.* EMNLP-CoNLL.

Venkatapathy, S., & Bangalore, S. (2009). Discriminative machine translation using global lexical selection. *ACM Transactions on Asian Language Information Processing, 8*(2). doi:10.1145/1526252.1526256

Verberne, S., Boves, L., Oostdijk, N., & Coppen, P. (2010). What is not in the bag of words for why-QA? *Computational Linguistics, 32*(2), 229–245.

Véronis, J. (2004). Hyperlex: Lexical cartography for information retrieval. *Computer Speech & Language, 18*(3), 223–252. doi:10.1016/j.csl.2004.05.002

Villavicencio, A., Ramisch, C., Machado, A., de Medeiros Caseli, H., & Finatto, M. J. (2010). Identicação de expressões multipalavra em domínios especícos. *Linguamática, 2*(1), 15–34.

Viterbi, A. J. (1967). Error bounds for convolutional codes and an asymptotically optimal decoding algorithm. *IEEE Transactions on Information Theory, 13*(2), 260–269. doi:10.1109/TIT.1967.1054010

Vivaldi, J., Màrquez, L., & Rodríguez, H. (2001). Improving term extraction by system combination using boosting. In *Proceedings of the 12th European Conference on Machine Learning (ECML)*, (pp. 515–526). ECML.

Vizine-Goetz, D. (1996). Using library classification schemes for internet resources. *OCLC Internet Cataloging Project Colloquium.* Retrieved October 8, 2010, from http://webdoc.sub.gwdg.de/ebook/aw/oclc/man/colloq/v-g.htm

Vogel, S., Ney, H., & Tillmann, C. (1996). HMM-based word alignment in statistical translation. In *Proceedings of COLING 1996: The 16th International Conference on Computational Linguistics*, (pp. 836-841). Copenhagen, Denmark: ICCL.

Voorhees, E. M., & Tice, D. M. (1999). The TREC-8 question answering track evaluation. In *Proceedings of the Text Retrieval Conference TREC-8*, (pp. 83-105). TREC.

Voorhees, E. M., & Tice, D. M. (2000). The TREC-8 question answering track evaluation. In E. M. Voorhees & D. K. Harman (Eds.), *Proceedings of the Eighth Text REtrieval Conference*, (pp. 83-105). TREC.

Voorhees, E. M. (1999). Natural language processing and information retrieval. In Pazienza, M. T. (Ed.), *Information Extraction: Towards Scalable, Adaptable Systems* (pp. 32–48). Berlin, Germany: Springer-Verlag.

Voorhees, E. M. (2001). The TREC question answering track *natural language engineering*. Cambridge, UK: Cambridge University Press.

Vossen, P., & Computer Centrum Letteren. (1997). Eurowordnet: A multilingual database for information retrieval. In *Proceedings of the DELOS Workshop on Cross-Language Information Retrieval*, (pp. 5–7). DELOS.

Vossen, P. (Ed.). (1998). *EuroWordNet: A multilingual database with lexical semantic networks*. Dordrecht, The Netherlands: Kluwer Academic Publishers.

Walker, D., & Amsler, R. (1986). The use of machine readable dictionaries in sublanguage analysis. In Grishman & Kittredge (Eds.), *Analyzing Language in Restricted Domains*, (pp. 69-83). LEA Press.

Walker, M., Whittaker, S., Laboratories, H. P., & Qz, B. (1990). Mixed initiative in dialogue: An investigation into discourse segmentation. In *Proceedings of the 28th Annual Meeting of the Association for Computational Linguistics*. ACL.

Wallach, H. M. (2004). *Conditional random fields: An introduction*. Technical Report MS-CIS-04-21. Philadelphia, PA: University of Pennsylvania.

Wallis, P. (2010). A robot in the kitchen. In *Proceedings of the ACL Workshop on Companionable Dialogue Systems*, (pp. 25-30). Uppsala, Sweden: ACL.

Walters, C. (2009). Facebook's new terms of service: "We can do anything we want with your content. Forever". *The Consumerist*. Retrieved September 15, 2010, from http://consumerist.com/2009/02/facebooks-new-terms-of-service-we-can-do-anything-we-want-with-your-content-forever.html

Walther, G., & Sagot, B. (2010). Developing a large-scale lexicon for a less-resourced language: General methodology and preliminary experiments on Sorani Kurdish. In *Proceedings of the 7th Workshop on Creation and use of Basic Lexical Resources for Less-Resourced Languages, (LREC 2010)*. Valetta, Malta: LREC.

Walther, J. B., & D'Addario, K. P. (2001). The impacts of emoticons on message interpretation in computer-mediated communication. *Social Science Computer Review, 19*, 323–345. doi:10.1177/089443930101900307

Walton, D., Reed, C., & Macagno, F. (2008). *Argumentation schemes*. Cambridge, UK: Cambridge University Press. doi:10.1017/CBO9780511802034

Wanas, N., Magdy, A., & Ashour, H. (2009). Using automatic keyword extraction to detect off-topic posts in online discussion boards. In *Proceedings of the First International Workshop on Content Analysis in the Web 2.0*. Madrid, Spain: ACL.

Wang, K., Ming, Z. Y., & Chua, T. S. (2009). A syntactic tree matching approach to finding similar questions in community-based QA services. In *Proceedings of the 32nd international ACM SIGIR Conference on Research and Development in Information Retrieval, (SIGIR 2009)*, (pp. 187-194). Boston, MA: ACM.

Wang, K., Ming, Z. Y., Hu, X., & Chua, T. S. (2010). Segmentation of multi-sentence questions: Towards effective question retrieval in QA services. In *Proceeding of the 33rd International ACM SIGIR Conference on Research and Development in Information Retrieval, (SIGIR 2010)*, (pp. 387-394). Geneva, Switzerland: ACM.

Wang, J. (2009). An extensive study on automated Dewey decimal classification. *Journal of the American Society for Information Science and Technology, 60*(11), 2269–2286. doi:10.1002/asi.21147

Wanner, L., Bohnet, B., & Giereth, M. (2006). What is beyond collocations? Insights from machine learning experiments. In *Proceedings of the EURALEX Conference*. Turin, Italy: EURALEX.

Wanner, L. (2004). Towards automatic fine-grained classification of verb-noun collocations. *Natural Language Engineering, 10*(2), 95–143. doi:10.1017/S1351324904003328

Way, A. (2010). Machine translation. In Clark, A., Fox, C., & Lappin, S. (Eds.), *The Handbook of Computational Linguistics and Natural Language Processing* (pp. 531–573). Chichester, UK: Wiley Blackwell. doi:10.1002/9781444324044.ch19

Webber, B., & Webb, N. (2010). Question answering. In Clark, A., Fox, C., & Lappin, S. (Eds.), *The Handbook of Computational Linguistics and Natural Language Processing* (pp. 630–654). Oxford, UK: Wiley-Blackwell. doi:10.1002/9781444324044.ch22

Webb, N., & Webber, B. (2009). Introduction. *Natural Language Engineering*, *15*(1), 1–8. doi:10.1017/S1351324908004877

Wechsler, M., & Schäuble, P. (1998). Multilingual information retrieval based on document alignment techniques. In *Proceedings of the Second European Conference on Research and Advanced Technology for Digital Libraries ECDL 1998*. Crete, Greece: ECDL.

Weeber, M., Mork, J. G., & Aronson, A. R. (2001). Developing a test collection for biomedical word sense disambiguation. In *Proceedings of the AMAI Symposium*, (pp. 746–750). AMAI.

Wei, X., & Rudnicky, A. (2000). Task-based management using an agenda. In *Proceedings of ANLP/NAACL Workshop on Conversational Systems*, (pp. 42-47). ACM.

Weisman, J. (2000, August 22). The making of e-commerce: 10 key moments. *E-Commerce Times*. Retrieved September 15, 2010, from http://www.ecommercetimes.com/story/4085.html?wlc=1284530145

WEKA. (2012). *The University of Waikato computer science department machine learning group*. Retrieved from http://www.cs.waikato.ac.nz/~ml/weka/index_downloading.html

Wermter, J. (2008). *Collocation and term extraction using linguistically enhanced statistical methods*. (Ph. D. Thesis). Friedrich-Schiller-Universität Jena. Retrieved from http://deposit.ddb.de/cgi-bin/dokserv?idn=993920594&dok_var=d1&dok_ext=pdf&filename=993920594.pdf

Wiebe, J. M., Bruce, R. F., & O'Hara, T. P. (1999). Development and use of a gold standard data set for subjectivity classifications. [College Park, MD: ACL.]. *Proceedings of, ACL-99*, 246–253.

Wiebe, J. M., Wilson, T., Bruce, R., Bell, M., & Martin, M. (2004). Learning subjective language. *Computational Linguistics*, *30*, 277–308. doi:10.1162/0891201041850885

Wilson, D., & Sperber, D. (1981). On Grice's theory of conversation. In Werth, P. (Ed.), *Conversation and Discourse*. New York, NY: St. Martin's Press.

Wilson, T., Wiebe, J., & Hoffmann, P. (2009). Recognizing contextual polarity: An exploration of features for phrase-level sentiment analysis. *Computational Linguistics*, *35*(5), 399–433. doi:10.1162/coli.08-012-R1-06-90

Witbrock, M. J., & Mittal, V. O. (1999). Ultra-summarization (poster abstract): A statistical approach to generating highly condensed non-extractive summaries. In *Proceedings of the 22nd Annual International ACM SIGIR Conference on Research and Development in Information Retrieval*, (pp. 315-316). Berkeley, CA: ACM.

Witten, I. H., Don, K. J., Dewsnip, M., & Tablan, V. (2003). Textmining in a digital library. *International Journal on Digital Libraries*, *5*, 1–4.

Witten, I. H., & Frank, E. (2005). *Data mining: Practical machine learning tools and techniques* (2nd ed.). San Francisco, CA: Morgan Kaufmann.

Wolfram, D., Spink, A., Jansen, B. J., & Saracevic, T. (2001). Vox populi: The public searching of the Web. *Journal of the American Society for Information Science and Technology*, *52*(12), 1073–1074. doi:10.1002/asi.1157

Woodward, J. (2003). *Making things happen: A theory of causal explanation*. Oxford, UK: Oxford University Press.

WordNet. (2010). *WordNet release 3.1*. Retrieved from http://wordnet.princeton.edu

Workshops, M. W. E. (2012). *Website*. Retrieved from http://multiword.sourceforge.net/PHITE.php?sitesig=CONF

Wright, von G. H. (2004). *Explanation and understanding*. Ithaca, NY: Cornell University Press.

Wu, D., & Fung, P. (2009). Semantic roles for SMT: A hybrid two-pass model. In *Proceedings of the Annual Conference of the North American Chapter of the Association for Computational Linguistics*, (pp. 13-16). Boulder, CO: ACL.

Wu, P. H.-J., Na, J.-C., & Khoo, C. S. G. (2004). NLP versus IR approaches to fuzzy name searching in digital libraries. In *Proceedings of the 8th European Conference on Digital Libraries*, (pp. 145-156). ECDL.

Xiao, C., & Rösner, D. (2004). Detecting multiword verbs in the English sublanguage of MEDLINE abstracts. In *Proceedings of the 20th international conference on Computational Linguistics (COLING 2004)*. Stroudsburg, PA: Association for Computational Linguistics.

Yaling, L., & Minghui, D. (2008). Lip contour extraction based on manifold. In *Proceedings of the International Conference on MultiMedia and Information Technology*, (pp. 229-232). Los Alamitos, CA: IEEE Computer Society.

Yamada, K., & Knight, K. (2001). A syntax-based statistical translation model. In *Proceedings of the 39th Annual Meeting of the Association for Computational Linguistics*, (pp. 523-530). Toulouse, France: ACL.

Yamada, K., & Knight, K. (2002). A decoder for syntax-based statistical MT. In *Proceedings of the 40th Annual Meeting of the Association for Computational Linguistics*, (pp. 303-310). Philadelphia, PA: ACL.

Yang, J., & Waibel, A. (1996). A real-time face tracker. In *Proceedings 3rd IEEE Workshop on Applications of Computer Vision (WACV 1996)*, (pp. 142-147). IEEE Press.

Yang, C. C., & Lam, W. (2006). Introduction to the special topic section on multilingual information systems. *Journal of the American Society for Information Science and Technology*, *57*(5), 629–631. doi:10.1002/asi.20325

Yang, Y. (1999). An evaluation of statistical approaches to text categorization. *Information Retrieval*, *1*(1-2), 69–90. doi:10.1023/A:1009982220290

Yarowsky, D. (1992). Word-sense disambiguation using statistical models of Roget's categories trained on large corpora. In *Proceedings of the 14th Conference on Computational Linguistics, COLING 1992*, (vol 2), (pp. 454–460). Stroudsburg, PA: COLING.

Yarowsky, D. (1994). Decision lists for lexical ambiguity resolution: Application to accent restoration in Spanish and French. In *Proceedings of the 32nd Annual Meeting of the Association for Computational Linguistics (ACL)*, (pp. 88–95). ACL.

Yarowsky, D. (1995). Unsupervised word sense disambiguation rivaling supervised methods. In *Proceedings of the 33rd Annual Meeting on Association for Computational Linguistics*, (pp. 189–196). Morristown, NJ: ACL.

Yashwanth, H., Mahendrakar, H., & David, S. (2004). Automatic speech recognition using audio visual cues. In *Proceedings of the IEEE India Annual Conference (INDICON 2004)*, (pp. 166-169). IEEE Press.

Yau, W. C., Kumar, D. K., & Arjunan, S. P. (2006). Voiceless speech recognition using dynamic visual speech features. In *Proceedings of the HCSNet Workshop on Use of Vision in Human-Computer Interaction (VisHCI 2006)*, (pp. 93-101). Canberra, Australia: VisHCI.

Yin, D., Xue, Z., Hong, L., Davison, B., Kontostathis, A., & Edwards, L. (2009). Detection of harassment on web 2.0. In *Proceedings of the First International Workshop on Content Analysis in the Web 2.0*. Madrid, Spain: ACL.

Yoo, I. (2006). A comprehensive comparison study of document clustering for a biomedical digital library MEDLINE. In *Proceedings of the 6th ACM/IEEE-CS Joint Conference on Digital Libraries*, (pp. 220-229). Chapel Hill, NC: ACM/IEEE.

Yoshida, K., Tsuruoka, Y., Miyao, Y., & Tsujii, J. (2007). Ambiguous part-of-speech tagging for improving accuracy and domain portability of syntactic parsers. [IJCAI.]. *Proceedings of, IJCAI-07*, 1783–1788.

Young, S., Schatzmann, J., Weilhammer, K., & Ye, H. (2007). The hidden information state approach to dialog management. In *Proceedings of Human Language Technologies: The Annual Conference of the North American Chapter of the Association for Computational Linguistics*, (pp. 27-28). ACL.

Youngs, G. (2009). Blogging and globalization: The blurring of the public/private spheres. *Aslib Proceedings*, *61*(2), 127–138. doi:10.1108/00012530910946884

Yuasa, M., Saito, K., & Mukawa, N. (2006). Emoticons convey emotions without cognition of faces: An fMRI study. *In Proceedings of CHI 2006 Extended Abstracts on Human Factors in Computing Systems*, (pp. 1565-1570). Montréal, Canada: CHI.

Yuhas, B. P., Goldstein, M. H. Jr, & Sejnowski, T. J. (1989). Integration of acoustic and visual speech signals using neural networks. *IEEE Communications Magazine, 27*(11), 65–71. doi:10.1109/35.41402

Yuille, A. L. (1991). Deformable templates for face recognition. *CogNeuro, 3*(1), 59–70.

Zajic, D., Dorr, B., & Schwartz, R. (2002). Automatic headline generation for newspaper stories. In *Proceedings of the ACL Workshop on Automatic Summarization and Document Understanding Conference,* (pp. 78-85). ACL.

Zelle, J., & Mooney, R. (1996). Comparative results on using inductive logic programming for corpus-based parser construction. In *Symbolic, Connectionist, and Statistical Approaches to Learning for Natural Language Processing.* Berlin, Germany: Springer Verlag. doi:10.1007/3-540-60925-3_59

Zhai, C., & Laffery, J. (2001). A study of smoothing methods for language models applied to ad hoc information retrieval. [SIGIR.]. *Proceedings of SIGIR, 2001,* 334–342.

Zhang, H., Zhang, M., Li, H., Aw, A., & Tan, C. L. (2009). Forest-based tree sequence to string translation model. In *Proceedings of the Joint Conference of the 47th Annual Meeting of the ACL and the 4th International Joint Conference on Natural Language Processing of the AFNLP,* (pp. 172-180). Singapore: ACL.

Zhang, J., Ackerman, M. S., & Adamic, L. (2007). Expertise networks in online communities: Structure and algorithms. In *Proceedings of the 16th International Conference on World Wide Web,* (pp. 221–230). New York, NY: WWW.

Zhang, M., Jiang, H., Aw, A., Li, H., Tan, C. L., & Li, S. (2008). A tree sequence alignment-based tree-to-tree translation model. In *Proceedings of the 46th Annual Meeting of the Association for Computational Linguistics and the Human Language Technology Conference,* (pp. 559-567). Columbus, OH: ACL.

Zhang, M., Jiang, H., Aw, A., Sun, J., Li, S., & Tan, C. L. (2007). A tree-to-tree alignment-based model for statistical machine translation. [Copenhagen, Denmark: MT Summit.]. *Proceedings of the MT Summit, XI,* 535–542.

Zhao, S. (2006). Humanoid social robots as a medium of communication. *New Media & Society, 8*(3), 401–419. doi:10.1177/1461444806061951

Zheng, D., & Li, F. (2009). Hot topic detection on BBS using aging theory. *Lecture Notes in Computer Science, 5854,* 129–138. doi:10.1007/978-3-642-05250-7_14

Zhou, B., Xiang, B., Zhu, X., & Gao, Y. (2008). Prior derivation models for formally syntax-based translation using linguistically syntactic parsing and tree kernels. In *Proceedings of the Second Workshop on Syntax and Structure in Statistical Translation (SSST-2),* (pp. 19-27). Columbus, OH: SSST.

Zhou, L., & Chaovalit, P. (2008). Ontology-supported polarity mining. *Journal of the American Society for Information Science and Technology, 69,* 98–110. doi:10.1002/asi.20735

Zhu, M., Hu, W., & Wu, O. (2008). Topic detection and tracking for threaded discussion communities. In *Proceedings of the International Conference on Web Intelligence and Intelligent Agent Technology,* (pp. 77-83). ACM.

Zobel, J., Moffat, A., & Ramamohanarao, K. (1998). Inverted files versus signature files for text indexing. *ACM Transactions on Database Systems, 23*(4), 453–490. doi:10.1145/296854.277632

Zollmann, A., Venugopal, A., & Vogel, S. (2008). The CMU syntax-augmented machine translation system: SAMT on Hadoop with n-best alignments. In *Proceedings of the International Workshop on Spoken Language Translation,* (pp. 18-25). Honolulu, HI: SLT.

About the Contributors

Sivaji Bandyopadhyay received the Ph.D. degree in Computer Science and Engineering from Jadavpur University, Kolkata, India in 1998. Since 1991, he has been a faculty member of the Department of Computer Science and Engineering, Jadavpur University. He is engaged with several national and international projects such as "Development of Cross Lingual Information Access (CLIA)," DIT, Government of India, August 2006 – 2010, "Development of English to Indian Languages Machine Translation Systems (EILMT)," DIT, Government of India, August 2006 – 2010, "Development of Indian Languages to Indian Languages Machine Translation Systems (IL-ILMT)," DIT, Government of India, August 2006 – 2010, "An Advanced Platform for Question Answering Systems," Indo-French Center for the Promotion of Advanced Research (IFCPAR), 2009 – 2012, "Multidisciplinary Research Field on Sentiment Analysis where AI meets Psychology (SAAIP)," Strategic India-Japan Cooperative Programme-Project in the area of Multidisciplinary ICT, DST, Government of India 2010 – 2013, "Answer Validation through Textual Entailment," CONACYT, Mexico, DST, India, 2010 – 2012. His research interests are in the area of natural language processing, machine learning, machine translation, sentiment analysis, question answering systems, and information extraction. He has had more than 100 publications in top conferences and journals and has served as program chair, workshop chair, and PC member of IJCNLP, NAACL, NLPKE, ICON, and others. He is a member of the ACL and AAMT.

Sudip Kumar Naskar is a Postdoctoral Researcher in the Centre for Next Generation Localisation (CNGL), at MT Research Group, National Centre for Language Technology, School of Computing, Dublin City University, Ireland. He obtained his PhD in Computer Science and Engineering from Jadavpur University, India. His research interests are focused around machine translation and word sense disambiguation.

Asif Ekbal is an Assistant Professor at Department of Computer Science and Engineering, Indian Institute of Technology, Patna, India. He finished his Ph.D. in Computer Science and Engineering from the Department of Computer Science and Engineering, Jadavpur University, India. Before joining to IIT Patna, he worked as a Postdoctoral Research fellow in the Department of Information Engineering and Computer Science, University of Trento, Italy, and Department of Computational Linguistics, Heidelberg University, Germany. His current research interests include information extraction, machine learning, and bio-informatics.

* * *

Rafael E. Banchs received the Ph.D. in Electrical Engineering from the University of Texas at Austin in 1998. Since then, he has conducted research in the areas of direct and inverse modeling and parameter estimation, as well as their application to practical problems in a variety of scenarios ranging from the oil industry to the media and communications industry. Currently, he works as a Research Scientist at the Human Language Technology Department of the Institute for Infocomm Research, a branch of the Agency for Science, Technology, and Research (A*STAR), Singapore, where his main research activity is focused on specific natural language processing problems such as machine translation, information retrieval, and automatic dialogue management.

Pushpak Bhattacharyya's research interests include natural language processing, machine translation, and machine leaning. He has had more than 130 publications in top conferences and journals and has served as program chair, area chair, workshop chair, and PC member of top fora like ACL, COLING, LREC, SIGIR, CIKM, NAACL, GWC, and others. He has guided 7 PhDs and over 100 masters and undergraduate students in their thesis work. Dr. Bhattacharyya plays a leading role in India's large-scale projects on Machine Translation, Cross Lingual Search, and Wordnet and Dictionary Development. Dr. Bhattacharyya has received a number of prestigious awards, including the IBM Innovation Award, United Nations Research Grant, Microsoft Research Grant, IIT Bombay's Patwardhan Award for Technology Development and Ministry of IT, and Digital India Foundation's Manthan Award. Recently, he has been appointed Associate Editor of the prestigious journal, *ACM Transactions on Asian Language Information Processing*.

Michael Carl is Associate Professor for Human and Machine Translation at the Copenhagen Business School. He studied Computer Sciences and Computational Linguistics in Berlin, Paris, and Hong Kong. He obtained his PhD from the University of the Saarland, Saarbrücken, in 2001. From 1994 until 2008, he was Researcher at the IAI (Saarbrücken, Germany) and involved in numerous NLP and Machine Translation projects. In 1999, he was on a PhD grant at the Hong Kong University of Sciences and Technology, and in 2002, he was a Post-Doctoral Researcher at RALI, Univerisité Montreal, Canada. He participated in several national and European projects and is author of more than 70 articles in international journals, books, and conferences. In 2008, he joined the Department of International Language Studies and Computational Linguistics (ISV) at CBS as an Associate Professor. His current research interest is focused around human and machine translation processes.

Miriam Lúcia Domingues received the MSc degree in Computer Science from Federal University of Rio Grande do Sul, Porto Alegre, Brazil, in 2003. She is a Researcher at the Federal University of Pará (UFPA), Pará, Brazil. She teaches the discipline of Data Mining in the Specialization Course of Database Systems of the Institute of Exact and Natural Sciences at the UFPA, Pará, Brazil. Her main research area is natural language processing, including Portuguese part-of-speech tagging, corpus-based acquisition, domain adaptation, and other intelligent computing related matters. MSc. Domingues is a member of the Brazilian Computer Society, and she joined the Latin American Researchers in Natural Language Processing and Computational Linguistics Group at the North American Chapter of the Association for Computational Linguistics.

Eloi Luiz Favero received his BSc and MSc (1990) degrees in Computer Science from Federal University of Rio Grande do Sul, Porto Alegre, Brazil, and the DSc degree in Computer Science from Federal University of Pernanbuco, Recife, Brazil, in 2000. He is an Associate Professor at the Federal University of Pará (UFPA), Pará, Brazil. He was a Coordinator of the Computer Science Graduate Program at the UFPA, Pará, Brazil. He is currently a Lecturer in the Faculty of Computer Science at the UFPA, Pará, Brazil. His current research interests include natural language processing, natural language generation, formal grammars, and intelligent computing. Dr. Favero is a member of the Brazilian Computer Society and the Academia Paraense de Ciências.

M. S. Gaur is presently Professor in Department of Computer Engineering, MNIT, Jaipur (India). He completed his B.E. (Electronics and Communication) from JNVU, Jodhpur (India) in 1988 and M.E. (Computer Science Engineering) from IISc, Bangalore (India) in 1993. He was awarded the PhD degree from University of Southampton (UK) in 2005. His research interests include network security, network on chips, and VLSI design.

Alexander Gelbukh holds M.Sc. degree in Mathematics and Ph.D. degree in Computer Science. Since 1997, he leads the Natural Language Processing Laboratory of the Computing Research Center of the National Polytechnic Institute (CIC-IPN), Mexico. He is academician of the Mexican Academy of Sciences, National Researcher of Mexico of excellence level 2, and the Secretary of the Mexican Society for Artificial Intelligence (SMIA). He is author or editor of more than 490 publications and co-author of four books in the areas of natural language processing and artificial intelligence. More information about him can be found on his personal page www.Gelbukh.com.

Mitesh M. Khapra is pursuing his PhD in the Computer Science and Engineering Department at the Indian Institute of Technology Bombay under the guidance of Prof. Pushpak Bhattacharyya and Dr. A. Kumaran (Microsoft Research India). His thesis work deals with overcoming the problem of resource scarcity in natural language processing by reusing existing resources across languages. Prior to enrolling for Ph.D., Mitesh did his M.Tech from the Computer Science and Engineering Department at the Indian Institute of Technology Bombay. Before that, he worked as Software Engineer and Senior Software Engineer at Infosys Technologies Ltd. and LGSoft, respectively. Mitesh submitted his thesis in January 2012.

Olga Kolesnikova obtained her M.Sc. degree in Linguistics from Novosibirsk State Pedagogical Institute, Russia, in 1989, and her Ph.D. in Computer Science from the Center for Computing Research of the National Polytechnic Institute (CIC-IPN), Mexico. Her research is in the area of computational linguistics; in particular, she is interested in text semantic analysis and computational lexicography.

Natalia Konstantinova is currently a PhD student at the Research Group in Computational Linguistics, University of Wolverhampton, UK. She got her degree from Saint-Petersburg State University in Mathematical Linguistics (2007). Her research is focused on information extraction from Wikipedia for interactive question answering under the supervision of Prof. Ruslan Mitkov and Dr. Constantin Orasan. It concentrates on information extraction and the ways it can be used in interactive question answering. Her fields of interests also cover ontology building, coreference resolution, machine learning for NLP, and machine translation. She was involved in the organisation of several events such as the RANLP conference series and is Editorial Assistant for the *Journal of Natural Language Engineering*. Her personal webpage is http://www.wlv.ac.uk/~in0988/.

Vijay Laxmi is currently Reader and HOD, Department of Computer Engineering, MNIT, Jaipur (India). She did her B.E. (Electronics and Communication) from JNVU, Jodhpur (India) in 1991 and M.Tech. (Computer Science Engineering) from IIT, Delhi (India) in 1992. She completed her PhD from University of Southampton (UK) in 2003. She has 15 years of teaching experience. Her research interests include security and image processing applications in surveillance.

Fernando López-Ostenero is Associate Professor at UNED and a member of the Natural Language Processing and Information Retrieval Group. His research interests are multilingual information retrieval, the development of translation resources for multilingual information retrieval, and user interaction in information retrieval tasks. Since 2001, he has been involved in the organization of iCLEF.

Aditya Mogadala is working as a Research Associate and also a Master of Science student working in the areas of natural language processing, machine learning, information retrieval, and text mining. He is particularly interested in cross language information retrieval and Multilingual Text mining.

Constantin Orasan is Senior Lecturer in Computational Linguistics at the University of Wolverhampton and Deputy Head of the Research Group in Computational Linguistics. He obtained his PhD in 2006 in the field of Automatic Summarization from the University of Wolverhampton. His main research interests are in fields related to information access, such as automatic summarization, question answering, and information extraction, but he has expertise in a wide range of fields of computational linguistics, including anaphora and coreference resolution, opinion mining and sentiment analysis, corpus building and exploitation, and technologies for machine translation. He has published over 60 papers in international conferences and journals, and has been invited to deliver talks at several international events. He has managed several projects including 2 EU-funded and 2 commercial projects. His personal webpage is http://www.wlv.ac.uk/~in6093/.

Carlos Rodríguez Penagos is a Senior Researcher in the Voice and Language Group at Barcelona Media Research Foundation. He has a Doctoral degree in Linguistics, with Computational Linguistics as specialty. His major areas of expertise are information extraction, opinion mining, natural language processing, knowledge engineering, and computer-aided translation. He has taught and coordinated various international research projects at the National Autonomous University of Mexico (UNAM), the Universitat Pompeu Fabra (UPF), and the National Cancer Research Center (CNIO), where he mined biomedical literature. He has been awarded various research grants by the National Science and Technology Council (Mexico) and the Generalitat de Catalunya Government (Spain).

Víctor Peinado is Researcher and PhD candidate at UNED's Natural Language Processing and Information Retrieval Group. His research interests focus on cross-language information access, more specifically on building linguistic resources and interactive information retrieval systems in multilingual scenarios. Since 2005, he has been involved in the organization of iCLEF, the interactive track at the Cross Language Evaluation Forum (CLEF).

Álvaro Rodrigo is Teacher Assistant at UNED and a member of the Natural Language Processing and Information Retrieval Group. His research interests are question answering, answer validation, and machine reading. He organized the answer validation exercises at CLEF, and he has been involved in the organization of QA@CLEF since 2006.

Patrick Saint-Dizier is a Research Director at CNRS. He heads a research group in NLP at IRIT in Toulouse, France. The main features are: natural language processing, discourse syntax and semantics, and reasoning. His main research themes merge foundational aspects with empirical studies and prototype development. The main topics are: (1) elaboration of a formalism (Dislog) and tools (TextCoop) for discourse analysis based on logic that include reasoning capabilities, lexical semantics, typography and some formal syntax aspects; (2) text clinic: improving the quality and contents of texts: application to grammatical error correction and style enhancement, and to procedure content improvements via risks analysis and prevention, elaboration of negotiation scenarios, requirement analysis (LELIE project); (3) cooperative access to information: cooperative question-answering, argumentation analysis, opinion analysis; and (4) extending the discourse analysis paradigm to other forms of communication: Western tonal music processing. He has published or co-authored a number of books, journal articles, and conference papers. He has also organized a number of workshops and summer schools on language processing.

Preety Singh did her B.E. (Electrical) at MNNIT, Allahabad (India) in 1989 and M.Tech. (Electronics) at IIT, Delhi (India) in 1990. She is currently pursuing her PhD from Department of Computer Engineering, MNIT, Jaipur (India). She is also working on a project on digital forensics. Her research interests include image processing related to surveillance applications.

Lucia Specia is Lecturer at Department of Computer Science, University of Sheffield, UK. She is part of the Natural Language Processing group. In the past, she has worked as Senior Lecturer at the University of Wolverhampton, and as Research Engineer at Xerox Research, France. She received a PhD from the University of São Paulo, Brazil, in 2007. Her research interests include statistical machine translation, quality assessment and estimation for machine translation, lexical semantics, and text adaptation.

Lyne Da Sylva has a multidisciplinary background (in Mathematics, Computer Science, Linguistics, and Computational Linguistics). Her doctoral thesis studied the use of default values in syntactic formalisms, in terms of theoretical linguistic aspects and formal implementation aspects. She is now Associate Professor at the École de Bibliothéconomie et des Sciences de l'Information (i.e. the School of Library and Information Science), at the Université de Montréal in Canada. Prior to this, she spent several years doing research and development work in natural language processing (syntactic analysis, grammar checking, and machine translation), including four years at Machina Sapiens Inc., a Montreal-based software development company. Her teaching includes indexing and abstracting (both manual and automated), thesaurus construction, computer-assisted document management, and semiotics of information systems. Her research focuses especially on the automation of indexing and abstracting through the use of natural language processing techniques, and especially automatic back-of-the-book indexing.

Vasudeva Varma is a Faculty Member at International Institute of Information Technology, Hyderabad, since 2002. His research interests include search (information retrieval), information extraction, information access, knowledge management, cloud computing, and software engineering. He is heading Search and Information Extraction Lab and Software Engineering Research Lab at IIIT Hyderabad. He is also the chair of Post Graduate Programs since 2009. He published a book on software architecture (Pearson Education) and over one hundred technical papers in journals and conferences. In 2004, he obtained young scientist award and grant from Department of Science and Technology, Government of India, for his proposal on personalized search engines. In 2007, he was given Research Faculty Award by AOL Labs. He was Visiting Professor at UPV, Valencia, Spain (Summer 2007), UBO, Bretagne, France (Summer 2009), and Language Technologies Institute, CMU, Pittsburgh, USA (Summer 2010).

Index

A

Active Appearance Models (AAM) 300
Active Shape Models (ASM) 300, 302
answer extractor 154
Artificial Intelligence Markup Language
    (AIML) 160
Audio-Visual Speech Recognition (AVSR) 292-293,
    303
Automatic Categorization 230, 232, 238-239, 248,
    261
Automatic Speech Recognition (ASR) 292

B

Bilingual Evaluation Understudy (BLEU) 98

C

CETENFolha 62-63, 65, 69, 72
chart parser 93
Chatspeak 231, 234-236, 248
chatterbots 150, 152, 166
Citation Analysis 270, 278, 289
Classification Scheme 239, 268, 273, 289
Commissariat à L´Energieatomique (CEA) 187
ComplementaryInfo (ComplInfo) 160
Compressed Word Format (CWFs) 191
Computational Learning in Adaptive Systems for
    Spoken Conversation (CLASSIC) 163
Conditional Random Fields (CRFs) 54, 191
Constraint-Based Problem-Solver (CBPS) 157
Constraint Grammar (CG) 54
Content Management Systems (CMS) 232
Content Processing 265, 271-274, 276, 289-290
context bag 24-26
Context Free Grammars (CFG) 91
Controlled Vocabulary 210, 228, 269, 279, 289-290
conversational agents 150, 155, 164, 166-168
conversational structure 151, 165

Co-Referencing 231, 234, 236-237, 248
CoreInformation (CoreInfo) 160
Corpus Co-Occurrence 35-37
Coupled Hidden Markov Model (CHMM) 301
Cross Language Information Access (CLIA) 171-
    172, 197
Cross-Language Information Retrieval (CLIR) 172,
    204-205, 221

D

Defense Advanced Research Projects Agency
    (DARPA) 100
Deutsches Forschungszentrum für Künstliche
    Intelligenz (DFKI) 187
Dialogue System 149-157, 162-164, 167-168, 261
Discourse analysis 132, 137-138, 142, 144, 177,
    270, 274, 280
Discourse Frames 141
Discrete Cosine Transform (DCT) 300
document processor 154-155
Document Summarization 174, 181-182, 230, 232,
    238-239, 248, 261, 280
Do It Yourself (DIY) 132
Dynamic Time Warping (DTW) 302

E

Education Resources Information Centre
    (ERIC) 267
Elementary Discourse Units (EDU) 131
Emoticons 231, 234-236, 248, 251, 257, 259-260
European Conference on Digital Libraries
    (ECDL) 266
European Multilingual Information Retrieval
    (EMIR) 187
Expectation Maximization (EM) 77, 297, 301
ExpectedAnswerType (EAT) 160
explanation function 141